Experiencing Jazz

Experiencing Jazz, Second Edition, is an integrated textbook with online resources for jazz appreciation and history courses. Through readings, illustrations, timelines, listening guides, and a streaming audio library, it immerses the reader in a journey through the history of jazz, while placing the music within a larger cultural and historical context. Designed to introduce the novice to jazz, *Experiencing Jazz* describes the elements of music, and the characteristics and roles of different instruments. Prominent artists and styles from the roots of jazz to present day are relayed in a story-telling prose. This new edition features expanded coverage of women in jazz, the rise of jazz as a world music, the influence of Afro-Cuban and Latin jazz, and streaming audio.

Features:
- Important musical trends are placed within a broad cultural, social, political, and economic context
- Music fundamentals are treated as integral to the understanding of jazz, and concepts are explained easily with graphic representations and audio examples
- Comprehensive treatment chronicles the roots of jazz in African music to present day
- Commonly overlooked styles, such as orchestral jazz, Cubop, and third-stream jazz are included
- Expanded and up-to-date coverage of women in jazz.

The media–rich companion website presents a comprehensive streaming audio library of key jazz recordings by leading artists integrated with interactive listening guides. Illustrated musical concepts with web-based tutorials and audio interviews of prominent musicians acquaint new listeners to the sounds, styles, and figures of jazz.

Richard J. Lawn recently retired as Dean of the College of Performing Arts at the University of the Arts in Philadelphia. You can see and hear him as saxophonist, composer, and bandleader for Power of Ten, playing in local clubs and on recordings.

Experiencing Jazz

Second Edition

Richard J. Lawn

Professor Emeritus, College of Performing Arts
at the University of the Arts

Routledge
Taylor & Francis Group

LONDON AND NEW YORK

Please visit the companion website at www.routledge.com/cw/Lawn

First published 2013 by Routledge

2 Park Square, Milton Park, Abingdon, Oxfordshire OX14 4RN
52 Vanderbilt Avenue, New York, NY 10017

Routledge is an imprint of the Taylor & Francis Group, an informa business

First issued in paperback 2019

First edition published 2007 by The McGraw-Hill Companies

Library of Congress Cataloging in Publication Data
Lawn, Richard, author.
  Experiencing jazz/Richard J. Lawn.—Second edition.
  pages cm
  Includes bibliographical references, discography, and videography.
  1. Jazz—History and criticism. 2. Jazz—Analysis, appreciation. I. Title.
  ML3506.L39 2013
  781.65—dc23   2012024753

ISBN: 978-0-415-65935-2 (pbk and online access card)
ISBN: 978-0-415-69960-0 (pbk)
ISBN: 978-0-415-83735-4 (online access card)
ISBN: 978-0-203-37981-3 (ebk and online access card)
ISBN: 978-0-203-37985-1 (ebk)

Typeset in Bembo, Helvetica Neue and Kabel
by Florence Production Ltd, Stoodleigh, Devon, UK

I am deeply indebted to my wife, Susan Lawn, for "putting her life on hold," not once but twice, while helping immeasurably to make this book become a reality. In addition, thanks to the many students who served as its inspiration.

Contents

List of Photos   xiv
List of Examples   xix
List of Figures   xxii
Preface   xxiii
Acknowledgments   xxviii

PART I **UNDERSTANDING JAZZ**   1

1 The Nature of Jazz   3

  Experiencing Music . . . Experiencing Jazz 4
  That Four-Letter Word 4
  Defining Jazz 6
  Chapter Summary 8
  Study Questions 9

2 The Elements of Jazz   13

  Rhythm 14
    Meter and Tempo 15
    Rhythmic Devices Important to Jazz 16
    Swing as an Aspect of Jazz Rhythm 18
  Melody 18
  Harmony 20
  Texture 21
  Form 22
  Improvisation 23
    Something Borrowed—The European Tradition 23
    Something New, Something Blue—The Jazz Tradition 24
    Blues 24
    Improvisation in Jazz 26
  Chapter Summary 29
  Key Terms 30
  Study Questions 31

3 Listening to Jazz   33

Performance Practice   33
 The Instruments of Jazz   34
 The Drum Set and Swing   34
 Orchestration and Instrumentation   36
 Instrumental Techniques and Special Effects   37
Understanding the Whole Performance   39
Describing the Performance   41
 Video Blues   42
Chapter Summary   43
Key Terms   43
Study Questions   44

4 The Roots of Jazz   45

Jazz in Perspective   45
 The Significance of African Music to Jazz   46
 African Musical Aesthetic   46
 Elements of African Music   47
 African Music as a Means of Communication   49
The Afro-Latin and Caribbean Tinge   49
 Background   50
 Early Fusions   52
Early American Vocal Music   54
The Innovators: Getting the Blues   56
 Robert Johnson (1911–1938)   57
 Bessie Smith (1894–1937)   59
 W.C. Handy—"Father of the Blues" (1873–1958)   61
Ragtime   62
Brass and Military Bands   67
Milestones: Chronicle of Historic Events   68
Chapter Summary   70
Key Terms   70
Study Questions   71

PART II   **CLASSIC JAZZ 1917–1945**   73

5 Jazz Takes Root   75

Jazz in Perspective   75
The Reception of Early Jazz   78
New Orleans—The Birthplace of Jazz   80
 Dixieland Jazz Band Instrumentation   81
The Innovators: Early Jazz   83
 Original Dixieland Jazz Band   83
 Kid Ory (1890–1973)   86
 Joe "King" Oliver (1885–1938)   86
 Lilian Hardin   86

Jelly Roll Morton (1890–1941)   89
Louis Armstrong (1901–1971)   91
Sidney Bechet (1897–1959)   94
Milestones: Chronicle of Historic Events   95
Chapter Summary   97
Key Terms   97
Study Questions   98

6 The Jazz Age: From Chicago to New York   99

Jazz in Perspective   99
South Side of Chicago   100
On the Other Side of Town   102
The Chicago Sound   103
The Innovators: A Few of the Many   104
New Orleans Rhythm Kings (NORK)   104
Bix Beiderbecke (1903–1931)   105
Frankie "Tram" Trumbauer (1901–1956)   106
Paul Whiteman (1890–1967) and Symphonic Jazz   108
Boogie-Woogie, Eight to the Bar   110
The Decline of the Chicago Era   111
Chicago Jazz in Retrospect   113
New York and the Harlem Renaissance   114
James P. Johnson (1891–1955)   115
Marketing Jazz   118
Milestones: Chronicle of Historic Events   120
Chapter Summary   121
Key Terms   122
Study Questions   122

7 The Swing Era: Jazz at Its Peak   125

Jazz in Perspective: The Depths of the Depression   126
The Country Recovers   127
The Anatomy of the Swing Era Jazz Band   127
Instrumentation   128
Repertoire and Arrangement   131
The Innovators: Swing on the East Coast   132
Fletcher Henderson (1897–1952)   133
Coleman Hawkins—"The Father of Jazz Tenor Saxophone" (1904–1969)   135
Duke Ellington (1899–1974): Music Was His Mistress   137
Benny Goodman—The "King of Swing" (1909–1986)   147
Popular White Swing Bands   151
Artie Shaw (Arthur Arshawsky) (1910–2005)   151
The Vocalists' Rise to Fame   153
Ongoing Latin Influences   155
Chapter Summary   155
Key Terms   156
Study Questions   157

8 Swinging Across the Country: The Bands, Singers, and Pianists   159

Jazz in Perspective   160
The Innovators: A Unique Kaycee Style   161
    Benny Moten   161
    William "Count" Basie (1904–1984)   162
    Lester Young (1909–1959)   164
Territory Bands   167
    Mary Lou Williams (1910–1981)   168
The Innovators: A Few of the Swing Era Singers and Pianists   170
    Billie Holiday (1915–1959): "Lady Day"   170
    Ella Fitzgerald (1918–1996): The "First Lady of Song"   172
    Art Tatum (1909–1956)   174
Traditional Jazz Revival   177
Swing Era Success   177
Milestones: Chronicle of Historic Events   181
Chapter Summary   184
Key Terms   185
Study Questions   185

PART III   **MODERN JAZZ**   187

9 The Bebop Revolution   189

Jazz in Perspective   189
The Lifestyle and Musical Characteristics   192
The Birth of Bebop: The First Recordings   194
    Characteristics of the Style   196
    Bebop Performance Practice and Instrumental Roles Redefined   197
The Innovators: Bop Stylists   199
    John Birks "Dizzy" Gillespie (1917–1993)   199
    Charlie Parker (1920–1955)   201
    Bud Powell (1924–1966)   203
    Dexter Gordon (1923–1990)   205
    J.J. Johnson (1924–2001)   206
The Innovators: Bebop Rhythm-Section Players   207
    Thelonious Sphere Monk (1917–1982)   207
    Oscar Pettiford (1922–1960)   209
    Kenny Clarke (1914–1985)   209
    Max Roach (1924–2007)   210
    Sarah Vaughan: "The Divine One" (1924–1990)   211
Modern Jazz Embraces the Afro-Cuban Spirit   213
    Dizzy Gillespie and the Birth of Cubop   213
The Decline of Bebop   217
Milestones: Chronicle of Historic Events   217
Chapter Summary   219
Key Terms   220

Appendix   220
Study Questions   223

10 The 1950s and Early 1960s: Cool, Intellectual, and Abstract Jazz   225

Jazz in Perspective   225
Characteristics of Cool Jazz   228
The Innovators: The Cool Sound on the East and West Coasts   231
    Miles Davis and Gil Evans: *The Birth of the Cool   231*
    Modern Jazz Quartet   233
    Gerry Mulligan (1927–1996) and Chet Baker (1929–1988)   233
    Dave Brubeck (1920–2012)   235
    Bill Evans (1929–1980)   238
The Brazilian Bossa Nova   241
    Stan Getz (1927–1991)   243
Third-Stream Jazz   245
    Lennie Tristano (1919–1978)   247
Who Was Popular   248
Milestones: Chronicle of Historic Events   249
Chapter Summary   250
Key Terms   251
Study Questions   252

PART IV   POSTMODERN JAZZ   253

11 Tradition Meets the Avant-Garde: Moderns and Early Postmoderns Coexist   255

Jazz in Perspective   256
The Innovators: The Characteristics and Artists of Mainstream Hard Bop   256
    Art Blakey (1919–1990) Carries the Message   258
    Other Hard-Bop Messengers   260
More About Funky, Soul Jazz and the 1950s and 1960s   264
Organ Trios and the Guitar   265
    Wes Montgomery (1923–1968)   265
    Jimmy Smith (1925–2005)   266
Everlasting Big Bands   268
Defining Postmodernism   270
    Ornette Coleman (1930–) and His Disciples   271
The Innovators: Postmodern Jazz Comes of Age   276
    Charles Mingus (1922–1979)—The Underdog   276
The End of Modern Jazz Heralded by the Beginning of the Postmoderns   278
Milestones: Chronicle of Historic Events   280
Chapter Summary   282
Key Terms   283
Study Questions   283

12 Miles and Miles of Miles: Miles Davis and His Sidemen Redefine Postmodern Jazz   285

Jazz in Perspective   286
The Music   287
The Early Miles   287
The First Great Quintet   289
Modal Jazz   290
    Miles and Gil   294
The Second Great Quintet   296
The Electronic Jazz–Rock Fusion Period   300
Davis Sidemen Become Major Forces   305
    John Coltrane (1926–1967)   306
    Wayne Shorter (1933–)   312
    Herbie Hancock (1940–)   313
Milestones: Chronicle of Historic Events   314
Chapter Summary   317
Key Terms   318
Study Questions   318

13 The Electric 1970s and 1980s   321

Jazz in Perspective   321
The Music   322
Jazz and Rock: The Two-Way Connection   323
The Innovators: Living Electric in the Shadow of Miles Davis   325
    Weather Report   325
    Herbie Hancock and the Head Hunters   329
    John McLaughlin (1942–) and the Mahavishnu Orchestra   331
    Chick Corea (1941–)   333
Soul and Pop Instrumental Jazz   336
    David Sanborn (1945–)   336
    The Brecker Brothers   336
    Grover Washington, Jr. (1943–1999)   337
    Chuck Mangione (1940–)   337
The Signs of the Times: New Technologies and Changing Business Models   338
Milestones: Chronicle of Historic Events   339
Chapter Summary   340
Key Terms   341
Study Questions   342

14 The Unplugged, Eclectic 1970s and 1980s   343

Long Live Acoustic Jazz   343
The ECM Sound   344
The Innovators: The Rebirth of Acoustic Jazz   345
    Keith Jarrett (1945–)   345
Return of Expatriates Unleashes a Rebirth of Acoustic Jazz   349

Wynton Marsalis (1961–) and the Young Lions   350

The Freedom Fighters Take Risks   352
       Cecil Taylor (1929–)   354

Old Bottles, New Wines—Long Live Big Bands   356

The Changing Jazz Landscape as the Millennium Comes to a Close   357

Milestones: Chronicle of Historic Events   358

Chapter Summary   360

Key Terms   361

Study Questions   361

15 Jazz for a New Century   363

Jazz in Perspective   364

Trends in Contemporary Jazz   365

Established Artists Offer Seasoned Jazz   367
       John Scofield (1951–) and Joe Lovano (1952)   367
       Michael Brecker (1949–2007) and Pat Metheny (1954–)   367

Popular Music Influences   371
       Tim Hagans (1954–)   372

Vocal Renaissance   374
       Esperanza Spalding (1984–)   375

Contemporary Women Emerging as Innovators   377
       Maria Schneider (1960–)   378

Jazz as a Global Music   382
       Afro-Cuban and Latin Jazz   382
       Danilo Pérez (1965–)   382

Jazz as an International Language   384
       Rudresh Mahanthappa and Vijay Iyer   387

The New Innovators: 21st-Century Emerging Artists   389
       Jason Moran (1975–)   390

Closing Thoughts   391

Milestones: Chronicle of Historic Events   392

Chapter Summary   396

Key Terms   397

Study Questions   397

Appendix I: Glossary of Terms   399

Appendix II: Suggested Jazz DVDs and Videos   411

Biographical   409

Historical Documentaries   410

Performance/Instructional   410

Important Feature Films   411

Appendix III: Chapter Notes and Additional Sources   415

Index   429

Photos

August Wilson Theatre (formerly Virginia Theatre)/Neil Simon Theatre 52nd Street, Manhattan, New York City. May 2007 ... xxiv

American bandleader James Reese Europe (1881–1919) poses (center, with baton) with members of his Clef Club Band, New York, 1914 ... 3

Original Dixieland Jass Band promotional photo ... 5

Jazz singer Joe Williams ... 7

The World Saxophone Quartet performing in 1992 ... 9

"Mother of the Blues" Ma Rainey on sheet-music cover ... 13

Old-style mechanical metronome ... 15

Gertrude "Ma" Rainey (1886–1939) and her Georgia Jazz Band, Chicago, 1923 ... 25

American jazz musician Louis Armstrong (1901–1971) smiles as he poses on stage with a band for the WMSB radio station in New Orleans, Louisiana, 1920s ... 26

Jazz musicians performing in a nightclub ... 33

The typical jazz drum set ... 35

April 16, 1912: The front-page *New York Times* newspaper headline announces the sinking of *The Titanic* ocean liner ... 45

Map tracing Christopher Columbus's voyages, which resemble slave-trade routes ... 51

Slaves returning from the cotton fields in South Carolina, c.1860 ... 54

Fisk Jubilee Singers ... 55

Bessie Smith, "Empress of the Blues" ... 59

Promotional photo, c.1930, of W.C. Handy, "Father of the Blues" ... 61

1899 sheet-music cover of Scott Joplin's "Maple Leaf Rag" ... 65

Portrait of American ragtime composer and pianist Scott Joplin (1868–1917), c.1910 ... 66

Player piano roll of Scott Joplin's "Maple Leaf Rag," patented September 13, 1904 ... 67

An American suffragette wears a sign proclaiming "Women! Use your vote," c.1920 ... 75

Portrait of the Buddy Bolden Band, New Orleans, Louisiana, c.1900 ... 81

The Original Dixieland Jass Band ... 84

Pianist, composer, arranger, singer, and bandleader Lilian Hardin Armstrong   86

King Oliver's Creole Jazz Band in the early 1920s   87

Composer and pianist Jelly Roll Morton at the piano   89

Louis Armstrong and his Hot Five   92

Sidney Bechet plays clarinet for a Blue Note Records session, June 8, 1939   94

Henry Ford and his son Edsel in front of their new model in New York in
    1927–1933   99

Marathon dance competitions were part of the growing phenomenon of youth
    culture in the 1920s, Chicago   101

Bix Beiderbecke and the Wolverines in the Gennett Recording Studios, in 1924,
    in New York   103

Cornetist Bix Beiderbecke (1903–1931) poses for a portrait, c.1925   105

Frankie Trumbauer and unidentified guitarist   107

Paul Whiteman and his orchestra   109

A crowd of depositors outside the American Union Bank in New York, having
    failed to withdraw their savings before the bank collapsed   112

Exterior of the Renaissance Casino ballroom in Harlem, New York, late 1920s   114

James P. Johnson poses for a studio portrait in 1921   115

Corner of Lennox Avenue and 147th Street in Harlem showing the exterior
    of the M&S Douglas Theatre and a sign for the Cotton Club a few doors
    down, 1927   125

Jazz pianist Teddy Wilson playing with a quartet during the set break of
    Benny Goodman's band, because racially mixed bands were not the rule in
    New York City at the "Madhattan Room" in the Hotel Pennsylvania   131

Bandleader, pianist, composer/arranger Fletcher Henderson   133

Coleman Hawkins, "the father of jazz tenor saxophone"   135

Duke Ellington and his band performing at the legendary Cotton Club   139

Dancers performing onstage at the Cotton Club   141

Composer Duke Ellington, singer Ivie Anderson, and drummer Sonny Greer pose
    for a portrait with the orchestra in 1943, in Los Angeles, California   143

Bandleader and clarinetist Benny Goodman (center) performs for a large crowd at
    Manhattan Beach, New York, August 11, 1938   148

The Benny Goodman Sextet   149

Guitarist Charlie Christian on stage with the Benny Goodman Orchestra, in
    New York, c.1940   150

Big-Band Leader Artie Shaw performs in 1945, Los Angeles, California   151

December 8, 1941: The front page of the New York World Telegram announces
    Japanese air attack at Pearl Harbor, commencing the U.S. entry into
    World War II   159

The Count Basie Orchestra performs on stage in Chicago in 1940   162

Count Basie with his "All American Rhythm Section"   163

Tenor saxophonist Lester Young performs while holding his instrument in his classic sideways style — 165

Pianist, composer, arranger Mary Lou Williams — 168

Billie Holiday singing at a Decca recording session, c.1946 — 170

Ella Fitzgerald, the "First Lady of Song," 1940 — 172

Art Tatum Trio — 175

Special edition of *Jazzmen*, produced by the Armed Services and designed to fit in soldiers' knapsacks — 177

The ruins of a cinema stand stark against the rubble after the atomic bomb dropped on Hiroshima August 8, 1945, brought World War II to a close — 189

The Onyx jazz club in New York, advertising singer Maxine Sullivan — 193

The club named after Charlie Parker, located at 1678 Broadway, New York — 195

Dizzy Gillespie, with characteristic puffed cheeks and upturned trumpet — 200

Jay McShann Orchestra in New York, 1942 — 201

Charlie Parker, with Miles Davis, trumpet; Tommy Potter, bass — 202

Pianist Earl "Bud" Powell — 203

Tenor saxophonist Dexter Gordon in Los Angeles, 1947 — 205

Thelonious Monk at Minton's Playhouse — 207

Drummer Max Roach — 210

Vocalist Sarah Vaughan — 211

Latin jazz singer and bandleader Machito (Frank Raul Grillo) holding maracas, while leading his band — 214

Saxophonist James Moody, Cuban conga player Chano Pozo, and trumpeter Dizzy Gillespie performing in 1948 — 215

Race riots and picketers in Birmingham, Alabama — 225

Miles Davis recording in 1959 — 231

The Dave Brubeck Quartet, with Brubeck at the piano, Paul Desmond on saxophone, Eugene Wright on bass, and Joe Morello on drums, in 1959 — 236

Pianist Bill Evans — 238

Stan Getz in a live performance — 244

Pianist Lennie Tristano — 247

American civil rights leader Dr. Martin Luther King Jr. (1929–1968) speaks at a rally held at the Robert Taylor Houses in Chicago, Illinois, 1960s — 255

Art Blakey and the Jazz Messengers play at the Birdhouse, a Chicago jazz club, 1961 — 258

Clifford Brown at a recording session — 262

Tenor saxophonist Sonny Rollins performs at the Berkshire Music Barn Jazz Festival in Lenox, MA, 1956 — 262

Guitarist Wes Montgomery, c.1960 — 266

Jimmy Smith sitting at the Hammond B3 organ — 266

Contemporary bandleader Stan Kenton rehearses his jazz band in London, in preparation for a performance at the Royal Albert Hall — 268

Saxophonist Ornette Coleman with trumpeter Don Cherry at the 5 Spot,
New York City 272

Jazz bassist and composer Charles Mingus 276

Apollo 11, the first manned lunar-landing mission, was launched on July 16,
1969, and Neil Armstrong and Buzz Aldrin became the first and second men
to walk on the moon 285

Miles Davis's nonet in a recording studio for the sessions released as
Birth of the Cool 288

John Coltrane, Cannonball Adderley, Miles Davis, and Bill Evans perform in the
studio, New York, May 26, 1958 292

Trumpeter Miles Davis and producer/arranger Gil Evans record the album
Quiet Nights in 1962 295

Miles Davis with Herbie Hancock, Ron Carter, and Wayne Shorter at the
1967 Newport Jazz Festival 297

Miles Davis performing in Copenhagen, 1973, wearing hip clothes of the day 304

John Coltrane performing on soprano saxophone with his quartet in West
Germany, 1959 307

Demonstrators march up Avenue of Americas on their way to Central Park in
New York as part of a rally against the Vietnam War, April 5, 1969 321

The rock band Blood, Sweat and Tears performs on stage at the Longhorn Jazz
Festival, Dallas, Texas 324

Weather Report performs on stage at the Playboy Jazz Festival at the Hollywood
Bowl, Los Angeles, June 1981 328

Herbie Hancock using a portable synthesizer keyboard 330

Guitarist John McLaughlin and violinist Jean-Luc Ponty from the Mahavishnu
Orchestra perform in Amsterdam, the Netherlands, in 1974 332

Return To Forever performs in May 1977 335

Popular Philadelphia soulful saxophonist Grover Washington, Jr. 337

Chuck Mangione playing his signature flugelhorn 338

A demonstration outside the Whitehouse in support of the impeachment of
President Nixon (1913–1994) following the watergate revelations 343

Jazz pianist Keith Jarrett, c.1975 346

Dexter Gordon and quartet performing in the UK 349

Trumpeter/composer Wynton Marsalis in 1982 351

Pianist Cecil Taylor performs at Ronnie Scott's in London 354

Jazz pianist and composer Toshiko Akiyoshi conducts her orchestra, c.1977 357

U.S. President Bill Clinton plays a saxophone along with musician Everett Harp
at the Arkansas inaugural ball 20 January 1993 363

Michael Brecker performing with the Brecker Brothers at the New Orleans
Jazz & Heritage Festival 369

Contemporary guitarist Pat Metheny 369

Popular smooth-jazz artist Chris Botti 371

Trumpeter/composer Tim Hagans at the 2008 IAJE Conference in Toronto, Canada   372

Diana Krall performing in 2004 at the Mountain Winery, in Saratoga, California   374

Esperanza Spalding performs at the 4th Annual Roots Picnic at the Festival Pier,
in Philadelphia, Pennsylvania, June 4, 2011   375

Maria Schneider conducts the Maria Schneider Orchestra on stage during the
Festival Internacional de Jazz de Barcelona at Palau De La Musica, in Barcelona,
Spain, 2011   379

Pianist Danilo Pérez   383

Jason Moran performs at Thelonious Monk Town Hall 50th Anniversary
Celebration, 2009   390

Examples

2.1   Graphic representation of "Happy Birthday"   14

2.2   Illustration of a simple syncopation in measure 1 that results from handclaps on off beats that create a tension between major beats represented by the foot tapping a steady pulse. By the second beat of the second measure, the handclaps are lined up precisely with the foot tapping on beats 2, 3, and 4, hence no syncopation and no tension   17

2.3   Using similar graphics, the following example illustrates a simple polyrhythm. In this case, the foot taps indicate a 3/4 meter and fundamental rhythm. The hand-clapping introduces a new rhythm in opposition to the foot tapping. If the foot tapping suddenly stops, the continuing handclaps give the illusion of 2/4 meter. The combined result when both are executed simultaneously is a polyrhythm   17

2.4   Two-octave C scale. Raised half-steps in between each scale note (black keys) are labeled above as sharps   19

2.5   Chord symbols in a typical progression that jazz musicians must learn to interpret   20

2.6   Visualization of monophonic texture. The light, horizontal, wavy line represents the melodic shape of a solo singer. There are no other layers present in this single-dimensional texture   21

2.7   Visualization of homophonic texture. The wavy, horizontal line represents the melodic shape of a solo singer. The vertical bars represent chords, with darker shades indicating major chords, and lighter shades representing minor chords   21

2.8   Visualization of polyphony. The light, horizontal, wavy lines represent the melodic shape of a solo singer and a second melodic voice complementing the primary vocal melody below it. The vertical bars represent chords, with darker shades indicating major chords, and lighter shades representing minor chords. Black dots represent a rising and falling bass line in counterpoint with the melody line. The entire texture, with multiple layers of activity, is described as polyphonic   21

2.9   Lowered third, fifth and seventh (E flat, G flat, B flat) are called "blue notes" and are indicated in the following keyboard example   24

2.10 Typical jazz chord progression illustrated by symbols   27

3.1   Swing ride cymbal pattern   36

3.2   Visual notations of special effects associated with jazz   38

Figures

1.1	Jazz styles timeline	10
7.1	Typical big-band seating arrangement	128
7.2	Memorable Swing Era hits and associated bands	153
7.3	Important artists to emerge from Woody Herman and Stan Kenton bands	154
7.4	Popular vocalists and associated bands	154
8.1	Cost of living index, c.1940	167
8.2	Well-known territory bands and their locales	167
9.1	Comparison of swing and bebop styles	198
10.1	Comparison of bebop and cool styles	230
11.1	Jazz Messengers Sidemen	259
11.2	Horace Silver Sidemen	259
11.3	A study in contrasts: A comparison in the characteristics of free jazz and more traditionally grounded, modern mainstream jazz styles	275
12.1	Miles Davis's innovations	305
12.2	John Coltrane's innovations	311
14.1	Distinguishing characteristics of Keith Jarrett's music	347
15.1	Late 20th- and early 21st-century trends and artists in jazz	366
15.2	21st-century women in jazz	380
15.3	21st-century emerging innovators	389

Preface

I do not agree that the layman's opinion is less of a valid judgment of music than that of a professional musician. In fact, I would often rely more on the judgment of a sensitive layman than that of a professional ...
—Jazz Pianist Bill Evans, from *The Universal Mind of Bill Evans*

Jazz is about America. It is American as apple pie and baseball, but surprisingly few people fully understand it or appreciate its wonder and appeal. Jazz represents the spirit and cultural fabric of America and has served as the basis of most popular music styles. Perhaps this is why our lives are invaded daily with jazz music – on television, in commercials selling everything from cars to banks and clothing, in films, in elevators and doctors' offices, in restaurants and shopping malls and countless other pubic places. It is music that evokes basic human emotions and can be soothing, chilling, sensual, raucous, uplifting, thought provoking, transformational, spiritual, meditative, annoying, or even jarring. Sometimes it strikes controversy among listeners. Anyone is capable of enjoying these fundamental feelings, but the experience is enhanced beyond expectation when one knows more about how the music is produced, its roots, developments and place in American history.

Pictured on the front cover is Swing Street, 52nd Street in New York City in 1948. It was *the* place to hear jazz in the mid-20th Century. Miles Davis, Charlie Parker, Billie Holiday Dizzy Gillespie, and performers from the earlier "Swing Era" could be heard in clubs like the Onyx and Three Deuces that lined the street between 5th and 7th Avenue as shown in the cover photo. Jazz in the 1930s and '40s was America's popular music. It was embedded in American culture and was the soundtrack for American life. The jazz musician helped to tell our country's story at nightclubs, dance halls, and on records and radio. Their music was accessible, daring and represented freedom to the outside world.

This same street shown in the 2007 photo overleaf by comparison looks quite different though still the home for aspects of the entertainment business. Jazz was associated with entertainment in its early years and considered forbidden fruit by some. Over time Jazz has gained a respect and stature shared by art music, studied and analyzed much like Western classical music. Jazz is now found in most university curricula, cultivated in high school and middle schools jazz bands, and no longer associated with underbelly of society. Jazz has become and international language recognized as an American tradition. We invite you to explore and experience this unique national treasure, listen to landmark recordings and hear the stories of the artists who changed American culture.

Experiencing Jazz, Second Edition, places the music in an historical, cultural, and social context of American society. By placing Jazz within the context of social history, students better understand

August Wilson Theatre (formerly Virginia Theatre)/Neil Simon Theatre 52nd Street, Manhattan, New York City. May 2007

its relevance. It also helps them to relate the music to their own interest areas, and to understand why, to some extent, the music may have developed as it did. In this way, *Experiencing Jazz, Second Edition*, goes beyond many textbooks.

COVERAGE

Experiencing Jazz provides clear explanations of each jazz style and how it contrasts or is similar to other styles. Each style is presented in association with its primary innovators. The material is presented in a logical chronological sequence, but art is never that clean and easy to categorize or sort out. The reader will find the occasional paradox within a single chapter created by the juxtaposition of one style against a polar opposite. This approach was chosen rather than compartmentalizing styles and artists and confining their discussions to nice, cleanly sectionalized chapters. The multiplicity of styles is precisely what was encountered at the time, particularly from about 1950 on, leaving audiences, critics and the musicians to make sense of it all. To frame the socio-cultural backdrop and keep its importance at the fore, each chapter begins with a section described as "Jazz in Perspective" and closes with a "Chronicle of Historic Events," serving as a reminder of the larger American fabric in which the music discussed throughout the chapter is an important thread.

Experiencing Jazz—the textbook and website with streamed music—provide the reader with an understanding of how jazz works, how and why it evolved, who its primary innovators were, how to listen to it, and how in some cases jazz has been informed by certain aspects of American society including the evolution of new technologies that parallel the growth of jazz. The book and website familiarize the student with the basic building blocks of music as they relate to a discussion of jazz. Without an elementary understanding of music construction and jazz performance practices, it is difficult to fully appreciate a jazz performance. It is for this reason that such topics are discussed in Chapters 2 and 3 rather than at the end of the book as appendices. *Experiencing Jazz* is designed to create educated listeners, not just to present facts, dates, figures, lists of tunes and performers.

Each style chapter includes a retrospective glimpse at the reception of jazz in America by providing the reader with some insight into how the music was perceived by critics, historians and fans.

CHAPTER ORGANIZATION

Fifteen chapters in all, the text is designed exclusively for the non-musician, carefully defining basic musical concepts as they relate to an understanding of a jazz performance. Such concepts are reinforced throughout the book.

- All key terms are shown in bold with immediate definitions. A comprehensive glossary of terms is included as an appendix.
- Explanations of fundamental musical concepts are often accompanied by graphic illustrations, making such concepts easier to understand by the non-musician.
- Each historic chapter begins with a section "Jazz in Perspective" that provides a context and historic backdrop for the music being discussed.
- Each historic chapter ends with a "Chronicle of Historic Events," once again reminding the reader of how jazz styles are woven into the fabric of American culture at the time.
- Specific references are made to the website where activities are provided to support the chapter.
- Each jazz style is carefully examined through discussion and comparison to performance characteristics of earlier jazz styles. Helpful quick reference comparative and descriptive tables are also provided to summarize salient characteristics.
- Chapters focus on the primary innovators including the bands and soloists and what made their work innovative.
- Listening guides are provided in each chapter to serve as road maps through each featured audio track. These guides focus on important points using laymen terms or terms that have been well defined and used throughout the text.
- Discussions of how jazz was received and marketed are also included.
- Chapter summaries and helpful study guides including a list of key performers, bands, terms and places along with review questions are found at the end of each chapter. Supplementary listening lists are also included at the close of each chapter.

NEW TO THIS EDITION

Since jazz is in a constant state of change it stands to reason that this second edition of *Experiencing Jazz* has been significantly revised:

- A final chapter addresses jazz at the close of the 20th century and the first decade of this new millennium.
- New sections about the internationalization of jazz as a global language and women in jazz have been added to the final chapter along with discussions and new recordings showing contemporary trends.
- Since a book about jazz should emphasize the music, a comprehensive collection of audio tracks—to accompany any text—is provided.
- Improved discussions of fundamental musical concepts as they relate to jazz performance are provided to cater to the needs of a non-musician in grasping basic musical concepts as they relate to a better understanding of jazz.
- Discussions of Afro-Cuban and Latin jazz trends are now integrated chronologically throughout the book.
- The narrative has been streamlined, reducing the page count.
- New links to historic recordings only recently made available by the Library of Congress.
- A new, greatly enhanced website providing streamed audio tracks, video, and additional supplementary materials including more listening guides for landmark recordings not provided in the companion audio collection.

MUSIC TRACKS

Experiencing Jazz offers a web streamed, comprehensive audio collection featuring landmark recordings by leading performers that illustrate the various styles discussed throughout the text. A complete list of tracks is included inside the covers. This collection is quite comprehensive, providing expanded coverage of women in jazz, Afro-Cuban and Latin jazz styles, and often overlooked styles or artists such as African music, rural blues, ragtime, organ trios, early symphonic jazz, vocalists and third-stream jazz. Some texts appear to be biased against certain styles, but *Experiencing Jazz* does not take sides and presents what listeners need to know in order to formulate their own aesthetic.

Listening guides that track each recording as it is streamed from the companion website clarify the listening experience. The website also includes additional listening guides for supplementary tunes easily found in most library collections or online suppliers. These guides are designed specifically for the non-musician and draw on skills acquired through readings about the elements of jazz and jazz performance practice presented in the first three chapters. Nothing has been assumed of the reader in terms of prerequisite knowledge. It is not enough to merely read about jazz, it must be keenly listened to and *Experiencing Jazz* provides all the necessary guidance to engage with the recordings and live performances.

A collection of audio recordings, combined with numerous video and audio tutorials found on the website reinforce the principles and performance practices associated with jazz. Emphasis is placed on artists who made and are making significant contributions to jazz rather than confusing the reader with lengthy lists of performers who, while their contributions to the evolution of jazz should be noted, are not considered in retrospect as major trendsetters or innovators. Special attention has been paid through the text design to emphasize one or two artists in each chapter who exemplify a particular style or trend. The decision to feature one artist over another was difficult but based logically on the artists innovative impact, longevity, and their overall impact and contributions to further developing the music. A case could certainly be made to highlight others.

LISTENING GUIDES

These are provided to most of the historically significant recordings streamed and from the companion website. The website also includes additional listening guides for supplementary study of tunes easily found in most library collections or online suppliers. These guides are designed specifically for the non-musician and draw on skills acquired through readings about the elements of jazz and jazz performance practice presented in the first three chapters. Nothing has been assumed of the reader in terms of prerequisite knowledge. It is not enough to merely read about jazz it must be keenly listened to and *Experiencing Jazz* provides all the necessary guidance to fully appreciate the recordings and live performance.

Not every significant recording or artist can be represented in any collection, no matter how extensive. The selection of recordings to include confronted the author with difficult choices as it does most teachers. In some cases recording companies were unwilling to license some landmark recordings, however, excellent alternatives were found and listening guides for others not included are found on the website.

ONLINE RESOURCES FOR STUDENTS AND TEACHERS

www.routledge.com/cw/lawn

Since this book embraces and recognizes the needs of non-musicians, web-based materials were developed to enhance student's understanding and appreciation of jazz by providing a more informed listening experience through audio, video and interactive tutorials. The companion website carefully parallels Chapters 1–3 in the text, providing audio and visual examples that bring to life the basic elements of music, jazz performance practices, improvisation styles, the instruments associated with jazz, and the concepts that help to define it. Chapters 4–15 provide suggestions for supplemental material found on the website such as interviews with innovative artists, YouTube links, and so on. A wealth of support material is included here that closely follows readings in the text. The website should therefore be considered as a closely integrated companion to the book. While it would be useful to have ready access to the website as each chapter is studied, it is not imperative or mandatory. All web-based activities are highlighted with icons throughout the text to direct students and teachers to additional information that can be found on the site.

This website provides a wide range of support for the students and teachers including:

- Interactive materials that clearly explain fundamentals of melody, rhythm, harmony, form, blues, and performance practice in jazz including improvisation
- Instructional videos to provide a keen awareness of form, the instruments associated with jazz including Latin percussion and their roles in an ensemble, solo jazz piano styles, and jazz drum-set performance techniques associated with jazz styles.
- An audio introduction to each instrument associated with jazz that also acquaints the user with special effects, performance techniques and brass mutes associated with the jazz style. There is an instrument identification quiz provided as well.
- Additional listening guides for recordings not provided in the streamed audio collection.
- Photos and documents that relate to each stylistic era.
- Numerous audio excerpts from interviews with noted musicians including Miles Davis, Gil Evans, Chick Corea, Keith Jarrett, Charles Mingus, Herbie Hancock, Pat Metheny, Charlie Parker, Dexter Gordon, Bud Powell, Stan Kenton, Stan Getz, John Coltrane, Billie Holiday,

Louis Armstrong, Gerry Mulligan, Dizzy Gillespie, and others bring authenticity to the text and the total experience.
- A condensed history of disc recording and discussion of the relationship of this medium to jazz.
- A glossary of terms that is linked to the any music specific terms used on the website.

Jazz has become a universal music that has gone global, recognized worldwide and identified with the United States, but no longer "owned" by Americans. It is a unique American nationalist style representing the most significant cultural contribution that the US has made to the global arts landscape. Jazz has become synonymous with modern American thought and is a metaphor for democracy and freedom of expression. It should be studied, experienced and treasured!

Richard J. Lawn
Summer 2012

ACKNOWLEDGMENTS

I offer my sincere thanks and appreciation to the following individuals for their significant contributions and assistance during various stages in the development of this text and companion materials.

Special thanks to: Dan Morgenstern, Tad Hershorn, and the staff of the Rutgers Institute of Jazz Studies; UT–Austin College of Fine Arts Information Technology staff Jim Kerkhoff, Frank Simon, Andy Murphy, and Tyson Breaux; Paul Young, Glenda Smith, Todd Hastings, and Paul White who, as students at The University of Texas, helped in the development of a CD-ROM as a prototype of the new website; David Aaberg for his tenacious editorial suggestions and concise chapter summaries; Ben Irom and Mark "Kaz" Kazanoff, who helped to create some of the listening guides; David Fudell and the staff of the Center for Instructional Technologies at The University of Texas; The Harry Ransom Humanities Research Center at UT-Austin; Jack Cooper for his composition *Video Blues*; Austin, Texas musicians Greg Wilson, Randy Zimmerman, Pat Murray, Mike Koenning, Craig Biondi, Paul Haar, John Fremgen, Steve Snyder, Chris Maresh, Eric Middleton, Russell Scanlon, and John Kreger for their recorded contributions; Charlie Richard, Steve Hawk, and the Hawk–Richard Jazz Orchestra, whose Sea Breeze Jazz CD (SB-2093) *The Hawk Is Out* provided a source for brief audio examples; Paul DeCastro, Jeff Benedict, and members of Rhumbumba for their self-titled Sea Breeze Jazz CD (SB-3067) that provided Afro-Cuban examples; members of the Third Coast Jazz Orchestra, whose Sea Breeze Jazz CD (SB-2116) *Unknown Soldiers* provided a source for additional audio clips; Marc Dicciani and Marlon Simon from the University of the Arts School of Music for their Afro-Cuban demonstrations; Sara MacDonald from the UArts Library; Wesley Hall for his assistance in gaining permissions for the website; Denny Tek for her perseverant photo research; and Constance Ditzel and the staff at Routledge, Taylor & Francis Group, for believing in the lasting value of this project.

PART 1

Understanding Jazz

CHAPTER 1

The Nature of Jazz

*Jazz isn't a noun. It's a verb. It's a process, a way of being, a way
of thinking.*[1]
—Pat Metheny

American bandleader
James Reese Europe
(1881–1919) poses
(center, with baton)
with members of his
Clef Club Band, New
York, 1914

EXPERIENCING MUSIC . . . EXPERIENCING JAZZ

Music is the most elusive, abstract, and in some ways most intangible of all art forms. It cannot be touched, felt, or seen. It does, however, evoke any number of emotional responses, which is why it has become such an important part of the human experience. The only way to truly understand music, like any art form, is to experience it. No art form can be genuinely appreciated without an intimate experience with it. By working with clay, one gains a new perspective on what the sculptor faces when creating a work of art. By closely examining jazz performance practice, one gains a new view and appreciation of the music-making process.

Jazz is a performance art—a spontaneous art designed for the moment. Although it can be described in words, analyzed, and placed in a historic continuum, it cannot be fully understood and appreciated without the music being experienced first hand. Yet words alone cannot do justice to the listening experience, and it is important to understand that it is the music that points to the words we use to describe it. Jazz is a work in progress, an ongoing experiment and music in constant evolution. To quote jazz guitarist Larry Coryell, "jazz is a workshop." One of the enduring qualities of jazz, and a defining characteristic, has been its ability to change, chameleon-like in nature, while absorbing every style it encounters, resulting in a new by-product.

Like any of the other art forms, music can be divided into numerous subcategories that, over time, have been described in great detail and consequently named. Words such as swing, bebop, cool, fusion, and smooth jazz have been coined in an effort to describe and compartmentalize jazz styles. It is the naming of these styles that often tends to confuse the listener, as there are often only subtle differences between them. The naming of various styles is the result of historians and critics attempting to better explain and describe the music. To some extent, these stylistic names are also the result of commercial marketing strategies. The term "jazz," used to describe this uniquely American music, is no less confusing than the terms "classical" or "pop" music. Each of these general headings can imply numerous substyles. What is unique about jazz compared with classical music, among other things, is the rate at which jazz styles have evolved. In a mere 100 years, this American music has been transformed to include countless innovations in performance practice. These stylistic changes are so significant that the jazz of today bears only subtle similarities to the earliest forms from 100 years ago, and yet buried beneath the surface are common threads binding all of the uniquely different styles together to form a rich tapestry. The fun lies in finding these common characteristics. The essence of jazz is its ability to absorb, transform, and change. Like any art form, it is periodically renewed by various influences. Throughout its development, jazz has been viewed variously as folk music, entertainment, and art music. All three views often existed simultaneously, a fact still true today. It is a music that crosses all social, economic, racial, and geographic boundaries. Centuries from now, only the unique American innovations will be recognized and remembered. These will be sports such as baseball, inventions such as the personal computer, and, no doubt, jazz. Its influence has endured, and it is a unique, original American art form that has been designated a national treasure by the U.S. government.

THAT FOUR-LETTER WORD

It wasn't that long ago we used to hear the word "jazz" frequently in common speech. It first appeared in American vocabulary in the early 1900s. Phrases such as "jazz up your wardrobe," "put some jazz in your savings account," "own the jazziest car on the road," and "quit jazzin' me!" came into being and were commonly heard. In the hit stage and film musical, *Chicago*, the most popular and most performed song is "All That Jazz." The storyline takes place in the "gangsta" days of Al Capone in the 1920s, when jazz was in the early stages of becoming America's popular music.

Existing as a slang term before it was used to describe music, its origins have puzzled historians for many years. Theories about the origins of the word jazz are largely unsubstantiated. Some have associated the word with the red-light district of New Orleans. Garvin Bushell, a circus band musician from New Orleans, offers the following observation:

> They said that the French had brought the perfume industry with them to New Orleans, and the oil of jasmine was a popular ingredient locally. To add it to perfume was called "jassing it up." The strong scent was popular in the red light district, where a working girl might approach a perspective customer and say, "Is jazz on your mind tonight, young fellow?"[2]

As late as 1947, Berry's *American Dictionary of Slang* cited the word under copulate. The term jazz was supposedly related to the act itself—"he's jazzin' her"[3] (a line from the musical *Chicago*). The *New York Times* used the term in its February 2, 1917 issue, in an advertisement taken by Reisenweber's club to promote "The First Eastern Appearance of the Famous Original Dixieland Jazz Band."[4] According to Nick LaRocca, the group's cornetist, "jass" was changed to "jazz" to discourage people from defacing signs by erasing the letter "j." The associations of the word jazz to vulgarity, sex, and the bordello, coupled with the many styles that the word could describe, probably explains why some jazz musicians rarely, if ever, use the word in discussing their own music.[5]

Others attribute the word's origins to linguistic variations. One writer points out the word's relationship to the French word *jaser*, which means "to chat," "to chatter," "to prattle," or "talk

Original Dixieland Jass Band promotional photo

a lot and say nothing." Prior to the Louisiana Purchase in 1803, the French owned the Mississippi Delta area, often referred to as the birthplace of jazz.

Creoles, a racial mix resulting from unions between French, African-Americans and sometimes Spanish, spoke a hybrid form of French. Some theorists suggest that the word "jazz" in Creole meant to speed things up. Another theory to consider is the claim that the term jazz is derived from West African languages, a natural conclusion because the Gold (west) Coast of Africa served as the point of origin for many slaves. Early jazz artists' names such as Charles and James morphed from their formal spellings to nicknames such as Chaz and Jas or Jazz.[6] A 1919 article in the *Music Trade Review* refers to the wild, barbaric music played by trumpeter Jasbo Brown after he'd had a few drinks. Patrons who enjoyed his musically gregarious behavior shouted, "More Jasbo," which eventually distorted to just "more jazz."[7] Jazz historian Robert Goffin attributed the word to a black musician named Jess who played in a "jerky, halting style." As early as 1904, James Reese Europe, a black society bandleader, believed the word was a distortion of the name of a New Orleans band known as Razz's Band. Other historians speculate that the term "jazz" stemmed from a vaudeville expression meaning to excite, stir things up, or make things go faster.[8]

As jazz developed into a more sophisticated, acceptable art form, efforts were even made to rename the music and discard "jazz," owing to its undesirable connotations. In 1949, *Down Beat* magazine sponsored a contest to find a new name for jazz. The publisher announced prizes and a distinguished panel of judges (including the well-known, contemporary big-band leader Stan Kenton and author S.I. Hayakawa). After months of deliberation, the winner was announced— CREWCUT. The winner collected her $1,000 first prize from the magazine and defended her entry as "simply the exact opposite of the slang name for 'classical' music—'Longhair'." Other winning selections were Amerimusic, Jarb, Syncope, Improphony, and Ragtibop. The results were announced in the magazine, but this surprising statement was added: "The judges were unanimous in the opinion, shared by the editors of *Down Beat*, that none of the hundreds of words submitted is adequate as a substitute for Jazz."[9]

Whatever the true story is about the derivation of this uniquely American word, the music and the word quickly gained recognition worldwide. One can fully experience jazz only by exploring how it is unique, how it can be described and identified, and how to evaluate and appreciate its forms and variety.

 Before reading the following section, visit the website to listen to the collage recording that traces approximately 80 years of recorded jazz. Make note of how different each excerpt is from the others, and make a list of the similar and distinctly different features. Repeat this exercise once you have read the following section.

DEFINING JAZZ

Jazz is a direct result of West African influences on European-derived music styles and popular American music. Since its beginnings at the turn of the 19th to 20th centuries, it has shown an ability to absorb aspects of other music styles and transform them into something entirely new and different. Jazz is, therefore, both a noun and a verb, as it is a way of interpreting music. In true West African tradition, jazz is shaped by the performers' individual musical gestures and spontaneous variations. It is a music in which the performers assume the most prominent role and bear the greatest responsibility. It features certain instruments and special effects that are synonymous with the style. Many of these instrumental affectations may have been an effort to emulate the flexibility and expressiveness of the human voice. These instrumental effects alter and color the sound in unusual ways and exerted an impact on 20th century "classical" music. Although jazz is closely associated with certain instruments, any instrument can be used to imply

Jazz singer
Joe Williams

the style. A wide range of instrumentalists and/or singers can present jazz, from solo performers to large orchestras. Self-proclaimed inventor of jazz Jelly Roll Morton advocated that almost any kind of music could sound like jazz, as jazz is a way of playing and interpreting music in an individualistic and spontaneous way.

Emerging in the first decades of the 1900s as an unpolished folk music, jazz reflected diverse influences. Among them are the blues, marching bands, polkas, field hollers and work songs, religious music, ragtime, and, of course, West African, Latin, and Afro-Cuban music, with an emphasis on individualistic expression through improvisation. Spontaneity, rhythmic complexity, and a close association with dance are other characteristics shared by African music and jazz. Jazz has been a chameleon even since the beginning, absorbing and reflecting the musical influences present in America at the turn of the century.

Although jazz is a distinctive style, recognizable worldwide, it has been difficult to define and has confounded many critics and historians. The difficulty of defining jazz is exacerbated because it remains in a constant state of change, influenced by popular culture, advancements in technology, and the musicians' own desire for change and self-improvement. Therefore, like the music itself, there is no absolute set of criteria for defining it. Nonetheless, different combinations of certain traits can always be found in jazz music. Jazz is a rhythmically vibrant and complex music that often includes a rhythm section (piano, bass, and drums). It is this rhythm section that eventually inspires other popular American music styles such as R & B, blues, and various rock styles. The rhythms of jazz are richly complex, creating an element of tension. Rhythm is not the sole source of this tension, for it is also found in the sometimes-dissonant harmonies and complex improvisations associated with jazz.

Some definitions of jazz assert that swing, a certain rhythmic phenomenon, and improvisation are two absolute criteria for authentic jazz. Although these can be important features, they are not entirely unique to jazz, nor are they required for the music to be considered jazz. Much contemporary jazz post-1970 does not swing in the same way jazz was played in the 1940s. Music in a jazz style may not contain much improvisation, but can still be identified as jazz. On the other hand, some non-jazz may contain jazz characteristics. For example, does jazz saxophonist Phil Woods's improvised solo on Billy Joel's pop hit "Just the Way You Are" make it jazz? It is not uncommon to hear improvisation in many pop and rock performances.

Jazz has become a truly eclectic music, embracing musical styles from around the world and transforming them into a uniquely American form of artistic expression that frequently requires the performer to improvise. The blues, in itself an individualistic and spontaneous form of expression, remains an important component of jazz and a significant contribution by black Americans. Black performers have been the primary developers of jazz and blues, although some white performers and composers contributed significantly to advancing the music and to developing it as a viable commercial product. At the dawn of the 21st century, jazz can easily be considered one of the most significant musical accomplishments of the previous century and one that shows promise for continued advancement.

In conclusion, the following elements and features characterize all jazz styles:

1. Jazz evolved in the US at the dawn of the 20th century by absorbing characteristics from African music, blues, ragtime, marching bands, polkas, field hollers and work songs, religious music, Afro-Cuban and Latin music, and American folk music.
2. Jazz is an ever-changing style of music with multiple substyles and is significantly influenced by an evolving popular culture.
3. African-American performers have been the principal innovators throughout the history of jazz.
4. Jazz is a way of performing that places emphasis on interpretation, improvisation, and individualistic expression, in the African tradition.
5. It is usually the performer who is most important to a jazz performance, not the composer.
6. Although jazz began as a folk music and became an important form of music associated with entertainment, it gradually matured to become art music, to be taken as seriously as classical music.
7. Until rock 'n' roll attracted younger Americans' attention, jazz had been the soundtrack for American life.
8. Rhythmic complexity, inspired by a rhythm section of piano, bass and drums, and sometimes guitar, is a predominant feature of jazz, including the special swing feel attributed to some styles.
9. Some instruments, such as the saxophone, guitar, drum set, and mutes used to color the sound of brass instruments, originated with jazz.
10. Jazz is the most unique and indigenous American art form.

 The subsection "Characterizing Jazz," found in the corresponding chapter of the companion website, provides an excellent supplement to this section and includes excerpts of interviews with many prominent performers. These artists offer their own insights into what makes this music so special. Note: All terms in bold are defined in the glossary included in Appendix I of this book and on the website.

CHAPTER SUMMARY

Jazz is a music that developed in America at the dawn of the 20th century. Many styles of music and music-making that influenced the beginnings of jazz reflect the melting pot that is America. This mix includes elements from both European and African music. A product of these diverse influences, jazz is a music containing a great variety of substyles, from early ragtime and blues-influenced jazz to free jazz and rock-influenced fusion.

Succinctly defining the word "jazz," considering its many substyles and the fact that jazz is constantly changing, is challenging. Origins of the word itself are also murky, with no single

The World Saxophone Quartet performing in 1992

explanation substantiated. A change in approach to improvisation is one of the most important factors in the development of the various styles of jazz, and yet examples of jazz containing little or no improvisation exist. At one time, jazz was played exclusively in a swing feel. Approaches to playing swing evolved with each new style of jazz, and, because jazz continues to evolve and adapt, embracing music styles from around the world, jazz is no longer played exclusively in a swing feel. Certain instruments and performance techniques have become associated with jazz, which can be played or sung by any number of performers. Individuality, spontaneity, and the importance of the performer instead of the composer have always been at the core of jazz.

What can be unequivocally stated about jazz is that it was pioneered primarily by black Americans, is often improvised, is rhythmically driven, and combines European, African, American, and, sometimes, Afro-Latin elements. Further, jazz continually evolves as it is influenced by technology, current events, different cultures, and music from throughout the world.

STUDY QUESTIONS

1. What are some of the theories regarding the origins and derivation of the word "jazz"?

2. Name some of the identifying or salient characteristics of jazz, regardless of substyle.

3. Jazz was the result of what primary non-European or American influence?

4. What other styles of music, European or American, were factors in the formation of early jazz styles?

5. Is the composer or performer more important to the jazz style?

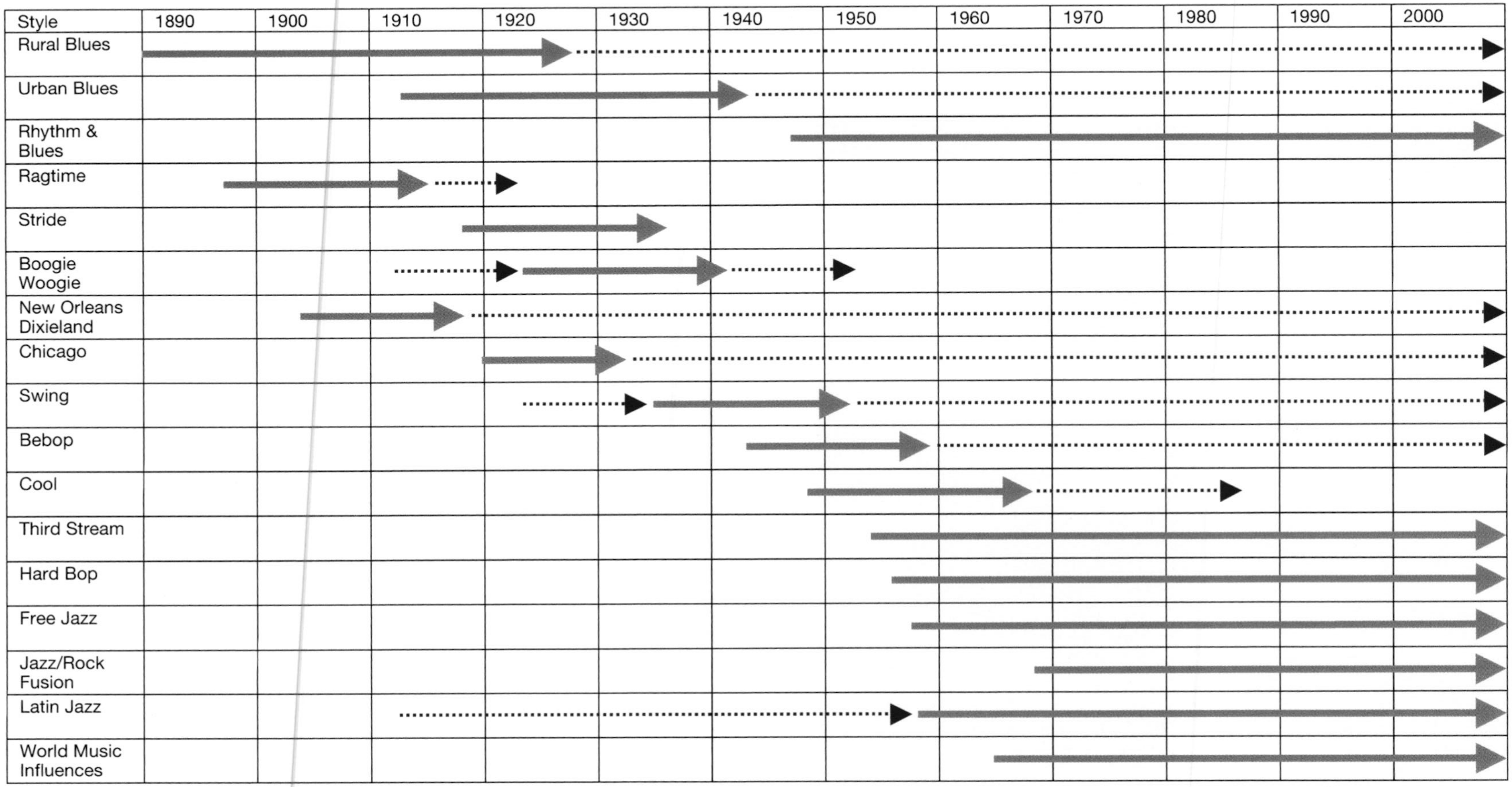

FIGURE 1.1 Jazz styles timeline

Solid line indicates dominant popular style, and dotted line indicates the beginnings of a style and/or its continuation beyond its period of peak popularity

6. Music from what continents or regions influenced the formation of jazz?

7. Can any piece of music that was not conceived as jazz be played in a jazz style? Explain your answer.

8. An aspect of rhythmic interpretation that is unique to jazz is called _____.

9. Define the term "Creole".

10. What style, born in America, is undoubtedly the most important African-American contribution to jazz?

11. What are the instruments or instrument groupings that are unique to jazz?

CHAPTER 2
The Elements of Jazz

Jazz did not exist until the 20th century. It has elements that were not present either in Europe or in Africa before this century. And at any of its stages it represents . . . a relationship among rhythm, harmony, and melody that did not exist before.[1]
—Martin Williams

"Mother of the Blues" Ma Rainey on sheet-music cover

Jazz, since its uncomplicated beginnings as a folk music, has evolved to become a complex and sophisticated music. Despite the many influences and changes that jazz has experienced over a century of development, and its uniqueness when compared with other music styles, jazz shares ingredients common to all forms of music.

 Although brief discussions of musical terms important to your understanding of jazz are provided throughout this chapter, you should refer to the website in order to more fully understand these concepts. The section entitled the "Elements of Jazz" provides audio demonstrations and more in-depth explanations of these terms and concepts.

Jazz can be examined and discussed in the same ways that apply to any style of music. All music is discussed in terms of rhythm, melody, harmony, form, and texture.

RHYTHM

Rhythm is accomplished through varying lengths of notes, combined with space, all in relationship to a steady pulse. Some notes in a melody last longer than others, and some move more quickly. So, duration is an expression of rhythm and time. Without rhythm, music has no sense of motion, and melodies would be monotonous and boring. It is the rhythm of music that propels it forward and ensures that it is not static. Without using complex musical notation, consider the graphic symbols in Example 2.1 that illustrates the familiar tune "Happy Birthday." Some notes are lower or higher in pitch (vertical scale), some are louder than others (indicated by darker images), and some are shorter or longer in duration (horizontal scale), indicating rhythm. Silence, or rests, seems to separate some of these notes. Sing the familiar tune to yourself as you move through the graphic from left to right.

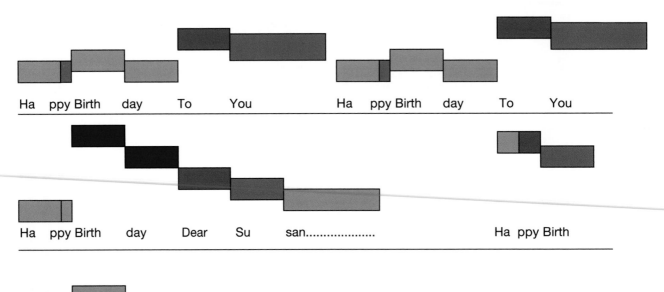

EXAMPLE 2.1 Graphic representation of "Happy Birthday"

Meter and Tempo

Meter defines the number of primary beats, or pulses, in each measure of music, and is the organization of rhythms. **Measure** (or **bar**) is a unit that serves as a container, holding a specific number of beats as defined by the meter. A waltz emphasizes a triple meter (1–2–3), where each measure has three beats, and a march features a duple meter (1–2), with two beats per measure.

Poetry has rhythm and meter. Sonnets, rhymes, and limericks all project rhythm and meter. Think of measures as inch marks on a ruler. In 4/4 meter, each beat would be represented by ¼-inch marks, as there are four quarters to each inch. The ¼-inch subdivision can be further divided into smaller increments, as is the case with music note values. To continue this analogy, how fast or slowly we move across a tape measure or yardstick, progressing from one inch to the next, is a measure of the tempo. **Tempo**, another concept important to the understanding of how music works, is an expression of pace or speed at which the music moves. It could also be compared to the pace of someone walking or running. Some songs seem to have no regular tempo, moving slowly and described as **rubato**.

It is safe to say that jazz performers and composers were content for decades to deal largely with music in duple meter—primarily 2/4 and 4/4 meters. For example, most ragtime piano music was written in 2/4 meter, and nearly all the instrumental jazz literature that followed well into the 1940s was in common time or 4/4 meter. Jazz musicians were most concerned during the first three decades of the formative years with honing skills as improvisers. Attention was focused on developing performance technique. It was not until the 1950s that jazz artists began to venture outside the safe confines of duple meters. Jazz waltzes were not popular until the 1950s and 1960s.

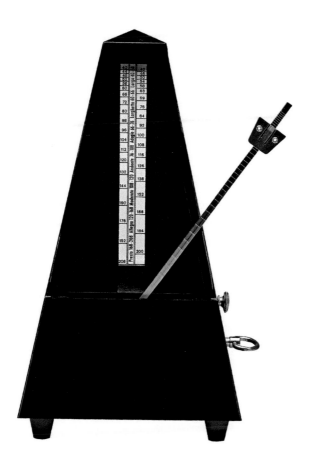

Old-style
mechanical
metronome

Listen to all or a portion of the following tracks, which serve as excellent examples of different meters. "Take Five," for example, is in 5/4 meter. Compare "Take Five" with "Every Tub," "Summertime," "Pent Up House" written in the more common 4/4 meter, or "La Fiesta," played in a fast 3/4 time. Also think about their differing tempos.

Symphony orchestras and bands have conductors to control the pace of the music—jazz ensembles have rhythm sections. There is flexibility in terms of tempo associated with a "classical" music ensemble performance. In larger ensembles such as symphony orchestras, the conductor controls the tempo. In smaller ensembles, the performers control the tempo and must work carefully together to adjust the tempo or risk a poor, disorganized performance. The rate of the steady pulse, or tempo, in a jazz or pop/rock group is consistent and generally maintained throughout the piece by the **rhythm section**, which is comprised of piano, bass, drums, and often guitar. Within this group of instruments, there is likely to exist a hierarchy of time-keeping responsibilities that may be somewhat dependent on the particular style of jazz. The other musicians in the ensemble must then strive to rhythmically coexist within this tempo. At times, performers in a jazz band may seem to rush or drag behind the rhythm section's steady pulse, but it is frequently by choice, not by error. The dragging sensation is described as **laying back** and is often associated with the sound of a particular band and helps to define its style.

The subject of rhythm as it relates to jazz is a thorny one that has provoked debate for many years. Attempts to define the special rhythmic qualities of jazz have sometimes ended in poetic metaphors and metaphysical phrases in attempts to make feelings and individual interpretations tangible. The very existence of a group of instruments described as the "rhythm section" points to the importance of this basic musical element to the jazz style. What other music ensemble, other than in related popular music styles that share similar roots with jazz (rock, R & B, pop), includes a group of instruments known as the "rhythm section"? The emphasis on steady rhythm is a distinguishing feature of this music, and, aside from the spontaneously improvised aspect of jazz, its unique rhythmic features are among the most important characteristics establishing jazz as a truly original style.

Listen to all or a portion of the following tracks from the online audio anthology, which serve as excellent examples of different tempos. Wynton Marsalis' "Delfeayo's Dilemma" presents the illusion of several different tempos. "Intuition" seems to have no set tempo, while "Poem for Brass" takes some time before a steady tempo is established. Compare these tracks with the slow, but steady, tempo of "Moon Dreams."

Rhythmic Devices Important to Jazz

The rhythmic terms syncopation and swing are synonymous with jazz. **Syncopation** occurs when a rhythm appears on a weak, normally un-emphasized portion of a beat (when your foot moves up), interacting with a regularly occurring rhythm or major beat emphasis (when your foot pats down). The rhythm that is normally un-emphasized becomes accented and creates a syncopation or tension.

A **polyrhythm** results when two or more different rhythms are played simultaneously, layered one on top of the other. One fundamental rhythm usually serves as the foundation, and other layers are added. The examples that follow clarify these two important concepts.

Much has been said about the predominance of syncopation in jazz, its importance in contributing to the unique nature of jazz rhythms, and the relationship to African music. To quote Gunther Schuller, from his book *Early Jazz*:

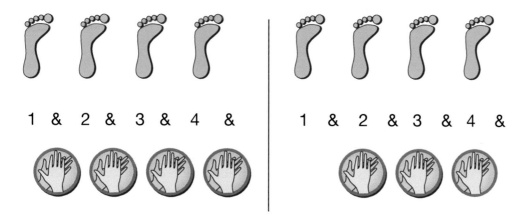

EXAMPLE 2.2 Illustration of a simple syncopation in measure 1 that results from handclaps on off beats that create a tension between major beats represented by the foot tapping a steady pulse. By the second beat of the second measure, the handclaps are lined up precisely with the foot tapping on beats 2, 3, and 4, hence no syncopation and no tension

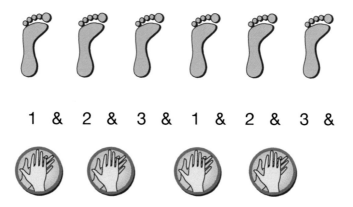

EXAMPLE 2.3 Using similar graphics, the following example illustrates a simple polyrhythm. In this case, the foot taps indicate a 3/4 meter and fundamental rhythm. The hand-clapping introduces a new rhythm in opposition to the foot tapping. If the foot tapping suddenly stops, the continuing handclaps give the illusion of 2/4 meter. The combined result when both are executed simultaneously is a polyrhythm

> By transforming his natural gift for against-the-beat accentuation into syncopation, the Negro was able to accomplish three things: he reconfirmed the supremacy of rhythm in the hierarchy of musical elements; he found a way of retaining the "democratization" of rhythmic impulses [meaning that any portion of a beat could have equal emphasis]; and by combining these two features with his need to conceive all rhythms as rhythmicized melodies, he maintained a basic, internally self-propelling momentum in his music.[2]

Schuller is also defining to some degree what **swing** is. It is this form of propulsion or forward momentum that we feel when something "swings."

Listen to the following track, which offers excellent examples of complex rhythms happening simultaneously and syncopations. The opening section of Keith Jarrett's "The Windup" (0:00–0:39) juxtaposes a regular rhythm played by one hand with improvised, syncopated rhythms that work against the regular rhythm and are played by the other hand. Listen to the "Bamaaya," the African music track in the online audio anthology, to hear complex polyrhythms played by the drummers.

Audio clips illustrating all of these terms used to describe various aspects of rhythm can be found in the corresponding chapter of the website. Here you can explore the subsection about rhythm.

Swing as an Aspect of Jazz Rhythm

Have you ever tried to explain how a food tastes to someone? It is almost impossible to truly appreciate the flavor of a particular food without actually tasting it. That same analogy is true for describing "swing." It is certainly one of the most difficult characteristics to define when discussing jazz rhythm. Musicians and analysts alike have struggled to respond to the frequently posed question—what is swing? Big-band leader Count Basie, when asked to define swing, said things such as, "pat your foot" or "tap your toe."[3] Jazz pioneer Louis Armstrong is reputed to have said, "If you have to ask, you'll never know."[4] Big-band Swing Era trumpeter Jonah Jones may have come closest when he implied that it was a feeling.[5] Duke Ellington defined swing as, "the un-mechanical but hard driving and fluid rhythm over which soloists improvise."[6] None of these responses, however, provides a precise, more scientific explanation of the rhythmic phenomenon that began to be described in the 1920s as "swing."

André Hodeir, author of the important 1956 publication *Jazz: Its Evolution and Essence*, said that: "jazz consists essentially of an inseparable but extremely variable mixture of relaxation and tension,"[7] and that the "feelings of tension and relaxation coexist at the same moment."[8] In other words, some performers are playing things on the beat, while others are simultaneously playing syncopated accents on other portions of the beat. The combined result is a forward momentum we describe as swing, and there can be many subtle variations of swing—as many variations as there are players. Swing can be compared to skipping. When we skip, we divide our even pace unevenly, which is a characteristic of swinging in jazz. We make an otherwise even-paced walk uneven; we make it skip, even though we may get from point A to point B in the same amount of time as it would have taken had we walked with an even pace (tempo).

A sound byte is worth 1,000 words in helping to define swing. Listen to The Count Basie Band play "Every Tub." This great band set the standard for swing, and the Basie rhythm section illustrates this concept at 0:32–0:55. You may be intrigued enough to listen to the entire track.

MELODY

Melody is the result of an organization of notes that move by varying distances—by step and leap—either ascending or descending, to form a musical statement. Melody is thought of as moving in a linear, horizontal fashion. A complete musical idea or statement is often termed a **phrase**. The term phrase can refer to a melodic, harmonic, or rhythmic statement. Short melodic phrases are strung together to create entire tunes.

The Count Basie recording of "Every Tub" on the companion website provides an excellent example of a musical phrase. Listen to 2:02–2:17 in this track to hear the repetitive melodic phrase played by the saxophones, with brass accompaniment.

Melody is by far the easiest ingredient to understand. Melodies can stand alone, be coupled with other melodies, or be sung/played with accompaniment. Melody is the aspect of most musical styles usually remembered more easily than harmony or even rhythm. A melody is often easy to recognize and remember because it may consist of only a few notes. Most listeners identify a lyric with a melody and hear them as one ingredient. Lyrics even help to clarify the overall form or architecture of a piece. Instrumental jazz is perhaps less easily grasped because it lacks a lyric to help listeners keep track of the various twists and turns of the melody. Remove the lyrics of a tune, and many listeners lose their way. The memorable melody of a show or pop tune that serves as the basis for an instrumental jazz treatment can become altered beyond easy recognition, as instrumentalists are not bound by lyrics. These show and pop tunes from the 1930s and 1940s were used in jazz improvisations. As jazz matured, performers discarded popular dance and show tunes from their repertoire, and the new, original jazz melodies became less easily recognized and more difficult to follow and remember.

Go to the website section entitled "Performance Practice" found under "Listening to Jazz." Good audio examples of homophony and polyphony can also be found as the first two excerpts on the second page of the subsection labeled, "Dissecting a Jazz Performance."

A piano keyboard is grouped into repeating sets of 12 different white and black notes, with each group of 12 defining an **octave**. A melody can begin on any of the 12 different notes. Singers often practice a song in different **keys**, dictating they begin on a different note, until they find the one that they feel most suits the mood of the tune and best accommodates their own voice range. Have you ever tried unsuccessfully to sing the "Star Spangled Banner" or a church hymn, struggling to make the highest or lowest note? You struggled because the tune was in the wrong key for you, forcing you to start on the wrong first note. This musical key falls into one of two categories that define a **tonality**, usually **major** or **minor**. The major or minor tonality helps to describe the aural character of a piece of music, a melody or a single harmony. Harmony and melody work together to establish a tonality. **Atonal** describes a piece that lacks any specific tonality and is therefore neither major nor minor. Only some very contemporary, avant-garde jazz music lacks tonality. A song may have more than one tonality, depending upon its complexity. Tonality could be compared to a painting where many colors may be used, but one seems dominant.

Most of the music presented in the online audio anthology is considered tonal and is in either a major or minor key. Duke Ellington's "Ko-Ko," for example, is in a minor key. Bill Evans's version of "Witchcraft" is an example of major key or tonality. The Ornette Coleman track "Mind and Time," however, is a good example of atonal improvisation, as Coleman pays no real regard to key, harmony, or prescribed melody. Begin your listening either at the beginning to listen first to the composed tune or at the start of his solo at 0:23.

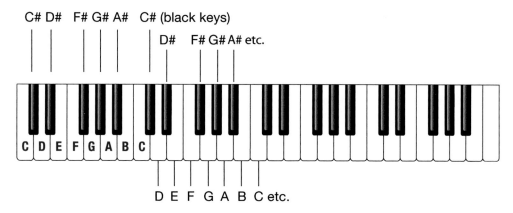

EXAMPLE 2.4 Two-octave C scale. Raised half-steps in between each scale note (black keys) are labeled above as sharps

For a more detailed explanation of melody and keys, along with musical examples, use the website and explore the section on melody found in the corresponding chapter "Elements of Jazz."

HARMONY

Harmony is a collection of two or more notes played together and, in contrast to melody, is viewed as a vertical event, as notes are stacked one on top of another and sounded simultaneously. **Chords** are similarly defined. The most basic of chords is the three-note **triad**. Harmony is typically used to accompany a melody. A succession of chords is called a **chord progression**, or just **progression**. The **harmonic rhythm** defines the pace at which chords move from one to another in a progression. Most jazz tunes feature a progression of chords that creates tension followed by resolution. This practice, known as **functional harmony**, is based on the notion that there are certain tendencies that lead one chord logically to another. This practice serves as the basis for a high percentage of jazz tunes and American popular music. We may feel unsettled when a chord progression does not follow this principle and seems to be unresolved.

The sense of **key**, or center of tonal gravity, is established by the tendencies of functional harmony and helps jazz players to create logical improvisations—melodies that relate back to this center of gravity. Jazz tunes often feature only one or two key centers, depending on how many uniquely different sections there are to the tune. It is essential that jazz improvisers are thoroughly conversant in functional harmony, as it is these principles that guide the soloist to create new melodies. The best soloists can identify the chords in a progression by hearing them, without the aid of printed music.

The harmonic language of jazz is largely borrowed from light classical, popular dance, religious, and various forms of entertainment music. Aside from the blues, the earliest forms of jazz were based on marches, cakewalks, quadrilles, and polkas—all dance forms popular in the 19th century.

Use the website to gain more insight into how harmony is constructed and functions. The section about "Harmony" is found in the corresponding chapter and includes many examples that can be played, helping you to understand these concepts.

Eventually, jazz adopted a more sophisticated harmonic vocabulary, including other altered tones that were not uncommon in 20th century "classical" music by composers such as Stravinsky, Debussy, and Bartók. Chords become richer and denser as more tones are added, often creating tension.

 On the website, listen to the lush, slow moving but changing harmonies (chord progression) used to support the melody of "Moon Dreams" from Miles Davis's *Birth of the Cool* recording. Listen to the entire track or just the opening section at 0:00–0:25.

B♭Maj7   Gmin7   Cmin7   F7   B♭Maj7

EXAMPLE 2.5 Chord symbols in a typical progression that jazz musicians must learn to interpret

TEXTURE

Music can be perceived as a mosaic or fabric where melodies and harmonies interact and intertwine, serving as the tiles or fibers in the completed work. The ways in which each musical tile or fiber interacts with one another—melody with harmony, or several melodies with one another—contribute to what is described as the music's **texture**. Texture can be dense or sparse, busy or static—transparent or dark and rich. These textures are further described as monophonic, homophonic, or polyphonic. **Monophonic** describes a single melodic line unaccompanied by harmony—for example, you singing by yourself in the shower. Music is **homophonic** when a melody line is supported by chord accompaniment. Homophonic textures are therefore denser than monophonic ones, because they have two layers—melody and chord accompaniment. **Polyphonic** music features two or more intertwined melodic lines. The different melodic lines are

EXAMPLE 2.6 Visualization of monophonic texture. The light, horizontal, wavy line represents the melodic shape of a solo singer. There are no other layers present in this single-dimensional texture

EXAMPLE 2.7 Visualization of homophonic texture. The wavy, horizontal line represents the melodic shape of a solo singer. The vertical bars represent chords, with darker shades indicating major chords, and lighter shades representing minor chords

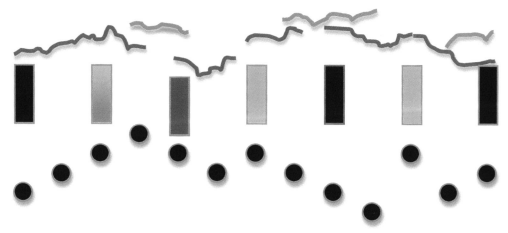

EXAMPLE 2.8 Visualization of polyphony. The light, horizontal, wavy lines represent the melodic shape of a solo singer and a second melodic voice complementing the primary vocal melody below it. The vertical bars represent chords, with darker shades indicating major chords, and lighter shades representing minor chords. Black dots represent a rising and falling bass line in counterpoint with the melody line. The entire texture, with multiple layers of activity, is described as polyphonic

said to be moving in **counterpoint** (literally, note against note) to one another. If you sang "Row, Row, Row Your Boat" as a round with staggered entrances, your friend beginning after you started, the resulting texture would be called polyphonic. The addition of chords, adding another layer to the texture, could also accompany the overlapping melodies in this round. Textures with a greater number of elements become increasingly challenging for the listener.

Excellent examples of these textural concepts can be heard on the companion website. For example, "Line For Lyons" offers an excellent example of polyphony or counterpoint at 0:00–0:45. Keith Jarrett's unaccompanied solo in "The Windup," beginning at 1:55–2:30, serves to further describe a monophonic texture, and "Take Five," beginning at 0:22, provides a good illustration of a homophony. More dense textures can be heard in J.J. Johnson's "Poem For Brass" excerpt.

Using Example 2.1, "Happy Birthday," you can see and hear illustrations of many concepts discussed to this point. For example, the melody continues to ascend in the first three phrases. The melody begins to descend in the third phrase. The melody, which constantly changes direction, is constructed of close steps and wider leaps. Where is the climax reached, at least in terms of the highest note? How many phrases comprise this familiar tune? If you sang it by your self, unaccompanied, the texture would be described as monophonic. If you were accompanied by piano chords, the texture would be described as homophonic. If, after singing it once, you began again on a different starting pitch, you would be changing the key. If another person improvised another melodic line with you, they would be adding counterpoint, creating polyphony.

FORM

Form in music describes its overall architecture—how many different melodies are there? Do they repeat, and if so how many times? Are sections repeated exactly or with variation? Form gives music structure similar to the organization we find in other art forms, in nature, everyday life and in architecture (suspension bridge, building, etc.). It is an important musical ingredient to comprehend in order to understand what you hear. Although form, on the surface, may seem to be the easiest element to understand, without the benefit of lyrics and a singer it may be difficult for the untrained listener to discern.

Most jazz compositions have more than one clearly defined section. A letter—A, B, C, etc.—defines each large section in the overall form. Each of these sections usually features a distinctly different melody and accompanying chord progression. For example, ragtime pieces are often based on the following formal scheme: AABBACCDD. This form is derived from the rondo form, a European "classical" model also evident in the march and the polka. The rondo describes a form where one section (A) reoccurs and is juxtaposed with contrasting sections (B, C, D). The consecutive letters in such a scheme (AA or BB) indicate that there is a repeat of that particular theme before the move on to a new one. Often, a piece that follows this model changes key at the C section.

Listen to the recording of Scott Joplin's "Maple Leaf Rag" on the companion website. It is close to resembling a rondo form, with multiple themes and changing keys. Can you determine when each new theme is introduced?

Many American popular songs that served as springboards for jazz improvisations followed the **song form** model, usually represented by ABA or AABA. One statement of the form is often called a **chorus**. The return to A to end the form gives one a sense of symmetry and finality. Each section (A and B) is typically 8 measures in length. Jazz musicians often refer to the B section as the **bridge** or **channel**. The blues is the simplest of all forms, as it is usually only 12 measures long, lacking a B or C theme.

Once again, "Take Five" on the companion website offers a good example of the classic song form—ABA. Each section of the form is divided up into two, 4-measure phrases. Following a brief introduction by the rhythm section, the A section begins at 0:22, with the second phrase occurring at 0:30 through repeat of the first. The first phrase of the B section begins at 0:38, with the second phrase following at 0:45. The A section returns at 0:52, and the second phrase occurs at 1:00. The improvised solo begins at 1:08.

The Billie Holiday rendition of "Body and Soul" and Stan Getz's recording of "Só Danço Samba," also included on the website, provide additional examples of AABA song-form structure that is easy to follow because of the lyric content. Can you identify the bridge in these two vocal pieces?

"James and Wes" is a good illustration of a 12-bar instrumental blues based on a repetitive melody and simple form.

> The section about form found in the corresponding chapter on the website provides a thorough explanation of form in music, with examples drawn from the jazz repertoire.

IMPROVISATION

Extemporaneous playing; spontaneous composition; creating music on the spur of the moment. These are simple phrases to describe the act of improvising. People now think of jazz at the mere mention of the term improvisation, although there are often improvised solos in pop tunes, and improvisation is often a component of Indian and other world music. Descriptions of jazz from almost any era agree that improvisation is a salient feature. Jazz historian Ostransky stated that, in jazz, "reading music is considered a lesser accomplishment than improvising it."[9] Discussing the importance of improvisation to jazz, noted jazz scholar James Lincoln Collier wrote that, "it is always the soloist that is written about, always the solo that is analyzed."[10] Earlier writings about jazz portrayed improvisation as a mysterious or divine process, adding to the music's mystique. Recently, more thoughtful discussions have helped understanding of the true process behind this unique form of creativity. As improvisation is an important feature of jazz, the intelligent listener needs to learn about its nature in order to develop skills for identifying and appreciating it.

Something Borrowed—The European Tradition

An early tradition of improvised music is found in medieval chants and in music from the Renaissance (c.1450–1600) and Baroque (c.1600–1750) periods. Composers were expected to deviate from the original melodies, as did Baroque composer Georg Philipp Telemann when he composed the *Methodical Sonatas*. He provided the basic melody on one line and, on another line, suggestions for improvisations not terribly different than those used by modern jazz soloist Charlie Parker.[11] In 1765, violinist and composer Karel von Dittersdorf wrote that: "A new custom developed . . . To show their improvisational creativity they [the soloists] start fantasias in which they play a simple subject which they then very artfully vary several times according to the best rules of composition."[12] Baroque composers J.S. Bach and G.F. Handel also included passages where improvisation was invited, and this practice continued until the beginning of the Romantic period (c.1820–1900). Although a fine improviser, Ludwig van Beethoven, an extraordinary composer from this period, began a new trend away from this improvisation. The increasing complexity of the music, the growth of music publishing businesses, and the increasing number of amateur musicians caused "classical" composers such as Beethoven to seek more control over their compositions. Franz Liszt, another composer and improviser, summed up this new trend by saying, "the most absolute respect for the masterpieces of the great masters has replaced the need for novelty and individuality."[13] More attention was paid to interpretation of the musical composition as written, and, by the late 1800s, the role of improvisation was diminishing in European music. However, at the same time, in the United States new styles of music were emerging that once again placed a high value on spontaneity and individuality.

Something New, Something Blue—The Jazz Tradition

The roots of American jazz can be compared to any folk tradition—impromptu, spontaneous, and simplistic. These characteristics, as well as rhythm, lyric, and melody, were of utmost importance in early vocal styles. Perhaps the closest thing to true improvisation in the late 1800s and early 1900s in America could be found in African-American vocal styles such as work songs and **field hollers** improvised by slaves and chain-gang workers, and especially in the **blues**. This vocal style featured **blue notes**, slightly altered tones where a special inflection was given to the third and seventh scale tones by lowering the pitch slightly. Instrumentalists later imitated this blues vocal style.

Blues

A distinguishing aspect of many jazz melodies, improvised and composed, is the blues. Blues melodies are based on alterations of a traditional scale. Some believe that the altered thirds, fifths, and sevenths of the blues scale can be attributed to certain African singing practices. A **scale** is a logical progression of ascending and descending notes, arranged in half- and whole-step intervals. The piano keyboard shown in Example 2.9 makes it easy to see these two basic intervals, which serve as building blocks for all scales. Note names are labeled. The distance from C to D is a whole-step interval, and the black key in between represents a half-step interval. Scales are comprised of eight consecutive notes, following a particular key signature, and are named in accordance with the starting note. On this keyboard, the C scale would be played as C–D–E–F–G–A–B–C. The third, fifth and seventh notes of this traditional scale are altered to form the **blues scale**, as shown in the example. The purple-shaded notes indicate the lowered third (E flat), lowered fifth (G flat), and lowered seventh (B flat) and are referred to as blue notes. There are gradations of blue notes, as singers and instrumentalists are capable of being less precise than a pianist when lowering these pitches.

The blues scale is almost an amalgamation of pitches from the major and minor tonalities. Leroy Ostransky, author of *Understanding Jazz*, felt that, "early jazz players probably saw little distinction between major and minor modes [scales] and used major and minor thirds interchangeably."[14] Whatever the origins, these slightly flatted pitches (third, fifth, and seventh scale degrees) became known as blue notes and are responsible for much of the special melodic and harmonic character in jazz that distinguishes it from other forms of music. Blue notes often

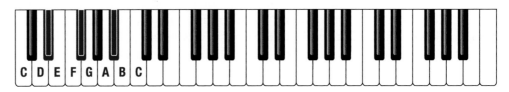

EXAMPLE 2.9 Lowered third, fifth and seventh (E flat, G flat, B flat) are called "blue notes" and are shaded in the following keyboard example

Gertrude "Ma" Rainey (1886–1939) and her Georgia Jazz Band, Chicago, 1923

help to communicate a melancholy feeling. Blues songs are sometimes associated with a depressed, downtrodden, or melancholy mood. The use of blue notes does not always, however, achieve this feeling, nor are these alterations always used to create this "blue" mood. They are merely one way to make a melodic line more personalized and expressive.

Some historians believe that the blues may have evolved as a result of African slaves attempting to reconcile their predominant five-note pentatonic scale with the Western eight-note scale and harmony they found in the US.

The similarity between blues and pentatonic scales is illustrated by an audio example found on the website in the corresponding chapter.

The most unique aspect of jazz harmony for many years was introduced through the application of blue notes to chords. Those altered tones that we identify with a blues melody were eventually incorporated into the harmonies to form more colorful and dissonant chords, beyond the simple three-note triad.

Go to the corresponding section of the website (Chapter 2) and you will find audio examples further helping you to hear what the blues sounds like. The online audio anthology includes examples of blues from two different periods of jazz history—"St. Louis Blues" and "Jimmy and Wes."

Improvisation in Jazz

As a whole, the earliest jazz instrumentalists were not known for their ability to improvise new solos each time they performed. Typically, these early musicians performed a piece nearly the same way each time, once their approach to a particular song had been refined. Their playing was largely a theme and variation style in which a melody was merely embellished and ornamented in new ways. Thematic variation is the simplest form of improvisation and is probably what Alphonse Picou (1878–1961), a New Orleans clarinetist, referred to when he described this early form of jazz as a "style of playing without notes."[15]

The study of the development of early instrumental jazz is difficult because, during this era, the music could be preserved only in a written format, or passed on aurally. No audible artifact remained for study, as recording technology had not yet been invented. As each jazz performance is an interpretation of a composition, the printed page could not totally capture the live performance and its unwritten subtleties. However, after the turn of the 20th century, jazz became perhaps the first music to be greatly influenced by the advent of sound recording, for it directly paralleled the growth of jazz. (See the brief history of recording included on the website.) Recordings provided lasting aural artifacts that faithfully reproduced the live performance other musicians could now be influenced by and could imitate. Recordings were also responsible for the very rapid changes in jazz, compared with the slower pace in previous musical history, where one style was popular for decades before a significant change occurred. Recordings, though, became both an asset and a disadvantage. On one hand, they quickly spread the music and were models for younger musicians trying to learn through imitation. On the other hand, musicians with a popular record now found that the public often wanted to hear live performances exactly

Photo of a jazz band in a radio studio, broadcasting, circa mid to late 1920s

as they remembered the recording. The pressures of popularity, customer satisfaction, and marketing could then discourage improvisation.

As jazz matured, largely through the work of Louis Armstrong in the mid 1920s, the concept and importance of improvisation solidified. There are many levels of improvisation at work within the hierarchy of a jazz ensemble. For example, drummers and bassists probably improvise the greatest percentage of the time, though often what they play is not new to them. They rely on familiar patterns that they have played many times. There is no precise duplication, however, and what they improvise often depends on the style of the tune, the tempo, and, of course, with whom they are playing. The amount of improvisational content in a particular performance is dependent, to a great extent, on the size of the ensemble and the intent of the music. Larger ensembles usually mean a lesser amount of improvisation, whereas small ensembles, such as trios and quartets, rely a great deal more on improvisation. Jazz aimed at a dance audience usually features less improvisation, because the music assumes a more subservient role.

Improvisation inspires a musical dialogue between the soloist and rhythm section, each complementing the other, while suggesting new ideas for elaboration as the improvisation evolves. Many performers have described the jazz solo as a story with a beginning, middle, and end. To tell a good story, there are characters; in musical situations, memorable melodic phrases serve the role of characters and are often repeated with some variation to provide continuity to an improvisation. The performer's duty is to take the listener on a journey. The more listeners are led to predict musical outcomes in this journey, the more engaged they are in the performance. But, if they can predict too much, they become bored and unchallenged. Listeners can easily tune out when a high percentage of what they hear is unpredictable or previously unexperienced.

Jazz soloists are faced with creating spontaneous, new melodies; however, they must adhere to certain guidelines. With each new style of jazz came new and often more challenging principles to which the soloist must adhere in order to gain the respect of peers and audiences while advancing the art form to a new level. Jazz players have learned about music theory and have developed the ability to hear harmonies. Each improvised solo, usually referred to as a chorus, should build as the musical story unfolds. The notes chosen must relate to the same progression of chords used to accompany the original melody. The only thing written out in the music for the soloist (and rhythm-section players) is a series of symbols that represent these chord structures. This form of abbreviated chord notation is shown in Example 2.10. It is the result of years of dedicated practice and inspiration that enables a jazz soloist, given only this simple, cryptic chart of information, to construct a moving, engaging, and coherent improvised solo.

To ensure that their improvisations are consonant with these harmonies, soloists use certain tools, such as scales and modes that relate to harmonies (chords), to help them negotiate a progression of chords in order to construct new, melodic improvisations. Soloists also use the notes of the chords themselves in order to improvise new melodies. It is a difficult process, as choices must be made on the fly. To allow the creative side of the brain time to recover from being spontaneous and consider what to play next, soloists often rely on "licks," or pre-learned patterns and phrases. These phrases, used throughout an improvised solo, often refer to the tradition, as they may be quotes of melodies played by another soloist years earlier. Even the great improviser

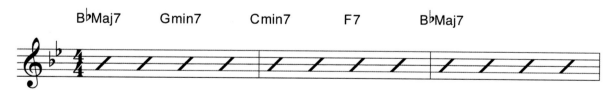

EXAMPLE 2.10 Typical jazz chord progression illustrated by symbols

Charlie Parker, in a bebop improvisation, quoted a Louis Armstrong solo recorded many years earlier. These quotes and memorized phrases can be strung together in many different ways to create new material. Phrases borrowed from the tradition could be compared to the many ways that we can express an idea in words. For example, take a phrase such as "The new-fallen snow is beautiful." This simple idea could be expressed and embellished in many different ways. One could have said, "The new snow that fell last night is beautiful," or "New snow like we got last night is really beautiful." These multiple means of expression are exactly what jazz players employ when they use a pre-learned phrase and put it to use in an improvised solo. In using a pre-learned phrase, the soloist creates the illusion of pure spontaneity for the listener. Although the sequences of pre-learned ideas are assembled and reassembled in new ways from performance to performance, many of the memorized ideas can be repeated. Ostransky wrote about this phenomenon in his book *The Anatomy of Jazz*. He said, "They [jazz improvisers] do not compose on the spur of the moment; their significant improvisations are the result of long practice and experience."[16] Through years of listening, borrowing, assimilating, analyzing, and imitating, soloists amass a collection of jazz phrases that suit their individual style and can be recalled at any time in the course of a solo. In other words, soloists play what they enjoy playing. Therefore, not everything played during a jazz solo is spontaneously created. These solos, more frequently than not, are based on a series of recreations—bits and pieces of pre-learned material coupled with newly created ideas to form fresh, new improvisations. In the fall of 1958, the then well-known swing band leader/composer Duke Ellington traveled to England for a tour with his orchestra. He expressed his thoughts and feelings about jazz improvisation in an article entitled, "The Future of Jazz" included in the souvenir program. In this article he said:

> There are still a few die-hards who believe there is such a thing as unadulterated improvisation without preparation or anticipation. It is my belief that there has never been anybody who has blown even two bars worth listening to who doesn't have some idea about what he was going to play, before he started. If you just ramble through the scales or play around the chords, that's nothing more than musical exercise. Improvisation really consists of picking out a device here, and connecting it with a device there; changing the rhythm here, and pausing there; there has to be some thought preceding each phrase, otherwise it is meaningless.[17]

Other forms of quotes used by jazz soloists include humorous ones, such as "Here Comes the Bride" (from the opera *Lohengrin* by Richard Wagner), which almost everyone knows, and melodies from other standard tunes that fit the particular chord progression. Quotes of this nature sometimes serve as homage to earlier players and a display of machismo, demonstrating to fellow musicians and informed listeners how much is known about the tradition. The player's ultimate objective is to have an effective dialogue with the other musicians, while creating exciting new ideas and incorporating appropriate aspects of the tradition. To quote contemporary trumpeter Tom Harrell, "He improves on his heritage, but he also tries to invent music that has never been heard before."[18] Only the greatest soloists, the true virtuosos on their instruments, are capable of spontaneously creating a high percentage of completely new material each time they improvise. The most innovative improvisers in the history of jazz were those who dared to break from tradition and forge new pathways that relied less on what had come before.

What most jazz players strive for is to find the "zone," which they describe as a mental state in which complete relaxation and intense concentration coexist. The late, great jazz pianist Bill Evans described his creative process to author and historian Dan Morganstern in a 1964 *Down Beat* magazine interview by saying that, "Everybody has to learn certain things, but when you play, the intellectual process no longer has anything to do with it . . . I am relying on intuition then. I have no idea of what is coming next."[19] Evans is describing the "zone" that so many jazz players have referred to and strive each night to attain.

With each style, a new improvisational language is developed. A new vocabulary is created initially by the innovators, and then further developed by the followers. Each style borrows from the vocabulary of a previous style(s), although it is inappropriate to use solely the improvisational vocabulary from one era on tunes from an entirely different style period. In other words, the improvised bebop style, which came about in the mid 1940s, is inappropriate to use in an authentic rendition of a Dixieland style tune from the 1920s, because bebop is too advanced, using devices not found in traditional Dixieland. The language of jazz improvisation is in continual evolution, always borrowing devices from previous generations.

Jazz players tend to copy and borrow from exceptional innovators. The great jazz soloists, such as Louis Armstrong, Charlie Parker, Dizzy Gillespie and John Coltrane, each created a new vocabulary and are still copied, years after their deaths. Nevertheless, there is a downside to learning from models, for originality can be sacrificed. The great Swing Era tenor saxophonist Lester Young spoke out in *Down Beat* magazine about the problem of "copy cats" in his 1949 interview with Pat Harris, entitled "Pres Talks About Himself, Copycats." Young told Harris,

> The trouble with most musicians today is that they are copycats. Of course you have to start out playing like someone else. You have a model or a teacher, and you learn all that he can show you. But then you start playing for yourself. Show them that you're an individual. And I can count those who are doing that today on the fingers of one hand.[20]

The problem of authenticity, originality, and re-creation through imitation in improvisation has been hotly debated, and each jazz improviser must evaluate how important it is to reflect the tradition when playing jazz and how much is too much. Pianist McCoy Tyner, in a clinic for college students, suggested that: "you should become proficient at taking chances,"[21] [rather than spending too much time copying other players, as that often only ends in losing your personal identity].

After reading this section, you should read and play the examples included in the sections on "Melody" and "Harmony" found in the corresponding chapter on the website. A tutorial about improvisation can also be found here.

It will be important, as you listen to examples of the various styles of jazz presented throughout the remainder of this book, to relate what you hear and read to the musical concepts presented in this chapter. You will find that the instrumental roles and performance practices change, and the application of musical concepts may also vary from style to style, helping to identify, define, and clarify each stylistic change, while making them uniquely different by comparison.

CHAPTER SUMMARY

Jazz, like all music, can be broken down into the basic elements of rhythm, melody, harmony, texture, and form. Of these elements, rhythm is significant in setting jazz apart from other styles of music. Included under the heading of rhythm are syncopation, meter, and swing. Swing refers both to a specific jazz style period and to a way of performing music. Jazz groups most often perform at steady tempos set by a rhythm section rather than by a conductor. The way in which the rhythm section plays and interacts has changed with each specific style of jazz. Tempo describes how quickly the music is played.

Harmony is represented by chords. Harmony supports, and is the basis for, composed and improvised melodies. Harmonies can be sophisticated or more basic, such as many examples of the early folk and jazz repertoire.

Texture describes the density of a piece of music. Texture is further defined as monophonic, homophonic, or polyphonic.

Form in music refers to its architectural construction. A piece of music may be constructed out of multiple themes, with sections that serve as transitions, introductions, and endings.

Improvisation is simultaneous composition and performance and is an important element of jazz. Although in no way exclusive to jazz, improvisation is a key ingredient of jazz. Many feel that some level of improvised content needs to be present for music to be considered jazz. Similar to the evolution of rhythm-section styles, approaches to improvisation have changed throughout the history of jazz. Early jazz performers often did little more than ornament the previously stated melody in their improvisations, whereas performers of other jazz styles may create an entirely new idea based on the same chord structure as the melody. In some styles of jazz, it may be difficult to differentiate a melody statement from an improvised solo.

The improviser creates new melodies using only chord symbols as a basic guide to the harmony of a tune. Although one might get the impression that the performer is creating entirely new music on the spot, typically, jazz musicians often create solos by interspersing countless short figures/phrases that they have played before with new, improvised material. In listening to alternate takes of recordings done by some of the great jazz masters, one often finds, not only similarities in the solos, but sometimes identical figures occurring at the same place in the form of the tune as other recordings of the artist playing that same tune. Specific figures/phrases are often closely associated with an artist, acting as a musical signature. In most styles of jazz, improvised solos follow the same form and harmony as the melody statement. Listeners can hum the melody to themselves during an improvised solo in order to keep track of the form.

The blues is undoubtedly the most important African-American contribution to the formation of American music. Inspired in part by certain African musical practices, blues inflections are both melodic and harmonic innovations associated with jazz.

Technology has had a profound effect on the development of jazz. As much of the evolution of jazz has centered on changes in approach to improvisation, the technology to record and preserve performances provided models from which new ideas could spring. Technology has also enabled longer and longer recordings of this highly improvised music.

KEY TERMS

Most important terms emboldened.

Atonal	Harmonic rhythm	**Monophonic**	Scale
Blue notes	**Harmony**	Octave	**Song form**
Blues	**Homophonic**	**Phrase**	**Swing**
Blues scale	**Improvisation**	**Polyphony**	**Syncopation**
Bridge (or channel)	Key	(polyphonic)	**Tempo**
Chord	Laying back	**Polyrhythm**	**Texture**
Chord progression	Major	(polyrhythmic)	Tonality
(progression)	**Measure** (bar)	Rhythm	Triad
Counterpoint	**Melody**	**Rhythm section**	
Form	**Meter**	Rondo	
Functional harmony	Minor	**Rubato**	

STUDY QUESTIONS

1. What is meant by syncopation?

2. Can you explain tempo and rubato?

3. The specific unit that serves as a container holding a specific number of beats defined by the meter is called a _____.

4. What does meter tell us?

5. What is the difference between a melody and a phrase, or is there any difference?

6. Discuss what is the significance of blues to jazz?

7. What three terms can be used in discussing the texture of a piece of music?

8. Tonality is described as _____, _____, or _____.

9. What section of the band has the responsibility of maintaining a regular pulse?

10. A group of chords is called a _____.

11. A logical progression of ascending and descending notes in whole and half-steps is called a _____.

12. In general, what is meant by functional harmony?

13. What are the most common forms used in jazz?

14. Is improvisation unique to jazz? Explain your answer.

15. Discuss the improvisational tradition in jazz.

16. In the standard song form, what term is used to describe the middle section?

Make sure that you also review material in the corresponding chapter of the website.

CHAPTER 3

Listening to Jazz

To appreciate music the listener must be actively involved. Passive listening to music does not bring about intelligent musical enjoyment, but active listening, which includes understanding and active participation with emotional responses, can foster musical enjoyment.[1]

Jazz musicians performing in a nightclub

PERFORMANCE PRACTICE

People often listen passively to music because they are bombarded daily by all kinds of it in so many different environments (doctor's office, elevator, supermarket, coffee shop, mall). Consequently, they become nearly oblivious to it. This book and its accompanying website are designed to enhance your ability to be a more active listener by increasing your level of appreciation and understanding of jazz, without detracting from the enjoyment of casually listening to music.

Everyone is entitled to their own opinion about music, but, in order to have a valid opinion, it is wise to have criteria to consider while listening to and evaluating a performance. Learn to be an observant member of the audience, know what to listen to and look for, and your experience will be substantially enhanced.

As jazz is considered an art form where so much is left to the personal interpretation of the performer and arranger, an overview of the techniques employed to personalize their performance is significant to our study of jazz.

The Instruments of Jazz

Different styles of music are often associated closely with certain instruments. We frequently can make an educated guess about the style of music that a band plays by merely looking at the band. We see a violin and we think of classical music, and a saxophone reminds us of jazz. Any instrument is capable of being played in a jazz style; however, the established tradition has drawn associations to certain instruments such as the saxophone and the drum set. Neither of these instruments is typically found in symphony orchestras. On the other hand, violins, cellos, violas, bassoons, oboes, and harps are rarely heard playing in a jazz style. When we see a group that consists of a three- or four-piece rhythm section, a saxophone, and a trumpet, it is very safe to assume that the music they play is associated in some way with jazz.

Some instruments have fallen out of favor in terms of their use in jazz. For example, the tuba, a hold over from brass bands, was commonplace in jazz ensembles well into the early 1930s, but is rarely used by more contemporary jazz groups. The clarinet was a very prominent instrument especially during the early jazz periods. Sidney Bechet first made the soprano sax popular in the 1920s. Instruments such as the drum set went through radical changes, stimulated both by technological advancements and by the musicians themselves. The guitar, which eventually became amplified, is a good example of how technology has had a direct impact on the music and performance practices.

The instruments associated with jazz are considered members of the brass, woodwind, percussion, and string instrument families. Members of the brass family include the cornet, trumpet, flugelhorn, trombone, tuba, and French horn. Only the cornet, trumpet, flugelhorn, and trombone are common to jazz. Brass players often use mutes in the jazz setting. Many different kinds of mute were actually first made popular by jazz players and later adopted by modern "classical" composers. The woodwind family consists of the flute, clarinet, oboe, saxophone, and bassoon. Those woodwinds most common to jazz are the saxophone, clarinet, and flute. The bass is a member of the string family, and, of course, the drum set and various Latin instruments are considered members of the percussion family. The piano was actually once considered a member of the percussion family, along with the pitched, keyboard percussion instruments such as the vibraphone and marimba. With the advent of electronic organs and modern synthesizers, the piano and its relatives might now best be associated with the keyboard family.

The Drum Set and Swing

Drummers, who serve to motivate the swing feel, have incorporated aspects of the African drum ensemble. These ensembles are comprised of many drummers, all playing different rhythms on different percussive instruments. The single jazz drummer on his drum set (also known as a "**kit**") is able to incorporate the rhythms played by many African drummers into one cohesive style. The fundamental or **ground rhythm** is maintained by the hi-hat cymbals (also known as the sock cymbal, played by a foot pedal) played on off beats 2 and 4, and sometimes by the bass drum that often defines each beat of the measure (1–2–3–4). The ride cymbal, typically played with the right-hand stick, also helps to keep steady time. The left hand is free to embellish this fundamental pulse and is expected to apply shifting accents on the other drums and cymbals as

The typical jazz drum set

the steady time flow is maintained by the hi-hat, ride cymbal, and bass drum. Done properly, the jazz drummer's one-man drum ensemble produces a swinging pulse of subtle, ever-changing tensions and relaxations created by the interactions of irregular patterns played by the hands and regular patterns played by the feet. Bear in mind, too, that the bass generally maintains the steady, predictable pulse of a tempo by playing notes on each beat of the measure (1–2–3–4). To quote Count Basie's long-time guitarist Freddie Green, in an interview with Stanley Dance, "the rhythm section is the foundation of it [swing]. If the rhythm section isn't swinging, then you can forget about it. If it isn't clicking, moving together . . ."[2] Jazz bassist Gene Ramey suggested that the rhythm section was the motor that propelled the band.

The swing **ride cymbal** rhythm, which gradually evolved as an additional means of providing a regular pulse, is as impossible to notate precisely as are many African rhythms. Many West African characteristics are evident in the shifting ride cymbal rhythm, which resembles the skipping analogy presented in Chapter 2. The ride cymbal is used to create a smooth, connected flow of skipping attacks that help to propel the music forward. Only recently have computer hardware and software enabled scientific studies to determine the true mathematical subdivision of each beat in various swing jazz styles. Suffice it to say here that, in a swing phrase, notes played on downbeats are lengthened and upbeats are shortened and accented slightly as they occur as anticipations of upcoming major beats or downbeats, much like the habanera rhythm. The exercise that follows will give you the sensation of swinging by emphasizing the second half of every other beat (2 and 4) with the "ga" syllable. Try using the syllables in Example 3.1 to verbally imitate the feeling of swing. The example represents 2 measures that can be repeated multiple times.

If a piece of music is described to musicians as a particular jazz style, then they will play it in the appropriate style, even though the proper jazz interpretation cannot be accurately notated.

Ding	Ding-ga	Ding	Ding-ga	Ding	Ding-ga	Ding	Ding-ga
1	2	3	4	1	2	3	4

EXAMPLE 3.1 Swing ride cymbal pattern

Tap a steady tempo with your foot and imagine the irregular punches and jabs of a boxer intermingled with this steady pulse. The exercise helps to portray the approach of the more modern drummer. Listen and watch the drummer on "Video Blues" found on the website to hear and see a good example of this style particularly during trumpet and saxophone solos.

Musicians must learn how to interpret music in the jazz style. Much has been said about the oral and aural traditions that are important to the very existence of various folk-music styles, and these same traditions have had a significant impact on the formation of jazz styles. It is not possible to swing if one has never heard it and learned first to duplicate it through imitation. In this way, jazz is very different than traditional Western European classical music. One of the primary reasons why "swing" has been so difficult to define is that jazz performance practices have changed significantly about every 10 years since the beginning of instrumental jazz in the early 20th century. The music has continued to swing as styles changed, but the actual interpretation of swing has changed. Swing means different things to different people, but the rhythmic spirit of jazz characterized by the swing phenomenon is identifiable in all of its numerous styles.

If you haven't already done so, examine the section in Chapter 2 on swing on the website. It can be found in the section about rhythm. The website also provides further detail about the drum set, including video clips that are found in the Performance Practice section of Chapter 3.

Orchestration and Instrumentation

Orchestration refers to which instruments are used to play the music. Orchestration, or **instrumentation**, can, and usually does, vary throughout a piece of music. Orchestration can contribute originality to a composition. A single composition can be rendered with many different orchestrations, although it is most often associated with the one originally conceived by the composer and/or arranger.

 Compare the orchestration of tracks included in the online audio anthology: "Summertime," arranged by Gil Evans, Stan Kenton's "La Suerte de los Tontos," or Charles Mingus's "Boogie Stop Shuffle." The differences should be striking.

The Arrangement

Although performers tend to occupy the most prominent position in jazz, the arrangers (who oftentimes are also the performers) also serve an all-important function. The **arrangement** refers to the way a group of musicians presents a particular piece of music when compared with the original model. The arrangement is considered an adaptation of the original. As much of the jazz repertoire during the first 50 years was based on popular songs of the day, adaptations were required to suit the needs of the jazz performer. These adaptations were, and continue to be, important in providing a unique identity for the performer or band. The "arrangement" is unique to jazz and American popular music. Although there are examples of arrangements in classical music, they are of much less significance to the history and development of the music.

As there is no standard instrumentation for jazz bands, and they can range in size from duos to large ensembles consisting of 16 or more musicians, it is necessary to organize the presentation of a song according to the specific instrumentation available. Arranging a song for a quartet or quintet is a simple task compared with arranging for a big band with five saxophones, ten brass and four rhythm instruments. Arrangers often add newly composed introductions, interludes, and endings to provide a fresh, new approach to the song they are arranging. There are many examples of arrangers who have changed the meter, the style, the tempo, and overall mood of a piece, transforming it into something entirely different than the original model. Arrangers also might embellish or alter the original chord progression (**reharmonization**), providing a more sophisticated version than the original. In some cases, these more complex reharmonizations provide more interesting challenges for the improvising soloist. Arrangers also develop a unique musical identity by the way in which they combine instruments and use brass mutes. Although the possibilities may not be endless, there are numerous instrumental combinations available to the arranger.

Excellent examples demonstrating the concept of arranging in jazz can be found in the online audio anthology. Search on YouTube for a jazz standard such as "All the Things You Are" and you will be astounded at the number of vastly different arrangements there are. Make a list of those versions you like best, citing specific similarities and differences between them. The online audio anthology also includes three versions of "Body and Soul." These versions are uniquely different. The vocal rendition by Billie Holiday is fairly true to the original, both harmonically and melodically. The Coleman Hawkins version, however, departs so radically from the original composition that it is barely recognizable. Esperanza Spalding's version is based on a different meter (5/4 rather than the traditional 4/4), and sections are added between each major section of the form (AABA).

Instrumental Techniques and Special Effects

Wind instrumentalists are influenced by a swinging rhythm section and vary their attacks, articulations, phrasing, and placement of accents in relation to the rhythm section's performance. **Articulation** refers to the way in which a note is attacked or initiated by the performer. It can be played harshly and with accent or without accent, or made short or long. A series of notes can be played smoothly and in a very connected, lyrical manner, or can be very separated. The way in which a melody is **phrased** can be compared to the way in which we read a sentence aloud, placing accents, slight emphasis, and so forth on particular words. Unlike "classical" musicians, jazz musicians are less bound by convention, and interpretive characteristics can vary drastically from player to player. By comparison, performance techniques such as articulation, phrasing, and accents are usually dictated to the "classical" musician by the composer and conductor and are played with near uniformity and precision.

It is difficult (if not impossible) for the instrumentalist or vocalist to swing if the rhythm section isn't swinging. It is the interplay between the horn players and the rhythm section that has created the essence of the jazz feel. Many agree that the first modern concept of swing was actually formulated, not by a rhythm player, but by a wind instrumentalist. Trumpeter and vocalist Louis Armstrong was, for many reasons, the first great jazz musician who, among his many achievements, established a clear concept of swing rhythmic interpretation.

Special Effects—The Sounds of Jazz

Special instrumental techniques are associated with jazz and help musicians to establish a personal identity on their instrument. The saxophone, the trumpet, and the trombone are capable of a wide range of special effects associated with jazz performance practice. In many cases, new words were created to describe the sound of these unusual and unorthodox techniques, such as:

- fall-off
- doit
- shake
- bend
- scoop
- gliss
- growl
- half-valve
- sub-tone.

Even though you may not read music, the graphics in Example 3.2 should help to provide a visual definition of these special jazz performance effects.

EXAMPLE 3.2 Visual notations of special effects associated with jazz

Brass instruments with valves can produce a choked, squeezed sound where no precise pitch is clear. This effect is described as the "half-valve," and soloists make use of this effect during their improvisations (trumpeter Lee Morgan does this on "Moanin'," included in the online audio anthology). Saxophonists and brass players can also superimpose a guttural throat "growl" on a tone. Any number of mutes can be added to brass instruments and in combination with any of these special effects. It is possible for saxophonists to play high notes beyond the normal upper range limit of their instrument. These are called "altissimo" notes and are capable of being produced on any member of this instrument family. They are difficult to play with control and finesse. The saxophonist can achieve a dark, subtle, wispy tone quality in the lower register by using a special technique called "sub-tone." Tenor saxophonists typically apply sub-tone in the lower range of this instrument, and it is a technique often used in ballads.

The best way to become acquainted with the instrumental sounds of jazz is to explore the "Instrumentation" and "Performance Practice" sections in the corresponding chapter on the website. Pictures and sound files of the instruments and mutes commonly found in jazz ensembles can be found in this section. A sound byte is worth a thousand words!

UNDERSTANDING THE WHOLE PERFORMANCE

There are common features in all jazz performances, and it can be helpful to review some aspects of the typical jazz performance, and the sequence in which they occur. Keep the following outline handy while listening to the music included in the online audio anthology. Many jazz performances adhere to the following scheme:

- introduction—often 4, 8, or 16 bars long (sometimes there is no introduction);
- tune statement—blues (12 bars), extended blues (16 or 24 bars), or song form (AABA, ABA, AAB);
- improvised solo(s)—usually adhering to the form of the piece, although sometimes abbreviated;
- interlude—interludes are sometimes used to link solos and are composed sections; often there is no interlude, only additional solos;
- shout chorus—newly composed material featuring the entire ensemble; this section is common in big band arrangements but often not found in small-group jazz performances;
- a return to the tune;
- ending—sometimes referred to as **coda** (musical term for ending) or **tag**.

"Take Five" or "Pent Up House," included on the audio anthology, provides a fine example of this classic small-group presentation formula.

There can be many exceptions to this scheme; however, a high percentage of performances follow this general model. Exceptions sometimes occur when the ensemble features a singer. Then, some tunes actually begin with a section identified as the "verse." This section is often played rubato and features a lyric that establishes the story line or context for the main body of the vocal tune that follows. This section is sometimes referred to as the chorus or refrain. In jazz "lingo," chorus also means one complete statement of the song's chord progression and formal scheme. This latter definition of the word represents how it is used throughout this book. It is usually the melody and lyric of the vocal refrain that we remember, and frequently the verse is omitted. Following the vocal, there is often a series of improvised solos, either by the singer, instrumentalists, or both. The singer may **scat** during the solo. Scat singing refers to the nonsense syllables used while improvising a melody vocally. Jazz trumpeter and singer Louis Armstrong popularized scat singing when he recorded "Heebie Jeebies" in 1926. Soloists may not improvise on the entire form, improvising only on the A section of a multi-theme song. The vocalist frequently returns at the B section, following an improvised solo on the A section. Solo sections may also include trading 4- or 8-bar phrases between soloists.

Big-band performances often include more than one **shout chorus** section separating improvised solos. This section is equivalent to the development section of a symphonic work and features the entire ensemble on newly composed material based on the tune's chord progression. These sections are often based on the chord progression of the original tune. There may be a section that features the saxophone, trombone, or trumpet section, described as a **soli**. In this case, a new melody is composed in an improvised style and then harmonized, so that each member of the section is playing a different note, while rhythmically following the lead melodic voice.

Watch the *Video Blues* movie provided in the corresponding chapter on the website and see if this presentation follows the prescribed format in the preceding outline.

The following guidelines will help while listening to the recordings required for this class. Don't try to answer all of the following questions in just one listening.

1. Because music is not stationary, memory is an essential factor in listening to it. Learn to remember what has been presented before. For example, if a short phrase is played, how many times is it repeated or slightly altered? Which instruments play the phrase? Is the phrase always played exactly the same? Is the phrase varied slightly or radically when it is repeated?

2. Are you focusing your attention on large musical ideas such as the main themes or soloists? This may sound like a simple task, but it can be difficult. Listening requires your complete attention and concentration.

3. Try to identify something new about a recording each time you listen to it. Taking notes on what you hear often helps you to remember more about the music.

4. Ask yourself the following questions: What size is the ensemble? Can you pick out the various instruments and identify their specific roles? Are there any unusual instruments heard not normally associated with jazz? Are typical jazz instruments used, but in unusual roles?

5. Pay particular attention to the soloists and what instruments they play. If brass instruments are used (trumpets, trombones, French horns, tuba), do they use mutes? Can you tell what kind?

6. What meter is the piece in (usually 4/4 or 3/4)?

7. As you become more acquainted with the various styles, how would you characterize the piece, or does the piece feature more than one style?

8. Is the tempo fast, slow, or moderate, or does the tempo change? Perhaps there is no strict tempo, and the tune is performed rubato.

9. What dynamic shadings—loud, soft, crescendos, diminuendos—add drama?

10. Can you describe the form of the piece? In what order do things occur? Is there an introduction before the initial statement of the melody? Is the melody clearly segmented— AABA? Are the soloists separated by some kind of ensemble section?

11. Does the piece invoke any particular non-musical impression or emotional response? Does it remind you of a place, a person, a situation, a mood, or other non-musical occurrence?

12. Does the quality of the recording say something about the technology used in the recording process and therefore help to approximately date the recording?

13. Can you distinguish the improvised sections from the composed sections of the piece?

14. Does the rhythm section create a spirited, buoyant, propulsive feel, giving the music a sense of forward motion?

15. Does the music "swing" in the traditional rhythmic sense?

16. Do the soloists make use of those characteristic sounds associated with jazz, i.e., bends, scoops, rips, growls, varying vibrato, extreme high registers or ranges, mutes, and other such devices used by wind players to "color" the sound and provide drama? Which instrumentalists used which of these devices?

17. Did the soloist gradually build the solo, as one would develop a story, or did the solo lack any apparent continuity, pacing, or structure?

18. Do the soloists seem to demonstrate mastery of their instrument? In what ways listed below do the soloists demonstrate their prowess?

- through display of technique (ability to play notes reasonably fast);
- by using the instrument's full range;
- by projecting a pleasing tone quality;
- by projecting an overall quality that fits the mood of the piece.

If necessary, review the sections about the instruments, in the corresponding chapter on the companion website, and about form, found in Chapter 2—"The Elements of Music in Jazz."

DESCRIBING THE PERFORMANCE

When evaluating a live performance, consider the following issues, as well as the preceding questions:

1. Experienced performers use aspects of their performance and subtle gestures to communicate with each other and the audience, in the true spirit of the African participatory tradition. Ensemble communication is essential for a good performance and, above all, to support the soloists in constructing an effective solo. Do you sense good communication during the performance?
2. Does the audience applaud? Unlike the case for soloists in a classical piece, audiences typically applaud a good jazz soloist before the end of a piece. This practice probably stemmed from the informal places in which jazz was presented for many years before entering the concert hall.
3. Is the performance spirited and does it seem sincere? Are the players involved in the performance, and do they hold your attention?
4. Did the singer improvise in a scat vocal style?
5. Do the soloists project self-confidence?

Originality and spontaneity are very important to a good jazz performance, although sometimes difficult to recognize and evaluate. The improvised nature of jazz is one area that makes it radically different from most other forms of music. Classical musicians are expected to be flawless and consistent in their presentation of a piece from performance to performance. Jazz musicians, on the other hand, are evaluated on their ability to be consistently spontaneous, uniquely different, and original. The ability to play entirely new improvisations from one performance to the next is risky, but makes a jazz musician stand out from the crowd. To do something unique, unusual, or unpredictable is often the mark of an exceptional jazz performer.

Author and jazz pianist Ted Gioia, in his book *The Imperfect Art*, points out that jazz, if measured against classical music performance standards, is often flawed. In jazz, the emphasis is placed on individual creativity and spontaneity, and, as a result, it is not uncommon to detect slight imperfections in a live performance. If the performers are really "going for it" and striving for an emotion-packed performance, mistakes can occur. The most polished performers, however, are skilled at masking mistakes in their improvisations, even turning them into creative ideas.[3]

The corresponding chapter on the website includes a number of examples to help you identify whether a performance is out of tune, rushes, drags, or is generally sloppy. These examples will help to further clarify these concepts and aid you in assessing the quality of a performance.

Video Blues

Video Blues, composed and arranged by Jack Cooper, is not a jam session played entirely by professionals. It represents a staged, instructional performance providing insight into many aspects of a jazz blues performance. This piece is a 12-bar blues arranged for three horns and a rhythm section. As you listen and watch, try to keep track of the 12-measure form that repeats throughout this video. To assist you in following the 12-bar blues form, conduct a simple 4/4 pattern (found on the website) or count silently as you tap your foot to the tempo: **1**–2–3–4 **2**–2–3–4 **3**–2–3–4 **4**–2–3–4 **5**–2–3–4, etc.

- The first chorus serves as an introduction and acquaints us with the members of the rhythm section. This introduction lasts approximately 22 seconds.
- The horn section makes the first statement of the main theme, from 0.22 to approximately 0.44. Can you explain what happens during this first chorus?
- The second statement of the tune features the trombone in call and response style with the other horns. This section lasts from approximately 0.44 to 1:05.
- The third chorus begins at 1:05 and features an ensemble "break," followed by a trumpet solo. This chorus ends at approximately 1:27.
- The fourth chorus, which begins at 1:27, features an improvised bass solo. The chorus ends at approximately 1:49.
- The alto sax is featured from approximately1:49 to 2:11.
- A drum solo begins the next chorus at approximately 2:12. The drummer exchanges solos in a dialogue with the piano. The chorus ends at approximately 2:33.
- The final chorus features the entire ensemble and begins at approximately 2:34. A final short ending, sometimes referred to as a "tag," is added following this last chorus. This tag begins at approximately 2:51.

After viewing this video you should be able to answer the following questions about the music:

- Did the bass player use an electric or acoustic instrument?
- What instruments accompanied the bass solo?
- What did the other horns do during the alto sax solo?
- Did the saxophonist play alto, tenor, or both?
- When did the drummer switch from sticks to brushes, and why?
- How many measures long was the ensemble "break?"
- What kind of mute did the trumpet soloist use?
- How many measures did the trumpet soloist play during the third chorus?
- Did the bass player use a bow, arco style?
- Was the guitar ever used as a single-line instrument as opposed to playing only chords?
- How many choruses of the blues were played, and specifically what happened during each chorus?

You should be familiar with the following terms and their use throughout this performance:

- call and response
- measure
- unison
- break
- fill
- comping
- pizzicato
- background figure
- syncopation
- trading fours
- phrase
- bar
- shout chorus
- kicks
- fermata.

Once you have completed this chapter, you should have a much clearer understanding of how the various elements of music work together in a jazz context, and how musicians communicate in a performance, interpret the music, and construct jazz music. This newly acquired knowledge will serve you well as you progress through this book, listen to jazz recordings, and attend live performances.

CHAPTER SUMMARY

In listening to jazz, it is very important to hone one's active listening skills. We have become a society of passive listeners, whether it is the way in which background music influences our shopping and eating habits or even the need some feel to have music in the background while doing other tasks (such as studying). Active listening involves noticing different details of a recording (the bass, the ride cymbal, the piano, etc.) during numerous listenings of the performance, as opposed to attempting to absorb all of the details of the performance simply by listening to the composite sound (everything at once).

Although it is possible for any instrument to be used in a jazz setting, some instruments (such as saxophone, flugelhorn, and drum set) are often associated with jazz, whereas others (such as violin, bassoon, and French horn) are more commonly associated with a symphony orchestra. In jazz, the way an instrument is played is much more important than the specific instrument being played. It is common for jazz artists to use techniques often foreign to the classical tradition. This may include such devices as growls, smears, and falls.

KEY TERMS

Accents	Kit	Shout chorus
Arrangement	Orchestration	Soli
Articulation	Phrased (or phrasing)	Tag
Chorus (or refrain)	Reharmonization	Trading fours
Coda (tag)	Ride cymbal	
Ground rhythm	Riffs	
Instrumentation	Scat	

STUDY QUESTIONS

1. Name the instruments usually found in the jazz rhythm section.

2. What wind instrument commonly associated with jazz is rarely heard in a classical music context?

3. Name the woodwind instruments commonly associated with jazz.

4. Name the brass instruments.

5. What is an arrangement, and its significance to jazz?

6. Name some of the special effects associated with jazz playing, especially wind instrument performance practice, and discuss why these affectations are important to jazz as a style. Can you find some of these special effects in recordings found in the companion collection?

7. Discuss the typical architecture that defines many jazz performances. Use letters and short musical terms to express the form and shape.

8. Describe those factors that you would attribute to an excellent jazz performance or recording.

9. When a singer scats, what are they doing?

10. What is meant by swing?

11. Discuss the roles of the rhythm-section instruments.

12. What is meant by orchestration?

CHAPTER 4

The Roots of Jazz

If you play a recording of American Jazz for an African friend . . . he may say, as he sits fidgeting in his chair, "What are we supposed to do with this?" He is expressing the most fundamental aesthetic of African music: without participation there is no meaning . . . The music of Africa invites us to participate in the making of a community.[1]
—John Miller Chernoff

April 16, 1912: The front-page *New York Times* newspaper headline announces the sinking of *The Titanic* ocean liner

JAZZ IN PERSPECTIVE

African slaves, brought to the US largely from the western shores of the continent, provided an indentured workforce for Southern plantations. This African influence provided the most essential catalyst for creating a new American music. Also landing in the US well before the 20th century were immigrants from throughout Europe, including Scots, Irish, English, French, Spaniards,

Background

A great number of pioneers in the jazz field are black and sought, with their music, to explore the roots of their African heritage. Previous discussions have underscored the connections between jazz and African-derived rhythms. The link between American jazz musicians of color and Afro-Latin and Caribbean music is also close, as many black immigrants and African slaves landed in Latin America and the Caribbean islands. It is understandable that jazz musicians from any era would be sympathetic and susceptible to the improvised nature of Afro-Latin and Caribbean music, with its syncopation and rhythmic complexities. The quest for knowledge about the diverse origins of black music has led jazz musicians to discover and assimilate aspects of Afro-Latin and Afro-Caribbean music styles ever since the beginnings of jazz in the Mississippi Delta region and New York. For example, the rich tradition of improvisation found in Cuban music forms a common link with jazz. Much Afro-Latin and Caribbean music is a form of folklore—music of the people. This style of music is a language based on the spontaneous expression of emotions, much like that found in African music. The emotional content of a song, which is frequently emphasized and brought about by rhythms, is of utmost importance to this music. Even the earliest jazz styles demonstrate this same quality, as jazz is a rhythmically rich music that has often been judged less on accuracy, unlike classical-music standards, and more on spontaneity, individual creativity, and raw emotional content. Jazz, like much folk music, including blues, is often assessed as much on emotional content as on sheer musicianship or virtuosity. In other words, you can be a terrific blues musician without having to be a fabulous guitarist or singer by traditional standards. Several common elements, therefore, exist between jazz and Afro-Latin music, serving as additional bonds. Such common bonds as spontaneity, rhythmic drive and complexity, improvisation, and individuality all contribute to an emotionally charged music.

Different drum styles are central to, and help define, different styles of Afro-Caribbean music, just as they contribute to identifying numerous different jazz styles, exemplifying another common bond between jazz and Afro-Caribbean music.

In terms of European influences, it was Spanish culture that most influenced Caribbean music, largely because its political influence ranged over this entire area for decades. Spanish culture is not one dimensional, but the result of the influence of many external cultures that at one time moved through this powerful European nation. These external influences included Arabic, Gypsy, Nordic, Indian, and Judaic. For example, the flamenco dance style is accompanied by music that is permeated with melodies derived from Middle Eastern and Indian scales, featuring a singing style that sounds Arabic in nature. As the Spanish explorers conquered the New World, their hybrid music found yet a new sphere of influence in South America, Central America, and the Caribbean islands. Latin American, Cuban, and other Caribbean music, therefore, is the result of influences from Spain and Africa and, much like early jazz styles, this music from the Caribbean and Latin America is derived largely from dance forms.

Since the 1500s, Cuban music demonstrated traits of European and African styles. Just as African slaves exerted their influences on American culture, they also brought music, religious ritual, and other African cultural practices to Cuba. African slaves came to Cuba from many of the same areas of the continent that supplied the slave trade to the US, namely Nigeria, Congo, Dahomey, and the Sudan. Almost exclusively, African immigrants inhabited several regions in Cuba, so that it is logical that a new music would emerge, identified as Afro-Cuban. African slaves had an impact on reshaping native Cuban music, particularly the rhythmic aspects.

Cuba became a safe haven, not only for Africans but also for Haitians in the 1700s and 1800s. Near the turn of the century (1900s) many Haitians, Cubans, and Puerto Ricans immigrated to New York City, settling in the eastern portion of the city's Harlem district. This area became known as "El Barrio," as it still is today. This term translates as "neighborhood" and became

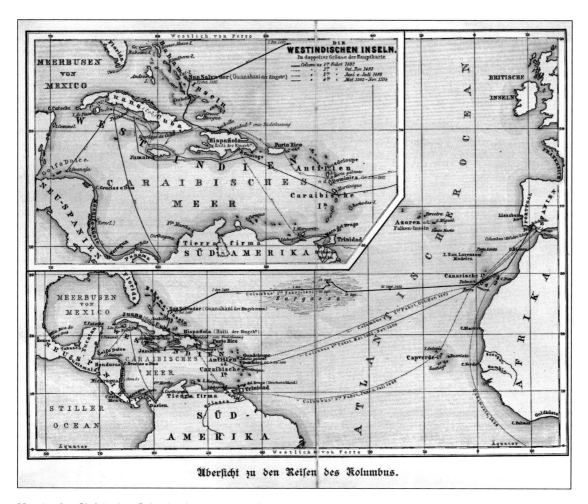

Map tracing Christopher Columbus's voyages, which resemble slave-trade routes

synonymous for Hispanic districts in cities throughout the US. Evidence of this influx of musicians to New York is obvious when one examines the personnel in James Reese Europe's military and society bands from the early 1900s.

In the early 1800s, nearly 10,000 Haitian refugees immigrated to New Orleans, commingling with the city's already culturally diverse population. Many Hispanic and Creole (French influenced) names appeared on the personnel rosters of bands active in New Orleans at the turn of the century. Louisiana was a melting pot of racial diversity, but, in 1894, new legislation changed racial codes, forcing Creoles to lose the social status they had once enjoyed. Consequently, the **Creoles**, who were a mix of French, Spanish, or black ethnicities, could no longer enjoy the educational and cultural benefits afforded them in the past as residents of the more upscale "downtown" area of the "Crescent City." As author Gene Santoro points out, this forced Creoles to mingle with blacks, introducing yet another multicultural flavor to an already rich gumbo in New Orleans. Public celebrations, including street dances and parades, particularly those associated with the Mardi Gras celebration in New Orleans' French Quarter, often featured Cuban- and Mexican-derived music and dance, or European music influenced by these non-European styles.[2] It should be no surprise to hear the similarity between a second line drum rhythm pattern associated with New Orleans street bands and a Latin American or Caribbean dance rhythm, as both often show a kinship with the habanera.

Drawing its heritage from African rhythms, the **habanera** is the basis for Caribbean rhythms and numerous Latin dance styles, including the merengue and conga. The habanera is also thought to be the forefather of the popular 1920s dance known as the Charleston.

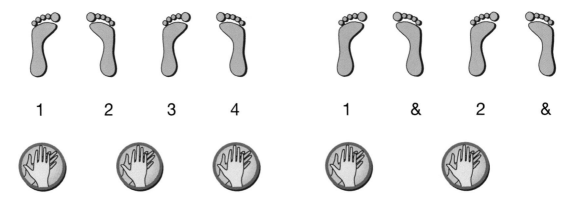

EXAMPLE 4.3
The habanera rhythm is represented in 4/4 meter for convenience, although it is usually found in 2/4 meter. Try to coordinate your hands and feet in a steady tempo. The handclap emphasizes the habanera rhythm, while the feet establish a basic tempo

EXAMPLE 4.4
Notice the close resemblance between this Charleston rhythm (for which an excerpt is available on the website) and the habanera at the middle of the measure

This identical rhythm and similar variations can be found in countless ragtime compositions and other early jazz and American music styles. Notice that all of these brief examples show the natural accent that occurs through anticipation created in the middle of the measure. You don't need to read music to see the resemblance between each of these examples. Each of these rhythmic examples presents a feeling of forward motion created by the anticipation of a major beat (the handclap in the middle of the bar). Anticipations of a major beat create a natural accent that helps to propel the music forward. Try tapping your foot in a regular tempo, while you clap your hands just before your foot comes down. If you clap consecutively in this manner, then syncopation occurs. The constant feeling of forward motion created by rhythmic anticipations (syncopations) played by one group, which collide with notes placed on the beat by other ensemble players, creates tension. It is this tension that provides the buoyant, swinging, bouncy feeling associated with jazz, usually referred to as "swing" and caused by syncopation.

Early Fusions

The first wave of popular Latin music to hit the US at a time when instrumental jazz was still in its infancy was the **tango**. The Christian establishment's reaction to the 1914 tango craze in the US deserves some consideration. The tango was thought to be decadent and barbaric by members of the Christian establishment. Those who participated in this dance craze, and there were many, were accused of loose sexual morals and drug and alcohol abuse. This reaction was not terribly different from reactions to jazz musicians and their music during this same time (for that matter, rock 'n' roll was initially received with similar mixed reviews by the more puritan community). A certain kinship existed, then, between Latin musicians and jazz performers, as both groups were victims of similar social and moral criticism. Jazz had borne the brunt of similar allegations even in the black New Orleans press.

Evidence of African, Afro-Cuban, Afro-Latin, and Afro-Caribbean music could be heard in numerous forms of popular American music in the early years of the 1900s in the US. The dancing and improvisation, key components of Afro-Cuban folk music, merged well with early jazz, also driven by these same forces. The aforementioned Charleston dance rhythm, associated with the flappers of the 1920s, is derived from the Cuban habanera and African rhythms from Ghana.

The rhythm that serves as the heart and soul of nearly all Latin- or Afro-Cuban-based jazz or dance music is the **clavé rhythm**, closely related to the habanera and to African bell patterns. Although the clavé pattern can be played on any percussion instrument, the instrument named after this rhythm often plays it. The clavés are two round, highly polished, hardwood sticks. Other, different rhythms are layered on top of the basic clavé pattern, which serves as a stabilizing anchor to the syncopated, complex, polyrhythmic mosaic that resembles similar concepts found in the rhythms of African music. The clavé pattern is presented as a 2-measure phrase (in 4/4 meter) arranged in subgroupings of either 3–2 or 2–3. In other words, the first measure of the pattern implies one rhythmic grouping (3 or 2), and the second, the opposite grouping. The grouping that outlines 3 provides an element of tension when played against a steady 4/4 pulse, because of the upbeat syncopation following beat 2 and the implied meter subdivisions. Once the clavé pattern begins, it never stops or changes until the song ends, and everything else throughout the song must always conform to the clavé, constructed around it and played in relationship to it. The clavé pattern is closely related to the habanera and appears as a fundamental, unifying rhythm to most Latin-jazz and folk styles. The clavé patterns are illustrated in Example 4.5. The first line shows the 3–2 grouping, with the second line illustrating the implied rhythmic subdivisions. The third line illustrates the 2–3 clavé grouping, and the bottom line shows the relationship of this rhythm to a rhythmic subdivision.

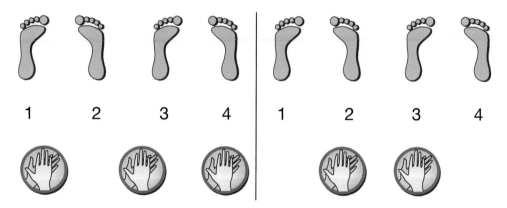

EXAMPLE 4.5 The clavé rhythm: The following illustrations are graphic representations of the 3–2 and 2–3 clavé patterns. The vertical line serves to delineate measures. You should try executing these rhythms with your hands and feet

There are many other similarities between dance rhythms that occur in Latin American and Caribbean folk music and rhythms found in jazz. Even the classic swing-style jazz drummer's ride cymbal rhythm (ding dinga ding dinga ding, etc.) can be traced back to origins in Afro-Latin and Caribbean rhythms.

The website includes demonstrations of the clavé rhythm. The clavé, as well as examples of numerous other indigenous Latin or Afro-Caribbean percussion instruments, can also be found in the corresponding chapter on the website.

EARLY AMERICAN VOCAL MUSIC

Some forms of African music promulgated in the US by slaves had a subtle impact on the formation of early jazz. For example, the performance of work songs and field hollers by slaves had little audience outside the plantations. Aside from the white overseers supervising the slave workforce, white listeners were likely unaware of such African-based music, unless they had an occasion to visit **Congo Square** in New Orleans (now known as Louis Armstrong Park). The square was a park-like place where blacks were permitted to congregate and participate in various ceremonies and rituals, both secular and sacred. Such gatherings often featured music and dance, improvisational in nature. Although it is true that the improvisatory nature of some of the work songs, designed

Slaves returning from the cotton fields in South Carolina, c.1860

to rhythmically mimic a work task and take one's mind off the drudgery of indentured slavery, may have eventually exerted some influence on American music, the influences on early jazz and blues are not obvious or well documented through recordings.

Slaves had the most contact with whites and European-derived music through their participation in religious-worship services, often sponsored, or at least encouraged, by their owners. Africans, who typically worshipped many gods, were comfortable with religious ceremony and ritual, and so they adapted easily to the Christian beliefs taught to them by their white masters. It was in this context that African musical influences were gradually exerted on traditional Christian hymns. Transformed, African-influenced religious songs eventually became know as **spirituals**, **gospels**, and **jubilees**. Spirituals were derived from white folk hymns and camp-meeting songs. They were often based on sacred themes or Bible scripture that illiterate slaves and whites attending the worship services could not read. To involve the congregation, the preacher intoned, or lined out, one phrase of text at a time. The parishioners responded by singing the line back, using some familiar folk or religious hymn tune of the day as a basis. Once again, the call–response format already familiar to Africans was put to use in the lining-out of religious text using song. As the tunes were slow, the congregation often embellished the melodies, singing them as they had remembered them or been taught by their elders, and in their own personal styles, often resulting in harmony. The themes were based on ridding themselves of the devil and returning to the Promised Land. Spirituals typically feature long, sustained melodies and communicate sadness. "Nobody Knows the Trouble I've Seen" and "Swing Low Sweet Chariot" are well known examples of the spiritual, which is often associated with, and influenced by, the blues. Gospels and jubilees, on the other hand, tend to be quicker in tempo, more rhythmic, and generally more high-spirited, featuring hand-clapping and other forms of rhythmic and instrumental accompaniment. The gospel, which developed some years later as an offshoot of the spiritual, was intended to be sung in harmony and without accompaniment by instruments. Blacks and

Fisk Jubilee Singers

Listen to examples of Fisk University vocal groups singing "Swing Low, Sweet Chariot," "Roll Jordan Roll," and "Great Camp Meeting" on the "Experiencing Jazz Playlist" at the Library of Congress Jukebox.

whites practiced spiritual and gospel styles, and, therefore, both styles were influenced by African and European musical traditions. In both cases, the bending of pitches and other, similar blues inflections were evident. Gospels might feature lyrics that are more secular in nature, or might project a message that could be interpreted with religious or secular overtones. The jubilee was a high-spirited song of praise and celebration. Most of us have heard "When the Saints Go Marching In," which is a fine example of what began as a jubilee, before being transformed into a widely performed New Orleans-style Dixieland instrumental piece. The Fisk Jubilee Singers, a product of Fisk University in the late 1800s, traveled widely, performing in these various vocal styles.

Mark Twain wrote to a friend in 1897 after hearing a performance by this group, saying: "I think that in the Jubilees and their songs, America has produced the perfect flower of the ages; and I wish it were a foreign product so she would worship it and lavish money on it and go properly crazy over it."[3] At this point, Americans still looked to Europe for inspiration, guidance, and approval when it came to the arts, and Twain seems to lament the fact that Americans could not yet appreciate the beauty and originality in their own, original product.

THE INNOVATORS: GETTING THE BLUES

Considering all the early black vocal styles, it is safe to say that the blues has had the most far-reaching impact. No one seems to know precisely how the characteristics of the blues came about, but it seems logical to assume that the blues was born as a consequence of the africanization of Western music.

The blues is perhaps as misunderstood a term as "jazz" or "swing." It can imply a mood or emotional state, a chord progression, or a tonality achieved by embellishing a melodic line. To make matters worse, blues became so popular in the early years of the 20th century that the word was frequently used in song titles even though the song bore absolutely no classic blues characteristics. The poetry of a blues lyric, in the case of a vocal blues, often tells the story of lost love, persecution, or any of life's other tribulations. The blues originated as a folk music with solo singers/songwriters who often improvised the melody and lyrics, accompanying themselves on a guitar or piano. Because these early blues songs were improvised by solo performers, there was a high degree of spontaneity, and there was no consistency in terms of length, chord progression, or meter. The rhythm, accent, and meter of the lyrics dictated how many beats to a measure and how many measures long the chorus would be. Through the use of vocal inflections such as bends, shakes, scoops, shouts, and varying vibrato speed, these early blues singers delivered emotionally charged performances. Hence, it was the high level of raw emotion projected, rather than the sophistication of the music, that was of most significance. The accompaniment, rather than consisting of a series of chords, might be little more than a single drone note on the guitar or a simple reoccurring melody, perhaps derived from a pentatonic or blues scale.

There are many styles of blues—classic, country, urban, and so on. There is not universal agreement on the character of each of these blues styles, and the lines that differentiate one from the other can be quite blurred. By the early 1920s, blues singers began to exert an influence on early jazz instrumentalists. This collaboration between singers and instrumentalists led to the gradual standardization of the blues form that continues to be recognized today.

For additional information on the blues and harmony, refer to these discussions on the website in Chapter 2—"The Elements of Jazz." If you haven't already done so, look at the *Video Blues* movie, also on the website and found in Chapter 3—"Listening to Jazz."

The classic blues form consists of 12 measures and essentially three primary chords—the I, IV and V chords. As jazz matured, this simple three-chord progression became only the skeletal outline for increasingly complex blues progressions, through the addition of many more chords connecting the three previously mentioned. Blues can be in a minor or major key, and the general tonality or lyric does not have to communicate melancholy. In fact, many blues pieces from the swing and bebop periods of jazz are actually quite uplifting. Some blues progressions have been extended to 16 measures, whereas others have been shortened to only 8. A bridge or middle section, usually 8 measures in length, can be added to extend the more typical 12-bar blues even further. In this case, the entire form would resemble the ABA song-form format for a total of 32 measures (each A is 12 measures in length, plus an 8-bar bridge).

The classic 12-bar blues is usually presented as three 4-measure phrases. The first line of text is usually repeated, followed by a third that acts as a contrast and summary to the first line. Each verse follows this same antecedent–consequent pattern. As the lyric typically occupies only about 2 measures, or half the length of each 4-measure phrase, an instrumentalist usually improvises during the second half of each phrase. The 2-measure improvisation serves as a "response" to the lyric, which represents the "call" in this African-derived format. Example 4.6 shows a template for this classic 12-bar-blues form.

Lyric   (Call)   Improvisation   (Response)

Lyric   (Call)   Improvisation   (Response)

Lyric   (Call)   Improvisation   (Response)

EXAMPLE 4.6 Classic 12-bar blues. Each block represents 1 measure

Robert Johnson (1911–1938)

Robert Johnson (1911–1938) is one of the foremost examples of this rich tradition, although his recordings were issued years after the blues emerged around the turn of the century. Only 11, 78-rpm "race" records were released during his lifetime, but his work has become recognized worldwide and was influential in the commercialization of rock 'n' roll and R & B styles years later. He lived in relative obscurity most of his life, but was canonized as an innovator in 1994, when the U.S. Postal Service issued a commemorative stamp with his portrait.

Johnson, known in some circles as "King of the Delta Blues," was as much a blues poet as he was a solo singer/songwriter. He wrote and sang about his own experiences as a musician wandering the Mississippi Delta region in hopes of establishing a reputation that would help him to escape a life of sharecropping and migrant itinerant fieldwork. In the early stages of his career,

LISTENING GUIDE

🔊))

Robert Johnson, *King of the Delta Blues Singers Vol. II*

"Ramblin' on My Mind" Take 2 (Robert Johnson) 2:33

Recorded San Antonio, Texas, 11/23/1936 for Vocalion Records

First released 1990; reissued on Columbia/Legacy CK 92579

Key and form: Blues, although not consistently 12 measures per chorus; F major (possibly E major, given inconsistencies in early 78-rpm pressings)

0:00–0:06	**Introduction—solo guitar**

0:07–0:36	First verse
	I
	I got ramblin', I got ramblin' on my mind
	     IV I
	I got ramblin', I got ramblin' all on my mind
	         V IV I
	Hate to leave my baby, but you treats me so unkind
	[Guitar ends verses with final phrase]

0:37–1:103	**Second verse**
	I
	And now babe, I will never forgive you anymore
	        IV I
	Little girl, little girl, I will never forgive you anymore
	        V IV I
	You know you did not want me, baby, why did you tell me so? [Guitar ends verses with final phrase]

1:04–1:28	**Third verse**
	I
	And I'm runnin' down to the station, catch that first mail train I see
	(spoken softly: I hear her comin' now)
	        IV I
	An' I'm runnin' down to the station, catch that old first mail train I see
	       V IV I
	I've got the blues 'bout Miss So-and-So, and the child got the blues about me
	[Guitar ends verses with final phrase]

1:29–1:55	**Fourth verse** I An' they's de'ilment,* she got devilment* all on her mind IV I She's got devilment, little girl, you got devilment all on your mind V IV I Now I got to leave this mornin', with my arm' fold' up and cryin' [Guitar ends verses with final phrase]
1:56–end	**Fifth verse** I I believe, I believe my time ain't long IV I I believe, I believe that my time ain't long V IV I But I'm leavin' this mornin', I believe I will go back home [Guitar ends with final phrase]

*Devilment means devilish, cruel or wicked behavior

© (1978) 1990, 1991 Lehsem II, LLC/Claud L. Johnson

Administered by Music & Media International, Inc.

he performed largely at jook joints and roadhouses that catered to loggers, migrant workers, and crews building roads for the Works Progress Administration (WPA) project. He became attracted to alcohol, gambling, and women, and it was his obsession with finding the right woman that led to his untimely death, supposedly at the hand of a jealous man who laced his whiskey with poison.

Although Johnson became well known in the Delta region, especially Mississippi and Arkansas, it wasn't until the release of his first recordings that his reputation spread, enabling him to tour outside the region, with performances in Chicago, New York, Detroit, St. Louis, and Canada. His first hit record for Vocalion Records, "Terraplane Blues," served to advance his career and no doubt led to John Hammond's quest to book him as an opening act for his 1938 "From Spirituals to Swing" extravaganza at Carnegie Hall. Hammond, a jazz impresario and champion of black performers, was unaware of Johnson's untimely death.

The recording included on the online anthology demonstrates this great rustic blues tradition. Johnson's original style marries his vocal poetry with a free-style guitar accompaniment that ranges from rhythmic chords in a boogie-woogie shuffle-like feel, to single-line, soloistic gestures that respond to his lyrics. By modern standards, his performance might be considered crude or rough around the edges, but there is an austere beauty, rhythmic savvy, and overall complexity to his emotionally charged performance that is unmistakable. Notice how he does not strictly adhere to balanced phrases, each with 4 measures of 4 beats. What comes naturally seems to be of greater importance, although one suddenly gets the sense that a beat was skipped here or there, or a measure added to the expected modern 12-bar-blues form. Johnson does adhere to the typical three-chord sequence (I–IV–V), and each chord has been noted above the lyric in the listening guide on p. 58. Each line is completed by solo guitar.

BESSIE SMITH (1894–1937)

Known as the "Empress of the Blues," Bessie Smith (1894–1937) is another classic blues singer from the period. In contrast to Johnson, she frequently shared the stage and recordings with jazz players who accompanied her. Listen to Bessie Smith's performance of "Lost Your Head Blues," included on early editions of the *Smithsonian Collection of Classic Jazz* (*SCCJ*), while following the lyrics provided below. Roman numerals and chord symbols have also been provided to help you follow the chord progression. Bessie begins singing after a brief 4-measure introduction improvised by cornetist Joe Smith. This performance follows the classic blues format outlined above, and, in this case, Joe Smith assumes the role of brilliantly improvising in a call and response format, following each lyric.

Bessie Smith, "Empress of the Blues"

LISTENING GUIDE

Bessie Smith

"Lost Your Head Blues"

Recorded 5/4/1926

Personnel: Bessie Smith, vocal; Joe Smith, cornet; Fletcher Henderson, piano. (Roman numeral chord symbols are indicated above the lyrics of each verse.)

	4-measure instrumental introduction	
Verse 1	I chord, 4 bars	
	I was with you baby when you did not have a dime	[J. Smith improvises 2 bars]
	IV chord, 2 bars	I chord, 2 bars
	I was with you baby when you did not have a dime	[J. Smith improvises]
	V⁷ chord, 2 bars	
	Now since you got plenty money you have throw'd your good gal down	
	[J. Smith improvises on I chord for 1 bar and V⁷ chord for 1 bar to end form]	
Verse 2	I chord, 4 bars	
	One things for always you ain't worth my while	[J. Smith improvises 2 bars]
	IV chord, 2 bars	I chord, 2 bars
	One things for always you ain't worth my while	[J. Smith improvises]
	V⁷ chord, 2 bars	I chord, 1 bar V⁷ /chord, 1 bar
	When you get a good gal you'd better treat her nice	[J. Smith improvises]
Verse 3	I chord, 4 bars	
	When you were lonesome I've tried to treat you kind	[J. Smith improvises 2 bars]
	IV chord, 2 bars	I chord, 2 bars
	When you were lonesome I've tried to treat you kind	[J. Smith improvises]
	V⁷ chord, 2 bars	I chord, 1 bar V⁷ /chord, 1 bar
	But since you're got money it done change your mind	[J. Smith improvises]
Verse 4	I chord, 4 bars	
	I'm gonna leave baby ain't gonna say goodbye	[J. Smith improvises 2 bars]
	IV chord, 2 bars	I chord, 2 bars
	I'm gonna leave baby ain't gonna say goodbye	[J. Smith improvises]
	V⁷ chord, 2 bars	I chord, 1 bar V⁷ /chord 1 bar
	But I'll write you and tell you the reason why	[J. Smith improvises]
Verse 5	I chord, 4 bars	
	Days are lonesome nights are so long long	[J. Smith improvises 2 bars]
	IV chord, 2 bars	I chord, 2 bars
	Days are lonesome nights are so long long	[J. Smith improvises]
	V⁷ chord, 2 bars	I chord, 1 bar V⁷/chord, 1 bar
	I'm a good ole gal but I just been treated wrong	[J. Smith improvises]

W.C. HANDY—"FATHER OF THE BLUES" (1873–1958)

William Christopher Handy (1873–1958), a bandsman, composer, and cornet player, is remembered as the "father of the Blues," following the publication in 1941 of his autobiography by the same name. Although there is some debate about this prestigious title, as others claim to publishing or performing in this style before Handy's "Memphis Blues" in 1912, history does show that it was W.C. Handy that brought the blues to widespread popularity. Handy was the son of a Methodist minister who had been freed from slavery. He readily admitted that he patterned his versions of the blues after black folk songs, with their roots in the South, though he also heard blues being sung on the streets of St. Louis well before his first publications. He heard these songs performed during his travels as a minstrel musician. **Minstrel shows** were early touring variety shows, popular during the mid 1800s. Traveling with small bands, actors, comedians, jugglers, and other entertainers, the shows offered humor, musical numbers, dancing, and often a parody play based on an *Uncle Tom's Cabin*-like theme. Minstrel shows are significant to a discussion of jazz, for they provided a means of employment for many early jazz musicians. Handy's travels with such shows took him all over the US and as far away as Havana, Cuba, where he initially heard the Afro-Latin rhythms that would later have a major impact on his compositions.

Promotional photo, c.1930, of W.C. Handy, "Father of the Blues"

As early as 1914, W.C. Handy incorporated a **tangana** (tango or habanera) rhythm in the first and third sections of his "St. Louis Blues" and in "Memphis Blues." It is the bass line from the "tango" section of Handy's "St. Louis Blues" that clearly borrows from this fundamental Afro-Latin rhythm.

Handy's first published composition was "Memphis Blues," originally written as a campaign song for a Memphis politician and titled "A Southern Rag." Handy and a partner formed a publishing company, one of the first black companies to enter this business. Although "Memphis Blues" enjoyed steady sales and has been recorded by numerous artists, it was Handy's "St. Louis Blues," published in 1914, that earned him the title "Father of the Blues." It was first recorded in 1915 and subsequently became the most widely recorded song in America. To quote David A. Jasen and Gene Jones, who authored *Spreadin' Rhythm Around: Black Popular Songwriters, 1880–1930*, "By 1930 ['St. Louis Blues'] was the most famous blues in the world. By 1930 it was the best-selling song in any medium—sheet music, recordings, and piano rolls."[4] Not only were its lyrics innovative, but "its harmonies literally put new notes into the pop music scale, and its structure showed writers a new way to build popular songs."[5] Handy actually used the blues scale in the body of this composition, which had never been done before in a published work. The success of this Handy original helped to pave the way for a blues sensation that swept the country in the early 1920s. Many new labels, or subsidiary labels of larger companies, were formed for the specific purpose of recording blues singers, including Bessie Smith.

In 1929, Handy's "St. Louis Blues" became the subject of a short film starring Bessie Smith, her only appearance on film. It was very likely her poignant recording of Handy's popular blues, also featuring Louis Armstrong, that led to her being selected for this role. This film is barely 15 minutes long but features an all black cast, including a large choir and stride pianist/composer James P. Johnson. Racial attitudes at this time prohibited mixing of blacks and whites on film, although it became increasingly common in the late 1920s to hear mixed companies of actors and/or musicians on radio, a faceless medium.

Every aspect of Handy's hit song "St. Louis Blues" was innovative, from the lyrics, which tell a frank tale of love lost, to the harmony, melody, and formal aspects of his composition. The formal structure is perhaps the most clearly innovative aspect of Handy's presentation of the blues. Most blues of the day were only 12 measures in length, with a formal scheme of simply A that was repeated numerous times. The formal scheme found in "St. Louis Blues," however, follows an AABA song form pattern, where each A represents a typical 12-bar-blues chord progression. The lyrics in these blues sections follow the same predictable pattern found in many blues tunes, including "Lost Your Head Blues," previously discussed. The first 2 measures of each 4-bar phrase in the A section are dedicated to lyrics, followed by impressive 2-measure improvisations by Louis Armstrong. This A-section architecture is typical in that it represents the classic question–answer or call and response format, in this case contrasting vocalist and improvising cornet soloist. The B section in this case is 16 measures in length, deviating from the blues norm. The chord progression in the final A section following B returns to the blues form; however, it is slightly different than the chord progression found in the initial A sections that begin the chorus. The B section departs from this standard blues sequence and features a tango-influenced rhythm, although barely discernible in this version. The form is sometimes changed, however, and performers have moved sections around, putting the B section before the A. For example, Handy's 1922 recording with his own band shows the tango B section first. Handy's earlier travels to Cuba and the 1914 tango dance craze in the US were no doubt responsible for this obvious influence. The formal outline, harmonic scheme, and lyrics that follow will help guide you through the performance of this historic recording on the companion website.

RAGTIME

The blues and **ragtime** styles actually emerged concurrently in the US, although the blues continues to exert significant influence on jazz, whereas ragtime does not. Ragtime enjoyed the limelight as a very influential style from about 1895 to 1915, although it is not considered more than an important precursor to jazz. It is considered to be the first style of American music to enjoy widespread popularity and demonstrate that a native form of American music, highly influenced by black performers and composers, could actually be the basis of commercial success. This music not only impressed many Americans, who bought sheet music versions, piano rolls, and pianos, but it also showed significant influence on classical composers of the day. In fact, one could say that this early jazz style found its greatest champions in those classical musicians of the day, who were enamored with its fresh and unique rhythmic qualities.

Racism in the US was born out of slavery, Jim Crow Laws, **minstrelsy** (an early form of variety show consisting of comical skits, dancing, and music, initially performed by whites in black face), and other forms of bigotry and stereotyping. **Coon songs** were often featured in minstrel shows. They were folk songs with lyrics that were generally derogatory of blacks and serve to exemplify racist attitudes of the time. In a sense, they were racist musical jokes that bore titles such as, "Every Race Has a Flag But the Coon," and "You're Just a Little Nigger, But You're Mine All Mine." White male and or female singers in black face often sang these songs, perhaps as minstrel-show entertainers. The same syncopated rhythms found in these early folk songs were the basis for similar syncopations and rhythmic vitality found in rags. Authors Jasen and Jones described the impact of this late 1800s coon song on ragtime as follows:

> Their constant use of syncopation attuned the public ear for the ragtime that would appear
> around the turn of the century. And their slangy, "low-class" lyrics took a big step away
> from politer European operatic song models. Their commercial success introduced "black"

LISTENING GUIDE 🔊

W.C. Handy

"St. Louis Blues" (W.C. Handy) 3:09

Bessie Smith, vocal; Louis Armstrong, cornet; Fred Longshaw, harmonium.

Recorded in New York, 1/14/1925

Columbia 14064-D

Key and form: D major; AA^1 (12-bars blues repeated); BB^1 (8 bars repeated in parallel key of D minor); A^{11} (12-bar blues back in original key of D major)

0:00–0:04	**Introduction**	

0:04 — First A section—12-bar blues

I	IV^7	V^7	I	I^7

I hate ta see the eve'nin sun go down   [Armstrong improvises second 2 measures]

| IV^7 | bVI^{7*} | V^7 | I | I^7 |

I hate ta see the eve'nin sun go down   [Armstrong improvises second 2 measures]

| V^7 | | ii* | V^7 | I^7 |

series of chords leading to V^7

It make me think I'm on my last go'round   [Armstrong improvises second 2 measures]

0:49 — Second A section—12-bar blues

| I | | IV^7 | V^7 | I | | I^7 |

Feelin' tomorrow like I feel today   [Armstrong improvises second 2 bars]

| IV^7 | bVI^{7*} V^7 | I | | I^7 |

Feelin' tomorrow like I feel today   [Armstrong improvises second 2 bars]

| V^7 | ii | V^7 |

string of chords leading from I^7 to V^7

I'll pack my grips [bags], 'n' make my get-a-way   [Armstrong improvises second 2 bars]

1:33 — B section (16 bars) (often played as a tango but not in this version)

| I | | V^7 |

St. Louis woman, with her diamond rings   [Armstrong improvises second 2 bars]

| V^7 | i (minor resolution) |

Pulls dat man around by her apron strings   [Armstrong improvises second 2 bars]

| i | V^7 |

Wasn't for powder an' the store-bought hair   [Armstrong improvises second 2 bars]

| V^7 | i | II^7 | V^7 |

The man I love wouldn't go nowhere, no . . . where . . .
I got dem
[Smith begins last verse as an anticipation of the next full chorus,
Armstrong begins accompaniment]

2:29 — Return to A section—12-bar blues

| I | V^7 | I | V^7 | I | V^7| V^7 | I | | | I^7 |

St. Louis Blues and as blue as I can be   [Armstrong improvises second 2 bars]

| IV^7 | | V^7 | I^7 |

He's got a heart like a rock cast in the sea   [Armstrong improvises second 2 bars]

| V^7 | bVI^{7*} | V^7 | I | I^7/F-sharp bass | IV^7 | bVIdim | D |

Or else he wouldn't have gone so far from me

* Denotes typical substitute chord for usual IV^7 chord

subject matter—and the work of many black songwriters—into middleclass white parlors on sheet music and cylinder records. In this time of families entertaining themselves at home around the piano, part of the fun was the naughtiness of playing at being black. Other ethnic groups took their lumps in songs but blacks got the worst of it.[6]

Both black and white musicians championed this piano style. Black pianist/composer Tom Turpin gained the first copyright for a rag in 1883, and white pianist/composer William Krell was the first to publish a ragtime composition in 1897, entitled the "Mississippi Rag." It was the black composers Scott Joplin and James Scott, however, who were perhaps most responsible for advancing the style.

Much like "blues," the term "rag" was frequently misused and often interchanged with the terms "blues," "two-step," and "cakewalk." The term "rag" supposedly stemmed from a black folk-dance style of the day, referred to as clog dancing. The word **ragtime** is thought to be a composite of two words—rag, meaning syncopated, and time, meaning rhythm. Therefore, ragtime implies a style of playing where rhythms are syncopated. The **cakewalk** was an upbeat, syncopated dance style popular prior to the beginning of the 20th century. Cakewalks continued to provide rousing finales to minstrel shows and often involved the entire cast dancing to rag-like music. Ragging was also considered a way of playing or interpreting music through the use of spontaneous syncopation.

What clearly differentiates a rag from a blues is the formal structure. Ragtime compositions have little resemblance to African styles, as the formal scheme and harmonic style for rags is clearly derived from European models. The AABBACCDD rondo form, or some close facsimile, is found in many rags and is closely related to the same form found in marches, reels, coon songs, polkas, and cakewalks of the day. Each section is usually 8 measures in length, and there is typically a modulation (key change) away from the primary key at the C theme, much like the key change found in marches at the trio. The "March King" and great American Bandmaster John Philip Sousa admired this style and often featured a "rag" or a "march and two-step" in his concert band performances.

Listen to examples of Sousa's band playing "Creole Belles" and "Chinese Blues" on the "Experiencing Jazz Playlist" at the Library of Congress Jukebox.

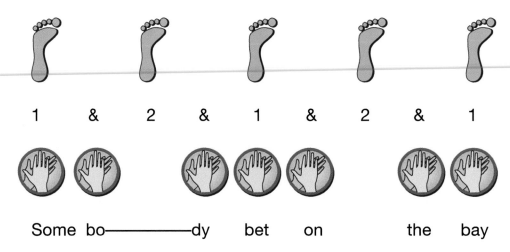

EXAMPLE 4.7 Final rhythm from Stephen Foster's "Camptown Races"

1899 sheet-music cover of Scott Joplin's "Maple Leaf Rag"

Rags also bore a remarkable similarity to tunes such as "Turkey in the Straw" (subtitled "Ragtime Fantasie") and "Camptown Races," composed by popular American folk songwriter Stephen Foster.

The classic rag was a strictly composed solo piano style that incorporated little or no improvisation or blues influences, at least by its early primary practitioners. Rags were composed in either 2/4 or 4/4 meter and featured a very regular, oompah-like left hand that supplied the fundamental rhythm while outlining the harmonies. The right hand added syncopated melodies to these regular, left-hand striding rhythms that served to emphasize strong beats (1 and 3). It was a percussive, mechanical style of syncopation though, and did not swing, as would be the case some years later. For example, listen to Jelly Roll Morton's recording of "Maple Leaf Rag" included on the *SCCJ* (editions before 2010). Not only has it been rhythmically transformed to swing, but Morton also altered the form and significantly embellished the melody (no doubt through improvisation) compared with the original Joplin recording included in the anthology that accompanies this text.

Portrait of American ragtime composer and pianist Scott Joplin (1868–1917), c.1910

Although the popularity of rags quickly spread from coast to coast, the geographic region that is generally considered as the epicenter of ragtime was the Midwest—specifically the cities of St. Louis and Sedalia. It was here that the major ragtime publishers began mass-producing sheet music in this style for distribution nationwide. Many of the next generation's band leaders/composers and jazz pianists, such as Duke Ellington, Fletcher Henderson, Fats Waller, and James P. Johnson, were first introduced to the piano through rags. It is believed that Duke Ellington first learned to play the piano by mimicking the key motion on a player piano spinning piano rolls of this kind of music.

Those composers deeply committed to the ragtime style were convinced that this was the new classical music of America, and that they were destined to achieve fame and fortune as its progenitors. Joplin, and later James P. Johnson, composed large-scale concert works including operettas, symphonies, choral works, and ballets in the ragtime style, although none of these efforts was successful, may never have been published, and in some cases they were never performed publicly. Joplin's operas "A Guest of Honor" and "Treemonisha" each saw only one self-produced public performance, and they were not well received. The latter was finally reproduced in 1976, winning the Pulitzer Prize that year. Joplin never recovered from the earlier failure, however, and, despite their best efforts to transform this style into a serious

LISTENING GUIDE

Scott Joplin

"Maple Leaf Rag" (Joplin) 3:19

Piano roll made by Scott Joplin in April 1916

Recorded from piano roll 6/1/1986 (Connorized piano roll #10265)

Form: AABBACCDD (16 bars of each theme)

0:00	A theme
0:23	A theme repeated
0:45	B theme—more rhythmic and syncopated with right-hand melody in octaves
1:07	B theme repeated
1:29	A theme returns
1:51	C theme in new key of D-flat major, richer harmonically in contrast with more right-hand chords
2:12	C theme repeated
2:34	D theme returns to key of A-flat major
2:57	D theme repeated

American national style, these composers began to witness the demise of public interest in ragtime around 1914. Although the influences of the ragtime piano style can be seen in the instrumental jazz of the era and it served as the direct predecessor of the stride solo piano style, ragtime had outlived its time and was eclipsed by the onslaught of instrumental jazz, featuring the daring, exciting, and virtuosic improvising soloist as the centerpiece.

Track 2 of the online audio anthology features a modern recording of Scott Joplin's performance of "Maple Leaf Rag." The original piano roll was made by the composer in 1916 and was re-recorded using a player piano and modern recording equipment in 1986. This recording, therefore, is not completely accurate in representing Joplin's performance skill. Nonetheless, it does give us a glimpse of his artistry as a composer and pianist. This popular rag follows the classic model, containing four uniquely different themes. The formal scheme is represented as AABBACCDD—not quite a classic rondo form. A key change occurs at the C theme. The time chart in the listening guide on p. 66 should help you follow these themes as they unfold.

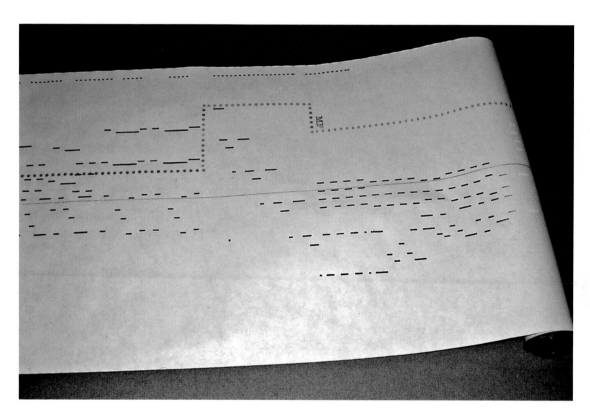

Player piano roll of Scott Joplin's "Maple Leaf Rag," patented September 13, 1904

BRASS AND MILITARY BANDS

Brass bands were an American tradition borrowed from Europe and popular in many towns around the US well before World War I and the beginnings of jazz. Some of the early jazz musicians began their careers as members of such bands, many situated in and around New Orleans. Early jazz instrumentalists Jimmy Noone, Sidney Bechet, Buddy Bolden, Bunk Johnson, and Joe "King" Oliver were all initially members of these brass bands. Brass-band repertoires included instrumental arrangements of piano rags, blues, marches, polkas, czardaszes (Slovakian folk dance), schottisches (Bohemian or Czech folk dance), cakewalks, and coon songs. Bands such as the

Olympia and Excelsior bands included cornets, clarinets, trombones, drums, tuba, and sometimes stringed instruments such as the banjo, guitar, and violin. It is believed that the banjo was actually derived from a similarly constructed African instrument.

These bands performed indoors and outdoors for various functions, including weddings, funerals, street parades advertising a touring show, a product or a business, and special occasions sponsored by various fraternal organizations.

On the East Coast, society bands and military bands began to reflect the influences of ragtime on instrumental music in the early 1900s. Syncopation was, no doubt, what James Reese Europe, an early black military and society bandleader, was referring to in 1919 when he talked about his band members "accenting notes which originally would be without accent."[7] It was the results of these early attempts at rhythmic interpretation that led to the beginnings of jazz, swing, and those subtle ingredients that cannot be notated accurately using the Western system of notation. Just like African music, jazz rhythms cannot be precisely notated. This fact no doubt frustrated the French musicians who tried, without success, to duplicate the sound of Europe's 1919 military band by merely reading the music he gave them. Hence, we can conclude that neither jazz nor African music can be played authentically by reading notes on the page. Traditional music notation must be translated by musicians familiar with the jazz style in order for the music to sound like jazz.

 Listen to an example of Europe's Society Orchestra performing "The Castles in Europe" on the "Experiencing Jazz Playlist" at the Library of Congress Jukebox.

Although James Reese Europe's and Will Marion Cook's society bands and orchestras in New York were recorded prior to the first jazz recording in 1917, no authentic recordings exist to document the sounds of these early New Orleans brass bands. There was no recording industry at the time, as the new technology for the preservation of sound had not yet been perfected. These bands served as a springboard for much smaller, more mobile ensembles that eventually became an essential ingredient of city nightlife.

MILESTONES

Chronicle of Historic Events

The timeline that follows will put the developments of jazz discussed in this chapter into a larger historical context, providing you with a better sense of how landmark musical events may relate to others that match your personal areas of interest.

1905	• The years leading up to the beginnings of instrumental jazz saw a tremendous influx of immigrants from Europe.
	• Oklahoma becomes the 46th state in 1907.
	• Women are not welcome in the workforce, though many are employed by the telephone company.
	• The light bulb is still being perfected by General Electric.
1908	• Long-distance radio broadcasts are still only dreamed about.

- A rebellious group of painters known as "The Eight" focuses on works depicting the coming of a new age—the industrialization and urbanization of America. Their touring show also focuses on the growing population of immigrants.

- President Theodore Roosevelt forms a commission to save natural resources.

- Competition begins between early auto manufacturers—Ford, Buick/GM.

- Jack Johnson becomes the first black boxer to win the world heavyweight championship.

- Gustav Mahler (composer) and Toscanini (conductor) make their U.S. debuts.

1909
- Admiral Peary reaches the North Pole.

- Psychologists Freud and Jung become well known for their theories and writings.

- W.C. Handy's ("Father of the Blues") "Memphis Blues" was composed for Edward "Boss" Crumps election campaign song. This is believed to be the first black-authored blues tune to be published.

- Architect Frank Lloyd Wright establishes his reputation.

- The first opera is broadcast live on radio from the MET by Lee de Forest, inventor of the radio vacuum tube.

1910
- The National Association for the Advancement of Colored People (NAACP) is founded.

- George Eastman develops the first easy-to-use portable camera.

- The Urban League is formed to help blacks migrating to northern cities from the South.

1911
- Irving Berlin's "Alexander's Ragtime Band" is a huge hit.

- Workers begin to unionize and strike for better wages.

1912
- A minimum-wage law is established.

- Wilson is elected president on the "New Freedom" slogan and human rights ticket.

- Jazz pianist/composer Jelly Roll Morton publishes "The Jelly Roll Blues."

- HMS Titanic sinks, killing 1,500 passengers.

- W. C. Handy published "Memphis Blues," the first published blues composition.

1913
- Congress passes an income-tax amendment.

- Buffalo Nickel makes its debut.

- Ford opens an assembly line to build the Model T automobile.

- A woman makes the first air flight as a passenger.

- Cecil B. DeMille produces the first full-scale Hollywood film at a cost of $47,000 for six reels.

1914–1916
- W.C. Handy publishes (1914) "St. Louis Blues," which is first recorded in 1915.

- The tango craze hits the US.

- War spreads throughout Europe, threatening to involve the US.

- Industry booms in the US.

- AT&T sends the first wireless message across the Atlantic Ocean in 1916.

- The first birth-control clinic signals new morals and the erosion of puritan Victorian ideals.

- Scott Joplin makes a piano roll of the "Maple Leaf Rag."

CHAPTER SUMMARY

The diverse influences of West African music, early American vocal music, blues, brass bands, and ragtime all contributed to the beginnings of jazz. From West Africa the use of polyrhythms was very important in the development of syncopated ragtime melodies and, later, to the swing feel of early jazz. Work songs, field hollers, spirituals, gospels, and other aspects of American vocal music contributed many of the inflections/effects that identify jazz.

Although not immediately obvious in some jazz styles, Afro-Latin and Caribbean music has had some kind of influence on many jazz styles. Like jazz, this music involves a mixing of elements from different cultures, including African and Spanish music that developed somewhat separately from that of the rest of Europe. Trade that brought many black immigrants and slaves to the US similarly affected Latin America and the Caribbean islands. One of the first jazz pieces to obviously fall under the influence of Latin music was W.C. Handy's "St. Louis Blues" (1914), which includes a tango section. The Argentinean tango was one of the numerous waves of dances that washed ashore from points south to excite dance-crazed Americans. The impact of Latin American dances can also be seen in the Charleston, a popular dance in the US in the 1920s that shows rhythms similar to the Cuban habanera. The clavé rhythm is also closely related to the habanera and of significant influence to developing jazz styles.

Ragtime is a composed music that flourished in the late 1890s and in the first decade and a half of the 20th century. It is a very syncopated music, written primarily for the piano. Its beginnings can be traced to the Midwest cities of St. Louis and Sedalia, MO. Although not actually jazz, ragtime bears a resemblance to the later, more improvised stride jazz piano style that featured similar left- and right-hand roles. Many jazz pianists and bandleaders had roots in ragtime, including Duke Ellington, Fletcher Henderson, Fats Waller, and James P. Johnson. In comparison with early jazz, ragtime was typically played in a stricter, more rigid manner than jazz. The best known of the ragtime composers is Scott Joplin. Other notable composers of the style include James Scott and Joseph Lamb.

Blues is a style especially dependent on vocalists and it developed at about the same time jazz emerged. The 12-bar-blues form has been used, not only by blues musicians, but also by the jazz community throughout the history of jazz. Although numerous early blues examples include a self-accompanied singer (Robert Johnson) performing often in variable/flexible tempos (rubato), other examples feature larger groups using musicians primarily associated with jazz (Bessie Smith). Portions of some of these early blues recordings are virtually indistinguishable from early jazz.

KEY TERMS

Important terms, people, ensembles, bands, and places:

Terms		People	Ensembles
Blues	Jubilees	Louis Armstrong	Eagle Brass Band
Brass bands	Merengue	Buddy Bolden	Olympia Brass Band
Cakewalk	Minstrel show	James Reese Europe	
Call and response	Motive	W.C. Handy	**Places**
Clavé rhythm	Ragtime (rags)	Scott Joplin	Congo Square
Conga	Spirituals	Ma Rainey	
Field hollers	Stride	Bessie Smith	
Gospels	Tango		
Habanera	Work song		

STUDY QUESTIONS

1. Discuss in brief the relationship of African music to jazz from the rhythmic standpoint.

2. Describe the form of a classic blues lyric.

3. The stride style generally refers to what instrument?

4. Who is known as the "Father of the Blues," and why?

5. Who is considered the "Empress of the Blues?"

6. Describe the essence of the ragtime style, discussing why it was influential to early jazz.

7. When was ragtime popular?

8. Describe the similarities between early jazz and African music.

9. Explain the difference between spiritual, gospel and jubilee.

10. Describe the typical blues form.

11. What non-American influence can be heard in "St. Louis Blues"?

12. What is the significance of early black vocal styles to instrumental jazz?

13. Aside from Scott Joplin, name two ragtime composers noted for their early work.

14. Clarify the meaning of call and response and discuss the heritage of this term and practice.

15. What is the significance of the habanera to jazz? What is its derivation? Name an early jazz tune that clearly shows its influence on jazz.

16. What is the clavé?

marched in the front line, and the percussion followed in the "second line." The rhythm section in these early jazz bands might consist of some combination of guitar or banjo, string bass or tuba, and drums. The banjo, eventually replaced by the piano and/or guitar, and a bass instrument were optional in the early rhythm sections, but became standard members of the jazz band by the mid 1920s. The bass instrument could be a tuba (sometimes called the "iron" or "brass" bass, which again was a remnant of the brass marching bands), bass saxophone, or a string bass. There is much recorded evidence from as late as the early 1930s to indicate that the transition from tuba to string bass was very slow, as was the abandonment of the banjo.

This instrumentation, as well as the roles these instruments played, is well exemplified by the recordings discussed throughout this chapter. The cornetist was often the star of the show, playing the syncopated main themes in brassy fashion. Gradually, the more brilliant trumpet replaced the cornet when jazz bands increased in size. The cornet, which came from the military and marching-band traditions, does not produce as much volume as the trumpet. The clarinetist provided more rhythmically active embellishments and filigree, elaborately ornamenting the cornet melodies. These clarinet passages, often played as rapid, scale-like patterns and **arpeggios** (chords outlined one note at a time), required technical mastery of the instrument. The trombone, which sounds below the cornet and clarinet, was used to outline the harmony by embellishing fundamental chord tones. The New Orleans Dixieland-style trombonist perfected the **"tailgate"** technique by using the slide to smear, or **gliss** (short for glissando, meaning to slide from note to note in a very smooth, legato fashion), from one pitch to the next. Early New Orleans bands often paraded through the streets on a horse-drawn wagon advertising a minstrel show or the opening of a new shop or saloon, or participating in a funeral procession. The trombonist required sufficient room to move his slide, which required that he sit on the tailgate of these wagons, hence the term "tailgate" trombone to describe this slippery style. As many early jazz bands did not have a banjo, guitar, or bass, the pianist was required to maintain the harmony and rhythm of the piece. Early drummers had discovered ways to emulate the marching-parade drum "second line," which typically included more than one player. By mounting a cymbal on a floor stand and creating a pedal arrangement to beat the bass drum with the foot, drummers were able to modify the marching configuration for indoor use by one player. Early drummers did little more than mimic the rudimentary techniques used by parade drummers and often employed gimmicky techniques and devices such as temple blocks, spoons, and other novelty instruments. Early drummers did very little that resembles our contemporary impressions of jazz drumming, and much of their performance consisted of antics such as twirling and throwing their sticks in the air. In their defense, we have no accurate evidence of how drummers performed live, as recording technology was still in its infancy in the early 1920s. Many tradeoffs were made during the early recording process, especially by drummers, as early acoustic recordings, prior to the advent of microphones and amplification, were unable to capture the same natural balance the bands achieved in live performance. One drummer or one loud cornetist could obliterate the sound of the other instruments and ruin a recording. These recording circumstances may also explain why early jazz cornet and trumpet players often used various mutes. We therefore do not know much about the performance practice of these early jazz drummers, who often were relegated to playing temple blocks and other quiet accessories for recording sessions.

 It may be helpful to review the section about "Instrumentation" included in Chapter 3, "Listening to Jazz," on the website. This section contains recorded examples of the various instruments and mutes, along with discussions about their construction and roles in a jazz band.

THE INNOVATORS: EARLY JAZZ

Original Dixieland Jazz Band

Despite the pioneering efforts made by black musicians in New Orleans and other parts of the South, the public's first widespread exposure to this new music would be through recordings made in New York by a white band calling themselves the Original Dixieland Jazz Band (ODJB). This band left New Orleans for Chicago in 1916, under the name Johnny Stein's Band from New Orleans, and enjoyed a successful engagement at Schillers Café. The group was billed as "Stein's Dixie Jass Band." The band broke up because of a disagreement among its members, and cornetist Nick LaRocca organized a new spin-off band he called the Original Dixieland Jasz [sic] Band. The success of Stein's band helped to encourage a gradual migration of New Orleans musicians to Chicago. LaRocca took his new band to New York in 1917, where they were booked to perform one week at Reisenwebers for $1000. They were an overnight sensation and changed the spelling of their name from "jass" to "jazz" to avoid having their advertisements defaced by the letter "j" being erased. Columbia Records, which had been accustomed to recording light classical music and opera, rushed to record them. The company was ill equipped to deal with the raucous new sounds produced by this group and consequently made inferior recordings that went unissued until after the very successful recordings made this same year by the Victor label. The ODJB recorded its first successful sides for the Victor label on March 7, 1917, which subsequently sold over 1 million copies, breaking all previous sales records. Consequently, this band, which played its own version of New Orleans black-inspired jazz, made the first case for the commercial potential of recorded instrumental jazz. At this time, the band consisted of a cornet, clarinet, trombone, piano, and drums. Their music was not written down, but boasted little or no improvisation. Some of their numbers, such as "Livery Stable Blues" and "Barnyard Blues," were novelty numbers, featuring animal sounds imitated by the wind instruments. Some referred to this style as "nut" music. The balance of their repertoire consisted of rag- and blues-based numbers, such as the popular "Tiger Rag," which bears a resemblance to the "National Emblem" march. The ODJB's repertoire and style were created for dancing and entertainment and were often misunderstood by those who attempted to write about it. For example, the New York *American* tried to describe the ODJB style in a November 1917 article that read: "The peculiar, somewhat discordant melody is said to be produced by tuning each of the instruments at a different pitch; and to end some of the strains they occasionally play what we have termed a crazy cadenza."[17]

On the strength of their success in New York, the ODJB traveled to England in 1918 and performed at the ball celebrating the signing of the Treaty of Versailles, which ended World War I. Cornetist Nick LaRocca was interviewed by the *Palais Dancing News* in England, where he claimed that,

> jazz is the assassination, the murdering, the slaying of syncopation. In fact it is a revolution in this kind of music [syncopated dance music] . . . I even go so far as to confess we are musical anarchists . . . our prodigious outbursts are seldom consistent, every number played by us eclipsing in originality and effect our previous performance.[18]

The band returned to New York, earning as much as $1,800 per week. It continued to perform and record and served as a model for many society dance bands that emerged in the 1920s. Like so many bands, the ODJB suffered from numerous squabbles, leading to various changes in personnel before it finally disbanded in 1938. In some ways, the ODJB's success at proving the commercial value of jazz became its own downfall, as emerging bands quickly showed that the style could be performed far better.

The Original Dixieland Jass Band

The track included here for discussion is an example of the work produced by the ODJB when this group first shocked New Yorkers with their new brand of music. It was billed by Victor as "a jass band, the newest thing in cabarets . . . it has sufficient power and penetration to inject new life into a mummy, and will keep ordinary human dancers on their feet till breakfast time."[19] While there is no real spontaneously improvised music, or at least any that is obviously improvised, the performance does feature a buoyant, swing rhythmic quality unlike any other recorded music of the time. Undoubtedly, the band reached this point through an improvisatory approach to developing the tune sometime prior to this recording. Their understanding of swing interpretation is proof that this aspect of jazz performance style was in practice in cities such as New Orleans and Chicago well before this recording was made. The ODJB was merely the first to capitalize on the new craze through the success of their early recordings.

The arrangement shows the typical New Orleans polyphonic style, popular during this period. The multisectional, rondo-like thematic structure reflects the strong influence that the ragtime style exerted on early instrumental jazz. The 4-measure introduction that is repeated during the statement of the initial A section is very similar to the beginning of many marches, and the 2-measure solo breaks by clarinetist Larry Shields were also typical of most jazz band arrangements of the day. It was often during these solo breaks that most, if any, of the real improvisation took place. In this case, it appears as though Shields is merely playing the same material he has probably played many times before, but it may have originated through the process of improvisation. The outline and timeline that follow will help you to navigate through this historic recording and understand more clearly how the song is constructed.

It is obvious in this 1917 recording by the ODJB that the New Orleans street bands, which played in a style similar to a marching parade band, left an impact on these white players who came from the same delta city. The initial march-like introduction reoccurs numerous times throughout the piece. Many of the other characteristics associated with the early New Orleans Dixieland style are heard throughout this seminal recording, including:

- sliding, tailgate trombone;
- dense polyphonic style featuring all three wind instruments playing simultaneously;
- florid clarinet **obligato** (prominent accompanying melody secondary to primary melody and often improvised) passages;
- drummer playing in a march-like style, including characteristic cymbal crashes and bass-drum hits;
- drummer's use of wood blocks, which were less distracting and invasive during this period of early recording technology;
- clarinet **solo breaks** (a point in a piece of music, lasting usually 2–4 measures, when everyone in the ensemble stops playing except the soloist);
- classic New Orleans instrumentation, although lacking any bass instrument such as tuba or string bass.

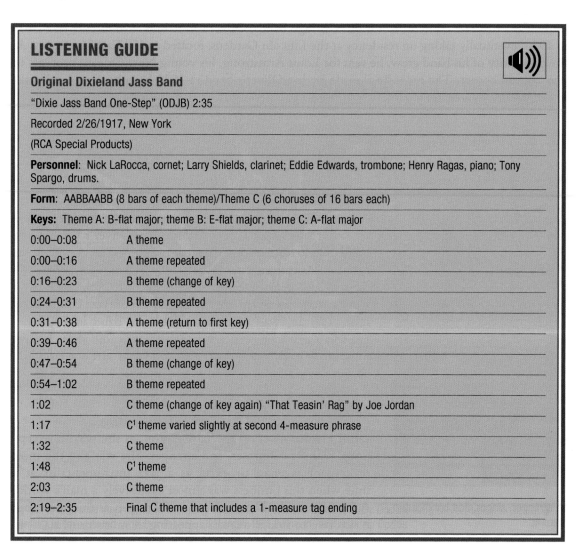

LISTENING GUIDE 🔊

Original Dixieland Jass Band

"Dixie Jass Band One-Step" (ODJB) 2:35

Recorded 2/26/1917, New York

(RCA Special Products)

Personnel: Nick LaRocca, cornet; Larry Shields, clarinet; Eddie Edwards, trombone; Henry Ragas, piano; Tony Spargo, drums.

Form: AABBAABB (8 bars of each theme)/Theme C (6 choruses of 16 bars each)

Keys: Theme A: B-flat major; theme B: E-flat major; theme C: A-flat major

0:00–0:08	A theme
0:00–0:16	A theme repeated
0:16–0:23	B theme (change of key)
0:24–0:31	B theme repeated
0:31–0:38	A theme (return to first key)
0:39–0:46	A theme repeated
0:47–0:54	B theme (change of key)
0:54–1:02	B theme repeated
1:02	C theme (change of key again) "That Teasin' Rag" by Joe Jordan
1:17	C¹ theme varied slightly at second 4-measure phrase
1:32	C theme
1:48	C¹ theme
2:03	C theme
2:19–2:35	Final C theme that includes a 1-measure tag ending

LISTENING GUIDE

Jelly Roll Morton's Red Hot Peppers

"Black Bottom Stomp" (Morton) 3:09

Recorded 9/15/1926, Chicago

(Victor 20221)

Personnel: Jelly Roll Morton, piano; George Mitchell, trumpet; Edward ("Kid") Ory, trombone; Omer Simeon, clarinet; Johnny St. Cyr, banjo; John Lindsay, bass; Andrew Hilaire, drums

Form: Theme A (16 bars); theme B (20 bars in new key)

0:00–0:07	8-measure intro (4 measures repeated) by full ensemble
0:08–0:21	A^1—8-measure section featuring call and response style; bass implies predominant 2-beat style with occasional 4-beat walking
0:22–0:36	A^2—trumpet alternates 4-measure phrases with full ensemble question–answer style
0:37–0:51	A^3—clarinet solo with banjo accompaniment
0:52–0:55	4-measure interlude and key change
0:56–1:14	B^1—6-measure ensemble phrase followed by short trumpet and trombone breaks; 12 measures of full ensemble follow for a total of 20 measures
1:15–1:32	B^2—clarinet solo with 2-measure break and rhythm section accompaniment; another 20-measure section is unusual
1:33–1:50	B^3—piano solo in stride-like style; section ends with full ensemble break that leads to next section
1:51–2:09	B^4—trumpet solo in stop-time; rhythmic break figures resemble displaced habanera rhythm
2:10–2:28	B^5—banjo solo includes 2-measure break; bass occasionally shows more modern 4-beat walking style
2:29–2:47	B^6—full ensemble returns to 2-beat style; 2-measure drum break followed by Dixieland ensemble style
2:48–end	B^7—final chorus features strong drum back-beat accents on 2 and 2-measure drum break before final 12-measure ensemble section and 2-measure coda or tag

Morton's music, daringly advanced for its day in demonstrating sophisticated orchestration and arranging techniques, was actually outmoded almost the day it was recorded. His style, largely based on ragtime, was quickly becoming eclipsed in the mid 1920s by a newer style of jazz that spotlighted the soloist as much as the ensemble. Ragtime, the basis for much of his work, was also becoming passé, and he found himself competing with younger musicians playing in a newer style. Although his music swung more, his ragtime-derived syncopated rhythmic style was not enough to sustain his reputation. Some of his later works, only recently discovered, seem to

You will find on the website several recorded excerpts of trombone, trumpet, and clarinet parts extracted from this composition and re-recorded. Try to find where these excerpts appear in the original recording. The website also contains a brief excerpt of the historic interview with Morton conducted by Alan Lomax.

reflect the work of big-band composers such as Duke Ellington, an ironic development as Morton never embraced the style and outwardly condemned the big-band swing movement. Like so many early jazz performers, Morton was largely forgotten at the time of his death and found it difficult to earn a living in the field he helped to create.

The recording of "Black Bottom Stomp" included in the companion anthology is considered to be the most seminal work by Morton and his Red Hot Peppers. Although the work itself could have been better rehearsed, it nevertheless not only demonstrates the high level of his artistry as a composer/pianist, but also features excellent solos for the day by Mitchell, Simeon, St. Cyr, and Ory. This track uncommonly uses a trumpet instead of the typical cornet, but of even more interest is the inclusion of a string bass, which at times actually plays quarter-note walking lines. More typical for this period would have been a tuba or bass saxophone, and so it is even more unusual to hear a **walking bass** line (ascending and descending scale-like bass lines, where one note is played on each beat of the measure), not a common practice until many years later in the Swing Era. Also recognizable is the call–response format featured in the first repeated A section of Morton's original. This recording also showcases numerous solo breaks and riffs, two ingredients that Morton was adamant about when he discussed the qualities of good jazz with Alan Lomax. The outline and timeline in the listening guide on p. 90 will help you to navigate through this historic recording and understand more clearly how the song is constructed.

See the website for excerpts of Armstrong discussing Buddy Bolden, Joe Oliver, and the early New Orleans traditions.

LOUIS ARMSTRONG (1901–1971)

You will find no argument in describing Louis Armstrong as the first truly exceptional virtuoso jazz soloist. Even those early recordings with Joe Oliver show that there was something special, not only about his rhythmic phrasing, but also about his choice of notes while improvising. His first encounter with the cornet came as a member of a band in a boys' school in New Orleans.

Growing up, he worked menial jobs at the New Orleans docks and played in local bands. His first significant employment as a musician was with Fate Marable's orchestra in 1919. Marable's small orchestra traveled up and down the Mississippi River on the SS St. Paul, a riverboat steam ship that carried passengers and goods between New Orleans and midwestern ports. This band included several of the musicians that would later team with him in Chicago to record his most influential early works. Armstrong stayed with Marable about two years before moving to Tom Anderson's cabaret band on Rampart St. in New Orleans. Soon after, he received word from his mentor Joe Oliver, now finding success in Chicago, to join his band as second cornet. It was Armstrong's first recordings with Joe "King" Oliver that introduced him to the world and, just like his mentor, he became widely known by several nicknames, including "Satchmo" and "Pops." His success with Oliver led to a short stint as featured soloist with Fletcher Henderson's New York band, which was pioneering the big-band sound, featuring more sophisticated arrangements for his larger band. Armstrong returned to Chicago in 1925 to form his most famous recording bands with his wife, pianist Lillian Hardin. These Hot Five and Hot Seven recordings are the most significant recordings made in the first 20 years of jazz history. These performances not only introduce a new way to structure jazz, in order to highlight the improvising soloist instead of the collective ensemble, but they also mark a distinct change in the interpretation of eighth notes. Armstrong's style moved away from the stiff syncopations associated with earlier ragtime-based performances toward a smoother, buoyant, driving swing style. Armstrong's solos swing like no other from this period and serve to instruct, not only future generations of wind players, but also drummers, in the art of swing-style playing. The following is a brief listing of those many aspects of Armstrong's style that characterize him as a true innovator:

• Armstrong demonstrated an ability to play higher notes than had previously been accomplished by other cornet players. He was one of the first musicians to discard the cornet in favor of the trumpet.

• Armstrong was a brilliant technician, who demonstrated his dexterity and flexibility by playing **double-time** solo breaks (playing notes twice as fast, three or four per beat instead of just two).

• Armstrong's choice of notes was also unique for the time, including altered tones that strayed from basic chord tones.

• Armstrong's rhythmic style swung harder than that of any musicians of the day, and, consequently, he influenced all instrumentalists—not just trumpet players.

• Armstrong's rhythmic phrasing was unique. He demonstrated the ability to treat a steady tempo in a more elastic manner by occasionally rushing, laying back slightly behind the beat, as well as implying polyrhythmic phrases (rhythmic groups of three against a 4/4 meter).

• His tone quality was brilliant, immediately captivating the listener as he soared above the rest of the band.

• Armstrong used various embellishments to his advantage. Inflections such as rips up to high notes and varying **vibrato** speeds were used to full advantage to add special emotional quality. (Vibrato colors a note by adding a vocal-like fluctuation to vary the pitch of a straight, pure tone.)

• Armstrong popularized vocal improvisation using nonsense syllables—a style later described as "scat" singing.

Louis Armstrong and his Hot Five. Left to right: Johnny Dodds, Louis Armstrong, Johnny St. Cyr, Kid Ory, Lilian Hardin Armstrong

He first demonstrated his scat vocal technique in his 1926 recording of "Heebie Jeebies." Armstrong's producer spread the rumor that he dropped the sheet music during the recording, while others claimed he just forgot the lyrics, forcing him to vocally improvise using nonsense syllables instead of words. Whatever the case, this recording launched an entirely new style of vocal jazz that has influenced jazz singers ever since.

Armstrong's popularity grew, not only in the US but also abroad, prompting him to tour worldwide. His ability as a charismatic entertainer, jazz trumpeter, and vocalist gave him the star power necessary for a minority to achieve the status and success that he enjoyed throughout his lengthy career. Although he became involved at various times in his career with more commercial music ventures and movies, he remained true to the art of jazz improvising, which he advanced further than anyone else had in this early jazz period.

There are so many outstanding recordings by Armstrong's Hot Five and Hot Seven bands that the inclusion of just one selection in the online audio anthology is difficult. "West End Blues" was chosen because it not only displays Armstrong's accomplishments as a trumpet and vocal soloist, but also displays the artistry of innovative pianist Earl Hines. Hines moved from his hometown of Pittsburgh to Chicago and became the first pianist to begin to discard the busy, two-hand ragtime and stride styles, in favor of a more single-line approach similar to that of wind players. Count Basie during the Swing Era and the many bebop pianists in the mid to late 1940s further honed this style. In this recording, Armstrong displays his clarion high-register ability, technical command in executing double-time solo breaks, and sense of rhythmic balance while playing streams of triplets, yet at times purposefully lagging behind the beat. His vocal solo here is far from an example of his best work as a scat singer, but it does show how similar his vocal and instrumental styles were. The outline and timeline that follow will help you to navigate through this historic recording and understand more clearly how the song is constructed.

"West End Blues" has often been described as the perfect example of Armstrong's virtuosic trumpet style. A more detailed description of this performance follows. Timings are approximate but will be helpful in delineating each section of this 12-measure blues.

LISTENING GUIDE

Louis Armstrong and His Hot Five

"West End Blues" (Oliver/Williams)

Recorded 6/28/1928

(Okeh 8597)

Personnel: Louis Armstrong, trumpet, vocals; Fred Robinson, trombone; Jimmy Strong, clarinet; Earl Hines, piano; Mancy Carr, banjo; Zutty Singleton, drums

Form: 12-bar blues

0:00–0:15	Introduction—Armstrong plays a rubato cadenza (solo without accompaniment and sometimes without strict tempo), followed by a brief sustained chord played by the ensemble of accompanying instruments. This introduction is followed immediately by Armstrong's entrance, which establishes the regular tempo and introduces the theme. These pick-up notes (notes that anticipate the actual beginning of a phrase of music) establish a symmetrical trend that is followed throughout the entire piece, as each new section begins as an anticipation using pick-up notes to begin each new chorus
0:15	Main theme—the main 12-measure theme is played by Armstrong with accompaniment by clarinet, trombone, and rhythm section. Pianist and banjo player place strong chords on each beat
0:50	Second chorus—this second 12-bar blues chorus features trombonist Robinson. It begins with a 1-beat anticipation at the end of the first chorus. Rhythmic accompaniment is provided by the drummer playing what sounds like spoons!

1:24	Third chorus—clarinetist trades phrases, in call and response style, with Armstrong in his scat vocal style. This chorus also begins with an anticipation at the end of the previous chorus
1:58	Fourth chorus—pianist Earl Hines is featured here in an unaccompanied solo, demonstrating why he is remembered as one of the most important pianists from this early period. His single-line right-hand melodies are reminiscent of those played by horn players. This more linear, horn-like style is in stark contrast to the busy, two-hand ragtime and stride-piano styles reflected by most pianists from this period. His left-hand style in this solo, however, does reflect the stride influence
2:32	Fifth chorus—Armstrong returns to the spotlight for the first 8 measures of this last chorus with a long, sustained high note followed by repetitive triplets, which he rushes and drags to provide a dramatic climax to the close of this piece. The piece concludes with a short, rubato-style ending featuring solo piano followed by the entire ensemble. The drummer adds the final touch with his spoons!

Sidney Bechet (1897–1959)

Although Sidney Bechet made significant contributions to jazz in the early years of its development, he remains a somewhat less prominent figure in its history. A New Orleans-born clarinetist, Bechet was largely self-taught, could not read music, and was known all his life as a somewhat discontented, migrant musician, constantly moving from one band and city to another. He never settled down with one band for any great length of time, and, consequently, there are many diverse recordings available. After moving to Chicago, where he performed with Freddie Keppard and King Oliver around 1918, he traveled to Europe with a large society orchestra led by Will Marion Cook. He stayed less than a year with Cook's Southern Syncopated Orchestra, but his travels to Europe with this group left an indelible mark on his career, for it was there that he discovered the soprano saxophone. He soon favored this instrument over the clarinet, and he is now not only remembered as the first **woodwind doubler** (one who plays several different woodwind instruments proficiently), but also is given credit for helping to popularize the soprano sax. Bechet's travels to Europe were also rewarded by his gaining recognition on both continents—no small claim for an early black jazz musician. Bechet's recordings with Clarence Williams's Blue 7 and the Red Onions bands, both of which also featured Louis Armstrong, are seminal and best show his blues- and ragtime-derived style.

Sidney Bechet plays clarinet for a Blue Note Records session, June 8, 1939

The impact that Oliver, Armstrong, Morton, and Bechet had on developing this new music called "jazz" is inestimable. They changed the course of history and the direction music would take, not just in America, but also worldwide. Their music became the soundtrack for American life, an emblem for freedom, and has changed forever the way we think about music-making.

MILESTONES

Chronicle of Historic Events

The timeline that follows will put the developments of jazz discussed in this chapter into a larger historical context, providing you with a better sense of how landmark musical events may relate to others that match your personal areas of interest.

1917	• The US enters World War I.
	• The ODJB issues the first 78-rpm recording, which sells 1.5 million copies. Victor Records and the New York press call it "jass."
1918	• Ironically, a New Orleans paper, the *Times-Picayune*, declares jazz "a musical vice," urging people of New Orleans to "be the last to accept the atrocity in polite society . . . and make it a point of civic honor to repress it."[24]
	• War ends in Europe.
1919	• The signing of the Versailles Treaty officially ends World War I, and the ODJB plays at the signing party.
	• Race riots mark the "Red Summer" in Chicago.
1920	• The census shows a growing urban population, with rural figures dropping to only 30% of the total. Illiteracy falls to 6%, and life expectancy increases to age 54.
	• Prohibition begins, making the production, sale, and transportation of alcoholic beverages illegal.
	• The negro baseball league is formed.
	• The Women's Suffrage Constitutional Amendment takes effect, wining them the right to vote.
	• Radio station KDKA begins regular weekly broadcasts from Pittsburgh, PA.
1921	• The jazz pianist Earl Hines makes the first live broadcast on KDKA radio.
	• James P. Johnson records "Carolina Shout."
	• The town of Zion, IL, bans public performance of jazz.
	• America experiences the worst economic depression since 1914.
1922	• The flapper marks the end of the Victorian age for U.S. women, who now smoke and drink in public places, often wearing flashy clothing.
	• Paul Whiteman's recording of "Whispering" sells 2 million copies.
	• Kid Ory's Sunshine Orchestra becomes the first black jazz band to make a recording.
	• Significant publications by authors James Joyce (*Ulysses*) and T.S. Eliot (*The Waste Land*) are issued.
1923	• The first jazz is broadcast live on the radio from Chicago.
	• A Russian inventor predicts television.
	• Joe "King" Oliver records "Dippermouth Blues" with his Creole Jazz Band, featuring Louis Armstrong.
	• The New Orleans Rhythm Kings become the first white jazz band to record with a musician of color.

	•	Officials around the country express concerns over teen dance marathons.
1924	•	Paul Whiteman's "Experiment in Modern Music" features George Gershwin's "Rhapsody in Blue."
	•	IBM is founded.
	•	The Teapot Dome Scandal occurs.
1925	•	Composer/conductor Igor Stravinsky makes his American debut conducting the New York Philharmonic in a program of his own music.
	•	Sinclair Lewis's *Arrowsmith* is published, and F. Scott Fitzgerald releases *The Great Gatsby*.
	•	The Florida State legislature requires daily Bible readings in all public schools.
	•	Tennessee passes a law forbidding the teaching of any evolutionary theories that deny creationism.
	•	Attorneys William Jennings Bryan and Clarence Darrow fight a court battle over the legality of teaching evolution.
1926	•	The first liquid-fuel rocket, pioneered by Robert Goddard, is launched.
	•	Hemingway authors his first novel, *The Sun Also Rises*.
	•	Langston Hughes publishes *The Weary Blues*.
	•	Jelly Roll Morton records "Black Bottom Stomp."
	•	NBC is incorporated.
	•	Movies are becoming the most popular form of American entertainment, making Douglas Fairbanks, Greta Garbo, John Barrymore, and Charlie Chaplin national figures. A new era of pictures with sound begins.
1927	•	Director Alfred Hitchcock releases his first film, *The Pleasure Garden*, in England.
	•	President Coolidge creates the Federal Radio Commission (FCC).
	•	The Academy of Motion Picture Arts & Sciences is formed.
	•	Henry Ford stops producing the Model T car; the first Model A Fords are sold for $385.
	•	The 18-station CBS radio network begins.
	•	Babe Ruth hits a record-setting 60th home run and becomes the highest paid athlete at $70,000 a year.
	•	*The Jazz Singer*, the first movie with a soundtrack, premieres in New York City.
	•	Duke Ellington opens at the Cotton Club in Harlem.
1928	•	Louis Armstrong records "West End Blues."
	•	"Amos & Andy" debuts on the NBC radio network.
	•	The first transatlantic flight from Europe to US takes place; other aviation milestones are set.
	•	The Pulitzer Prize is awarded to Thornton Wilder for *Bridge of San Luis Rey*.
	•	General Electric opens the first TV station in Schenectady, NY.
	•	Amelia Earhart becomes the first female to fly across the Atlantic Ocean.
	•	The first all-talking motion picture is shown in New York.
	•	Herbert Hoover is elected U.S. president.

CHAPTER SUMMARY

The 1920s represented a time of social, technological, and economic change in America that greatly influenced the growth of early jazz. The newly established recording industry, the advent of radio, a quickly growing music-publishing industry, and improvements in transportation enabled this new music to spread quickly. Those rebelling against Victorian values embraced the freedom expressed by improvised music. Prohibition was a conservative reaction to this freedom and, as jazz musicians often played in clubs illegally selling alcohol, they became linked in the minds of conservatives to organized crime and general moral decay.

Early jazz groups were composed of a front line (most typically cornet, clarinet, and trombone) and a second line (the early rhythm section), as they evolved from street-parade and funeral bands. The instrumentation of the second line varied considerably, but generally included a bass instrument (tuba, bass sax, or string bass), a chording instrument (banjo or guitar, with or without piano), and drums. Because of limitations in the recording technology of the day, the drummer would often play wood blocks and other softer sounds, to avoid distortion and balance problems. The groups tended to play in a very contrapuntal style (more than one important musical line played simultaneously).

The ODJB, a group of white musicians originally from New Orleans, made the earliest-known instrumental jazz recording in New York in 1917. Their music featured very little improvisation, but they enjoyed tremendous popularity. Cornetist Joe "King" Oliver, on the other hand, led an important early jazz band (Creole Jazz Band) that placed emphasis on improvisation. Jelly Roll Morton (Ferdinand LaMothe) was an early jazz pianist/bandleader and the first notable arranger, who may be best known for his claim to be the inventor of jazz.

Louis Armstrong is universally acknowledged to be the first great jazz soloist. His technique, range, and rhythmic feel on cornet (later trumpet) were far beyond those of any of his contemporaries. More importantly, Louis Armstrong's improvisations showed an understanding of harmony and rhythm without peer. He also is recognized as the father of scat singing (improvising vocally using nonsense syllables). Having performed around the world, Louis Armstrong became an international star.

KEY TERMS

Important terms, people, places, and bands:

Terms
Arpeggio
Creole
Diatonic
Double-time
Gliss (abbreviation for glissando)
Legato
Obligato
Prohibition act
Scat
Solo break
Tailgate
Vibrato
Walking bass
Woodwind doubler

People
Louis Armstrong
Sidney Bechet
Buddy Bolden
F. Scott Fitzgerald
Lilian Hardin
Earl Hines
Langston Hughes
Jelly Roll Morton
Joe "King" Oliver
Kid Ory

Places
Cotton Club
Storyville
Tin Pan Alley

Bands
Creole Jazz Band
Hot Five and Hot Seven
Original Dixieland Jazz Band
Red Hot Peppers

STUDY QUESTIONS

1. How was jazz perceived and received in the 1920s? Make sure that both opinions are presented.

2. New businesses and technologies in the 1920s supported the growth, dissemination, and rapid spread of jazz. Discuss these innovations and how jazz was closely intertwined with them.

3. Describe the social mood of the "jazz age."

4. Why was New Orleans such an ethnic, cultural melting pot?

5. What evidence supports the notion that many early New Orleans jazz musicians were Creoles, or at least had French ancestry?

6. What is meant by the second line?

7. What cities other than New Orleans supported the early growth of jazz?

8. What instruments might have filled out the rhythm section in an early New Orleans jazz band?

9. What were the usual wind instruments heard in an early New Orleans jazz band and what were their musical roles?

10. What is the significance of the Original Dixieland Jazz Band? Describe the band's style.

11. Where and when was the first instrumental jazz recording made?

12. Who was one of the first successful woman instrumentalists in jazz?

13. "Dippermouth Blues" bears some of the characteristics associated with many pieces from the period. What are they?

14. Who is considered the first important jazz composer/arranger?

15. What aspects of Jelly Roll Morton's music made it unique and original for the times?

16. Who is considered to be the first great jazz soloist?

17. What characteristics made Louis Armstrong a true innovator?

CHAPTER 6

The Jazz Age
From Chicago to New York

The first World War had been fought, and in the back-wash conventions had tumbled. There was rebellion then, against the accepted, and the proper and the old. . . . The shooting war was over but the rebellion was just getting started. And for us jazz articulated . . . what we wanted to say.[1]
—Hoagy Carmichael

Henry Ford and his son Edsel in front of their new model in New York in 1927–1933

JAZZ IN PERSPECTIVE

Although New Orleans was the epicenter of jazz, the aftershock was felt far and wide. Other cities that did most to support this new wave in American music were Chicago and New York. Both of these northern cities supported a tremendous influx of African-Americans between 1916 and 1930. About 500,000 sought a better way of life and moved from southern locations to northern cities between 1916 and 1919. More than 1 million more left the South in the decade that followed. Chicago and New York had become ethnic melting pots, with a more diverse collection of European immigrants, blacks, and whites than any other place in the world.

SOUTH SIDE OF CHICAGO

The south side of Chicago, known as the "vice district" or the "Levee," became the new home for many enterprising blacks during the 1920s. They launched business ventures catering to leisure-time activities. Many of these establishments supported black entertainers and fostered a sense of racial pride in the south side. The cabarets and saloons were often referred to as **black and tans**, as they catered to a mixed black and white clientele. In a 20-block area of Chicago's vice district, one could find a staggering number of saloons, variety theaters, gambling houses, pool rooms, and bordellos.[2] It is no small wonder that the south side of Chicago in the 1920s was a magnet for black entertainers, who found plentiful well-paying jobs. Many transplanted New Orleans jazz musicians practiced their trade in the Levee district, such as Freddie Keppard, Kid Ory, Joe Oliver, Louis Armstrong, Jelly Roll Morton, Lilian Hardin, Earl Hines, and Jimmy Noone, among others.

There was always a threat of police raids in the Levee district, which, as author William Kenney points out, "seemed to contribute just the right note of excitement to Chicago's jazz scene, mixing the new styles of personal liberation . . . [and] adding drama to the new music."[3] If it wasn't the police, it was the Juvenile Protective Association (JPA) that was making life difficult for those who frequented the vice district. Essentially a temperance society, the JPA had made it its mission to curb the sins of Chicago's youth, whom it perceived as negatively influenced by the lure of the Levee district. The south-side black and tans were in the business of selling "suggestive African-American musical entertainment which helped customers to create an atmosphere of inter-racial sensuality," according to Kenney.[4] This atmosphere did draw a good deal of negative press from right-wing groups with conservative ideologies. For example, the New York-published *American* issued the following warnings in its January 22, 1922 article entitled "Jazz Ruining Girls, Declares Reformer: Degrading Music Even Common in 'Society Circles,' Says Vigilance Association Head."

> Moral disaster is coming to hundreds of young American girls through pathological, nerve-irritating, sex-exciting music of jazz orchestras, according to the Illinois Vigilance Association. In Chicago alone the association's representatives have traced the fall of 1,000 girls in the last two years to jazz music. Girls in small towns, as well as the big cities, in poor homes and rich homes, are victims of the weird, insidious, neurotic music that accompanies modern dancing.
>
> "The degrading music is common not only to disorderly places, but often to high school affairs, to expensive hotels and so-called society circles," declares Rev. Phillip Yarrow, superintendent of the Vigilance Association. The report says that the vigilance society has no desire to abolish dancing, but seeks to awaken the public conscience to the present danger and future consequences of jazz music.[5]

This New York press was not alone, as many other articles appeared in newspapers and music-trade magazines that denigrated the increasingly popular new music. They often carried similar vigilante themes and rarely offered any real analysis or specific criticism of the music. *Etude* ran an article in the January 1925 edition entitled, "Is Jazz the Pilot of Disaster?", and *Metronome* printed the following in a 1923 article:

> I can say from my knowledge that about 50% of our young boys and girls from the age 16 to 25 that land in the insane asylum these days are jazz-crazy dope fiends and public dance hall patrons. Jazz combinations—dope fiends and public dance halls—are all the same. Where you find one you will find the other.[6]

Although jazz was not without its critics in the 1920s, it also had its champions. Some writers about jazz made an effort to discriminate between "high-brow" and "low-brow" jazz. In other words, they differentiated between good and bad jazz. The *Musical Quarterly* published an article in 1926 by Edwin J. Stringham in which he attempts to set the record straight about good and bad jazz. He says that:

> there are two sides to the Jazz question. This form of music . . . has been denounced far and wide as being of immoral character. I have in mind only the better type of jazz; that which is composed by understanding musicians, that which is well conceived and written according to ordinary esthetical and technical standards.[7]

Like so many early writers on the subject of jazz, Stringham failed to see that this music could not be judged and held to the same standards and practices associated with traditional European classical music, and that it must be assessed by different criteria. His appreciation of jazz was obviously directed at the more symphonic style associated with Paul Whiteman. Regardless of the growing press and public debates inspired by jazz, the appeal and lure of the music were far too great for a few negative articles to abate its attraction to young Americans.

Marathon dance competitions were part of the growing phenomenon of youth culture in the 1920s, Chicago. First prize was $500

ON THE OTHER SIDE OF TOWN

The north and west side of Chicago, inhabited by middle- and upper-class whites, offered dance halls and cabarets. A few bands even employed black performers, although they were far from fully integrated. Many of these nightspots featured dance bands that included some jazz-like numbers as part of their repertoire, as this was the music that many young whites wanted to hear. Social dancing was a driving force of the entertainment industry in the 1920s and was a primary form of entertainment for upwardly mobile white audiences. By the 1920s, there was already a distinction between the ensembles that included orchestral instruments such as strings and those that did not. Those ensembles featuring orchestral instrumentation and a largely dance-oriented repertoire were categorized as "sweet" bands, and the black south-side bands were termed "hot" jazz bands. The sometimes-bitter debates that continue to rage among fans and critics advocating for one of these two sides actually began at the advent of instrumental jazz. Some gave little credence to those white bands that largely played sweet dance music with little improvisation but billed themselves as jazz bands. In order to appease both sides of this debate, many bandleaders, such as Isham Jones, who played popular dance halls in Chicago frequented by white clientele, employed a few jazz soloists so that they could respond to the growing request for hot jazz by the younger generation. These younger white patrons demanded music similar to what they had heard in the south-side cabarets.

> School dances, fraternity parties and the like became major venues for jazz and dance bands in the late 1920s. Many of the major college campuses gave birth to their own bands organized by students with or without the sanction of school officials. For example, Princeton, Harvard, Yale, Texas University and the University of Chicago all spawned jazz bands during the late 1920s.[8]

The JPA and other urban reform groups actively monitored many of the Chicago dance halls. They actually urged dance-hall managers to speed up the tempos in order to encourage respectable dancing at arm's length. There was a demand for fast-paced dance music that was morally sterile. "Cooperation between dance hall entrepreneurs and urban reformers shaped the commercialization of the dance craze and created a demand for fast paced 'peppy,' but morally sanitary, jazz age social dance music."[9] Some say that these sanctions are largely responsible for the faster tempos that are generally agreed upon to be an identifying characteristic of Chicago jazz. According to New Orleans banjoist Johnny St Cyr, "the fastest numbers played by old New Orleans bands were slower than . . . the Chicago tempo."[10] Organizations such as the JPA considered a night of dancing for their young people less harmful than a bout with liquor or associations with "people of color" on the south side.

Dance orchestras led by Paul Whiteman, known eventually as the "King of Jazz" thanks to his publicists, Guy Lombardo (Royal Canadians), Vincent Lopez, and Art Hickman, who frequented Chicago hotel ballrooms and north-side dance halls were paid thousands of dollars for a week-long engagement. This was no small sum, considering the fact that an automobile could be purchased for well under $1,000! Those few "hot" jazz players who were hired to add spice to the dance repertoire played by these "sweet" bands often used this opportunity to refine their basic music-reading skills and put good money in their pockets, as they were often paid some of the highest salaries.

Young, white Chicago musicians idolized the black New Orleans musicians for their free spirit and ability to play unencumbered, "real" jazz. To many of these young north- and west-side Chicago youth, jazz represented freedom and a breaking away from the authoritarian demands of their elders. "Jazz seemed to express artistic alienation from middle-class materialism,"[11] according to William Kenney. Some of these young, white musicians, such as clarinetist Mez Mezzrow, strove to emulate their black idols in every way—adopting their speech patterns and general life styles. Many young, white Chicago musicians, such as Benny Goodman, the son of immigrant parents, and Bud Freeman, had a distinct advantage over the black New Orleans musicians. Being schooled musicians, able to read and execute difficult music as well as play jazz, their background opened up numerous opportunities that were unavailable to some black musicians who may have lacked formal training. These young, white players nevertheless did everything they could to emulate the best of black jazz they had heard in the south-side establishments, especially influenced by transplanted New Orleans musicians such as Joe "King" Oliver, Jimmie Noone, Freddie Keppard, and Kid Ory.

THE CHICAGO SOUND

Bud Freeman, Jimmy McPartland, Frankie Teschemacher, and Dave Tough were all members of Chicago's white middle class and became known as the Austin High Gang. For some reason, much has been made in the jazz history annals about the Austin High Gang, when in fact many of the musicians actually responsible for what became identified as the Chicago jazz sound had no relationship to this middle-class, suburban high school. Many came to Chicago from elsewhere, and many others actually became known only after leaving Chicago to perform and record elsewhere. It is these white musicians, regardless of their origins, who created the Chicago sound. As you will see in the following pages, the Chicago style serves as a transition to the big-band Swing Era that follows and, in some ways, serves as a distant prelude to the "cool" jazz sounds of the 1950s. The following list of characteristics helps to define the Chicago jazz style.

Bix Beiderbecke and the Wolverines in the Gennett Recording Studios, in 1924, in New York

- Although there is some debate, there is evidence to support that the average tempo increased during the Chicago period, as compared with the earlier New Orleans style.
- The saxophone appeared as a regular, new member of the bands.
- Most Chicago bands featured some New Orleans-style polyphony, but the soloist begins to emerge, relegating other band members to more background roles during a solo.
- Chicago bands reflected a refinement of style and instrumental polish not associated with many early New Orleans bands.
- Individual musicianship appeared to be on the rise in terms of technique, tone production, and the ability to read music.
- The ensembles seemed less haphazard, with a greater emphasis placed on the arrangement and well-rehearsed ensemble performance.
- Rhythm sections were significantly more advanced, and playing techniques improved. The tuba was gradually replaced by the string bass, and the guitar began to emerge as a solo voice. This transition, however, was slow, and the banjo and tuba could still be found in early 1930s big bands.
- The earlier New Orleans 2-beat rhythm-section style, reminiscent of the marches and rags, was transformed by featuring walking bass lines and accents that imply 4/4 meter, instead of the earlier 2/4 meter common to rags.
- The cornet was gradually phased out in favor of the trumpet.
- Chicago bands began to expand in size and instrumentation.

THE INNOVATORS: A FEW OF THE MANY

New Orleans Rhythm Kings (NORK)

Perhaps the most influential group of white musicians to emerge in the early 1920s that helped define a new Chicago sound was the New Orleans Rhythm Kings (NORK). The NORK based their sound in part on the black New Orleans style of polyphonic jazz, but their arrangements tended to favor a more sophisticated and organized sound. The group's cornetist, Paul Mares, is quoted as saying, "we did our best to copy the colored music we'd heard at home [New Orleans]. We did the best we could, but naturally we couldn't play real colored style."[12] Their influence was widespread, and they made significant improvements in playing a smoother, more legato-phrased style of jazz; however, as a group, they did not make a major impact at the time.

Their repertoire was an amalgamation of blues, rag-based and dance tunes. Some feel that many of the white bands, such as the NORK, that emerged during the Chicago period were little more than dressed-up, more-polished, and, in some cases, watered-down versions of the New Orleans black style. Others viewed the new sound as a natural progression in refining what had gone before.

The NORK, in 1923, became the first white band to record with a musician of color, when it invited Jelly Roll Morton to record several sides with the group, including his own "Mr. Jelly Lord" and "London Blues." Black and white musicians may have associated with one another in the black and tans of Chicago's south side or, for that matter, in the Harlem district of New York, but it had been largely forbidden for people of color to mix publicly on the bandstand until Benny Goodman broke the unwritten ban on racially mixed bands in the late 1930s.

The NORK, first known as the Friars Society Club Orchestra, made its first recording in 1922, becoming the first Chicago-based jazz band to record. Isham Jones's society, "sweet" dance band actually recorded a few months earlier, but its repertoire was more for dancing and not considered jazz. With cornet, trombone, clarinet, saxophone, piano, banjo, bass, and drums, the NORK was a fairly large band, sporting eight musicians.

The first NORK recordings predated those made by Joe "King" Oliver by seven months, but there is no doubt that he, along with other New Orleans musicians who had moved to Chicago, provided the primary inspiration for the formation of the Chicago jazz sound. The recordings made by Louis Armstrong's Hot Five and Hot Seven bands in the mid 1920s embodied both the spirit of earlier New Orleans bands and the new trend to spotlight the soloist more than had been the case in the earlier New Orleans groups.

BIX BEIDERBECKE (1903–1931)

Cornetist Leon Bix Beiderbecke and saxophonist Frankie Trumbauer are undoubtedly the most well-known Chicago-era musicians. Ironically, neither Beiderbecke nor Trumbauer was a native Chicagoan. Beiderbecke was a transplanted Iowan, whose parents had sent him to a private academy in Chicago in hopes of bringing some discipline to their son and curbing his "unnatural obsession" with music. Beiderbecke had been a truant child in Iowa, where he studied piano and became infatuated with jazz. Chicago was certainly the wrong city for him to learn about discipline and take his education seriously, as the vibrant jazz atmosphere on the south side was a distraction and only encouraged him to further pursue his musical obsessions.

Although Beiderbecke had access to formal music training, he largely rejected it in favor of his own, unorthodox style that was in part responsible for his unique tone quality and identity on the cornet. For example, he often used the wrong fingerings to produce certain notes on his cornet. He played both piano and cornet largely by ear and only learned to read music later in his career, when the demands of reading written-out arrangements in large ensembles required it.

His first school band was the Rhythm Jugglers, but he was not heard around town until he joined the Wolverines. The Wolverines played at school dances and parties, imitating the sounds of black bands they had heard in the south-side cabarets, and white bands such as the NORK. Beiderbecke was actually never recorded in Chicago, and, in 1925, he left the Wolverines, moving to Detroit to take a job with the Jean Goldkette Orchestra. Goldkette commanded a large stable of society bands that performed throughout the Midwest and was based in Detroit. At one time, he controlled as many as 20 bands, and his primary ensemble was known to have squarely beaten the great Fletcher Henderson's New York band in a battle of the bands. Beiderbecke's position with the Goldkette orchestra was merely a steppingstone before he moved on to record with saxophonist Frankie Trumbauer's small group. The two had become acquainted in Goldkette's Orchestra and both joined the popular Paul Whiteman Orchestra, along with a number of other renegades from the Goldkette outfit.

By the time Beiderbecke made the move to the Whiteman Orchestra, he had become known for his unique style that was in stark contrast to the hot players of the day such as Louis Armstrong. Beiderbecke had a more lyrical sound that projected a sense of "subdued passion." In contrast to the

Cornetist Bix Beiderbecke (1903–1931) poses for a portrait, c.1925

flashy, double-timing Armstrong, his solo breaks might consist of only one note, repeated with slight shadings or inflections. Most consider Beiderbecke to be the first in a long line of "cool" style musicians that represented a departure from the "hot" school of playing associated with Armstrong. His long-time friend and popular songwriter Hoagy Carmichael (who composed "Stardust" and often booked Beiderbecke at Indiana University) described his sound as "pure, resembling a chime struck by a mallet."[13] You would never hear him adding a buzzing growl or thick, wide vibrato to his sound, as was the case with most black players of the day.

He had an obvious knowledge, or at least a keen natural sense of harmony, that he demonstrated in several piano compositions that reflect the popular 1920s French Impressionistic, classical style of composition. His composition "In a Mist," notated for publication by Whiteman arranger Bill Challis, as Beiderbecke was unskilled at such things, serves as an excellent example of this sophisticated, almost classical piano style, which was never evident in his jazz cornet playing.

Ironically, it is the recordings that Beiderbecke made with Frankie Trumbauer, and a few with Whiteman, that made him famous, but not until long after his untimely death in 1931 at age 28. Tuberculosis, alcoholism, and a generally reckless, bohemian lifestyle contributed to his poor health during the last several years of his life. Although he was greatly admired by black and white musicians, he was not particularly well known by the general public during his lifetime. This obscurity may seem undeserved, as his recordings, although not made in Chicago, have ultimately surfaced as those that help to signify and define the Chicago jazz sound.

 Listen to Wiedoeft's "Saxophobia" and the Brown Brothers' "Down Home Rag" on the "Experiencing Jazz Playlist" at the Library of Congress Jukebox.

FRANKIE "TRAM" TRUMBAUER (1901–1956)

Whereas Beiderbecke lives on in the annals of jazz history as the first great white performer, his bandmate Frankie Trumbauer enjoyed a less illustrious career, even though his contributions were significant. Frankie "Tram" Trumbauer (1901–1956) played the alto and C-melody saxophones. The C-melody, which was considered by many the black sheep of the saxophone family, sounds between the E-flat alto and the B-flat tenor, although its size more closely resembles the tenor sax. It was known for its unique tone quality, somewhere in between the alto and tenor. The C-melody was popular among amateurs because it did not require any music transposition. It was pitched in the key of C, enabling the performer to read from piano music and making it a good choice for at-home, family-parlor sing-a-longs. Another saxophonist of note was Rudy Wiedoeft, who, along with the Brown Brothers saxophone ensemble, popularized the saxophone in the US from about 1917 to 1927. Wiedoeft was a popular radio and vaudeville performer who, along with the Brown Brothers, was the first to record a section of saxophones. Wiedoeft's technique and articulation were impressive, as were the flashy showpieces that he composed to showcase the instrument and his facility. Saxophone historian Ted Hegvik wrote that Wiedoeft "took the saxophone—an instrument without a style, a literature, or an artistic example—and, in supplying it with all of these, created the 'saxophone craze' of the 1920s."[14] It is only recently that historians have begun to realize the great influence that Wiedoeft, who was not a jazz saxophonist, exerted on early jazz players such as Trumbauer.

Trumbauer recorded his first important solo in 1923 and, through this recording, had an immediate influence on black and white saxophonists. Like Beiderbecke, Trumbauer's sound was smooth, lyrical, and cool, and his rhythmic phrasing rarely demonstrated much syncopation or thick, wide vibrato. He was a brilliant technician, following the path that Wiedoeft so deftly cleared. His solos were so well crafted they appeared premeditated and had a gracefulness that served as an antithesis to the hot school of jazz playing. Richard Sudhalter, author of *Lost Chords*, described his playing as "elegant and debonair."[15] He was of great influence on a future generation of jazz saxophonists such as Lester Young, who carefully studied and memorized his recorded solo on "Singin' the Blues," included in the online audio anthology. This single solo turned the saxophone world on its ear and became the subject of future arrangements where the entire solo was quoted note for note. Every saxophonist, black or white, learned this solo and frequently quoted from it in their solos. Most historians believe that Trumbauer's best work occurred during his 4-year association with Bix Beiderbecke as members of the Goldkette and Whiteman Orchestras. The small group recordings that stemmed from these associations showed a unique musical kinship that Beiderbecke and Trumbauer shared. They not only complemented each other, but also seemed to feed off of the contrasts that they created.

Frankie Trumbauer and unidentified guitarist

A number of features are apparent in the classic Trumbauer–Beiderbecke recording "Singin' the Blues," namely the prominent use of the saxophone, greater solo space with less reliance on Dixieland-style full ensemble, a clear 4-beat emphasis that begins with Beiderbecke's solo, and the elevated role of the guitar, as compared with the earlier use of banjo.

Trumbauer left the Whiteman Orchestra in 1936 to strike out on his own, following Beiderbecke's early death. He performed and recorded briefly with the Three T's, a group of Whiteman sidemen consisting of the Texas trombone sensation Jack Teagarden and his brother Charlie Teagarden, who played trumpet. Trumbauer's contributions to jazz, however, waned after Beiderbecke's death, and he retired from the music business in 1940 for a career in aviation.

Eddie Lang (1902–1933), who is remembered as the "father of jazz guitar," also recorded with Trumbauer and Beiderbecke. He was born in Philadelphia, PA, and also performed in Chicago, New York, and London. His recording of "For No Reason At All in C" is legendary and unusual, in that it features a trio of Beiderbecke on piano, Trumbauer on saxophone, and Lang on guitar. Trumbauer ignores the theme in favor of improvising on the chord scheme of this old standard tune. Although it is certainly not bebop, one could consider this recording an early predecessor of this style, which was years away from blossoming, and deserves to be considered as supplementary listening.

LISTENING GUIDE

Frankie Trumbauer and His Orchestra

"Singin' the Blues" (McHugh–Fields) 2:59

Recorded 2/4/1927

(Okeh 40772)

Personnel: Frankie Trumbauer, C-melody saxophone; Bix Beiderbecke, cornet; Bill Rank, trombone; Jimmy Dorsey, clarinet, alto saxophone; Paul Mertz, piano; Eddie Lang, guitar; Chauncey Morehouse, drums	
Key and form: E-flat major; 32-bar theme divided into four 8-bar sections (ABA¹C)	
0:00–0:06	4-bar instrumental intro without rhythm section
	First chorus
0:07–0:20	Trumbauer solos on C-melody sax, accompanied by piano and guitar (8 measures total)
0:21–0:34	Second section—Trumbauer continues his solo, ending the section with 2-bar solo break (8 measures total)
0:35–1:02	Final section—Trumbauer continues in improvised style solo (notice how guitarist mimics fast sax triplet passage moments later); 2-bar break ends first chorus (16 measures total)
	Second chorus
1:03–1:16	Beiderbecke solos on cornet for 8 measures
1:17–1:31	Beiderbecke continues solo, ending the section with 2-bar break, which begins with a double-time phrase and ends with an Armstrong-like rip to anticipate the last phrase of the chorus
1:32	Beiderbecke continues to solo for the final 16 measures of the form
	Final chorus
2:00–2:13	Dixieland polyphonic-style full ensemble section
2:14–2:28	Dorsey plays clarinet solo quoting Hoagy Carmichael's famous "Stardust" at 2:22–2:24
2:29–2:42	Full ensemble, Dixieland style
2:43–end	Full ensemble with a 1-measure guitar solo break

Paul Whiteman (1890–1967) and Symphonic Jazz

In the words of jazz historian Marshall Stearns, "If the ODJB [Original Dixieland Jazz Band] made jazz a household word in 1917, Paul Whiteman made it semi-respectable in 1924."[16] When Paul Whiteman founded his orchestra in 1919, he wisely employed Ferde Grofé, stealing him away from Art Hickman's West-Coast band. Pianist and arranger for Whiteman, Grofé is credited as a pioneer in developing concepts in arranging and composing for the large dance and symphonic orchestras. Both Whiteman and Grofé had similar backgrounds, having been schooled in the European classical tradition, and so it is no surprise that this training became the basis of their style. Grofé's arrangements for Whiteman of "Whispering," "Japanese Sandman," "Avalon," and scores of other songs became enormous sellers in 1920 and the years just after, and they made Whiteman the most celebrated bandleader of the period. Numerous examples of Whiteman's recordings, including "Whispering," can be found at www.LOC.gov/jukebox.

Perhaps the most acclaimed performance by the Whiteman Orchestra was his 1924 "Experiment in American Music," at which he premiered Grofé's orchestration of George Gershwin's "Rhapsody in Blue." In this concert, Whiteman dressed jazz in more respectable clothes, making it more appealing to the masses by shedding the barroom atmosphere and ragged musicianship that had been associated with some jazz of the times. Henry Osgood, who penned one of the first books about jazz in 1926, suggested that it was safer and less risky for the public to enjoy Whiteman's brand of jazz, and, with his "experimental" concert, he had taken "the very first step toward the elevation of jazz to something more than accompaniment for dancing."[17]

The overwhelming press that surrounded the premier of "Rhapsody in Blue" and Whiteman's syndicated book served to add some credence to the title "King of Jazz," coined by his publicist. Whiteman's orchestra, and others that followed his model, reported weekly payrolls in excess of $5,000 per week, a great deal of money in the twenties. (See the Whiteman payroll sheet found in the companion website.)

Historians have not always been kind to Whiteman, and he has often borne the brunt of criticism from jazz purists. For example, Robert Goffin described Whiteman's recordings as "essentially banal music, but played beautifully by first-rate musicians."[18] According to jazz scholar James Lincoln Collier, these criticisms are unfounded and unfair, as about half of Whiteman's recordings featured jazz solos. Had it not been for Whiteman, Chicago-school artists such as Beiderbecke, Jimmy Dorsey, Eddie Lang, Jack Teagarden, and Frankie Trumbauer, to mention a few, might never have received the widespread exposure that eventually proved to be important to the ongoing development of jazz. Collier also points out that it was Whiteman who introduced the idea of featuring vocalists along with symphonic, jazz-style arrangements, a concept that was capitalized on some years later during the peak of the big-band Swing Era.[19] The idea of using both singers and strings in the dance-band context became a model, laying the groundwork for the success of jazz-informed singers such as Frank Sinatra, who enjoyed great acclaim years later. Whiteman and his arrangers also demonstrated that jazz improvisation could coexist within the tightly arranged framework designed for the large, symphonic-style ensemble. Although conservative compared with the authentic jazz combo, the Whiteman symphonic prototype has had a lasting impact on the history of jazz since the 1920s.

"Mississippi Mud" serves as an excellent example of the Whiteman style, demonstrating an amalgamation of African-American jazz, popular music, and a European style of orchestration. This particular tune also illustrates many of the classic devices discussed previously and associated with this orchestra—the vocal solo and group, "scat" singing, the improvised "hot" jazz solo, and orchestrations inspired by the large, European classical-like ensemble.

Paul Whiteman and his orchestra

LISTENING GUIDE 🔊

Paul Whiteman and His Orchestra

"Mississippi Mud" (Barris–Cavanaugh, arr. Satterfield) 3:22

Recorded 2/18/1928, New York

(Columbia)

Personnel: Bix Beiderbecke, cornet; Charlie Margulis, trumpet; Bill Rank, trombone; Irving "Izzy" Friedman, clarinet; Chester Hazlett and Charles Strickfaden, alto saxophones; Frankie Trumbauer, C-melody saxophone; Nye Mayhew, tenor saxophone; Mike Trafficante or Minton Leibrook, tuba; Tom Satterfield, piano; Mike Pingitore, banjo, guitar; Steve Brown, bass; Harold McDonald, drums; Irene Taylor, Bing Crosby, Al Rinker, Harry Barris, Jack Fulton, Charles Gaylor, and Austin Young, vocals

Key and form: A theme—E-flat major (A—10 bars, A^1—12 bars); B theme—C minor (4 bars)/E-flat major (4 bars)

0:00–0:07	6-bar vocal introduction based on second B theme, with Crosby scat singing final phrase
0:08–0:020	Beiderbecke paraphrases A theme for an unusual 10-measure section
0:21–0:35	Beiderbecke continues his variation of the A theme, this time for a more logical 12 measures
0:36–0:45	B section features low brass playing stop time phrases in call and response with full ensemble played Dixieland style with cornet lead (8 measures)
0:46–0:57	B repeats
0:57–1:08	Friedman plays clarinet solo with rhythm-section accompaniment. Tuba switches to string bass and occasionally walks. A clarinet solo break in measures 7–10 (A section 10 measures)
1:09–1:23	A^1 clarinet solo continues for 12 measures
1:24–1:28	4-measure instrumental break serves as an interlude leading to vocal that follows
1:29–1:41	Taylor sings A section with vocal chorus as background (10 measures)
1:42–1:57	Taylor vocal continues for second A—12 measures long
1:58–2:07	Crosby sings B section with alternating scat phrases
2:08–2:17	Same scheme is repeated for second B section
2:18–2:32	Taylor sings A theme with vocal choir as backdrop
2:33–2:46	Beiderbecke leads orchestra in Dixieland-style polyphonic arrangement with fills and a saxophone solo break at the end of the phrase by Jimmy Dorsey. Notice the ascending rip à la Armstrong played by Beiderbecke
2:47–3:06	Ensemble style continues with an additional 4-measure phrase, making the entire section 16 measures long
3:07–end	Final coda sung by Taylor in rubato style, with male-choir accompaniment leading to splash cymbal abrupt ending

BOOGIE-WOOGIE, EIGHT TO THE BAR

Solo pianists learned how marketable they could be in the 1920s, as they had the advantage of being employable in almost any venue. The stride style, discussed in more detail in the preceding chapter, was the basis for much of the piano jazz, solo and ensemble, heard throughout the 1920s. Prior to the advent of talking motion pictures, many jazz pianists found employment in movie theaters, where they improvised accompaniments to silent films.

Boogie-woogie was a rhythmically charged, blues-inspired solo piano style that initially surfaced, to no great attention, in the mid-to-late 1920s. This gregarious, highly improvised style was spawned in roadhouses, barrooms, honky-tonks and at rent parties. The style utilizes the basic 12-bar-blues harmonic scheme and features a strong, repetitive left-hand motive that can resemble a walking bass line. This left-hand pattern usually consists of four pairs of eighth notes—hence the "eight to the bar" description often used (8 eighth-notes complete one 4/4 measure or bar). Pianists added elaborate right-hand melodies to this left-hand accompaniment pattern. As one hand might employ a different meter than the other, this style requires much independence between right and left hands, as is the case with the stride style.

Pine Top Smith, who recorded "Pine Top's Boogie Woogie" in 1928, helped to popularize this style, which enjoyed a revival in 1938 and flourished well into the early 1940s. Chicago gave birth to several important second-generation contributors to this style—namely Albert Ammons, Meade "Lux" Lewis, and Jimmy Yancey. Along with work by Pete Johnson and Joe Turner, the Lewis and Ammons recordings were successful enough to encourage the later adoption of this style by the big bands of Count Basie, Tommy Dorsey, and Charlie Barnet, among others. The style was diluted during these years, although it was absorbed into the lasting Chicago blues tradition. Even today, the blues tradition, including boogie-woogie, is maintained in clubs throughout this northern city.

A short video demonstration of boogie-woogie can be found in the corresponding chapter on the website.

THE DECLINE OF THE CHICAGO ERA

There are many factors that led to the steady decline of jazz in Chicago at the close of the 1920s. The most catastrophic economic event, sending a shock wave through the entire nation, was the stock-market crash on "Black Thursday," October 29, 1929, marking the beginning of the **Great Depression**. No single event has eclipsed this economic disaster in the history of the United States. The tremendous losses, which effectively crippled Wall Street, led to a run on banks, with millions of Americans withdrawing their life savings for fear of losing them all. For many, it was too late, as banks and businesses across the country failed, leaving record numbers of Americans unemployed and concerned about the well-being of their families. A tremendous new industry had developed around the steady growth in popularity of jazz, and much of it came tumbling down. Record and publishing companies, radio manufacturers and networks, cabarets, dance halls and speakeasies, theaters, booking agents, and of course musicians all suffered—no one was insulated from this American economic tragedy. For example, the Gannett record label, which at one time had under contract many of the top performers, totally collapsed in 1929, as did a number of other labels.

But the Depression was not the only factor responsible for dimming the lights on Chicago's nightlife. By the late 1920s, musicians had begun to steadily migrate to New York, where more opportunities existed, especially for recording, and recordings were perceived as a musician's ticket to mass popularity. For many musicians, New York was perceived as the place to be. There certainly were numerous opportunities for employment in dance orchestras that were taking advantage of the widespread dance craze. Some jazz musicians flocked to dance bands, such as those led by Paul Whiteman, among others.

A crowd of depositors outside the American Union Bank in New York, having failed to withdraw their savings before the bank collapsed

Prohibition, politics, urban reform groups, movies with soundtracks, the closing of some cabarets, and police raids on mob-run speakeasies all contributed to musicians' desires to look for greener pastures. Although the Chicago mob, with bosses such as Al Capone, helped to provide an environment in the clubs that encouraged the music, their illegal activities also brought unending attention to many establishments that were raided on a regular basis. Some musicians found that the underworld could be your best friend one minute and turn into your worst enemy the next. Pianist Fats Waller was supposedly escorted at gunpoint from his dinner table to a waiting car, driven to Al Capone's headquarters in East Cicero, and ordered to play at a surprise birthday party for the gangster. He was tipped handsomely for his trouble, but the money may not have outweighed the mental anguish. Joe Glaser, who eventually became Louis Armstrong's manager, had ties to the Chicago mob. The club that he managed was, in reality, run by the mob. It was raided so frequently that Armstrong's pianist Earl Hines claimed that he ran for the police paddy wagon at the first sign of a raid so that he could get a good seat![20] The government and the courts had closed many of the cabarets by 1928, and, as a result, many of the musicians were forced to look for work in larger dance bands or other cities. By 1928, "250 cabaret entertainers and 200 musicians had lost their jobs."[21]

The attraction to New York and the appeal of Kansas City, fast becoming a wild town in the image of Chicago, lured many away from the windy city. Larger dance-oriented bands and symphonic jazz-style orchestras began to win the battle for public attention in the mid-to-late 1920s. There was still an audience for smaller, New Orleans- and Chicago-style groups, but the public's interest was the larger dance bands. The country was primed for the big-band Swing Era, but Prohibition would have to be repealed, and the nation would need to recover from the economic ravages of the Depression, before the climate would be right to encourage the most popular and lucrative times ever enjoyed by the jazz musician.

CHICAGO JAZZ IN RETROSPECT

Since the mid 1930s, there has been a plethora of books written about jazz, each author with an individual take on the history of jazz. There is no doubt that the "longer view" offers a better perspective to historians and critics. The following viewpoints about F. Scott Fitzgerald's "Jazz Age" will provide some insight into the significance of this period.

Wilder Hobson published *American Jazz Music* in 1939. He offered the following opinions about the Chicago period:

> The Chicago jazz players, Negro and white, of the twenties were for the most part still, in effect, in a folk-musical environment, playing spontaneous music in obscure dance halls and moving on later for impromptu sessions in still more obscure speakeasies. Their music had a very limited white audience and little or no commercial value or publicity. By the late twenties fine jazz playing emerged somewhat into the commercial spotlight. But there was nothing which might have been called a public demand for, or recognition of, the jazz language.[22]

Hobson went on to describe Chicago jazz as "a blend of the negros' personal intensity and a linear economy suggestive of Bix Beiderbecke."[23] Although some of Hobson's comments about the 1920s are valid, many of his observations serve to show that he was out of touch with the reality of the 1920s and what it meant to the advancement of jazz. Hobson's book is, nevertheless, considered the first jazz criticism book of real value to be published by an American. French author Hugues Panassié first published *Hot Jazz* in America in 1934. The French author insisted that Chicago jazz was a "white appropriation"[24] of music created by black musicians. It is important to mention that Panassié never traveled to the US to witness jazz first hand, prior to the writing of his first book on the subject. Author Rudi Blesh agreed with Panassié and referred to Chicago jazz as "white imitations of Negro jazz, sincere but not profound."[25] Blesh also felt that many good "negro" musicians had been tainted and spoiled by the commercial influences of white jazz. Last, contemporary jazz scholar, composer, and conductor Gunther Schuller, author of *Early Jazz*, classified the Chicago style as "commercial performances geared to a thriving mass market requiring a consumer's product."[26]

Looking back at jazz criticism is interesting, as it provides a glimpse and perspective on the music's reception at the time. We often find in such writings shortsighted perspectives from authors who lacked hindsight and the advantage of the longer view. Every new trend, regardless of its long-term effects, is valid and contributes to the ongoing evolution of an art form, adding to the continuum. No one has the foresight to know where it may be going, but history has shown that we must let it go there along its own natural course, unencumbered by criticism, and enjoy the ride—wherever it takes us.

NEW YORK AND THE HARLEM RENAISSANCE

While Chicago had its south side, New York City had **Harlem**, an area that served as a hot house for the germination of black intellectualism, cultural development, and community pride during the 1920s. On one hand, Harlem was the center of a growing sense of black pride, and yet, at the same time, conditions continued to deteriorate, as more and more blacks fled the south to this northern city in search of work and a better life. The influx of newcomers into this concentrated area gradually caused conditions that led to the creation of slums and ghettos.

While some black intellectual leaders, such as writer Langston Hughes, were champions of jazz and reflected this attitude in their writings, other church-going black community leaders looked down on the music and its practitioners. This group considered the music to be "low brow," representing a part of black heritage that should be repressed and forgotten, rather than encouraged. Despite these conflicts within the community, Harlem produced some of the finest jazz musicians of the day.

The ragtime style served as a springboard for the creation of a looser, more swinging style that developed initially in the Harlem section of Manhattan. James P. Johnson, who was also a highly skilled ragtime pianist and composer, is considered to be the "father" of this new **"stride" piano** solo style. There were other pianists associated with this style, and together they are remembered as the "**Harlem Pianists**." This group included Eubie Blake, Willie "The Lion" Smith, Duke Ellington, Fats Waller, and Art Tatum, among others. The left-hand technique associated with this style is clearly related to the oompah, 2-beat style of ragtime, providing a

Exterior of the Renaissance Casino ballroom in Harlem, New York, late 1920s

steady, regular rhythm. The left hand leaps in large "strides" across the keyboard, stating chord roots on strong beats and basic chord tones above the root on the weak beats. In counterpoint to the regularity of the left hand, the right hand creates single-line melodies and interacts with the regularity of the left hand in most unusual and irregular ways, setting up syncopations and polyrhythms. Rhythmically, the stride style is more sophisticated, with more intricate rhythms and a smoother sense of swing than the rather rigid, predictable syncopations associated with rags. There is a greater tendency toward improvisation, application of blues inflections, and generally faster tempos than in most classic rags, which called for no improvisation and were not informed by the blues. (Chapter 3, "Listening to Jazz," on the website provides a video example of stride piano found in the "Instruments–Piano" section.)

Many of these Harlem Pianists earned their living supplying accompaniment for silent films and blues singers, such as Bessie Smith. They also performed at cabarets, rent parties, and for Tin Pan Alley publisher shops to help market new music. Informal competitions, sometimes referred to as "cutting contests," were staged at a musician's home. A modest admission fee was charged, and this income was used to help the tenant pay his rent. These rent parties became fairly commonplace, not only in Harlem, but also in Kansas City and Chicago.

James P. Johnson (1891–1955)

The "father of stride piano," educated in the classical tradition and trained by Eubie Blake, James P. Johnson served as musical director for the black film "St. Louis Blues" and arranged some 16 musical reviews for Broadway. Despite his reputation among musicians as a superior pianist, composer, and accompanist, Johnson never enjoyed great commercial success. His popular tunes such as "The Charleston" became standards, but were in sharp contrast to his love for more serious works in the stride style. These works include an opera, a symphony, a concerto, and a symphonic suite. Each of these major, multi-movement works was designed "to tell a story, the story of America's ethnic heritage, especially the distinctive role of his race."[27] Unfortunately, the white world of serious music was not ready to accept semi-serious, orchestral music by a black composer; consequently, much of his work in this vein was rejected by publishers. Ironically, in 1935, George Gershwin, a white, Jewish composer, created *Porgy and Bess*,

James P. Johnson poses for a studio portrait in 1921

a successful and more lasting American opera based on similar themes. Johnson's work as a stride pianist nevertheless was of great influence on Fats Waller, Duke Ellington, and the bebop-era pianist/composer Thelonious Monk.

Johnson's "Carolina Shout" is included in the online audio anthology. It is truly one of the most inspired stride-piano performances on record and shows a radical departure from ragtime. As the title implies, it is based on an old New Orleans ceremonial ring-shout, featuring contrasting themes. The piano roll of this piece supposedly served to instruct a young Duke Ellington, who placed his fingers on the player piano keyboard to follow the piece note by note. This particular

MILESTONES

Chronicle of Historic Events

The timeline that follows will put the developments of jazz discussed in this chapter into a larger historical context, providing you with a better sense of how landmark musical events may relate to others that match your personal areas of interest.

1922	• The flapper marks the end of the Victorian age for U.S. women, who now smoke and drink in public places, often wearing flashy clothing.
	• Paul Whiteman's recording of "Whispering" sells 2 million copies.[32]
	• Kid Ory's Sunshine Orchestra becomes first black jazz band to record
1923	• The first jazz is broadcast on radio live from Chicago.
	• A Russian inventor predicts television.
	• Joe "King" Oliver records "Dippermouth Blues" with his Creole Jazz Band, featuring Louis Armstrong.
	• The New Orleans Rhythm Kings become the first white jazz band to record with a musician of color.
1924	• Paul Whiteman's "Experiment in Modern Music" features George Gershwin's "Rhapsody in Blue."
	• IBM is founded.
1925	• Composer/conductor Igor Stravinsky makes his American debut conducting the New York Philharmonic in a program of his own music.
	• Sinclair Lewis's *Arrowsmith* is published.
	• The Florida State legislature requires daily Bible readings in all public schools.
	• Tennessee passes a law forbidding the teaching of any evolutionary theories that deny creationism.
	• "The Prisoner's Song" and "The Wreck of the Old '97," recorded by Vernon Dalhart, become the first million-selling country-music recording.
1926	• The first liquid-fuel rocket, pioneered by Robert Goddard, is launched.
	• Hemingway authors his first novel, *The Sun Also Rises*.
	• NBC is incorporated.
	• Movies become the most popular form of American entertainment, making Douglas Fairbanks, Greta Garbo, John Barrynore, and Charlie Chaplin national figures. A new era in pictures with sound begins.
1927	• The first public demo of TV takes place.
	• CBS is founded.
	• Lindbergh makes the first flight across the Atlantic, from New York to Paris.
	• Al Capone makes millions from illegal rackets in Chicago.
	• Babe Ruth hits his 60th home run, breaking previous baseball records. His salary is $20,000.
	• Ford launches the Model A car.
	• Bix Beiderbecke and Frankie Trumbauer record "Singin' the Blues (Till Daddy Comes Home)."
	• Work begins at Mt. Rushmore of a sculpture of four presidents.
1928	• Louis Armstrong records "West End Blues," which sells for 75 cents.
	• There is a rise of negro intelligentsia during the Harlem Renaissance (Langston Hughes and Alain Locke).

- Duke Ellington enjoys success at the Cotton Club.

- Pianist Pine Top Smith records "Pine Tops Boogie Woogie."

- "King of Jazz" Paul Whiteman records "Mississippi Mud."

1929
- The Museum of Modern Art opens.

- The Valentine's Day mob battle takes place in Chicago.

- Commercial passenger air travel begins.

- Black Tuesday—the Wall Street Stock Market crash marks the beginning of the Great Depression.

- Author William Faulkner publishes *The Sound and the Fury.*

CHAPTER SUMMARY

With plentiful jobs available, including good paying jobs for musicians, Chicago became a destination for many black Americans migrating from the south in the 1920s. Many important New Orleans musicians, including Freddie Keppard, Joe Oliver, Louis Armstrong, and Kid Ory, made the move to Chicago. The Prohibition Act imposed by the government made the sale and manufacture of alcoholic beverages illegal. During Prohibition, nightclubs known as speakeasies illegally sold alcohol and were run by racketeers. Some conservative groups, notably the JPA, sought to lessen the impact on youth of what they felt was sexually provocative music.

Jazz in Chicago in the 1920s served as a transition from the New Orleans jazz style to the swing of the 1930s. In addition to the transplanted black New Orleans musicians, a generation of primarily white, Chicago-based musicians became important contributors. One such group, the NORK, helped to define the Chicago sound by adding a saxophone and playing more sophisticated arrangements, in a smoother, more connected style. In 1923, the NORK recorded with Jelly Roll Morton, becoming the first white group to record with a musician of color. Probably the most significant musicians of this new generation were Frankie Trumbauer and Bix Beiderbecke. Frankie Trumbauer was a stellar technician on the C-melody sax. Beiderbecke was accomplished as a pianist, but is best known as a cornetist. He is generally considered the first great, white soloist of jazz, whose subdued approach served to foreshadow the cool jazz of the 1950s. Sadly, an unhealthy lifestyle led to Beiderbecke's early death at age 28.

The jazz of Chicago tended to place more focus on the individual soloist, compared with the collective improvisation of New Orleans jazz. The saxophone was much more commonly used, as was the string bass. Many of the white musicians were associated with "sweet" bands, which included strings and played primarily dance music. Some sweet groups, such as the Paul Whiteman Orchestra, were immensely popular, sometimes selling in excess of 1 million copies of a single recording.

Around the same time, New York City's Harlem was becoming an important center of black culture. The Cotton Club, Savoy Ballroom, and Apollo Theater featured performers who would help shape the next style of jazz. It also became known as the neighborhood of the "Harlem Pianists," with James P. Johnson remembered as the "father of stride piano," the direct successor of the earlier ragtime style.

Boogie-woogie, a style of piano playing that was different from stride, developed, not in Chicago, but initially in the more rural areas in the mid 1920s. A key ingredient of this blues-inspired style was the repetitive rhythm in the left hand, often referred to as "eight to the bar." It became popularized in later years.

KEY TERMS

Important terms, places, people and bands:

Terms
Black and tans
Boogie-woogie
Great Depression
Race records
Stride piano

Places
Cotton Club
Harlem
Levee district
Roseland
Savoy

People
Albert Ammons
Bix Beiderbecke
Duke Ellington
Benny Goodman
Harlem Pianists
Fletcher Henderson
Earl Hines
Langston Hughes
James P. Johnson
Pete Johnson
Eddie Lang
Meade "Lux" Lewis

Pine Top Smith
Frankie Trumbauer
Paul Whiteman
Rudy Wiedoeft

Bands
New Orleans Rhythm Kings
Paul Whiteman
Wolverines

STUDY QUESTIONS

1. What characteristics distinguish "hot" bands from "sweet" bands? Can you name some representative bandleaders in each style?

2. What features distinguish Chicago-style jazz from its earlier New Orleans Dixieland predecessor?

3. Of what significance was the JPA to jazz in Chicago?

4. What was the first Chicago-style white jazz band to record?

5. Bix Beiderbecke played which two instruments proficiently?

6. Which Chicago-style musician is often considered an early pioneer of the "cool" jazz sound?

7. Why was Frankie Trumbauer influential, and which instrument did he play?

8. Who was the first important guitarist to emerge during the Chicago period?

9. What instrumentation changes or additions occurred in the Chicago jazz band?

10. Which symphonic-jazz bandleader introduced the notion of using vocalists with the jazz ensemble?

11. Describe the boogie-woogie style and name two premier artists associated with the style.

12. When and where was the first live jazz radio broadcast made?

13. Was Paul Whiteman's book at all accurate in its predictions about the future of jazz?

14. By the mid 1920s, what cities were considered to be the centers for jazz activity? Specifically, what areas within these two cities?

15. Jazz was widely criticized during this period. Why and what specifically were the stated objections?

16. Which white band became the first jazz group to record with a person of color, and who was he?

17. Name some of the well-known "Harlem pianists."

18. What are the primary differences between the ragtime and stride styles?

19. Who is remembered as the "father of stride piano"?

20. What effect did Prohibition, the Depression, new technologies, and the underworld have on jazz in the mid-to-late 1920s?

21. In what ways was jazz marketed during this period, helping to spread its popularity and serving to create a new industry?

22. What led to the decline of the Chicago jazz era?

CHAPTER 7

The Swing Era

Jazz at Its Peak

It is not very difficult to understand the evolution of Jazz into Swing. Ten years ago this type of music was flourishing, albeit amidst adverse conditions and surrounded by hearty indifference.[1]
—Duke Ellington, 1939

Corner of Lennox Avenue and 147th Street in Harlem showing the exterior of the M&S Douglas Theatre and a sign for the Cotton Club a few doors down, 1927

JAZZ IN PERSPECTIVE

The Depths of the Depression

By 1930, jazz had established itself as more than just a passing fancy, but the effects of the Depression were nearly devastating. Had it not been for the resilient spirit of the American people, there is little doubt that the musicians and their music would not have survived. By 1932, the Depression had left 15 million Americans unemployed—one-quarter of the workforce. This depressed economic environment nearly eradicated the jazz and popular music movement, even though there was an increasing demand for inexpensive entertainment. Entertainment provided relief from stress and a chance to forget troubled times. The movie industry boomed during the 1930s, and, for only pennies, patrons were treated to live entertainment that could include singers, dancers, comedians, jugglers, and magicians, in addition to a newsreel about current events, a serial (the predecessor of the TV series), and the feature film. The movie house was the logical successor to vaudeville, providing good entertainment for little money. According to author Burton Peretti, record production, which had soared in the 1920s, fell 96% in the early 1930s. By 1932, even major labels such as RCA Victor, and Warner Brothers were close to bankruptcy.[2]

Americans' leisure time was occupied by inexpensive activities that they could afford—listening to the radio, parlor sing-a-longs, movies, board games such as Monopoly, and, of course, inexpensive dance halls. Ballroom dancing was the craze, and, without this popular social ritual in the 1930s and early 1940s, there would not have been a big-band Swing Era. The larger dance halls demanded larger bands, capable of filling the room with the dynamic sounds dancers craved. The small groups of the 1920s would have been incapable of projecting enough volume to entertain dancers in the large dance halls and hotel ballrooms. Although the move toward larger jazz bands began in the 1920s, it took a complete economic recovery before the halcyon days of the big bands would be fully realized.

The Depression affected blacks more than whites, and racial unrest escalated in the decaying ghetto communities of major cities throughout the US. Civil rights grievances increased, and the first major race riot occurred in Harlem in 1935. It is no wonder that a job in the entertainment industry, even with its drawbacks, was an attractive alternative to more traditional employment, where few opportunities were available, especially for blacks.

For big-band musicians who were fortunate enough to continue to work through the Depression years, there were numerous hardships. The lives of traveling black musicians were especially arduous. They played successive one-nighters, traveling hundreds of miles between engagements, eating meals irregularly, and often encountering prejudices that required them to sleep in cars, busses, and local homes rather than the hotels at which they might have been performing. Even long after the Depression had subsided, popular white bands enjoyed plush accommodations at hotels where they were booked for extended engagements, while black bands continued to tour. Popular black bandleader Jimmy Lunceford is reported to have said that, in 1942, his band logged "a couple of hundred one-nighters a year, 15–20 weeks of theaters [typically a week in each theater], maybe one four week location, and two weeks of vacation."[3] Needless to say, many of these musicians never enjoyed a normal home life, but it was something they were willing to sacrifice.

THE COUNTRY RECOVERS

Prohibition was repealed in 1933, and, by 1935, thanks to the efforts of President Franklin D. Roosevelt and his "New Deal," the country saw economic recovery and began to experience a new sense of optimism about its future. Roosevelt's comprehensive New Deal provided numerous federal relief programs, created public-works jobs, and offered farm credits and housing assistance —all designed to relieve the country from the effects of the economic Depression. His **WPA** (Works Projects Administration) even offered programs to help the arts by providing assistance for musicians, writers, and theater projects. The First Lady recognized the growing problems of racial inequality and publicly endorsed equal rights. This civil rights movement would continue to escalate once the US entered World War II.

The "common man," according to author Burton Peretti, became a central theme, and, spontaneously, the country became focused on developing a new sense of nationalism. Classical composers such as Aaron Copland (who composed "Fanfare For The Common Man"), Virgil Thompson, and Roy Harris created pieces that incorporated American folk songs, and authors such as John Steinbeck contributed books such as *The Grapes of Wrath*, which underscored the "common man" theme.[4]

The Prohibition Act that prohibited the sale and consumption of alcohol until 1933 actually added some impetus in the early years to what eventually became known as the Swing Era. Teens and young adults, until the repeal of Prohibition, freely attended dance halls across the "dry" American midland. It was the teenage and college crowds that created the first demand for swing music and were largely responsible for big-band jazz becoming a lasting symbol of American society and culture. Even during the Depression years, bands maintained a working schedule by booking dances at high schools and college campuses. During this period, alcohol was not a factor in determining if young people could or couldn't attend popular venues. The music could, therefore, thrive in this benign environment, contrary to its beginnings in brothels, roadhouses, nightclubs, and cabarets, where drinking was commonplace.

THE ANATOMY OF THE SWING ERA JAZZ BAND

By 1934, the groundwork for the success of big-band swing style had been laid by the likes of Paul Whiteman, Glen Gray, Ben Pollack, Fletcher Henderson, Don Redman, and Duke Ellington. These early masters cultivated the jazz arrangement for larger bands, building on the accomplishments of Jelly Roll Morton and those arrangers in the employment of sweet or symphonic bandleaders, such as Paul Whiteman.

Armstrong's Hot Five and Hot Seven recordings, as well as his brief stay in New York with the Henderson band, revolutionized the way musicians began to think, not only about improvisation, but also about the swing rhythmic feel. Musicians followed Armstrong's lead during the Swing Era, smoothing out their articulation and producing less choppy, clipped phrases. Slurred passages became more practiced, rather than the earlier staccato-tongued approach.

Although establishing categories can be misleading in the clarification of any art form, as exceptions always exist, and artists frequently cross lines, it is safe to say that most of the many big bands could be generally categorized as follows:

- Sweet bands that made few attempts to play real jazz and focused on society dance repertoire: Guy Lombardo's Royal Canadians fits well into this category.
- Swing-style dance bands featured a well-rehearsed repertoire performed by exceptional musicians, playing arrangements informed by the swing style, but geared largely for the dance

audience. These bands were often the most popular but featured little improvisation. Glenn Miller's band fits this description.

- "Hot jazz dance bands" were successful at compromising by performing music that clearly captured the essence of hot jazz by featuring stellar soloists, while appeasing the dance crowd by including a more tempered, danceable repertoire and vocalists. The great Benny Goodman and Artie Shaw bands are included in this group.
- "Hot" jazz big bands based their repertoires largely on pure hot, swing jazz, with ample room for improvising soloists. Some of the arrangements grew out of an improvised process rather than stemming from a concerted effort by composers/arrangers. Jimmy Lunceford, Jay McShann, and Count Basie led this type of band.

Although a few bands, such as Duke Ellington's, defied categorization, for the most part the bands could be placed in one of these four categories.

Instrumentation

The big bands all sported the same basic instrumentation as those early jazz bands that had preceded them—just more of them. Now, instead of just one of each of the wind instruments, there were sections of them. By the mid 1930s, the average big band had grown in size to include three or four saxophones, two or three trumpets, two or three trombones, and a three- or four-piece rhythm section. The saxophone, which first emerged in the mid 1920s, became the instrument of choice in most big bands. Gradually, the saxophone eclipsed the clarinet in popularity, although many of the saxophonists were called upon to play both instruments and may have started their careers as clarinetists. They were called woodwind doublers, or simply "doublers." The cornet players gradually converted to trumpet, a transition that started during the Chicago period. The trumpet delivered a more brilliant, powerful sound. The trumpet, therefore, lent itself more readily to the demands of the dynamic music performed by the powerful big bands. The single trombone, common to most New Orleans and Chicago jazz bands, was reinforced with the addition of one or more. The modern big band usually includes five saxophones, four

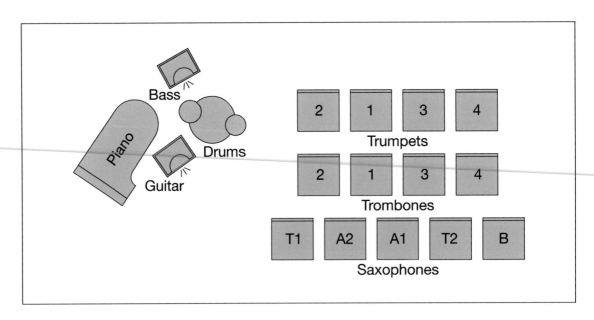

FIGURE 7.1 Typical big-band seating arrangement

or five trumpets, and between three and five trombones. Most bands set up in three parallel rows, with the saxophonists seated in the front row, closest to the audience, as they have the least ability to project. The trombones sit behind the saxophones, and the trumpets are in the back row. The brass section, the term often used to describe the collective trumpet and trombone sections, was often placed on tiered risers. The rhythm section is usually situated on the right side of the band (the audience's left). There are alternatives to this traditional seating arrangement, but often they were used to accommodate special circumstances.

Many of the big-band leaders also fronted small groups, which became a necessity during World War II, when it was difficult to staff a full big band. Goodman, Shaw, and Basie, among others, had small groups as well as big bands. In some ways, the small group could be an enticement for the best soloists in the big band, as it provided much more room for extended solos and additional recording opportunities. Most big-band arrangements, particularly those by the popular white dance bands, included only short improvised solos, and the best soloists often felt this to be a confining, creatively stifling atmosphere. This limitation was particularly true if the band recorded a hit that included an instrumental solo. In this case, audiences expected the soloist to duplicate the recorded solo in live performances, defeating any sense of spontaneity or creativity. Even today, over a half a century after the popular big-band hit "In the Mood" was recorded, audiences still expect to hear exactly the same original solo, even though it was initially an improvisation.

The rhythm section, which always seemed to be at the heart of major stylistic changes in jazz performance practice, was most responsible for the swing feeling associated with this style. It has always been somewhat confusing, as the term "swing" in this case has a double meaning— it describes a certain rhythmic phenomenon associated with jazz interpretation, and it is also a term used to describe this particular period in the history of jazz. When compared with the Chicago or New Orleans styles, the swing rhythm sections manifested several radical departures from earlier practices. First and foremost were the changes in instrumentation. Gradually, rhythm sections embraced the string bass, moving away from using wind instruments such as the tuba or bass saxophone. Although the string bass was much quieter than its early counterparts, it was significantly more agile and capable of playing smooth, "walking" lines on all four beats and at fast tempos. The "walking" bass line is a performance practice still used today and was first associated with the Swing Era. Amplification, a Swing Era innovation, later helped the acoustic bass to balance properly with the rest of the band.

The transition from tuba to bass was slow. As late as the early 1930s, it was not uncommon to see rhythm sections in swing bands still using the tuba and banjo in their rhythm sections. The guitar was largely used as a rhythm and time-keeping instrument, with chords strummed on the unamplified instrument on every beat of the measure.

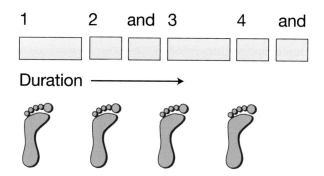

EXAMPLE 7.1 A graphic representation of 1 measure in 4/4 meter showing alternation between a full quarter note of full value on beats 1 and 3, followed by even eighth-note divisions of beats 2 and 4. This rhythm pattern does not swing

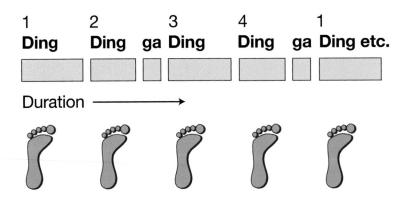

EXAMPLE 7.2 A graphic representation of 1 measure in 4/4 meter showing the uneven division of beats 2 and 4, causing a feeling of anticipation of the following beats (3 and 1). This was the typical pattern played by the drummer on the cymbals, expressed below by the syllables. This rhythm helps to create the basis of the "swing" feel. Horn soloists and pianists would likely also swing in this uneven fashion

By the 1930s, drum-set design and construction had significantly improved, as had recording techniques that allowed Swing Era drummers to play for recordings much as they did in live performances. As they developed more technique, dexterity, and independence of limbs, they began to create an approach to time keeping and rhythmic embellishment that more closely resembles what we hear today. Armstrong's rhythmic style did much to influence how drummers during this period played, as they eventually adopted his rhythmic style, transferring it first to the hi-hat and later to the "ride cymbal" to create what we now identify as the classic swing-style pattern.

The bass drum was used on all beats to reinforce the bass line. The snare drum and tom toms were used to embellish and decorate the arrangement, highlighting certain rhythms played by the horns. A good drummer would play a brief improvised rhythmic figure described as a **fill** to set up a response played by the horns, or to underscore a particular high point in the arrangement (often termed **chart**).

Make sure that you review the sections about Performance Practice in Chapter 3, "Listening to Jazz," found on the website. It might also be helpful to view the short video entitled *Video Blues*, paying particular attention to the rhythm section. If you haven't already done so, you should also examine the section about rhythm found on the website in Chapter 2 — "The Elements of Jazz."

As the bass and guitar players were playing on each beat, and the drummer was also emphasizing every beat, often embellishing in between major beats, pianists were forced eventually to create a new style of harmonic accompaniment. In previous years, pianists had followed the earlier stride, boogie-woogie, and ragtime models that were best suited for solo performance or for bands that had no bass or guitar (banjo). Pianists found that these busy, early soloistic styles, which were centered around filling up every beat in every measure, were inappropriate for the swing-style rhythm section, as the other instruments had well-defined roles that duplicated much of what earlier jazz pianists used to play. Eventually, pianists developed a sparser style of harmonic accompaniment, as it was no longer necessary to carry the added burden of keeping steady time— now the responsibility of the bass and drums. The new piano accompaniment style to emerge from the Swing Era was termed **comping**, an abbreviation of complement. It is Count Basie's rhythm section that is given much of the credit for developing these more modern rhythm-section techniques.

Jazz pianist Teddy Wilson playing with a quartet during the set break of Benny Goodman's band, because racially mixed bands were not the rule in New York City at the "Madhattan Room" in the Hotel Pennsylvania

Repertoire and Arrangement

Throughout the history of jazz, each era has been responsible for contributing to a growing repertoire. This repertoire, along with established performance practices associated with the proper interpretation of this music, has resulted in what could be considered the "jazz canon." The first generation of jazz performers and composers contributed pieces to the canon such as "Tiger Rag," "St. Louis Blues," "King Porter Stomp," and "Sugar Foot Stomp," to name just a few titles. The Swing Era gave birth to an astounding list of songs that were added to this expanding canon. One can view this repertoire, particularly from this period, as a list of works that fall into one of three basic categories—(1) the standard pop tunes that were readily adopted by jazz performers and arrangers, (2) **head charts** that were based largely on a series of improvised repeated motives ("**riffs**"), often in call–response style, that outlined blues or "rhythm changes" ("I've Got Rhythm" model), and (3) the jazz standard, written by jazz players and initially performed by them. This was the age of the great American popular song, written by composers such as Irving Berlin, Cole Porter, and George and Ira Gershwin. These songs were usually composed for the theater or film. Jazz arrangers and performers were quick to adopt songs such as Gershwin's "Lady Be Good" and "I've Got Rhythm" or Irving Berlin's "Blue Skies" and recast them in their own new molds. In addition to these Tin Pan Alley composers, Swing Era jazz composers also contributed immeasurably to the growing jazz repertoire. Duke Ellington, of course, was one of the most prolific, writing thousands of pieces during his lifetime. Ellington, sometimes with help from his band members, composed jazz standards such as "Perdido," "Don't Get Around Much Anymore," "Mood Indigo," and "In a Sentimental Mood." Ellington, like others, also borrowed from the earlier tradition, for example using portions of "Tiger Rag" as the basis for his new compositions. But Ellington was not the only composer contributing to the repertoire. Bix Beiderbecke's old friend Hoagy Carmichael, for example, wrote the timeless ballad "Stardust," and Benny Goodman composed "Stompin' at the Savoy," both of which serve as excellent examples of jazz standards that continue to be performed today.

All the swing bands had theme songs, many of which became charted by the trade journals that tracked record sales and other means of measuring a band's popularity. Fans immediately identified a theme song with the band that created it—for example, Count Basie's "One O'Clock Jump," Lionel Hampton's "Flying Home," and Duke Ellington's "Take the 'A' Train." Once a band popularized a song, it was not uncommon for other bands to create their own arrangements of it.

It has already been established that the arranger assumed a great deal of responsibility for developing a big band's particular sound. It was during this era that the jazz arranger first rose to high status. The arrangers and soloists gave each band its unique musical identity—its DNA. It was the arrangers' job to promote the particular strengths of the bands they wrote for, showcasing the best soloists and capitalizing on special attributes that might be available to give the band its special musical signature. Although some arrangers wrote for more than one band, they were able to adjust their writing style to suite the individual strengths of each band. Arrangers determined what key a piece should be in, the tempo, the style, which soloists and sections would be featured, how each section of the piece would be orchestrated (what instruments were assigned to what notes and roles) and harmonized, and other details. A good arranger would not only find a unique way to orchestrate and harmonize the original tune, but might also add entirely new material that would appear as the introduction, coda, or even in the main body of the arrangement. Although the big bands may have been relatively similar in terms of their instrumentation and general repertoire, the ways in which this repertoire was presented differed widely from band to band, and the arrangers controlled the presentation.

THE INNOVATORS: SWING ON THE EAST COAST

As jazz music was so widespread by the 1930s that no single city served as a Mecca, the Swing Era can be viewed geographically, examining the hotbeds of musical activity throughout the country and the musicians associated with these areas.

As discussed in the previous chapter, New York had become a Mecca for jazz and the developments in big bands of the early 1920s. It is no surprise that this trend continued during the Swing Era, when New York supported any number of swing and sweet dance bands, both black and white. Gigs at the Savoy and Roseland Ballrooms in New York, for example, attracted bands from across the country, as these engagements marked a level of accomplishment and achievement they all sought.

 Listen to the brief discussion with Gene Ramey about Eastern and Western swing. This interview is found in the corresponding chapter on the website.

Fletcher Henderson (1897–1952)

The frequently told story about many black jazz pioneers is that many were simply street-trained musicians. This "noble savage" myth of unschooled, innate talent was perpetuated by many of the early jazz writers. On the contrary, many of those jazz musicians, such as Fletcher Henderson, although not completing higher-education degrees, sought training beyond high school. Admittedly, his training as a mathematician and chemist may not have formally prepared him for the career path that he ultimately chose, but he was nevertheless an articulate, intelligent representative of the black arts community in Harlem. He initially found work in New York as a song peddler, working for W.C. Handy's jointly owned publishing company. This employment was supposed to be temporary until Henderson found work as a pharmacist. Whether it was a poor market for pharmacists or his initial success as a pianist that led to his career change is irrelevant, but he found himself in much demand as an accompanist for blues singers in race recordings and live performances. He recorded with Bessie Smith (see "Lost Your Head Blues," included on the *SCCJ*) and performed extensively with Ethel Waters. His first band was little more than an ordinary dance band, but it did earn him a local reputation as the "black Paul Whiteman." When it became apparent that hot jazz was what was attracting public attention, particularly in Harlem, he began to employ more soloists who were exploring improvisation. In 1924, he brought in Louis Armstrong from Chicago.

Bandleader, pianist, composer/arranger Fletcher Henderson

Armstrong stayed barely a year, but left an indelible impression on Henderson's men and all New York musicians. Saxophonist Don Redman became Henderson's musical director about this same time, and together they began to develop a formula for big-band arranging that became the archetype for many others to follow. Together, these arranging pioneers built upon devices that were pioneered by Whiteman and Jelly Roll Morton. Those characteristics and techniques that define this arranging style are as follows:

- call–response style, setting brass and saxophones in opposition;
- arranged by choirs, keeping like instruments together, rather than mixing brass and woodwind;
- harmonized soli sections achieved by composing a lead voice in an improvised style and creating parallel harmony, using secondary instrumental voices to follow the same melodic rhythm as the lead voice;
- stock swing rhythmic patterns scored (written) for wind players.

Henderson continued to improve his band, adding more top-flight soloists, but his rising star never reached a zenith. "A Study in Frustration" was the name that Columbia Records attached to their reissue of Fletcher Henderson big-band recordings, and this title aptly defines much of his career. Although he and his alto saxophonist Don Redman did much to establish the arranging formula that was followed for years to come, neither of these men ever enjoyed great success.

with the tongue). Hawkins's recordings in the early 1920s with the Henderson band showed a very choppy, articulated style of tonguing (as did many early jazz players), but, by the end of that decade, falling under Armstrong's influence, he showed the smoother phrasing evident in his 1939 recording of "Body and Soul." Hawkins was the first tenor saxophonist to bring this more modern approach to the instrument.

His understanding of music theory enabled him to create and negotiate elaborate chord progressions. He flaunts these impressive skills on "Body and Soul," included in the online audio anthology. Throughout this improvised solo, he demonstrates his inventive and skillful use of chord substitutions and embellishments, replacing chords in the original progression with more harmonically colorful and rich alternatives. Hawkins also introduced a new sense of **dissonance** (clash created by notes that do not fit a given harmony) and resolution by surrounding **chord tones** (notes that are part of a chord) with more dissonant neighbor tones (notes that are not part of the basic chord), eventually resolving them to consonant chord tones. This approach later became the foundation of the bebop improvisational style.

Although it is limiting to place narrow, blanket descriptions on a soloist's improvisational style, it is generally agreed that Hawkins took a largely vertical, or arpeggiated, rather than linear, approach to improvising. **Arpeggiated** refers to the way a wind instrument plays a chord by playing each pitch, one at a time, in ascending or descending order, rather than playing them simultaneously, like a piano, to sound the chord. The arpeggiated approach is in contrast to a more horizontal, scalar, or linear style associated with some other performers, such as Lester Young, Hawkins's most well-known counterpart, discussed in the following chapter (see Example 7.3). No soloist conforms exclusively to either approach, but uses a combination of both. Hawkins negotiated his way through chord progressions by outlining the chords, playing chord tones in ascending and descending sequences, creating arpeggios. He had attended Wasburn College in Topeka, Kansas, studying music theory and composition for 2 years, so it is no wonder that he excelled in his knowledge of harmony. As a result of these stylistic traits, his playing bore little resemblance to that of the instrument's early pioneers.

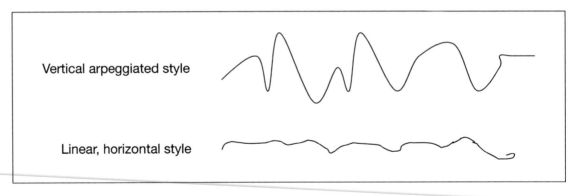

EXAMPLE 7.3 Contrast between arpeggiated and linear styles

In 1939, a *Down Beat* magazine reader's poll showed Hawkins in the top spot on his instrument, enabling him to assemble fine big bands and small groups filled out with some of the most modern musicians of the day. This popularity led to his sponsorship of what many consider to be the first landmark bebop recording session, in 1941, featuring young upstarts Dizzy Gillespie on trumpet, Oscar Pettiford on bass, and Max Roach on drums. Bebop, however, was not yet an established or recognized style.

LISTENING GUIDE

Coleman Hawkins and His Orchestra

"Body and Soul" (Green-Sauer-Heyman-Eyton) 2:59

Recorded 10/11/1939 Bluebird B-10253

Reissued on The Smithsonian Collection A5 19477

Personnel: Coleman Hawkins, tenor saxophone; Joe Guy, Tommy Lindsay, trumpets; Earl Hardy, trombone; Jackie Fields and Eustis Moore, alto saxophones; Gene Rodgers, piano; William Oscar Smith, bass; Arthur Herbert, drums

Form: 32-bar song form choruses (AA^1BA^2 = chorus)

0:00–0:09	Introduction—4 bars, solo piano
0:10–1:30	First chorus—32 bars, tenor chorus melody and solo
0:10–0:29	A section—8 bars, tenor plays chorus melody with simple, restrained piano, bass, and drums accompaniment
0:30–0:50	A^1 section—8 bars, tenor begins improvised virtuoso solo over chorus chord changes, only hinting at melody, with piano, bass, and drums
0:51–1:10	B section—8 bars, tenor improvises freely over bridge chord changes, with rhythm
1:11–1:30	A^2 section—8 bars, tenor continues solo over chorus chord changes, with rhythm
1:31–2:59	Second chorus—34 bars, improvised tenor solo on AA^1BA^2 chord progression
1:31–1:50	A section—8 bars, tenor continues virtuoso improvisation over chorus chord changes, with sustained background chords in trumpets and saxes, simple rhythm section accompaniment
1:51–2:11	A^1 section—8 bars, similar to A section
2:11–2:31	B section—8 bars, tenor continues solo, trumpets and saxes tacet, continued simple rhythm
2:32–2:59	A^2 section—10 bars, tenor climaxes improvisation over sustained chords in trumpets and saxes, short tenor solo cadenza followed by ending chord in trumpets and saxes

DUKE ELLINGTON (1899–1974): MUSIC WAS HIS MISTRESS

As the title of John Edward Hasse's book implies, Edward Kennedy "Duke" Ellington was "Beyond Category." Ellington was more than a composer and bandleader; he became an institution and has been the subject of more books than possibly any other jazz musician. A prolific writer, Ellington is considered one of America's foremost composers, whose catalogue contains approximately 2,000 works, including film scores (*Anatomy of a Murder*, *Paris Blues*, with Louis Armstrong, and *The Asphalt Jungle*), musicals, sacred music, popular dance tunes, and episodic concert works. His work was and is recognized worldwide, receiving France's highest award—The Legion of Honor, and the U.S. Presidential Medal of Honor for his contributions to the American art form. Four countries issued postage stamps to honor his accomplishments.[6]

Ellington followed a destiny instilled in him as a youngster by his family. He was the child of a proud black family who earned an honest living in Washington, DC. As a youngster, he was taught that he was special and should carry his head high, so it is no surprise that he eventually earned the royal title of the "Duke" of jazz. In DC, he studied piano and learned about the dance-band business, performing with local bands and organizing his own, which he called the Washingtonians. Ellington was articulate, sophisticated, witty, elegant, and, most of all, had the self-confidence to believe in himself and his potential for greatness. He believed that, despite his blackness, he was heir to a throne. As a child, he showed talent as a painter, although he ultimately chose to follow another artistic calling. However, he continued, throughout his career, to pursue painting as a form of relaxation, while traveling with his band and performing in over 20,000 engagements, living out of a suitcase in hotels and backstage dressing rooms for most of his life. His visual mind clearly influenced his music and is evident in many of his impressionistic, moody works, which often seem like tone paintings.

With his early success in New York at the famed Cotton Club (1927–1931), Duke Ellington continued to sustain a working big band for nearly 56 years, until his death in 1974. His uncanny ability as a leader is a testament, not only to his leadership, but also to his genius and charisma. Why else would some members of his band remain for over 40 years—virtually their entire careers? Although he was a pianist, his real instrument became the band. Ellington developed a sound palette comparable to no other composer or bandleader, learning to combine instruments in unusual ways and relying on the unique abilities of his band members. Even in the face of bebop and other stylistic trends in jazz following the Swing Era, Ellington stayed his course, following his own lead.

To fully appreciate Ellington's recordings, one needs to become more closely acquainted with the following characteristics that make the Ellington sound so unique:

1. The 4 years that Ellington spent at the Cotton Club represent what could be termed his workshop period. With an ever-changing floorshow, often involving exotic choreography and singers depicting African scenarios, Ellington learned to create new music, or revise old music quickly, to accommodate the needs of new shows. He had to create moods that reinforced the jungle atmosphere by creating special, unique orchestrations and by using drums to provide a jungle-like scenario, with African-American entertainers performing in exotic, native-like costumes.

2. Although the catalogue of Ellington compositions is almost mind-boggling, it is not difficult to find pieces that are strongly influenced in some way by the blues. Another primary source of inspiration was train travel. As Duke and his band often traveled by train, the sounds and rhythms associated with this mode of transportation permeate his scores. An early composition entitled "Daybreak Express" is an excellent example of his use of the train theme.

3. With the help of his exceptional musicians, such as trumpeter Bubber Miley and trombonist "Tricky Sam" Nanton —outstanding brass soloists who had developed unique performance techniques—he learned to make use of the special sounds of muted brass instruments.

4. Ellington's orchestration during the Cotton Club period began to demonstrate a special flare for combining instruments from different families—termed cross-section orchestration—and using mutes to alter the open, unmuted sound of a brass instrument. In this way, he left an indelible and unique signature on every composition. Most bands followed the orchestration model made popular by Fletcher Henderson and Don Redman, who arranged by choir—keeping like families of instruments together in their statement of melodic and harmonic passages. Instead of following this already shopworn path, Ellington favored combining instruments from different families, carefully assigning notes to instruments in less expected registers or ranges to achieve new sound colors. For example, in "Mood Indigo," he scores the clarinet in its lowest register, sounding under the trombone, which usually plays under the higher-pitched woodwind instrument.

5. Recognizing the strengths of his individual musicians, Ellington wrote specifically for them. His music never sounds quite the same when played by other bands, although many did play it, because they lack the special musical personalities necessary to duplicate the Ellington sound.

6. Most music produced during the Swing Era, even by the best-established, most polished bands, never displayed much harmonic originality—if any at all. Ellington developed a harmonic style all his own, constructing unusual chord progressions that often broke the rules of convention that dictated which chords should precede and follow one another. He frequently presented harmonically ambiguous introductions and interludes connecting main themes.

Duke Ellington and his band performing at the legendary Cotton Club

These ambiguous sections defy a descriptive tone center and provide no clear sense of key, while breaking rules of functional harmony.

7. Harmonically speaking, Ellington also favored creating dissonances by adding tones outside the ordinary three-note triads and four chords typically found in the run-of-the-mill swing-band arrangements of the day. His penchant for dissonance was evident in both his piano and arranging styles. It is not uncommon to hear Ellington play closely grouped, dissonant clusters of notes at the piano, and this same harmonic sense found its way into his band arrangements. His dissonant piano style can be heard clearly in "Ko-Ko," included in the online audio anthology.

8. As discussed and illustrated in the section on form found in the "Elements of Jazz" chapter on the companion website, most popular music follows a rather predictable structure based on phrase groups in multiples

of 4 and 8 measures. For example, the A section of a typical jazz or popular song from this period is generally 8 or 16 measures in length. Ellington broke free of this stereotypical template, sometimes composing phrase groups of 5 and 10 measures, as is the case in his "Concerto For Cootie," included in the *SCCJ* (editions prior to the 2010 release).

9. Other big-band composers were not particularly known for revising their work to create new, improved versions. Rarely did they extrapolate a section from one piece and use it as the basis for a new composition. Throughout his career, Ellington followed both of these practices. "East St. Louis Toodle-o" was later revised as "New East St. Louis Toodle-o" and is a good example of this Ellington practice. The more popular swing ballad "Do Nothin' Till You Hear From Me" was later extrapolated from "Concerto for Cootie." Ellington rarely performed anyone else's music, as was common practice in many other big bands from the period. Other bands played arrangements of Ellington's music, but the reverse was rarely true.

Although it is always dangerous to categorize art into neat cubbyholes, it does serve an instructional purpose. In the case of Duke Ellington, his prolific career offered him opportunities to compose for numerous occasions, people, and surroundings, and to express his own beliefs and convictions. Categorization will help you to understand the depth and breadth of this man's talent and legacy. His music can be loosely divided into five categories: (1) jungle styles; (2) popular dance tunes; (3) atmospheric mood pieces; (4) miniature solo concertos; and (5) multi-movement, extended-form concert works. Although he was not an active member of the civil rights movement, nor a militant, outspoken activist, Ellington was deeply committed to his race and proud to be black. As a result of this personal dedication, he often wrote on African-American themes, including tributes to prominent members of the race. "Black, Brown, and Beige," "Black and Tan Fantasy," "Creole Rhapsody," and numerous others suggest this theme and attest to his commitment. A closer examination of the works in each of these five categories follows.

1. **Jungle pieces**: Ellington's first formative period as a composer/bandleader was during the band's Cotton Club engagement. During this time, he wrote a number of what are often classified as "jungle pieces." In these, he used drums, muted brass, and sometimes-bizarre instrumental effects, along with special orchestrations to project the jungle atmosphere depicted by the floorshow. "Caravan," co-composed with his valve trombonist Juan Tizol, serves as a good example of this early style.

2. **Popular dance pieces**: Perhaps in an effort to remain popular, Ellington composed a number of tunes designed to capture the attention of the dance-crazed public. Some were set to words composed by his manager, Irving Mills. He had hopes that the recordings of these songs would become hits. Many of them did, but, ironically, other bands' arrangements of them were often more successful than his own recordings, which may have suffered because of the more extended improvised solos, which were too sophisticated for the average dance crowd. "In A Mellow Tone," "Don't Get Around Much Any More," "It Don't Mean a Thing if it Ain't Got That Swing," "Sophisticated Lady," and "Prelude to a Kiss" are fine examples of Ellington's more popular composition style. The somewhat angular, leaping melodies and wide range in these last two titles, along with their unusual chord progressions, were daring as far as pop tunes of the day went, making them less attractive to the casual listener who liked best those melodies that were easily remembered.

3. **Mood pieces**: A number of Ellington's works are categorized as "mood" pieces. These compositions establish an atmospheric, pastel sense, and often use the term "mood" in their titles, such as "Mood Indigo" or "In a Sentimental Mood."

4. **Solo features**: Ellington composed a number of miniature concertos to feature the various soloists in his band. Perhaps the most famous of these solo features is "Concerto for Cootie."

Dancers performing onstage at the Cotton Club

5. **Episodic concert works**: The final category of Ellington compositions is by far the most daring, as these works broke away from the established tradition of the big band by serving a secondary function—providing music for dance or shows. Although the two musicians were vastly different in many ways, Ellington followed Paul Whiteman's lead in believing that jazz and related American popular music could serve as the basis for more serious concert or symphonic works that would establish a new, purely American tradition. There is evidence to support the idea that Ellington was so enthralled with the European high art that he worked to elevate his own music to the same stature. He was once asked what few recordings he would want if he were "fleeing from this or that wicker city." (The author Robert Goffin was a French-speaking Belgian who wrote his book about jazz during World War II, when he had to flee leaving behind thousands of records.) Ellington's initial response to Goffin's question included classical pieces by Ravel, Debussy, Delius, and Holst. Upon further consideration, he added six jazz works and his own composition, "Something to Live For."[7] The technology of the time worked against his early efforts to create extended-form, multi-movement pieces that exceeded the typical, established, 3-minute 78-rpm record model. His first effort, "Creole Rhapsody," was recorded in 1931 and broke new ground. Despite its innovations, including unusual phrase lengths, the piece was marred by poor thematic structure and was not well received. We can only imagine that he was forced by the limitations of available recording technology to make certain compromises in this work, which was nearly 6½ minutes long and occupied two sides of a 78-rpm record. His

A listening guide for an excellent example of a piece from Ellington's "mood" category can be found in the corresponding chapter on the companion website.

subsequent efforts were spotty; nonetheless, the most important consideration was that he was making major strides in elevating his music to the level of art music, on a par with multi-movement classical works. Along these lines, he contributed numerous extended concert works, a dance suite, and three sacred concerts. A few of his many works in this category include: the "Far East Suite," "Such Sweet Thunder," inspired by Shakespeare's plays and sonnets, "Suite Thursday," "Drum is A Woman," the "Perfume Suite," "The River," commissioned by the Alvin Ailey Dance Company, "Togo Brava Suite," "The Liberian Suite," and the "New Orleans." As is evident from many of these titles, his travels, along with people he had met, often inspired these lengthy compositions. Although some of these works were criticized for their discontinuity and absence of sufficient jazz improvisation, there is little doubt that they helped to elevate jazz to a status on a par with European concert music.

Ellington was an enigma without peer. He stands as somewhat of an anomaly, as he was able to sustain a big band well beyond the years of their general popularity. Only a few other bands, some of which were latecomers, were able to continue beyond the true heyday of this great music. Count Basie, Woody Herman, Stan Kenton, Buddy Rich, and Maynard Ferguson are among the very few bandleaders who were able to keep their big bands touring and recording long after 1945 by adding new arrangements that captured current popular and jazz trends. On the other hand, Duke Ellington stayed on course, relatively unaffected by changing tastes and stylistic trends. Bebop, cool, and funk are all styles that passed him by later, leaving no real impact on his own style. Although other big bands of the day relied heavily on the popularity of their singers, many of whom went on to stellar solo careers, not one of Ellington's singers rose to such heights. Ellington never relied heavily on vocalists for popular appeal. He was his own master and is "beyond category."

Not only was he responsible for contributing a huge body of work to the jazz canon, but he was also as a leader who helped to introduce some of the most individualistic soloists to the world. These include the lyrical and bluesy alto saxophonists Johnny Hodges and Russell Procope; baritone saxophonist Harry Carney; trumpeters Bubber Miley, Cootie Williams, Clark Terry, Ray Nance (who also played violin), and Cat Anderson; drummers Sonny Greer and Louis Bellson; and trombonists "Tricky Sam" Nanton (heard prominently in the featured selection "Ko-Ko") and Lawrence Brown.

Significant Ellington Sidemen

Trumpets	Bubber Miley, Cootie Williams, Rex Stewart, Clark Terry, Cat Anderson
Alto Sax	Russell Procope, Johnny Hodges
Tenor Sax	Ben Webster, Paul Gonzalves
Bass	Jimmy Blanton, Oscar Pettiford
Trombones	"Tricky Sam" Nanton, Juan Tizol, Lawrence Brown
Tenor Sax and Clarinet	Barney Bigard, Jimmy Hamilton
Baritone Sax	Harry Carney
Drums	Sonny Greer, Louis Bellson

Many of these sidemen revolutionized the way in which their instruments were played, making people realize potentials that had never before been imagined. For example, one of the most important jazz bassists in the development of this instrument was Jimmy Blanton, who performed with Ellington's rhythm section in the early 1940s. As a soloist, Blanton was perhaps without peer at that time, consequently bringing the bass into the solo spotlight and out of its more obscure role as a member of the rhythm section. His strong walking bass lines, which

Composer Duke Ellington, singer Ivie Anderson, and drummer Sonny Greer pose for a portrait with the orchestra in 1943, in Los Angeles, California

can be heard on "Ko-Ko," included in the accompanying anthology, provided the foundation for some of the finest recordings by this band. Baritone saxophonist Harry Carney was also often spotlighted as a soloist in Duke's arrangements and assigned colorful notes in **chord voicings** (the way pitches are organized to state a particular chord) that would capture Carney's fat, luscious sound on the baritone. Prior to Carney's development on this instrument, the baritone sax had been relegated to playing tuba or bass-like parts, usually emphasizing chord roots. Last, and certainly not least, was Ellington's alter ego, composer/arranger Billy Strayhorn. Strayhorn's first piece for Ellington was "Take the 'A' Train," written in haste to show Ellington what he could do. It not only became the band's theme song, but also marked the beginning of a life-long relationship. Strayhorn so closely captured the Ellington sound that it became difficult to tell which of the two had actually written some of the music.

"Ko-Ko" is generally agreed to be one of Ellington's most outstanding showpieces, conceived and recorded during one of his prolific periods and by one of his best bands. This piece is one of many he based on a simple blues progression—in this case, in a minor key. Although it is a commonplace blues (discussed in Chapter 2), it is in the very unusual key of E-flat minor. His ability as a composer and orchestrator to develop a short, 3-minute masterpiece that transcends the simplicity of this simple, almost shopworn harmonic form is a testament to his genius. According to Martin Williams, "Ko-Ko" "was originally dedicated to the drum ceremonies that centered in Congo Square in pre-Civil War New Orleans, survivals of African worship."[8] The tom-tom rhythm pattern stated in the introduction lays the groundwork for the rest of the pieces and captures this old New Orleans scenario. Ellington also makes use of the timeless African call–response form, with Juan Tizol starting the call on his valve trombone, which invokes the response from the ensemble. This effect continues throughout much of the arrangement, with different instrumental groups assuming the role of the "caller" and "responder." Bassist Jimmy Blanton demonstrates clearly in this recording why he is considered to be an important link in the lineage of jazz bassists, providing strong, well-balanced walking lines and short solo fills throughout the arrangement.

Ellington Firsts

1. First black band to broadcast nightly on the radio;
2. First composer to merge jazz with film to create the film short *Black and Tan Fantasy*;
3. First black jazz band to appear in a full-length feature film—*Check and Double Check*;
4. First black jazz composer to score a musical theater production and use his band in the production;
5. First jazz composer to create extended concerts pieces that required more than one side of a 78 rpm record to produce—*Creole Rhapsody* being the first;
6. First jazz composer to compose for full-length feature films.

Although all of the Ellington multi-movement suites offer something interesting, perhaps one of the more widely acclaimed is the "Far East Suite," a major work created collaboratively with Billy Strayhorn and released in 1967. The suite is the result of a 1963 Ellington Orchestra tour of what was actually the Middle East, sponsored by the U.S. Department, including stops in Amman, Nabul, New Delhi, Ceylon, Tehran, Madras, Bombay, Baghdad, and Ankara. Other cities were on their itinerary, but the tour was cut short by the assassination of President John F. Kennedy. In March of 1964, Ellington wrote in *Music Journal*, in an article titled "Orientations" (quoted in the original liner notes that accompanied the LP), that:

> The tour was a great adventure for us on what is indeed the other side of the world. Sometimes I felt it was this world upside down. The look of the natural country is so unlike ours and the very contours of the earth seem to be different. The smell, the vastness, the birds, and the exotic beauty of all these countries make a great inspiration. I hope much of this will go into the music, but doing a parallel to the East has its problems. From my perspective, I think I have to be careful not to be influenced too strongly by the music we heard, because there is a great sameness about it, beginning in the Arabic countries and going through India all the way to Ceylon.

Why the suite was mis-titled in terms of the geographic reference is anybody's guess, but the music Ellington and Strayhorn created is enchanting and projects a mood equal to the best classical program music.

"Isfahan," the third movement from the Ellington/Strayhorn "Far East Suite," is by far one of the most striking and celebrated Ellington Orchestra ballads. Recent scholarship has suggested that this particular piece, although copyrighted under both composers' names, was actually written by Strayhorn and initially titled "Elf."

Composed in 1963, before the completion of the suite in 1965–1966, this atmospheric ballad features the sensuous alto saxophone of Johnny Hodges, who makes pure poetry out of the haunting melody. His ability to smear and bend notes, connecting them seamlessly in liquid fashion, made him one of the most identifiable soloists of all time. Harry Carney's thick, lush baritone saxophone can be heard on composed fills at 1:29 and 3:04.

The tune, which could be considered one of Ellington's "mood" pieces, was renamed for use in the suite after the band's U.S. State Department-sponsored tour of the Middle East, which included a stop off at this city in Iran, south of Teheran.

There is no introduction to "Isfahan," and Hodges's opening, unaccompanied descending solo line immediately lays out the most important phrase in this composition. There is nothing superfluous in this entire, brief 4-minute piece, which includes very little improvisation on the part of the soloist. The solo breaks, in the early jazz tradition, and sudden pauses, which are always in tempo, supply surprising tension and anticipation to this otherwise relatively straightforward ballad. On closer examination, however, there are surprising changes made to the typical song form.

Although Ellington may have been the "Duke" and the first to achieve the many accomplishments cited above, someone else claimed the crown of "King" of swing. It is important to point out that none of the black bands captured the commercial spotlight and financial success to rival the best of the white swing bands. Benny "the King" Goodman led certainly one of the best of the white bands, without overly compromising his standards to satisfy the dance-crazed public. His crown was earned only after many years of struggling and failing as a freelance musician and bandleader.

Be sure that you use the website to review the high points of this chapter and access a wealth of supplementary material. There are some fascinating excerpts of interviews with Duke Ellington and others that feature in the corresponding chapter heading.

LISTENING GUIDE

Duke Ellington and His Famous Orchestra

"Ko-Ko" (Ellington) 2:40

Recorded 3/6/1940, Chicago

(Victor 26577)

Personnel: Duke Ellington, piano; Wallace Jones and Cootie Williams, trumpets; Rex Stewart, cornet; Joe Nanton, Lawrence Brown, and Juan Tizol, trombones; Barney Bigard, clarinet and tenor saxophone; Otto Hardwicke and Johnny Hodges, alto saxophones; Ben Webster, tenor saxophone; Harry Carney, baritone saxophone; Fred Guy, guitar; Jimmy Blanton, bass; Sonny Greer, drums

Form: 2-bar minor blues

0:00–0:11	Introduction—8 measures featuring trombones over single bass note (pedal point) played by bass and baritone sax
0:12–0:31	First chorus—theme played by muted trombone in call–response with sax section
0:32–0:50	Second chorus—muted trombone solo (different from first mute), with sax line and brass syncopated brass punches as background texture
0:51–1:07	Third chorus—trombone soloist continues for another chorus
1:08–1:25	Fourth chorus—Ellington plays piano solo featuring dissonant chords and cascading lines over brass punches and sax unison line
1:26–1:44	Fifth chorus—trumpets play melody, with sax and trombone figures in contrast
1:45–2:03	Sixth chorus—2-bar exchanges between full band and solo bass
2:04–2:21	Seventh chorus—most climactic section termed the "shout chorus," when entire ensemble plays new material at high dynamic level
2:22–2:33	Return of 8-measure introduction
2:34–end	4-bar coda

LISTENING GUIDE

Duke Ellington Orchestra

"Isfahan" (Ellington/Strayhorn) 4:02

From "The Far East Suite"

Recorded 12/20/1966

Bluebird 07863 (reissue 66551–2)

Personnel: Reeds: Johnny Hodges, alto sax; Russell Procope

Trumpets: Cootie Williams, Cat Anderson, Mercer Ellington, and Herbie Jones; trombones: Lawrence Brown, Buster Cooper, Chuck Connor

Rhythm: Duke Ellington, piano; John Lamb, bass; Rufus Jones, drums

Form: A (8 bars); B (8 bars); A (8 bars); plus 8-bar coda

This structure is unusual, because each 4-bar phrase within the A sections begins with the end of the previous 4-bar phrase. This descending line that serves as the most prominent feature of the melody begins each phrase as a pickup or anticipation of the first bar of each phrase. This feature is evident from the very first line played by the soloist. The final return to the A section is also unusual, as it is extended beyond the expected 8-bar reprise of A. At this point, an additional 4-bar section of brand new material occurs, before the return to the main 4-bar theme to end the form, making the final A section following the bridge a full 16 bars rather than 8.

0:00–0:16	A theme begins immediately, stated by Hodges on alto sax
0:17–0:32	Second phrase of A theme
0:33–1:04	B theme for 8 bars ends with pickup to A theme
1:05–1:20	Return to A theme, first phrase
1:21–1:37	Second phrase of A theme
1:38–1:48	Extension of A theme consisting of new material
1:49–1:52	Break
1:53–2:05	Return to final 4-bar phrase from A theme
2:05–2:08	Bass solo break
2:09–2:32	Full band plays new material based on A-section harmony; Hodges improvises solo fills
2:33–2:39	Alto sax plays solo break, ending with pickup to return of melody
2:40–2:55	Return to A theme
2:56–3:11	Second A-theme phrase
3:12–3:22	Extension to A theme for 4 bars
3:33–3:26	Break—silence
3:27–3:28	Reprise of A theme, leading to a false sense of ending
3:29–3:40	Break—silence
3:41–end	Hodges plays alto sax pickup to repeat of final phrase, leading to ending chord where Hodges plays opening five notes of melody as a final

BENNY GOODMAN—THE "KING OF SWING" (1909–1986)

A child of Russian–Jewish immigrants, Goodman was a product of the urban acculturation process in Chicago in the 1920s. Here, he learned to borrow both accepted and unorthodox techniques from black and white musicians. Goodman associated with members of the Austin High Gang. He most likely learned the value of practice and maintaining a good work ethic from his parents. His efforts were rewarded with a polished and flawless technique, along with a pure tone and vibrato that could at times be considered an anticipation of the "cool" sound developed years later in the 1950s. Because of his classical training, he developed a classical approach to the clarinet, unlike many of the more freewheeling, untrained jazz players of the day. This background no doubt led to his association with classical composers and performers later in his career.

His early Chicago experiences with society dance bands led by Ben Pollack and in recording studios as a freelance musician earned him a reputation as a consummate musician, comfortable in any number of musical situations. His solo work, as pointed out by historian Gunther Schuller, often sounded safe, or risk free, no matter how difficult the passage, lacking the tension and daring so often associated with great jazz performances. He was such a superior musician in every way that his music suffered at times from a lack of edge and urgency. In short, Goodman and his band were often just too perfect. His style was therefore contrary to the hallmark "hot" black soloists of the day.[9] As a result of this criticism, his early work is not considered to be profound or entirely original. This criticism, whether justified or not, followed him much of his life.

As Goodman's reputation as a recording soloist grew, he formed his own band in the early 1930s to honor several recording contracts. Although these early groups were not entirely successful, they did record several rewarding arrangements penned by Glenn Miller in 1931. Chicago drumming sensation Gene Krupa was instrumental in the success of the early Goodman band. This band also featured the brilliant Texas trombonist Jack Teagarden, who would eventually take this instrument to new heights, away from the earlier tailgate style. However, like most musicians, Goodman struggled through the effects of the Depression in the early 1930s. As much of the recording work had disappeared during these years, he took to performing live for radio broadcasts. Because radio provided free entertainment, it became even more popular during those difficult economic times.

His first successful recordings were made with the English Columbia label. By then, he had formed an alliance with John Hammond, who was one of the most successful promoters and champions of jazz to emerge during this period. Hammond, who was an active civil rights spokesman, convinced him to use the best possible talent for these recordings, including the up-and-coming Billie Holiday. Holiday made her first recording with the Goodman band. It was also Hammond—who exerted a major influence on Goodman for much of his career—who urged Goodman to form an allegiance with Fletcher Henderson. Goodman hired Henderson as his chief arranger, which not only saved Henderson's decaying career, but also eventually attributed to Goodman's overwhelming success. Goodman, who had experienced more than one failure, had all but abandoned any hope of fronting a successful jazz band and was bored with the run-of-the-mill dance-band arrangements. It was Hammond's commitment to Goodman and Hammond's ability to secure engagements, including extended radio broadcasts, that kept his band working in the face of failure. Goodman employed some of the finest musicians and soloists of the day, including Krupa, trumpeter Bunny Berigan, and pianist Jess Stacy.

The Goodman band struck out on what proved to be a lackluster tour across the country in 1935. By the time the band had reached Denver, he was almost ready to abandon all hope for success. His "Let's Dance" radio contract had been dropped, and he had succumbed once again to what he perceived as commercial pressures by playing more and more pedestrian arrangements of popular dance tunes. Most of these arrangements avoided improvisation, and all sounded much the same. Something happened, however, when the band arrived at the Palomar Ballroom in Los Angeles, California. That night, there was a young crowd on hand whose tastes had apparently caught up to the adventuresome Goodman and the more daring side of his band that featured "hot" arrangements by Fletcher Henderson. This young crowd craved Goodman's most demanding literature, which actually featured more improvisation. The young crowd was enraptured by Goodman's set of "hot," danceable

Bandleader and clarinetist Benny Goodman (center) performs for a large crowd at Manhattan Beach, New York, August 11, 1938

arrangements, and their enthusiastic acceptance, which was broadcast nationwide on radio, sparked the beginning of the great Swing Era. It was ironic that these same Henderson "hot" arrangements that turned Goodman's career around had been recorded only a few years earlier by Henderson's band, but failed at that time to generate any real notice. On that particular night, however, Goodman and his band became an overnight success, and he ultimately captured the title of "King of Swing." The differences between the Henderson and Goodman bands are obvious, but do not explain Goodman's overnight success. The Henderson band often featured higher-caliber soloists and swung harder, but it was difficult to match the level of precision and polish that Goodman, who was known as a taskmaster, had achieved.

Goodman and his band rode the crest of the wave that he had created until 1942, when he broke up his band. By then, he had posted an amazing list of accomplishments in the 7 years since his overnight success at the Palomar.

Like many other big-band leaders, Goodman found that he could also be successful surrounding himself with all-star casts in small group settings. His small groups, which included Lionel Hampton on vibes, Charlie Christian on guitar, pianist Teddy Wilson, and Gene Krupa on drums, may have actually contributed more to jazz in terms of a lasting influence than his big bands. Goodman's trios, quartets, and sextets brought a chamber-music element to jazz at a time when bombastic big bands were the thing. Throughout his career, Goodman showed a penchant for classical music, commissioning Igor Stravinsky and performing classical repertoire with the New York Philharmonic and the Budapest String Quartet.

John Hammond, who eventually became Goodman's brother-in-law, recognized the growing importance of bringing the best soloists into Goodman's band. Motivated by his empathy with black musicians struggling for equality and recognition, he persuaded Goodman to become the first white bandleader to employ black musicians in public performance. Goodman's first step towards integrating his bands led other bandleaders such as Charlie Barnet to follow. Goodman's first historic trio, formed in 1935, broke precedence by featuring black pianist Teddy Wilson, a native Texan, who 1 year later became a regular member of Goodman's small groups. Wilson was a polished pianist who had incorporated elements of Earl Hines's and Art Tatum's styles. The trio soon became a quartet with the addition of vibraphonist Lionel Hampton, another aspiring black musician. Hampton began his career as a drummer and had recorded with Louis Armstrong's big band. Hampton switched to vibes, seeing more opportunity for notice on this unusual instrument. (Make sure that you become acquainted with the vibraphone, which can be found on the website in the instruments section of Chapter 3—"Listening to Jazz.") Wilson left Goodman in 1939 to form his own band and, for a time, was singer Billie Holiday's musical director. Hampton too eventually left Goodman to form his own small and big bands and became one of the most important early innovators on his instrument. As a dedicated performer, he was known for his showmanship and tireless energy.

The last great black performer to be added to Goodman's small group was the revolutionary guitarist from Oklahoma, Charlie Christian. Christian was a major talent by the time he hit New York at the age of 23. The blues background that is apparent in his playing reinforced the importance of this heritage at a time when it could easily have been forgotten, amid the craze for popular big-band dance tunes. Most importantly, Christian engineered a solo style on guitar that brought the instrument into a more prominent role in jazz. Prior to his work in jazz, the instrument had been largely relegated to playing chords, providing regular rhythmic accompaniment. Christian's father performed throughout Texas and Oklahoma in bands that could be described as the predecessors of the western swing style. Many of these players actually pioneered the use of amplified guitar, but it is Christian who is justifiably given credit for bringing amplified guitar to widespread attention and use. The amplification helped him to break away from the traditional chording role and create a more linear, single-note solo style, similar to that of the saxophonists of the day. Jazz historian Gunther Schuller described his style as possessing "uncluttered lines, often arching shapes, flawless time, and consistently blues-inflected melodic/harmonic language."[10]

The Benny Goodman Sextet. L–R: Lionel Hampton, Artie Bernstein, Benny Goodman, Nick Fatool, Charlie Christian, Fletcher Henderson

Woody Herman Sidemen	Stan Kenton Sidemen
Nick Brignola, baritone sax	Art Pepper, alto sax
Stan Getz, tenor sax	Maynard Ferguson, trumpet
Zoot Sims, tenor sax	Peter Erskine, drums
Joe Lovano, tenor sax	Frank Rosolino, trombone
John Fedchock, trombone	Marvin Stamm, trumpet
Bill Chase, trumpet	Anita O'Day, vocalist
Neal Hefti, arranger	June Christy, vocalist
Ralph Burns, arranger	Pete Rugolo, arranger
Al Cohn, tenor sax	Kai Winding, trombone
Nat Pierce, piano	Mel Lewis, drums
Pete and Conti Candoli, trumpet	Gerry Mulligan, baritone sax
Dave Tough, drums	Bud Shank, alto sax
Sal Nestico, tenor sax	Tim Hagans, trumpet
Tom Harrell, trumpet	Conte Candoli, trumpet

FIGURE 7.3 Important artists to emerge from Woody Herman and Stan Kenton bands

Vocalists	Bandleader Affiliation
Jo Stafford	Tommy Dorsey
Rosemary Clooney	Tony Pastor
Billie Holiday	Benny Goodman Artie Shaw
Helen Forest	Artie Shaw, Benny Goodman and Harry James
Helen O'Connell	Jimmy Dorsey
Peggy Lee	Benny Goodman
Kay Star	Charlie Barnet
June Christy	Stan Kenton
Frank Sinatra	Tommy Dorsey
Anita O'Day	Gene Krupa
Bing Crosby	Paul Whiteman

FIGURE 7.4 Popular vocalists and associated bands

By the mid 1950s, the tide began to turn again, gradually diminishing the careers of all but the biggest of these stars, with yet another new wave of American popular music—rock 'n' roll.

ONGOING LATIN INFLUENCES

Using Jelly Roll Morton's words, the "Spanish tinge" continued to flourish during the Swing Era. America's infatuation with Latin dances came in waves, one after another, each popularized by Latin musicians who had taken up residence in the US. Pérez (Prez) Prado, for instance, was a Cuban-born musician who helped popularize the mambo. The samba was also known among early jazz and popular musicians. Carmen Miranda, famous for her fruit-cocktail headdresses, helped to further popularize this dance form in 1946, and it was reborn in the 1970s. The rumba entered the American scene in 1929, followed by the popular conga in 1937 through its promotion by noted Cuban bandleader Desi Arnaz (Lucille Ball's husband and of *I Love Lucy* TV fame). Many of these traditional dance rhythms underwent simplification or alteration to accommodate the demands of the dance-oriented American public. Xavier Cugat was largely responsible for some of this popular simplification. His great success enabled him to continually import Cuban musicians to replace those who left his employment to seek opportunities with other jazz bands.

The growing popularity of Latin music, combined with the increasing number of Latin musicians migrating to the US, led jazz musicians to continue with experiments to integrate the two styles. Valve trombonist Juan Tizol performed with the Duke Ellington Orchestra in the 1930s. It was during this period that Ellington collaborated with Tizol to compose and record "Caravan," "Conga Brava," and "Bakiff," all possessing obvious Afro-Cuban rhythmic qualities. Another east-coast Swing Era bandleader, Cab Calloway, recorded "Doin' the Rumba" in 1931. From time to time, he employed Latin American-born musicians such as trumpeter Mario Bauza. Bauza, who had played in the trumpet sections of big swing bands led by Chick Webb, Fletcher Henderson, and Don Redman, became an important catalyst in the formation of new Latin-jazz styles in the late 1930s and throughout the 1940s. His friendship with jazz trumpeter Dizzy Gillespie later becomes significant to the growth of Latin jazz and Cubop in the late 1940s, discussed in more detail in Chapter 9.

CHAPTER SUMMARY

In the first half of the 1930s, the Great Depression had a profound effect on life in America and on jazz. Twenty-five percent of the workforce was unemployed, with minorities being especially impacted. The recording industry slowed to a near standstill, as all but the most established record labels went bankrupt owing to plummeting record sales. Looking for inexpensive forms of entertainment as a way to forget their troubles, many Americans turned to radio, the movies, parlor games, and ballroom dancing.

As the popularity of ballroom dancing increased, so did the size and number of dance halls. At a time when sound reinforcement was still in its infancy, larger musical groups were needed to fill these larger halls with music. Instead of the three-musician front line of the previous decade, bands expanded to have entire sections of trumpets, trombones, and saxophones, in addition to the three- or four-piece rhythm section. Fletcher Henderson and his arranger Don Redman are often credited with the standardization of big-band instrumentation and arranging techniques still in use today.

CHAPTER 8

Swinging Across the Country

The Bands, Singers, and Pianists

No previous form of jazz had come even close to the immense popularity of the swing bands, which thoroughly dominated the hit charts during the years 1936 through 1945.[1]
—Bernard Gendron

8th December 1941: The front page of the *New York World Telegram* announces Japanese air attack at Pearl Harbor, commencing the U.S. entry into World War II

JAZZ IN PERSPECTIVE

Kansas City, or "Kaycee" as the locals knew it, was the midwestern big-city hub for cattlemen and wheat farmers selling their wares. They came to this city starved of the various forms of entertainment that were hard to come by in the more remote, rural plains. Cabarets, gambling houses, nightclubs and bars, opera houses, and dance halls were plentiful in this big city, near the confluence of the Missouri and Kansas Rivers. Kaycee had its special brand of music, much of which was derived from blues and ragtime styles. As was the case in other big cities during this period, there was a shady side to Kansas City. Gangsters not only owned many of the establishments, but also saw to it that illegal alcohol flowed freely, supporting nightlife activities. Just as Al Capone controlled much of the Chicago scene, Kansas City flourished from dawn until dusk during the reign of political boss Tom Pendergast. Pendergast gained control of the rough-and-tumble immigrant district known as the First Ward. This appointment was a stepping-stone, leading to his eventual control of much of the politics in the city, and eventually the entire state, until the federal government brought him down in 1938 on charges of tax evasion, among others. He enjoyed close ties to the gangster community. His demise came only after he did much to ensure the unencumbered operation of clubs selling illegal alcohol and every other imaginable vice during Prohibition years. Much like Chicago and New York, there were the black and white sides of town in Kansas City, each supporting dozens of nightclubs and gambling houses. Kansas City, described as a "wild town" during these years, could satisfy any desire and was a magnet for musicians who willingly came to provide their brand of music. During the Depression years, the numerous clubs that supported live music sustained many of the Kansas City musicians.

In a radio interview with jazz radio DJ Art Vincent, bassist Gene Ramey made the following observations and comments about the scene in Kansas City:

> It was back in 1932 when I came from Texas to Kansas City. At that time Benny Moten had his band. They had those fabulous battles of bands and I think that's the thing that impressed me the most about Kansas City. Those guys were dressed in the sharpest clothes. In those days it seemed like every big time musician owned a Hudson car. I remember George E. Lee [Kansas City territory bandleader] had two of them. And they would have these battles of the bands . . . I can't name all of them . . . Andy Kirk's 12 Clouds of Joy, Walter Page's Blue Devils, Harlan Leonard's Rockets, Julius and Carl Banks, Clarence Love, and of course the mighty Benny Moten. On holidays, Labor Day or Christmas Eve, they'd have a ballroom battle of all those bands and it would start at 7 o'clock and go to about 5 o'clock in the morning. Just one band after another until whoever won that contest and of course Benny Moten always won.[2]

THE INNOVATORS: A UNIQUE KAYCEE STYLE

Although there are some similarities in terms of the nightlife and corruption, there are many differences that distinguish Kansas City and other southwestern cities from New York in the 1930s. Remote southwestern and midwestern towns were less subject to the influences of New Orleans, and, as author Ross Russell put it, musicians in these towns "were left to their own musical devices."[3] The plain states were slow to absorb the more sophisticated musical styles evolving in Harlem and to participate in the growing music industry developing around Chicago and in these eastern urban areas. Consequently, ragtime and blues styles continued to flourish during the Swing Era and exerted a strong influence on music in the southwest. Many of the eastern-based groups developed in ways that identified them with a more sophisticated approach compared with the bands from the Midwest and Southwest. Bassist Gene Ramey, who traveled to New York as a member of the Kansas City-based band led by Jay McShann, was in a good position to assess the differences between bands from these two locales. He offered the following explanation: "lots of those [bands] that came from the east were [featuring] unnecessary interludes and modulations. KC bands [on the other hand] had a certain ruggedness, roughness that swung hard."[4]

The east-coast band with the most sophistication was of course Duke Ellington's. Ramey also pointed out that eastern rhythm sections lacked the "laid-back," behind-the-beat, "Baptist" beat that he associated with midwestern and southwestern bands. He felt that the eastern bands played with a very precise, "metronome beat."

Benny Moten

It was the popular Benny Moten band that is most associated with jazz in this city during the Pendergast reign. The Moten band captured much of the choice work, and, when bookings became sparse and travel difficult for Walter Page's Blue Devils band, many of Page's top bandsmen were lured to the Moten band. The Blue Devils, out of Oklahoma City, were a fine outfit that, at one time, employed Lester Young on saxophone, pianist William Basie, Walter Page on bass, and vocalist Jimmy Rushing. It was this southwestern band, along with Moten's, that perfected the blues riff, head-style arrangement. By 1932, nearly all of these fine Blue Devils musicians, including the leader, had left to join the Moten band. Listen to Moten's recording of "Moten Swing," included on the *SCCJ* (editions prior to 2010), to hear this band at the top of its game.

Benny Moten started his band in 1923, but at this point the area was still heavily under the influence of ragtime, brass bands, and vaudeville-style music. His first recording, released in 1923 and coinciding closely with those issued by King Oliver in Chicago and Fletcher Henderson in New York, featured a New Orleans-like instrumentation to project an arranged ragtime-ensemble style. Over the years, Moten built his Kansas City-based band to be rivaled by no other from the area. He gradually expanded the instrumentation, while moving away from the rag-based style. Up until the addition of the Blue Devils' personnel, his band lacked the secure soloists that the eastern bands boasted, and he had difficulty producing arrangements that would adequately showcase his expanded band. The recruitment of those stellar Blue Devils soloists, however, turned this situation around. Bill Basie, one of the first to leave the Blue Devils, replaced Moten at the piano, enabling the leader to concentrate on conducting and the business of running his band. Historian Ross Russell called bassist Walter Page "the single most important addition to the Moten band during this period."[5]

WILLIAM "COUNT" BASIE (1904–1984)

A tragedy struck Moten and his band in 1935, just as they were at the top of their game. Moten died on the operating table while undergoing a simple tonsillectomy. In short order, Bill Basie, capitalizing on his old friendships with members of the Moten and Blue Devils bands, brought together a new band under his leadership. At this point, he declared himself the "Count." Basie's band was first discovered by impresario John Hammond, who heard a radio broadcast of the band. He was so impressed that he brought the band to New York in 1936.

It is doubtful at this point that Bill Basie, the "Kid from Redbank," New Jersey, realized that he had begun a legacy that would continue even today under the leadership of band alumni. With the exception of a brief 2-year period from 1950 to 1952, when economics forced him to reduce his band to a smaller group, Basie maintained his career as a big-band leader for 49 years. The Basie band brought together the finest musicians from this area and codified the relaxed, swinging blues-riff style that is associated with bands from the Midwest and Southwest. The blues was at the core of this band's style, and, in these early years, much of the arranging was accomplished by Eddie Durham, who was gifted at constructing "head" arrangements based on riffs to serve as a framework for Basie's superb soloists. Head arrangements came about as the result of musicians improvising simple riffs (a short, repeated musical phrase described as motive), usually blues-based, that were memorized and eventually

The Count Basie Orchestra performs on stage in Chicago in 1940. Seated at far right: Lester Young; others: Walter Page (bass), Buddy Tate, Tab Smith, Jack Washington (saxes), Joe Jones (drums), Freddie Green (guitar), Vic Dickenson, Dicky Wells, Dan Minor (trombones), Buck Clayton, Ed Lewis, Harry Edison (trumpets)

Count Basie with his "All American Rhythm Section"—Walter Page, bass; Jo Jones, drums; Freddie Green, guitar

served to codify a particular arrangement. The arrangers utilized simple motives (short, melodic phrases that serve as the primary basis of a tune) as riffs, which served to characterize a loose, improvised style. The arrangers who have provided "charts" (accepted term for arrangement) for the band over the years have always maintained Durham's concern for economy of style. These motives and riffs were orchestrated for brass and saxophones and served both as **backgrounds** (secondary material that serves as accompaniment to a solo) behind soloists, as well as primary material for the main themes. The various riffs were often tossed about from section to section, in a call–response format. The arrangements also took advantage of the large dynamic range of a big band, contrasting quiet rhythm-section moments with bombastic surprises in the form of full band blasts. The Basie band, although never specializing in sophisticated and elaborate compositions, attracted listeners who were caught up in the relaxed swing and simplicity that became the hallmark of this great band. Basie had eliminated all that was superfluous, leaving only those essential ingredients that appealed to man's basic instincts by creating an infectious brand of toe-tapping swing. Late in his career, he was asked in a *Sixty Minutes* television interview to describe his music. After a brief pause, he replied succinctly by saying, "tap your toe." His brief description was as streamlined and to the point as his music.

It was the Basie rhythm section that generated the undercurrent that contributed to a unique brand of swing. Known as the "All-American Rhythm Section," these four men revolutionized and modernized the approach to rhythm-section playing by the late 1930s. They were the first rhythm section to redefine the roles of their

Many Swing Era "territorial" musicians went their entire lives without being recorded, whereas some were recorded, but with limited circulation, and others, such as Benny Moten and Jay McShann, became nationally known initially through their regionally produced records. Most of these bands were deeply rooted in a blues tradition, and much of their repertoire was based on improvised head arrangements. Many of these black performers came to jazz from a strong foundation in gospel and spiritual music, as religion was an important part of their upbringing in this part of the country. Many of the greatest musicians of the Swing Era, such as Ben Webster, Lester Young, Charlie Christian, Count Basie, and Mary Lou Williams apprenticed early in their careers with territory bands. Although many of these exceptional soloists moved on to successful careers, the ravages of the Depression years were too much for many of the territory bands to overcome, as they relied so heavily on the ability to travel, and for this reason many migrated to Kansas City in search of employment.

Mary Lou Williams (1910–1981)

With the exception of vocalists, the jazz profession remained largely a male-dominated world. Of course, there were exceptions, such as Ina Rae Hutton's Sweethearts of Rhythm and Phil Spitalny's "All-Girl" orchestra, but more often than not they were treated like novelty acts, playing watered-down jazz with window dressing. Some female orchestras became popular during wartime, when many male musicians had been drafted. Mary Lou Williams was, however, an exception. Her accomplishments are even greater when you consider the general attitude towards women in jazz, which was encouraged by the press. For instance, *Down Beat* magazine, founded in 1934 on the strength of the growing enthusiasm for swing, ran an article in 1938 titled, "Why Women Musicians are Inferior." The author was coldly unsupportive of the "fairer sex," citing that "women should be able to play with feeling and expression and they never do." He went on to say that, "women don't seem to be able to develop a lip" to withstand the endurance required to play jazz on a wind instrument. "The mind may be willing but the flesh is weak."[7] This same magazine printed rebuttals written by women in the field, but it was difficult to further their minority opinion. Other writers expounded that women were not hired for their musicianship as men were, but were employed because they were attractive to men. Women were "not well suited to the hard life of touring and playing in 'gin joints,'"[8] other writers claimed. The scales in the jazz gender battle have unfortunately always tipped on the side of the male musicians, and only recently have women begun to be recognized for their artistic contributions to jazz. Consequently, it has taken decades for Mary Lou Williams's contributions to be fully appreciated and touted.

She was raised in Pittsburgh, where she developed an early flare as a solo pianist and arranger. She was hired by Andy Kirk's Kansas City-based 12 Clouds of Joy and remained with Kirk from 1930 to 1942, before moving to New York. By this time, her reputation as a first-rate arranger and composer earned her commissions from Benny Goodman, Earl Hines, Tommy Dorsey, and even Duke Ellington. In an unprecedented move, the New York Philharmonic Orchestra premiered a portion of

Pianist, composer, arranger Mary Lou Williams

LISTENING GUIDE

Mary Lou Williams with Andy Kirk and His 12 Clouds of Joy

"Mary's Idea" (Mary Lou Williams)

Recorded 12/6/1938

New York City

Decca 2326

Andy Kirk: Director

Personnel: Harry Lawson, Clarence Trice, Earl Thompson, trumpet; Ted Donnelly, Henry Wells, trombones; John Harrington, clarinet, alto saxophone; Earl Miller, alto saxophone; John Williams, alto and baritone saxophone; Dick Wilson, tenor saxophone; Mary Lou Williams, piano; Ted Brinson, guitar; Booker Collins, bass; Ben Thigpen, drums

Soloists: Donnelly; Trice; M.L. Williams; Harrington, clarinet; Donnelly

Form: AABA song form repeated

0:00–0:05	Introduction for 4 measures
0:06–0:16	First chorus—brass section plays punctuated, harmonized tune with unison sax line as secondary melody
0:17–0:27	Second A
0:28–0:38	B section featuring harmonized saxes followed by solo trombone
0:39–0:50	A section from top of chorus repeats
0:51–1:12	Second chorus—trumpet solo on first two A sections
1:13–1:35	Piano solo by Williams on B section and final A section of chorus. Note more modern, single-note style following in the early Hines tradition
1:36–1:59	Third chorus—clarinet solo with muted brass accompaniment
2:00–2:24	Ensemble chorus featuring brass and saxes in rhythmically sophisticated riff style
2:25–2:35	B section with trombone solo on first 4 bars followed by muted brass
2:36–2:43	Final A section closely resembling first A theme
2:44–end	Coda

her "Zodiac Suite" in Carnegie Hall, in 1946. The merging of jazz and symphonic styles in this work was by itself unique and groundbreaking, and the fact that the suite was composed by a woman added to the significance of its premier.

In New York, Williams adapted her style as a pianist and composer/arranger to the new bebop idiom emerging in the mid 1940s, contributing works to Dizzy Gillespie's big band. Before her career came to a close, she had composed numerous jazz pieces, sacred works for chorus and orchestra including three masses, and many recordings. She stands as an exceptional example of the highest accomplishments by women in jazz, claiming a list of awards of which any artist would be proud.

Like Ellington, Mary had a habit of revisiting her compositions, as she was always learning, growing, and absorbing the latest jazz innovations. The track in the listening guide above, initially created in 1930, is just one of those updated arrangements. It demonstrates exceptional architectural craftsmanship and sets up a series of tensions and relaxations as it moves from section to section. You may guess right that the alto saxophonist listed in the personnel is her husband.

THE INNOVATORS: A FEW OF THE SWING ERA SINGERS AND PIANISTS

As the Basie band's style was molded largely by the blues, it stands to reason that the band would feature blues singers. A long line of exceptional blues singers, mostly males, performed with the Basie band during its lengthy history. Jimmy Rushing and Joe Williams best exemplify this style. One of the most famous of all jazz singers began her career with the Basie band, although her stay was brief, and commenced what became a lengthy relationship with Lester Young. Her name was Billie Holiday.

Billie Holiday (1915–1959): "Lady Day"

Lester Young gave her the nickname "Lady Day," but Lester called everybody "Lady," even the men. Gene Ramey, who performed and recorded with Lester Young and worked with "Lady Day," offered the following insight into these two compatible and compelling artists:

> Louis Armstrong showed us that you could play a melody and not actually play the melody. You could play the harmonic structure of a melody which made it more pleasing. I think she [Billie Holiday] got some from Louis Armstrong—the idea of how to make songs, even the worst songs, so appealing. And along with that you'll notice that Lester Young got his idea from that, so I would say that Billie Holiday kept the thing going, the sound that was actually created by Armstrong; but she is the only one to this day that put it through with the voice like that. She would sing a note with so much appeal. She was the greatest singer with the worst voice. If you'll notice her voice—it sounded like nothing, but she had so much control of the way to put a song over. It would sound like, as they would say, a bluesy singer. It was appealing—she was begging. She would take a halfways good song and make it wonderful. I was one of the pall bearers at Prez's funeral and the last time I saw her was about three or four months before he died.[9]

Ramey was both complimentary and a bit harsh in his assessment of Holiday, but another bassist, John Levy, who worked with Holiday seemed to confirm Ramey's opinions:

> Billie was a complete stylist. When you listen to her sing, you feel she has lived that experience and she is telling a story about it. I don't think anyone can express a story better than Billie. She didn't have great range or any of that stuff, but most of the tunes she sang had good melody lines and good stories, and they're not easy to sing or play.[10]

Billie Holiday singing at a Decca recording session, c.1946

Information about her early life is somewhat obscure and blurred by inaccuracies, but we do know that Billie Holiday's father played guitar with Fletcher Henderson's band. Although her life was clouded with problems, including prostitution and drug and alcohol addiction, which eventually led to her arrest, her talent should not be obscured by these details. Like other black performers, she owed her initial discovery and subsequent first recordings with Benny Goodman to John Hammond. It was through this association that Holiday met Teddy Wilson, who served as musical coordinator for her outstanding recordings from the mid 1930s. Her long association with Lester Young, whose wispy, light sound complemented Holiday's, is well known, as is her fairly short stay with Artie Shaw's big band, which followed her even shorter stay with the Basie band. She joined the Shaw band in 1938 to become one of the first black singers to appear with a white band. This arrangement was not without problems, and there is evidence that Shaw, who stood by Holiday, became frustrated and disgusted with racially prejudiced attitudes. Her best work is considered to have been accomplished from about 1939 to 1944, before her life was turned to chaos by drugs, alcohol, and ensuing legal problems. Although the movie about her, *Lady Sings the Blues*, gives one the impression that she was primarily a blues singer, much of her repertoire does not confirm this. She claimed Louis Armstrong as a significant influence, and preferred popular tunes and love songs. Her style was certainly informed by the blues style, and she was a fine blues singer, although she might be more accurately labeled a torch singer. Her untrained voice projected a certain plaintive cry, a forlorn quality that went beyond the accomplishments of most singers of the day. She became quite popular as a singer who could deliver passionate, poignant performances. She phrased much like an improvising instrumentalist and rarely interpreted the melody strictly as it was written—so one could say in this way she improvised; however, she is not known for scat singing or straying completely away from the melody. Holiday always took great liberty in reinterpreting the rhythm of a melody so as to find just the right way to give the lyric its greatest

LISTENING GUIDE

Billie Holiday

"Body and Soul" (Heyman-Sour-Eyton-Green) 2:57

Recorded 2/29/1940 Vocalion 5481

Reissued on Columbia Legacy K 65757-S1

Personnel: Roy Eldridge, trumpet; Jimmy Powell, Carl Frye, alto saxophones; Kermit Scott, tenor saxophone; Sonny White, piano; Lawrence Lucie, guitar; John Williams, bass; Jo Jones, drums

Form: 32-bar-song form choruses (AA¹BA² = chorus)

0:00–0:11	Introduction—4 bars, trumpet solo over sustained chords in saxes, rhythm-section accompaniment
0:11–1:44	First chorus—32 bars, vocal chorus melody:
0:11–0:34	A section—8 bars, vocal chorus melody over sustained sax section lines, rhythm accompaniment
0:35–0:57	A¹ section—8 bars, similar to A
0:58–1:21	B section—8 bars, vocal chorus bridge over long moving trumpet and sax section lines
1:22–1:44	A² section—8 bars, vocal chorus melody over moving sax section lines
1:45–2:57	Second chorus—24 bars, trumpet solo (Eldridge), vocal bridge and chorus:
1:45–2:07	A¹ section—8 bars, improvised trumpet solo, over moving sax section lines, rhythm section
2:08–2:30	B section—8 bars, vocal bridge over moving sax section lines, rhythm section
2:31–2:57	A² section—8 bars, vocal chorus over trumpet and sax section sustained moving lines, rhythm section

impact. Listen to her rendition of "Body and Soul," included in the accompanying anthology, and pay particular attention to the way in which she accents or emphasizes certain words, syllables, and phrases to give the lyrics special meaning and maximum impact. She is accompanied by an all-star cast, including some members of the Basie band, such as Roy Eldridge, who was the most important Swing Era trumpet soloist to serve as a link between Louis Armstrong and the more modern Dizzy Gillespie.

You should go back and listen to the Coleman Hawkins recording of this same song, paying particular attention to how radically Hawkins departs from the original melody, which is more closely adhered to by Holiday.

Holiday's performance of "He's Funny That Way," included on the *SCCJ* (editions prior to 2010), also serves as an excellent illustration of her uncanny ability to deliver a lyric with an impact even greater than any composer or lyricist could imagine or hope for. This particular recording, as Martin Williams indicates, also reveals the rapport that Holiday enjoyed with Lester Young, who weaves beautiful counterpoint to her emotionally charged lyricism. Her life was ultimately overcome by the effects of her substance abuse, which eventually took over her life, leaving her nearly destitute in her final days. Fortunately, her music has stood the test of time, transcending this tarnished aspect of her life.

 Make sure that you review the corresponding chapter on the website, which includes several short interviews with Billie Holiday and Lester Young.

ELLA FITZGERALD (1918–1996): THE "FIRST LADY OF SONG"

A case can be made that Coleman Hawkins and Lester Young served to represent two contrasting sides of jazz playing during the Swing Era—hot and cool, respectively. Of equal contrast were singers Billie Holiday and Ella Fitzgerald. Holiday represented the cool, lyrical, and melancholy plaintive cry of the era, whereas Fitzgerald represented the hot, boisterous, gregarious, macho side of jazz singing. Orphaned as a child, she moved to New York, where she was initially discovered at a talent contest sponsored by the Apollo Theater. Black bandleader and drummer Chick Webb hired her, and she became a near overnight success with her 1938 recording of "A-Tisket, A-Tasket." Her popularity enabled her to assume the leadership of Webb's band when he died in 1939, a position that she held for 3 years before striking out on her own. Her partnership with promoter Norman Granz in the years to come was legendary and led to a series of "songbook" recordings featuring the repertoire of America's finest popular songwriters. Fitzgerald also became a headline attraction on Granz's Jazz at the Philharmonic tours, and recordings helped her to achieve international status as a performer. It didn't hurt that she was accompanied by some of the very best instrumentalists of the day.

Ella Fitzgerald, the "First Lady of Song," 1940

Fitzgerald was a consummate performer who never failed to astound her audiences with her amazing range, vocal flexibility, and sense of rhythmic swing. As was the case with Holiday, she has served as a model for all future jazz singers to follow, particularly those who improvised in the scat style (an improvised jazz singing style using wordless syllables), unlike Holiday's style, which did not favor significant improvisation or scatting. Armstrong no doubt served as her influence in this regard (and they recorded more than once together), but she elevated the art of scat singing to new heights. Her improvisations were as sophisticated as those of any instrumentalist, and they admired her ability to interact with them using a similar, horn-like language. Fitzgerald was equally skilled at improvising lyrics, as illustrated by the track included on the accompanying anthology. She enjoyed a long and very productive career performing in every imaginable setting worldwide. Once again, trumpeter Roy Eldridge is showcased.

LISTENING GUIDE

Ella Fitzgerald

"Honeysuckle Rose" (Fats Waller–Andy Razaf) 4:32

Recorded live, July 1964, at Juan-Les-Pins, France

"Ella Fitzgerald Live" Verve Compact Jazz 833 294–2

Personnel: Ella Fitzgerald, vocal; Roy Eldridge, trumpet; Tommy Flanagan, piano; Bill Yancey, bass; Gus Johnson, drums

Form: Repeated 32-bar-song form (AA^{1}BA = chorus) in F major

0:00–0:07	Introduction—4-bar piano solo
0:07–0:54	First chorus—32-bar-song form: vocal chorus:
0:07–0:18	A section—8-bar vocal verse, original melody, with trumpet improvisation
0:19–0:30	A^1 section—8-bar vocal verse, with trumpet continuing "ad-lib" improvisation
0:31–0:42	B section—8-bar vocal bridge, with trumpet improvisation
0:43–0:54	A section—8-bar vocal verse, with trumpet improvisation
0:55–1:42	Second chorus—32-bar song form: improvisation:
0:55–1:06	A section—8-bar vocal improvisation, repeated scat musical ideas or "riffs," with trumpet and rhythm section-accent answers
1:07–1:18	A^1 section—8-bar vocal improvisation, repeated scat "riffs," with band answers
1:19–1:30	B section—8-bar vocal free scat improvisation, with rhythm, trumpet drops out
1:31–1:42	A section—8-bar vocal scat mimicking rapid "trumpet-like" melodies
1:42–2:29	Third chorus—32-bar-song form: improvisation:
1:42 1:53	A section—8-bar vocal improvisation, bluesy scat "riffs," with band accents, trumpet reenters
1:54–2:05	A^1 section—8-bar vocal scat, repeated "riffs," with rhythm and trumpet accents
2:06–2:17	B section—8-bar vocal and trumpet free simultaneous improvisation
2:18–2:29	A section—8-bar vocal free scat, also using words, trumpet drops out
2:29–3:15	Fourth chorus—32-bar song form: shout chorus:

2:29–2:40	A section—8-bar vocal and trumpet "shout" melody, with band accents	
2:41–2:52	A¹ section—8-bar vocal and trumpet "shout" melody repetition with variation	
2:52–3:03	B section—8 bars (bridge), vocal and trumpet trade 1 bar improvisations	
3:04–3:15	A section—8-bar vocal and trumpet "shout" melody as in previous A section	
3:16–4:25	Fifth chorus—32-bar-song form with tag: vocal verse	
3:16–3:27	A section—8-bar vocal verse variation, improvised words and new melody, trumpet fills	
3:27–3:38	A¹ section—8-bar vocal verse variation, more improvised words	
3:39–3:50	B section—8-bar vocal bridge variation, improvised words, new melody, trumpet fills	
3:51–4:25	A section—8-bar vocal verse variation, extended 15-bar vocal tag, trumpet improvisation	

Art Tatum (1909–1956)

Art Tatum was an anomaly among pianists. The art of solo piano playing, although certainly not disappearing, had at the very least become less prominent during the "swing" years. The focus had shifted away from solo pianists, most of who, like Earl Hines, had jumped on the bandwagon and formed their own big bands in hopes of riding the popularity wave. Tatum was truly an exception and is considered to represent the epitome of solo jazz piano in the 1930s and 1940s. Legally blind, Tatum concentrated on developing a solo and trio style during the Swing Era that was without equal. Although he received some early formal schooling in music, his impaired vision made formal training less practical, and his self-taught approach seemed more appropriate. His early inspiration was Fats Waller, although he showed more of a penchant for classical music than his elder. Idolized by critics and musicians, Tatum never gained widespread popularity with fans or in the magazine readers' polls, probably because he strayed away from the Swing Era mainstream. His most striking recordings in the solo and trio format show his total mastery of the keyboard and illustrate an unparalleled technique that awed both jazz and classical pianists. He was in total control, with unprecedented facility, a rich sense of harmony, an uncanny ability to improvise long lines, and a grasp of the earlier stride tradition. Although he was a masterful improviser, he was sometimes criticized for repeating himself, working out arrangements and improvisations in advance, and often duplicating his recordings in live performance. Whether performing solo or with his famous trio, which included Tiny Grimes on guitar and bass specialist Slam Stewart, he preferred to perform arrangements rather than original material, and his arrangements were incredibly intricate. His style was unique and, in many ways, chameleon-like, featuring frequent shifts from one mood to another, frequent chord substitutions, rhythmic, metric and tempo shifts, thematic variation, and counterpoint between left and right hands. Consequently, he was difficult to play with, as observed first hand by bassist Gene Ramey:

> I worked with Tatum, though I never did satisfy him. Tatum wanted a bass player to stay at home [play simply, outlining the basic harmony]. He would really rather have you play 2-beat (only 2-notes out of every 4-beat measure) no matter how fast the tempo. He had a thing where he would play one song with his right hand and another song with his left. I might get carried away with what he was playing with his right hand and go right along with that and he would get so mad . . . Slam Stewart took my place with him. No bass

player should be playing with Tatum. He's a solo player. A solo pianist can go anywhere he wants to.[11]

One cannot overemphasize how far he raised the bar, influencing generations of jazz pianists who followed, such as Bud Powell, Lennie Tristano, and more contemporary pianists, such as Oscar Peterson and Herbie Hancock, to mention but a few discussed in upcoming chapters. His sheer virtuosity and technical mastery of his instrument, however, had an impact on many instrumentalists of the day, not just pianists. The recorded example included in the online audio anthology provides evidence of his incomparable virtuosity and illustrates why he had such an impact on so many pianists who followed. An additional listening guide through his performance of "Tiger Rag" can be found in the corresponding chapter on the website.

Art Tatum Trio. L–R: Tiny Grimes, Slam Stewart, and Art Tatum

LISTENING GUIDE

Art Tatum

"Tea For Two" (Caesar-Youmans) 3:11

Original issue: Brunswick 6553, Reissue: Best of Jazz 4022

Recorded New York, 3/21/1933

Art Tatum, solo piano

Form: Repeated 32-bar-song form (ABA^{1}C = chorus)

0:00–0:06	Introduction—4 measures
0:07–0:52	First chorus—32-bar-song form: melody or theme
0:07–0:17	A phrase—8 bars, piano plays song melody
0:18–0:29	B phrase—8 bars, piano plays song melody
0:30–0:41	A^1 phrase—8 bars, piano plays song melody
0:42–0:52	C phrase—8 bars, piano plays song melody
0:53–1:38	Second chorus—32-bar-song form: improvised solo:
0:53–1:04	A phrase—8 bars, piano solo over song chords
1:04–1:15	B phrase—8 bars, piano solo
1:16–1:27	A^1 phrase—8 bars, piano solo
1:27–1:38	C phrase—8 bars, piano solo
1:39–2:24	Third chorus—32-bar song form: improvised solo explores upper range of piano:
1:39–1:50	A phrase—8 bars, improvisation
1:50–2:01	B phrase—8 bars, continue improvisation
2:01–2:12	A^1 phrase—8 bars, continue improvisation
2:13–2:24	C phrase—8 bars, continue improvisation
2:24–3:11	Fourth chorus—32-bar song form: improvised solo;
2:24–2:35	A phrase—8 bars, improvisation
2:36–2:46	B phrase—8 bars, improvisation
2:47–2:57	A^1 phrase—8 bars, improvisation
2:58–3:11	C phrase—8 bars, improvisation

TRADITIONAL JAZZ REVIVAL

Although swing reigned supreme during the late 1930s and early 1940s, it was not without contenders for public attention. There were some who spoke out against what they thought was overly commercialized, stagnant dance music and expressed their support for the "authentic," "hot" jazz styles of the 1920s. The nostalgic rebirth of interest in New Orleans- and Chicago-style jazz led to the establishment of two record labels devoted to recreating this earlier tradition. H.R.S. and Commodore, along with other established labels such as RCA Victor and the newly formed Blue Note, rushed to record Bunk Johnson, Sidney Bechet, Johnny Dodds, Jelly Roll Morton, Kid Ory, and other nearly forgotten artists who had forged early instrumental jazz. The Yerba Buena Jazz Band from the San Francisco Bay area also contributed to what became an international revival movement.[12] Perhaps it was new books on the subject of early jazz, such as Frederick Ramsey's *Jazzmen*, issued in 1939, or the numerous articles in upscale magazines such as *Esquire* that helped to spark this revival.

Benny Goodman and John Hammond sponsored the landmark "From Spirituals to Swing" concert at Carnegie Hall in 1938, featuring a lineup of blues, spiritual, boogie-woogie, and New Orleans performers offering a jazz retrospective that kindled interest in historic jazz and the roots of swing. The concert was also unique because jazz and related forms were presented for the first time in a hallowed concert hall that had previously showcased only classical music. For nearly 8 years, a sometimes-bitter feud waged between traditionalist fans, labeled **moldy figs**, the swing crowd, and the new modernists, who sided with the newer music challenging swing for attention and described as bebop.

Special edition of *Jazzmen*, produced by the Armed Services and designed to fit in soldiers' knapsacks

SWING ERA SUCCESS

For the first time in the history of American music, from 1935 until about 1945, popular music was in complete resonance with American society and thought. Whether one lived on the East Coast, West Coast, or somewhere in between, swing was the thing. Attending dances was so much a part of the American way that it was often an important stage in the adolescent courtship ritual. Many young women and men met their lifelong partners on the dance floor. This is the only time in the history of jazz that the music was in sync with the American psyche. As the country came out of its worst depression, Americans gained a sense of confidence, and their renewed spirits yearned for the enjoyable things in life to occupy their leisure time. Never before, and never since, has jazz experienced such financial success, public acceptance, and worldwide acclaim. For almost 10 years, big-band swing music was America's pop art, and nearly any reasonably capable musician was working, and for good money. New magazine publications such as *Down Beat* (which first hit the newsstands in 1934), *Esquire*, and *Metronome* followed the music and its creators, sponsoring polls to determine the most popular musicians and bands of the day. Fans debated as to which was the best band or hottest soloist. Hot clubs sprang up in this country and abroad, formed for the sole purpose of providing a meeting ground for enthusiasts who collected and enjoyed listening to jazz recordings. Between 1937 and 1940, *Metronome* magazine posted nearly 300 big-band entries for its readers to rank in their polls. This number represented only a portion of the number of working bands throughout the nation. They were to be ranked in one of three categories—"Swing," "Sweet," and "Favorite of All."[13] These same magazines also began ranking individual soloists and choosing "all-star" bands, based on input from their writer-critics and readers. The critics and fans did not always agree, and, as history proves, sometimes both parties were wrong in their selections, at least if we consider which musicians ultimately had a lasting impact on the music.

During the peak years of the Swing Era (c.1935–1945), it was not uncommon to see long lines of fans clambering to gain entrance to a dance where a name band was performing, or crowding the bandstand or stage to get a closer look at their favorite band. Imagine being swept up in the frenetic enthusiasm of a throng of crazed fans, rushing the stage to get a closer look at their swing idols, and struggling to get close enough to feel the throbbing pulse of the big band. This exchange of energy between musician and exuberant audience made the often-difficult life of the big-band musician all worthwhile.

At times, these crowds were almost uncontrollable in their enthusiasm, much like reactions in the 1960s to rock groups such as the Beatles, Cream, or the Rolling Stones. New dances, including the shag, shim-sham, and big apple emerged overnight to become the next sensation. Dance marathons and contests, staged battles between bands, and "cutting contests," where soloists challenged one another on the bandstand, were all familiar scenes during this era. Radio stations broadcast band battles live from ballrooms, adding to public exposure, helping to sell recordings, and promoting future engagements.

Successful leaders, particularly white bandleaders such as Glenn Miller, Artie Shaw, and Benny Goodman, became wealthy icons, enjoying reputations on a par with the most famous movie stars and much like those of pop, rock, or country-music headliners today. For that matter, some bandleaders married movie stars, and the most successful bands were occasionally featured in films. Bandleader Artie Shaw married both Lana Turner and Ava Gardner. The Swing Era also produced its share of bluebloods—even royalty, or at least their nicknames suggested such status. Edward Kennedy Ellington, for example, was dubbed the "Duke," and Benny Goodman was known as the "King of Swing;" William Basie was referred to as "Count," Billie Holiday was known as "Lady Day," and Lester Young had bestowed upon him the title of the "President," or "Prez" for short.

A new cult language began to emerge during the Swing Era. Developed largely by the black jazz community, this new jargon was quickly adopted by white musicians. New words and expressions such as "crib" (dwelling), "chick" (female), "hip" (wise, aware and sophisticated), "bread" (currency or money), and "it was a gas" (impressive, satisfying, enjoyable) were born and helped to create an even more cult-like environment in which these musicians lived and worked.[14] Gene Ramey reminisces about some of the extra-musical slang expressions that developed, particularly among jazz musicians:

> Now we always had lots of smoke signals that we used in conversation. Say you and your wife are sittin' over there and me and my wife are sittin' over here and you're talking in a different language. Now we can't understand what you're saying, but we can watch by the expression that you must be talkin' about us. So then I would say to her "You know, it's kind of drafty in here. Do you feel that draft." She's got the message right away.
> We started using anti-language. We would say something was "bad" which really meant it was good. Lester Young and Cab Calloway had a whole bunch of those expressions. They really personalized it.[15]

The expression "feel a draft" was also coined as an expression of racial prejudice and attributed to Lester Young. Jazz lingo has motivated American slang for decades, and it is not unusual to find more than one meaning associated with a particular word.

Many of the successful star soloists left the employment of one band to strike out on their own, forming a new band under their leadership. One successful band often led to several other spin-offs. For example, Gene Krupa, Teddy Wilson, Lionel Hampton, Harry James, Jack Teagarden, Bunny Berigan, Buddy Rich, and Cootie Williams formed their own bands after serving apprenticeships with Benny Goodman, Glenn Miller, the Dorsey Brothers, Artie Shaw, Duke Ellington, and others. It was not uncommon for those most in-demand soloists to move from one band to another, following the best wage, best working conditions, and best public exposure. The most in-demand musicians were bartered and traded from band to band like professional athletes.

There were several factors that were responsible for the success or failure of a big band during the Swing Era.

- Arrangers and musical directors established a band's identifiable sound. Their particular treatment of a song gave the band its unique sound. Fans could often identify a particular band after listening to only a few measures of music.
- Soloists contributed significantly to the overall success of a band, explaining why bandleaders typically paid them the highest salaries.
- The leader's personality, stage presence, and charisma also contributed to the band's public appeal, and, for that matter, a few leaders such as Cab Calloway did not play an instrument, although most did.
- Vocalists added an extra element of popular appeal, as everyone could appreciate a lyric, even if they did not understand or relate to the more involved instrumental arrangements. Consequently, every band had at least one vocalist and it might feature two—a male and a female. In some ways, the overwhelming success of some of these singers, such as Frank Sinatra, actually contributed to the gradual downfall of big-band jazz.
- Businessmen, booking agents, and promoters helped bandleaders make their careers. Without them, a great band would languish unknown in its quest for notoriety.
- The quality of the band's dance music attracted fans.
- The band's exposure on radio, record, and in major venues helped immeasurably to popularize a band.

Although these factors promoted a band's success, any one factor could also lead to its demise, as suggested with the growing popularity of some singers. For example, bassist Gene Ramey, along with many black musicians, was very much against many of the white managements and their business practices, feeling that they placed too many conditions on employment and often worked against a band's success:

> Moe Gale was intent on breaking up the [Jay] McShann band after he found he couldn't bring us into his fold. You see Moe Gale owned the Savoy [Ballroom] and he owned the Golden Gate and he had control of the Rockland Palace, Apollo Theater, and Audubon Ballroom. I remember they had us set up to be one of the first black bands to play in a white hotel. That hotel was down on 43rd and Broadway. I forget the name of it but it's nothing but a dump now. Anyway, this was the come-on, now the stipulation they came up with—McShann would give them complete authority over the band [including] hiring and firing. This was the thing they tried to do when they got rid of Charlie Parker.
> We were a band with only one record out and I was making $16 a night and the other guys were making $13. They even sent us out with phony booking agents who would run away and we would have to pay for the dance hall, bouncer, ticket-takers and everything. That happened to us in Georgia, Virginia and South Carolina. They had that attitude:

"We can help you and without us you're nothing. We can do whatever we want to do with you and if you don't like it we won't help you." We had lots of that sort of thing happening, so the musician who went to New York expecting to really make it found that he was at their mercy—somebody else was the master of his fate.[16]

The record industry, which had all but collapsed during the Depression years, made a tremendous rebound during the peak years of the Swing Era. For example, 10 million records were sold in 1933, and by 1938 that figure climbed to 33 million. By 1941, the record industry boasted sales in excess of 127 million! In only 1 year during the swing peak, the number of jukeboxes (a term for coin-operated record players derived from "**juke joint,**" a slang expression for a black brothel) in use soared from 25,000 to 300,000, serving to promote black artists at a time when there were few featured on radio broadcasts. This music had truly captured the attention of most Americans and was no longer the focus of harsh criticism. Swing music had, in fact, become impossible to ignore, and to some degree the popular singers had much to do with the record industry's rebound.[17]

As is the case with any fad, "swing" spawned its own industry, which revolved around the making and marketing of this music. By 1940, there was, for the first time, a clear jazz tradition, a developmental timeline that could be examined, dissected, and debated among journalists, historians, critics, and fans. As a result, numerous articles about jazz ran in trade magazines, journals, and newspapers. Magazines devoted to jazz began to flourish, drawing the attention of jazz fans lured to the print debates and encouraged to participate in readers' polls. A new generation of writers contributed several new books on the subject, and, as one would expect, each offered their own views on jazz—some optimistic and some less so about the future of jazz. For example, English-born critic and historian Leonard Feather wrote that there was an obvious differentiation between commercial and authentic jazz. For example, in 1945, he asserted that,

Among the outright commercial bands, Tommy and Jimmy Dorsey and Harry James and the rest of them, there were the customary assortment of good jazz, bad jazz and music that does not pretend to be jazz by my standards or anyone else's.

In this same article he cited the young Woody Herman and Billy Eckstein bands as exciting surprises for the year. He closed the article saying that: "By the time the musicians in uniform come marching home [from WWII], the music business will be ready, both artistically and commercially, to hit a new all-time high in jazz history."[18] If this was a prediction about the decline of swing bands and the upsurge of a new kind of jazz, he was right. If he was predicting ongoing health for the big bands and the jazz business in general, then he was wrong.

There was a false sense of security that surrounded the big-band movement, but not everyone was lulled into believing that they could ride the crest of this commercial wave indefinitely. Some critics took a hard line on many of the swing bands that made little effort to challenge the listener. Author Wilder Hobson called swing a fad that had been encouraged by the repeal of Prohibition. Like so many writers on the subject, he was concerned about over-commercialization. He said, in his 1939 book *American Jazz Music*, that the bands

follow the usual practice of mixing many compromise arrangements of popular songs with its jazz orchestrations; this is undoubtedly a necessity if a band wishes to maintain such an extraordinary wide popularity as Goodman has had. It is no small wonder that talented jazz musicians in general regard their playing as a livelihood and make their best music in small, impromptu sessions. As working men, they may appreciate the swing fad, but as musicians they dislike it intensely.[19]

The rapid changes that had occurred in jazz styles throughout its relatively short history had already led critics to expect periodic change to occur, and, at this point, some were becoming impatient. But Hobson agreed that "in the midst of the 'swing' salesmanship a good deal of excellent music [had] been made," citing Goodman's small groups and the best of the black bands as high points. He added though that, "The swing fad has encouraged just about every imaginable kind of commercialization of the jazz language."[20] Even Duke Ellington recognized that, by 1940, the fad had run its course, and he too publicly expressed concerns about the music's future. It had clearly become shopworn and, at least with many bands, too predictable.

By the mid 1940s, big-band swing in most cases had become a cliché, a caricature of itself. Although there were a few new bands that arrived on the scene during this time, most of the bands began to dissolve, leaving only a few, led by Count Basie and Duke Ellington in particular, to carry on the tradition. The new, younger bands led by Stan Kenton and Woody Herman had embraced the newer style of jazz emerging from New York along with the Afro-Cuban forms. Although they never flourished as they had in the 1930s and early 1940s, the big-band tradition would be carried forward into the next century, at least in terms of the general sound and instrumentation, but discussion of this will be delayed until a future chapter. By the mid 1940s, it was time for a change, and there was a line of young musicians in New York waiting to forge a new path for jazz that was radically different than the big-band-swing brand of jazz. The big-band Swing Era, although not forgotten, was destined to become a lasting, but faded, memory.

MILESTONES

Chronicle of Historic Events

The timeline that follows will put the developments of jazz discussed in Chapters 7 and 8 into a larger historical context, providing you with a better sense of how landmark musical events may relate to others that match your personal areas of interest.

1929	• The Museum of Modern Art opens.
	• The Valentine's Day mob battle takes place in Chicago.
	• The beginnings of commercial passenger air travel are seen.
	• Black Tuesday—the Wall Street Stock Market crash marks beginning of the Great Depression.
1930	• The planet Pluto is discovered.
	• George Gershwin's musical *Girl Crazy* opens, featuring "I Got Rhythm," which serves a role as important to jazz as the blues.
	• Nancy Drew books about a teenage female sleuth become popular with young female readers.
1931	• More bank failures create an even more unstable economy.
	• The "Star Spangled Banner" is declared to be the national anthem.
	• The Empire State Building is completed as the world's tallest building.
	• The Dick Tracy cartoon begins.
	• The George Washington bridge is completed—the longest suspension bridge in the world.

1932
- Roosevelt is elected president on "New Deal" promises.
- Radio City Music Hall opens as the largest theater in the world.
- Amelia Earhart becomes the first woman to fly solo across the Atlantic in a small plane.
- Greta Garbo and John Barrymore star in *Grand Hotel*.

1933
- *Newsweek* and *Esquire* magazines are founded.
- The Chicago Exposition showcases the "Century of Progress."
- The 21st Amendment repeals Prohibition after nearly 14 years.
- Jazz pianist Art Tatum records "Tea For Two."
- Adolph Hitler becomes Chancellor of Germany.

1934
- Cole Porter's musical *Anything Goes* opens.
- F. Scott Fitzgerald publishes *Tender is the Night*.
- Comic Strip "Li'l Abner" makes its debut.
- Legendary blues singer Leadbelly is pardoned from prison term.
- The Securities Exchange Commission and Federal Communications Commission are established to regulate the stock market and communications.
- The Disney character Donald Duck is born.
- *Down Beat* magazine, dedicated to jazz, is founded.

1935
- George Gershwin's American opera/musical *Porgy and Bess* opens.
- The WPA is formed in an effort to put America's 11 million jobless back to work. This affects one-quarter of American families.
- President Roosevelt establishes the Rural Electrification Administration to electrify rural America.
- Dancer Martha Graham gains notice as a pioneer of modern dance.
- The Social Security Act becomes law.
- Germany imposes anti-Semitic laws.

1936
- American morals loosen as a *Fortune* magazine poll shows 67% favor birth control.
- Babe Ruth and Ty Cobb are inducted into the newly founded Baseball Hall of Fame.
- F.D.R. wins reelection in a landslide vote.
- Child actor Shirley Temple is a box-office smash.
- Margaret Mitchell's book *Gone With the Wind* sells a record 1 million copies in 6 months.
- Benny Goodman enjoys a hit with "Goody-Goody."

1937
- Margaret Mitchell wins a Pulitzer Prize for *Gone With the Wind*.
- The first NBC Orchestra performance takes place with Toscanini conducting.
- General Motors gives in to striking workers and union demands.
- Amelia Earhart disappears in a single-engine airplane.
- The Golden Gate Bridge in San Francisco opens.
- Right-wing political movements attract some American interest because of the Depression.
- Walt Disney releases the film *Snow White and the Seven Dwarfs*.

1938
- Benny Goodman and a racially mixed all-star band perform at Carnegie Hall.
- Dupont Company makes first products with Nylon. Teflon and fiberglass are introduced in the same year.

- Austria falls to Nazi Germany.

- The minimum-wage law is established, along with a 40-hour workweek. The same law prohibits wage discrimination based on sex.

- H.G. Wells's radio hoax has millions of Americans believing in a Martian invasion.

- Ella Fitzgerald launches her career with a successful recording of "A-Tisket, A-Tasket."

- Count Basie's band records "Every Tub."

- Andy Kirk's 12 Clouds band records Mary Lou Williams's "Mary's Idea."

- *Superman* is introduced as an action comic.

1939
- The US hosts the 60-nation Worlds Fair.

- War erupts in Europe, as the US attempts to remain neutral.

- Einstein reports on atomic-power potential for weapons.

- Negro performers, athletes, writers, and politicians continue the fight for equality.

- The first baseball game is televised to only 400 viewers with TV sets.

- As the Depression fades, Hollywood capitalizes on the renewed American spirit, making 388 films. These included: *Gone With the Wind*, with Clarke Gable and Vivian Leigh; *The Wizard of Oz*, with Judy Garland; *Stagecoach*, with John Wayne; *Wuthering Heights*; *Goodbye Mr. Chips*; *Mr. Smith Goes to Washington*, with Jimmy Stewart; *Pinocchio*; and *Gunga Din*, with Cary Grant.

- The dance team of Ginger Rogers and Fred Astaire becomes popular on stage and screen.

- Radio dramas, soap operas, comedies, and variety shows become popular, with *Search for Tomorrow*, *Burns and Allen*, and *The Jack Benny Show*.

- Author Frederick Ramsey publishes *Jazzmen*.

- Author John Steinbeck publishes *The Grapes of Wrath*.

- Coleman Hawkins records "Body and Soul."

1940
- Hattie McDaniel becomes the first black woman to win an Oscar for her performance in *Gone With the Wind*.

- Social security is first received.

- John Steinbeck wins a Pulitzer Prize for *The Grapes of Wrath*.

- The American Negro Exposition in Chicago celebrates emancipation.

- Hemingway authors *For Whom the Bell Tolls*.

- War in Europe escalates with the fall of France.

- A draft lottery is created to bolster the U.S. armed services. Males aged 21–36 must register for the draft.

- Billie Holiday records "Body and Soul."

1941
- Automakers cut production to aid the war effort.

- President Roosevelt establishes the Fair Employment Practices Commission to end discriminatory practices.

- NBC and CBS compete on commercial TV.

- Pearl Harbor is invaded by Japanese air strikes on December 7, prompting the US to declare war.

- Orson Wells writes, directs, produces, and stars in the film *Citizen Kane*.

- President Roosevelt wins the U.S. presidency for an unprecedented third term.

- Swing-dance bandleader Glenn Miller records the timeless hit "In the Mood."

1942
- Large numbers of women enter the U.S. workforce to aid the war effort and replace drafted men.
- Automobile production is halted for 3 years as a consequence of World War II. There is rationing of petroleum products, sugar, meat, and other products.
- Singer Frank Sinatra becomes the new king of American pop music, although wartime hits by the big swing bands are still selling.
- Jackson Pollock has a one-man art show.
- The movie industry vows to no longer restrict blacks to comic and menial roles.
- *Casablanca*, an all-time American film hit, stars Ingrid Bergman and Humphrey Bogart.
- Bing Crosby records "White Christmas" from the movie *Holiday Inn*.

1943
- The war death toll reaches 60,000 Americans, although the US turns the tide on the Pacific, Africa, and European fronts.
- Rodgers and Hammerstein enjoy a hit with the Broadway musical *Oklahoma*.
- Racial tensions lead to riots in New York, Los Angeles, and Detroit.
- T.S. Eliot publishes *Four Quartets*.

1944
- *Esquire* magazine publishes the first jazz poll and sponsors an all-star concert at the Metropolitan Opera House.
- The cost of living escalates by almost 30% in 12 months.
- Playwright Tennessee Williams publishes *The Glass Menagerie*.
- Americans salvage discardable goods for the war effort.
- D-Day: American troops storm the beaches in Normandy, forcing the Germans to retreat from France.
- American composer Aaron Copland premiers *Appalachian Spring*, and Sinatra continues to woo young audiences with his popular vocal stylings.
- Franklin D. Roosevelt wins a record fourth term as U.S. president.
- Major Glenn Miller, the popular swing bandleader, is lost in an apparent plane crash. He was known for "In the Mood," "Moonlight Serenade," and "Tuxedo Junction."

CHAPTER SUMMARY

Being rather isolated from Chicago, New York, and the other main population centers, big bands developed somewhat independently in Kansas City and the Southwest. Groups performing primarily in this territory tended to rely on the blues and ragtime as a basis for their repertoire. Head arrangements, made up primarily of various riffs (repeated phrases), were much more common in this region than the more sophisticated arrangements of East-Coast groups. Using some key players from these southwestern territory bands, such as the Blues Devils and Benny Moten's band, William "Count" Basie formed his band, which rose to national and international notoriety, surviving well beyond the life of its founder. The rhythm section of the Basie band of the late 1930s, sometimes referred to as the All-American Rhythm Section, helped to redefine the roles of the rhythm-section instruments, not only for the Swing Era but also for future jazz styles.

In the 1930s, Kansas City was a hub for farming and ranching communities and also offered opportunities for musicians beyond those of many other cities, owing, in part, to political boss

Tom Pendergast. Under his control, clubs were able to operate openly, serving alcohol during Prohibition and offering many other forms of daring entertainment. This situation made Kansas City a wild town, with many clubs featuring some of the area's top groups, including the bands of Jay McShann, Andy Kirk, Benny Moten, and Count Basie.

Tenor saxophonist Lester Young was probably the most influential of the many great soloists in the Basie band of the 1930s. His light, airy sound and linear improvisations were in sharp contrast to the assertive and angular solos of Coleman Hawkins. Just as Coleman Hawkins's approach had an important impact on bebop, Lester Young's approach influenced many cool-jazz musicians of the 1950s.

The styles of vocalists Billie Holiday and Ella Fitzgerald paralleled those of Lester Young and Coleman Hawkins. Billie Holiday was not known as an improviser, but created interpretations of melodies that hardly resembled the originals and were made even more compelling by her understated voice. Fitzgerald, on the other hand, had magnificent technique and was an exceptional improviser. Her assertive approach would align her more with Coleman Hawkins's style.

The Swing Era was a golden age for jazz in that big-band music was the popular music of the day; however, not all big bands placed emphasis on hot-jazz solos. Generally, the most popular of the big bands were dance bands, precisely performing arrangements that left little space for improvisation.

KEY TERMS

Important terms, people, and bands:

Terms	People	Bands
Arpeggiations	William "Count" Basie	Count Basie
Backgrounds	Ella Fitzgerald	Blue Devils
Juke joint	Billie Holiday	Andy Kirk
Moldy figs	Benny Moten	Benny Moten
Motives	Walter Page	Artie Shaw
Riffs	Art Tatum	
Territory bands	Mary Lou Williams	
	Lester "Prez" Young	

STUDY QUESTIONS

1. Was there a discernible difference between midwestern, southwestern and East-Coast bands? If there was a difference, what was it?

2. Who was Tom Pendergast and what was his significance to jazz and where?

3. Why did jazz flourish in Kansas City, just as it had in New York and Chicago?

4. Which midwestern band is said to have perfected the blues riff, head-style arrangement associated with this regional brand of swing?

5. Describe the musical character of the Basie style.

6. What does the "All American Rhythm Section" refer to, and what was its significance to jazz?

7. Compare and contrast the styles of Lester Young and Coleman Hawkins.

8. Who was "Lady Day"?

9. Can you describe Billie Holiday's style?

10. Can you explain how Louis Armstrong influenced two important Swing Era female jazz singers?

11. What was a territory band? Can you name several?

12. Who is considered "the first lady of song"?

13. Compare and contrast Ella Fitzgerald's and Billie Holiday's styles.

14. What was so amazing about Art Tatum, and which more modern-day pianist did he influence?

15. What is the significance of the "moldy figs"?

PART 3

Modern Jazz

CHAPTER 9

The Bebop Revolution

It is the repetition and monotony of the present-day Swing arrangements which bode ill for the future. Once again it is proven that when the artistic point of view gains commercial standing, artistry itself bows out, leaving inspiration to die a slow death.[1]
—Duke Ellington

The ruins of a cinema stand stark against the rubble after the atomic bomb dropped on Hiroshima August 8, 1945, brought World War II to a close

JAZZ IN PERSPECTIVE

No single event or action was responsible for the gradual decline in big-band popularity. The big-band Swing Era was by far the most lasting, influential, and commercially successful period in all of jazz history. The influences of the Swing Era and big bands continue to this day; however, this music gradually succumbed to the pressures of entertainment and became a commodity—

a business that relied on basic principles of supply and demand. There was an astounding demand for this music just prior to the U.S. entry into World War II, and there were hundreds of bands ready to supply the popular music. Once the US was drawn into the war with the bombing of Pearl Harbor on December 7, 1941, both the demand and supplies necessary to sustain the big-band swing movement were cut off, or, at the very least, the supply lines were dramatically reduced. An examination of the specifics of this decline around 1944 will help you to understand the complexities of the situation that caused the downfall of the most successful times for jazz and the rise of a new, more rebellious music, described as bebop.

1. The music became one of the many casualties of wartime, and for less than obvious reasons. Although, to many fans, the life of a jazz musician may have seemed glamorous, it wasn't. Long hours spent traveling in between gigs, and a generally unstable and irregular lifestyle tended to discourage a normal family life. Consequently, many big-band musicians were young, single, and very vulnerable to the armed-services draft. Many were drafted, and others voluntarily enlisted. Successful bandleader and arranger Glenn Miller enlisted, as did many of his band's members. Their duty was to entertain the troops in the Great Britain area. His plane disappeared during a flight over the English Channel and was never found. Bandleaders who did not join the armed services were left with the difficult task of staffing their bands. Some leaders formed small combos, or ultimately gave up, disbanding their bands until after the war, and others never regrouped. Dances became less popular because of the reduced male population, and women were recruited into the workforce to help stimulate the wartime economy and contribute to the war effort. "Rosie the Riveter," portrayed in posters and movie newsreels, served as an example to women across the country of women's capabilities, doing what previously was considered men's work in factories. With such a shortage of men, and women's leisure time curtailed by their new work-a-day lives, it is obvious why dance halls began to close their doors. Even the famous Cotton Club fell victim to these circumstances and was gradually forced to close. As dance halls became scarcer, it was difficult for the bands to maintain a reliable, steady work schedule. If they had released a new record, it would sell only on the strength of their personal appearances, and it became more and more difficult to book the necessary number of engagements to sustain the bands and the sale of their recordings. In some cases, promoters could not fill engagements because they could not find a band to book, or the band was unable, owing to the transportation crisis, to travel to the engagement. In the summer of 1942, *Variety* magazine reported that there was a shortage of bands available to fill bookings. As a result, musicians' salaries escalated, making it even more difficult for bandleaders to employ those most in-demand musicians.

2. Petroleum and its by-products were key to the war effort. Gasoline, oil, and rubber were much in demand, as these precious resources were essential for a successful military campaign, abroad and at home. Consequently, travel became much more difficult, and many of the swing bands relied on automobile or bus transportation to get from one engagement to the next. The rationing of petroleum products particularly hurt the black bands. According to author and historian Scott DeVaux, the National Association For the Advancement of Colored People (NAACP) complained after the Department of Defense banned the use of buses for travel not related to the war effort. For a short time, the government conceded, allowing five buses for the transportation of 45 bands. This arrangement failed for obvious reasons and was curtailed in 1943, leaving the traveling black bands in the lurch.[2]

3. In 1940, James Petrillo was elected president of the American Federation of Musicians (AFofM). Petrillo rose to this position as national union head after serving as chief of the Chicago local

musicians' union. By 1942, Petrillo determined that musicians had been selling themselves short in terms of their payment for recordings. Recordings, for which musicians were paid only once, were played countless times on the radio, and the popularity of jukeboxes, which offered no return to musicians, provided Petrillo with a convincing argument. His claims that the record companies were getting rich at the musicians' expense were not unfounded. In 1942, claiming that recording musicians were "playing for their own funerals,"[3] Petrillo called for a ban on all recording by union members. The timing, in some ways, was good, in that record companies had been forced to reduce their production, as records were made from a petroleum by-product that was in short supply. The only records made for nearly 2 years, aside from bootlegged sessions, were "V-Discs," made exclusively for U.S. troops abroad and sanctioned by the Defense Department. Gradually, the major record companies succumbed to Petrillo's pressure and signed the union agreement, which established a royalty structure. Monies paid by the record companies to the AFofM were used to establish the Music Performance Trust Fund, a fund that is still in existence and is used to subsidize free public performances by union musicians. Not all of the union members supported the spirit of this strike, however, as careers were definitely stalled or even halted by Petrillo's actions.

4. As previously discussed, the presence of vocalists became increasingly important to the success of a big band (see sales information included at the close of this chapter). It stands to reason that the general public would warm to the good-looking male and female singers who delivered heart-rending ballads and uplifting swing tunes. People untrained to appreciate instrumental music are quick to follow and appreciate the universality of a lyric—something everyone can understand and enjoy without any special knowledge of music. It was this widespread appeal of the vocalists and their success with popular songs that eventually contributed to the steady decline of big-band jazz. Singers were less affected by the AFofM recording strike, as they were not union members and consequently were offered some limited recording opportunities during the strike. If they used union instrumentalists to back them, they didn't dare give them credit on the record, for fear of repercussions from the union for breaching the ban—in effect, crossing the picket line. Frank Sinatra, whose career rose to fame following the strike, is considered a pop singer with phrasing and overall style informed and influenced by jazz. During the strike, he issued a record that featured his vocal solos with choral accompaniment. At this point in the history of American music, the pop singer begins to take the lead, gradually eclipsing the popularity of the swing big band.

5. A growing artistic unrest among some of the more prominent soloists and younger musicians such as Coleman Hawkins, Dizzy Gillespie, and Charlie Parker began to manifest itself concurrently with the U.S. entry into World War II. Big-band arrangements, particularly those designed for recordings, rarely left sufficient room for the improvised solo. These 78-rpm records supported only about 3 minutes of music per side, which amounted to only 8–16 measures of solo space in the arrangement. Many of the fine soloists spotlighted in these bands began to enjoy the musical freedom provided by the after-hours jam session more than their regular, salaried position with a big band. In the eyes of some of the musicians, a few fans, and some critics, jazz had strayed off the path pioneered by its first great soloist—Louis Armstrong. Many younger players sought to establish jazz as a serious art form, a style that stood on its own and did not serve at the pleasure of some other popular entertainment form. Critic Roger Pryor Dodge said, in 1945, that, "the demands of the listening public could never create an art. Its demands are not creatively inciting to the musicians."[4]

6. Immediately following the end of World War II, the future of big-band jazz seemed questionable at best. By the end of the 1940s, jazz had endured a second recording strike and faced the growing onslaught from pop singers and R & B performers vying for popularity. The number of outlets for

big-band swing entertainment had substantially diminished, and a new social paradigm seemed to be taking root. Men had returned from the war eager to start families, reclaim lives that had nearly been lost, and in many cases take advantage of the GI Bill, which provided government financial assistance to those who wanted to pursue a higher-education degree or specialized vocational training. A new focus on family, planning for the future, and buying a house took precedence over partying, dancing, or club hopping. Many Americans who served in the war had put their lives on hold for several years and, following the war, needed to grow up as responsible adults quickly. There was much less room in this generation's lives following World War II for the music they had so loved and left to defend democracy. They grew up in the face of war and, at its conclusion, found that it had engendered new goals and dreams. The music of the big-band Swing Era just didn't fit in any more.

7. Although there were more musicians working as sidemen than at any other time in the history of jazz during the big-band Swing Era, many of these musicians were left behind by the new bop style. Many musicians were unable to cope with the innovations associated with the bop style and were quick to criticize it. They did not possess the skills necessary to confront the demands of this complex new style.

Although some musicians were left behind by bop, so too were many fans. Fans who had followed the more listenable, danceable, big-band style were shocked to find, after the AFofM recording ban, that the music had so radically changed. Some fans felt that it had become a self-indulgent music for "insiders" and no longer related to the masses. In many cases, they were right. You had to be "hip" to understand it and willing to hang out in the small clubs where it was played. Despite this controversy, it is safe to say that the bebop style has had a lasting influence on jazz, as even today it serves as the basis for studying and teaching the language and craft of jazz improvisation.

THE LIFESTYLE AND MUSICAL CHARACTERISTICS

An underground, cult-like, rebellious music, bebop, or "rebop" as it was first called, lacked the commercial appeal of the big dance band. Instead, its appeal was based on new challenges for listeners and practitioners, who strove to create a new form of jazz that demanded the attention of its listeners and was not subservient to any other form of entertainment. Although there were several big bands that played danceable, bop-like music, bop music was largely played by small bands and made no effort to pander to the dance-hungry public, as had been the case during the previous decade. The new, younger-generation black musicians sought to reclaim their music, reshaping it as an art-music through a combination of experimentation and repackaging of certain aspects of the earlier jazz tradition.

Some thought bebop was a frantic music that reflected the chaos associated with wartime and the beginnings of the modern atomic age. In every way, this new modern music challenged the old ways and traditions, much as the earliest forms of jazz had done. Even the dress, mannerisms, speech, and general bohemian (someone in the arts who disregards conventional behavior) lifestyle of the bebop musician worked against the old ways and accepted norms. The bop musicians were well dressed, often sporting dapper suits, berets, and goatees. Their demeanor on stage often projected a more detached, aloof attitude toward their audiences. For example, dark sunglasses hid their eyes from full view, and musicians often left the stage after their solo. This behavior

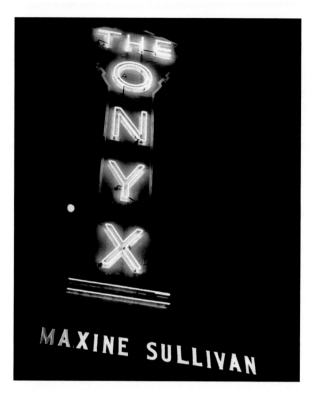

The Onyx jazz club in New York, advertising singer
Maxine Sullivan

was often considered arrogant by the uninitiated public, but more often than not was merely a gesture of respect for the other musicians who were subsequently featured. Bebop jazz was an insider's music, played initially by musicians for musicians, in a jam-session atmosphere.

There were other aspects of this new style that unfortunately served to attract a good deal of negative press. Beboppers seemed to have a reputation for loose sexual mores and consumed a wide array of alcohol, drug stimulants, and depressants. Although mild drugs such as marijuana had been in use years before, bebop musicians turned to more deadly, addictive drugs that ruined the careers of some of the music's greatest innovators. For the first time in jazz, we see black and white musicians resorting to heroin and other illegal substances as a form of escape from everyday discriminations or in an attempt to reach new heights of artistic creativity. For some, drugs seem to offer a false sense of confidence and a euphoric relief from the trials of their everyday existence. Drug use for many became a badge of hipness and a talisman of their lifestyle, and many young musicians felt that, in order to play like their heroes, they must act like them in every way, including in the use of addictive drugs. Saxophonist Stan Getz, in an interview with National Public Radio's Fresh Air host Terry Gross, spoke candidly about drug use among musicians:

> As I look back on it, musicians used drugs and alcohol for two reasons. One is the same reason why doctors use morphine, because when you get tired morphine is a work drug. As long as you don't take too much of it, it will keep you going. Alcohol is a temporary stimulant before it is a depressant. I think that was one reason because we traveled and worked very hard. I didn't look to any idols as a reason to take drugs or [because] it would make me play better. That's nonsense. The other reason is that there is a state of mind that you need to do anything in the art forms. It's called the alpha state . . . Alpha is the state of mind [that you need] to create something. It's sort of thinking off the top of your

head—relaxed concentration, and when you can't get that naturally, you're too tired or
something, you might resort to alcohol, drugs, chocolate, food—anything that will give you
a chance to get into alpha—to relax and think but not like an accountant would think.
Think in the artistic sense. That's the reason I used stuff.[5]

Bop musicians were sometimes labeled as communists, anti-American, and unpatriotic, but
it was racism, economic exploitation, poverty, and other forms of discrimination that they
protested, not a political ideology. Some turned to religion, particularly Islam for solace, as it
seemed that Muslims saw no difference in the color of their comrades. Bebop to some was the
expression of a newfound militancy by black musicians and one that would prove to escalate in
the years ahead.

Bebop, not for "squares" or the unhip, created a civil war in the music scene. For the
first time in the history of jazz, there is no single popular style. A few swing bands, based on a
now shopworn tradition, still existed alongside a handful of more modern, new big bands, led
by Billy Eckstine, Dizzy Gillespie, Stan Kenton, and Woody Herman. These musicians, along
with beboppers and traditional jazz musicians such as Louis Armstrong, all vied for attention from
the industry and public. Musicians and critics were outspoken in their assessments of bebop,
declaring that its creators, Dizzy Gillespie and Charlie Parker, were either jazz music's saviors or
its destroyers. For example, Norman Granz, a well-known promoter, producer, and jazz
entrepreneur, initially said, in a 1945 *Down Beat* magazine interview, that, "Jazz in New York
stinks,"[6] referring to the small clubs that had sprung up on 52nd Street that supported small bebop
bands. Granz went on to criticize Charlie Parker's sets at the Three Deuces club as rigid and
repetitive. Some years later, Granz embraced this music and its associated artists and packaged
successful tours featuring all-star casts, including bop figures Parker and Gillespie. Louis Armstrong,
whose own brand of jazz in the mid 1920s was revolutionary, criticized bop in a 1948 *Down
Beat* magazine article entitled "Bop will Kill Business Unless it Kills Itself First." Here, he described
bop as "crazy mixed-up chords that don't mean nothing at all" and attacked bop musicians as,

young cats who want to carve everyone because they're full of malice, and all they want to
do is show you up. . . . [At] first people get curious about it because it's new, but soon
they get tired of it because it's really no good and you got no melody to remember and no
beat to dance to.[7]

Some years later, Armstrong made peace with the younger generation, appearing on the same
stage with Gillespie and other younger-generation musicians. Other more traditional jazz and
swing musicians, such as Chicago "Moldy Fig" Mez Mezzrow, called bebop "frantic, savage,
frenzied, and berserk,"[8] and Swing Era bandleaders such as Benny Goodman were equally harsh.
Goodman, for example, initially accused bop musicians of "faking it," but later employed them
in his band and hired arrangers to write in the bop style.[9]

THE BIRTH OF BEBOP: THE FIRST RECORDINGS

Although it is true that Charlie Parker and Dizzy Gillespie are considered the founding fathers
of bebop, the birth of this new style was actually encouraged, supported, and embraced at a few
New York clubs by several older musicians during the AFofM recording ban. Uptown Harlem
nightspots such as the Club Onyx, Clark Monroe's Uptown House, and Minton's Playhouse
became the staging ground for jam sessions attended by guitarist Charlie Christian, bassist Oscar
Pettiford, and tenor saxophonist Coleman Hawkins. Younger upstarts such as trumpeters Dizzy

The club named after Charlie Parker, located at 1678 Broadway, New York

Gillespie and a young Miles Davis, drummer Kenny Clarke, and pianist/composer Thelonious Monk also frequented these clubs, particularly Minton's, which many consider to be the most important laboratory for the creation of this new music. These loose jam sessions allowed for experimentation, unencumbered by the demands of an audience wanting to dance. Old melodies were discarded in favor of creating new ones, using their associated chord progressions as a springboard for lengthy improvisations. Against the musicians' union, club owners charged an admission to those curious patrons who wanted to enjoy the fruits of these experimental jam sessions. Only the most exceptional musicians dared to participate and sit in at these sessions, as the music presented challenges that demanded virtuosic command of their instruments and a thorough understanding of music theory. Musicians frequented these clubs after they finished their more sedate, big-band dance jobs, in search of a more challenging, artistic stimulus. The popularity of these few uptown clubs opened up opportunities for new clubs downtown on 52nd Street, which became know as "Swing Street" or just "the Street." These clubs offered steady, well-paid employment for many small groups in the mid-to-late 1940s, once the idea of a small, intimate club to showcase jazz for listening caught on.

Characteristics of the Style

Bebop, the onomatopoeic (a word or use of a word that sounds like what it is meant to describe) term that was eventually used to describe the scat sung rhythms associated with this new music, was a radical departure from big-band swing jazz. These characteristics can be summarized as follows:

- Bebop featured smaller combos (trios, quartets, and quintets), rather than large ensembles.
- Although swing typically required arrangements for large bands with little improvisation, bop arrangements were simple, following a predictable scheme: theme–solo–solo–solo–theme, which allowed ample space for improvised solos. The arranger's role, therefore, became less important in bebop.
- The emphasis therefore returned to improvisation, as it did when Louis Armstrong recorded his Hot Five and Hot Seven discs.
- Bebop showed little concern for the dancing public and was intended to challenge both the serious listener and musician.
- Bebop repertoire was based on:

  - blues forms;
  - the George Gershwin **"rhythm changes"** model derived from his popular song "I've Got Rhythm," featured in his 1930 Broadway show *Girl Crazy*;
  - new melodies composed over chord progressions borrowed from other songs (described as **contrafacts**), which enabled bebop musicians to make additional royalties from their recordings (copyright laws do not protect chord progressions);

 An excellent example of a bebop "contrafact" composed and recorded during the bebop period can be found in the corresponding chapter on the website.

  - new tunes designed using the new style and vocabulary by composers such as Charlie Parker, Thelonious Monk, and Dizzy Gillespie.

- When bebop artists did perform a popular tune, they often completely disregarded the original melody, sacrificing it in the interests of improvisation. As historian Marshall Stearns once said, "Bop made a practice of featuring variations upon melodies that were never stated."[10]
- The saxophone surpassed the clarinet in terms of popularity, and the clarinet began to fall out of favor, in sharp contrast to earlier decades and jazz styles.
- The guitar became a less essential instrument in the bop combo. Although excellent soloists began to develop during this period, as long as there was a pianist, the guitar was a non-essential ingredient in bop small groups.

- Bebop music was virtuosic in its musical demands on the performer in that it often featured: (1) fast tempos and very slow ballads; (2) technically difficult "heads" (jazz lingo for tune); and (3) more sophisticated and challenging chord progressions.

Bebop Performance Practice and Instrumental Roles Redefined

When compared with earlier styles, bebop shows obvious and subtle differences in performance techniques attributed to all the instruments associated with this style. For example:

- The horn players used noticeably less vibrato than had previous generations.
- There was less obvious and predictable swing or unevenness in the melodic lines associated with bop, as compared with the swing style. The de-emphasis on exaggerated swing was no doubt due to the faster tempos that made it more difficult to facilitate an exaggerated swing eighth-note emphasis. Try skipping fast: the faster you go, the more difficult this uneven gait becomes.
- Horn players demonstrated increased technical facility, enabling them to improvise complex, fast passages.
- In some cases, bebop instrumentalists pushed the upper, useful range of their instruments. Trumpeter Dizzy Gillespie serves as a good example of pushing this envelope.
- Bebop instrumentalists became more aware of music theory, which enabled them to negotiate the more advanced harmonies and dissonances associated with the style.
- There was no such thing as a sideman in bebop small groups, as each member soloed and carried great ensemble responsibilities.

As was the case with every major stylistic innovation throughout the history of jazz, changes in rhythm-section performance practice lie at the heart of advances during the bebop era. The bass, which had largely been relegated to the role of time keeping and outlining harmonies, begins to emerge during the bop period as an instrument that, in the hands of a master, was capable of creating meaningful improvised solos. The groundwork for the bass to emerge as a solo instrument had been laid by the previous generation of swing players, such as Jimmy Blanton with the Ellington band, Slam Stewart with Benny Goodman and Art Tatum, and, of course, Walter Page with the Count Basie band.

By the close of the Swing Era, drummers had begun to move the well-defined swing pattern from the hi-hat to the ride cymbal and were occasionally featured in solo spots. Their solos, however, were usually predictably rudimental in construct and more rhythmic than melodic. Using saxophonists and trumpet players as their model, bebop drummers began to shape their solos in a more melodic fashion, even though the drums are not considered to be melodic instruments. Bebop drum-set innovators Kenny Clarke and Max Roach also discarded the use of the bass drum on every beat, in favor of using it only for occasional punctuation and to prod the soloist. The earlier concept of playing the bass drum on every beat could obscure the bass player's walking lines. Clarke is given much of the credit for this modern innovation, claiming that he dropped the regular bass drum thumping by accident when he realized he could not maintain the fast bop tempos for any length of time.

Pianists followed the comping style that had been pioneered by Count Basie and singer/pianist Nat "King" Cole, who played sparse chord accompaniments in non-repetitive and unpredictable rhythmic gestures. The intent of this comping style was to accompany and complement the soloist and not be distracting by over-playing. This style was a radical departure from the earlier, busy stride and ragtime styles. Bebop pianists developed their right-hand single-line technique, enabling them to play long, improvised lines in the same style as bebop horn players.

Swing Style Characterisics	Bebop Style Characteristics
1. Big Bands personified the swing era and style.	1. Bop bands were small combos of 3–5 pieces.
2. The elaborate arrangement brought attention to the ensemble rather than the soloist. Solos were often brief, especially on recordings.	2. Arrangements were not elaborate. Bop combos placed the emphasis on the improvising soloist. Consequently the greatest percentage of recordings was dedicated to improvisation.
3. Swing era soloists at times were required to play the same solo that they played on recordings.	3. Bop soloists prided themselves in spontaneous creativity, striving to be different each time they play a tune.
4. Vocalists became prominent during the swing era.	4. Vocalists were rarely featured with bebop bands.
5. Swing bands were often subservient to commercial pressures aimed at entertainment dancing.	5. Bop bands played music for artistic sake. Bop was aimed at listeners not dancers.
6. The bass played walking lines, fulfilling a time keeping role in the rhythm section.	6. The bass continued to maintain time keeping roll, but emerged as solo instrument.
7. Drummers emerged as soloists, but still relied on technical, rhythmic rudiments. Responsibility was largely time keeping using bass drum on all beats.	7. Drummers became more melodic in their approach and further developed as soloists. Bass drum was reserved for explosive punctuation rather than used on all beats.
8. Guitar often used in big bands but largely in rhythmic, chording contexts.	8. Guitar was infrequently used in bebop bands. A few performers advanced the instrument's soloistic potential.
9. Performances always placed emphasis on presenting recognizable and memorable melodies.	9. Melodies were often obscured beyond recognition in favor of fresh variation and improvisation.
10. Repertoire was based on arrangements of pop and show tunes of the day.	10. Repertoire placed emphasis on blues and "rhythm changes" formats that inspired the composition of new tunes.
11. Clarinet was a popular instrument especially in the hands of bandleaders.	11. The saxophone eclipsed the clarinet in bop. No prominent bop innovators were known for their clarinet playing.
12. Swing was the popular music of the day, leading record sales and radio play.	12. Bop did not enjoy the mass appeal of swing.
13. Performers could be good musicians and work in a big band without ever soloing.	13. Bop bands featured only the best virtuosic soloists.
14. Vibrato was usually obvious.	14. Vibrato became less emphasized especially as tempos increased.
15. Uneven eighth-note swing was quite noticeable.	15. Uneven swing eighth-note became de-emphasized especially as tempos increased.

FIGURE 9.1 Comparison of swing and bebop styles

Review Chapter 3—"Listening to Jazz"—on the website and explore the Performance Practice subsection. Here you will learn to recognize many of the concepts that relate to the bebop style. Specifically, the sections to be reviewed under Performance Practice are Piano, Bass, Drum Set, Interpretation, Dissecting a Jazz Performance, and Improvisation.

In some cases, pianists only occasionally played left-hand chords to accompany their right-hand improvisations.

Figure 9.1, above, provides a quick reference and comparison of swing and bebop styles, serving to summarize the aforementioned discussion.

THE INNOVATORS: BOP STYLISTS

Although there were many outstanding musicians associated with the bebop movement, only a few have ultimately been considered real innovators who pushed the boundaries and reached new heights. The following section will focus primarily on those instrumentalists who made significant contributions to the evolution of their particular instruments in the jazz continuum.

Dizzy Gillespie and Charlie Parker are considered to be the founding fathers of the bebop style. Their first meeting was as members of the Earl Hines big band, before it was taken over by singer Billy Eckstine. Unfortunately, the recording ban is responsible for there being no lasting evidence of their work together in this band. Although musically there were similarities that brought these two artists together, there were as many contrasts, particularly in lifestyle, that ultimately sent them in different directions. Despite their differences, both musicians left an indelible imprint on the future of jazz.

A supplementary listening guide for "Koko," recorded by Parker and Gillespie at the outset of bebop in 1945, can be found on the website in the corresponding chapter.

JOHN BIRKS "DIZZY" GILLESPIE (1917–1993)

John Birks "Dizzy" Gillespie was born to a large family in South Carolina. He left school at age 18 to join his family in Philadelphia, and it was here that he met his first mentor, trumpeter Charlie Shavers. Shavers, like Gillespie in his early years, closely followed Roy Eldridge's swing-style model. Gillespie, who was known for his practical jokes and clownish behavior, became known in the Philadelphia area as "Dizzy," a nickname that stayed with him the rest of his life. Gillespie made the move to New York in 1937 and, like most of the bebop artists, found employment in big bands. In his case, Teddy Hill and Cab Calloway provided big-band opportunities for Gillespie to travel to Europe and to record. Gillespie began to surpass the influences of swing-style trumpeters by the early 1940s. He met Charlie Parker at Minton's jam sessions, and they both became members of the Billy Eckstine big band. The Eckstine big band became a home for many of the younger-generation bop players. The band was short lived, however, and failed to provide the kind of danceable entertainment that was appealing to most jazz fans. Despite the appealing vocals by Eckstine and Sarah Vaughan, the band's repertoire was too modern for the dance-oriented audience.

It was perhaps Gillespie's relationship with Coleman Hawkins in the early 1940s that is most significant to his own advancement and to the birth of bebop as a new style. The early 1940s collaborations of these two artists, immediately following the AFofM recording ban, led to recording sessions that produced the first bop records and served to introduce listeners to the new style. The overwhelming and unexpected success of Hawkins's "Body and Soul" (released in 1939), which boldly presented improvisations without ever stating the original melody, no doubt served to inspire and give hope for commercial success to the next generation of younger bebop artists.

Gillespie and Parker formed their history-making quintet in 1945, shortly after the Hawkins sessions. It fizzled, in part owing to Parker's personal battles with drug and alcohol addition, and in no time at all Gillespie returned to the big-band format, while Parker continued to struggle, developing his reputation as a small-group performer. This situation underscores two major differences between these two artists: (1) Although economics often encouraged him to work in smaller bands, Gillespie favored big bands throughout his life, whereas Parker always favored small groups; and (2) Parker struggled with drug addiction and alcoholism most of his life, which drove him and Gillespie (the more clean-living of the two) apart more than once.

Dizzy Gillespie, with characteristic puffed cheeks and upturned trumpet

Like Louis Armstrong and Roy Eldridge who had preceded him, Dizzy Gillespie was an innovator. Many of the characteristics that define his style as a composer and performer became the heart and soul of the bebop style. He claimed his signature, upturned trumpet was the result of an accident when a birthday-party guest sat on it. He liked its newfound acoustical properties, and so he had future instruments designed with an up-flared bell. All innovators are known for very specific contributions, and Gillespie is no exception:

- He further developed the extremely high register of the trumpet, executing improvised lines in the stratosphere.
- He fused bebop and swing-style jazz with Afro-Cuban rhythms, forging the Cubop style.
- Gillespie possessed a blinding technique that, along with his high-register abilities, made him one of the flashiest performers on the instrument.
- He was a ferocious trumpet player, but, despite his high notes and fast technique, he was known to invoke shocking surprises by sudden changes in dynamics and range, and by slowing down or speeding up his technique. His style was dramatically captivating and dynamic, based on contrasting extremes—from soft to loud and high; and from subtle, simple melodies to long bursts of rapidly played notes.
- There was a new element of harmonic sophistication in Gillespie's compositions as well as his improvisations. He began to incorporate notes from the blues scale (flatted thirds and fifths) into chords, and composed unusual chord progressions to accompany his sometimes-exotic melodies. These notes were considered dissonant before the bebop period.
- Many of his compositions are now important landmarks in the repertoire, e.g. "Woody n' You," "Bebop," "Manteca," "A Night in Tunisia," "Groovin' High," and "Con Alma."

Gillespie's discography indicates that he lived a great deal longer than Parker. Once again in contrast, Parker, with his voracious appetite for life, somehow compressed at least one full lifetime of creativity into a significantly shorter lifespan. On the other hand, Gillespie's durability, showmanship, musicianship, and resilience earned him countless honors and awards, and his legacy will live for years to come.

CHARLIE PARKER (1920–1955)

Charlie Parker was nicknamed "Yardbird," which became simply "Bird." He earned the nickname while traveling by car through the Ozarks with a local territory band. The car swerved and hit a chicken crossing the road, and Parker insisted they retrieve it for dinner! From that moment on, he was known as Yardbird, or Bird for short.

Born in Kansas City, Parker's life was in stark contrast to that of Gillespie, who had experienced a normal childhood and upbringing. For most of his life, Parker knew no father, and his male role models were those traveling jazz players who passed through Kansas City. Parker hung out whenever he could to get a glimpse of his heroes, such as Lester Young, whom he claimed as one of his greatest influences. By 15, Parker had switched from the baritone horn to the alto saxophone, had become involved with various addictive drugs, and had married his first wife. In contrast to Gillespie, who was raised in an upstanding family and more privileged by educational opportunities, Parker learned only the basics in school and was largely a self-taught musician. He nevertheless developed an innovative style that was to become the model and inspiration for generations of players. For years after his premature death at age 35, subway walls and billboards were painted with the words "Bird Lives," the title of Ross Russell's captivating Parker biography. Parker became a cult hero and was idolized by the many young musicians who were inspired by his new, modern approach to improvising.

Parker's first recordings were made with Jay McShann's Kansas City swing-style big band. Like most bands from the Midwest, the McShann band was deeply rooted in the blues tradition, and Parker's style was based in part on this tradition throughout his career. Germs for at least one of his later small-group compositions can be heard in these early McShann recordings, but his mature style did not gain widespread exposure until the small-group recordings made in 1945–1946 with Dizzy Gillespie surfaced. Following a nervous breakdown in California brought on by family problems and drug abuse, Parker resurfaced with his second quintet, featuring the young trumpeter Miles Davis, whom he hired to replace Gillespie. Although still in the very early stages of development, Davis's style was in many ways radically different than the bravado style of Gillespie. Parker enjoyed great success throughout the late 1940s and early 1950s, earning awards in various jazz magazine polls and increased record sales. He enjoyed a fertile period of recording and live performances with his own small groups, Afro-Cuban bands,

Jay McShann Orchestra in New York, 1942. L–R: McShann far left; Gene Ramey, bass; Walter Brown at microphone; Gus Johnson, drums; Charlie Parker, second saxophone from left

string ensembles, and various all-star bands. His recording of *Just Friends* with a small chamber ensemble of strings, woodwinds, and rhythm was his biggest-selling record. He looked back on this series of recordings as one of his proudest accomplishments. Despite what appeared on the surface to be a successful career, his life was always in a state of chaos, living as he did in the fast lane and on the edge, both musically and personally. His reputation as a known drug user, however, cost him deeply, and, in 1951, the New York authorities revoked his cabaret card, banning him from performing in the city's nightclubs. Until several years later, he could not even perform in Birdland, the club that bore his name. Parker attempted suicide several times and was nearly always in debt to friends or the pawnshop, where more than once he hocked his alto for quick cash. His last engagement was at Birdland only seven days before his death. He was a tormented artist who never fulfilled many of his dreams, not the least of which was to study classical composition.

Parker's style, although based in great part on the blues, was entirely unique and one that redirected the path of jazz for decades to follow. As a composer and performer, he charted a new course for many to follow. His style and contributions can be summarized as follows:

- Like Gillespie, Parker patterned many of his new compositions off the chord progressions and formal schemes of old standard tunes and 12-bar blues, i.e., "Anthropology" (Gershwin's "I've Got Rhythm"), "Ornithology" ("How High the Moon"), "Scrapple From the Apple" ("Honey Suckle Rose"), "Now's the Time," and "Billie's Bounce" (blues).
- Parker eliminated or severely curtailed the use of vibrato (except in ballads), in comparison with Swing Era styles. His lean tone had an edge.
- Like Gillespie, Parker possessed blazing technique that enabled him to negotiate complex chord progression at very fast tempos and gave him the ability to play fast, double-time lines.
- Parker played in a more legato style (less articulation, or tonguing, of notes) than most players from the previous generation of saxophonists.
- Parker's improvisations were newly created, complex melodies that rarely bore any resemblance to the tune. Each improvised chorus was a newly created masterpiece, often with little repetition or reference to previous material.
- As an improviser, Parker had a rare gift that enabled him to render two completely different solos from performance to performance, as demonstrated by the two takes of "Embraceable You" featured on the *SCCJ* (editions prior to 2010). These solos were recorded only moments apart but are entirely different.

Charlie Parker, with Miles Davis, trumpet; Tommy Potter, bass

- Parker was particularly gifted at taking simple chord progressions such as the 12-bar blues or an old standard tune and embellishing it by adding chords to link the original skeletal framework. (Listen to "Blues For Alice" as an example of a complex blues approach, as compared with King Oliver's "Dippermouth Blues.")
- Parker introduced new possibilities that existed by improvising lines based on pitches found in the upper structures of chords, beyond basic, fundamental chord tones (1,3,5,7).

Despite his untimely death in 1955, his music exerted a major force for the next several decades. Young musicians hung on every phrase he played and sought to emulate him in every way. Bassist Charles Mingus told *Down Beat* magazine, at the death of Parker, "Most of the soloists at Birdland had to wait for Parker's next record to find out what to play next. What will they do now?"[11] They not only copied his playing, note for note, but also sought to follow his lifestyle, leading many to experiment with drugs in an effort to reach the same creative state. His improvisations were conceived of a new and innovative musical language that remains at the core of jazz musicians' education, even today.

Bud Powell (1924–1966)

"The Amazing Bud Powell" (1924–1966), to borrow the title of his multi-volume set of recordings on the Blue Note label, is considered the most eminent of bebop pianists, known for his incredible right-hand technique and sparse left-hand comping style that was rhythmically freer than that of earlier pianists. Like so many artists from this period, he struggled with racial prejudices, various addictions, and mental disorders. Powell jammed at Minton's Playhouse, where he met and was influenced by pianist Thelonious Monk. Ellington trumpeter Cootie Williams was first to employ Powell as his pianist, from 1942 to 1944, and it was this band that laid claim to being the first to record a Monk composition ("Epistrophy" in 1942).

Powell suffered a severe head injury in 1945 as the result of a racial incident during which he was beaten. Coupled with his already quirky personality, this injury led to a series of emotional breakdowns, alcoholism, and numerous stays in medical institutions, where he even underwent electric-shock treatments. Poor physical and mental health plagued Powell for much of his adult life, hampering his career and causing erratic performances. Eventually, Powell moved to Paris, where audiences were more accepting of black performers and very receptive to jazz. Here, he teamed with another expatriate, Kenny Clarke, who had been the house drummer at Minton's, and French bassist Pierre Michelot. Although his recordings from this period tend to be spotty compared with his earlier standard, he was still capable of displaying the virtuosic talent that had earned him a reputation as the best of the bebop pianists.

Powell's style was original, yet based on a synthesis of Art Tatum's technique and Teddy Wilson's lyricism. He preferred to play rapid, Parker-like right-hand lines in counterpoint and contrast to a sparse, rhythmically jagged and irregular, low-register, and often dissonant left-hand chordal accompaniment that resembled Monk's style. His technique allowed him to play fast, double-time lines at will. Like Earl Hines had done decades before in copying Armstrong, Powell preferred a style that was

Pianist Earl "Bud" Powell

LISTENING GUIDE 🔊

Dexter Gordon and Fats Navarro

"Index" (Dexter Gordon) 3:02

From *Nostalgia*

Recorded 12/22/1947, Newark, New Jersey

Savoy MG12113 SV 0123

Personnel: Fats Navarro, trumpet; Dexter Gordon, tenor saxophone; Tadd Dameron, piano; Nelson Boyd, bass; Art Mardigan, drums.

Form: 12-bar blues

0:00–0:17	First chorus—12-bar-blues riff tune played by sax and trumpet in cup mute
0:18–0:34	Second chorus—repeat tune
0:35–0:51	Third chorus—tenor sax improvisation on form
0:52–1:09	Fourth chorus—sax continues improvising on blues form
1:10–1:27	Fifth chorus—sax solo continues
1:28–1:45	Sixth chorus—final sax chorus
1:46–2:03	Seventh chorus—trumpet begins soloing on blues form
2:04–2:21	Eighth chorus—trumpet continues soloing
2:22–2:39	Ninth chorus—last trumpet solo chorus
2:40–end	Last chorus—Return to "head" for final chorus with ending fermata

---

J.J. Johnson (1924–2001)

J.J. Johnson (1924–2001), who can be heard in recordings with all of the above bop artists, is considered the first trombonist to absorb the new harmonic and melodic language fostered by Parker and Gillespie. However, unlike Parker, Gillespie, Powell, and Monk, Johnson travelled in many musical directions throughout his career, venturing far beyond his roots in bop. His fluid technique, ability to negotiate the faster bop tempos, rhythmic inventiveness, fast articulation, yet light tone and reserved vibrato, accommodated the new, post-war style. The trombone is perhaps the most difficult of the wind instruments to master from the technical standpoint, and Johnson's technique allowed him to master the bebop style. His first important recorded solo was as a member of Parker's small group on a 1947 recording of "Crazeology." In the 1950s, he collaborated with trombonist Kai Winding to form an unusual small group that featured the trombone duo. Johnson eventually also became as well known for his arrangements and compositions, spending many years in Hollywood composing for film and television before returning to the jazz scene as a performer in his later years. His activities at the center of the cool and third-stream styles will be discussed further in the next chapter.

THE INNOVATORS: BEBOP RHYTHM-SECTION PLAYERS

Thelonious Sphere Monk (1917–1982)

Thelonious Sphere Monk (1917–1982) was perhaps the most enigmatic personality to gain attention as a pianist and composer in the late 1940s. Monk became the house pianist at the after-hours club Minton's, where he performed with Parker, Gillespie, Charlie Christian, Kenny Clarke, and many of the other pioneers of the new bop style. Ironically, however, Monk's own piano style eventually became the antithesis of what bop represented and encouraged—fast, flashy, notey passages, all characteristics exemplified by Bud Powell. Although his harmonic concepts were very advanced for the day, his style was deeply rooted in the older stride tradition, and he did not seem to possess the right hand technique required to play the fast lines typically associated with the bop style of improvisation. Everything about Monk, his music, and persona was unorthodox and eccentric, from his hand position at the keyboard to the way he dressed. Monk's style was rhythmically driving, percussive, harmonically rich, and quirky to say the least. Bassist Gene Ramey, who participated in early Monk recording

Thelonious Monk at Minton's Playhouse

sessions, theorized that Monk purposely sought to create a style that was less easily mimicked, as, by the mid 1940s, most of the younger musicians on the scene were overtly copying the Parker–Gillespie–Powell style. Improvisational clichés were quickly becoming common practice, and it is no wonder that Monk's more obtuse, almost avant-garde style caused the jazz world to initially overlook him. Consequently, he is often referred to as a rediscovery figure, not widely recorded or recognized until the 1950s and 1960s. It was difficult for Monk to get work in his early years because of this unique style, which was contradictory to the current trends. His sparse accompanying style and unusual chord voicings comprised a style that was often criticized by horn players looking for the ideal accompanist. Monk never wasted a note, and his solos were often masterful understatements, sounding like an edited improvisation in which all extraneous material had been omitted. He used the entire range of the keyboard and often approached the instrument in a percussive fashion.

Ex-Ellington trumpeter Cootie Williams was the first to record an arrangement of a Monk composition, although it seemed out of character to be performed by this swing-style big band. Monk also performed and recorded with tenor saxophonist Coleman Hawkins. Monk's most significant compositions from this bebop period were collected on two LPs for Blue Note Records. Each tune illustrates a perfect marriage between melody, harmony, and rhythm, making the whole better than the sum of these individual components. Monk's compositions are very difficult to perform, as the musicians must completely internalize the composition, being willing to give up a certain amount of themselves in order to project the essence of the tune through their improvisations. His later recordings for the Prestige and Riverside labels, although not big sellers at the time, were later identified as landmark recordings. Some believe that his much touted 1957 "Brilliant Corners" release planted further seeds for the not-yet-realized avant-garde movement in jazz.

Monk was one of the few jazz artists to be pictured and written about in *Time* magazine and, after his death, was the subject of more than one film. His legacy, which includes compositions such as "Straight No Chaser," "Ruby My Dear," "'Round Midnight," "Criss Cross," "Well You Needn't," and "Epistrophy," among others, can be summed up by his own quotation from *Harper's* magazine:

> Maybe I've turned jazz another way. Maybe I'm a major influence. I don't know. Jazz is my adventure. I'm after new chords, new ways of syncopating, new figurations, new runs. How to use notes differently. That's it. Just how to use notes differently.[12]

He chose his own path and was unaffected by the press or current trends, passing this attitude and uncompromising ethic on to those, such as avant-garde pianist Cecil Taylor (featured in Chapter 14), who would follow.

In the recording of "Epistrophy," Monk demonstrates many of the quirky elements of his unique style as a composer and pianist. The composition and performance are somewhat abstract and angular, although they include a good deal of repetition that helps to make them recognizable and listenable. His pianistic style is equally unique for the period—loose, not flashy like Powell, rhythmically choppy and irregular, and with a comping style often based on unusual chord voicings that sometimes seem muddy and harmonically unclear. Also evident is his penchant for the descending, exotic-sounding whole-tone scale evident throughout his solo and again at the very end, serving as a final signature.

LISTENING GUIDE

🔊))

Thelonious Monk

"Epistrophy" (Thelonious Monk) 3:05

From *The Genius of Modern Music Vol. 2*

Blue Note CDP7–81511–2

Recorded 7/2/1948

Personnel: Thelonious Monk, piano; Milt Jackson, vibraphone; John Simmons, bass; Shadow Wilson, drums

Form: 32-bar form A(4)–A^1(8)–A^1(4)–B(8)–A^1(4)–A(4). Although the A sections are similar, they are different enough to be designated as such in the formal outline (A and A^1). Parentheses above indicate the number of bars. The soloists never improvise on the bridge (B) of the tune.

0:00–0:07	Introductory piano vamp implies 3/4 meter against 4/4, creating a polymetric situation
0:07–0:34	Jackson plays similar A themes for a total of 16 bars
0:35–0:49	Contrasting B section
0:50–1:02	Final A section completes first full chorus and statement of tune
1:03–1:31	Jackson improvises vibes solo on A section only
1:31–2:00	Monk improvises piano solo on A section
2:01–2:29	Head returns played on vibes
2:30–2:44	B section—Jackson avoids melody on second half and improvises
2:45–end	Return to final A section—Monk plays signature, whole-tone descending scale to end performance

Oscar Pettiford (1922–1960)

Oscar Pettiford (1922–1960) was the first modern bassist to serve as a link between Swing Era bassists Slam Stewart and Jimmy Blanton and the more modern demands of bebop. Pettiford, who was first schooled as a pianist, toured with a family band as a teenager. His first major positions were held in swing bands led by Charlie Barnett (1942), becoming the first black musician to join this band, and Roy Eldridge (1943). It was Coleman Hawkins's important transitional recordings that brought Pettiford to the center of attention in terms of the new bop movement, and he soon found himself co-leading a quintet with Dizzy Gillespie in 1944. He returned to working with big bands, holding down the bass chair in Duke Ellington's band from 1945 to 1948 and, a year later, with the Woody Herman band. Throughout the next decade, he recorded with most of the significant personalities of the bebop era, including Monk, Art Blakey, Stan Getz, and Bud Powell. Later in his career, he adopted a jazz-playing technique for the cello. He passed away suddenly in Copenhagen, his home away from home, as a result of a polio-like virus. Pettiford is remembered for bringing the bass into a better-defined solo role and is considered the first modern jazz bassist.

Kenny Clarke (1914–1985)

Kenny Clarke (1914–1985) is considered the true father of the modern bebop style of drumming. Clarke was the first of this new breed of bop drummers to disregard the regular use of the bass drum. Drummers in the earlier styles played in a chunky, less-flowing style than what evolved in the mid 1940s, thanks to the efforts of Clarke, Roach, and Art Blakey (Chapter 11). The most immediate predecessors of this new modern style were Jo Jones (with Basie's band), Cozy Cole, and Sid Catlett. Both Cole and Catlett had cut some of the first early bop sides with Gillespie and Parker. Bop drummers, along with bass players, still carried the burden of maintaining the steady pulse and time feel; what changed was how they maintained the time. Swing-style drummers used the bass drum on every beat, often very aggressively, whereas Clarke and his followers transferred this every-beat pulse from the bass drum to the lighter, more flexible ride cymbal, where it was easier to achieve more variety. Clarke, who also played piano and vibes, which may explain his more melodic approach to the drums, is credited as the first drummer to overtly avoid using the bass drum on every beat. He claimed to have developed this approach by accident when playing the faster bop tempos, which made it tiring to use the bass drum on every beat and slowed the tempo down on extended tunes with long solos. He developed a more independent, less rigid style of drumming where all limbs were free to embellish the basic beat and inherent rhythms of the melody. This new style is akin to the punching and jabbing of a boxer, who continues to move in a flowing rhythm around the ring. Teddy Hill, who once fired Clarke from his big band for playing in this wilder style, took over the management of Minton's Playhouse, where he later hired Clarke as house drummer. It was here, in the years that followed, that Clarke perfected this new style. Max Roach elaborated on it by adding even more complex syncopations and cross-rhythms. Hill described this new, accented approach to playing—using the bass drum only to "drop bombs" as musical punctuation marks—as "Klook-mop music," a name that stuck, and Clarke earned his new nickname—"Klook."

Before taking up permanent residence in Paris in 1955, Clarke became a dominant figure in the New York scene, performing with Miles Davis, Monk, Tadd Dameron, Ella Fitzgerald, Gillespie, and many others. After serving time in the Army, Clarke returned to the States to become a regular member of Gillespie's big band, before leaving to help found the Modern Jazz Quartet with pianist John Lewis (Chapter 10). Clarke was less intrigued by Lewis's new brand of "cool" jazz and termed it "too bland and pretentious." He left New York for Paris where he cofounded the Kenny Clarke–Francy Boland big band. Clarke was a well-rounded musician, who brought his knowledge of composition and melodic instruments to the drum set to create a new way of playing time by engaging in a dialogue with the performers, in ways that had never been done before.

Max Roach (1924–2007)

Drummer Max Roach (1924–2007) represents one of the newer breeds of schooled musicians that surfaced during the bebop period. By day, he studied percussion and composition at New York City conservatories and by night he sat in at Minton's and Monroe's Uptown House. Roach and Kenny Clarke, his mentor, are considered to be the best representatives of the explosive new drumming style that emerged in the mid 1940s and complemented what the bop horn players were doing melodically and rhythmically. Roach is considered the earliest and most fluent member of the modern school of drumming, less concerned with mere time keeping and more concerned with a melodic approach to drumming and rhythmically complementing the tune and soloists. Roach was the first to approach the drums in a more melodic fashion.

Roach replaced Clarke at Minton's, later recording with Hawkins, Gillespie, and Parker, where he showed off the new style of drumming. At home in small groups and big bands, including those led by Ellington, Benny Carter, and Gillespie, Roach co-led the famous hard bop group in the mid 1950s with trumpet virtuoso Clifford Brown (Chapter 11). From then, he performed and recorded with most noted jazz soloists of the past several decades. In the 1970s and 1980s, he pursued composition with more fervor, writing for new and interesting amalgamations of instruments, including string quartets and choirs, while always remaining true to the basic tenets of the jazz tradition. Roach, a vocal spokesman for equal rights, also explored more fringe styles of jazz in the 1960s and 1970s with artists such as pianist Cecil Taylor, and saxophonists Archie Shepp and Anthony Braxton, all movers and shakers in the avant-garde jazz style. His *We Insist— Freedom Now* suite, recorded in the 1960s, showed his awareness and deep commitment to the civil rights movement, with which he was actively involved. The claims that there is little relationship between sociopolitical issues and the arts are clearly mistaken. He composed, performed, and taught for decades, exerting an influence on young drummers for nearly seven decades. His influence on the years since the mid 1940s cannot be overstated, and he can be heard on "Moon Dreams" and "Pent Up House," found in the online audio collection and discussed in the upcoming chapter.

Drummer Max Roach

Sarah Vaughan: "The Divine One" (1924–1990)

Sarah Vaughan was one of several singers, along with Carmen McRae and Betty Carter, to fall under the influence of the bop generation of instrumentalists and serve as an example of the vocalist's side of this movement. A contralto, she earned the nickname "The Divine One" because of her incomparable vocal technique and mastery, often compared with those of the best of opera singers. She negotiated her exceptional four-octave range with ease, and her signature swoops from the height of her range to the extreme low register and back are legendary and hallmarks of her individualistic style. Vaughan used her rich, resonant vocal quality, strong, controlled vibrato, sudden changes in dynamics, and flare for the daring and dramatic to advantage, bringing her praise from vocalists and instrumentalists. In contrast to Billie Holiday, her incredible vocal technique at times inspired her to ignore the interpretation of a lyric in favor of exploring and flaunting her vocal talent, but, if doing the unexpected with utmost sincerity and virtuosic artistry is the mark of a truly great performer, then Sarah Vaughan earned her reputation. Vaughan's talent shone on sultry ballads and, like Fitzgerald and Holiday, she did not favor blues, but did enjoy a romping, swing, or bop-style tune.

Sarah Vaughan began her love affair with music as a child, singing and playing organ and piano in a Newark, NJ, Baptist church. Like

Vocalist Sarah Vaughan

Ella Fitzgerald had done 8 years earlier, she won a competition at an Apollo Theater Amateur Night and captured the attention of pianist–bandleader Earl Hines. Hines put her to work serving as second-string pianist and vocalist in his band, sharing that spotlight with baritone Billy Eckstine. It was here, and later with Eckstine's own bop-oriented band, which splintered off from the Hines band, that she encountered the horn players who would write the new bebop language, including its finest authors, Charlie Parker, Dexter Gordon, Dizzy Gillespie, Fats Navarro, and others. Gillespie called her, along with Carmen McRae, a "musician's singer. Both of them can play the piano and accompany themselves. They know all the flat fives and modern progressions and can do them vocally."[13] As a scatting improviser, something she did with less abandon or flash than Ella Fitzgerald, Vaughan took full advantage of her training as a pianist, enabling her not to only embrace the melodic side of improvisation, as is the case with most singers, but also to get inside the complex bebop harmonies in much the same way as the horn players. "You had to sing within whatever the chords were they were playing. You had to know a little about music or have a hell of a good ear," according to Vaughan.[14]

In 1944, she became one of the first singers to record in the bop vein, immediately after the AFofM recording strike was settled. *Down Beat* magazine recognized her in their polls from 1947 to 1952, and she won top vocalist in 1950. Her most exceptional recorded work is undoubtedly those sides preserved on the Mercury/Emarcy label and those made later in life for the Mainstream and Pablo labels. Despite these successes in the 1950s, recording with the likes of the Count Basie Band, Miles Davis, saxophone hard bopper Cannonball Adderley, and trumpeter Clifford Brown, she found herself jumping from label to label and producer to producer. She was trying her hand at becoming a more mainstream, popular success, at a time when the general public had lost track of jazz in favor of following pop trends. Her volatile, diva-like personality earned her a second nickname, "Sassy," and this may partially explain her label/producer hopping. For the most part, even amidst the backdrop of over-produced orchestral arrangements, or in lavish productions of pop tunes, including Beatles tunes, of later years, she remained true to her roots as a jazz singer, emerging later and throughout her career to record exceptional jazz. Along with Bessie Smith, Billie Holiday, Ella Fitzgerald, Betty Carter, and Carmen McRae, Sarah Vaughan stands as one of the most original and identifiable jazz singers, serving as an important model for generations of singers to follow.

"Easy Living," included in the online audio anthology, is an example of Vaughan in the later stage of her career but still in impeccable form, demonstrating her flare for slow ballads and operatic-like technique. Some of the finest rhythm-section players of the 20th century, each in their own right noted soloists, provide exquisite accompaniment on this Pablo recording, produced by jazz impresario Norman Granz.

LISTENING GUIDE

Sarah Vaughan

"Easy Living" (L. Robin/R. Rainger) 4:36

From *How Long Has This Been Going On?*

Recorded 4/25/78 in Hollywood, CA, Pablo PACD-2310–821–2

Personnel: Sarah Vaughan, vocals; Oscar Peterson, piano; Joe Pass, guitar; Ray Brown, bass; Louie Bellson, drums

Form: 32-bar-song form (AABA)

0:00–0:16	Introduction—pianist Oscar Peterson provides rubato introduction
0:17–0:56	Chorus begins with first A section sung in tempo with rhythm-section accompaniment
0:57–1:35	Repeat of A section
1:36–2:12	Bridge or B section of form
2:13–2:40	Return to final A section to complete first full chorus; bass and drums drop out (2:41–2:49) in final bars of chorus as tempo deteriorates to rubato
2:50–3:31	Piano and voice in duet return to bridge, breaking from expected form by eliminating first two A sections
3:32–4:02	Band reenters in tempo to state final A section
4:03–end	Vaughan improvises a short rubato coda; listen for bowed bass

MODERN JAZZ EMBRACES THE AFRO-CUBAN SPIRIT

A smooth blending of jazz and Latin or Afro-Latin music was not accomplished overnight. Both sides were forced to overcome challenges encountered by the union of styles. Latin musicians were faced with jazz rhythms, similar to, yet different from, their native styles, and a more advanced harmonic and melodic vocabulary. Latin percussionists, using various drums such as congas and timbales, gradually learned how to coexist with jazz rhythm sections. Example 9.1 is an example of a variation of the Cuban Son rhythm. This same rhythm is frequently played in jazz on the conga drum with only one small change—leaving out the initial downbeat of each measure, as shown in Example 9.1. Chano Pozo plays this rhythm on the conga drum in the introduction of "Manteca," discussed in the following pages and included in the online audio collection.

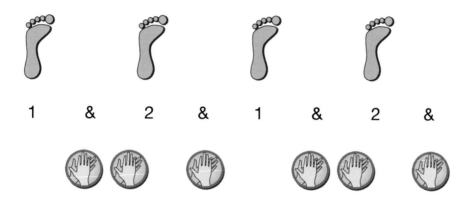

EXAMPLE 9.1 Graphic representation of the jazz conga drum variation. Tap your left foot in a steady tempo following the graphic, while clapping the conga-drum pattern

The increasing popularity of Latin dance music urged jazz artists to discover ways to incorporate the complex Latin rhythms into their own styles. Eventually, the exchange became mutual, and Latin bands began exploring the more advanced harmonic and melodic possibilities that the jazz language presented. Machito's band of the 1940s was probably the most stable and successful in the integration of styles during this period. Jazz bands began hiring Latin musicians, and vice versa, making for a healthy exchange of ideas. For example, Latin bandleader Rene Touzet hired jazz arranger Johnny Mandel, who had arranged for many artists, including Frank Sinatra. Mandel then persuaded Touzet to employ former Stan Kenton jazz artists to complement his Latin band. Eventually, the entire horn section of this band consisted of jazzmen, and Mandel conducted extensive experiments superimposing Latin rhythms on the jazz repertoire. The result was frequently referred to as "Cubop." "Barbados," recorded by Charlie Parker, is an excellent example of this style, as is Bud Powell's "Un Poco Loco." Parker also recorded the album *South of the Border* for the Mercury label, featuring a bop approach to traditional Latin tunes.

Dizzy Gillespie and the Birth of Cubop

Dizzy Gillespie was the prime force in the blending of jazz and Afro-Latin styles in the middle and late 1940s. Gillespie's early association with the Cab Calloway band served to introduce him to fellow trumpet-section mate and arranger Mario Bauza. Gillespie and Bauza, who later became Machito's arranger, became friendly on and off the bandstand, attending after-hours sessions together at New York Latin music clubs. Gillespie's experiences sitting in with these Latin bands

	• John Hersey wins a Pulitzer Prize for *A Bell For Adano*.
	• Germany surrenders.
	• The US drops an atomic bomb on Hiroshima—Japan surrenders.
1946	• The US begins space exploration.
	• The "Iron Curtain" signals the beginning of "cold war" conflict between democracy and communism/socialism.
	• The US begins atomic testing at Bikini Atoll (Island).
	• Irving Berlin premiers his new musical, *Annie Get Your Gun*.
	• The ENIAC computer ushers in a new age.
	• Popular films include *The Postman Always Rings Twice* and *The Best Years of Our Lives*.
1947	• Robert Penn Warren wins a Pulitzer Prize for *All the King's Men*.
	• Author James Michener publishes *Tales of the South Pacific*.
	• Tennessee Williams premiers *A Streetcar Named Desire*.
	• The GI Bill provides housing, education, and business opportunities for former armed-services members in an attempt to stimulate the post-war rebuild.
	• Jackie Robinson becomes the first African-American to play professional baseball.
	• There are growing concerns about communist activities in the US—10 Hollywood personalities are blacklisted.
	• Dexter Gordon records "Index."
	• A tape recorder is produced for home use.
	• Dizzy Gillespie's bebop big band records Afro-Cuban tinged "Manteca," defining the Cubop style.
1948	• Toscanini conducts the first NBC Orchestra concert on TV.
	• The transistor is developed by Bell Labs to replace the vacuum tube.
	• The Supreme Court rules that race may not be used to consider law school admissions at the University of Oklahoma, and President Truman attempts to halt racial discrimination in the military.
	• James Michener wins a Pulitzer Prize for *Tales of the South Pacific*.
	• The Supreme Court forbids prayer in schools.
	• *Candid Camera* and *The Milton Berle Show* top the list of popular new TV shows.
	• Monk and Jackson record "Epistrophy."
1949	• Rodgers and Hammerstein create the Broadway musical *South Pacific*.
	• Harry S. Truman wins the presidential election.
	• Arthur Miller's play *The Death of a Salesman* wins a Pulitzer Prize.
	• Miles Davis and company launch the cool jazz style.
1950	• Senator McCarthy denounces communism and begins efforts to purge the US of all members of this party, blacklisting 205 well-known personalities.
	• The U.S. backs South Korea against North Korea, and the war with Korea begins.
	• William Faulkner wins the Nobel Prize for Literature, and Ralph Bunch wins the Peace Prize.
	• The U.S. census indicates there are 150 million Americans.
	• Parker, Gillespie, and Powell record "Anthropology" live at Birdland.

1951	• The U.S. detonates an H-bomb.
	• The UNIVAC electronic, digital computer is unveiled.
	• *I Love Lucy*, staring Lucille Ball, is an instant TV success.
	• Author J.D. Salinger's *Catcher in the Rye* is a tale of teenage alienation.
	• Charlie Parker, Dizzy Gillespie, and Bud Powell peform "Anthropology" at Birdland.

CHAPTER SUMMARY

In the early 1940s, numerous factors combined to cause the demise of many of the big bands. America's entry into World War II necessitated a military draft that claimed many big-band musicians. Others, wanting to do something for their country, enlisted. Those still in the US had to cope with the rationing of petroleum-related products, including gasoline and tires, making travel very difficult. Even records depended on petroleum products that were being reserved to support the war effort. On the home front, with so many men away fighting the war, women took on many of the jobs traditionally held by men, leaving very little leisure time. Add to this situation the recording ban of the early 1940s imposed by the musicians' union, and it becomes clear that big bands could no longer thrive as they had.

At the same time, top jazz soloists continued to seek more artistically rewarding avenues to express themselves, beyond the confines of the big band. At after-hours clubs such as Minton's Playhouse, where musicians could play music for themselves, rather than for the public, a return to the early jazz ideal emphasizing improvisation fostered a new music—bebop. Although older musicians (notably, Coleman Hawkins) were important in helping to bring about this new style, trumpeter Dizzy Gillespie and alto saxophonist Charlie Parker are considered the true founders of bebop. Typically, a bebop group was small (three to five performers), allowing each member ample time to solo. As a music for musicians, bop tended to use much more complex harmonies and could be played at very fast tempos, as dancers were no longer a consideration. Pianist Bud Powell and tenor saxophonist Dexter Gordon made significant contributions to developing the bop language on their instruments, and only the very best musicians were capable of playing this music.

The musical partnership and friendship between Dizzy Gillespie and Mario Bauza helped forge Cubop. This hybrid style was the result of the merging of certain aspects of bebop with Afro-Cuban styles.

Pianist/composer Thelonious Monk contributed a sophisticated and original harmonic approach to bop. Although he served as the house pianist at Minton's, participating in many important bop sessions, his quirky, unorthodox style does not fit the bop ideal. At the time, his music and performance style defied classification and mainstream trends.

Not all of the bebop innovations involved solo styles. Changes took place in the rhythm section to accommodate this new style. Drummers used primarily the ride cymbal to maintain pulse, rather than the hi-hat and bass drum, as, at some of the fast tempos, it became physically impossible for drummers to maintain a steady pulse with the bass drum. Bop drummer Kenny Clarke is normally credited with this development. He and Max Roach were the trend-setting bebop drummers. Pianists abandoned the timekeeper role in favor of a punctuated style known as comping, and the guitar was often omitted from bop rhythm sections. Bass players still frequently played walking bass lines, but some, notably Oscar Pettiford, used the bass more and more as a solo instrument. This new approach gave the rhythm section a more open, less cluttered feel.

Year	Title	Artist
1943*	Besame Mucho	Jimmy Dorsey Orchestra (I)
4-I	Artistry in Rhythm	Stan Kenton Orchestra (I)
	Is You Is or Is You Ain't?	Louis Jordan Orchestra (I)
	Cow-Cow Boogie	Freddie Slack Orchestra (I)?
1944	White Christmas	Frank Sinatra with H. James Orch. (V)
7-V	You Always Hurt the One You Love	Mills Brothers (V)
5-I	Begin the Beguine	Eddie Heywood Orchestra (I)
	Cocktails For Two (novelty)	Spike Jones Orchestra (I)
	Opus No. 1	Tommy Dorsey Orchestra (I)
	On the Sunny Side of the Street	Tommy Dorsey Orchestra (I)
	Swingin' On A Star	Bing Crosby (V)
	Don't Fence Me In	Bing Crosby (V)
	Too-Ra-Loo-Ra-Loo-Ra	Bing Crosby (V)
	Sentimental Journey	Les Brown Orchestra (I)
	Rum and Coca Cola	Andrews Sisters (V)
	Into Each Life Some Rain Must Fall	Ella Fitzgerald (with the Ink Spots) (V)
1945	Till the End of Time	Perry Como (V)
7-V	If I Loved You	Perry Como (V)
3-I	Dig You Later	Perry Como (V)
	Temptation	Perry Como (V)
	I Can't Begin To Tell You	Bing Crosby (V)
	Cottage For Sale	Billy Eckstein (V)
	Prisoner of Love	Billy Eckstein (V)
	Laura	Woody Herman Orchestra (I)
	Tampico	Stan Kenton Orchestra (I)
	Shoe-Fly Pie	Stan Kenton Orchestra (I)
1946	Prisoner of Love	Perry Como (V)
12-V	I'm Always Chasing Rainbows	Perry Como (V)
4-I	South America, Take it Away	Bing Crosby (V)
	McNamara's Band	Bing Crosby (V)
	Alexander's Ragtime Band	Bing Crosby (V)
	To Each His Own	The Ink Spots (V)
	The Gypsy	The Ink Spots (V)
	April Showers	Al Jolson (V)
	Rockabye Your Baby	Al Jolson (V)
	You Made Me Love You	Al Jolson (V)
	Sonny Boy	Al Jolson (V)

Year	Title	Artist
	Anniversary Song	Al Jolson (V)
	Glow-Worm	Spike Jones Orchestra (I)
	Humoresque	Guy Lombarde Orchestra (I)
	Christmas Island	Guy Lombarde Orchestra (I)
	Choo Choo Ch' Boogie	Louis Jordan and His Tympani 5
1947	By 1947 nearly every million seller was either a vocal, novelty number, or instrumental by a sweet band bearing no resemblance to jazz aside from instrumentation. The big band era had clearly come to a close at least in terms of capturing the attention of throngs of Americans as it had only a few years earlier.	

* In 1943, the recording industry was hit hard by the AFofM recording ban, hence fewer million-selling hits, most of which were recordings issued from archived, previously unreleased stock

Information is based on statistics cited in Peter A. Soderbergh's *Old Records Price Guide 1900–1947*, Des Moines: Wallace-Homstead Book Company, 1980, pp. 176–180

STUDY QUESTIONS

1. Cite the reasons for the gradual decline of swing-style popularity.

2. Compare and contrast bebop with swing style.

3. Describe the social atmosphere that surrounded the bebop style.

4. Can you name some of the older swing musicians who helped to develop and promote the earliest forms of small-group bebop?

5. What changes occurred in the bass's role and performance style during the bebop period?

6. Which three bassists had laid the groundwork for a more modern style that emerged during the bebop period?

7. Bebop drummers initiated what significant changes in their playing during the bebop period? Which two drummers were most instrumental in making these changes?

8. Who are the two pianists given much of the credit for modernizing the jazz pianist's accompaniment style?

9. Who was the first trombonist to embrace the more modern bebop style?

10. What was Cubop and who was largely responsible for it?

11. List the musical characteristics that define Dizzy Gillespie's unique style.

12. List the musical characteristics that define Charlie Parker's revolutionary and unique style.

13. Who are considered the originators of the bebop style?

14. Who was the tenor saxophonist given much of the credit for incorporating Parker's bebop alto style?

15. Which tenor saxophonist was heralded as the leading tenor saxophonist of the post bop school?

16. Who was the preeminent bebop pianist?

17. What kind of repertoire did bop bands concern themselves with?

18. Describe the typical bebop tune in terms of the overall form or architecture of its presentation.

19. Which eccentric bop-era pianist was equally recognized as a composer?

20. In what ways did Monk's style make him an anomaly in the bebop period?

21. Who was the bassist who served as a link between swing-style bassists Jimmy Blanton and Slam Stewart and the more modern, soloistic demands of the bebop style?

22. Which two drummers are considered to be the best representatives of the explosive new drumming style that emerged in the mid 1940s and complemented what the bop horn players were doing melodically and rhythmically? In what ways did these two drummers modify their playing, compared with earlier Swing Era drummers?

23. Who is considered the true father of the modern bebop style of drumming?

24. Name one preeminent vocalist from this period and describe her style.

25. Were there any bebop-style big bands? If so, who were their leaders?

26. How can the decline of bebop be explained?

27. Was bebop an art music, or music that supported entertainment?

Make sure that you also review material on the corresponding chapter of the website.

CHAPTER 10

The 1950s and Early 1960s

Cool, Intellectual, and Abstract Jazz

The first time in history that a jazz drummer's solo was so soft that you had to whisper or be conspicuous.[1]
—Ralph Gleason

Race riots and picketers in Birmingham, Alabama

JAZZ IN PERSPECTIVE

On the surface, the 1950s appeared to be a period of great prosperity and tranquility in the US. In many ways this was true. Americans had survived the ravages of World War II. Those who returned to a normal life were realizing the American dream—starting families, owning a TV, a car, and a house in suburbia, and perhaps profiting from a college education funded by the GI Bill for those who had served in the armed forces. However, beneath this rosy surface lay the beginnings of a cold war, essentially a battle between democracy (the US) and communism, represented by Russia and the Iron Curtain communist bloc countries. Many actors, writers, and artists were victimized for their freethinking ideas and blacklisted by the radical conservative Senator Joseph McCarthy. The growing cold war fueled anti-communist sentiments, and McCarthy was the most vocal advocate for democracy. He singlehandedly led a crusade to rid the country of all suspected communists or, worse, anyone who spoke of liberal ideas freely. Many artists, actors, and writers were blacklisted because of mere accusations about communist sympathies, and McCarthyism ran unchecked, ruining careers for some time.

Racial tensions, although largely non-violent during the 1950s, continued to escalate, despite some progress being made toward desegregation of schools and public places. The U.S. State Department, however, saw in jazz the perfect counter-offensive to thwart communism and the cold war. Construction on the Berlin Wall began in 1961 and was designed to separate communist East Germany from the Free World. The Bay of Pigs incident between Cuba and the US underscored the growing tensions between communist bloc countries and the Free World. Communism was painted to represent repression, oppression, and rigid structure, whereas jazz was cast as the perfect weapon—the Western embodiment of democracy, freedom of choice, and expression. Tours abroad were sponsored by the State Department, making use of Louis Armstrong and Dizzy Gillespie as jazz ambassadors. Willis Conover hosted a regular jazz program targeted at the Iron Curtain countries by the Voice of America radio station, operating on shortwave frequencies. Ironically, African-Americans, who continued their quest for equality in the US more earnestly than ever before, had still not earned the very democratic freedoms they were asked to promote. Despite the 1954 Supreme Court ruling against school segregation, President Eisenhower was reluctant to send federal troops to Arkansas to enforce the high court's ruling. Louis Armstrong, who rarely made his political views public, openly criticized the president and was so unnerved that he canceled an upcoming State Department goodwill trip to Russia. Armstrong stated publicly that: "The people over there ask me what's wrong with my country. What am I supposed to say? It's getting almost so bad a colored man hasn't got any country."[2] Two years later, Miles Davis, stepping outside Birdland in New York for a smoke, was assaulted and bludgeoned by the police. The NAACP was forced to activate its forces against the courts again in 1956, and the Reverend Martin Luther King rose to be the most effective leader and spokesman for the growing civil rights movement.

Not only was there increasing political tension between the US and Russia, but the race to stake out new frontiers in space eventually found these two superpowers even more at odds. The National Aeronautics and Space Administration (NASA) was formed in 1958, and the US launched the first artificial, unmanned earth satellite that same year. Extraterrestrial activity and science fiction were in the minds of many Americans, and some jazz performers reflected this new obsession in their record titles, such as the Riverside release *Clark Terry In Orbit* and George Russell's *Jazz in the Space Age*. The atomic bombs dropped on Hiroshima and Nagasaki to end World War II launched the nuclear age, causing great concern for many Americans. The University of Chicago developed the first nuclear power plant in 1956, and there came the realization that the same tool that had provided peace through destruction was now also the key to new scientific discoveries. This new reality caused many Americans to reassess the very nature of life itself.

Young people once again found the need to re-evaluate life and look inwardly for solutions to living in a world that was becoming increasingly stressful. No longer were their parents' values always desirable models. In some ways, a new cycle, much like in the 1920s, had begun, especially with the under-30 generation. Some turned to Eastern philosophical teachings and the offbeat writings of poets who represented the new beat generation. Langston Hughes, for example, became identified as the poet laureate of the late 1940s and 1950s, and other writers also emerged and found a kinship with the spontaneity of improvised jazz. For many, it became increasingly important to learn how to "stay cool" and find new ways to enjoy life while controlling their emotions.

By the mid 1950s, jazz had not only become an art, it had become a way of life and, to some, a science, with a unique subculture somewhere to the left of mainstream society. Not everyone supported the new, cool, intellectual jazz movement. Some felt that jazz was running parallel to what had happened to classical music when the serial 12-tone composers took over, applying too many formulas for music to be enjoyable. Jazz in the hands of these so called "mathematicians" (referring to the third-stream crowd and Lennie Tristano's early free jazz experiments) had become more of a science than an art, and it was this criticism from those who appreciated more mainstream black jazz from the same period that served to chill some of the cool experimentalists.

The new, more abstract attitude could be seen in other artistic arenas as well. Painters no longer cared to portray lifelike objects, for example Jackson Pollock, who preferred to drip paint on his canvas in more spontaneous, abstract gestures, often improvising as he created. Architects began to use more functional designs that were sometimes criticized for their tendency to be too stark and pessimistic. The titles of some jazz recordings seemed to capture this mood and project a sense of moving forward into uncharted territory. Stan Kenton, who for a time called his band the "Innovations Orchestra," featured works such as the "City of Glass" (composed by Robert Grettinger) or "Opus in Abstract." Keeping with the more intellectual, academic trend among the new breed of 1950s jazz musicians was composer George Russell, who, in 1953, published the first major theoretical treatise about jazz harmony and melody. He called it his *Lydian Chromatic Concept of Tonal Organization*. Perhaps it was the more intellectual jazz known as third stream, which combined elements of jazz improvisation and rhythm with European art music, or the more cerebral, sedate, and sophisticated sound of cool jazz, or simply the then 40 years of jazz tradition that explains the steady flow of more scholarly publications such as Russell's that emerged in the 1950s. Serious efforts by Marshall Stearns—*The Story of Jazz*—and French author/composer André Hodeir—*Jazz, Its Evolution and Essence*—marked the beginning of writings about jazz that were more informed than ever before.

The literary world reflected similar attitudes, and many closely allied themselves with jazz—both bebop and cool. In 1955, Jack Kerouac wrote the novel *On the Road* about the wanderings of impulsive young adults, often at loose ends and out of sync with mainstream society. His representation of the West-Coast scene, though, depicted a more carefree, relaxed, and affluent lifestyle. For that matter, the names of new jazz record labels, such as Fantasy, Contemporary, and Pacific Jazz, helped to reinforce the Californian "LA LA Land" stereotype. The Walt Disney, Hollywood, expansive beach images helped to sell millions of newcomers on the opportunities available in the sunny state with a mild climate. As a result, the state's population nearly doubled during the 1950s. Allen Ginsberg, Norman Mailer, William Burroughs, and Lawrence Ferlinghetti, like Kerouac, aligned themselves with the jazz subculture, even on occasion performing with its members. Some labeled this group of artists, musicians, and writers as deviants, but their freer ideas about race, religion, and sexuality were resonant with the younger generation's modern, "hip" new attitudes. Thespians used the jazz performer as a metaphor to represent the struggling, repressed minority, viewed as second-class citizens by respectable society and caught in an anguished struggle to gain acceptance and respectability. It is no small wonder that a bebop-derived score was used as a backdrop for the film version of Tennessee Williams's *A Streetcar Named Desire*.

Home entertainment and rock 'n' roll had a negative effect on jazz popularity. Television became the center of family entertainment, and the improved "hi-fi" stereo recordings that could be enjoyed in the confines of one's living room often became a reasonable substitute for live, late-night entertainment. The "baby boomer" generation was cradled during the 1950s, and home entertainment was a must in order to stay close to the nest after a hard day's work. The younger set turned on to emerging rock 'n' roll and folk, a rage that began to sweep the nation in the 1950s, but not without protest from the more mature generation, who reacted to it in the same way their parents had to jazz decades earlier. Rock 'n' roll represented immoral, sexual behavior, as jazz had in the 1920s. The Coasters, Little Richard, Fats Domino, Jerry Lee Lewis, the Platters, Bill Haley and the Comets, Chuck Berry, and of course Elvis Presley rose to star status, while jazz began to take more and more of a back seat. Television also had a direct impact on record sales. A survey of 1950s hits shows a direct relationship to television exposure. For example, Tennessee Ernie Ford, with his country brand of religious-tinged music, Jackie Gleason, Pat Boone, Perry Como, Mitch Miller, the Kingston Trio, Rick Nelson, Harry Belafonte, and Johnny Mathis enjoyed gold-record sales and were simultaneously regular TV personalities.

Somehow, amidst the slump in live entertainment and despite the popular rock 'n' roll phenomenon, the jazz festival concept was successfully born at this same time, serving to salvage many jazz careers. George Wein produced the successful Newport Jazz Festival in 1954, which started a new trend. Even some of the older jazz acts were rejuvenated by such festivals. For example, Duke Ellington made headlines at this festival in 1956, at a time when he was being accused of becoming passé. Norman Granz began his Jazz at the Philharmonic series and successfully booked all-star groups on tours throughout Europe and Japan. Both promoters were champions of racial equality and insisted that people of all races be permitted to attend these performances. Many of Granz's Philharmonic concerts were recorded and are still available on CD reissues.

CHARACTERISTICS OF COOL JAZZ

If bop was hot, muscular, and macho, then cool was the subtler, more romantic, more feminine reaction. Whereas vivid reds, yellows, and orange shades might best represent bebop, a painter might use light pastel shades to represent the sound of much cool jazz. The following musical attributes are typically associated with this 1950s, restrained, more intellectual style:

- Cool jazz featured toned-down dynamics accomplished through a variety of means, including drums that were often played by brushes instead of sticks. Bands played more quietly, brass players often added mutes, and trumpet players might choose the mellower flugelhorn.
- Tempos were often, but not always, slower than bop tunes.
- More emphasis was placed on improvising listenable melodies, rather than playing fast, technical passages.
- Trumpet players placed less emphasis on playing screaming high notes and, in contrast, focused on playing mellow melodies in the middle register.
- Vibrato is a useful device in expressing emotions, and cool horn players often projected a steely, colder emotional style by discarding or nearly removing vibrato from sustained note values. Bop players had already significantly reduced the amount of vibrato compared with the previous swing generation.
- Although cool musicians didn't abandon the previous repertoire and forms, the blues was nearly forgotten in favor of experimenting with new forms. Compositionally speaking, they stretched boundaries by mixing meters within a song (going from 4 beats a measure to 3) and using unusual phrase lengths. (Most songs up until this time were constructed of typical patterns, where melodies were grouped in 2- or 4-measure subdivisions).

- Arrangers and band leaders began to make use of instruments that had not been previously associated with jazz, i.e. French horn, tuba, flute, and oboe. There are other instances where instruments that had previously been considered indispensable were omitted, such as the piano.
- The influence of sophisticated, European-derived composition devices is increasingly noticeable in cool-style jazz.
- Although the ensembles were never larger than 9 or 10 players, tightly defined arrangements even for trios and quartets became very important, much as they had been during the big-band period.
- General experimentation was the motto of many cool-jazz instrumentalists.

Cool jazz in the 1950s reflected a complete reexamination of what had come before. Without being so radical as to throw the baby out with the bathwater, the musicians associated with this school broke new ground. Predictable rhythmic patterns and forms were dismantled and reassembled in new ways. Although improvisation was still important, and integral to jazz, in the cool sound it sometimes occupied an equal role to composition and arrangement, as had been the case in the big band era. It was a musical style that was practiced by more white per-formers than black. It may be that white performers were subconsciously trying to get back in the game by producing a new brand of jazz that was more destined for the concert hall, more polished and sophisticated, and less intrusive than bop. White musicians, who had enjoyed such a prominent role in the commercial success of the big-band Swing Era, lost ground during the bebop period to black artists, who refocused jazz as an improvisational art, not as entertainment and dance accompaniment. Cool served to bring white musicians back into the foreground by offering a menu of jazz that, in some cases, was more accessible and easy to market to the casual listener.

The images displayed on the covers of many of the cool recordings sent a different message as well, depicting beautiful women, beaches, men and women posed with fast cars, and the general sunny California beach vibe. This cool-jazz imagery was in stark contrast to that shown on recordings released by black artists of the period, who continued to follow the bebop tradition. These musicians were portrayed with sweat pouring off their brows in dimly lit nightclub scenes, surrounded by cigarette smoke. Cool jazz, therefore, projected a much cleaner image to the consumer.

The terms "cool" and "West-Coast" jazz have been used interchangeably, causing some confusion and misunderstanding about this period. Although it is true that many of the musi-cians associated with the new 1950s style were based on the West Coast, this should not give the impression that all cool jazz originated here. For that matter, the West Coast at this time was simultaneously a source for the hotter, bop style of jazz. Easterners also became involved in the cool sound and approach. It is important to note that many musicians who were associated with cool jazz were not devoted to it exclusively. It was a time of experimentation, and, unlike the earlier periods of jazz where one or two styles dominated, musicians in the 1950s often moved freely from one style to another, perhaps even within the confines of one recording. This chameleon-like activity becomes commonplace in jazz from this time on. For example, tenor saxophonist Stan Getz contributed several burning bop recordings in the late 1940s, but is often considered in discussions of cool jazz. Pianist Bill Evans, discussed in this chapter, also defies categorization under any one single style.

A summary of the fundamental characteristics that define cool jazz, along with a direct comparison with the bebop style, is presented in Figure 10.1 on p. 230. The figure offers a quick reference, making clear how these two styles served to contrast with one another.

Bebop Style Characteristics

1. Aside from ballads, bop was a garish, flashy, dynamic, "in your face" music.

2. Drummers were aggressive and primarily used sticks.

3. Bop tunes often featured fast tempos and technically demanding "heads".

4. Trumpet soloists developed macho, technical flare, exploring the extreme upper register.

5. Heavy vibrato was less popular with bop soloists than it had been with previous generations.

6. Bop style was dominated by black musicians.

7. Experimentation in terms of composition, orchestration and instrumentation was of little significance and takes a back seat to the soloist.

8. Bop bands were usually small combos.

9. The blues continued to dominate bop repertoire.

10. European classical influences were virtually nonexistent in bebop.

11. In its day, bebop did not prove to be commercially viable.

Cool Style Characteristics

1. Cool was softer dynamically and less intrusive than bop.

2. Drummers popularized brushes to help inspire a more mellow, relaxed approach.

3. Tempos were generally slower with greater emphasis placed on listenable melodies.

4. Trumpeters were less concerned with playing high notes and tone down their approach by using mutes and the more mellow flugelhorn.

5. Vibrato became even less predominant in the cool style with some players nearly discarding it completely.

6. The cool style was popularized largely by white musicians.

7. Innovative compositions featuring experimentation with orchestration and instrumentation became increasingly important.

8. Cool bands, with a few exceptions, were usually small combos.

9. The blues is much less important to cool repertoire.

10. European classical influences became embraced including compositional techniques like counterpoint.

11. Cool was more commercially successful than bop. One artist who emerged from this period was featured on the cover of *Time* magazine.

FIGURE 10.1 Comparison of bebop and cool styles

THE INNOVATORS: THE COOL SOUND ON THE EAST AND WEST COASTS

It was Gil Evans and Miles Davis on the East Coast and Dave Brubeck, Chet Baker, and Gerry Mulligan on the West Coast who were said to be the progenitors of this new direction in jazz. San Francisco became the center for their activities and, ironically, was also the city that harbored the "moldy figs" revival of traditional, early jazz styles. Many new record labels were formed to capitalize on the new west-coast artists and their experimental music.

Miles Davis and Gil Evans: The *Birth of the Cool*

Gil Evans grew up on the West Coast, where he started his own swing band, which never quite made the leap to star status. He actually used progressive big-band leader Stan Kenton as an occasional sub-pianist in this early band. Just before and after World War II, Evans worked as an arranger for the most influential of the "Johnny-come-lately" east-coast big bands, led by pianist Claude Thornhill. Thornhill encouraged his arrangers to experiment. Evans and other arrangers, such as Gerry Mulligan, who also wrote for Thornhill's band, were the first to add French horns and tuba to the standard big band, often juxtaposing this rich brass sound with the dark, reedy sound of a section of clarinets instead of saxophones. These orchestrations laid the groundwork for the innovations that soon followed, serving as the catalyst for the first major cool-style recording.

Evans moved to New York, taking up residence in an apartment that became a hangout in the late 1940s for trumpeter Miles Davis, baritone saxophonist Gerry Mulligan, and others who were instrumental in forming the nonet that would define the new cool sound. They collectively decided to form a band with an unusual instrumentation, designed to emulate the Thornhill sound, but with only nine players. Their new ensemble would have one of each member of the brass family (French Horn, trumpet, trombone, and tuba), alto and baritone saxes, and a three-piece rhythm section. The group's pianist, John Lewis, along with trumpeter Miles Davis, arranger Johnny Carisi, Evans, and Mulligan contributed arrangements to this historic series of recordings, eventually issued as *Birth of the Cool* by Capitol Records. No other movement in jazz was announced so abruptly, with the release of a single recording, as was the case in 1949–1950. This band defined the cool style, but without abandoning all that had come before. Their music projected an air of sophisticated, "restrained chamber music" to the astute, well-prepared audience. Mulligan, altoist Lee Konitz, and Davis served as the prominent soloists, and they all sought to shed the trappings and "**licks**" (stock melodic patterns or phrases, derived initially from an improvisation, that become adopted by others) that had become bebop's clichéd language. Mulligan was a gifted soloist and arranger, who was the first noted baritone sax soloist to come forward since Ellington's Harry Carney. As an earlier member of the Thornhill band, Konitz had already displayed his willingness to blaze new trails as an improviser, emerging from Bird's

Miles Davis recording in 1959

long shadow. Davis had been somewhat out of character in Parker's bop bands, as he lacked the aggression associated with the Gillespie trumpet style and seemed to prefer a more mellow, minimalist approach as he matured. The band performed live in New York for only a short time, but the impact they had on the future of jazz, particularly the cool style, was immeasurable. Davis's association with Evans would spark even greater collaborations in the future. Most of the cool players who followed captured the essence of this first model.

 Listen to the interviews with Miles Davis and Gerry Mulligan, who discuss the *Birth of the Cool* sessions. They can be found on the corresponding chapter on the website.

Although "Moon Dreams," one of several contributions by Evans to the *Birth of the Cool* sessions, is not representative of every song on this landmark recording, it does exemplify Evans's flare for orchestration and personifies many aspects of the cool sound. His ability to cast moody tone paintings through unusual instrumental textures defied earlier arranging doctrines practiced by most large-ensemble arrangers. Solos by Davis, Konitz, and Mulligan are very characteristic of the cool sound, often vibrato-less, stark, and spare in technique. Other pieces on the recording, such as "Boplicity," are clearly more upbeat, offering a renewed look at the still-omnipresent bop influences.

LISTENING GUIDE

Miles Davis

"Moon Dreams" (MacGregor–Mercer) 3:17

Recorded 3/9/1950 in New York City

Reissued on Capitol Jazz *Birth of the Cool* CDP 7 92862 2

Personnel: Miles Davis, trumpet; J.J. Johnson, trombone; Gunther Schuller, French horn; John Barber, tuba; Lee Konitz, alto saxophone; Gerry Mulligan, baritone saxophone; Al McKibbon, bass; Max Roach, drums

Form: 32-bar-song form (ABA^{1}C = chorus) with extended coda

0:00–0:25	A section—8 bars; theme—played by ensemble with trumpet lead
0:25–0:50	B section—8 bars; theme—4 bars, alto sax plays theme with background chords and answering lines in ensemble
0:25–0:36	4 bars—ensemble plays theme with trumpet lead
0:51–1:16	A^1 section—8 bars; theme—played by ensemble with trumpet lead (2 bars), then trombone lead (6 bars)
1:17–1:43	C section—8 bars; theme—4 bars, alto sax plays theme with background chords and lines in ensemble
1:17–1:29	4 bars, trumpet lead over moving parts and lines in ensemble
1:44–2:12	C^1 section—9 bars baritone sax solo; ensemble—4 bars, baritone sax solo with moving background ensemble lines
1:44–1:57	4 bars, ensemble with trumpet lead, baritone and alto sax fills
2:13–3:17	Coda—trumpet leads overlapping, cascading, descending ensemble lines

Modern Jazz Quartet

No discussion of the cool style would be complete without including the Modern Jazz Quartet (MJQ), the longest-running group in jazz, with the fewest personnel changes, and the cool-jazz standard bearer from the East Coast. The original members of this quartet served as the nucleus of Dizzy Gillespie's bebop big-band rhythm section in 1947. The quartet became known for its polished chamber-jazz approach, counterbalanced by Milt Jackson's more aggressive, blues-influenced style on the vibes. First known as the Milt Jackson Quartet, it changed its name in 1953 to the more co-op sounding MJQ. Their first recording as the MJQ in that year showed an early penchant for an arranged sound, in contrast to the freewheeling nature of most bop-influenced groups. They avoided the theme–solo–solo–solo–theme predictability and favored a more structured, at times classically influenced, light sound. Improvised counterpoint in the tradition of European classical-music composers became the MJQ's hallmark, as was their dapper attire of smartly styled, tailored suits—an influence, no doubt, years later on Wynton Marsalis and his cohorts in the 1980s. "I am an American Negro," MJQ pianist John Lewis said, and "I'm proud of it and want to enhance the dignity of that position."[3] Duke Ellington and Lewis were similar bedfellows in this regard, and both produced dignified jazz suitable to the most elegant concert halls. "Django," dedicated to the Belgian guitarist, is one of the best-known works by the MJQ and it appeared on their second recording. "Django" is included on the *SCCJ* (any edition). Their dignified, refined, and polished brand of jazz made them attractive to a wide range of audiences and performance venues. On the other hand, some felt their music was pretentious, but, under the musical leadership of John Lewis, the quartet broke new ground for many years. Lewis, like Gunther Schuller and J.J. Johnson, was serious in his efforts to elevate jazz to the same high plateau as European art music. All three of these musicians were at the center of the third-stream movement, born in the mid 1950s, to bring together elements of jazz and aspects of European concert music. At the time, this style had little impact, influence, or following, and it was not until years later that its repercussions would be of value.

Gerry Mulligan (1927–1996) and Chet Baker (1929–1988)

Baritone saxophonist Gerry Mulligan and West-Coast-native son Chet Baker on trumpet are justifiably also given much credit for advancing the cool-jazz style on the West Coast. Mulligan was a stylistically versatile baritone saxophonist who could mix comfortably, jamming with musicians from any era. He played an unusual instrument mastered by very few and, coupled with his gift as a composer/arranger, left an indelible mark on jazz history. Pianist/composer George Russell called him "the most important innovator of the 1950s."[4] Like so many musicians from the 1950s, Mulligan cut his teeth as a member of numerous big bands. He met Gil Evans as a result of his employment as an arranger for the Thornhill band, after a stint with Gene Krupa's mid 1940s big swing band. Following his collaborations with Evans on the *Birth of the Cool* sessions, Mulligan moved to sunny California, where he conceived the piano-less quartet. His first quartet featured the young Chet Baker, recently discharged from the armed services. Baker had sat in with Charlie Parker earlier in his career, but had begun to formulate a more lyrical, wistful style than that associated with bop. Baker's romantic, abbreviated vocal and instrumental style helped to define the new cool style, while also serving to make him and the quartet very popular. Baker, who struggled through life with drug addiction, could be compared to James Dean, the young, good-looking 1950s actor who played the youthful, troubled soul on the silver screen. The resemblance between the two was remarkable, and both projected the misunderstood, rebellious, brooding, sensitive image that represented the anti-establishment ideals of the younger generation. Many lived on the fringe, as did Baker. Baker's success as a trumpet player and vocalist prompted

LISTENING GUIDE

Gerry Mulligan Quartet with Chet Baker

"Line for Lyons"

Recorded 9/2/1952, Fantasy EP 4028

Reissued on OJC, OJCCD-711–2

Personnel: Gerry Mulligan, baritone saxophone; Chet Baker, trumpet; Carson Smith, bass; Chico Hamilton, drums

Form: Repeated 32-bar-song form (AA^{1}BA^2 = chorus), in G major

0:00–00:22	First chorus—32 bars, melody:
0:00–0:11	A section—8 bars, trumpet plays melody, with accompanying sax counter-line and swinging bass and drums
0:11–0:22	A^1 section—8 bars, trumpet plays slightly varied melody, with sax and rhythm similar to A section
0:23–0:34	B section—8 bars, trumpet plays bridge melody with answering sax counter-line and swinging bass and drums
0:35–0:46	A^2 section—8 bars, trumpet plays slightly varied melody, with sax and rhythm similar to A section
0:46–1:33	Second chorus—32-bar sax solo/trumpet solo:
0:46–0:57	A section—8 bars, sax improvises solo over chorus chord changes, with swinging bass and drums, trumpet tacet
0:58–1:09	A^1 section—8 bars, sax continues improvised solo
1:10–1:21	B section—8 bars, trumpet improvises solo over bridge chord changes, with sustained descending sax counter-line, swinging rhythm section
1:22–1:33	A^2 section—8 bars, trumpet continues solo, with long sax counter-line
1:34–2:30	Third chorus—35-bar sax/trumpet solo and melody with tag:
1:34–1:45	A section—8 bars, sax and trumpet improvise solo together, using fragments of the melody
1:45–1:57	A^1 section—8 bars, sax and trumpet improvise, similar to previous A section
1:57–2:09	B section—8 bars, trumpet plays bridge melody similar to first B section, with answering sax counter-line and swinging bass and drums
2:10–2:30	A^2 section—8 bars, trumpet plays melody as in first A section, with accompanying sax counter-line and swinging bass and drums; 3-bar ending tag repeats last line of melody

Listen to the interviews with Gerry Mulligan, who talks about Chet Baker and the famous piano-less quartet. These excerpts can be found on the website in the corresponding chapter.

him to strike out on his own, performing and recording in Europe and the US with a number of different partners and rhythm sections. He was replaced in the Mulligan quartet by valve trombonist/composer Bob Brookmeyer and, later, flugelhornist Art Farmer. Brookmeyer has distinguished himself since as one of the foremost modern jazz composers, frequently working in Europe and teaching in his later years.

The Mulligan–Baker quartet was unique in that there was no piano or guitar, leaving only single-line performers. Mulligan felt that the absence of a chording instrument freed the soloists to become more melodically inventive, as they would not be bound to the pianist's chords. The result was pure melody in counterpoint between bass and the two horns. Their style was relaxed, detached, and rhythmically subdued. Melodic clichés that had become associated with the bop style were almost completely absent in the Baker–Mulligan quartet performances. Mulligan described his music to *Down Beat* magazine as,

> Pipe and slipper music. I like jazz that is easy and quiet with a subtle swing. Lester Young used to get a sound on his horn that I would like to get with my whole group. Jazz is an art of many emotions; ours is to relax and build from a comfortable position.[5]

"Line for Lyons," included in the online audio anthology, was composed as a tribute to west-coast jazz entrepreneur and festival promoter Jimmy Lyons. Their performance on this track is exemplary of the improvisational style associated with this period of jazz, where the **contrapuntal** dialogue between the two instrumentalists almost makes the listener forget that there is no piano or guitar accompaniment. Their improvisations are reserved, lyrical, and not overbearing.

Mulligan appeared in several movies, including *I Want to Live* (1958) and the 1960 beatnik flick *The Subterraneans*. By the early 1960s, Mulligan abandoned the small group and founded the Concert Jazz Band, which played challenging, big-band compositions featuring some of the finest New York musicians of the day, including trumpeters Clark Terry and Doc Severinsen of television's *Tonight Show* fame. He also appeared on record with numerous pairings, including record dates with Ben Webster, Stan Getz, Thelonious Monk, Johnny Hodges, and Paul Desmond. The *Two of a Mind* recording with Paul Desmond is one of the finest examples of improvised duet playing in a piano-less quartet setting.

DAVE BRUBECK (1920–2012)

Although it is true that many of the players who became involved in the cool movement were based on the West Coast, Mulligan, Davis, J.J. Johnson, and others involved in the *Birth of the Cool* sessions were part of the New York scene and key players in the bop trend a few years earlier. Unlike these Easterners, Dave Brubeck was a west-coast native son. Born and raised in the northern farmlands of California, Brubeck attended the University (then College) of the Pacific in Stockton, studying classical composition and piano. It is here that his archives now reside and here that he formed his first groups. Very few recordings of his early octet exist, but we do know that its style was the precursor of what Brubeck eventually became famous for—merging jazz with "classical" techniques. Perhaps no one is more closely associated with the west-coast style, and no one was more successful and controversial at the same time. Critics have either loved or despised his brand of jazz, but it was all this publicity, pro and con, that helped to catapult him to fame in the mid 1950s. Not many other jazz artists can lay claim to being on the cover of *Time* magazine—an honor bestowed on Brubeck in 1955. In retrospect, his music was more important then than it is now, but he nevertheless served as an important link in the history of jazz. Most critics who leveled criticism at his quartet claimed that it did not swing and had not assimilated the roots of jazz. His critics felt that his music was too compositionally derived and lacked the improvisational spontaneity of the jazz-jam-session atmosphere. Such criticism is often directed at new jazz that breaks from mainstream traditions, as was the case with Brubeck and avant-garde artists who followed.

When Brubeck was praised, it seemed almost begrudgingly, but it is irrefutable that his quartet was rhythmically charged, producing unexpected accents, heavy-handed piano accompaniments, and experiments in odd meter signatures. For example, he was known to play in one meter and tempo, while the rhythm section forged ahead in another, creating mesmerizing polymetric tensions. His piano style was very chordal, using big blocks of chords, rather than the fast, single-line passages associated with the bop pianists. In contrast, Brubeck's quartet avoided the now cliché-ridden bop style, favoring modern "classical" composition devices such as contrapuntal interplay, and he relied on saxophonist Paul Desmond to help inspire improvisational dialogue. They resorted to blues tunes later in their careers, but Brubeck's earlier music was harmonically rich and fresher, drawing from a contemporary "classical" palette, which he used to influence arrangements of standard tunes. He studied "classical" composition with renowned French composer Darius Milhaud, who himself had been influenced by jazz, and so the influences went full circle. (See the supplementary chapter included on the website for additional information about the marriage of jazz and classical music. Third-stream jazz is discussed later in this chapter.)

Like other white bands before his, led by Beiderbecke, Trumbauer, and Goodman, Brubeck's quartet brought jazz out of the urban taverns that had spawned it, developing a marketable niche on the college concert circuit. His success encouraged others to follow suit, including the important cool-style black combo the MJQ, featuring pianist John Lewis and Milt Jackson on vibes. The campus market for jazz grew greatly during the 1950s, and Brubeck's quartet cashed in before the market was swept away by the rock 'n' roll phenomenon of the 1960s.

The tune that served to make Brubeck and his quartet familiar to households worldwide was "Take Five," composed by his long-time associate, alto saxophonist Paul Desmond. Contemporary pop artist Billy Joel is reputed to have said that this tune was as important to him as "Sergeant Pepper's" was to the Beatles and rock 'n' roll, nearly a decade later.[6]

Paul Desmond (1924–1977) was an anomaly in the continuum of jazz saxophonists. His playing was in direct opposition to the trend of creating an edgier, harsher, and more aggressive, brittle tone. Instead, he chose to model his serene, demure, lyrical, and dry sound on the earlier black tenor saxophonist Lester Young. A would-be writer, Desmond was intelligent, well read, and witty, often poking fun at his own playing. He once said that he was "unfashionable before anyone knew who he was. I wanted to sound like a dry martini."[7] Although, to some degree, he may have been right in his self-assessment and criticism, he influenced at least one generation of

The Dave Brubeck Quartet, with Brubeck at the piano, Paul Desmond on saxophone, Eugene Wright on bass, and Joe Morello on drums, in 1959

young players and has never really been copied. Writer Gene Lees described him as "the loneliest man [he] ever knew,"[8] and at times his playing is melancholy. His high register is unmistakable in its crystalline, almost classical-sounding purity, which in some ways made him the perfect partner for Brubeck, counterbalancing his own flowing, perfectly developed melodic lines with the pianist's rhythmic, chordal, and percussive style.

Despite its unconventional approach to jazz, the Brubeck quartet, collectively and as individuals, soared in popularity, releasing a new record every 4 months or so and winning polls in *Down Beat*, *Metronome*, and *Playboy* magazines. It is amazing to realize that the quartet not only survived the 1960s, but also flourished, despite the rock 'n' roll sensation that had begun to take the country by storm.

"Take Five" represents the more popular side of the Brubeck Quartet, and the track was released as a longer LP version and a shorter, edited, ready-for-radio 45-rpm record. Although some critics may not have accepted this track as great jazz, millions of listeners, including some who may not have been aware of jazz, turned on to the tune's memorable melody and rhythm vamp that served as a bed for improvisations by Desmond and drummer Joe Morello. What makes the success of this song even more phenomenal is that it was written in 5/4 meter, rendering it a non-danceable form of jazz. Desmond was as surprised as anyone that it was so widely acclaimed, as his only goal had been to compose a simple tune to serve as a canvas for a drum-solo feature.

LISTENING GUIDE

Dave Brubeck Quartet

"Take Five" (Desmond) 2:52 (short version)

Recorded July 1959, New York City, "Time Out", Columbia

Reissued on Sony Legacy Records

Personnel: Dave Brubeck, piano; Paul Desmond, alto saxophone; Gene Wright, bass; Joe Morrello, drums

Form: 24-bar-song form melody (ABA) in 5/4 time

0:00–0:22	Introduction—12 bars, drums, piano, bass: 4-bar staggered entrances of drums, piano, and bass set up 5/4 groove
0:22–1:06	Opening melody section—24-bar melody:
0:22–0:36	A section—8 bars, alto sax plays melody in two similar 4-bar phrases, with continuing swinging 5/4 piano, bass, and drum groove on vamp
0:37–0:51	B section—8 bars, alto sax plays bridge melody in two similar 4-bar phrases
0:52–1:06	A section—8 bars, alto sax plays melody similar to opening A section
1:07–1:58	Solo section—28-bar alto sax solo: improvised sax solo over tonic (E flat) chord, and swinging 5/4 rhythm-section accompaniment
1:59–2:18	Solo section—11-bar drum solo: improvised drum solo, with continuing piano and bass 5/4 swinging groove
2:19–2:33	Closing melody section—8-bar melody: sax plays A section of melody, similar to opening A section
2:33–2:52	Ending tag—9 bars, sax repeats last melody fragment over 5/4 tonic chord groove in rhythm section

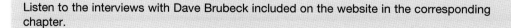

Listen to the interviews with Dave Brubeck included on the website in the corresponding chapter.

Bill Evans (1929–1980)

Pianist Bill Evans, one of a long line of pianists who served with Miles Davis's bands, revolutionized the jazz trio of piano, bass, and drums. In addition, his innovations as a pianist served to influence future generations of pianists, including Herbie Hancock, Chick Corea, and Keith Jarrett, among others. His first important collaboration was as a member of composer George Russell's small groups, where he premiered Russell's famous "Concerto For Billy the Kid." In 1958, he joined the Miles Davis Quintet during the pivotal years when the new modal approach (discussed in Chapter 12) was being developed. It was with this quintet, and in his prior work with Russell, that Evans began to demonstrate a mastery of the keyboard, technically and harmonically unique in the development of jazz-piano styling. Although he had the facility to "burn" like Bud Powell at fast tempos, he also favored a sensitive touch in

Pianist Bill Evans

the ballad tradition. Ballads were Evans's forte, and he was known for very slow tempi that benefited his lush, sensuous, harmonic approach. His trios featured a revolving collection of bassists and drummers over his lifetime, setting a new standard in modern jazz. They developed a sense of improvised interplay by liberating the bassist from playing walking bass lines for involvement in a more melodic dialogue with the pianist. Evans's technique was refined and fluid, although he varied his right-hand melodic approach with a more rhythmic, close block-chord solo style known as **locked hands style**. This more rhythmic, chord style of playing, along with his penchant

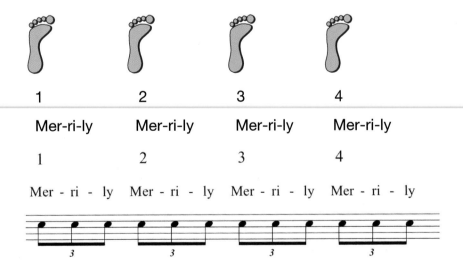

EXAMPLE 10.1 Eighth-note triplets

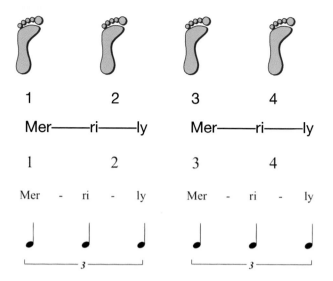

EXAMPLE 10.2 Quarter-note triplets

for juxtaposing one meter or tempo with another, showed a certain kinship with Brubeck's work, although Brubeck tends to have a heavier touch at the keyboard. Evans favored the tension created by long lines of triplet patterns (groups of three) over the relentless pulse laid down by bass and drums emphasizing 4/4 meter, creating a polymetric illusion. Try tapping your feet in a regular pulse while saying *mer-ri-ly, mer-ri-ly, mer-ri-ly, mer-ri-ly*, as shown in the exercises in Examples 10.1 and 10.2.

The space that Evans left in his improvised phrases was purposeful, allowing the drums and bass to provide their own musical commentary. The lines were often blurred, and at times it was difficult to tell who the featured soloist was. The titles of Evans's recordings not only reflected his musical style, but also captured his muse, by projecting his forward-looking, introspective, experimental, and cerebral creative process. Titles such as *Explorations, Interplay, Intuition, Quintessence*, and *Moonbeams* are good examples, along with the popular solo recording *Conversations with Myself*, where Evans took advantage of new multi-track recording technologies, enabling him to improvise in counterpoint with his previously recorded tracks, the result sounding like three pianists playing simultaneously.

The Evans trio style developed to its most advanced stage with young bassist Scott LaFaro. With LaFaro and drummer Paul Motian, Evans's trio developed a sense of free rhythmic and melodic interplay that was truly telepathic—like three minds thinking as one. The polyphonic, contrapuntal dialogue between Evans's and LaFaro's irregular, non-walking bass lines illustrated a unique collaboration never before achieved. LaFaro, with his classical training, was perhaps the most important new voice, as he brought into focus an entirely new concept of bass playing that was more melodic and horn-like. While the walking style had been the most important innovation to occur during the Swing Era, LaFaro's more liberated, soloistic style is viewed as the next most important change in jazz-bass performance practice.

The website includes an excellent audio example, along with the tune discussed below, that exemplifies the interactive-dialogue improvised style developed by pianist Bill Evans and bassist Scott LaFaro. This example is the last example under the discussion of the bass in the "Performance Practice" section of the "Elements of Music" section.

LISTENING GUIDE

Bill Evans Trio

"Witchcraft" (Leigh-Coleman) 4:30

Recorded 12/28/1959 New York City,

CD: Riverside 12–315

Personnel: Bill Evans, piano; Scott LaFaro, bass; Paul Motian, drums

Form: Repeated 40-bar-song form choruses (ABCDA[1])

0:00–0:52	**First chorus**—40 bars
0:00–0:10	A section—8 bars, piano plays song melody in block chord style, with improvised bass fills and swinging groove with brushes on drums
0:11–0:21	B section—8 bars, piano continues song melody in block-chord style, with bass fills and swinging drums
0:21–0:31	C section—8 bars, piano plays melody in single-note style, with syncopated repeated pattern in bass, swinging groove in drums
0:31–0:41	D section—8 bars, piano plays melody in single-note style, bass walks with swinging drums
0:42–0:52	A[1] section—8 bars, piano returns to block-chord-style melody, with improvised bass fills
0:52–1:44	**Second chorus**—40 bars, piano and bass solo
0:53–1:02	A section—8 bars, piano and bass solo together over song chord changes, creating interweaving lines in conversational style, with swinging drums
1:03–1:13	B section—8 bars, continues as in previous A section
1:14–1:23	C section—8 bars, piano continues improvised solo, with repeated bass pattern similar to first chorus C section
1:24–1:34	D section—8 bars, piano continues solo, with walking bass and swinging drums similar to first chorus D section
1:34–1:44	A[1] section—8 bars, piano and bass solo continues as in previous A section
1:45–2:36	**Third chorus**—40 bars, piano solo
1:45–1:55	A section—8 bars, piano continues solo with walking bass and swinging drums
1:55–2:05	B section—8 bars, piano continues solo with walking bass and swinging drums
2:06–2:15	C section—8 bars, piano continues solo with repeated syncopated bass pattern similar to previous C sections
2:16–2:26	D section—8 bars, piano solos with walking bass and swinging drums, similar to previous D sections
2:26–2:37	A[1] section—8 bars, piano solos with walking bass and swinging drums
2:37–3:29	**Fourth chorus**—40 bars, bass solo: bass improvises with occasional piano "comments," swinging drums
3:29–4:32	**Fifth chorus**—47 bars
3:29–3:39	A section—8 bars, piano plays varied melody in block-chord style, similar to first chorus A section
3:40–3:50	B section—8 bars, piano plays melody in single-note style, with walking bass
3:50–4:00	C section—8 bars, piano continues single-note melody with repeated syncopated bass pattern, similar to previous C sections
4:01–4:10	D section—8 bars, piano continues single-note melody, with walking bass
4:11–4:32	A[1] section with ending tag—15 bars, piano plays varied melody in block-chord style, with improvised bass fills, similar to first-chorus A section; added 7-bar ending tag

Drummer Marty Morrell, who performed and recorded extensively with Evans's trio in the mid 1960s, recently commented:

> Bill was a complete musician, totally immersed in his music and deeply committed to it. He was incredibly organized and planned his sets very carefully to ensure that one tune flowed into another so the performance was as musical an experience as possible. Bill's music was the perfect projection of his personality—sensitive and highly emotional. Nothing about his music was superfluous. Each solo was well paced, never too long and with every note perfectly placed within each phrase making for a perfectly balanced and organized improvisation. He played like a painter—every stroke had special meaning and contributed to the whole picture.[9]

In terms of repertoire, Evans, like most cool-style musicians, avoided the blues and focused on original material coupled with reworked, obscure standards not usually performed. Outside the trio context, his collaborations with Getz, guitarist Jim Hall, and singer Tony Bennett represent the highest level of performance. Despite his problems with drug addiction, Evans continued to play a significant role in jazz up until his premature death in 1980, at the age of 51. Although he may not be the classic cool artist, he emerged during this period, and his music reflects some of the characteristics of this style. Bill Evans never produced a mediocre recording, maintaining the highest level of musical integrity throughout his abbreviated career.

Listen to the interview with Bill Evans included on the companion website and found in the corresponding chapter.

THE BRAZILIAN BOSSA NOVA

Slavery of Africans in Brazil existed for over three centuries, until it was abolished in the late 1800s. African rhythmic practices are, therefore, evident in much Brazilian music. For example, the Brazilian **samba** can be traced to dance forms from Africa's Angola and Congo regions. Syncopated ostinato rhythm patterns shown in the following example serve as the foundation of what became a popular ballroom dance style in the 1930s and 1940s and served as the foundation for the creation of the bossa nova. The samba style also became popular among 1970s jazz artists. The last of these examples is clearly related to the habanera, introduced in an earlier chapter.

The fact that Brazilian music is rhythmically rich, harmonically wealthy, and in part African derived, is no doubt why jazz artists were eventually drawn to this music.

The bossa nova is a later derivative of the samba, and the term is Portuguese slang for the "new wrinkle" or the "new touch." It is played at various tempi, but rarely very fast. Although, at times, there can be an almost subliminal similarity between the clavé, samba, and the bossa nova rhythm patterns, the bossa nova is actually a discretely different rhythmic style. The basic bossa nova rhythm, which is highly syncopated, is shown in Example 10.4 on p. 243. Both the samba and bossa nova are dance styles associated with Brazil's four-day *Carnaval* celebration, which features a countrywide celebration of street dances, parties, and parades, culminating in Mardi Gras. The Mardi Gras tradition has spread to many parts of the US, especially the southernmost cities.

The pattern shown in Example 10.4 represents a graphic interpretation of a fundamental bossa nova rhythm pattern. Try tapping your foot and clapping the syncopated accents that capture the essence of the bossa nova rhythm.

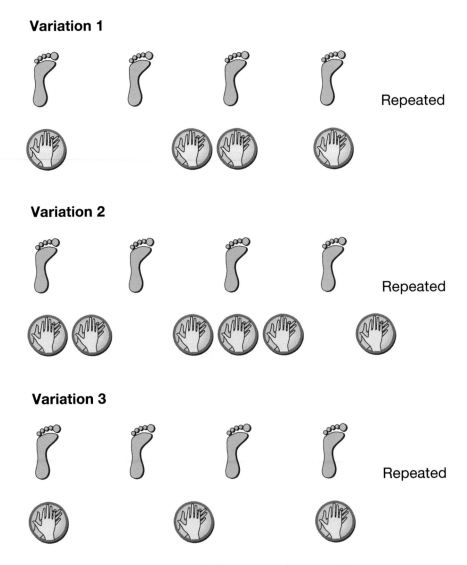

Variation 1

Repeated

Variation 2

Repeated

Variation 3

Repeated

EXAMPLE 10.3 Samba rhythmic ostinato patterns; the foot image represents downward taps

Traditionally, the guitar maintains the fundamental, highly syncopated bossa nova rhythm pattern, reinforced by the drummer. The Stan Getz recording included in the companion anthology follows this scheme. Although the pattern can vary, as is the case on this recording, the essential syncopated rhythms that serve as the foundation of this style continue without interruption, helping the music to glide along.

Antonio Carlos Jobim was known to have been influenced by the cool, West-Coast jazz style, as was Brazilian guitarist Laurindo Almeida, who took up residence in Los Angeles during the peak cool years. The stage was set so the marriage between jazz and sophisticated Brazilian popular music seemed almost inevitable. Jobim and his guitarist/singer João Gilberto are accredited with developing the samba-related bossa nova style. This style had an impact on a number of American jazz artists, such as flutist Herbie Mann, Stan Kenton, and Dizzy Gillespie, who tried to exploit the use of Brazilian elements in American jazz even before they skyrocketed to widespread popularity in the US in the early 1960s. Almeida also teamed with west-coast artists such as saxophonist Bud Shank, Kenton, and others, but it wasn't until Stan Getz and his comrades,

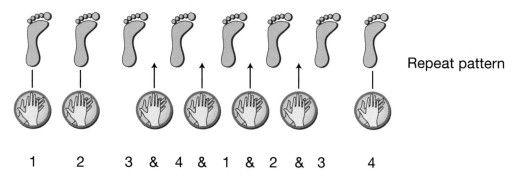

Repeat pattern

1   2   3 & 4 & 1 & 2 & 3   4

EXAMPLE 10.4 Hand clapping syncopated bossa nova rhythm—syncopated tensions occur when hand claps fall between the foot taps. There are numerous variations on the ostinato bossa nova rhythm patterns

including guitarist Charlie Byrd, traveled to Central and South America in 1961 on a State Department tour that the marriage between these styles became consummated and commercially successful. In 1962, they recorded *Jazz Samba*, which rose to be a number 1 hit on the *Billboard* magazine pop charts. Its unexpected, overwhelming success launched the bossa nova craze in America. According to *Jazz Times* author David Adler, the bossa nova served as a bridge between the fading influences of the great American songbook composers, such as George Gershwin and Cole Porter, and the rise in popularity of rock 'n' roll.

STAN GETZ (1927–1991)

Stan Getz was a tenor saxophonist who, like baritone saxophonist Mulligan, was at home in many different jazz styles. Perhaps it is his musical connection to Lester Young's melodic style and sound that explains why Getz is so often considered in discussions of the cool sound. Young, along with Bix Beiderbecke, is often considered one of the earliest forefathers of the cool sound, offering an alternative to the Coleman Hawkins and Louis Armstrong hot heritage. Getz first appeared on the scene, however, in the midst of the bebop revolution, gaining widespread exposure initially through his association with the more modern Woody Herman big band. It was here that he helped to establish the famous "Four Brothers" Herman saxophone section. His hit solo on Herman's recording of "Early Autumn" served as the necessary springboard to leader status, and he recorded his first quartet sides in the late 1940s. Like so many white, cool-era players, Getz had learned to create a style that was fresh and free of many of the clichéd bopisms associated with Parker and his crowd. What makes Getz somewhat difficult to classify is his chameleon-like style, for he could comfortably play hot, swinging solos, and yet was equally at home in the more subdued, cool style of the 1950s. He was fairly inactive for much of the 1950s, as he struggled to conquer drug addiction, and it was his ingenious recording of Eddie Sauter's *Focus*, a suite for strings and rhythm, that helped to restart his career.

Although Getz was instrumental in launching the bossa nova jazz craze, initially with his recording of "Desafinando" from the successful *Jazz Samba* album, it was his follow-up recordings with Brazilian singers such as Astrud and João Gilberto that pushed his career over the top, winning him Album and Record of the Year for the ever-popular "The Girl From Ipanema." *Billboard*'s pop charts only showed the Beatles' *A Hard Day's Night* ahead of this initial Getz/Gilberto collaboration. The bossa nova soundtrack of the award-winning film *Black Orpheus* also played a significant part in raising American audiences' awareness of this popular, native Brazilian folk style. "Corcovado" (also known as "Quiet Nights"), "One Note Samba," and "How Insensitive" were all popular recordings that followed, introducing the Brazilian samba, a number of Brazilian musicians, and a battery of native percussion instruments to American audiences. Getz's light, airy sound was a wonderful complement to the wispy, vibrato-less sound of the Brazilian vocalists. An analogy could be made to the musical rapport that also existed between Lester Young and Billie Holiday, whose two sounds were symbiotic. Getz had always had a penchant for romantic ballads and was drawn to the similar sultry, romantic quality in Brazilian music. It is the combination of lyrical, romantic, and twisting melodies with the busy rhythms that provides an element of tension that is the essence of the bossa nova style.

The jazz bossa nova recordings released by Getz, and by a host of others who capitalized on the "easy listening" nature of this music, were a huge success in the US, selling millions of records. Even AM radio stations aired 45-rpm single versions of these hits. It is difficult to achieve commercial success without compromising artistic integrity, but Getz did just this with his immensely popular bossa nova recordings. Getz, in a 1990 interview with Terry Gross on her NPR syndicated *Fresh Air* program, explained why he was drawn to this Brazilian style: "[The bossa nova] is very beautiful music with suggestive, laid back rhythms. The melodies are beautiful, sad and romantic. It's a folk music and all folk music is beautiful and it goes perfectly with jazz."[10]

In the following song, included in the online audio anthology, Getz demonstrates his ease at improvising in this genre and is accompanied by the famous Brazilian guitarist/singer João Gilberto. Although the title suggests that it is a samba, the guitar and drum patterns more closely resemble the rhythmic style of a medium-fast bossa nova. The bossa nova and samba are Brazilian folk-dance rhythms. Getz's solo is certainly one of the happiest on record in this style, demonstrating his facility in improvising complex double-time phrases, tempered by sultry blues-derived lines. Also of note in this session is the participation of pianist Antonio Carlos Jobim, who is undeniably the most recognized composer of Brazilian bossa novas and sambas.

Stan Getz in a live performance

LISTENING GUIDE

Stan Getz/João Gilberto

"So Danço Samba" (de Moraes, Jobim) 2:33 (excerpt)

Recorded New York City, 3/18–19/1963, Verve LP 8858651

CD reissue, Verve 810 048

Personnel: Stan Getz, tenor saxophone; Astrud Gilberto, vocals; João Gilberto, guitar, vocals; Milton Banana, drums; Tommy Williams, bass; Antonio Carlos Jobim, piano	
Form: Repeated song form (AABA = chorus)	
0:00–0:05	Introduction—4-bar guitar and piano sets up bossa nova groove
0:06–0:51	First chorus—32-bar vocal melody:
0:06–0:16	A section—8-bar vocal (João Gilberto) in Brazilian Portuguese, with guitar, bass, and drums accompaniment
0:17–0:28	A section—8-bar vocal, similar to A section
0:28–0:39	B section—8-bar vocal bridge, similar to A section
0:40–0:51	A section—8-bar vocal, similar to previous A sections
0:52–1:38	Second chorus—32-bar tenor sax solo: improvised tenor sax solo with bossa nova rhythm-section accompaniment, key change to F major
1:39–2:25	Third chorus—32-bar tenor sax solo: continued tenor sax solo, key change to A-flat major
2:25–2:33	Fourth chorus—(fades out) tenor sax returns to melody

THIRD-STREAM JAZZ

The fact that significant jazz and classical composers as well as performers (Miles Davis, J.J. Johnson, John Lewis, Duke Ellington, Charles Mingus, and Gunther Schuller) were attracted to the idea of merging certain aspects of the jazz tradition with classical composition techniques and instrumentations lends credibility to the third-stream jazz movement. Although the product of this movement in the mid and late 1950s through early 1960s was not particularly attractive to the general public, nor for that matter to many of the mainstream jazz musicians, it was a movement that has endured, had lasting influence, and gained some momentum as time passed.

Two landmark recordings from the mid 1950s serve to document the work of crossover composers. J.J. Johnson, Gunther Schuller, John Lewis, Milton Babbit, Charles Mingus, Duke Ellington, and George Russell represent the wide range of possibilities for composers who are open to the influences of both music styles. It was Schuller, a true Renaissance man in this age of specialization, who participated in the movement and coined the term "third stream" to describe it. As European classical art music is labeled the first stream, and American jazz the second, the term "third stream" seemed appropriate to describe a style of music that combined elements of both traditions. It was a logical direction for jazz composers to pursue, as, by the late 1950s, jazz had developed a strong tradition, with an identity and repertoire that could now withstand the risk of affiliations with the music from which its founders had initially sought distance. Jazz pianist/composer John Lewis described it as a "hybrid," while Schuller used the term to include music that "attempts to fuse the essential characteristics of jazz and so called 'classical' music."[11] Although third-stream jazz was far more structured and organized from the compositional standpoint than any other style of jazz, composers who work in this style seek to create pieces that present the illusion or impression of spontaneity that is so essential to good jazz. The problem these composers faced was in creating music that was tightly controlled, while also allowing the important elements of jazz—rhythmic vitality, spontaneity, and the essential element of improvisation—to rule. As many of the pieces from the heart of this period show, this union was a tall order and one that often went unsatisfied. Consequently, much of the original music labeled "third stream" was not well received by either the jazz audience or the classical crowd. In Schuller's own words:

Tristano was praised as *Metronome* magazine's "Musician of the Year" in 1947, but his recordings were largely unsuccessful from a commercial standpoint, and Tristano turned to teaching. His music was an anomaly in the midst of bebop and cool. His style was based on long improvised lines, often played without swing and devoid of any reference to bop clichés. His tunes were sometimes harmonically complex, forcing the soloists to radically depart from the well-trodden path laid by the bop generation. Much like Art Tatum, Tristano and his music defied categorization, although he is generally associated with this period of increased intellectual developments and cool jazz.

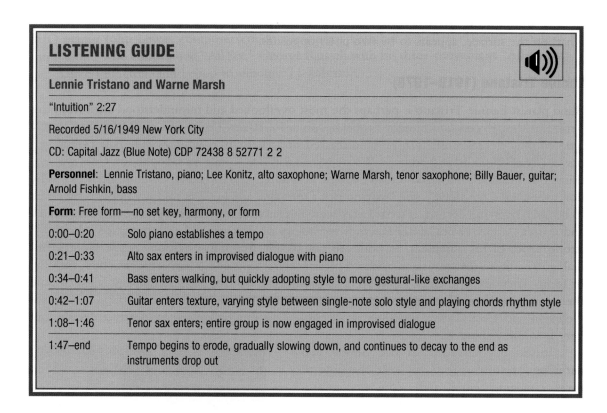

LISTENING GUIDE

Lennie Tristano and Warne Marsh

"Intuition" 2:27

Recorded 5/16/1949 New York City

CD: Capital Jazz (Blue Note) CDP 72438 8 52771 2 2

Personnel: Lennie Tristano, piano; Lee Konitz, alto saxophone; Warne Marsh, tenor saxophone; Billy Bauer, guitar; Arnold Fishkin, bass

Form: Free form—no set key, harmony, or form

0:00–0:20	Solo piano establishes a tempo
0:21–0:33	Alto sax enters in improvised dialogue with piano
0:34–0:41	Bass enters walking, but quickly adopting style to more gestural-like exchanges
0:42–1:07	Guitar enters texture, varying style between single-note solo style and playing chords rhythm style
1:08–1:46	Tenor sax enters; entire group is now engaged in improvised dialogue
1:47–end	Tempo begins to erode, gradually slowing down, and continues to decay to the end as instruments drop out

WHO WAS POPULAR

Others who contributed to the West-Coast, cool sound found that being based in the Hollywood area led to more lucrative careers in film and television studios and ended their careers as full-time jazz musicians. The popular poll winners throughout this decade were Dave Brubeck, the MJQ, Miles Davis, Paul Desmond, J.J. Johnson, drummer Shelly Manne, Gil Evans as arranger, Stan Getz, Gerry Mulligan, Chet Baker, and the progressive, adventuresome big band fronted by Stan Kenton. In the vocal categories, Ella Fitzgerald continued to capture the attention of fans and critics, along with Frank Sinatra, whose style and demeanor wowed the women and sold millions of records in the 1950s.

MILESTONES

Chronicle of Historic Events

The timeline that follows will put the developments of jazz discussed in this chapter into a larger historical context, providing you with a better sense of how landmark musical events may relate to others that match your personal areas of interest.

1949	• Rodgers and Hammerstein create Broadway musical *South Pacific*.
	• Harry S. Truman wins the presidential election.
	• *The Lone Ranger* debuts on TV.
	• Arthur Miller's play *Death of a Salesman* wins a Pulitzer Prize.
1950	• Senator McCarthy denounces communism and begins efforts to purge the U.S. of all members of this party, blacklisting many well-known personalities.
	• The U.S. backs South Korea against North Korea.
	• William Faulkner wins a Nobel Prize for Literature, and Ralph Bunch wins the Peace Prize.
	• The U.S. census indicates there are 150 million people in the US.
	• The cold war begins.
	• Miles Davis and cohorts record the famous *Birth of the Cool* sessions.
1951	• The US detonates an H-Bomb.
	• The UNIVAC electronic, digital computer is unveiled.
	• *I Love Lucy* is an instant TV success.
1952	• *Mad Magazine* is first published.
	• Dwight "Ike" Eisenhower is elected 34th president.
	• Gerry Mulligan and Chet Baker record "Line for Lyons" with their piano-less quartet.
	• Author Ralph Ellison's *Invisible Man* presents the black man's underworld.
1953	• McDonald's fast-food hamburger chain begins.
	• McCarthy and the House Committee on Un-American Activities continue to persecute many artists, poets, writers, actors, and other intelligensia.
	• After 3 years, the Korean War draws to a close, but not before there are 3 million casualties.
	• Marilyn Monroe becomes a film sex symbol.
1954	• The Brown Vs. Board of Education decision by the courts is a key victory for the NAACP and desegregation movement—the Supreme Court rules against school segregation.
	• Ernest Hemingway wins a Nobel Prize for Literature.
	• McCarthy and the communist witch-hunt are condemned.
	• The first Newport Jazz Festival is a success.
1955	• The minimum wage is set at $1.
	• African-American Rosa Parks is arrested in Alabama for not giving up her bus seat.
1956	• Civil rights advocate Martin Luther King has his home bombed.
	• *Peyton Place* by Grace Metalious becomes a bestseller.
	• The musical *My Fair Lady* hits Broadway.

- Top films include *Invasion of the Body Snatchers*, *The Ten Commandments*, and *Bus Stop*.

- The University of Alabama is sued for banning blacks from enrolling.

- Elvis Presley becomes a rock 'n' roll idol.

- Bus segregation is declared unconstitutional.

- The University of Chicago develops the first nuclear power plant.

1957
- John F. Kennedy is awarded a Pulitzer Prize for *Profiles in Courage*.

- Count Basie's band becomes the first black band to perform at New York City's Waldorf-Astoria Hotel.

- President Eisenhower sends federal troops to assist the integration of Little Rock, Arkansas, schools.

- Leonard Bernstein enjoys a hit with his musical *West Side Story*.

- Beat author Jack Kerouac publishes *On the Road*.

1958
- Texan Van Cliburn wins the Tchaikovsky Piano Competition.

- NASA is created to bolster the U.S. position in the space race against the USSR.

- The Kingston Trio, Everly Brothers, Little Richard, Rick Nelson, and Chuck Berry are pop music successes.

- A Texas Instruments engineer invents the micro-chip.

1959
- Coast-to-coast flight becomes a reality, along with passenger flights to Europe.

- Jazz singer Billie Holiday dies at age 44.

- Integrated schools open in Little Rock, Arkansas.

- Dictator Fidel Castro takes control of Cuba.

- The Dave Brubeck Quartet becomes popular with its recording of "Take Five."

- Alaska and Hawaii become the 49th and 50th states, respectively.

- *Some Like It Hot* and *Ben Hur* are popular films.

- The Bill Evans trio records "Witchcraft."

CHAPTER SUMMARY

The 1950s was a time of prosperity, but also unrest, in America. The space race, the cold war, the first nuclear power plant, and court rulings in favor of school desegregation all mark the 1950s. Advances in technology with the huge growth of television and hi-fi audio equipment gave parents of the baby-boom generation more reasons to stay home in their leisure time, rather than going out to clubs. These factors and the birth of rock 'n' roll increasingly diverted the public's attention from jazz. One development that served to renew interest in some of the more established jazz groups was the jazz festival, notably the Newport Jazz Festival, which began in 1954 and became an annual event.

Although Miles Davis's *Birth of the Cool* album signaled the beginning of cool jazz, the majority of important cool-jazz artists/groups were white. California was home to a number of influential cool-jazz musicians, leading to the somewhat inaccurate term "West Coast," which, for many, was synonymous with cool jazz. This style, in comparison with bebop, tended to be more subdued and delicate, with few instances of especially loud, high, or fast playing. Other differences contrasting with earlier styles included the use of instruments not normally associated with jazz (French horn, tuba, flute, etc.), very little use of the blues form, mixed meters, and, in some cases, a return to emphasizing the arrangement and ensemble playing.

The quartet featuring baritone saxophonist Gerry Mulligan and trumpeter/vocalist Chet Baker gained much popularity in the 1950s. This group used no piano or other chording instruments, deriving harmony instead from the counterpoint between the bass and two wind instruments. The Dave Brubeck Quartet achieved worldwide fame, especially for selections in odd meters, including "Take Five" (in 5/4 meter) and others. The Modern Jazz Quartet was an important black cool-jazz group, which remained virtually intact for many years. Lennie Tristano led groups in the late 1940s and 1950s that, in addition to playing in a cool style, also recorded the first examples of free jazz, "Intuition" and "Digression," in 1949. Tenor saxophonist Stan Getz was a contributor to numerous styles of jazz, but is best known for his part merging the bossa nova, a Brazilian style, with jazz. Defying classification, Bill Evans's influence as a pianist and leader is undeniable. His trios explored a new concept in rhythm-section playing in which interaction was more important than the traditional roles of piano, bass, and drums.

The term "third stream," coined by Gunther Schuller, refers to a music combining elements of the European classical tradition and jazz. It was a music that lacked much popular appeal and emerged during this period of greater intellectualism in jazz.

Sadly, the 1950s marked the end of a number of brilliant jazz careers and left fans looking for new heroes. Charlie Parker, Fats Navarro, Billie Holliday, Lester Young, Art Tatum, the Dorsey Brothers, Frankie Trumbauer, James P. Johnson, W.C. Handy, Walter Page, and the great young trumpeter discussed in the next chapter, Clifford Brown, all passed on in the 1950s, leaving room for new voices and new directions in jazz. However, before we look too far into the next decade, it is important to examine the other side of jazz in the 1950s, discussed in the next chapter—the African-American mainstream jazz that stemmed from the bebop tradition in the previous decade.

KEY TERMS

Important terms, people, and bands:

Terms
Bossa nova
Contrapuntal
Locked hands style
McCarthyism
Samba
Third stream

People
Chet Baker
Dave Brubeck

Miles Davis
Paul Desmond
Bill Evans
Gil Evans
Stan Getz
Milt Jackson
Antonio Carlos Jobim
J.J. Johnson
Lee Konitz
Scott LaFaro
John Lewis

Warne Marsh
Gerry Mulligan
Lennie Tristano

Bands
Bill Evans Trio
Dave Brubeck Quartet
Gerry Mulligan Quartet
Modern Jazz Quartet

STUDY QUESTIONS

1. What new and unusual instruments not typically associated with jazz were sometimes heard in cool-style bands?

2. What was the first cool recording, and when was it made? What was unique about its instrumentation? Who were the principal musicians, including arrangers, involved in creating this new sound?

3. What was unique about the Mulligan/Baker quartet?

4. Did cool-style jazz attract primarily black or white musicians?

5. Describe and characterize the cool-jazz sound.

6. In what way did Bill Evans change the approach to jazz trio performance?

7. What Chicago-style musicians are credited as early pioneers of the more cool approach to jazz?

8. What is the significance of the MJQ?

9. Describe the political, social, and literary climate during the 1950s, and how there was a parallel to what transpired in the jazz community.

10. Who coined the term "third stream," and what is meant by this term?

11. What great arranger partnered with Miles Davis to contribute some of jazz's most serious concert works?

12. Why was Lennie Tristano important to jazz?

13. Who is the jazz saxophonist identified with the bossa nova jazz movement?

14. Which Dave Brubeck Quartet recording sold over a million records to become one of the most widely recognized instrumental jazz recordings of all time? Can you explain this success?

15. Which quartet was the most popular to emerge from this period?

PART 4

Postmodern Jazz

ART BLAKEY (1919–1990) CARRIES THE MESSAGE

No leader or group better exemplifies the music and attitude of this period than drummer Art Blakey and his Jazz Messengers. Tadd Dameron's late-1940s bebop band, with his identifiable style of composition, is considered the precursor of the Messengers and other like bands in the 1950s and through the early years of the following decade. Art Blakey, along with his first pianist Horace Silver, deserves much of the credit for building on Dameron's tradition and establishing the fundamental 1950s hard-bop sound. Both rhythm-section players are also noted for mentoring generations of young players who, under their tutelage, became leaders in their own right. Blakey was already a veteran by the time he hooked up with Silver, as he had played with many of the important bebop figures. The Jazz Messengers experienced several changes in personnel before it became an established co-operative band in the mid 1950s. The group was first billed as Horace Silver and the Jazz Messengers. Silver by now had also become an established, sought-after sideman, performing and recording with Stan Getz, Oscar Pettiford, and Coleman Hawkins. The group's first outing at Birdland in 1954 produced a two-volume recording entitled *A Night at Birdland with the Art Blakey Quintet*. The quintet featured the amazing young trumpeter Clifford Brown, and this landmark recording set the tone for at least the following decade. Later that year, Blakey and Silver reorganized the band, bringing in seasoned Texas-born trumpeter Kenny Dorham and Philadelphia tenor saxophonist Hank Mobley. This group's first recording for the Blue Note label bore its new name on the cover—*Art Blakey and the Jazz Messengers*—and included Silver's gospel-tinged "The Preacher," along with other toe-tapping, rhythmically driving pieces. Although the personnel stayed intact for only a year, they served their purpose, establishing Blakey as the leader of a dynasty that would reign for four decades. Silver struck out on his own and accomplished similar success with his own quintets. The list of Blakey and Silver sidemen who carried their tradition into the future is as long as it is impressive.

Art Blakey and the Jazz Messengers play at the Birdhouse, a Chicago jazz club, 1961. L–R: Wayne Shorter on saxophone, Art Blakey on drums, and Lee Morgan on trumpet

The group's music was always fresh and original, dictated by these strong horn players and pianists such as Silver and Bobby Timmons, who also composed material for the band. It is Silver and Timmons who are justifiably given credit for developing a major current within the hard-bop mainstream, known as funky jazz, or soul jazz. The Messengers' seminal 1958 recording featuring Timmons's title track "Moanin'" capitalized further on groundwork already established by Silver in his "The Preacher." Listen and follow the analysis of this classic tune included in the accompanying anthology. Its three salient features—(1) a call and response using a church-like amen response; (2) a very definite and aggressive rhythmic style that encourages the listener to tap the beat; and (3) an apparent blues roots—typify the "funky" style. Lee Morgan's trumpet solo on "Moanin'" is drippy with soulful, bluesy gestures, smears, and half-valve techniques that add to the greasy appeal of his solo.

Alto Sax:	**Lou Donaldson**, Gary Bartz, Donald Harrison, **Jackie McLean**, Bobby Watson, **Kenny Garrett**
Tenor Sax:	**Sonny Stitt**, **Benny Golson**, Ira Sullivan, **Johnny Griffin**, **Hank Mobley**, Carter Jefferson, Billy Pierce, Dave Schnitter, **Wayne Shorter**, **Branford Marsalis**, Jean Toussaint, Javon Jackson
Trumpet:	**Clifford Brown**, **Lee Morgan**, **Kenny Dorham**, **Freddie Hubbard**, Bill Hardman, Donald Byrd, **Woody Shaw**, Ira Sullivan, **Chuck Mangione**, **Terence Blanchard**, Wallace Roney, Philip Harper, **Wynton Marsalis**, Brian Lynch, Valery Ponomarev
Trombone:	**Curtis Fuller**, Julian Priester, **Steve Turré**, **Robin Eubanks**
Piano:	**Horace Silver**, **Bobby Timmons**, Sam Dockery, Joanne Brackeen, **Cedar Walton**, Walter Davis, Jr., Ronnie Mathews, **Keith Jarrett**, George Cables, James Williams, Donald Brown, Bennie Green, Mulgrew Miller, Geoff Keezer
Bass:	Spanky DeBreast, Jymie Merritt, Victor Sproles, Doug Watkins, **Charles Fambrough**, Lonnie Plaxico, **Peter Washington**, **Reggie Workman**, Dennis Irwin

FIGURE 11.1 Jazz Messengers Sidemen (**bold** indicates most influential. Recommended recordings at close of chapter)

Alto Sax:	**James Spaulding**
Tenor Sax:	**Bob Berg**, **George Coleman**, **Joe Henderson**, **Hank Mobley**, **Michael Brecker**, Junior Cook, Clifford Jordan, Tyrone Washington
Trumpet:	**Randy Brecker**, **Art Farmer**, Carmell Jones, **Woody Shaw**, **Donald Byrd**, **Tom Harrell**, **Blue Mitchell**, Charles Tolliver, **Kenny Dorham**
Bass:	**Bob Cranshaw**, **Larry Ridley**, **Gene Taylor**, John Williams, **Teddy Kotick**, Teddy Smith, **Doug Watkins**
Drums:	**Art Blakey**, **Louis Hayes**, Mickey Roker, John Harris, Jr., Roger Humphries, **Billy Cobham**, Roy Brooks, **Al Foster**

FIGURE 11.2 Horace Silver Sidemen (**bold** indicates most influential. Recommended recordings at close of chapter)

LISTENING GUIDE

Art Blakey and the Jazz Messengers

"Moanin'" (Bobby Timmons) 3:02 (excerpt)

Recorded 10/30/1958, Blue Note BST 84003

Reissued: "The Blue Note Years" 7243–4–96375–2-8

Personnel: Lee Morgan, trumpet; Benny Golson, tenor saxophone; Bobby Timmons, piano; Jymie Merritt, bass; Art Blakey, drums

Form: Repeated song form (AA¹BA)

0:00–0:59	First chorus—32 bars, theme:
0:00–0:14	A section—8 bars, piano plays melody theme (call), answered by stop-time response
0:15–0:29	A¹ section—8 bars, trumpet and saxophone play melody theme, answered by stop-time band response
0:30–0:43	B section—8 bars, trumpet and saxophone play bridge melody over rhythm section, no stop-time
0:44–0:59	A section—8 bars, piano plays A theme melody, answered by stop-time band responses
1:00–1:59	Second chorus—32 bars (AABA), trumpet solo, with rhythm accompaniment, in straight 4/4 shuffle-style time
2:00–3:01	Third chorus—34 bars (AABA), trumpet solo, with rhythm accompaniment. First 2 measures of fourth chorus set up tenor sax solo at fade

Other Hard-Bop Messengers

Horace Silver (1928–)

It would be unfair not to acquaint you with the work of a few of Blakey's outstanding Messengers, who left their own legacy as leaders following their association with the drummer. Horace Silver (1928–) is undoubtedly one of the most noted not discussed in later chapters. His own brand of jazz relied heavily on strong and often repetitive bass lines, simple but strong melodies, blues-influenced chord progressions, and musical influences from outside the US, in particular his native Cape Verde. Silver's recordings *Cape Verdean Blues* and *Song For My Father* reflect his Portuguese ancestry and interest in calypso music. Through his compositions, Silver's recordings often gave the listener a sense of continuity from track to track, e.g. *Cape Verdean Blues* and his most popular recording, *Song For My Father*. The titles of many of his other fine recordings used wordplays based on his name that suggested musical continuity throughout, such as *Silver 'n Wood*, *Silver 'n Brass* and *Silver 'n Voices*. Like Blakey, he relied heavily on the strengths of outstanding sidemen, a list of which is a who's who of contemporary jazz (see Figure 11.2 on p. 259). Although now in semi-retirement, Silver still occasionally releases a new recording. "Jazz had a little better shot [then] than today," Silver said, "precisely because they would take a jazz tune and put it on the jukebox where it had more potential for people hearing it. Also because [the tunes] had that danceable thing."[5]

"Strollin'," the Silver track included in the online audio anthology, is a fine representation of the hard-bop sound. The chord progression is quite sophisticated and far more complex than his blues- and Latin-influenced tunes. The tune is based on two contrasting 8-measure phrases that, for analysis purposes, will be labeled A and B. Each of these 8-measure phrases can be further divided into two 4-measure sections—the first serving as the antecedent and the second the

LISTENING GUIDE

Horace Silver

"Strollin'" (Silver) 4:57

Recorded New York City 7/8/1960

Blue Note Records *Horace-Scope* CDP 7 84042 2

Personnel: Blue Mitchell, trumpet; Junior Cook, tenor saxophone; Horace Silver, piano; Gene Taylor, bass; Roy Brooks, drums

Form: 32-measure tune in four 8-measure phrases—ABAB¹; Key of D-flat major

0:00–0:01	Begins with short bass pick-up
0:02–0:15	First chorus—trumpet and tenor sax state first theme (A) in harmony; rhythm section plays in 2-beat style
0:16–0:30	B theme stated in similar fashion
0:31–0:44	Return to first theme (A) with exact repetition
0:45–0:59	B¹ second theme, second 4 measures entirely different than earlier B
1:00–1:56	Second chorus—Blue Mitchell's trumpet solo on entire form
1:57–2:53	Third chorus—Junior Cook's tenor sax solo on entire form (notice lack of vibrato); quotes tune at close of solo (2:40), ending with a bluesy descending line
2:54–3:49	Fourth chorus—Silver's piano solo begins; aggressive left-hand low register jabs are similar to Thelonious Monk's style; quotes from Sonny Rollins "St. Thomas" at 3:36–3:40
3:50–4:45	Fifth chorus—trumpet and sax return to state tune with rhythm-section 2-beat style accompaniment
4:46–end	Coda is additional 2 measures

Listen to the interviews with Horace Silver that can be found in the corresponding chapter on the website.

consequent response. The body of the tune is a good illustration of the older **"2-beat" swing** style, with the drummer playing the signature open–closed hi-hat cymbal pattern, while the bass emphasizes primarily beats 1 and 3—hence, the "2-beat" identification. It isn't until the solos begin that the bassist begins walking a 4-beat line, more typical of this era. The relaxed gait, as the tempo suggests, and infectious melody make "Strollin'" one of the many unforgettable Silver tunes.

Clifford Brown (1930–1956) and Sonny Rollins (1930–)

Clifford Brown was critically acclaimed for his uncompromising work in elevating the hard-bop style to a higher level. He was lauded as the next Dizzy Gillespie—the torchbearer for the next generation of jazz trumpeters—and he most likely would have had an even more lasting impact had he not died in an automobile accident at the age of only 25.

After brief apprenticeships with bands led by Lionel Hampton and Tadd Dameron, Brown joined up with drummer Max Roach to form the Clifford Brown–Max Roach Quintet in 1954,

Clifford Brown at a recording session

Tenor saxophonist Sonny Rollins performs at the Berkshire
Music Barn Jazz Festival in Lenox, MA, 1956

etching their first recordings in California. This recording is evidence that more than just the
"cool" sound was emanating from the West Coast during the 1950s. Roach, who was a veteran
drummer from the bebop generation, had impeccable credentials, never swaying from the straight
and narrow artistic path and always uncompromising in his social and political doctrines. As an
artist, he did what he could to express through music dissatisfaction with the black man's status
in America's society.

The first generation of the Roach–Brown Quintet featured Richie Powell, Bud Powell's
younger brother, and west-coast tenor saxophonist, Harold Land. The few recordings that this
band made, and the 1956 version with saxophonist Sonny Rollins replacing Land, stand alone
as some of the best that hard bop had to offer. Brown's musicianship was unparalleled, with
flawless technique and a trumpet sound that was controlled and fat and flowed like warm butter
from his bell. His style was based in part on Fats Navarro, but his improvisations show originality
and an uncanny ability to play long, meaningful improvised lines that make so much sense one
has to wonder how they could have been created spontaneously. Land was an able counterpart,
but Rollins was more than his equal.

Tenor saxophonist Sonny Rollins (1930–) is often mentioned in discussions of the hard-bop
style, although his climb to critical acclaim began in the latter days of the bebop era. Although
Dexter Gordon is considered the first tenor saxophonist to incorporate Bird's bop alto style, the
younger Sonny Rollins in many ways is perhaps a better example of the first modern, post-war
tenor saxophonist to take this instrument to new heights in later years. His recordings with Parker,
the MJQ, J.J. Johnson, Fats Navarro, Miles Davis, and the Clifford Brown–Max Roach Quintet

put him at the center of bebop and the hard-bop explosions. In later years, Rollins, or "Newk" as he was nicknamed, preferred the trio setting in the 1950s. With the absence of piano or guitar in his trios, he followed the same path as those piano-less groups led by cool-style saxophonist Gerry Mulligan and the subsequent free-jazz experimentalist Ornette Coleman. In recent times, Branford Marsalis has followed this same model, preferring the melodic freedom encouraged by the absence of chord-playing instruments. Rollins is recognized by his fat sound, reminiscent of Dexter Gordon and the elder statesman Coleman Hawkins. According to Gunther Schuller, he was the first of the modern improvisers to create long-winded solos that consisted of a series of logically developed motives. In contrast to most soloists from this period, who based their solos

LISTENING GUIDE

Sonny Rollins

"Pent Up House" (Sonny Rollins) 8:52

From *Sonny Rollins Plus 4*

Recorded New Jersey 3/22/1956

Prestige PRCD-30159-2

Personnel: Sonny Rollins, tenor saxophone; Clifford Brown, trumpet; Richie Powell, piano; George Morrow, bass; Max Roach, drums

Form: A (8) A¹ (4) A (4) for 16 total bars per full chorus

0:00–0:19	Theme
0:20–0:39	Theme repeated
0:40–0:58	First chorus—Clifford Brown improvises with bass
0:59–1:18	Second chorus—drums join in; Brown improvises long line through almost entire chorus
1:19–1:38	Third chorus—piano adds sparse comping; ends chorus with blues lines
1:39–1:57	Fourth chorus—trumpet builds solo by high-register shouts and double-time phrases
1:58–2:18	Fifth chorus—trumpet continues to improvise
2:19–2:39	Sixth chorus—trumpet continues to improvise, gradually winding down solo
2:40–2:58	Seventh chorus—Rollins begins sax solo, logically building on Brown's last phrase
2:59–3:19	Eighth chorus—Rollins shows skill in developing improvised motives using repetition and sequences
3:20–3:39	Ninth chorus—Rollins displays technical ability with double-time passages
3:40–4:21	10th chorus—soloist uses motivic development techniques—repetition, sequence, and thematic variation
4:22–4:42	11th chorus—final improvised sax chorus
4:43–6:45	Six more choruses—piano improvises using blues, riffs, alternating with longer, bebop-inspired lines
6:46–7:05	Two choruses of drums trading 2-bar phrases with sax and trumpet
7:27–7:43	Drums solo on 16-bar form
7:44–8:06	Second drum solo chorus
8:07–8:27	Return to "head"
8:28–end	Final repeat of "head" and short tag to end

on a series of unrelated ideas, guided solely by the progression of chords, Rollins developed solos that were based on thematic developments of his improvised ideas. His improvisations could be considered more melodically driven, in the style of Lester Young, rather than directed by Coleman Hawkin's style, which was geared more to harmony.

By the late 1950s, following a long list of outstanding collaborations, recordings, and compositions, Rollins was heralded as the leading tenor saxophonist in the bop, post-bop tradition. He contributed a number of compositions now considered as staples in the jazz repertoire, including "Valse Hot," "Blue 7," "St. Thomas," "Oleo," "Airegin," and "Doxy." Of particular interest are his "Valse Hot," for its 3/4 meter (an unusual digression for the times from the predictable 4/4 meter), and the popular "St. Thomas," which featured a calypso rhythmic feel. It is no wonder that Rollins enjoyed a mild obsession with this brand of Caribbean music, as his parents hailed from the West Indies.

One of the most compelling recordings made during this period is "Pent Up House," which Rollins recorded with the Clifford Brown–Max Roach Quintet and which is included in the online audio collection. The solos by Brown, Rollins, and Roach represent the most creative and fluid playing from the era. Listen to the long lines that Brown spins out in his improvisation, without pausing for a breath. Rollins demonstrates his evolving mastery of motivic development and cliché-free improvisations on this recording. Take note of how he develops simple ideas before moving on to a new musical thought.

Other fine examples of Clifford Brown at his peak in the quintet, with Harold Land on saxophone, are "Daahoud," with a listening guide included on the companion website, "Joy Spring," "Jordu," and "Sandu." These recordings represent some of the most memorable moments from this great quintet.

MORE ABOUT FUNKY, SOUL JAZZ AND THE 1950s AND 1960s

Funky jazz, or soul jazz as some call it, is a style that united jazz with the down-home qualities of the black community and popular music: R & B, gospel, and sanctified, holy-roller music. It was a time for black musicians to reconnect with a heritage that had, in some ways, been previously shunned because of memories of repression and slavery. Time had provided some distancing, and black musicians could once again be proud of their rich culture and history. It was particularly significant that their efforts to renovate these musical roots came in the midst of the biggest push for civil rights since emancipation. Funky jazz raised the black communities' awareness of their cultural heritage, and white audiences appreciated it for its memorable melodies, slower tempos, and strong rhythmic basis, which rendered some of the material almost danceable.[6] The more popular and danceable recordings found their way into jukeboxes across the country.

The titles of hard-bop recordings and tunes often gave away the funky punch line, even before a first playing. For example, Horace Silver's "The Jody Grind," "Sister Sadie," "Serenade to a Soul Sister," and "The Preacher"; Cannonball Adderley's album *Them Dirty Blues*, featuring "Work Song" and "Dat Dare," *Mercy, Mercy, Mercy*, and *Why Am I Treated So Bad*; Jimmy Smith's *The Sermon*, *Home Cookin'* and *Back at the Chicken Shack*, and, in the 1960s, Herbie Hancock's popular "Watermelon Man." The themes of these titles all relate to "soul foods," religious activities, black slang, or comments on their earlier years of slavery and repression. Other titles invoking black slang terms or hip language, such as "blue(s)," "dig," "boss," "funky," "mojo," "workin'," and "cookin'," were also commonplace.[7] This music, some of which was marketed on the 45-rpm record designed for the popular music market, reached a large audience through jukeboxes and radio play. Alto saxophonist and Blakey alumnus Jackie McLean referred to the popularization of this style of jazz as "a banner of racial self-affirmation."[8] Musical values for black and white musicians, as well as audiences, had changed radically by the mid 1960s, caused largely by the surge in popularity of commercially viable pop groups such as the Beatles, Rolling Stones, Cream, Jimi Hendrix, and others. Since the earliest recordings by the Original Dixieland Jazz Band, the recording industry has shown interest in promoting white popular styles that are sometimes imitations or renditions of black music.

Although funky jazz was popular with many fans, who accepted it as an honest effort to make an artistic endeavor commercially palatable, many critics felt differently. For example, Martin Williams felt that the movement was largely "regressive, self-conscious, monotonous, and even contrived."[9] But the musicians fought back. Saxophonist Cannonball Adderley, well known for his commercially successful funky recordings in the early 1960s, countered with his own rebuttal:

> We just played music we enjoyed. There was nothing calculated about it. However, I feel a responsibility to the man who's paying the freight, and I try to be reasonably entertaining by playing music I think they want to hear—and music I think they should hear. In addition to this responsibility to the audience, you have a responsibility to yourself, the band, [and] your art. I see no reason why jazz musicians should not live well simply because they're jazz musicians and artists. Responsibility to the art doesn't mean you have to be hungry.[10]

Critics, in some cases, were more prone to write favorably about hard-bop musicians, who they viewed as not catering to commercial tastes. For better or worse, critics have always sided with music that is less influenced by public taste and more likely to have an impact on the long-range artistic development of the music. To be commercially successful as a jazz artist is often, but fortunately not always, the kiss of death when it comes to critical favor. The popular, funky brand of jazz sold records, engaged audiences, and was commercially viable. It resurfaced in the 1990s as the basis for what has been termed "acid jazz." Many of the early recordings in this new genre were little more than facelifts of tunes from the late 1950s and 1960s.

ORGAN TRIOS AND THE GUITAR

Two instruments emerged as powerful forces in jazz during the1950s and 1960s and collaborated to capitalize on the jazz-soul movement. Although the guitar had been a standard member of the rhythm section through the swing years, it wasn't until Charlie Christian arrived on the scene, along with modern amplification technology in the 1940s, that the instrument became viable as a solo instrument. The organs used by Count Basie and Fats Waller in earlier years were of older design and remnants of silent-film theaters. New electronic technologies enabled this instrument to become more viable in contemporary settings.

Wes Montgomery (1923–1968)

Guitarist Wes Montgomery was raised in Indianapolis, where he worked with his brothers and other local musicians. His first opportunity for more widespread exposure was as a member of Lionel Hampton's band. Hampton is remembered for giving many young, unknown musicians their first opportunity for broader exposure. Riverside Records enabled Montgomery to strike out on his own, and his first recording for that label quickly established him as one of the leading innovators on this instrument. It seems that self-taught musicians, as was Montgomery, often discover revolutionary new techniques, as they are not bound by accepted conventions. This was the case with Montgomery, who employed thumb picking, chord soloing (in contrast to single-note), and octave techniques (two notes an octave apart played simultaneously) that had never before been used.

Guitarist Wes Montgomery, c.1960

Jimmy Smith sitting at the Hammond B3 organ

These techniques are evident in the recording found on the accompanying anthology. He quickly became known as the most important guitarist since Charlie Christian and was signed by Verve records. Although this label offered better exposure, its producers favored slicker, poppish, commercial productions, framing Montgomery with lush string backup arrangements of pop tunes of the day such as "California Dreamin'" and "Goin' Out of My Head."

The other important aspect of Montgomery's brief career that was significant to the development of jazz styles was his organ-trio sessions, the basis of his first recordings for the Riverside label. Organ trios, coupling the instrument with guitar or saxophone and drums, became a popular configuration in the late 1950s, as they were easy to record and inexpensive to book. The organ's bass pedals eliminated the need for a bass player. The sound of the electronic Hammond organ, with its broad, dynamic range and versatile tone quality, resonated with the new wave of pop music stemming from the R & B and rock 'n' roll community. To quote author David Rosenthal: "There was something raucous, something down and dirty in its array of electronic growls, wails, moans, and shrill **ostinato** [persistently repeated rhythmic and/or melodic phrase, sometimes a bass line] tidal waves that immediately appealed to black ears,"[11] and many white followers of mainstream jazz. The organ is considered the immediate predecessor of the synthesizer, which rose to popularity in the 1970s.

Jimmy Smith (1925–2005)

Montgomery's first recordings paired him with organist Melvin Rhyne, but Montgomery's overnight success led to a recording partnership with another rising star—organist Jimmy Smith. Smith, who began his career as a Philadelphia-area pianist, was influenced by contemporary blues organists Wild Bill Davis and Bill Doggett and ultimately found more success as an organist.

He developed a ferocious right hand and can be recognized by his rapid-fire bursts of notes. He used the instrument to full advantage, playing it like a powerful orchestra, capable of projecting a wide range of moods, from electrifying to more subtle. Like other black artists from the period, Smith rode the crest of the popular funky-soul tidal wave, releasing numerous recordings that featured secular, modern versions of sanctified, down-home, and dirty blues. The organ was a natural for this style, as it was so often a part of worship in the sanctified churches. Other organists followed Smith's lead, capitalizing on the new trend. They included Richard "Groove" Holmes, "Brother" Jack McDuff, and the queen of jazz organ, Shirley Scott. In addition to his work with Montgomery, Smith recorded with other solid guitarists, such as Kenny Burrell and Quentin Warren, who earned popularity during this era. The organ trios from this period can be considered as the genesis of many of the more modern "groove" bands, popularized in the late 1990s and early part of this new century by guitarists John Scofield, the group Medeski Martin & Wood, and second-generation Philadelphia organist Joey DeFrancesco.

The "James and Wes" excerpt from a critically acclaimed recording that is included in the online audio anthology features Smith and Montgomery in a straight-ahead, swinging blues tune, demonstrating their muscular style as soloists and showing off the aforementioned personal stylistic traits. Notice that, in this trio, there is no bass instrument, and Smith's feet, playing bass lines on the organ bass pedals, fulfill this role. Organists could also use one of the keyboards to play fast, up-tempo bass lines.

LISTENING GUIDE

Jimmy Smith and Wes Montgomery

"James and Wes" (Smith) 2:48 (excerpt)

Recorded 9/28/1966, Verve "Jimmy and Wes: The Dynamic Duo" SVLP 8678

Reissued Verve Master Edition Series

Personnel: Jimmy Smith, organ; Wes Montgomery, guitar; Grady Tate, drums

Form: Repeated blues 12-bar blues

0:00–0:16	First chorus—12-bar melody: organ plays riff melody with guitar, organ bass pedal, and drum accompaniment
0:17–0:33	Second chorus—12-bar melody: organ repeats riff melody with similar accompaniment
0:34–0:50	Third chorus—12-bar guitar solo: improvised guitar solo, with organ and drums accompaniment
0:51–1:08	Fourth chorus—12-bar organ solo: improvised organ solo with guitar, organ bass pedal, and drums accompaniment
1:08–1:25	Fifth chorus—12-bar guitar solo: improvised guitar solo with organ sustained chords, organ bass pedal, and drums accompaniment
1:26–1:42	Sixth chorus—12-bar organ solo: improvised organ solo with organ bass pedal and drums accompaniment, guitar tacet
1:42–1:59	Seventh chorus—12-bar guitar solo: improvised guitar solo (octaves), with organ sustained chords, organ bass pedal, and drums accompaniment
2:00–2:17	Eighth chorus—12-bar melody: organ plays riff melody with guitar, organ bass pedal, and drum accompaniment, octave guitar fills at end
2:18–2:48	Ninth chorus—12-bar melody: organ plays riff melody with guitar, organ bass pedal, and drum accompaniment, octave guitar fills at end

EVERLASTING BIG BANDS

It is important to realize that, although the sun had set on big-band popularity, there were a number who survived the onslaught of popular new music trends and small-group jazz innovations. One such survivor was pianist and arranger/composer **Stan Kenton** (1911–1979). Kenton first surfaced in the late 1940s, leading his own band, which was labeled "progressive" even for those times. Stan Kenton and arranger Johnny Richards were also pioneers in the mingling of jazz and Afro-Latin styles during the 1940s and 1950s. Machito supplied the percussionists for Kenton's first band that enjoyed success with this new format. "Peanut Vendor" was Kenton's first recording success in this new vein and utilized a version of the Cuban bolero. The following quote from Stan Kenton accurately describes the atmosphere during this period of Afro-Latin influence:

> Rhythmically, the Cubans play the most exciting stuff. We won't copy them exactly, but we will copy some of their devices and apply them to what we're trying to do. The guys in our rhythm section are doing just that. So are the guys in Woody's [Herman]. And while we keep moving toward the Cubans rhythmically, they're moving toward us melodically. We both have a lot to learn.[12]

Contemporary bandleader Stan Kenton rehearses his jazz band in London, in preparation for a performance at the Royal Albert Hall

LISTENING GUIDE

Stan Kenton

Cuban Fire Suite

"La Suerte de los Tontos" (Fortune of Fools) composed/arranged by Johnny Richards, 4:17

Recorded 5/22–24/1956, New York City

Capital Jazz (Blue Note) CDP77962602

Soloists: Lennie Niehaus, alto sax; Vinnie Tanno, trumpet

Personnel: *Trumpets*: Ed Leddy, Sam Noto, Lee Katzman, Phil Gilbert, Al Mattaliano, Vince Tano; *Trombones*: Bob Fitzpatrick, Carl Fontana, Kent Larson, Don Kelly; *French horns*: Irving Rosenthal, Julius Watkins; *Tuba*: Jay McAllister; *Saxophones*: Lennie Niehaus, alto; Bill Perkins, Lucky Thompson, tenors; Billy Root, baritone; *Rhythm section*: Stan Kenton, piano; Ralph Blaze, guitar; Curtis Counce, bass; Mel Lewis, drums; *Percussion*: Saul Gubin or George Gaber, tympani; Willie Rodriguez, bongo; Tommy Lopez, conga; George Laguna, timbale; Roger Mozian, clavés; Mario Alvarez, maracas

Form: Song form (ABA¹) in D major

	Introduction:
0:00–0:10	Contrapuntal brass playing variations to main theme
0:11–0:24	French horns enter, followed by saxes, trombones, tuba, and baritone sax stating initial motive
0:24–0:28	Tuba solo
0:28–0:33	Percussion and brass enter
0:34–0:38	Percussion and rhythm section establish Latin tempo
0:39–1:13	Contrapuntal layering: bass (0:39), saxes (0:43), trombones (0:50), trumpets plus additional sax line (0:59); section crescendos as each new part enters
	First chorus:
1:14–1:29	Primary A theme
1:30–1:45	B section featuring trumpets and French horns
1:46–1:57	A¹, variation on first A theme
	Transition:
1:58–2:04	Percussion interlude with French horns, trombones, and rhythm serves as transition to sax solo that follows
	Second chorus:
2:05–2:44	Lennie Niehaus plays alto sax solo on ABA form with brass background figures added
	Interlude:
2:45–2:49	Short interlude links alto solo to trumpet solo that follows
	Third chorus:
2:50–3:28	Trumpet solo on form with sax backgrounds
	Interlude:
3:29–3:33	Brief brass and percussion interlude
	Fourth chorus:
3:34–3:41	A theme only partially restated
3:41–end	New material features exchanges between brass and percussion and represents the high point of the piece

Kenton's dynamic recording entitled the *Cuban Fire Suite* followed "Peanut Vendor." The suite of compositions on this recording are all composed by Johnny Richards (John Cascales) and are the product of his extensive study in Latin America, Mexico, Cuba, and the Latino sections of New York City. Each composition is based on a traditional Latin rhythm of predominantly Cuban origin. *Cuban Fire* represents a landmark recording in his lengthy Kenton discography and served to launch Richard's career as an arranger/composer. "La Suerte de los Tontos," the sixth movement from the suite, demonstrates the power and machismo that Kenton's band was known for.

Kenton not only incorporated the influences of bebop and Cubop, but also ventured into the realm of jazz influenced by contemporary classical music with his LA Neophonic Orchestra. As was the case with most big-band leaders, Kenton helped to launch the careers of a host of notable jazz performers and arrangers, including cool-style saxophonists Art Pepper, Lee Konitz, Lennie Niehaus, Stan Getz, and Zoot Sims (the latter two also played with Woody Herman). Additionally, brass men Frank Rosolino, Carl Fontana, and Maynard Ferguson, among many others, did tours of duty with Kenton's band. Kenton was a champion, in the 1960s, of the still-young jazz-education movement, sponsoring camps and clinics throughout the US and employing exceptional young college graduates. Kenton passed on in 1979, and his will prohibited the formation of "ghost bands" to recreate his music.

DEFINING POSTMODERNISM

Although much of the 1950s and 1960s was consumed with modern mainstream jazz, at the close of the 1950s, Ornette Coleman stood the jazz world on its head, signaling with much fanfare a new age of postmodern jazz. It isn't exactly clear when postmodernism began, nor is there unanimous consensus about what the term means. There are some generalities that can be used in an effort to clarify how the term can be applied to the jazz that follows Coleman's path and emerges in other art forms in the mid-to-late 1960s and beyond. Typically, postmodernism refers to art that features a mixture of historical styles and new approaches, warped through various forms of reinterpretation and purposeful misrepresentation. The result is considered unconventional and sometimes produces what could be considered a parody. Such performances are not governed by the same rules used to create the original art, and as such are not subject to analysis by applying familiar, traditional criteria. Instead, postmodern artists attempt to force the development of entirely new sets of criteria by creating works that defy analysis by traditional means. These artists develop new processes for the making of art by bringing diverse elements together in new and different ways. In some situations, the creative process can be more important than the product.[13] Postmodern art also tends to reflect the influences of new techniques and technologies, particularly those associated with electronics and the information age. The postmodern age stands as a time of great diversity, when no singular trend is evident, but instead many different directions are being pursued simultaneously. Diversity is an important trend to remember as we progress through the 1960s and beyond, tracing further developments in jazz.

ORNETTE COLEMAN (1930–) AND HIS DISCIPLES

California-based alto saxophonist Ornette Coleman, a transplanted Texan with a strong grounding in bebop and R & B, turned the jazz world upside down, causing international debate and controversy in 1958–1959 with the release of his first recordings on the Contemporary and Atlantic labels. He delivered an entirely new kind of jazz that was well suited to the new, postmodern age.

In the early years, Coleman kicked around his native area of Fort Worth, Texas, and nearby states playing in R & B and circus bands. As a saxophonist, he was largely self-taught and preferred to play a plastic alto sax. Coleman uses a mouthpiece and reed combination that helps him control pitch and produce a vocal quality that, at times, simulates crying, shouting, and moaning and is akin to early blues and African vocal styles. "You can always reach into the human sound of a voice on your horn if you're actually hearing," Coleman said, "and [trying] to express the warmth of the human voice."[14] Not everyone was impressed with his originality, however, and he endured unimaginable abuses, simply because he chose to play in a non-traditional manner. Some found his sound and sense of pitch to be offensive, annoying, unschooled, and inappropriate. He suffered beatings and had his horn destroyed because of his quest for individuality.

He left Texas for Los Angeles, where he hoped to find a more supportive environment, but found it necessary to sustain himself by taking low-paying odd jobs that enabled him to seek out nightly jam sessions. The local musicians found Coleman to be eccentric, brazen, and without any inhibitions, and most refused to let him sit in, often asking him to leave the bandstand. In time, however, Coleman encountered a small group of kindred spirits who recognized that he offered something entirely new, not based on the laws laid down by the bebop crowd that everyone was bound to at the time. For example, trumpeter Bobby Bradford cited Coleman's penchant for playing "outside the harmony." (The term "outside" is often used to refer to avant-garde, free jazz that denies most prescribed rules of functional harmony, form, and melody.) "I was very impressed that he had the courage and audacity to test Charlie Parker's law," Bradford said. "That's when I began to think of him as a genius."[15]

So what made Coleman and his music so controversial and different than what had come before? For the jazz neophyte or newcomer to experimental free jazz, Coleman's music presents a challenge, for it is difficult to draw relationships to other, familiar musical experiences. His music defies predictability. Aside from occasional reoccurring melodic and rhythmic fragments that are composed and serve as springboards for improvisation, nothing can be labeled as formulaic. There are several important aspects of Coleman's legacy to become acquainted with before hearing his music:

- His compositions, although often folksy in quality, frequently introduced shifting meters, changing tempos, and odd phrase groupings.
- Bass and drums sometimes played in different, opposing tempos.
- Although Coleman's composed themes sometimes imply a tone or key center, his improvisations are polytonal, in that they constantly shift from one tonality to another.
- Coleman and Don Cherry, his longtime trumpeter, did not adhere to conventional ideas of intonation. By traditional standards, they often played out of tune.
- Their improvisations did not rely on prescribed chords or formal structure and were based solely on melody and its development.
- Although his main themes are composed and often demonstrate a sense of form, his improvisations are often free of any allegiance to the form and are rather unpredictable departures from his theme.
- Coleman's group concept was revolutionary from the standpoint of liberating the rhythm section from its earlier roles. The bassist was free to follow his own muse rather than playing rigid, walking bass lines that implied specific chords in a progression. The drummer was equally free to interact in a free-form dialogue with the other members of the quartet.

Coleman's music could be compared to **aleatoric** classical music, as the outcomes of his quartet's improvisations were based somewhat on chance and total spontaneity, without premeditation. On the other hand, there is an intentional dialogue in Coleman's performances, although unrestrained by traditional guidelines. Such planned group interchange does not exist in aleatoric, "chance" music. Coleman said:

> When our group plays, before we start out to play, we do not have any idea what the end result will be. Each player is free to contribute what he feels in the music at any given moment . . . I don't tell the members of my group what to do. I let everyone express himself just as he wants to.[16]

As his tunes are based on melody for its own sake, without reference to prescribed harmony, his improvisations too were melodically derived, with no concern for chords or a set harmonic progression. Consequently, and like no other jazz before, each performance of a tune was radically different and comprised of a higher degree of pure improvisation than ever before.

Coleman termed the theory that drove his music "**harmolodics**," but it is a term more widely known than understood. In essence, it was his way of describing the ever-shifting relationships that can occur when freely improvised melodies interact with one another, implying different accidental harmonies and tonalities. Shifting key centers helped to ensure that any harmonic relationship that might exist between melody and bass line was strictly accidental. Imagine the result of a three-voice vocal group, all singing the same song, but with each singer changing keys at will and using different rhythms. A melody, or a melodic phrase, can be set to any number of different chords, and he wanted his bassists to be free and sensitive to any of the possible relationships that they could help to imply. To ensure that harmony never influenced his players' decisions, he did not use a pianist or guitarist. In many ways, Coleman's seminal quartets demonstrated a further extension of earlier works by (1) Gerry Mulligan's

Saxophonist Ornette Coleman with trumpeter Don Cherry at the 5 Spot, New York City

piano-less quartets; (2) Bill Evans's trios, which sought to liberate the bass from its time-keeping responsibilities; (3) early New Orleans jazz, which often featured improvised counterpoint between instruments; (4) Thelonious Monk's free-spirited compositions and performance style; and (5) Lennie Tristano, who pioneered free jazz in 1949.

Coleman's improvisations, and those of his other quartet members, were almost entirely unpredictable, although based in part on the more conservative and predictable rhythmic style of Charlie Parker. Coleman's rhythmic style was more irregular than earlier beboppers and kept the listener constantly off balance. There were no traditional signposts to guide the listener, just pure emotion. Some critics and musicians criticized him for being a charlatan who had no training. In the 1958 *Down Beat* readers' poll, the year Brubeck Quartet saxophonist Paul Desmond won, Coleman received only 21 votes following the release of his first two recordings on the Contemporary label. Many other critics and musicians, on the other hand, such as Nat Hentoff, Amiri Baraka, Schuller, and Lewis, felt that Coleman was making a "unique and valuable contribution to tomorrow's music."[17]

As a true postmodern, Coleman forced the listener to abandon old standards and means of comparison and evaluation. His music made it necessary to re-evaluate the way jazz was judged. Coleman and his producers were convinced that his new brand of jazz was a beacon for those looking for a new direction, and his first album titles illustrate his commitment to predicting and pioneering the future—*Something Else*, *Tomorrow Is the Question*, *The Shape of Jazz to Come*, and *Change of the Century*.

Listen to "Mind and Time," included in the online audio anthology. See if you can identify the unusual characteristics of Coleman's quartet style. This track is from his second release on the Contemporary label and was the first recording to demonstrate the true essence of his style, which led to a contract from the major, New York-based Atlantic label. Despite its freshness, the tune itself adheres closely to a standard riff-like call–response format. Trumpeter Don Cherry described it as a 10-bar form,[18] but it is actually 11½ measures in all, divided into an initial 6½-measure phrase, followed by a 5-measure phrase in 4/4 meter. The entire 11½-measure tune is repeated before improvised solos begin.

Coleman's greatest accomplishment is, perhaps, the 1960 Atlantic Records recording entitled *Free Jazz* (an excerpt of which is included on the *SCCJ* (editions prior to 2010)), which featured two quartets playing 36 minutes of uninterrupted, improvised music. An appropriate painting 'White Light' by abstract expressionist painter Jackson Pollock is featured on the cover of this landmark recording. Pollock's postmodern abstract expressionism offered a perfect visual association with Coleman's music.

Aside from a few composed, but loosely played, ensemble passages that serve as interludes between solos, the balance of *Free Jazz* features entirely improvised dialogues between the two quartets. The result is a mind-boggling stream-of-consciousness mosaic of ever-changing textures. It can be compared to a group of people at a party, all having conversations, interacting, some voices sounding more predominant at times than others. Although some of the rhythm instruments essentially fulfill traditional roles as timekeepers, others are free to interact, comment, and react to the horn players' gestures. The horn players, in turn, base their background riffs on ideas that began as improvisations stated by the primary soloist at the moment. *Down Beat* magazine played it safe when it reviewed this recording, electing to straddle the fence by printing opinions that represented both camps. For example, Pete Welding gave the recording a five-star rating—the highest possible. He said that the recording "does not break with jazz tradition; rather it restores to currency an element that has been absent in most jazz since the onset of the swing orchestra—spontaneous group improvisation."[19] Welding went on to say that Coleman's music was "relentless in its re-examination of the role of collective improvisation, and this is, in many respects, where the work is most successful."[20] Critic John Tynan, who had been one of Coleman's cheerleaders, contributing rave reviews following the release of his first two recordings, had a different impression of Coleman's *Free Jazz*. He wrote:

> Collective improvisation? Nonsense. The only semblance of collectivity lies in the fact that these eight nihilists were collected together in one studio at one time and with one common cause: to destroy the music that gave them birth. Give them top marks for the attempt.[21]

Tynan's refusal to give any stars in his review of *Free Jazz*, the recording that coined the term and set a new course for jazz, also known as the "new thing," will no doubt continue to be disputed. It cannot, however, be disputed that Coleman's music exerted a magnetic force that attracted and influenced many musicians, changing the way in which they thought about playing jazz. Coleman and his music laid the foundation for the formation of the non-profit Association for the Advancement of Creative Music (AACM), centered in Chicago and devoted to supporting black, avant-garde jazz. Muhal Richard Abrams founded the organization in 1965, following a landmark series of sold-out concerts the year before, organized by Bill Dixon and billed as "The October Revolution in Jazz." The AACM can be directly linked to the formation of such contemporary avant-garde bands as the Art Ensemble of Chicago and Anthony Braxton's various ensembles. A similar organization in St. Louis, known as the Black Artists Group, was formed in 1968 in the image of the AACM and later helped to foster groups such as the adventuresome World Saxophone Quartet.

The less-informed listener often finds free jazz difficult to understand or appreciate, for its practitioners took so many liberties, breaking away from well-established traditions. Any new art form or style becomes difficult to understand when there is no frame of reference, causing one to lose the ability to relate it to something that is understood. Free jazz, therefore, threw many listeners off balance, as it continues to do even today. Figure 11.3, opposite, should help to put this style in sharper focus, making the juxtaposition and contrast of styles and approaches clearer.

LISTENING GUIDE

Ornette Coleman

"Mind and Time" (Coleman)

Recorded 1/16/1959, Contemporary 7569

Reissued on OJC OJCCD-342-2

Personnel: Ornette Coleman, alto sax; Donald Cherry, trumpet; Percy Heath, bass; Red Mitchell, bass; Shelley Manne, drums

Form: 11½-measure melody

0:00–0:22	Melody
0:00–0:06	A section—6½ bars, alto sax and trumpet play melody in unison, with rhythm-section accompaniment
0:06–0:11	B section—5 bars, sax and trumpet play melody in unison, with rhythm-section accompaniment
0:11–0:17	A section—6½ bars, sax and trumpet repeat A-section melody in unison, with rhythm-section accompaniment
0:17–0:22	B section—5 bars, sax and trumpet repeat B-section melody in unison, with rhythm-section accompaniment
0:23–1:52	Open "free" alto sax solo, exploring the melodic and harmonic material of the melody section, with bass and drum swinging accompaniment
1:52–2:36	Open "free" trumpet solo, exploring the melodic and harmonic material of the melody section, with bass and drum swinging accompaniment
2:36–end	Melody with 3-bar ending tag, sax and trumpet play melody in unison, similar to opening melody section, with ending tag inverting last phrase of melody

	Free	**Modern Mainstream**
Repertoire	New compositions, often lacking chord progressions. Based more on melody and rhythm than harmony. If supporting harmony is used, rules governing functional harmony are ignored.	Blues, tunes based on "rhythm changes" harmonic scheme, contrafacts, recreations of standard pop and show tunes, and newly composed tunes by jazz artists. Melodies clearly derived from harmonies.
	Form and structure may be less obvious or completely absent.	Form and structure fairly obvious, frequently based on modern song form.
Instrument Roles	*Bass* – Freed from walking bass lines derived from prescribed chords. Not always in sync with drums.	*Bass* – walking bass lines derived from prescribed chord progression and in sync with drums.
	Instrument emerges with equal stature as potential soloist.	Instrument emerges with equal stature as potential soloist.
	Piano – At times absent from ensemble altogether, or freed from traditional comping roles defined by traditional chord progressions.	*Piano* – Bound by prescribed chord progression. Supplies harmonic backdrop to melody. Comping technique employed to accompany soloists.
	Drums – Played in unconventional ways, sometimes out of time, out of sync with bass, and without traditional swing style.	*Drums* – Played in conventional synchronized fashion. Along with the bassist, defines steady tempo, and style.
	Solos in a more melodic fashion and often not bound by tempo or form.	Modern drummers begin to solo in a more melodic fashion. Often bound by tempo and form of composition.
	Horns – State melody, if one exists, followed by improvisations often not bound by traditional chord progressions, or any chords whatsoever.	*Horns* – Statement of melody followed by improvisations. Improvisations bound completely by prescribed chord progression.
Performance Practice	Horn players redefine traditionally accepted standards in intonation, phrasing, sound and articulation. Use of bop inspired rhythms, but free of melodic clichés.	Intonation and overall sound derived from traditionally accepted European performance practice, but with ample room for personal expression.
	Performance practice less bound by the jazz tradition and reflecting past practices.	Performance practice heavily influenced by the jazz tradition and past practice.
	Impromptu, seemingly ragged, or under-rehearsed performances as compared to traditional standards.	Cohesive, well-rehearsed performances.
	Overall performance presentation is less prescribed and expected. Focus on group textures – soundscapes – rather than consistently well-defined individual solos. (There are exceptions to this in free jazz however)	Performance presentation is well defined, prescribed by past practice. Clearly defined sections with each instrument fulfilling a well-understood role including that of soloist.
	Simultaneous dialogue, like the many conversations of a crowd, and similar to the collective polyphonic improvisations heard in early New Orleans jazz but less governed by traditional harmonies and bass lines. Individual instrument voices often blurred.	Clearly defined musical dialogue where main characters are well defined and individual instrument voices easily separated.

FIGURE 11.3 A study in contrasts: A comparison of the characteristics of free jazz and more traditionally grounded, modern mainstream jazz styles

Mingus's ensembles were always harbingers for exceptionally innovative soloists, who were encouraged to go out on a limb, experiment, and express their blackness. Although mixed about Coleman's "new thing," Mingus was clearly intrigued by it. After hearing a Coleman recording among a group of more traditional recordings, he commented later that,

> His [Coleman's] notes and lines are so fresh. It made everything else he was playing, even my own record that he played, sound terrible. I'm not saying everybody's going to have to play like Coleman. But they're going to have to stop playing like Bird.[23]

This was an important revelation, considering Mingus had begun his career playing traditional jazz with Louis Armstrong and Lionel Hampton and bop with masters such as Parker, Powell, and Gillespie.

To capture the looseness and improvised feel and ensure that members of the band could contribute their own personal sounds and emotions, Mingus preferred to teach the musicians their parts rather than write them down. He even referred to his bands as the Jazz Workshop. He was public in showing his respect for the jazz tradition, and especially for Jelly Roll Morton, Monk, and Ellington. His compositions bore some resemblance to Ellington's, in that each composer shared a similar flaw—Mingus's more lengthy compositions were at times fragmented and lacked continuity, but this was a common trait (some considered blemish) of much postmodern art and, in some ways, helps to define it.[24]

Like Monk, Mingus is considered a rediscovery figure, in that his music has gained more respect and popularity in the years following his death than during his lifetime. Pop star Joni Mitchell completed a project that was intended as a collaboration with Mingus but ended as a tribute recording following his death. Some years later, composer Gunther Schuller recreated from Mingus's sketches a 2-hour, multi-movement concert work entitled *Epitaph*. The bass line that begins Mingus's famous "Haitian Fight Song" became the backdrop for a 2001 automobile TV commercial, although it is doubtful that most viewers were aware of the origins. The contemporary Mingus Big Band tribute band, formed years after his death, has been most successful in recreating his music while capturing recent polls and public attention in the process. They have established themselves as one of the most significant big bands of the early 21st century and are helping to keep this great tradition alive.

Mingus's brand of loose, driving hard bop is well defined by "Boogie Stop Shuffle," included in the online audio collection. It is classic Mingus in that it draws on important aspects of the black tradition—in this, the blues and a riff style associated with bands from the earlier years of jazz. As the title implies, the piece is built on a foundation of boogie-woogie-style riffs. Mingus had a penchant for also using ensemble riffs to accompany soloists, and this particular piece is no exception.

THE END OF MODERN JAZZ HERALDED BY THE BEGINNING OF THE POSTMODERNS

There were two stylistic strata moving in parallel during the 1950s and 1960s, and it is important to realize that both modern jazz and emerging postmodern styles coexisted and will continue to do so for quite some time, with many artists participating in many styles.

There seems to be no single reason why hard bop became of less interest, any more than there is a reason why any popular art form falls out of favor. Styles inevitably decline for any number of reasons. Hard bop was designed to attract and hold black and white audiences, at a time when attentions were being drawn toward new emerging pop styles, such as R & B and

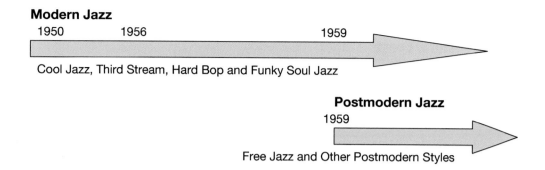

EXAMPLE 11.1 Modern and postmodern jazz coexist

rock 'n' roll. Television had also become affordable and, along with movies and musicals, became the frequent source of leisure-time activity. For example, recordings of TV personalities, Broadway musicals, and movie themes contributed to nearly half of the top 50 gold (sales of 500,000 or more) and platinum (sales of 1 million or more) recordings produced in the 1950s. The balance of these hit recordings are attributed to Elvis Presley, Frank Sinatra, Johnny Mathis, Nat "King" Cole, Harry Belafonte, and two jazz artists—Dave Brubeck for *Time Out* (with "Take Five") and Miles Davis for *Kind of Blue*. (Davis's *Kind of Blue* has sold over 5 million copies worldwide since its release, but, at the time of its release in 1959, was not even charted by sales polls.)

Numerous problems plagued the performers of this time, not least of which was their highly publicized drug use. Jazz journalist Leonard Feather pointed out that, "of the 23 *Down Beat* poll winners, nine were known narcotics users and five had arrests and convictions on record."[25] An alarmingly high percentage of hard-bop artists were junkies, causing many to ask why. Saxophonist and Blakey alumnus Jackie McLean suggested that drugs were a "form of self-medication—trying to cool yourself out. It's the pain of being so creative and not having avenues to express it, or having your work considered less than important that could drive a man to many things."[26] Not all artists felt this way, however. Pianist Oscar Peterson offered an alternative view:

> I have seen how players can succumb to this false crutch, especially when their careers seem stagnated or suspended. I have observed the raft of famous but misguided players follow their idols into drug-abuse, and often into death as a result . . . If I had to advise any young musician, I'd say that your instrument should be your needle, and music your addiction. It is mine.[27]

For many musicians participating in the hard-bop scene, notoriety was fading by the early 1960s, as they lost their battle for acceptance by young audiences to the rock 'n' roll bands. *Down Beat* magazine reviewer John S. Wilson gave Blakey's Messengers' recording *Big Beat* a lackluster review, stating that it was nothing more than a repetition of "material that has been gone over time and time again."[28] In 1978, author and historian James Lincoln Collier agreed with Wilson in writing that, "the hard bop style was exhausted [by 1960], worn out by overuse. . . . The central problem was a lack of musical intelligence, a failure of imagination on the part of the players in the style."[29] Dave Brubeck and Miles Davis are examples of two exceptionally successful musicians who survived the transition from modern jazz to the postmodern era. As Davis—a successful hard-bop musician—spanned so many decades, all the while serving as a steward for so many new directions in jazz and introducing, along with them, new young artists, his career will be discussed in detail in the upcoming chapter.

MILESTONES

Chronicle of Historic Events

The timeline that follows will put the developments of jazz discussed in this chapter into a larger historical context, providing you with a better sense of how landmark musical events may relate to others that match your personal areas of interest.

1956	• Civil rights advocate Martin Luther King has his home bombed.
	• *Peyton Place* by Grace Metalious is a bestseller.
	• The musical *My Fair Lady* hits Broadway.
	• Top films include *Invasion of the Body Snatchers*, *The Ten Commandments*, and *Bus Stop*.
	• The University of Alabama is sued for banning blacks from enrolling.
	• Elvis Presley becomes a rock 'n' roll idol with the release of "Heartbreak Hotel."
	• Bus segregation is declared unconstitutional.
	• Stan Kenton records *Cuban Fire Suite*.
	• Clifford Brown, Sonny Rollins, and Max Roach record "Pent Up House."
1957	• John F. Kennedy is awarded the Pulitzer Prize for *Profiles in Courage*.
	• The nuclear arms race heats up.
	• The Count Basie band becomes the first black band to perform at New York's Waldorf–Astoria Hotel.
	• Vocalist Pat Boone enjoys popularity.
	• President Eisenhower sends federal troops to assist the racial integration of Little Rock, Arkansas, schools.
	• The US races Russia in space exploration.
	• Leonard Bernstein enjoys a hit with the musical *West Side Story*.
1958	• Texan Van Cliburn wins the Tchaikovsky Piano Competition.
	• NASA is created to bolster the U.S. position in the space race with Russia.
	• The Kingston Trio, Everly Brothers, Little Richard, Rick Nelson, and Chuck Berry are pop music successes.
	• Art Blakey's Jazz Messengers records the funky jazz tune "Moanin'."
1959	• Coast-to-coast flight becomes a reality, along with passenger flights to Europe.
	• Richie Valens, Texan Buddy Holly, and "The Big Bopper" die in a plane crash.
	• Jazz singer Billie Holiday dies at age 44.
	• Integrated schools open in Little Rock, Arkansas.
	• The ill-fated Ford Edsel hits the market.
	• Alaska and Hawaii become the 49th and 50th states.
	• *Some Like It Hot* and *Ben Hur* are popular films.
	• Avant-garde-jazz artist Ornette Coleman records "Mind and Time."
1960	• Martin Luther King becomes a prominent civil rights leader—protests, sit-ins, and other forms of non-violent protest against segregation and discrimination are held.
	• Free-jazz artist Ornette Coleman records the revolutionary *Free Jazz*.

- The birth-control pill is approved.

- Cold war tensions escalate following the U2 spy plane incident. Tension mounts in Cuba.

- J.F. Kennedy defeats Richard Nixon for the presidency by a narrow margin.

- *Camelot* opens on Broadway.

- Charles Mingus records "Boogie Stop Shuffle."

- Horace Silver records "Strollin'."

1961
- Rock 'n' roll is a success with teenagers. The *American Bandstand* TV show and Chubby Checker's "The Twist" are hot with teens.

- Fears of Armageddon increase as the missile race and atomic testing escalate.

- Harper Lee wins a Pulitzer Prize for *To Kill a Mocking Bird*.

- The US continues giving assistance to South Korea, defending democracy against communism.

- Freedom Riders are attacked as they tour the South to evaluate compliance with desegregation acts.

- The American astronauts Shepard and Grissom are the first to explore space, helping the US to catch up with Russia in the space race.

1962
- Astronaut John Glenn orbits Earth.

- John Steinbeck wins a Nobel Prize for *The Winter of our Discontent*. Other bestsellers included Helen Gurley Brown's *Sex and the Single Girl* and *One Flew Over the Cuckoo's Nest* by Ken Kesey.

- The US sends a small force to Laos.

- Popular films include *Lawrence of Arabia*, *Dr. No*, *Days of Wine and Roses*, *To Kill a Mocking Bird*, *What Ever Happened to Baby Jane?*, *Long Day's Journey into Night*, *The Manchurian Candidate*, and *How the West Was Won*.

- Russia agrees to withdraw missiles from Cuba.

1963
- Violent demonstrations in Birmingham, Alabama, lead to desegregation of lunch counters and integration of schools.

- Four young girls are killed in a Birmingham, Alabama, church bombing, which, along with other racial incidents of the period, inspired jazz composer Charles Mingus to compose "Fables of Faubus."

- Martin Luther King is jailed for his civil-disobedience actions.

- President Kennedy lends support to racial equality.

- The first blacks graduate from the University of Mississippi.

- The popularity of folk music soars through work by singers Bob Dylan, Joan Baez, Pete Seeger, and Peter, Paul & Mary.

- Martin Luther King addresses the largest ever civil rights rally and declares, "I have a dream."

- Pop artists such as Andy Warhol gain popularity for controversial postmodern art, breaking traditional barriers.

- JFK is assassinated in Dallas, Texas—Lyndon B. Johnson is sworn in as president.

- William Faulkner wins a Pulitzer Prize for fiction.

- James Baldwin publishes *The Fire Next Time*.

1964
- The British rock group the Beatles is widely accepted by American youth.

- Folk musicians such as Dylan continue to express themes of social injustice and the horrors of war in lyrics.

- Congress passes the Civil Rights Act prohibiting racial discrimination.

- Student unrest on the University of California Berkley campus and race riots in New York lead to deaths and arrests.

	• Julie Andrews stars in *Mary Poppins*. Other popular films included *The Pink Panther* and the Beatles' *A Hard Days Night*.
	• Martin Luther King wins a Nobel Peace Prize.
	• Lyndon B. Johnson wins the presidential election handily.
1965	• The US takes the offensive in Vietnam, despite divided public opinion.
	• Dances such as the Frug and Watusi are popular, along with mini dresses and go-go boots.
	• Black Muslim sect leader Malcolm X is shot by a member of an opposing sect.
	• 25,000 blacks organize a march on Montgomery, Alabama, to affirm their right to vote.
	• An astronaut walks in space.
	• President Johnson signs the Voting Rights Act favoring African-Americans.
	• Racial tension explodes in the Los Angeles Watts district.
	• Timothy Leary advocates use of drugs to "tune in, turn on, and drop out."
1966	• The war in Vietnam escalates amid waves of antiwar protests.
	• Race riots erupt in Chicago and Atlanta.
	• Pop music matures, with the Beatles, Bob Dylan, the Beach Boys, the Byrds, and Motown groups the Supremes and the Miracles.
	• President Johnson launches a war at home on urban decay, awarding grants to cities for reconstruction.
	• Top films include *Blow Up*, *A Man For All Seasons*, and *Who's Afraid of Virginia Woolf*.

CHAPTER SUMMARY

In the 1950s, fans had numerous jazz listening options. While the cool reaction to bebop was taking place, most notably on the West Coast, a new generation of musicians continued the development of the bop tradition, creating hard bop. Within the hard-bop movement was a smaller faction, playing not only bop-inspired jazz, but also a more commercial, sometimes danceable music. Influenced by gospel music and R & B, this brand of jazz was labeled "funky jazz" or "soul jazz." By the mid 1950s, important early third-stream works were recorded, and, by the end of the 1950s, free jazz took listeners to entirely new destinations, while other groups continued to play cool jazz and hard bop.

Art Blakey, Horace Silver, Clifford Brown, and Max Roach led important early hard-bop groups. Originally, drummer Blakey and pianist Silver worked together, forming the Jazz Messengers. Horace Silver later went on to lead his own groups, and both leaders had a knack for finding and developing young talents who became important contributors to jazz. Young trumpet sensation Clifford Brown teamed with bop veteran drummer Max Roach to form the Clifford Brown–Max Roach Quintet. Brown would tragically die in an automobile accident at age 25. Outstanding hard-bop alto saxophonist Cannonball Adderley was better known to the general public for his funky jazz hits, as was guitarist Wes Montgomery for his renditions of pop tunes. Selections by both artists could be heard on the radio and on jukeboxes throughout the country.

The postmodern movement is probably best illustrated by free-jazz alto saxophonist Ornette Coleman. His 1959 recording *Free Jazz* announced the dawn of a new era in jazz, just as Miles

Davis's *Birth of the Cool* had done 10 years earlier. In a way, free jazz reestablished the emphasis on group or collective improvisation that was important in early New Orleans jazz. Unlike early jazz, however, free jazz did not rely on meter, melody, or chord changes. A free-jazz performance might contain some basic kind of theme statement, but, beyond that, the performers were welcome to add comments to the improvised conversation as they saw fit. Free-jazz artists also frequently treated pitch/intonation in a completely different way, resulting in what sounds out of tune by traditional standards. It should come as no surprise that, in general, free jazz has probably the least commercial appeal of any jazz style.

Bassist/composer Charles Mingus, an important pioneer of late modern and postmodern jazz, defies categorization. His diverse background includes work with Louis Armstrong, serving as bassist for the important bebop concert of Charlie Parker and Dizzy Gillespie at Toronto's Massey Hall, and performing and composing third-stream works. Mingus's reputation gained more notoriety in the years following his death. Much of his music lives on in the work of the Mingus Big Band.

KEY TERMS

Important terms, people, places, and bands:

Terms	People	
Aleatoric	Cannonball Adderley	Jimmy Smith
Funk	Art Blakey	Bobby Timmons
Harmelodic	Clifford Brown	
(harmelodics)	Don Cherry	**Places**
Mainstream	Ornette Coleman	Watts
Ostinato	Charles Mingus	
Pendulum theory	Wes Montgomery	**Bands**
Postmodernism	Max Roach	Clifford Brown–Max Roach
	Sonny Rollins	Quintet
	Horace Silver	Horace Silver Quintet
		Jazz Messengers

STUDY QUESTIONS

1. How would you describe the hard-bop style?

2. What size bands are associated with hard bop, and what is the typical instrumentation?

3. Name the various styles of jazz that could be heard during the 1950s.

4. What cities seemed to be the strongholds for hard-bop bands and musicians?

5. Name some of the stable small groups that emerged during the hard-bop period.

6. Who is given credit for developing the funky style of hard-bop jazz?

7. Discuss the essence of the funky-jazz style.

8. Which guitarist, who is known as the most important player of this instrument since Charlie Christian, teamed up with organists, and in what ways did he make his playing style unique?

9.   What was unusual about the instrumentation of Ornette Coleman's revolutionary bands, and how did this instrumentation help him to forge a new style?

10. Although Ornette Coleman's style attracted a great deal of attention in the late 1950s, many characteristics of his music were not entirely new or unique. Which artists paved the way and followed similar musical paths?

11. What was so unique about Charles Mingus's music?

12. Compare and contrast the hard-bop style to free jazz, including a discussion of instruments' roles.

13. Discuss the meaning and implications of the term "postmodern."

14. What is the significance of Isaac Newton's "pendulum theory" to jazz at this point in time?

15. What kind of music had become popular with the American public in the 1950s, gradually replacing jazz, and why?

CHAPTER 12

Miles and Miles of Miles
Miles Davis and His Sidemen Redefine Postmodern Jazz

I don't want to sound like nobody but myself. I want to be myself, whatever that is.[1]
—Miles Davis

Apollo 11, the first manned lunar-landing mission, was launched on July 16, 1969, and Neil Armstrong and Buzz Aldrin became the first and second men to walk on the moon

JAZZ IN PERSPECTIVE

The 1960s were tumultuous times in America and an age of conflicting values—peace, love, rock 'n' roll, and war. Jazz experienced many changes as a result of these influences and vied for attention with new trends in popular music. This decade is perhaps the most unsettled, at least on home soil, as any on record, and the music in many ways reflects the tension and restless atmosphere. Political and social unrest was sparked and fueled by the war in Vietnam (1965–1973), the missile and space race with the Soviet Union, a soft and sagging economy, a volatile civil rights movement, the rock 'n' roll music explosion, and the rise and eventual assassinations of two of America's greatest leaders and orators—President John F. Kennedy (1963) and Reverend Martin Luther King (1968).

In retrospect, Stanley Kubrick's film *2001: A Space Odyssey* may have done more to summarize the 1960s than may have been apparent at the time. His 1968 episodic film, complete with dramatic special effects by 1960s standards, is a study in contrasts of mankind's frailties and accomplishments. A year later, U.S. astronaut Neil Armstrong became the first human to set foot on the moon, where he announced to the world that his was "one small step for man" but a "giant leap for mankind." Although this may have been true in terms of scientific advancements and outer-space exploration, on Earth it seemed like mankind was taking backward steps at an alarming rate. The U.S. involvement in the war between North and South Vietnam drew mass protest, inspiring musicians such as Bob Dylan to express political commentary at concerts and on recordings. Peace marches to protest the war and young males burning their draft cards were common occurrences. Some radical college students, who were enraged by the war, the draft, social injustices, and racial inequalities, joined the Students for a Democratic Society (SDS) organization. Other young people tried a less volatile means of protest, marching 50,000-strong to San Francisco one summer for a "love-in." Dressed in their tie-died clothing, with males sporting hairdos that made the Beatles look conservative, these young men and woman sought both to escape from the harsh realities of life and to end political and social injustices with peaceful solutions. Their peaceful demonstration at the 1968 Chicago Democratic convention against the war in Vietnam, however, turned to bloodshed, with 700 injuries and 650 arrests.

During these same years, the civil rights movement escalated, bringing new focus to racial prejudices. The famous phrase "I have a Dream," spoken by civil rights champion Reverend Martin Luther King, who preached non-violent resistance, was intended to incite peaceful protest for equal rights, but public gatherings often led to violence in American cities and on college campuses. Riots in Watts lasted 5 days, leaving behind a charred community that saw 34 dead, 1,000 injured, and 4,000 arrested. Riots erupted in other major cities across the country, including Birmingham, Philadelphia, Boston, Chicago, and Detroit, where 38 died in 1967. Dr. King, who was awarded the Nobel Peace Prize in 1964, was assassinated only 4 years later. Other black leaders, such as Black Muslim Malcolm X, led more violent demonstrations, following his civil-disobedience credo, but he too was struck down by an assassin's bullet in 1965. Women, led by spokespersons such as author Gloria Steinem, were also vocal in the 1960s, demanding equal treatment. The women's liberation movement was born in the 1960s and encouraged the symbolic burning of bras to make a case for an end of male supremacy.

The 1960s was a time when drugs, sex, and rock 'n' roll seemed to permeate college campuses, breeding a new sense of social unrest and revolution, much as had been the case about 40 or 50 years earlier, when Victorian ideals were put on trial and rejected by the younger generation. Just as jazz became the theme song for this earlier generation, rock 'n' roll was adopted as the anthem of 1960s youth. Beatlemania struck American youth in 1964, when the British pop group first appeared in 73 million homes via the Ed Sullivan TV show. Young people experimented with LSD, marijuana, and other mind-expanding hallucinogenic drugs as they listened to Janis Joplin sing "Women is Losers," the Beatles' John Lennon with "Give Peace a Chance," or guitar sensation Jimmy Hendrix with "Are You Experienced." For many teens and college-age students, it was time to turn on and tune out—the "age of Aquarius," peace and love, flower people, hippies, non-conformity, and a time to drop out from an intolerant, flawed society. It was impossible for the jazz world to go untouched by such significant developments in the evolution of American society and thought.[2]

THE MUSIC

The jazz purists felt that the "three Ms," referring to Monk, Mingus, and Miles (Davis), kept "real" jazz alive through the 1950s and early 1960s, in the midst of soulful, funky jazz, cool jazz, and third-stream fads. The jazz world had lost its spiritual leader and guiding light with the death of Charlie Parker in 1955, and many were waiting, looking for the next messiah to show them the way. The three Ms created original, adventuresome forms, harmonies, rhythms, and new compositions, not forged merely by borrowed chord progressions stolen from earlier compositions, as had been the case with much of the bebop repertoire. These new approaches challenged soloists to dig out of the predictable ruts left by those who had sculpted the modern bebop style. Mingus and Monk were both significant bridges linking past jazz traditions to the artist soon to be recognized as the new messiah. In 1955, no one yet knew that Miles Davis, the child of an East St. Louis dentist, who had first come to New York to study classical music at the Juilliard School of Music, would ultimately be the one to achieve such recognition. He cultivated or made significant contributions to seven periods of jazz development, including bebop, hard bop, cool, modal, third stream, progressive, and jazz–rock fusion. No other jazz artists can lay claim to such an accomplishment and contribution. His music was as provocative as his stylish, at times flamboyant, dress, and his elusive, sometimes militant behavior only fueled his rise to notoriety, adding to the mystique that will always be a part of his legacy. In time, Davis would transcend his status as merely a preeminent musician to become a cultural icon, a man whose art never remained static and always reflected the current state of an ever-changing American culture.

THE EARLY MILES

Without the advantage of the broader perspective that we now enjoy, Miles Davis's career could easily have ended, or been doomed to relative obscurity, by the early 1950s, and he would have been remembered as just another trumpet player. In many ways, his less flamboyant trumpet style, as compared with the macho Gillespie, Navarro, or Brown approaches, characterized many of his earliest recordings, where he was featured as the youngest member of Parker's late-1940s bebop band. These early solos were often undeveloped and lacked the virtuosic traits that were the hallmark of bebop. His technique was at times unsteady, his sound small by comparison, and he rarely played bravado-like high-note passages, preferring the middle to lower registers of the instrument. He was no doubt preoccupied with finding his own voice, while feeling pressure to conform to the accepted style at the time. There was an element of insecurity and inconsistency in many of these early solos, and yet they also possessed an austere, melodic beauty that was often absent in bop. Although it is true that he did not demonstrate a commanding, in-your-face style compared with notable bop artists, Davis did demonstrate in these early solos a desire to be different, following his own path and muse. Historian Martin Williams aptly described Davis's first entry into the jazz scene as Parker's sideman: "Davis was an effective foil for Parker's technical and emotional exuberance."[3] Davis was preoccupied with finding a lyrical, more subdued approach to improvisation, caressing the harmonies rather than setting fire to them, as was the case with Parker, Gillespie, and the other hot-bop soloists. In his autobiography, comparing bebop artists' approach with his different, cooler style, Davis described Gillespie's and Parker's music as,

> this hip, real fast thing, and if you weren't a fast listener, you couldn't catch the humor or the feeling of their music. Bird and Diz were great, fantastic, challenging—but they weren't sweet. The *Birth of the Cool* was different because you could hear everything and hum it also.[4]

The cooler side of Davis, exposed briefly in the 1949 *Birth of the Cool* recordings and short-lived nonet club engagements, served to launch the cool style, a movement that many artists devoted entire careers to exploring. The music recorded by the nonet seemed to frame Davis in a much more comfortable setting, as illustrated by his exceptional solos throughout these recordings. His solos were as revolutionary as the arrangements and compositions.

The *Birth of the Cool* was just a way station, and Davis kept moving, always in search of something new and more in sync with his own personal feelings about jazz. Everything about his playing, particularly his sound and attack, was different than what had come before. Although one hears the earlier tradition in his playing, there is also a very clear, new message being given.

Miles Davis's nonet in a recording studio for the sessions released as *Birth of the Cool*. Pictured are, clockwise from left: Bill Barber, Junior Collins, Kai Winding, Max Roach (obscured behind screen), Al Haig (at piano), Joe Shulman (standing at rear), Miles Davis, Lee Konitz, Gerry Mulligan

The very fact that his style didn't fit well into the bebop context provided a framework for him to emerge as perhaps the most influential jazz artist of the postmodern era. However, Davis's career was nearly derailed by an addiction to heroin, a 4- or 5-year habit that he eventually conquered only through his own perseverance and abstention. During the early 1950s, he was under contract with the Prestige label and recorded a number of fine discs, but with no real, established group. In every case, these recordings featured headline performers from the era, including the MJQ. The Prestige recordings all offer some shining examples of brilliant playing. Davis's solos during this period showed a newfound maturity, a new personalized trumpet sound, and a sense of pacing and confidence where the element of space was becoming as valuable, if not more so, than a rapid burst of notes à la Gillespie. He had effectively learned to edit out all the unnecessary notes from the bebop style, simplifying improvisations down to the most essential, melodic ingredients. The result was a poignant and to-the-point musical statement. Economy of style, along with his frequent use of the metallic harmon mute, became his trademarks as he developed a more mature style. Additional characteristics associated with Davis's sound that separated him from dozens of trumpet players were his unique attack and preference for a straight tone with no vibrato. In his autobiography, he said that: "People tell me that my sound is like a human voice and that's what I want it to be."[5]

Without a band he could call his own, and with a bad habit that was consuming much of his life, it was difficult to see Davis in the early 1950s going much further, despite his unique approach to the instrument. By 1955, both became non-issues, as Davis found new freedom from his drug addiction and formed his first stable quintet, including John Coltrane on tenor saxophone (who replaced Sonny Rollins), Red Garland on piano, Paul Chambers on bass, and Philly Joe Jones at the drums. From this point on, Davis never looked back, and each personnel change to the quintet added a new dimension and often inspired him to pursue an entirely new musical direction. Perhaps his greatest attribute of all was his uncanny ability, as a leader, to identify and nurture new, young talent, in a sense returning the favor many times over that Parker had done for him. "I have always said that what the group does together is what makes music happen," he said. "My gift [was] having the ability to put certain guys together that would create a chemistry and then letting them go; letting them play what they knew and above it."[6] The list of alumni from Miles Davis's bands is a list of the most significant innovators in the past four decades of jazz. Topping this list are John Coltrane, Cannonball Adderley, Bill Evans, Herbie Hancock, Tony Williams, Wayne Shorter, Chick Corea, John McLaughlin, Joe Zawinul, Keith Jarrett, and Jack DeJohnette.

THE FIRST GREAT QUINTET

Miles's first great quintet followed the pattern established by the all-stars dates he had fronted or participated in earlier in the decade. This repertoire included a balance of original jazz compositions and transformations (and at times abstractions) of standards such as "I'll Remember April," "Easy Living," "Alone Together," "The Man I Love" and "There is No Greater Love." By the mid 1950s, however, Davis's own quintet was devoting more and more attention to creating new works, and typically over half of the pieces included on these recordings were new jazz compositions, as opposed to face-lifts of older standards. The group hit its stride during its performance at the 1955 Newport Jazz Festival. Its performance at Newport of "Walking," a composition Davis had recorded 2 years earlier with J.J. Johnson, Horace Silver, and Kenny Clarke, brought the group long-overdue recognition. This successful performance served to mark the rebirth of Miles Davis and earned him a top spot in the *Down Beat* magazine's critics' poll that same year. He relinquished the top spot in this annual poll for only 2 years during the next 17 years.

MODAL JAZZ

Several personnel changes at the close of the 1950s added more depth to Davis's quintet and brought a more modern sound to the group. These changes included Bill Evans, the replacement for the older-style pianist Red Garland, and the addition of Julian Cannonball Adderley to the front line, making the quintet a sextet. The two saxophonists—Adderley on alto and John Coltrane on tenor—were stylistically different enough that they served to complement one another. Adderley was deeply rooted in the blues and hard-bop traditions, projecting a wonderful, bouncy, and happy sound, while Coltrane was the more contemporary player who, like Miles, shunned vibrato, making his sound more metallic, brooding, and coldly passionate. The late 1950s also marked the beginning of a long-time relationship Davis enjoyed with Columbia Records, which successfully catalogued nearly every major innovation in his career from this point on. The new sextet recorded two significant albums, in 1958 and 1959, that served to revolutionize both the compositional and improvisational sides of jazz and, in many ways, led Davis down a path that he would walk for the balance of his career. The new concept displayed on these recordings was labeled "**modal**" and was first introduced by the title track of the quintet's 1958 recording *Milestones* (although the original title was just "Miles"). Although this track was the only modal composition included on the *Milestones* recording, it established new concepts that would revolutionize future generations of jazz players and composers and served as the central theoretical basis behind Davis's next landmark 1959 release, *Kind of Blue*. Over time, this album sold more copies than any other Davis recording, totaling more than 5 million worldwide. "I wanted the music this new group would play to be freer, more modal, more African or Eastern and less Western,"[7] he said. The modal concept was not new, but it was certainly new in terms of its applications to jazz in 1958. The theory of modality originated with the Greeks and medieval church music, where entire pieces were based on one or two scales, also called modes. There are seven modes that can easily be seen by relating them to the white notes of the keyboard—see Example 12.1.

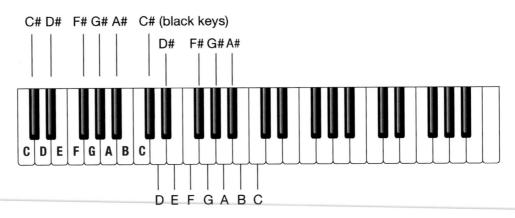

EXAMPLE 12.1 Piano with whole and chromatic half-steps indicated over two octaves, C to C

The modal eight-note scale that begins on C and ends on C (an octave higher or lower) is called the Ionian mode. It is also called the C major scale. If one begins on D and plays all the same white notes ascending to the next D, the Dorian mode is defined. If we began on E, then we would construct the Phrygian mode. The Lydian mode begins on F, and so on, with each new mode using the same pitches but defining a new mode. Each of these seven "church modes," as they were called in ancient times, can begin on any of the 12 different notes (C, C sharp, D, D sharp, E, E sharp, and so on) on the keyboard—so that one could begin any of the seven modes on a black key or a white key by following the same pattern.

Traditional tunes are constructed of melodies derived from a progression of different chords. The progression of chords is created by the tendency of one chord to move to another. Each different chord dictates a different relative scale and has a somewhat different quality. Modal music, on the other hand, lacks these typical harmonic sequences and exists when melodies and harmonies are derived from pitches contained in a single scale that usually last for long periods (8 measures or more). Modal tunes center around one or two tones or key areas (D Dorian, for example), occasionally shifting from one key center, or mode, to another (D Dorian to E-flat Dorian, as is the case in Davis's "So What"). Tunes of this nature establish a sense of tonality through long durations of one mode. The harmonies played as accompaniments to solos on modal tunes are all constructed exclusively from the notes found in the particular mode, even though there is an illusion of the pianist changing harmonies or chords. It is easier to grasp this concept and hear a modal tune when you focus on the bass, which is rather static.

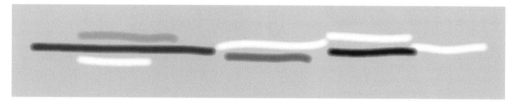

(A) Visual conceptualization of a modal texture. There is a sameness about this visual texture, much like there is in a modal section of music, where all notes, whether used vertically as a chord or horizontally to form melodic lines, stem from the same essential set of pitches (color, in this example)

(B) Visual conceptualization of functional harmony: Each horizontal bar represents a changing chord in a progression. Some chords are related, whereas others serve a quite different role. The black represents the strong chords that supply more variety than the above example

EXAMPLE 12.2   By using different shades to represent sound, it is possible to differentiate between modal and functional harmony, as shown in the above illustrations.

By taking jazz in an entirely new modal direction, away from what had become dominated by increasingly complex chord progressions, Miles Davis and his sextet made a bold statement in the late 1950s that provided newfound freedom to the improvising soloist—a freedom that would resonate in and influence the next decades of jazz. Improvisations became freer and driven more by the importance of spinning out endless melodic lines through constant variation, rather than concern for adhering to ever-changing chords. No longer were soloists confined by chord progressions that presented harmonic signposts to help guide or map them in specific directions through a maze that represented the form of the piece. Without fixed, repetitive chord progressions, modal tunes presented more uncharted maps, lacking fixed repetitive chord progressions, and encouraging the soloists to go in any number of directions, forcing them to place more emphasis on melodic invention. One entire section of a modal tune might dwell on one mode for 16 measures, before changing to another mode or key. One structural similarity between more traditional and modal tunes exists, however, in that both are often based on the song-form architectural plan (AABA or ABA).

John Coltrane, Cannonball Adderley, Miles Davis, and Bill Evans perform in the studio, New York, May 26, 1958

 If necessary, review the sections about harmony and melody found on the website in Chapter 2—"The Elements of Jazz"—to further clarify your understanding of these concepts. There is an example to further clarify the difference between modal and functional harmony found in the section about harmony.

The classic song form, defined as AABA, was the model that Davis used for the first two modal jazz pieces—"Milestones" (1958) (listening guide included on the website) and "So What" (1959). Either tune serves as an excellent example of this new style, and "So What" is included in the online audio anthology as it offers other distinguishing features and presents some of the finest listening from this period. It is from the album *Kind of Blue*, one of the biggest-selling jazz recordings of all time. Each track is a gem, suggesting a new direction in jazz, away from earlier well-established pathways, yet building on the tradition. "So What" is unusual in featuring the bass playing the tune. Although it pioneers new ground in the possibilities offered by modal tunes, it also draws on the African tradition and roots of jazz by once again using the call–response format in presenting the tune. You will recall that this organizational practice dates back to the roots of jazz and is evident in nearly every style. Compare this tune with "Moanin'," discussed in the previous chapter, to hear similarities in the use of the call–response form. See if you can keep track of the A and B sections and hear when the mode changes from D Dorian to E-flat Dorian, helping to identify these sections.

Coltrane and Adderley left Davis's quartet after the recording of *Kind of Blue* to pursue their own careers as leaders. The competent tenor saxophonist Hank Mobley replaced Coltrane, who, along with other personnel rotated into the quintet's lineup, served during this transitional phase that linked Davis to perhaps his greatest, most prolific years, with the second stable quintet. This quintet, as well as the significant careers of Davis's sideman will be discussed later in this chapter.

LISTENING GUIDE 🔊

Miles Davis

"So What" (Miles Davis) 9:26	
From *Kind of Blue*	
Recorded 1959	
Columbia CL 1355	

Personnel: Miles Davis, trumpet; John Coltrane, tenor saxophone; Cannonball Adderley, alto saxophone; Bill Evans, piano; Paul Chambers, bass; Jimmy Cobb, drums

Form: 32-measure AABA song form. Tune derived from D-Dorian and E-flat-Dorian modes.

0:00–0:32	Rubato introduction by piano and bass
0:33–0:48	Solo bass enters in tempo with A theme based on ascending D-Dorian mode (the call or question) with piano 2-chord descending response
0:49–1:01	8-measure A section repeats; saxes added to piano response
1:02–1:15	B section features bass on same theme, moves up to new key of E-flat Dorian; sax and piano 2-chord response continues
1:16–1:30	Return to A section (D Dorian) to complete full chorus of tune
1:31–1:59	Second chorus—Miles Davis improvises on A sections in D Dorian
2:00–2:13	B section of first chorus; change up to E-flat Dorian
2:14–2:27	Final A section of first chorus; return down to D Dorian
2:28–3:24	Third chorus—trumpet improvisation continues for 32 measures on AABA form
3:25–4:19	Fourth chorus—Coltrane improvises on tenor sax for 32 measures on form (out of time "sheets" of sound can be heard at 3:29 on second A section, with long sustained piano accompaniment
4:20–5:14	Fifth chorus—tenor sax improvisation continues for 32 measures on form
5:15–6:09	Sixth chorus—Adderley begins alto sax improvisation on form
6:10–7:04	Seventh chorus—improvisation continues over 32 bar AABA form.
7:05–8:01	Eighth chorus—Evans improvises one chorus with horn background figure used during tune; first A features chord solo; Evans plays simple single note line in 2nd A section; B section and return to A feature dissonant 2-note intervals and closely grouped chord clusters
8:02–8:15	Ninth chorus—bass, piano, and drums, with bass improvising on first A section
8:16–8:29	Bass returns to A theme; piano and bass play 2-chord response
8:30–8:43	B section features bass on same theme transposed up half-step; piano and bass play 2-chord response
8:44	Final A theme; piano and bass play 2-chord response
8:45–end	Ending: piano, bass, and drums fade away following repeat of A theme to end

MILES AND GIL

Miles Davis had many interests, and, at times, he was involved simultaneously in more than one artistic direction.

> I met Gil Evans for the first time when he approached me about arranging "Donna Lee." I told him he could do it if he got me a copy of Claude Thornhill's arrangement of "Robbins' Nest." . . . I liked the way Gil wrote music and he liked the way I played.[8]

Miles was particularly fond of the lush orchestrations that Thornhill favored. Evans and Thornhill parted ways in 1948, and it was during this time that Evans and Davis began formulating a plan that led to the *Birth of the Cool*. "Gil and Gerry had decided what the instruments in the band would be before I really came into the discussions," Miles said. "But the theory, the musical interpretation and what the band would play was my idea."[9] This collaboration would not be the last, and, in 1957, while John Coltrane was off serving his 1-year informal apprenticeship with Thelonious Monk, they collaborated again to produce the first of several critically acclaimed recordings. It is these recordings that established Evans as the new Svengali (anagram of Gil Evans and title of a later Evans recording) of the arranging world, a title he still holds, long after his death in 1988. The Davis–Evans partnership is perhaps the best known in jazz history and comparable with that of Duke Ellington and Billy Strayhorn. The 1957 project for the Columbia label was titled *Miles Ahead* and, like the *Birth of the Cool* sessions, featured an unusual combination of instruments and adventuresome arranging of an eclectic group of pieces. The orchestra included a full complement of brass, including French horns and tuba in the Thornhill tradition; but, in place of the traditional saxophone section, Evans substituted flutes, clarinets, bass clarinet, and oboe—all instruments more closely associated with a classical-music setting. This instrumentation created a tone palette that became the Evans trademark for years to come. Evans, much like Ellington, handcrafted each part with the knowledge that exceptionally gifted musicians would interpret them. In the case of the Evans–Davis collaborations, these musicians were the best studio musicians in New York, comfortable in classical and jazz idioms. Only such training would enable them to meet the challenges that Evans presented in his scores. Evans, once again like Ellington before, demonstrated a gift for mixing brass and woodwinds in unusual and previously untried combinations. The results were wonderful sonic pastels in which all of the individual sounds of the instruments lost their identity while contributing to the creation of an entirely new sound color. Evans's biographer Stephanie Stein Crease stated that, "Evans [had the ability] to orchestrate a mood." And Davis had an uncanny ability "to respond to the ambiance Gil created for him."[10] There was a special, symbiotic relationship between the black soloist and white arranger, which first bloomed with the *Miles Ahead* project. This recording was based on a carefully sequenced group of pieces that represented an integrated suite or musical panorama, as compared with the typical jazz recording that was often nothing more than a random collection of unrelated pieces. Evans had conducted extensive research in various Latin–Spanish forms, and his interest in Spanish flamenco and other Spanish and Latin American dance forms was apparent throughout this recording and many others that followed. Davis embraced such ethnic influences, surfacing periodically throughout his entire career following his collaborations with Evans. Although these Davis–Evans jazz hybrids were very different from Cubop, they illustrate the ease with which elements of jazz can mix with various world music styles to form something entirely new and fresh.

The episodic suite format in *Miles Ahead* became the foundation for two additional collaborations that followed—*Porgy and Bess* in 1958 and *Sketches of Spain* in 1959. Each project became more adventuresome. *Porgy*, George Gershwin's seminal work that premiered in 1935, was in some ways a misfit, as it was neither an opera nor a Broadway musical. *Porgy* fit somewhere in the middle and could best be described as a purely American opera. Gershwin had already established himself as a somewhat controversial composer of symphonic jazz, who blended together elements of jazz, blues, and classical traditions such as "Rhapsody in Blue," premiered by Paul Whiteman. *Porgy* was Gershwin's most daring work, at least in terms of crossing boundaries. The Jewish-born Gershwin composed the pseudo opera *Porgy and Bess*, which was based on black themes and set in a ghetto wharf known as "Catfish Row." What could have been more controversial in 1935? *Porgy* did survive the controversy and enjoyed successful revivals in 1943, 1952, and again in 1959, when Hollywood made the film version, featuring Sidney Poitier, Dorothy Dandridge, Sammy Davis Jr., Pearl Bailey, and Diahann Carroll. "The film's production and release (June 1959) coincided with the rapidly growing Civil Rights movement" that was gaining momentum, and, "once again, *Porgy* attracted criticism in the black community due to increasing sensitivity to racial stereotyping [and exploitation]."[11] The Davis–Evans remake of *Porgy* could not have been better timed, and Davis's brooding, plaintive, vocal-like trumpet sound was the perfect instrumental sound to substitute for the traditional vocals in the original opera. *Porgy* is a masterpiece in terms of arranging, orchestration, and melding of soloist to ensemble. Davis used a complete arsenal of instruments, including the trumpet, flugelhorn, and trumpet with a harmon mute—the sound that became his signature throughout his career. Some critics, though, openly objected to the lack of swing and presence of jazz tradition in Evans's arrangements. They felt that it was too orchestral to be real jazz.

Both *Miles Ahead* and *Porgy* are also significant from a technological standpoint, as both made use of stereo recording and the overdub process, at this point still a new technique. Overdubbing allowed Davis to play his solo parts after a polished recording of all the underlying instrumental accompaniments was completed. This technique marked the beginning of a new era in recording. *Porgy and Bess* sold more copies immediately surrounding its release than any other Miles Davis recording until his *Bitches Brew* release in 1970. "Summertime" is no doubt the most famous track from the *Porgy* recording, and this Evans arrangement has been the source for many other imitations since. The lush orchestrations use combinations of instruments that, at times, lose their individual identity and, when mixed together, represent an entirely new tone color.

Miles Ahead, *Porgy and Bess*, and the 1959 release of *Sketches of Spain* established Miles as a crossover artist, attracting many non-jazz record buyers.

Trumpeter Miles Davis and producer/arranger Gil Evans record the album *Quiet Nights* in 1962

If necessary, reacquaint yourself with the sound of the harmon mute. This mute, along with examples of other brass-instrument mutes, can be found on the website in Chapter 3—"Listening to Jazz." Excerpts of interviews with Evans and Davis, among others who discuss their collaborations, are also included on the companion website in the corresponding chapter.

LISTENING GUIDE

Miles Davis/Gil Evans

"Summertime" (G. Gershwin, I. Gershwin, D. Heyward) 3:17

Recorded 8/18/1958, New York

Porgy and Bess, Columbia CL 1274, Reissued Columbia CK 40647

Personnel: Miles Davis, trumpet; *Trumpets*: Louis Mucci, Ernie Royal, John Coles, Bernie Glow; *Trombones*: Jimmy Cleveland, Joseph Bennett, Richard Hixon, Frank Rehak; *Saxophones*: Julian Adderley, Daniel Banks; *French Horns*: Willie Ruff, Julius Watkins, Gunther Schuller; *Flutes*: Philip Bodner, Romeo Penque; *Tuba*: Bill Barber; *Bass*: Paul Chambers; *Drums*: Philly Joe Jones

Arranged by Gil Evans

Form: Repeated 16-bar song choruses (AA') with ending tag

0:00–0:35	First chorus—16 bars, theme played by muted trumpet, with repeated ascending French horn line, answering trombone, and woodwind descending lines, swinging rhythm section
0:35–1:10	Second chorus—16 bars, muted trumpet solo, with continuing repeated ascending French horn line (add flutes), answering trombone, and woodwind descending lines, swinging rhythm section
1:11–1:46	Third chorus—16 bars, muted trumpet solo continues, with repeated ascending line now played by flutes and muted brass, answering trombone, and woodwind descending lines, new closing ensemble melody (mm.15–16) based on ascending brass line, swinging rhythm section
1:46–2:21	Fourth chorus—16 bars, muted trumpet solo continues, with backgrounds similar to second chorus, closing ensemble melody (mm.15–16) similar to third chorus, swinging rhythm section
2:22–2:57	Fifth chorus—16 bars, muted trumpet solo continues, with repeated ascending-line woodwind, answered by new tuba figure, trombone and saxophone descending lines, swinging rhythm section
2:58–3:17	Tag—4 bars, bass tacet, trumpet closes on long note over first repeat of ascending line, with answering tuba; second repeat slows down to final ensemble chord

THE SECOND GREAT QUINTET

Just as was the case in the formation of Miles Davis's first stable quintet, personnel for his second and most adventuresome group did not take shape immediately. His *Seven Steps to Heaven* recording from 1963 features two different pianists, two drummers, as well as a new saxophonist and bassist. *Seven Steps* is therefore a transitional recording and includes only two original compositions, yet serves to introduce his new trio that will become the nucleus of this revolutionary new quintet— Herbie Hancock on piano, Ron Carter on bass, and the amazing young drummer Tony Williams. Tenor saxophonist George Coleman rounds out the quintet that followed with two additional recordings before Davis makes one final personnel change. These two live recordings—*My Funny Valentine* and *Four and More* show enough of the new band to indicate that a significant change in performance practice is underway, but it is not until Davis replaces the less adventuresome

Coleman with Wayne Shorter that the quintet begins to soar in an entirely new direction. Davis recruited Shorter from Art Blakey's Jazz Messengers, where Shorter had earned the title of musical director, shaping much of the Blakey band's repertoire. Pianist Hancock was also already a seasoned player, with a recording contract for Blue Note Records and a modern approach to harmony and melodic invention. His recordings with hard-bop trumpet ace Freddie Hubbard, another Blakey alumnus, have become legends on their own. *Maiden Voyage*, in particular, is a must for every serious jazz collector, as is his *The Prisoner* and *Empyrean Isles*, where he combined funky tunes with a very modern repertoire. All three new, youthful rhythm mates were not afraid to go out on a limb, and all were keenly aware of the importance of developing telepathic communication to attain the cohesive, yet seemingly loose, free sound they were searching for. They sought to go on an entirely new journey each time they performed a piece, and they took their listeners with them. This quintet revolutionized small-group improvisation and ensemble playing. Drummer Tony Williams, only 17 years old when Davis hired him, had developed an entirely new way of playing that relied on total independence of each limb, so that he could interject a constant barrage of polyrhythmic jabs, playing all around the fundamental beat but without interfering with the regularity of it. He didn't just play time, as had been the tradition with all drummers before him; he played around the pulse without destroying it and could always rely on the steady bass lines played by Ron Carter to provide the necessary glue to keep things together. As a protagonist in the group, Williams instigated constant interplay and dialogue. Williams was the first contemporary drummer to utilize the sock cymbal (hi-hat) on all four beats, as had been done years earlier with the bass drum. By this time, most postmodern drummers had elected not to use the bass drum on every beat. Each member of this rhythm section became recognized as the next important player in the jazz developments of their instruments.

Miles Davis with Herbie Hancock, Ron Carter, and Wayne Shorter at the 1967 Newport Jazz Festival

jazz world by storm. "Hip," informed soloists in small jazz groups around the nation were quoting from this simple tune. "Jean Pierre" became the rage and was evidence of Davis's continued ability to be musically charismatic.

During his final years, Miles performed a mixed repertoire that even included an arrangement of pop-artist Cyndi Lauper's "Time After Time." His most successful performances during these final years were the result of collaborations with guitarists Mike Stern and John Scofield, along with bassist/composer/producer Marcus Miller. Often sophisticated, this modern repertoire still showed roots in the jazz tradition. For instance, Scofield's title track from *You're Under Arrest* (perhaps referring back to Davis's illegal bust in front of Birdland in the 1940s) was based essentially on the time-tested Gershwin, AABA "I've Got Rhythm" model. Davis's *Tutu*, produced in collaboration with Marcus Miller, is reminiscent of the highly orchestrated, textural style of Gil Evans, only not achieved in this case by acoustic instruments, but with layers of orchestrated electronic sounds.

Davis's final 1992 studio recording, *Doo Bop*, once again proved that he had his ear to the street. This collaboration with rapper Easy Moe Bee bears all the signs of street music, with infectious, machine-like, throbbing bass and drum grooves providing the landscape for Davis's improvisation. Dance grooves permeate the recording, along with a few more seductive tempos. Although Davis was in good form, the repetitive vamps and sampled drums that surround him are a bit tiresome and lack the spontaneity that lies at the heart of good jazz and earlier work by Davis.

Miles Davis performing in Copenhagen, 1973, wearing hip clothes of the day

No other instrumentalist in the history of jazz had such a presence and lasting impact on this music. Davis ranks with a select few, including Armstrong, Ellington, and Parker, as a true innovator. But, unlike any of these icons who had preceded him, Davis was a chameleon, always changing his course and updating his approach. Davis was always on the move, never so deeply rooted in one particular tradition that he was not able, willing, and eager to change. In many ways, this one man's career represents the essence of what jazz was and should be—music in constant transition and evolution, borrowing from the past, but not stuck in it.

Figure 12.1, summarizing Miles Davis's unique style that defined his artistry and his contributions to jazz, will be helpful in further clarifying his importance to the history of jazz.

Miles Davis Innovations

1. Was active in seven different styles – bebop, cool, third stream, modal, hard bop, progressive or post-hard bop, and fusion.
2. Preferred the middle and low register rather than the extreme high register, though at times spikes and flares into the high register were used as an element of surprise and tension.
3. Employed an economy of style where space was often favored over long, notey passages.
4. Often used the harmon mute.
5. Developed a unique and identifiable sound and attack. His sound could change like the weather and varied from dramatic to passionate, cold and militant.
6. As a melodic improviser was less concerned about harmony and often played phrases of unusual length.
7. Avoided bebop clichés, though vocal-like blues influences can be found in his playing.
8. Had a lyrical tone that frequently lacked noticeable vibrato.
9. Preferred a linear, scalar approach instead of the vertical, arpeggiated style.
10. Demonstrated an element of angularity and preference for chromatic, more dissonant passages as his style matured.
11. Was ever evolving, never resting on prior accomplishments – the most significant innovator in the post-modern jazz era.

FIGURE 12.1 Miles Davis's innovations

DAVIS SIDEMEN BECOME MAJOR FORCES

One should not underestimate the contributions Miles Davis's sidemen made in reshaping jazz, during and after their apprenticeships with the great master. The following chapter will look more closely at these and other Davis sidemen, who continued to exercise a significant influence on shaping the future of jazz.

JOHN COLTRANE (1926–1967)

Tenor saxophonist John Coltrane was as important to the development of jazz in the postmodern period as Parker was to the moderns. Every player who followed Coltrane, or "Trane" as he was nicknamed, has been significantly influenced by the repertoire he created and his new approaches to the instrument. Like Parker, he was equally comfortable with blues, ballads, standards, and up-tempo repertoire. He added to this older canon a new repertoire that included complex, fast-paced tunes, harmonically fresh ballads, free-form atonal pieces, modal music (after Miles), and cross-culturally influenced works that moved jazz in several new directions.

Coltrane was born in North Carolina, but began to mature as a saxophonist while playing in the Philadelphia area with blues and dance bands. Although his roots were in blues and hard bop, he was destined to be a major voice in the later developments of modal and free jazz. Coltrane rose to prominence as a member of Miles Davis's first great quintet. At this point in his development, he was considered a disciple of bop saxophonists Dexter Gordon and Sonny Stitt, but with more technique and a tendency towards more jagged phrases. He left the Davis quintet in 1957 to take up with pianist Thelonious Monk, for a period that proved to be one of the most rewarding experiences in his training. Monk taught him more about harmony and melodic development. "Working with Monk," Coltrane said, "brought me close to a musical architect of the highest order. Monk was one of the first to show me how to make two or three notes at the same time [multiphonics]."[23] Their live recordings together are significant in the documented evolution of both careers.

Coltrane first encountered the modal style upon his return to the Miles Davis band in 1958 and subsequently participated in both recordings that served to introduce the style to the world—*Milestones* and *Kind of Blue*. Perhaps it was these encounters with modal music that led him to develop a new technical approach to improvising on a harmony. Ira Gitler, writing for *Down Beat* magazine, was the first to describe this technique as **"sheets of sound."**[24] Coltrane played such rapid bursts of notes (usually ascending) that each individual note was indistinguishable, and the by-product was as close to the sound of a chord as a saxophone was capable of producing. Chords can be played on a keyboard instrument, guitar, or vibes, but wind instruments are nearly incapable of producing more than one note at a time (aside from multiphonic techniques). Coltrane's "sheets" of notes, always played as a rapid gesture, are as close as one can come to sounding a complete harmony on the instrument. The effect is akin to running your thumb up the strings of a harp or piano keyboard. Another striking aspect of these gestures is that they did not swing, because the notes were played so fast, and this was a very new concept to jazz, as previously it was thought that everything one played should swing and fit within the context of the rhythm section's steady pulse. One could say that he played against the time or pulse, or simply ignored it. These techniques became part of Trane's musical signature—his style. His "sheets of sound" led to explorations of other new devices, many of which were adopted by serious, contemporary classical saxophonists and composers. Later in his career, for example, Coltrane began utilizing both harmonic fingerings and **multiphonics**. Harmonic fingerings enabled him to produce an unusual **timbre** (tone quality) on certain notes by using unorthodox fingerings to produce them. The principle relates to simple laws of physics that govern the vibration of a string. When a string is set in vibration and then divided at certain points, different, higher pitches above the fundamental pitch established by the string length will result. These pitches above the fundamental note are called **harmonics**. All musical instruments make use of this basic principle. Multiphonics are produced by special fingerings that enable the instrument to sound more than one note at a time. It was a logical progression for Coltrane to move from his "sheets of sound" effect to multiphonics.

Even before he left Davis's group, Coltrane had secured the interest of major record labels. In Miles's own words: "The group I had with Coltrane made me and him a legend."[25] Coltrane recorded two landmark recordings under his own name while still performing with Miles—*Blue Train* (Blue Note, 1957) and *Giant Steps* (Atlantic, 1959). Ironically, both of these recordings are the antithesis of the modal style he had been introduced to by Davis at this same time. These recordings mark the culmination of Coltrane's involvement in the post-hard-bop style and are considered to be the penultimate conclusion of his immersion in tunes that presented complex harmonic

John Coltrane performing on soprano saxophone with his quartet in West Germany, 1959

progressions. In both recordings, most notably *Giant Steps*, he explores complex chord changes derived by substituting new chord sequences for more typical, expected ones. He was clearly concerned, at this time, with developing total control of his instrument, practicing obsessively to develop a virtuosic technique that allowed him to address any challenge, harmonic or technical. Both the title track from *Giant Steps* and "Countdown" from the same recording are excellent examples of this advanced period in Coltrane's development. Although neither tune is a beautiful work of art, as both served as technical exercises for Coltrane, both tunes continue to be important yardsticks in measuring saxophonists' progress, prowess, and level of achievement. The ability to improvise on "Giant Steps" and "Countdown" has become a necessary rite of passage for all saxophonists.

In stark contrast to this complex harmonic style on this album, Coltrane includes "Naima," which is far more static and modal in conception, featuring a pedal-point bass line with slow-moving harmonies. *Down Beat* magazine awarded five stars to this recording, and a retrospective review pointed out that: it was his first recording to include completely original tunes; on "Naima," he introduced the pedal point (repetitive bass tone with changing harmonies above) as an effective compositional device in jazz; and he reached a new plateau of virtuosic control that has taken nearly 30 years to equal and surpass.[26] With these two recordings at the close of the 1950s (*Blue Train* and *Giant Steps*), Coltrane took hard bop to the brink in terms of harmonic complexity and sheer virtuosity.

"Lazy Bird," a Coltrane composition included in the online audio anthology, is a fine example of this complexity and the ease with which Coltrane negotiated challenging chord progressions at brisk tempos. The sidemen on this record are in good form, representing some of the finest hard-bop soloists of the day, and two-thirds of the rhythm section (Chambers and Jones) had worked with Coltrane as members of Miles Davis's quintets, so there was good chemistry. Trombonist Curtis Fuller clearly descends from the earlier J.J. Johnson bebop trombone style.

LISTENING GUIDE

John Coltrane—*Blue Train*

"Lazy Bird" excerpt (Coltrane) 4:31

Recorded 9/15/1957 in New York

Blue Note Records reissued on CDP 7243 8 53428 0 6

Personnel: John Coltrane, tenor sax; Lee Morgan, trumpet; Curtis Fuller, trombone; Kenny Drew, piano; Paul Chambers, bass; Philly Joe Jones, drums

Form: repeated 32-bar-song form (AABA = chorus)

0:00–0:07	Introduction—8 measures featuring piano
0:08–0:15	First chorus—A section theme played by trumpeter Lee Morgan
0:16–0:23	Trumpet repeats A theme
0:24–0:31	Bridge or B theme played by trumpet with tenor sax/trombone counter line in call–response style with trumpet
0:32–0:38	Trumpet ends first chorus with repeat of A theme
0:39–1:08	Second chorus—improvised trumpet solo on entire AABA form, with rhythm-section accompaniment
1:09–1:39	Third chorus—trumpet solo continues on form with rhythm section
1:40–2:10	Fourth chorus—trombone solo featuring Curtis Fuller, with rhythm-section accompaniment
2:11–2:40	Fifth chorus—trombone solo continues
2:41–3:11	Sixth chorus—Coltrane enters with first of several choruses
3:12–3:42	Seventh chorus—tenor sax continues solo
3:43–4:14	Eighth chorus—Coltrane plays final solo chorus
4:15–end	Excerpt ends with beginning of piano solo

LISTENING GUIDE

John Coltrane—*Live at Birdland*

"Afro Blue" (Mongo Santamaria) 6 (excerpt)

Recorded 10/8/1963 live at Birdland, New York

Impulse Records IMPD-198

Personnel: John Coltrane, soprano sax; McCoy Tyner, piano; Jimmy Garrison, bass; Elvin Jones, drums

Form: Two contrasting phrases, each 8 measures (AB improvised interlude A¹B)

0:00–0:28	Pianist McCoy Tyner builds the end of his solo to a climax
0:29	Coltrane enters in the extreme high register of the soprano sax
3:08	Coltrane returns to the first section of the original melody
3:22	Coltrane begins improvising again
4:19–4:34	Coltrane plays the second portion of the main theme
4:35	Quartet begins to wind down dynamically
5:46	Group states last phrase of tune in dramatic rubato style

Coltrane eventually left Davis to strike out on his own, abandoning the dense, complex harmonic web in which he had become entangled and immersing his new quartet in a steady diet of modal music. He pursued this new style as if it were a religion, seeking more and more freedom to express new emotions. With pianist McCoy Tyner, drummer Elvin Jones, and bassist Jimmy Garrison, he popularized modal jazz to an extent that undoubtedly surprised even the record label executives. *My Favorite Things*, the quartet's first, highly acclaimed 1960 recording, featured Coltrane on soprano saxophone as well as tenor. Previously, Sidney Bechet had been the only other jazz instrumentalist to use the soprano with any regularity or success. The soprano had become little more than a footnote, until this recording revived interest in the instrument. Improvements in its design made it more acceptable, and, since the 1960s, the instrument has become standard in the saxophonist's arsenal. Coltrane's sound on this instrument was as unique and personal as it was on tenor. He evoked an eastern or North African flavor on the soprano, at times producing a sound similar to the nasal quality of Indian reed instruments or the oboe, developed centuries earlier in Europe to perform classical music.

The intensity of this quartet, with Coltrane on soprano sax and tenor and Tyner and Jones in the rhythm section, is remarkable—spellbinding in its intensity and without comparison at the time, at least for a small group. "My Favorite Things," included in the online audio anthology, is no exception, comparing favorably with his other modal work at the time. He seemed to prefer up-tempo 3/4 meters for the lengthy soprano sax excursions, and this recording, along with "Inch Worm" and "Afro Blue," all share this quality. Drummer Elvin Jones is explosive, constantly prodding pianist Tyner and Coltrane, dropping salvos with bass drum and cymbals, while injecting machine gun-like chatter with his other hand. The excerpt begins at the close of Tyner's solo, propelled by the trio to a fevered pitch that requires Coltrane to begin his solo at this precipice and build from there. As the excerpt begins mid-track, you may want to first listen to the return of the tune from 3:08 to 4:34, before listening to the entire track.

Coltrane's modal repertoire and recordings, including the highly touted *A Love Supreme*, demonstrated a growing spirituality. Many of the pieces on these recordings, including the originally released version of "Impressions," were long incantations—lengthy improvisations that kept building in hypnotic intensity, much like "My Favorite Things." Critics and listeners were captivated, awarding him Jazzman of the Year, Record of the Year, and first place in the tenor saxophone category, and electing him to the *Down Beat* Hall of Fame, all following the release of *A Love Supreme* in 1965. This recording was one of his most compelling and lasting works, selling a million copies by the close of the 1970s, 20 years after it was recorded.[27] Supplemental listening guides to "Acknowledgement" from *A Love Supreme*, "Impressions," and "Afro Blue" are provided in the corresponding chapter on the website.

Following an all-too-familiar bout with drug and alcohol addiction, Coltrane had turned towards religion and philosophy to seek inner peace and to help him on his personal and musical journey. He is the first jazzman to overtly present his music as a religious offering, as was the case with *A Love Supreme*. The music on this recording, and others that followed, borders on meditations or prayers, such as "Alabama," his elegy for four small girls who lost their lives in the 1963 Birmingham church bombing. "Alabama" is a riveting testament to the mood of the times, when the eyes of the nation were riveted on individuals such as Governor Faubus, who sent National Guard troops to keep young black school children from attending school. This situation, and many others like it, was reflected in the music of many black artists during this time. His search for spirituality led him to the study of Indian music, and he also showed an interest in Latin, Arabic, and African music. Hence, Coltrane is often considered the first jazz musician to seriously pursue world-music styles and consciously weave them into his new brand of American jazz. These influences are most evident in *Africa Brass*, *Olé Coltrane*, and "India," among others. One gets the impression, after hearing Coltrane's performances from this modal period and beyond, that he is searching, at times desperately reaching and crying out with his distinctive vocal-like wails, for something that was unattainable. With its folk-like quality, there is a sense of both deep passion and inner torment in his music. His tone was unique, often lacking vibrato, projecting a steely quality and a vocal-like, primordial cry, as if he were in pain. The metal mouthpiece he used instead of the hard rubber or plastic variety no doubt contributed to his ability to deliver his unique and identifiable tone. His sound has been described as hard-edged, metallic, and brittle. As Wayne Shorter once said, "he had a sense of urgency like he couldn't get everything he wanted out [of the horn]."[28] At other times, as shown on his *Ballads* recording, he could be more caressing, rarely straying far from merely interpreting the beautiful melodies of these tunes.

Coltrane's quartet continued to push the boundaries in the early 1960s, and, in 1961, he added multi-reed player Eric Dolphy to the quartet. Although Dolphy played flute and alto saxophone, he is most remembered for unleashing the potential of the bass clarinet, an instrument that had rarely been explored for its potential as a jazz solo instrument. Now a quintet, their performances became more and more abstract, featuring relentless, long solos. One tune could last an entire set in a live performance, or occupy the entire side of a recording. Some labeled the group's new direction, and that of other black experimentalists, as the "new thing" or "outside" jazz. Coltrane defended their long solos: "they're long because all the soloists try to explore all the avenues that the tune offers. They try to use all their resources."[29] However, many audiences became alienated and turned off by what they perceived as a self-indulgent attitude. After attending a live club date, a *Down Beat* correspondent wrote:

> I heard a good rhythm section . . . go to waste behind the nihilistic exercises of the two horns . . . Coltrane and Dolphy seem intent on deliberately destroying swing. They seem bent on pursuing an anarchistic course in their music that can be termed anti-jazz.[30]

Dolphy expanded his possibilities with the flute, sometimes deriving his inspiration from birdcalls and the ¼-tone whistles that they sometimes sing. Both instrumentalists seemed to want to begin with a blank easel that could be totally open and responsive to their feelings and surroundings. Their music was about finding new ways to communicate with their instruments, in an effort to convey their innermost feelings to the listener. "The main thing a musician would like to do is to give a picture to the listener of the many wonderful things he knows of and senses,"[31] Coltrane said. The "new thing" put off some critics and listeners, and some were openly critical, accusing the artists of abandoning the tradition, including "swing." "It's kind of alarming to the musician," Dolphy said, "when someone has written something bad about what the musician plays but never asks the musician anything about it."[32]

Coltrane continued to push the boundaries of jazz, and, by 1965, it seemed that he had exhausted the possibilities that modal jazz presented, just as he had several years before with harmonically complex hard bop. The only logical alternative for Coltrane was to venture into completely unknown and unpredictable territory, as Ornette Coleman had done several years earlier. "In the early 60s he was studying with me," Coleman said. "He was interested in non-chord playing, and I had cut my teeth on that stuff."[33] The work Coltrane had done with Coleman and the new breed of black musicians experimenting with the "new thing" no doubt all had a major impact on Coltrane, moving him toward his final phase of exploration—free jazz. Perhaps it was the sense of chaos that everyone who lived through the 1960s felt that also motivated Coltrane to move further outside of tradition, motivating him to assemble one of the most important recordings in this history of jazz—*Ascension*. In this recording, Coltrane abandoned predictability, as Coleman had done with his *Free Jazz*. The roles of meter, pulse, melody, harmony, and form were redefined, as they were nearly non-existent. Ironically, it was released the same year that he was awarded Jazzman of the Year for his work on the *Love Supreme* recording, but *Ascension* was far less accessible to the average listener. Listeners often have more difficulty appreciating recorded free jazz, regardless of the artist, compared with the energy of the live experience. *Ascension* featured four saxophonists, two trumpets, two bassists, one drummer, and a pianist. Nothing was pre-composed, aside from the opening five-note melody introduced by Coltrane. What follows is 38 minutes of unstructured improvisation, an orgiastic free-for-all that portrays the contrast between group chaos and free-form solos by the individual instrumentalists. The solos, like that of saxophonist Pharaoh Sanders, were at times streams of shrieks, squawks, screams, squeaks, shouts, hollers, cries, moans, yells, wails, and occasional blues-infected melodies. The soloists were not bound by any prescribed or accepted syntax, making them free of melodic, rhythmic, harmonic, and structural conventions. It was this blatant attack on accepted standards and the very tradition itself that enraged many. The non-musical effects served to turn off many listeners and incited their "anti-jazz" allegations. The release of this recording was the most controversial event in jazz since Coleman's *Free Jazz*, eliciting such criticism as "unattractive" and the result of Coltrane "going off the deep end."[34] But the jazz community was polarized, as others felt *Ascension*, and the other free-jazz works that followed, were inspirational and challenging, elevating jazz to a new plateau of art music. *Down Beat* magazine, in 1966, came out in favor of the recording, describing it as "possibly the most powerful human sound ever recorded."[35]

Figure 12.2 offers a summary of the stylistic innovations that made Coltrane the most important saxophonist in modern jazz at this point.

John Coltrane lived a relatively brief life considering his impressive achievements, passing away as the result of liver cancer in 1967. His death shook the jazz world much as the loss of Parker had. His candle had burned quickly, and perhaps that is why he had been so compulsive and obsessive about accomplishing so much in such a short time. His influence has been pervasive in much of the jazz produced after 1960, and he exerted a significant influence on contemporary saxophonists such as Branford Marsalis, Michael Brecker, James Carter, Kenny Garrett, Joshua Redman, Joe Lovano, and Chris Potter, among others.

Coltrane Innovations

1. Was active in three different phases of jazz–hard bop, modal and free.
2. Had a penchant for lengthy improvisations.
3. Produced a highly original tone quality that often lacked vibrato, projecting a plaintive quality.
4. Reintroduced and popularized use of the soprano saxophone
5. Favored developing smaller motives or melodic cells rather than improvising long unrelated lines.
6. Was one of the first jazz musicians to overtly incorporate music of other cultures, Western and non-Western.
7. Played music that was deeply inspired and informed by the blues tradition.
8. Developed new saxophone performance techniques including "sheets of sound," multiphonics, and harmonic fingerings in addition to extending the range of the instrument.
9. Sometimes played purposefully dissonant lines that were outside the given key (chord). This practice is often referred to as "side-stepping" or playing "outside."
10. Significantly raised the bar for all future performers through his sheer virtuosity and challenging compositions.
11. Established a new approach to freer, open modal playing.
12. Openly used music to express his religious and social beliefs.
13. Was the most important post-modern tenor saxophonist.

FIGURE 12.2 John Coltrane's innovations

Wayne Shorter (1933–)

Born in Camden, New Jersey, Wayne Shorter pursued and completed a BA degree in music education at New York University before joining the armed forces. By the time Shorter made his first appearance with Miles Davis in 1964, he had already established himself as an important voice, working with Horace Silver, Art Blakey, and Maynard Ferguson. Like so many saxophonists in the early 1960s, Shorter was profoundly influenced by Coltrane, but he also bore similarities to both Lester Young and the more contemporary Sonny Rollins in terms of his gift for melodic development. In comparison with Coltrane, his tone was softer and lighter, more in the Young tradition, and somewhat broader. Shorter, like Coltrane, used vibrato only sparingly, which made it that much more poignant when he did. The most unique aspect of Shorter's style was his sense of rhythm. Although he could lock into the groove of a rhythm section and swing with the best of them, he often chose not to, floating over the top of the regular pulse and upsetting the listener's equilibrium. His preference for long tones and space over blinding bursts of notes often gives one the impression that he is playing "slower than the rhythm sections that accompanied [him]."[36] Shorter rarely quoted anyone except himself, and his improvisations are barren of any clichés. Much like Miles Davis, Shorter tended to spin melodies that were grouped in odd numbers of measures, and his choice of notes also contributes to his unique, original approach. He was a guiding force as a saxophonist and composer in the famous Davis quintet of the mid 1960s, just as he had been with Art Blakey's Jazz Messengers in prior years. "Wayne was the idea person, the conceptualizer of a whole lot of musical ideas we did,"[37] Miles said.

> Wayne has always been someone who experimented with form instead of someone who did it without form [referring no doubt to the free jazz movement]. That's why I thought he was perfect for where I wanted to see the music I played go. He understood that freedom in music was the ability to know the rules in order to bend them to your own satisfaction and taste. That's why I say he was the intellectual musical catalyst for the band.[38]

His compositions often broke rules when compared with previous jazz repertoire. Unusual forms and chord progressions, dictated more by melody and improvisation than functional harmony, are his trademarks. His tunes often do not adhere to simple and predictable architectures (4-, 8-, 16-, 24-, or 32-measure units), but take the shape of 14, 18, and 20 measures. He sees composition and improvisation as closely intermingled, and, consequently it is not unusual when a Shorter composition flows freely and seamlessly between written and improvised material, blurring the lines between composition and improvisation. "Paraphernalia" (*Miles in the Sky*), "Dolores" (*Miles Smiles*), and "Masqualero" (*Sorcerer*), and of course "Orbits," the featured track in this chapter, serve as excellent examples of this approach. An intellectual artist, Shorter's compositions are often motivated by non-musical occurrences. For example, his 1964 *Speak No Evil* recording was inspired by folklore, black magic, and legends. Shorter says,

> I was thinking of misty landscapes with wild flowers and strange, dimly seen shapes—the kind of places where folklore and legends are born. I'm getting stimuli from things outside of myself. Before I was concerned with . . . my ethnic roots, but now I'm trying to fan out, to concern myself with the universe instead of just my own corner of it.[39]

His improvisations are as thoughtful as his compositions and are always perfectly conceived in terms of their reference to the original tune. In contrast to Coltrane, who played obsessively long, self-indulgent solos, Shorter was the master of the understatement, often producing short compositions and even more abbreviated solos, with no unnecessary excess.

Shorter left Davis's quintet at the close of the decade to enable a more focused pursuit of his own career. When we examine his impact throughout the 1970s, discussed in more detail in the following chapter, you will see why Wayne Shorter is considered one of the most influential jazz musicians of the late 20th century.

Herbie Hancock (1940–)

Herbie Hancock was the most important jazz pianist to hit the scene, following Wynton Kelly and Bill Evans. The bond between all three was not only stylistic, as Hancock borrowed from both artists who preceded him, but also because each performed with Miles Davis. His stylistic diversity, another characteristic he shares with many of the Davis sidemen, has earned him fans from the pop, jazz, and, to some degree, classical worlds, because, as a child prodigy, he performed with the Chicago Symphony. Since then, Hancock has somehow managed to maintain multiple careers, freely moving between solo piano performances, producing and recording in the pop and jazz worlds, film scoring, experimenting with the latest electronic technology, and performing with cutting-edge jazz groups, both mainstream and avant-garde.

Hancock was already an established musician when he signed with the Miles Davis Quintet. While working with Davis, he continued to maintain a profile as a leader on records and as a highly sought after sideman. It would be difficult to find a pianist who has participated on more recordings and in more diverse settings than Hancock, who lists numerous collaborations on his vast discography.

His pianistic style is derived from two distinct genealogy lines—the harmonically rich style associated with Bill Evans, and the right-hand technical approach fostered by a long line of pianists, beginning with Bud Powell. Hancock's comping style is also highly personal and identifiable for its crispness and rhythmic agility. Hancock's solos are often contrasting in terms of dynamics, density, and texture, juxtaposing dense harmonic passages with single-note lines. One can often sense his classical training, which gives him the facility to perform the most difficult passages with ease.

Hancock's first recording as a leader in 1962 featured the funky, gospel-tinged "Watermelon Man," one of the most widely performed pieces from his repertoire, along with the modal "Maiden Voyage" from his 1965 recording by the same name. "Watermelon Man" and "Cantaloupe Island," from his 1964 release entitled *Empyrean Isles*, were revived and became part of the foundation of the acid-jazz movement of the later 1990s. Other compositions by Hancock that were penned in the 1960s and have since become part of the jazz canon include "Dolphin Dance," featured on his *Maiden Voyage* album, and "Speak Like a Child," the title track from his 1968 release. Hancock was a major force in shaping jazz over the next several decades, particularly the 1970s, during which time his Jekyll and Hyde musical personality was difficult to track.

MILESTONES

Chronicle of Historic Events

The timeline that follows will put the developments of jazz discussed in this chapter into a larger historical context, providing you with a better sense of how landmark musical events may relate to others that match your personal areas of interest.

1957	• John F. Kennedy is awarded a Pulitzer Prize for *Profiles in Courage*.
	• The nuclear arms race heats up.
	• The Count Basie band becomes the first black band to perform at New York's Waldorf–Astoria Hotel.
	• Vocalist Pat Boone enjoys popularity.
	• President Eisenhower sends federal troops to assist the racial integration of Little Rock, Arkansas, schools.
	• The US races with Russia in space exploration.
	• Leonard Bernstein enjoys a hit with his musical *West Side Story*.
	• John Coltrane records "Lazy Bird."
1958	• NASA is created to bolster the U.S. position in the space race.
	• The Kingston Trio, Everly Brothers, Little Richard, Rick Nelson, and Chuck Berry are pop-music successes.
	• Miles Davis's Sextet records the modal composition "Milestones."
	• Miles Davis collaborates with Gil Evans to create *Porgy and Bess*, featuring the popular "Summertime."
1959	• Coast-to-coast flight becomes a reality, along with passenger flights to Europe.
	• Richie Valens, Texan Buddy Holly, and the "Big Bopper" die in a plane crash.
	• Jazz singer Billie Holiday dies at age 44.
	• The Miles Davis Quintet records "So What" on *Kind of Blue*.
	• Integrated schools open in Little Rock, Arkansas.
	• Alaska and Hawaii become the 49th and 50th states.
	• *Some Like It Hot* and *Ben Hur* are popular films.
	• Barbie Doll is released, inspiring the comic strip *Kathy*.
1960	• Protests, sit-ins, and other forms of non-violent protest against segregation and discrimination take place.
	• Martin Luther King becomes a prominent civil rights leader.
	• The *Fantastics* is a hit on Broadway.
	• The birth-control pill is approved.
	• Cold war tensions escalate following the U2 spy-plane incident. Tension mounts in Cuba.
	• JFK defeats Nixon for the presidency by a narrow margin.
	• *Camelot* opens on Broadway.
1961	• Rock 'n' roll is a hit with teenagers. The *American Bandstand* TV show and Chubby Checker's "The Twist" are hot with teens.

- People fear Armageddon as the missile race and atomic testing escalate.

- Harper Lee wins a Pulitzer Prize for *To Kill a Mocking Bird*.

- The US continues assistance to South Korea, defending democracy against communism.

- Freedom Riders are attacked as they tour the South to evaluate compliance with desegregation acts.

- Astronauts Shepard and Grissom are the first to explore space, helping the US to catch up with Russia in the space race.

1962
- Astronaut John Glenn orbits Earth.

- Hollywood starlet and silver-screen sex symbol Marilyn Monroe dies.

- John Steinbeck wins a Nobel Prize for *The Winter of Our Discontent*. Other bestsellers included Helen Gurley Brown's *Sex and the Single Girl* and *One Flew Over the Cuckoo's Nest* by Ken Kesey.

- The US sends a small military force to Laos.

- Popular films include *Lawrence of Arabia*, *Dr. No*, *Days of Wine and Roses*, *To Kill a Mocking Bird*, *What Ever Happened to Baby Jane?*, *Long Day's Journey into Night*, *The Manchurian Candidate*, and *How the West Was Won*.

- Russia agrees to withdraw missiles from Cuba.

- Early "women's lib" author Betty Friedan writes *The Feminine Mystique*.

1963
- Violent demonstrations in Birmingham lead to desegregation of lunch counters and integration of schools.

- Martin Luther King is jailed for his civil disobedience actions.

- President Kennedy lends support to racial equality.

- The first blacks graduate from the University of Mississippi.

- The popularity of folk music soars through work by singers Bob Dylan, Joan Baez, Pete Seeger, and Peter, Paul & Mary.

- John Coltrane records "Afro-Blue."

- Martin Luther King addresses the largest ever civil rights rally and declares: "I have a dream."

- Pop artists such as Andy Warhol gain popularity for controversial art that breaks traditional barriers.

- President John F. Kennedy is assassinated in Dallas, Texas—Lyndon B. Johnson is sworn in as president.

- William Faulkner wins a Pulitzer Prize for fiction.

- James Baldwin publishes *The Fire Next Time*.

- The British rock group the Beatles release their first album.

- JFK's assassin, Lee Harvey Oswald, is murdered by Jack Ruby while in custody.

1964
- The British rock group the Beatles is widely accepted by American youth after an appearance on TV.

- Folk musicians such as Dylan continue to express themes of social injustice and the horrors of war in lyrics.

- Congress passes the Civil Rights Act prohibiting racial discrimination.

- Race riots in New York lead to deaths and arrests; there is student unrest on the University of California Berkley campus.

- Julie Andrews stars in *Mary Poppins*. Other popular films include *The Pink Panther* and the Beatles' *A Hard Day's Night*.

- Martin Luther King wins a Nobel Peace Prize.

- John Coltrane records his ever popular *A Love Supreme*.

- Lyndon B. Johnson wins the presidential election handily.

1965
- The US takes the offensive in Vietnam, despite divided public opinion.

- Dances such as the Frug and Watusi are popular, along with mini dresses and go-go boots.

- Black Muslim sect leader Malcolm X is assassinated by a member of an opposing sect.

- 25,000 blacks organize a march on Montgomery, Alabama, to affirm their right to vote.

- An astronaut walks in space.

- President Johnson signs the Voting Rights Act, guaranteeing blacks the right to vote.

- Racial tension explodes in Los Angeles' Watts district—there are 5 days of riots.

- Timothy Leary advocates the use of drugs to "tune in, turn on, and drop out."

1966
- The war in Vietnam escalates amid waves of anti-war protests.

- Race riots erupt in Chicago and Atlanta.

- Pop music matures with the Beatles, Bob Dylan, the Beach Boys, the Byrds, and Motown groups the Supremes and Miracles.

- The Miles Davis Quintet records "Orbits."

- Lyndon B. Johnson launches a war on urban decay at home, awarding grants to cities for reconstruction.

- Top films include *Blow Up*, *A Man For All Seasons*, *Who's Afraid of Virginia Woolf*.

1967
- Sports fans enjoy the first football Super Bowl—the Packers against the Chiefs.

- Race riots in Detroit are the worst in U.S. history.

- Long hair (males), hippies, and rock bands such as Otis Redding, the Beatles, the Mamas and the Papas, the Byrds, Jefferson Airplane, Grateful Dead, the Who, Janis Joplin, Jimmie Hendrix, and the Doors create music that represents the times.

- College enrollments show a 100% increase since 1960.

- Bare skin and mini skirts reflect growing hedonist attitudes in American youth.

- Public Broadcasting Networks are established.

- Growing anti-war sentiment is directed at U.S. involvement in Vietnam.

- *The Graduate* is the top film.

1968
- Growing anti-war sentiment influences Lyndon B. Johnson's decision not to run for reelection.

- Civil rights leader Martin Luther King is assassinated.

- Robert Kennedy is assassinated.

- The government issues a report exposing a trend toward a two-society nation divided by race.

- The rock musical *Hair* reflects the times.

- 5,000 radical student members of SDS take over Columbia University campus.

- Riots take place at the Democratic national convention in Chicago.

- Stanley Kubrick's movie *2001: A Space Odyssey* reflects the nation's infatuation with space travel.

1969
- The Supreme Court orders an end to all school segregation.

- Top films are *Midnight Cowboy*, *Easy Rider*, *Butch Cassidy and the Sundance Kid*.

- Norman Mailer wins a Pulitzer Prize for *The Armies of the Night*.

- President Richard Nixon takes steps to pull the US out of Vietnam, amidst continued anti-war rallies.

- Astronaut Neil Armstrong walks on the moon.

- The Woodstock event is the largest rock concert ever. Thousands of youth enjoy music, sex, and drugs in a peaceful display for peace.

- Miles Davis records the landmark *Bitches Brew* recording, released the following year.

- Campus demonstrations against the war in Vietnam become increasingly heated.

CHAPTER SUMMARY

The 1960s was a decade of both tremendous challenges and achievements for America. Wars often unify a country, but military involvement in Vietnam instead polarized Americans, causing both peaceful and deadly protests against the war. Civil rights and women's rights issues came to the forefront, sparking yet more protests and demonstrations. U.S. president John F. Kennedy was assassinated, as was civil rights leader Martin Luther King and presidential hopeful Robert F. Kennedy. The Cuban missile crisis, another chapter in the continuing cold war with the Soviet Union, nearly started World War III. In science, man first set foot on the moon, while, in the world of music, British rock 'n' roll bands, most notably the Beatles and the Rolling Stones, changed the American popular music scene. The turmoil of the 1960s is also reflected in the many concurrent new approaches to jazz that developed in the 1960s and through the styles that continued along paths established years earlier.

Miles Davis stands apart from all other great innovators in jazz preceding him, in that, unlike Louis Armstrong or Charlie Parker, Davis was an important contributor to more than one style of jazz. After playing his version of bebop with Charlie Parker, Miles announced the arrival of cool jazz with his 1949 *Birth of the Cool* album. Had Miles been like most of the other great jazz innovators, he would have continued to play and refine cool jazz for the balance of his career. On the contrary, Miles Davis continued to change, identifying and nurturing young talent, while pioneering new styles of jazz. The group described as Davis's "first great quintet," later a sextet, featuring John Coltrane (tenor sax), Cannonball Adderley (alto sax), and Bill Evans (piano), brought a new modal approach to hard bop. This group's *Kind of Blue* album (1959) has sold more than 5 million copies since its release. During this time, Davis also worked with arranger Gil Evans, recording three third-stream albums with large ensembles. When Coltrane, Adderley, and Evans departed to form their own groups, the personnel in Davis's group became unsettled, finally stabilizing with the group known as the "second great quintet." This group featured Wayne Shorter (tenor sax), Herbie Hancock (piano), Ron Carter (bass), and Tony Williams (drums). This quintet played a more progressive jazz, often playing music that used odd phrase lengths, disguised meter, and unconventional chord changes and forms. Many feel that this was Davis's most creative period. As the group matured, the music became less structured, influenced by the free-jazz approach of Ornette Coleman, but sometimes played with a straight eighth-note feel, rather than a more traditional swing feel. By the late 1960s, the group had expanded, adding guitar and using as many as three electronic-keyboard players. This music, combining the instruments and grooves of rock with jazz, became known as fusion and reflected a more postmodern spirit. Many of Davis's sidemen would go on to become leaders of important fusion groups. For health reasons, Davis went into retirement in 1974. Coming out of retirement in 1981, he formed a new group that continued to play in a pop-influenced fusion style. His final project was a hip-hop–jazz album produced by rapper Easy Moe Bee.

John Coltrane pushed the tenor saxophone to new limits in technique and improvisation and also reintroduced the soprano saxophone to the jazz world. His use of multiphonics (playing more than one note at a time), rapid-fire runs (described as sheets of sound), facility in the extremely high register, and his ability to navigate complex chord changes set a new standard against which saxophonists today still measure themselves. Coltrane played with Miles Davis in the late 1950s, but also served as leader for recordings during that time. After leaving Davis, Coltrane assembled a quartet that played primarily modal jazz. With his spiritual awakening, Coltrane incorporated more eastern elements into his music. In his final years, Coltrane's music became much freer and was clearly influenced by Ornette Coleman's work.

Wayne Shorter and Herbie Hancock were both members of Miles Davis's second great quintet. Shorter's importance is not just as a saxophonist, but also as a composer. He brought new, unconventional ideas to Davis's group, before leaving to cofound the very important fusion group Weather Report. Herbie Hancock, well established before joining the Davis group, has continued to play in a diverse range of settings, from mainstream to pop.

KEY TERMS

Important terms and people:

Terms	People	
Harmonics	Cannonball Adderley	Herbie Hancock
Modal (or modes)	Ron Carter	Keith Jarrett
Multiphonic	Paul Chambers	Philly Joe Jones
Pedal point	George Coleman	John McLaughlin
Sheets of sound	John Coltrane ("Trane")	Hank Mobley
Timbre	Chick Corea	Wayne Shorter
	Bill Evans	Tony Williams
	Red Garland	Joe Zawinul

STUDY QUESTIONS

1. The 1960s was a tumultuous time in the US, and it was perhaps the most productive and innovative decade for Miles Davis. What was the social, political, and cultural mood of the times, and what issues dominated American thought?

2. Miles Davis first surfaced as a visible performer as a member of whose small group, and playing what style of music?

3. How did Davis's style contrast to that of Dizzy Gillespie?

4. Discuss Davis's involvement in the "cool" style.

5. Who were members of Miles Davis's "first great quintet," and what kind of music did they play?

6. When were the first modal-jazz recordings made, and what were the titles?

7. Describe the difference between modal jazz and more traditional jazz, based on functional harmony.

8. What was the formal scheme of the first modal tunes recorded by Davis?

9. What impact did modal jazz have on the improvising soloist?

10. What mute became synonymous with Davis's sound?

11. Who was the arranger who collaborated with Davis to create some of the most significant works in the history of jazz? Name some of these important recordings.

12. Who was the earlier Swing Era bandleader who had some influence on Gil Evans and the concepts presented on the *Birth of the Cool* recording?

13. Name the Davis recording that remains the leading-selling album in the history of jazz.

14. Name the musicians who became members of Davis's "second great quintet." What instruments did they play?

15. Who became one of the most significant composers to contribute to Davis's second quintet?

16. Did Ornette Coleman show any influence on the original music produced by Davis's second quintet?

17. Davis's *Filles De Kilimanjaro* recording marks the beginning of his adventures in incorporating aspects of popular music in forming a new direction in jazz. What are several new characteristics apparent on this recording that point to pop-music influences?

18. The merging of popular-music elements with jazz marked a new style of jazz called _____.

19. What popular rock bands or artists served as inspiration to Miles Davis and Herbie Hancock?

20. Which two Davis recordings mark the beginning of the last period of Davis's musical growth?

21. What are the similarities and differences between Davis's music heard on *Bitches Brew* and Ornette Coleman's *Free Jazz*?

22. Why did Davis choose to merge jazz with popular rock styles of the time?

23. Miles Davis participated or was at the forefront of which seven jazz styles?

24. What was so unique about Miles Davis's style and remained a constant throughout his career?

25. Which member of the saxophone family was popularized by John Coltrane?

26. Which two members of the saxophone family is Coltrane noted for?

27. Describe the term "sheets of sound" and what was unique about this technique.

28. Coltrane left Miles Davis briefly to join which pianist's group?

29. Could John Coltrane be classified as someone who was interested in world music? Explain and defend your answer.

rivaled that of the1940s created an air of doubt, cynicism, and suspicion among all classes of Americans. Society as a whole became more bifurcated, and, as the 1970s gave way to the 1980s, the economic gap between classes widened. More subgroups formed, particularly as the US offered a safe haven and land of opportunity for numerous ethnic-minority groups who emigrated. With each subgroup came a uniquely different brand of culture that encouraged a more fractured American music scene. Perhaps the only area that showed progress and had improved by the 1980s was racial relations. Blatant segregationist policies had been all but eliminated, and, through new equal-opportunity and affirmative-action programs, more African-Americans were seeking and completing education beyond high school. Consequently, an increasing number of blacks entered the workforce in various professional roles, including science, medicine, law, and politics. African-Americans became mayors of major cities and visible leaders in other aspects of public service. The study of black history and culture was suddenly elevated to a new, high level of importance. Black artists in all fields, including television, theater, literature, and music, were making greater strides than ever toward achieving equal footing with other groups in the US. There was a noticeable increase in TV shows starring all-black casts. Isaac Hayes became the first black composer to win an Academy Award for his score to the film *Shaft*, and a record number of Americans watched Alex Haley's TV mini-series documentary *Roots*, depicting the struggles of a black family in America over many generations. These trends had a positive effect in raising the awareness of jazz, paving the way for a new wave of young black artists, who reclaimed their birthright to this music and gave it a greater degree of respect than ever before.

THE MUSIC

Up until the 1950s, jazz had followed a traceable, linear progression of developments, with only one or two being predominant at any given time; but, by 1970, the rich tradition, which now included numerous styles and influences, seemed to yield to no single musical direction. The 1970s was an age of synthesis on all levels and, in the true spirit of postmodern culture, performing artists drew from all available sources for new inspiration. The tremendous amalgamation of styles was emblematic of an ever-increasing multicultural society, with growing immigrant populations from Asia and south of the border. This expanding minority population no doubt appreciated jazz's willingness to embrace and absorb musical influences from non-Western cultures, many of which counted improvisation as a key ingredient in their native music. Rhythm sections also evolved and were augmented by the addition of percussionists during the 1970s. Although a few groups had made use of Afro-Cuban drummers during the Cubop days of the late 1940s, most jazz bands, until this period, carried only a drum-set player. Additional percussion instruments enabled these new 1970s bands to absorb and reflect Brazilian, Afro-Cuban, Indian, and other world-music styles. Jazz became a more global music in the last decades of the 20th century, owing in part to improved means of communication and because of the postmodern-jazz artists' quest for new ways to express themselves. Jazz from this point on was a fractured, splintered genre. It became increasingly difficult to tell what was meant by the application of the word "jazz" to describe the music. The menu for fans in the 1970s and 1980s included the following styles and representative artists:

- electric, jazz-fusion bands in the Miles Davis *Bitches Brew* tradition—Weather Report;
- soul, R & B-style jazz inspired by the black tradition—Grover Washington, Jr.;

- the first wave of instrumental-pop, easy-listening, or smooth-jazz artists—George Winston, Spyro Gyra, and Chuck Mangione;
- a new European sound pioneered by the German Editions of Contemporary Music (ECM) label—European saxophonist Jan Garbarek and American pianist Keith Jarrett;
- rebirth of forgotten mainstream hard-bop artists, some of whom had become expatriots in Europe and now returned to the US playing what was termed neo- or progressive bop—saxophonists Phil Woods and Dexter Gordon;
- emerging young black artists eventually labeled as the "**Young Lions**" and led by an amazing trumpeter Wynton Marsalis; most of these newcomers follow the progressive or neo-bop course;
- free jazz patterned after earlier work by Ornette Coleman, Eric Dolphy, and John Coltrane—Art Ensemble of Chicago, Cecil Taylor, and Anthony Braxton;
- modern big bands likened to Count Basie and Duke Ellington but representing all that had happened in jazz since the 1940s, necessitating an update of the older model—Toshiko Akiyoshi and Thad Jones/Mel Lewis;
- world-music-influenced jazz styles—Herbie Hancock, Pat Metheny, Don Ellis, Mahavishnu John McLaughlin, and Weather Report, among others.

After considering this menu, there is no wonder that listeners, critics, journalists, and promoters were more confused than ever by the "jazz" label. Following the deaths of Albert Ayler, John Coltrane, and Eric Dolphy, and the retirement of Miles Davis in the mid 1970s, the jazz world was at a loss for a single guiding force. As there was no single beacon to light the way, the music that was practiced throughout the final decades of the 20th century moved in many different directions simultaneously, with no single trend or leader outstanding. This chapter presents the electric mix of trends and artists who contributed significantly to the jazz tradition during the 1970s and 1980s. Chapter 14, which follows, will examine the trends in acoustic jazz during this same period.

JAZZ AND ROCK: THE TWO-WAY CONNECTION

By 1970, jazz was under the influence of a new wave of popular rock bands, some of which incorporated certain aspects of jazz. Even *Down Beat* magazine proclaimed, as early as 1967, that, although it would continue to cover jazz, it would also cover rock music.[2] Pop bands, just like the Swing Era big bands of the 1930s and 1940s, captured the public's attention by featuring vocalists. Major record labels such as Columbia dropped acoustic jazz artists such as Charles Mingus, Ornette Coleman, and Keith Jarrett, because the average younger listener disconnected from established, more traditional instrumental jazz and was attracted to the new electric "fusion" brand. However, older fans of bop and swing styles felt disenfranchised. The word "fusion," most often used in association with a style of hybrid electric–jazz–rock music, actually had a much broader application during the 1970s, including new fusions of world- and classical-music styles with jazz.

Many of the 1970s rock bands found success by adding jazz-style horn sections to the usual collection of electric guitars, bass, drums, keyboards, and vocals. For the most part, these horn bands could be placed in one of two categories—those that were essentially rock bands, but played music featuring horn arrangements that were sometimes informed by certain aspects of the jazz tradition, and those that employed authentic, jazz-trained horn players performing repertoire that harkened back to the jazz and R & B traditions. Chicago Transit Authority (CTA), or Chicago as they became known, fit into this first category, never claiming much in the way of a jazz heritage. BS&T and Chase, on the other hand, often featured improvisation and modern swing

The rock band Blood, Sweat and Tears performs on stage at the Longhorn Jazz Festival, Dallas, Texas. L–R: guitarist Steve Katz, bass guitarist Jim Fielder, singer David Clayton-Thomas, trombonist Jerry Hyman, and trumpeters Chuck Winfield and Lew Soloff

grooves in their presentation of original material, as well as remakes of classic jazz pieces such as BS&T's rendition of Billie Holiday's "God Bless This Child." BS&T's trumpet star, Lew Soloff, best remembered for his stratospheric bop-influenced solo on "Spinning Wheel," left the band to become one of the most important jazz players on the New York scene, a position that he still enjoys. He was a mainstay of the later Gil Evans Orchestras and many other prominent jazz and pop groups. There emerged a free exchange of players from both camps, beginning in the 1970s.

Although it is difficult to generalize rock-inspired bands from this period, it is safe to say that they absorbed and reflected one of two fundamental traditions, but rarely both—white English rock groups, or black R & B bands and the Motown sound. The rock bands, whether they sported jazz-like horn sections or not, rarely based their music on the kind of spontaneity associated with jazz. The jazz–rock fusion bands, on the other hand, often featured some element of spontaneity.

While John Travolta's film *Saturday Night Fever* and the public's craving for disco-style dance music swept the nation, jazz was morphing into new styles rooted in Miles Davis's music of the late 1960s and early 1970s. The overriding texture in this new brand of jazz was electronic. The synthesis of electronic and acoustic sounds provided the perfect soundtrack for an ever-changing American society. Even horn players adopted electronic gadgets that enabled their wind instruments to compete in a landscape increasingly dominated by electronic instruments. The electronic piano, the electric guitar, with all the possible special-effects gadgets, and the electric bass became ever present. For that matter, the acoustic bass became nearly forgotten, eclipsed by its electric cousin, a less expensive and more easily played instrument. Even many well-established acoustic jazz bassists found it necessary to add this new instrument to their arsenal. Being a good acoustic bassist was not enough in the 1970s.

The music world was rocked in the 1980s by the digital revolution, a tremor brought on by the increased accessibility of desktop computing, the compact disc, and the release of the **Musical Instrument Digital Interface (MIDI)** standard—a new way for musical instruments to be controlled and information to be distributed using a simple binary computer code. The music industry may not have realized, in 1983 when it first unleashed the MIDI standard, that this invention would have as sweeping an impact on the industry as had the phonograph, tape recorder, LP, and electric guitar and bass in earlier years. MIDI implementation allowed computers to control instruments, amplified acoustic instruments to control electronic ones, and permitted computer-generated music to interact with live musicians. "It's a whole new ballgame," said guitarist Pat Metheny in a 1985 *Down Beat* magazine interview. "Now my guitar can be a harp, it can be vibes, it can be anything. It's unlimited in the sense that it's up to your imagination."[3] The guitar came of age in the 1970s fusion bands, no doubt owing to the focus on this instrument in rock 'n' roll styles. Since then, the instrument has become a major voice and enjoys a role in the jazz ensemble as important as that of any other instrument.

Like most jazz and pop styles, the electric fusion-jazz style began to short-circuit by the late 1970s, as the market became saturated with clones of the artists and bands that had pioneered the style. Eventually, even the pioneers became caricatures of themselves. Raw fusion became more and more sanitized, and the watered-down versions at the end of the decade and into the 1980s and 1990s became known by various names—"happy jazz," "hot tub jazz," "fuzak," and, most recently, "smooth jazz" and "acid jazz." Whatever the name, and although there are differences that are addressed more thoroughly in Chapter 14, all of these different breeds are related to similar seeds, cultivated first in the late 1960s and early 1970s.

THE INNOVATORS: LIVING ELECTRIC IN THE SHADOW OF MILES DAVIS

Former Miles Davis sidemen continued to impact jazz trends in the 1970s, leading bands such as Weather Report, Return to Forever, the Mahavishnu Orchestra, and the Head Hunters. A significant difference between leaders of the fusion movement and their mentor Miles Davis is that, although Davis had moved jazz forward by initiating numerous stylistic changes, he generally pursued only one or two styles at a time. In contrast, this new breed of 1970s Davis protégés wore many hats, often simultaneously.

Weather Report

Two Davis sidemen founded this groundbreaking group—keyboardist **Joe Zawinul** (1932–2007), who had first come under the spotlight as a member of Cannonball Adderley's Quintet in the 1960s, and Davis alumnus **Wayne Shorter** (1933–) on soprano and tenor saxophone. Following his stint with Adderley, during which time he composed the popular funky hit "Mercy, Mercy, Mercy," Zawinul composed the title track for Davis's *In a Silent Way* and added his electronic-keyboard voice to *Bitches Brew*. The genesis of Weather Report dates back to 1970 and the release of their initial, self-titled recording. Although there were many personnel changes throughout the group's 16-year career, it remained true to several important doctrines:

- spontaneity and invention;
- improvisation as a paramount virtue in achieving spontaneity;
- deviation from predictable AABA forms and melodic phrase lengths;
- percussion as an important ingredient, in addition to the drum set;

LISTENING GUIDE

🔊

Chick Corea

"La Fiesta" (Chick Corea) 8:21

From *Captain Marvel*

Recorded 3/3/1974

Columbia/Legacy 986086–2

Personnel: Stan Getz, tenor saxophone; Chick Corea, electric piano; Stanley Clarke, acoustic bass; Tony Williams, drums; Airto Moreira, percussion

Form: 3/4 meter; introduction (24 bars) AA (16 bars) interlude (16 bars) BB (32 bars) CC (16 bars) interlude (8 bars) D (18 bars) D^1 (24 bars) AA (16 bars)

0:00–0:06	Piano alone sets tempo
0:07–0:12	Piano joined by bass, drums, and percussion
0:12–0:17	Rhythm section completes introduction
0:18–0:22	Tenor sax plays first 8-bar A-section theme
0:23–0:28	Repeat of A theme for 8 bars
0:29–0:40	Rhythm-section interlude featuring piano solo
0:41–0:52	Sax states B theme for 16 bars
0:53–1:03	B theme played twice
1:04–1:15	C theme played twice by sax for 16 bars
1:16–1:21	Rhythm-section interlude featuring piano solo
1:22–1:33	D theme in new key; rhythmic feel changes (18 bars)
1:34–1:51	D^1 nearly identical to D theme, but with 6-bar extension (24 bars)
1:52–2:02	A theme played twice for 16 bars
2:03–4:14	Sax improvised solo with rhythm section comping on repeats, 8-bar chord progression
4:15–4:32	C theme reoccurs plus rhythm-section 8-bar interlude
4:33–4:44	D theme reoccurs
4:45–5:02	D^1 theme
5:03–5:13	AA (16 bars)
5:14–6:48	Piano solo over same 8-bar vamp
6:49–7:06	Ensemble returns to C theme plus 8-bar rhythm-section interlude
7:07–7:18	D theme restated for 18 bars
7:19–7:31	D^1 theme with extension restated for 24 bars
7:32–7:55	Coda is vamp on 2 chords with sax improvising
7:56–end	Gradual retard to final resting point

Listen to excerpts of interviews with Chick Corea that are included in the corresponding chapter found on the website.

Corea's recording *Leprechaun* was released in 1976 and was awarded two Grammy Awards, along with a five-star review in *Down Beat* magazine. Orchestral instruments, in addition to a battery of synthesizers, make this recording even more dynamic. Like Hancock, Corea sought to do what was necessary to get the uninformed listener to take notice. In a 1974 interview, Corea told *Down Beat* writer John Toner that,

> A project of ours is familiarizing people with what we do. If we play as an opening act to a well-known rock group, 80 percent of the audience doesn't know us from Adam, and doesn't know anything about John Coltrane, Miles, and jazz. All they are familiar with is the sound of our instruments, the electric instruments; and that we have a beat.[21]

Like so many bands from the electric phase of the 1970s, Corea's RTF ran out of creative rope in its efforts to create popular crossover music that also satisfied the musician's creative side. However, by the time he disbanded RTF, Corea had left an important legacy and an indelible mark on jazz. His creations constitute the best examples of the fusion of jazz, electronics, rock, classical, Brazilian, and Spanish elements.

Return To Forever performs in May 1977. L–R: Lenny White, Stanley Clarke, Al Di Meola, Chick Corea

SOUL AND POP INSTRUMENTAL JAZZ

A new wave of R & B, blues, and gospel-inspired musicians swept through the 1970s and into the 1980s, offering listeners a milder dose of instrumental jazz than the aforementioned Davis sidemen. Although the style seems to personify black music, it was not limited to black musicians.

David Sanborn (1945–)

Alto saxophonist David Sanborn (1945–), for example, represents one of the most influential, soulful, and identifiable voices from this era. He initially received widespread exposure through his membership of the *Saturday Night Live* TV band, frequently spotlighted on camera during one of his passionate, sometimes screaming, high-octane solos. Additional cameo solo performances on recordings by James Taylor, David Bowie, and Stevie Wonder helped him become one of the most copied players during this time. There is always an intense, gospel quality to his solos, and his unique sound, musical mannerisms, well-paced solos, and unusual, "harmonica-like phrasing"[22] (perhaps inspired by Stevie Wonder) brought him widespread recognition and popularity. His Grammy Award in 1981 in the R & B category is evidence of his success, popular appeal, and influence on a crop of young saxophonists, who rushed to purchase the unusual metal mouthpiece in their efforts to copy his style.

The Brecker Brothers

Brecker brothers Michael and Randy have been protagonists in pop and jazz circles since their pioneering efforts to fuse elements of both traditions in the 1960s. In 1975, they regrouped to establish the Brecker Brothers band as a sequel to earlier bands they had been involved with, such as Dreams and Mahavishnu drummer Billy Cobham's band. There were a number of pop bands that included horn sections along with vocals in the mid 1970s that may have helped to inspire the Brecker Brothers' band sound, along with influences from jazz groups such as John McLaughlin's Mahavishnu Orchestra. Tower of Power, The Average White Band, James Brown, and of course the *Saturday Night Live* TV band, founded in 1975, all captured certain elements of soul, funk, and other black-influenced styles that also became part of the Brecker Brothers' sound. All of these groups shared several musical characteristics: (1) hard-driving rhythm sections and rock-like grooves that frequently emphasized back beats (beats 2 and 4); (2) complex "heads" featuring intricate, technically busy, and jagged melodic lines; (3) melodies that were largely based on syncopated rhythms; (4) heavily articulated, short staccato lines; and (5) ballads often reminiscent of the Motown black pop tradition. The Brecker Brothers band stood out from the field of pop bands, distinguishing itself with more adventuresome compositions featuring angular melodies, unusual harmonies, odd meters, and rapid-fire, virtuosic solo improvisations out of the jazz tradition. Randy Brecker experimented with various electronic devices to alter the sound of his trumpet, helping him to compete with the era's electronic sound of synthesizers and guitars that had drawn listeners away from acoustic instruments. A long list of important studio-session and pop musicians from the period, including David Letterman's Paul Schaeffer, David Sanborn, and Frank Zappa drummer Terry Bozzio, augmented the core band, helping to establish the Brecker Brothers' sound. The band enjoyed a 7-year run, recording six albums for Arista Records, until the group disbanded in 1982. Their efforts were rewarded with seven Grammy nominations, confirming the crossover appeal to pop and young jazz fans. The GRP label celebrated the nostalgic rebirth of the Brecker Brothers band in 1992 with the release of *Return of the Brecker Brothers*. The band's second recording for GRP, *Out of the Loop*, came in 1994 and was recognized with two Grammy Awards. Randy continues to be an important force in the contemporary jazz scene, in the US and abroad, recently rekindling the Brecker Brothers band in 2011, but without his brother, who passed away in 2007.

Grover Washington, Jr. (1943–1999)

Philadelphia tenor saxophonist Grover Washington, Jr. (1943–1999) could be considered a new breed of transplanted Texan, as his soulful brand of jazz can be traced back to the school of "Texas Tenors," a group of saxophonists from the 1940s, well oiled by the southwest blues tradition. Complementing the organ trio was his early preference, along with R & B groups that kept him working regularly through the mid 1960s. His first major recording date took place in 1971, when he released *Inner City Blues*. His subsequent 1975 *Mister Magic* recording was charted as the number 1 record on several polls. A number of other gold and platinum records followed, each offering his unique blend of jazz and soulful blues, while often featuring other prominent studio musicians of the day. Like other pioneers of the "smooth-jazz" movement, Washington was an accomplished musician who was capable of playing jazz with more substance than required by the soulful style he popularized.

Popular Philadelphia soulful saxophonist Grover Washington, Jr.

Chuck Mangione (1940–)

Not all those artists who enjoyed popular success for their palatable brand of instrumental jazz were saxophonists. Call him a sell-out, call him the creator of "smooth jazz," describe his music as instrumental pop, whatever the rhetoric, trumpeter/flugelhornist Chuck Mangione (1940–) enjoyed pop-star status from the mid 1970s through the early 1980s. Most fans that followed his career then had no idea of his earlier achievements—tours and/or recordings with Art Blakey's Jazz Messengers, trombonist Kai Winding, and high-note trumpeter/bandleader Maynard Ferguson. Most listeners are more familiar with the lyrical, memorable melodies, pleasing jazz-inspired harmonies, and Latin-inspired grooves that were the hallmark of Mangione's 1970s hits, such as "Land of Make Believe," "Bellavia," "Chase the Clouds Away," and, of course, the hugely successful "Feels So Good," which reached number 2 in the 1977 pop charts. This was no small accomplishment for a jazz-inspired instrumental recording that often featured bebop-grounded improvisations. Mangione's commercial success was confirmed by the Grammy he received in 1977. His successful score for the unreleased film *The Children of Sanchez* brought him a second Grammy Award in 1978 and a Golden Globe nomination. His large-scale orchestral collaborations produced the 1970 recording *Friends and Love* and *Together* in 1971, both unique for the time. It was during this time that Mangione became identified with the flugelhorn, developing a signature sound that helped to popularize the instrument in the years that followed.

Chuck Mangione playing his signature flugelhorn

"I think that categories are becoming meaningless," Mangione said in a 1977 interview, "because of the boundaries that are being crossed. People who get into the artists that are popular now will go back and check out other records they've made in the past."[23] It would be tempting, but misleading, to declare Mangione as the pioneer of 21st-century "smooth jazz." The glaring difference between Mangione, Washington, or Sanborn and some of the smooth-jazz performers is that the popular smooth artists have no recordings from the past to check out, as Mangione suggests doing. They have no heritage for fans to trace back—no roots in the jazz tradition.

Mangione left the scene in 1989, and there followed a hiatus from music that lasted about 5 years, before he announced his return in 1994. His more recent recordings on the Chesky label prove that he still writes melodies that are "hard to resist,"[24] according to *Down Beat's* John McDonough. He now seems to be in semi-retirement, performing occasionally with a small group or recreating his full orchestra material from the 1970s.

THE SIGNS OF THE TIMES: NEW TECHNOLOGIES AND CHANGING BUSINESS MODELS

The digital revolution occurred in the last decades of the 20th century, brought about by the miniaturization of electronic components and less costly production processes. The impact of these new technologies can be roughly compared with that of electrification in the early 1920s. Apple pioneered the small, personal computer when they first unveiled the Apple II computer in 1977. A few years later, new technologies that had already been available to high-end professional users were brought to the average household in the form of the VCR. The first units cost about $1,000, and blank videotapes averaged $15 each. Although the cassette format dominated the audio marketplace in the 1970s, this format was eclipsed by the compact disc, which first hit the consumer market in 1982. This new format did much to encourage reissue campaigns of treasures that had been, in some cases, locked in vaults for years, tragically unavailable to a new, younger generation of jazz enthusiasts. Major labels began reissue campaigns that brought about a renewed interest in standards, the classic jazz repertoire, and the piano trio format, along with the rediscovery of artists who had, in some cases, been nearly forgotten. Unfortunately, major labels focused more on inexpensive reissues that guaranteed sales and incurred minimal production costs, rather than taking risks with new artists. The only new artists to receive major media attention at the end of the decade were those "Young Lions" who essentially played music similar to that heard on older, reissued material. As the cost of CD production fell, some of the best music was issued by a growing number of small, independent US and European labels, all trying to cash in on the new marketable CD format with newly discovered artists. Many of the small "indie" labels, however, lacked widespread distribution and marketing tactics, and so exceptional music was often lost in a sea of unknown releases.

MILESTONES

Chronicle of Historic Events

The timeline that follows will put the developments of jazz discussed in Chapters 13 and 14 into a larger historical context, providing you with a better sense of how landmark musical events may relate to others that match your personal areas of interest.

1970	• Kent State University student riots protesting war end in four deaths. Students strike for peace in 450 US colleges.
	• Women march for equality in New York.
	• Drug-culture rock stars Jimmy Hendrix and Janis Joplin die of drug overdoses.
	• The Beatles break up.
1971	• Andrew Lloyd Webber's rock musical *Jesus Christ Superstar* creates a stir.
	• Astronauts further explore the lunar surface.
1972	• Movies of the year include *The Godfather, Cabaret, Last Tango in Paris*, and *Play it Again Sam*.
	• Nixon is reelected amidst the Watergate affair.
1973	• Francis FitzGerald is awarded a Pulitzer Prize for *Fire in the Lake*.
	• The US ends its role in Vietnam following approximately 55,000 deaths.
	• The courts allow abortion in the Roe Vs. Wade case.
1974	• Robert Lowell wins a Pulitzer Prize for *The Dolphin*.
	• President Nixon is forced to resign over his role in Watergate; Gerald Ford assumes the presidency.
	• Stan Getz records "La Fiesta" with Chick Corea's group.
1975	• President Ford declares the Vietnam era officially over.
	• *The Wiz* wins awards as the new musical sensation.
	• President Ford saves the city of New York from bankruptcy.
1976	• Hit films are *Rocky* and *Network*.
	• Steve Jobs and Steve Wozniak launch Apple Computer with only $1,300 capital.
	• Americans celebrate the bicentennial.
1977	• American rock idol Elvis Presley dies.
	• John Travolta's *Saturday Night Fever* helps to popularize discos.
	• Other popular films include *Star Wars, Annie Hall*, and *Close Encounters of the Third Kind*.
	• Weather Report records "Palladium," along with its popular hit "Birdland."
1978	• The retirement age is raised to 70.
	• Carl Sagan is awarded a Pulitzer Prize for *Dragons of Eden*.
	• The Jonestown cult mass suicide shocks the nation.
1979	• Award-winning films include *Kramer vs. Kramer, Norma Rae, All That Jazz, Manhattan, Star Trek*, and *Apocalypse Now*.
	• Iran seizes the U.S. embassy, taking 80 hostages.
1980	• The government admits to recession—the auto and steel industries continue to lose money.
	• Race riots erupt in Miami.

	•	John Lennon is killed.
1981	•	Ronald Reagan takes office as U.S. president.
	•	The Iranian hostages are released.
1982	•	Andrew Lloyd Webber's *Cats* is a Broadway musical hit.
	•	The recession sets industry back to its lowest levels in 34 years.
1983	•	Sally Ride becomes the first woman in space.
	•	A national committee determines that the US is at risk owing to mediocre education performance.
	•	MIDI binary language is developed by electronic musical-instrument manufacturers—it creates a boom in electronic-instrument sales.
1984	•	Democrats pick Geraldine Ferraro as the first woman candidate for vice president.
	•	Reagan wins reelection.
1985	•	Madonna, a new pop singing sensation, performs in the Live Aid pop concert to benefit African relief efforts.
	•	Hit movies include *Out of Africa* and *Kiss of the Spider Woman*.
1986	•	The Chernobyl nuclear-reactor incident in the USSR alerts the world to the dangers of nuclear energy plants.
	•	The space shuttle Challenger explodes, killing all the astronauts on board.
	•	The US bombs Libya.
	•	A secret mission to send arms to Iran (Iran Contra Affair) is revealed.
	•	FOX is created as the fourth TV network.
1987	•	Author Tony Morrison publishes *Beloved*, a story about slavery.
	•	A nuclear arms treaty is agreed between the USSR and US.
	•	Madonna and Bon Jovi top the pop-music charts.
	•	August Wilson's *Fences* wins a Pulitzer Prize for drama.
	•	*Les Misérables* wins a Tony award for best musical.
1988	•	For the first time, CDs outsell vinyl records and cassettes.
	•	Prozac is introduced as a drug to treat depression.
	•	The Soviet Union withdraws troops from Afghanistan.
1989	•	The Berlin Wall separating East and West Germany falls, signaling the end of the cold war.
	•	Thousands of Chinese student protestors are killed in Tiananmen Square.

CHAPTER SUMMARY

In the 1970s and 1980s, the term "jazz" continued to encompass more and more substyles, some representing further development of previous styles and some exploring new directions. The line between jazz and rock became blurred with the advent of rock bands that included jazz-like horn sections (Chicago or BS&T) and jazz bands that featured rock rhythm sections (Chase). The development of electronic instruments, notably synthesizers, led to a vastly expanded sound palette. Five former Miles Davis sidemen continued to explore the heavily electronic approach that served as the foundation of the *Bitches Brew* album in the formation of four significant jazz-fusion groups—Weather Report, RTF, the Head Hunters, and the Mahavishnu Orchestra.

Weather Report, founded by keyboardist Joe Zawinul and former Miles Davis saxophonist Wayne Shorter, was a major contributor to jazz fusion for 16 years. A perennial *Down Beat* magazine award winner, the group initially played with a jazz-inspired freedom similar to that heard on the Miles Davis *Bitches Brew* album. Over time, however, the group developed a more commercial approach. In 1976, fretless-electric-bass phenomenon Jaco Pastorious was added to the group. Weather Report then recorded "Birdland," its biggest hit. This tune has been arranged for, and performed by, countless big bands, marching bands, and drum corps.

Pianist Herbie Hancock first gained widespread recognition for his 1962 funky-jazz hit "Watermelon Man." After working with Miles Davis, he tried other, different settings before forming the fusion group the Head Hunters, which recorded the hit "Chameleon" in 1973. In 1983, his hit "Rocket" won a Grammy Award and five music-video awards. In addition to film scoring, Hancock continues to be involved with the commercial side as well as the bop-inspired mainstream of jazz.

Bitches Brew guitarist John McLaughlin founded the Mahavishnu Orchestra in 1971, adding electric violin to the typical fusion instrumentation. The band was known for its very complex music, including changing, odd time signatures.

After playing in free- and mainstream-jazz settings, former Miles Davis keyboardist Chick Corea founded the group RTF. Initially, RTF played Latin- and Spanish-inspired jazz, some of which had been commissioned by saxophonist Stan Getz. The group eventually replaced the saxophone with electric guitar, enabling a repertoire with more commercially appealing rock grooves, many of which featured very complex, tight orchestrations and sophisticated, large-scale forms. Since the breakup of RTF, Corea has played both in fusion settings, notably his Elektric Band, and numerous mainstream neobop settings, including his own Akoustic Band.

A number of other jazz artists have continued to cross and blur the line separating jazz and rock. Saxophonist David Sanborn was highly visible on television and copied by many young players. The Brecker Brothers (Michael and Randy) produced complex funk-influenced jazz with innovative soloists. Grover Washington, Jr. gained much popularity playing a soulful predecessor of smooth jazz. His 1975 recording *Mr. Magic* was a huge hit. Trumpeter Chuck Mangione at one time played burning hard bop with Art Blakey and the Jazz Messengers. In later years, he became better known for his easy-listening flugelhorn hit "Feels So Good," which, in 1977, reached number 2 on the pop charts. The trends in pop-influenced jazz did not begin and end with the 1970s, as will be shown in the final chapter.

KEY TERMS

Important terms, people, and bands:

Terms		Bands
MIDI	Herbie Hancock	Blood, Sweat and Tears
Young Lions	John McLaughlin	The Brecker Brothers
	Chuck Mangione	Chicago
	Jaco Pastorius	The Head Hunters
People	David Sanborn	Mahavishnu Orchestra
Michael Brecker	Wayne Shorter	Return to Forever
Randy Brecker	Grover Washington, Jr.	Weather Report
Chick Corea	Joe Zawinul	

STUDY QUESTIONS

1. Name two popular rock bands that featured jazz-like horn sections.

2. What are some of the key characteristics that describe Weather Report's style?

3. Who was the electric bassist who brought this instrument to the attention of the jazz community? What was so unique about his approach to the instrument?

4. Herbie Hancock explored the funky side of jazz (considered the predecessor of acid jazz and hip-hop) in the 1960s with what hit tunes?

5. Hancock's Head Hunters band released what hit recording that changed the sound of jazz in the 1970s?

6. What popular-music artists helped influence Hancock's Head Hunters band sound?

7. Like so many former Miles Davis sidemen, Hancock has worn many musical hats since the early 1970s. Discuss some of his other stylistic adventures, aside from the fusion style expressed by the Head Hunters.

8. What instrument in the 1970s becomes one of the prominent voices of fusion jazz?

9. Like Herbie Hancock, Chick Corea has explored many different styles of jazz. Discuss this aspect of Corea's musical split personality.

10. Certain aspects of non-American music permeate the music produced by Corea's Return to Forever Band. What world music influenced this band?

11. In what ways did new recording technology and changing business models change the landscape for the jazz musician?

12. Soul jazz became popular in the 1970s. Can you describe this jazz in terms of its roots?

13. Name two popular saxophonists who championed soul jazz.

14. Before turning to the more popular side of jazz, with whom had Chuck Mangione performed?

15. Who was the flugelhorn player who did much to popularize instrumental jazz in the 1970s?

CHAPTER 14

The Unplugged, Eclectic 1970s and 1980s

[I'm] almost thinking of retiring and waiting for the '80s. There's such a sense of stagnation and a lack of direction now, a shying away from possibilities rather than an embracing of them.[1]
—Pat Metheny

A demonstration outside the Whitehouse in support of the impeachment of President Nixon (1913–1994) following the Watergate revelations

LONG LIVE ACOUSTIC JAZZ

The voice of acoustic jazz musicians was nearly drowned out by the omnipresent electric jazz style of the 1970s. These two decades appear to be the most fractured period in the history of jazz to this point, where "anything goes" was the unspoken motto. The deaths of many earlier jazz pioneers made this an even more uphill struggle for the jazz musician who was more informed by the acoustic tradition. The 1970s saw the passing of Duke Ellington and his premier saxophonists

Johnny Hodges and Harry Carney. Other artists who passed away during this period included Paul Desmond, Lee Morgan, Charles Mingus, Louis Armstrong, Bobby Timmons, Lennie Tristano, and Cannonball Adderley, among others. Although the work of living artists who clung to the jazz tradition was somewhat eclipsed by fusion-style jazz (rock, electronic-influenced jazz), there were several more traditional acoustic jazz trends and significant artists that did not go unnoticed or without lasting influence.

A debate surrounded the renewed interest in acoustic jazz, occupying most of the 1980s and casting a long shadow into the next millennium. The controversy wasn't about whether jazz should be nurtured; it was more about which kind of jazz should receive our support. Two factions emerged—those who championed imitation (acoustic musicians old and young) and those who represented innovation (acoustic and electric musicians). Wynton Marsalis became the mouthpiece and chief advocate for the preservation of those elements he deemed most important to jazz—swing and the blues. Yet some accused Marsalis and his "Young Lions" of merely shoplifting music that had already been patented by the mid 1960s. Meanwhile, other artists tried to steer jazz away from what they saw as stale, shopworn traditions. They were the postmodern renegades, who found nothing sacred and borrowed freely from any musical style they felt worthy. Eclecticism became this group's motto.

THE ECM SOUND

German classical bassist and part-time production assistant Manfred Eicher launched the independent label ECM in 1969, initially specializing in recordings by innovative and free-jazz artists such as Paul Bley and Marion Brown. ECM (Editions of Contemporary Music) established a new trend in independent labels, eventually serving as a successful model for the many "indies" that would follow. Free of commercial restrictions and contractual obligations, ECM artists found freedom to follow their creative muse. ECM promoted quiet, chamber jazz at a time when volume had been increased to rock-level decibels by the electronic–jazz fusion movement. In Eicher's words, "people had to learn to listen again. We tried to channel the chamber music esthetics of written classical music into the improvisational aspect."[2] Consequently, "ECM was not recognized as a jazz label only, but as a stream of music [notice he uses Gunther Schuller's term appropriately here, as much of the ECM music merged jazz with other styles] where we combined improvisational fields with written fields—of course with the jazz tradition."[3] Eicher wanted to duplicate the efforts of the finest European classical record labels by providing the same high-quality sonic reproduction for jazz, and he successfully set a new standard in recording. "I wanted to get that element of transparency."[4] The music captured by the label soon became described as "the ECM sound." This sound is characterized by pastel, modal melodies that are often folk-like in quality. Improvisation was abundant on ECM recordings, and non-swung 8th-note rhythm grooves were more commonplace than the more traditional jazz post-bop swing style.

Even the artwork on ECM record jackets promoted a quiet, pensive, and introspective quality. Unlike U.S. labels, which typically featured portraits or photos of the artists in action, ECM covers presented landscapes, abstracts, and other panoramas. "We try to capture much more atmospheric waves than any title," said Eicher.[5]

The label became known for its uncompromising releases and, contrary to large American labels, artistic freedom for its artists. This freedom lured some of America's finest artists, along with a growing pool of European artists who were experimenting with jazz and improvised music. Canadian expatriot Kenny Wheeler made his mark as a trumpet player and composer released on ECM. His albums *Gnu High, Double, Double You,* and *Music For Large and Small Ensembles,* featuring a mix of American and European artists, established his unique musical voice while helping to elevate the label's reputation. Guitarists Pat Metheny and Ralph Towner, along with pianists Chick Corea and Keith Jarrett and drummer Jack DeJohnette, also helped the label to grow. Jarrett's success almost single-handedly brought ECM into the global market. Both Corea and Jarrett recorded solo albums for the label, and the success of these recordings breathed new life into the art of solo jazz piano playing, once again extending a long tradition that had enjoyed an earlier rebirth through the work of Bill Evans.

Once again, however, some jazz purists criticized the label for its classical-music sentimentality and for abandoning the real roots of jazz. Thanks to Eicher's label though, a number of American and European artists were afforded widespread exposure throughout Europe, Japan, and the US, at a time when their efforts could have easily gone unnoticed because of the emphasis on jazz–rock fusion. In addition to those American musicians previously mentioned, ECM served to launch the careers of a new, emerging breed of European musicians, profoundly influenced by jazz, such as saxophonist Jan Garbarek, pianist Bobo Stenson, guitarist Terje Rypdal, and bassist Eberhard Weber. ECM continues to be a source of interesting music that crosses boundaries.

The website includes an interesting assessment and discussion of European jazz that began to emerge with some direction in the 1970s. This discussion with a former member of Amsterdam's Willem Breuker Kollektief, as well as interviews with Tim Hagans, can be found in the corresponding chapter on the website.

THE INNOVATORS: THE REBIRTH OF ACOUSTIC JAZZ

KEITH JARRETT (1945–)

A child prodigy who was determined to have a genius IQ before he entered public school, Keith Jarrett (1945–) has been an important force in the sunset years of the 20th century. Jarrett, like Hancock, is a classically trained pianist. He gave his first full-length concert performance, complete with original compositions, at age 6. His intense interest in jazz and improvisation did not bloom until he was a teenager, and, by this time, he had already demonstrated amazing technical facility and musicianship. Discovered by Art Blakey at a New York jam session, Jarrett joined Blakey's Jazz Messengers, sharing the stage with Chuck Mangione. He was quickly catapulted to public prominence after joining saxophonist Charles Lloyd's quartet. Jarrett gained widespread recognition for his amazing solo performances on Lloyd's most successful recording, *Forest Flower* (1966). Jarrett left Lloyd to work with his own trio, which included ex-Ornette Coleman bassist Charlie Haden and former Bill Evans drummer Paul Motian. An awareness of these associations is important to understanding of Jarrett's somewhat "outside," free trio music from this period, which also featured saxophonist Dewey Redman, who was an Ornette Coleman disciple.

Jarrett, yet another alumnus of the Davis band's keyboard chair, initially turned down Miles's first offer to join his band in favor of continued pursuit of his own trio. He eventually did join the Davis group at the height of his electronic–funk phase, serving alongside Chick Corea as a second electronic keyboardist and later occupying the sole keyboard chair. Jarrett, a dedicated purist and committed acoustic musician, later commented that there was only one person he would ever have played an electronic instrument for—Miles Davis. There was a mutual respect between these two great musical forces, despite Jarrett's lack of respect for Davis's 1970s band sound:

> I thought the band was the most egocentric band I had heard musically . . . except for Miles. Miles was still playing nice, beautiful things, and the rest of the band was in boxes [not listening to one another or communicating]. I just wanted to do a little bit to change the feeling.[6]

A man of few words, Davis once asked Jarrett, "Keith, how does it feel to be a genius?"[7] and, years later, Miles characterized Jarrett as "the best pianist I ever had."[8] This was no small compliment, given the others under his consideration.

Jarrett's mind is a sponge, absorbing every kind of music he ever encountered, and his tonal memory enables him to recall things in an instant. Consequently, he often amazes listeners by the full range of his eclectic creative process. He can instantly shift gears from playing bebop one moment to a romantic, Bill Evans style the next, with European classical devices and bombastic avant-garde gestures lurking, to emerge at any moment. Jarrett has always been motivated by folk music, something he shared with Davis and a commonality that no doubt drew them together.

Jarrett left Davis following the loud, electric Fillmore years, in order to pursue musical directions that couldn't have been more contrasting—his progressive acoustic trio, as well as his works for solo piano. It was Jarrett's partnership with Manfred Eicher and the ECM record label that had jumpstarted his unparalleled success as an acoustic jazz musician, at a time when nearly everyone else was focused on fusion. *Facing You*, his first successful ECM solo piano release, led to his overwhelming successful *The Köln Concert* (1975), which sold 600,000 copies in the first 5 years and continues to sell consistently. Jarrett approached the keyboard with a completely blank slate, nothing performed with premeditation, much as he does today with his trio, which rejects rehearsing. He used improvised, folk-like melodies, rhythmic riffs, and down-home gospel-like vamps in improvisations that typically lasted 30–45 minutes without pause. Never once does he falter, totally immersing himself in the physical and spiritual aspect of piano playing and the creative process itself. In Jarrett's own words, "The ideal state to be in, just before I make a sound, would be a state where there is nothing to gain, no ideas to purge. You can only make music when there isn't anything first."[9] His technique is flawless and, coupled with his lyrical romanticism, produces a captivating performance that leaves audiences breathless. Jarrett's technique has been compared to that of Art Tatum and Oscar Peterson, but with a more modern sensibility that puts him in a category by himself.

Jazz pianist Keith Jarrett, c.1975

The unexpected success of his solo, trio, and quartet recordings was proof that an audience still existed for acoustic, adventuresome jazz that challenged the listener and found a universality with the folk tradition. Jarrett rekindled the art of solo jazz piano playing and, in his ECM trio and quartet recordings, he helped to expose a number of emerging European artists. Jarrett's discography is more diverse than one could imagine, including chamber works (*In the Light*), works for soloist and orchestra (*Luminescence* and *Celestial Hawk*, commissioned by the Boston Symphony), and, of course, more recent recordings of classic standards by his second regular combo, known simply as the Standards Trio. This group has dedicated itself to keeping a tradition and great repertoire alive. Their performances and recordings are completely impromptu—no rehearsals, no set lists, and only one take for recordings—preserving the live and spontaneous aspect of the performance. Many consider his trio to be one of the best, rivaling those led by the great pianists he has been compared to—Bill Evans and Oscar Peterson.

"The Windup," found in the accompanying collection, is an excellent example, not only of Jarrett's unique personal style from this period, but also of the kind of company he kept with an emerging breed of new European musicians. The track begins with a syncopated, gospel, folksy vamp that serves to introduce the melody, played by soprano saxophonist Jan Garbarek and Jarrett. The loose, rhythmic feel and placement of accents in the melody provide an illusion that the meter is changing, but, in fact, the piece is not that unusual metrically. A simple 4/4 meter is nearly consistent throughout, with only one 2/4 measure occurring, just prior to the second theme. Although the piano solo may imply harmonies, much as was the case with Ornette Coleman's free-jazz repertoire, there are none whatsoever for Jarrett to follow. Drums and bass are added, and yet there is still no set form nor chords, which makes his solo completely improvised, inspired by the flow of thought and motivated solely by his improvised melodic direction.

As Jarrett's music offers such a wide range of features, Figure 14.1 offers a summation of characteristics that might help you to identify and appreciate what his music is all about. See if you can identify some of these characteristics in "The Windup."

- Unusual chord progressions in trio tunes
- Use of pedal points (a sustained or reoccurring bass pitch around which harmonies change)
- Free form solos, sometimes with no clear tonality
- Down-home, gospel-like vamps (short sections repeated multiple times) and syncopations
- Rock and Latin tinged straight-8th note tunes in the 1970s
- Unusual phrase groupings and lengths in composed and improvised melodies that cause meter and form to often sound unconventional even if they are not
- Spectacular, flawless, virtuosic technique and execution
- Penchant for folk-like melodies especially in solo repertoire
- Minimalist aspect of some solo music where lengthy sections are dependent on repetitive figures that often serve as underpinning to more elaborate improvisations
- Emotionally charged, romantic and classically influenced passages
- Athletic and physical performances—rising off the bench, groaning and singing along with his improvisations
- Occasionally reaches inside the piano to play the strings directly
- Ventures into free jazz

FIGURE 14.1 Distinguishing characteristics of Keith Jarrett's music

LISTENING GUIDE 🔊

Keith Jarrett

"The Windup" (Jarrett) 4:57 (excerpt)

Recorded 4/24–25/1974, Oslo, Norway

Belonging ECM 1050 422 829 115–2

Personnel: Keith Jarrett, piano; Jan Garbarek, soprano saxophone; Palle Danielsson, bass; Jon Christensen, drums

Form: AABA¹C in C major, in 4/4 meter

0:00–0:39	Introduction—gospel-like vamp with staggered entrances by piano, bass, and drums; bass and left-hand piano play repetitive ostinato figure
0:39–1:22	First chorus:
0:39–0:47	A section—soprano sax enters with A theme
0:47–0:55	A section—soprano sax repeats A theme
0:55–1:01	B section—contrasting theme yet still surrounding the pitch C
1:01–1:06	A¹ section—soprano restates a theme that closely resembles the first A theme
1:06–1:13	C section—rhythmically punctuated melody
1:13–1:22	Vamp—much like intro but trio repeats figure for only 8 bars
1:22–1:56	Second chorus:
1:22–1:30	A section—soprano sax returns with A theme
1:30–1:37	A section—soprano sax repeats A theme
1:37–1:42	B section—contrasting theme yet still surrounding the pitch C
1:42–1:47	A¹ section—soprano restates a theme that closely resembles the first A theme
1:47–1:56	C section—rhythmically punctuated melody
1:56–2:30	Piano solo—free, unaccompanied piano solo, not based on any preconceived chord progression
2:30–4:36	Piano solo continues—joined by bass and drums in free-flowing, almost timeless playing; bass does not walk, neither does drummer play in a strict tempo
4:36–4:42	B section—piano solo seamlessly returns to B theme
4:42–end	C section—soprano sax plays final C theme before abrupt end (original, unedited recording includes a soprano sax solo before the group returns to play the entire tune)

RETURN OF EXPATRIATES UNLEASHES A REBIRTH OF ACOUSTIC JAZZ

Dexter Gordon's triumphant return to the US in 1976 was heralded by the two-record set *Homecoming*, recorded live at New York's famed jazz club, the Village Vanguard. His no-nonsense, hard-bop-derived band featured one of the bright lights of postmodern trumpeting—Woody Shaw. Shaw introduced a new vocabulary to jazz-trumpet playing, borrowed from contemporary pianists such as Corea, but his unfortunate early death interrupted the natural conclusions and potential of his innovative style. Gordon's follow-up studio recording *Sophisticated Giant* sold an amazing 100,000 copies during this time when acoustic, mainstream jazz was poorly marketed amidst the fusion boom. Gordon's successful repatriation was followed by the return of two other saxophone titans who had sought refuge in Europe from fusion and pop disco trends—Johnny Griffin and Phil Woods.

Dexter Gordon and quartet performing in the UK

Although there was significant attention paid to rediscovered musicians such as Gordon, the buzz was loudest, not over the rebirth of older, established musicians such as Gordon, but over the young trumpet prodigy who first gained widespread exposure through his work with Art Blakey's Jazz Messengers—Wynton Marsalis. The successful return of the older expatriates and acceptance of their music (the same they had played years before, when people stopped listening) no doubt had a great deal to do with paving the way for the success of what eventually became described as the "Young Lions." Marsalis and a large, new crop of outspoken, well-trained, impeccably dressed, and bountifully talented young black performers came to be known as the Young Lions following the title of the 1982 Marsalis recording. Giving new life to progressive bop, neo-bop, post-bop, neo-classic, or whatever label you choose for the movement, his success is undeniable and has changed the jazz landscape. Wynton Marsalis and his sax-playing brother Branford drew much attention in the 1980s, paving the way for a steady stream of other young, black and white artists. Branford toured with British pop artist Sting and served for a time as musical director for Jay Leno's *Tonight Show* band. A long line of other newcomers followed closely, taking advantage of the Marsalis wake helping to rekindle what some felt was an old flame dressed up in new clothes. Marsalis and company dismissed free jazz and electric–jazz–rock fusion styles, claiming that many of the artists associated with these styles were little more than carnival barkers, ungrounded in the important roots of jazz and strayed too far from the tree. The die had been cast, and these artists signaled a full-scale, successful revival of acoustic jazz, firmly rooted in the bop tradition and the sound of Miles Davis's mid 1960s progressive quintet. Their champions applauded them for reclaiming the rich jazz heritage and bringing it back to the rightful owners—the black artists who had largely created it—while their detractors criticized them for embalming jazz, stagnating its progress, and curating it for the museum.

WYNTON MARSALIS (1961–) AND THE YOUNG LIONS

Despite some negative press, brought about in part by Marsalis's own outspoken convictions and preferences, he has single-handedly done more to raise an international awareness of the importance of jazz than anyone else in the past 20 or 30 years. He has been tireless in the pursuit of his own convictions and has succeeded, where many have failed, in securing significant support and visibility for jazz.

Born in the birthplace of jazz, his training as a youth in New Orleans prepared him for study at the world-renowned Juilliard School of Music in New York. Art Blakey was impressed by the young upstart and, before Marsalis turned 20, hired him and his saxophonist brother Branford to form the front line of his acclaimed Jazz Messengers. Aside from Miles Davis's small groups, Blakey's band had given birth to more leaders in the field than any other. Before long, Marsalis was fronting his own band and made his recording debut as a leader in 1982, with an exciting, young quintet. His group at that time was known for its adventuresome new compositions and reinterpretations of standards that often ended in obscuring the original beyond recognition. Modeled in many ways after Davis's second great quintet in the mid 1960s, Marsalis's musicians played on the edge, with drummer Jeff "Tain" Watts doing everything he could to build on the Tony Williams tradition of blurring meters, power playing, and unparalleled intensity.

The group shared a telepathic sense of communication, much like Davis's classic mid 1960s quintet, capable of playing at any tempo and seamlessly shifting gears from one tempo to the next. Marsalis is a gifted trumpeter, with flawless technique, warm, liquid, buttery sound, a sense for dramatic contrast, a strong background in the tradition, including the skillful use of various mutes, and the unusual ability to perform classical music as well as jazz. He never fails to demonstrate his complete and total command of the instrument, enabling him to control his sound much as a vocalist does to interpret a lyric. His brother, saxophonist Branford Marsalis, is an extension of Wayne Shorter and is equally equipped on the soprano saxophone. Drummer Watts, with his prize fighter-like punching and jabbing, keeps things heated up in "Delfeayo's Dilemma" and is guilty of being a constant sparkplug in this quintet.

Since the early 1980s, Marsalis has been a powerful and articulate spokesman for jazz, backing up an overconfident attitude and opinions by producing an astounding catalogue of jazz and classical recordings and winning nine Grammy Awards at the time of writing. In 1983, he became the first and only artist to win a Grammy Award in both jazz and classical categories, an amazing accomplishment that he duplicated 2 years later. Perhaps his most treasured accomplishment was the coveted Pulitzer Prize in music composition, bestowed upon him in 1997, the same year he was named Artistic Director of Jazz at the Lincoln Center. Marsalis became the first jazz composer to receive the Pulitzer, which was awarded for his massive, 3-hour *Blood on the Fields*. This work almost defies classification, but most closely resembles a cantata, as it involves a big band, vocal soloists, and narration to tell the story of slavery in America. In size and breadth alone, it was a Herculean accomplishment, brilliantly performed and recorded by Marsalis's Lincoln Center Jazz Orchestra. This orchestra now tours regularly, carrying its musical message to large and small communities alike, worldwide. The orchestra has also served as a catalyst for numerous commissions and collaborations, primarily with dance companies and choreographers, including Alvin Ailey's American Dance Theater, the New York City Ballet, Garth Fagan, Twyla Tharp, and the New York Philharmonic. His episodic work *All Rise* parallels an Ellington sacred concert, in that the underlying message has religious overtones. The work, which seamlessly interweaves jazz and various styles of classical music, is in 12 parts, composed for orchestra, big band, chorus, and vocal soloists. To completely appreciate this work, one must be at least casually acquainted with some of the most important 20th-century classical works, by Igor Stravinsky, Charles Ives, and Paul Hindemith, as well as aspects of the Ellington tradition. Marsalis has clearly studied the many facets of music in order to absorb and reflect all of these traditions in something that is altogether new. *All Rise* is the culmination of intensive study, and it is clear that Marsalis is a highly motivated, still youthful artist who has already left an indelible mark on the history of jazz.

Marsalis's artistic output is equal to that of at least several artists, especially when one realizes his additional commitment to the production of educational programs, fund-raising for jazz at the Lincoln Center, TV specials such as the Ken Burns epic documentary *Jazz*, and the publication of an array of instructional materials. It is not difficult to understand why *Time* magazine named him one of "America's 25 Most Influential People."[10] There seems to be no end to Marsalis's capability to accomplish seemingly insurmountable projects, and therefore it would be foolish to predict his potential for amazing future feats. Perhaps most important to this discussion is Marsalis's apparent realization that it will be through composition and the new challenges presented to performers and listeners that jazz will advance to new, unknown vistas in the century that is just now unfolding.

Trumpeter/composer Wynton Marsalis in 1982

LISTENING GUIDE 🔊

Wynton Marsalis

"Delfeayo's Dilemma" (Wynton Marsalis) 6:46

Recorded January 1985, New York

"Black Codes (From the Underground)" Columbia CK40009

Personnel: Wynton Marsalis, trumpet; Branford Marsalis, tenor saxophone; Kenny Kirkland, piano; Charnett Moffet, bass; Jeff "Tain" Watts, drums

Form: Repeated choruses (ABC) predominantly in 4/4 meter, each section varying in length from 23 to 28 bars (section C always includes one 3/4 bar, even during solo sections). Each section (A, B, and C) of the choruses is divided in half, with the first half presenting thematic material, and the second half an improvised (ad lib) solo.

0:00–0:27	First chorus—27 bars (includes a 3/4 bar), theme
0:00–0:11	A section—11 bars: 5-bar theme played by trumpet, sax, piano, with bass and drums tacet; then 6 bars of swinging bass and drums, with piano ad lib solo
0:11–0:19	B section—8 bars: 4-bar theme played by trumpet and sax, with rhythm-section accompaniment; then 4 bars of swinging bass, drums, with piano ad lib solo
0:19–0:27	C section—8 bars: 4-bar unison theme (the fourth bar here is 3/4), played by trumpet, sax, over bass pedal point; then 4 bars of swinging bass and drums, with ad lib piano solo
0:27–0:52	Second chorus—25-bar theme similar to first chorus, but last 4 bars of C section are abbreviated here to 2 bars
0:53–1:20	Third chorus—28 bars, trumpet solo, following chorus (ABC) solo form (A = 12 bars, B = 8 bars, C = 8 bars), with swinging rhythm-section accompaniment
1:21–3:07	Fourth–seventh choruses—28 bars each, trumpet solo continues
3:08–3:34	Eighth chorus—28 bars, tenor sax solo, following chorus solo form, with swinging rhythm-section accompaniment
3:34–4:26	Ninth and tenth choruses—28 bars each, tenor sax solo continues
4:27–4:52	Eleventh chorus—28 bars, piano solo, following chorus solo form, with swinging rhythm-section accompaniment
4:53–5:45	12th and 13th chorus—28 bars each, piano solo continues
5:45–6:11	14th chorus—27 bars, theme similar to first chorus
6:12–6:46	15th chorus—23+ bars, theme similar to second chorus, but last 4 bars are a closing sustained chord

THE FREEDOM FIGHTERS TAKE RISKS

While it was Thelonious Monk, Lennie Tristano, Ornette Coleman, John Coltrane, Eric Dolphy, and Charles Mingus, along with bandleader Sun Ra and pianist Cecil Taylor, who pioneered the early free jazz movement, new faces arrived on the scene in the 1970s who joined this community, pushing the envelope. Some of these artists emerged from the Jazz Composers' Orchestra Association in New York or the Chicago-based Jazz Composer Guild and used their music to make personal statements about civil rights with albums such as *Things Have Got to Change, Cry of My People* and *Attica Blues*. In New York, it was the loft scene that became a bastion of experimental, risky music that pushed jazz in new directions, although some of the music born in these loft performances did not stray far off paths already forged by pianist Cecil Taylor or saxophonists Ornette Coleman and John Coltrane. Chicago was the other hothouse of creativity during this period, germinating a number of cutting-edge artists. The Art Ensemble, formed in 1969, best exemplified the Chicago avant-garde style. This collective transformed the expected concert into a musical happening, a theatrical event at which, to the shock of some audiences, the musicians sported tribal African garb, face paint, and masks. In contrast, trumpeter Lester Bowie wore a medical lab coat. Their music, in some ways much like the older Sun Ra, represents a mosaic of numerous styles of music and at times bordered on the comical and absurd. Ra served as the mentor, model, and instigator of the Art Ensemble's own unique style. To be fair to this experimental and adventuresome group, to see them live, as is the case with many free styles of jazz, is far more meaningful than listening to recordings which is often the downfall of much new, experimental jazz. It is so much in the moment, about process, group interaction, and theatrics that much is lost in the translation to a solely audio medium. Fringe artists also risked being labeled "charlatans" by many traditional artists and critics, who expressed the opinion that "the emperor has no clothes." On the other hand, other critics came forward to support the efforts made by experimental artists and placed more hope in their efforts than they did in the new-traditionalists, obsessed with recreating what, in their opinions, had already been done.

Of all the fringe performers to surface in the 1970s and 1980s, it was the Art Ensemble, the World Saxophone Quartet (WSQ), Anthony Braxton, and pianist/composer Cecil Taylor who undoubtedly left the most lasting impression. For example, the Art Ensemble's ECM release *Nice Guys* was awarded four and a half stars, a near-perfect assessment, by *Down Beat* critics. The WSQ can take much of the credit for introducing the notion that ensembles that do not resemble a jazz band, at least in terms of the expected instrumentation, could perform jazz. They often performed without a rhythm section and, in doing so, paved the way for many other groups to follow, for instance the Kronos and Turtle Island String Quartets.

Anthony Braxton's *Creative Orchestra Music 1976* is another recording that has stood the important test of time. This particular recording continues to be a favorite of many critics and demonstrates that the traditional big band could be dressed in an entirely new wardrobe to provide a fresh new look at this very traditional ensemble.

A supplemental listening guide of a Braxton recording from *Creative Orchestra Music* can be found on the companion website.

Some of these adventuresome artists, such as Anthony Braxton, were deconstructionists in the true spirit of the postmodern ethic. The deconstructionists took earlier styles of music and tore them apart, salvaging certain aspects that served as the basis for their own redesigned renditions. These artists borrowed from old and new forms, ranging from marches and polkas to punk rock, R & B, Monk, Mingus, Jelly Roll Morton, Scott Joplin, blues, and Duke Ellington, forming a new music that put a different spin on these earlier traditions. In many ways, their new slant on jazz could be viewed as parodies or satires on what had already transpired in jazz. At times, these artists seemed as much concerned about process as they were about product and were sometimes accused of being irreverent in their reinterpretations of earlier styles. They had no fear of exploring new ground and were immune to the possible outcome of their efforts—it was the creative process and what it led to that counted. Although the new brand of experimental jazz sometimes drew on familiar traditions and often was based on discernible forms, the ways in which these traditions were warped often left listeners confused about the value of this new music. This deconstructionist approach often left impatient listeners with too little that was familiar, and unfamiliarity in the arts often breeds discontentment. However, more curious listeners give time and the "benefit of the doubt" to experimental artists who establish credibility by demonstrating that they have the tools and backgrounds to ensure valid music-making. In the case of many of these new artists, no two projects were the same, and they have been known to pursue more than one direction at a time, using different ensembles to satisfy their various creative musings.

As suggested, some of the active avant-garde jazz artists in the 1970s and 1980s were not so new to the scene, as was the case with Cecil Taylor.

Cecil Taylor (1929–)

Pianist Cecil Taylor's (1929–) career in some ways followed Monk's in that, although he had an impact in the early stages of his career, he was far better received in later years. Taylor, caught up in the wake of a new wave of experimental artists receiving better press in the 1970s and 1980s than ever before, was rediscovered and appreciated for his obtuse, abstract style. He studied serious music and jazz at the New England Conservatory, where he fell under the influence of black and white, classical and jazz artists, such as pianists Horace Silver, Thelonious Monk, Dave Brubeck, and Lennie Tristano, along with composers Duke Ellington and Igor Stravinsky. Taylor developed an awesome piano technique that was as much percussive as it was pianistic. His amazing technique and facility have impressed both jazz and classical pianists. He uses his fists, forearms, elbows, and palms to create dense, dissonant clusters of sounds that defy analysis and, for some listeners, are like fingernails on a blackboard. *Down Beat* magazine awarded him "Best New Star" in 1962, but there was no significant support for his odd brand of jazz that placed "unrelenting demands . . . on the listener,"[11] according to pianist and educator Bill Dobbins. His music is more about texture and rhythm, sound and organization, than it is about European-derived harmonies and recognizable melodies. Although Taylor described his music as an "extension of period

Pianist Cecil Taylor performs at Ronnie Scott's in London

music—Ellington and Monk,"[12] and tried to "imitate on the piano the leaps and space a dancer makes,"[13] his style more closely resembles European avant-garde classical music than jazz, and he was virtually unemployed through much of the 1960s. As audiences began to catch up to the avant-garde in the 1970s, Taylor's career was rejuvenated, along with that of other, older fringe artists.

Taylor's music has remained far from mainstream, often without steady tempo or, for that matter, the traditional elements of music and listening signposts. A good example is his "Jitney No. 2" from the critically acclaimed *Silent Tongues* album, recorded live at the 1974 Montreux Jazz Festival. This track is an encore and spin-off, along with one other track on the record, from the featured five-movement solo piano suite displaying Taylor's incredibly virtuosic and percussive style that is so at odds with other music discussed throughout the text. At first, it may appear as completely free-form, with random gestures and bursts or clusters of notes that have no relationship. However, after repeated listening, one begins to hear how the ascending two-tone clusters stated at the outset resurface throughout the short piece, serving as a unifying motive. Also noticeable is how the gestures and sound textures in between this reoccurring motive are contrasting. There is, therefore, architecture to this piece, with contrasts between vertical, cluster-like textures and rapid, sonic streams of single-note lines that connect the reoccurring two-tone motive. The listening guide that follows is less specific than others throughout the book, as the music is less traditionally organized, but it will point to some landmarks throughout the piece, enabling you to hear some of the architectural structure that gives this piece coherence.

"Jitney No. 2" provides clear evidence of Taylor's facility, his technical prowess at the keyboard, and his creative improvisational powers. It therefore is no surprise that he continues to serve as an inspiration to many contemporary, younger pianists.

LISTENING GUIDE

Cecil Taylor

"Jitney No. 2" (Cecil Taylor)

Recorded 7/2/1974 Montreux, Switzerland

Cecil Taylor, piano

Form: Free-form and highly improvised

General statements will point out the reoccurring two-tone motive, as well as the introduction of improvised episodes that connect reoccurrences of the motive.

0:00–0:05	Introduction of main motive
0:10–0:16	Main motive reoccurs
0:26	Main motive reappears briefly
0:29	Main motive reappears briefly
0:35	Section based on rapid scalar lines
0:45–0:46	Main motive reappears briefly
0:48	New improvised gesture based on multi-note trill
0:57	Another new texture
1:06–1:12	Main motive reappears briefly
1:11	New improvised passage, with rapid, single-note lines and chord clusters
1:48–1:59	Vague references to main motive
2:00–2:22	Rapid, single-note lines with occasional multi-note jabs
2:23–2:44	Reference to two-tone motive that now begins to expand to three-, four- and five-note rhythmic groupings with improvised lines in between
2:45–end	Further references to main motive as piece builds to a climax

OLD BOTTLES, NEW WINES—LONG LIVE BIG BANDS

As more and more educational institutions began to embrace the study of jazz throughout the 1970s and 1980s, the market became saturated with young players looking to establish careers. Many of the more fortunate ones found spots in bands led by graying big-band leaders who had somehow survived the Beatles, Janis Joplin, Jimi Hendrix, and the jazz-fusion movement. Others started their own bands or became sidemen in new bands established by younger leaders, trying to keep the tradition alive while moving it forward. The older leaders who came out of the Swing Era, such as drummer **Buddy Rich** (1917–1987), clarinet saxophonist **Woody Herman** (1913–1987), stratospheric trumpeter **Maynard Ferguson** (1928–2006), and pianist **Stan Kenton** did their best to remain relevant by employing vital, younger sidemen and arrangers who kept their repertoire fresh with big-band versions of pop and film music of the day. In hindsight, these bands became important to the future of jazz by providing training grounds for young musicians who, in many cases, have become important voices in the new century.

The two most important big bands to emerge in the late 1960s and mid 1970s, at least in terms of advancing a new standard, were the New York-based **Thad Jones** (1923–1986)/**Mel Lewis** (1929–1990) Jazz Orchestra and the West Coast **Toshiko Akiyoshi/Lew Tabackin** Jazz Orchestra. The Jones/Lewis organization began as a rehearsal band, driven by an interest among New York's finest studio-recording and theater musicians to play more challenging music than they typically encountered in the recording and TV studios. The band's first book consisted of a group of 10 originals that Count Basie had commissioned his former trumpeter **Thad Jones** to score. Basie's band found them too modern and out of character, and so they were rejected. Although Jones and Lewis have both passed on, their legacy continues with the Vanguard Jazz Orchestra, still performing at the Village Vanguard every Monday night. Most historians agree that it was Jones's writing, realized by his exceptional band, that revitalized the conventional big band, breathing new life into it so that it could survive beyond the 20th century.

Who could ever imagine that a female Japanese jazz pianist would also play a significant role in the 1970s revival of the sleeping giant—the big band, which some had pronounced a dead dinosaur years earlier. Pianist **Toshiko Akiyoshi** (1929–) was inspired by the late Bud Powell, and she became the first Japanese jazz musician to be recorded by an American record company. She and her husband, saxophonist and flutist **Lew Tabackin** (1940–), took up residency in Los Angeles in 1972, where she formed her first big band to perform her own music, recorded by the RCA label from 1974–1976. Her unique style broke away from many accepted writing conventions and has often been compared to that of Duke Ellington, who found his unique sound in part by ignoring conventions and allowing the special talents of his bandsmen to influence the way in which he composed and arranged. To quote Tabackin,

> Toshiko is never afraid to try devices that haven't been used. The woodwind aspect [flutes and clarinets] is particularly noteworthy; her saxophone voicings have a heavier sound than most reed sections; like Thad Jones she uses five-part harmony [there are usually five saxophonists in a big band] rather than let two instruments double the same note [as had been the standard rule up until Jones and Akiyoshi].[14]

Tabackin continues to point out how his wife "draws so much on her own culture, not fighting it like so many foreign jazz musicians who try to prove themselves by being ultra-Americans."[15] Her ethnic background brought an entirely new viewpoint to big-band composition, as shown by "Children in the Temple Ground," "Kogun," and "Tanuki's Night Out." Akiyoshi's music also shows her own unique sense of rhythm and phrasing, no doubt an additional result of her Asian descent. The Akiyoshi/Tabackin big band was the rage in the late 1970s, winning Grammy

Jazz pianist and composer Toshiko Akiyoshi conducts her orchestra, c.1977

nominations from 1976 to 1994. *Down Beat* magazine named her Best Composer for four straight years in the early 1980s, and she won the Best Arranger category in 1984. She has also been the recipient of numerous other awards, commissions, and prizes, both in the US and abroad. In the early 1980s, she relocated her band to New York, where she and her husband continue to create, although she retired the big band, with a final Carnegie Hall performance in 2003. Aside from vocalists, no contemporary woman in jazz had captured so much attention prior to Akiyoshi's rise to popularity.

THE CHANGING JAZZ LANDSCAPE AS THE MILLENNIUM COMES TO A CLOSE

By the close of the 1980s, jazz had lost an even greater number of important artists, including big-band leaders Thad Jones, Woody Herman, Count Basie, Benny Goodman, Gil Evans, Buddy Rich, and Harry James. In most cases, their deaths signaled the end of opportunities for young musicians who, in years past, found their entry point to begin a life in jazz as members of these big bands. Other innovative performers and composers who passed on during the decade included Thelonious Monk, Woody Shaw, Joe Farrell, Jaco Pastorius, Chet Baker, Mary Lou Williams, Bill Evans, Philly Joe Jones, and Kenny Clarke. *Down Beat* magazine columnist Art Lange wrote, in a retrospective column about the 1980s, "If jazz is the home of the individual, the repository of the unique, and personal expression is to be prized above all else, the music lost a measure of authenticity that will be hard to replace."[16]

Although some moaned that jazz was dying a slow death, some progress was being made. Despite the raging debates in the press between Marsalis and his Young Lions and the opposition, which included other musicians along with some critics, jazz musicians began to achieve what they strove for since the beginning—respectability and equality with high-art forms. Since Scott Joplin and James P. Johnson, Jelly Roll Morton and Duke Ellington, W.C. Handy and James Reese Europe, efforts to elevate jazz to the same high plateau as classical music had succeeded. Much like classical music, jazz had become institutionalized. The growing jazz-education movement corresponds to the rekindled interest in what jazz composers and arrangers had brought to the tradition, and what new inspiration could be ignited by a modern generation of composers. There was a renewed interest, in part inspired by jazz educators and the Young Lions, in the music of Duke Ellington, Charles Mingus, Tadd Dameron, Gil Evans, and Thelonious Monk. The jazz-education movement, spearheaded by the International Association for Jazz Education, gained significant ground in the 1970s and 1980s, as music programs nationwide jumped to employ specialists to deliver instruction in a wide range of courses. Even U.S. government legislators stood up to recognize jazz in 1987, when they passed a resolution designating jazz as a "rare and valuable national American treasure to which we should devote our attention, support, and resources to make certain it is preserved, understood, and promulgated." The resolution's sponsor, Michigan State Representative John Conyers, Jr., cited jazz as "a unifying force, bridging cultural, religious, and age differences." Conyers also pointed out that jazz "makes evident to the world an outstanding artistic model of individual expression and democratic cooperation within the creative process thus fulfilling the highest ideals and aspirations of our republic."[17] The National Endowment For the Arts, along with state and private foundations, awarded major grants to promote jazz festivals, composers, and touring ensembles. New ensembles were created for the specific purpose of perpetuating earlier jazz by recreating the works of Ellington, Henderson, Mingus, and others. But, once again, these efforts were criticized by some, who felt that, by concentrating on the preservation of the past, a stranglehold was put on the music's continued growth, and it would be doomed to the same fate as classical music in the 1980s and 1990s. Perhaps that which was fought to be attained for so long, the elevation of jazz to a status of high art, in the end would not prove to be worth the fight, as, along with classical-music sales, jazz began to hit a serious slump. The unanswered question appeared to be—would the new millennium offer anything better for jazz, its practitioners and listeners?

MILESTONES

Chronicle of Historic Events

The timeline that follows will put the developments of jazz discussed in Chapters 13 and 14 into a larger historical context, providing you with a better sense of how landmark musical events may relate to others that match your personal areas of interest.

1970	• Jean Stafford wins a Pulitzer Prize for *Collected Stories*.
	• The American Medical Association votes in support of abortions in some cases.
	• *Patton*, *M*A*S*H**, and *Woodstock* are popular films.
1971	• Bussing supports integration of schools.
	• The 26th Amendment allows 18-year-olds to vote.
1972	• Liberated women publish *Ms. Magazine*.
	• The Senate ratifies the Equal Rights Amendment.

1973	• The Watergate conspirators are convicted; Nixon declares his innocence.
	• Herbie Hancock enjoys success with the Head Hunters band, and the recording of "Chameleon" is a popular hit.
1974	• President Nixon is forced to resign over his role in Watergate; Gerald Ford assumes the presidency.
	• Jazz composer and bandleader Duke Ellington dies.
	• Pianist Keith Jarrett records "The Windup" for the German ECM label.
	• Pianist Cecil Taylor records "Jitney No. 2."
1975	• The VCR becomes a common home appliance.
	• Top films include *One Flew Over the Cuckoo's Nest* and *Jaws*.
1976	• The stagnant economy hampers and frustrates U.S. citizens and government.
	• Jimmy Carter is president.
	• Satirist Tom Wolfe declares the 1970s as the "Me Decade."
1977	• Alex Haley wins a Pulitzer Prize for *Roots*.
	• The space shuttle Enterprise makes a test flight.
	• President Carter declares there is an energy crisis.
	• Detroit car makers feel the pinch from Japanese competition.
1978	• Hannah Gray becomes the first woman university president at the University of Chicago.
	• The economic malaise continues, and President Carter announces an anti-inflation plan.
1979	• Divorce rates continue to escalate.
	• There is a nuclear disaster at the Three Mile Island power plant.
	• 99% of Americans own a TV set, says a *Washington Post* poll.
1980	• The prime rate soars to 21.5%.
	• The popular "Pac Man" video game launches a new trend in leisure-time activity.
	• Ted Turner launches the all-news CNN network.
1981	• The Columbia shuttle flight orbits earth.
	• IBM makes first-generation personal computers available.
1982	• John Updike wins a Pulitzer Prize for *Rabbit is Rich*.
	• The national debt reaches an all-time high.
1983	• Poverty in Mexico and Central America causes an increase in illegal immigrants.
	• Alice Walker wins a Pulitzer Prize for *The Color Purple*.
1984	• The most American banks fail since 1938.
	• Top films include *Ghostbusters*, *Amadeus*, and *Beverly Hills Cop*.
1985	• Wynton Marsalis's quintet, which includes his brother Branford, records "Delfeayo's Dilemma."
	• British scientists discover a hole in the ozone layer above Antarctica.
1986	• A secret mission to send arms to Iran (Iran Contra Affair) is revealed.
	• FOX is created as the fourth TV network.
	• Nintendo games are introduced.
	• Grammy Song of the Year is "We Are the World"—US supporting African social-reform issues.

1987	• The stock market plummets on Black Monday.
	• *Dirty Dancing* and *Beverly Hills Cop III* are among the top movies.
	• *Les Misérables* wins a Tony award for Best Musical.
	• Grammy record of the year is Paul Simon's African-inspired *Graceland*.
1988	• Pan Am Flight 103 explodes over Scotland; Libyan terrorists are suspected.
	• Le Chunnel, the world's largest undersea tunnel, is completed connecting France with the UK.
	• The Soviet Union withdraws troops from Afghanistan.
1989	• George Bush is elected U.S. president.
	• The Exxon Valdez oil-tanker disaster occurs near Alaska.
	• Arsenio Hall, Oprah Winfrey, and Colin Powell forge new ground for black entertainers and politicians.

CHAPTER SUMMARY

Although jazz–rock fusion music received much public attention and airplay in the 1970s and 1980s, a core of musicians continued to play and develop various aspects of acoustic jazz. With the popularity of fusion, major record labels dropped many lower-selling acoustic-jazz artists. Fortunately for a few musicians, the German independent label ECM was established in 1969, primarily as an alternative to fusion, featuring quiet, acoustic jazz. Pianist Keith Jarrett, who had played hard bop with Art Blakey in the mid 1960s and later electrified jazz with Miles Davis, went on to become one of ECM's most important artists. Jarrett is both a technician and improviser of the highest order, performing primarily in solo-piano and small-group settings.

The 1970s also saw the return of some jazz masters to America. Dexter Gordon had opted in earlier years, along with other, more senior performers, to live overseas in order to make a living playing the music they enjoyed, rather than give in to commercial pressures. Their return to the US in the 1970s rekindled interest in mainstream jazz, focused not only on returning jazz giants, but also on a new, young generation of bop-inspired players, often referred to as the "Young Lions." Trumpeter/composer Wynton Marsalis became the spokesman for the very talented and well-trained musicians representing this movement. Marsalis is not only an expert improviser but is also an outstanding classical trumpeter. In an amazing feat, he won Grammy Awards in both jazz and classical categories in the same year—and he did that twice (1983 and 1985)! Additionally, Marsalis became the first jazz composer to be awarded the Pulitzer Prize. As director of the Lincoln Center Jazz Orchestra, Wynton Marsalis has also committed himself to jazz education.

Some view the work of the "Young Lions" as an "imitation" of mid 1960s progressive jazz, and look to the free-jazz work of Ornette Coleman and other free-jazz experimentalists as the "innovation" of 1970s and 1980s in jazz. Anthony Braxton, Sun Ra, the Art Ensemble of Chicago, and the World Saxophone Quartet represent a few of the many contributors to this style. Pianist Cecil Taylor, an active free-jazz artist for five decades, may be one of the most under-appreciated of these performers.

A few big bands from previous eras (including the bands of Buddy Rich, Woody Herman, Stan Kenton, and Maynard Ferguson) continued to perform in the 1970s and beyond. These groups were able to continue because they changed with the times, adding arrangements of current tunes and hiring talented young sidemen. Two outstanding new big bands, the Thad Jones/Mel Lewis Big Band and the Toshiko Akiyoshi/Lew Tabackin Jazz Orchestra emerged during the late 1960s and 1970s. Both bands featured fresh new approaches to big-band writing, tight ensemble work, and outstanding soloists.

The many "schools" and events of jazz of the 1970s and 1980s may, in some ways, reflect other events and developments of the time. During the 1970s, President Richard Nixon resigned as a result of the Watergate cover-up, the US continued waging war in Vietnam and eventually withdrew without victory, inflation and unemployment grew at alarming rates, and the personal computer was introduced. In the 1980s, the development of the VCR, the compact disc, and MIDI had a tremendous impact on the entertainment industry. Some of the great jazz legends died, and the "Young Lions" emerged on the scene to provide momentum in preserving and advancing their rich jazz heritage.

KEY TERMS

Important terms, people, and bands:

Terms
ECM
Vamp

People and bands
Toshiko Akiyoshi
Anthony Braxton

Ornette Coleman
Manfred Eicher
Dexter Gordon
Keith Jarrett
Thad Jones
Mel Lewis
Young Lions

Branford Marsalis
Wynton Marsalis
Cecil Taylor
Phil Woods

STUDY QUESTIONS

1. Jazz became fractured in the 1970s and 1980s in part because of the prevalence of so many different styles—name them.

2. What style of jazz seemed to take the lead during much of the decade, and why?

3. Describe what became known as the ECM sound and what its significance was to jazz.

4. Although pianist Keith Jarrett has been involved in several different jazz styles, he has an individual approach that can be characterized by what traits?

5. Who was the older tenor saxophonist who is, in part, responsible for rekindling interest in acoustic, modern jazz in the mid 1970s?

6. Who was the hard-bop bandleader who provided a training ground for many of the important young artists of the 1980s, including the Marsalis brothers?

7. Who became the first jazz musician to win the Pulitzer Prize? What composition won him this unprecedented distinction?

8. In what ways has Wynton Marsalis been compared to Duke Ellington?

9. Which six artists are given credit for pioneering free jazz in the earlier decades?

10. Name several artists who carried the torch for free jazz in the 1970s and beyond.

11. Why, in some cases, has it been difficult for free jazz to gain supportive listeners in any significant numbers?

12. Which were the two more contemporary big bands to gain some exposure in the 1970s?

CHAPTER 15

Jazz for a New Century

The ultimate achievement for any culture is the creation of an art form.[1]
—Wynton Marsalis

The student has to absorb, and make discriminating choices about what he thinks is good or bad, and not let somebody else tell them.[2]
—Keith Jarrett

U.S. President Bill Clinton (R) plays a saxophone along with musician Everett Harp (L) at the Arkansas inaugural ball 20 January 1993. Earlier in the day, Clinton was sworn in as the 42nd president of the United States

JAZZ IN PERSPECTIVE

A strong economic climate during the 1990s provided Americans with what became, in retrospect, a false sense of security and prosperity. Economic prosperity abruptly ended in 2008, when the financial, auto, home industry, and virtually all aspects of the U.S., and eventually world, economies witnessed the worst collapse since the Great Depression. Unemployment topped 10%, and the government attempted to right the ship through financial bailouts and unemployment payment extensions. The year 2008 will be remembered as the beginning of the Great Recession, highlighted by turmoil in the mortgage industry and in politics prompting the grass-roots Occupy Wall Street movement. Its members protested in groups throughout the US, bringing attention to the growing economic divide between classes and associated inequities. It is, therefore, not surprising that all aspects of the entertainment industry have suffered, including the clubs and concert venues that support jazz. Even major symphony orchestras have faced bankruptcy and reorganizations requiring significant salary and benefit reductions. Jazz festivals in the US and abroad continue to be a viable source of employment for musicians, but the shortage of jazz clubs in some cities makes it increasingly difficult for jazz artists to find regular work. It has become almost economically impossible for big bands to maintain regular touring schedules, and, for that matter, very few big bands exist on any regular basis, aside from those sponsored by the armed services. The Mingus Big Band, Basie Band, and the Lincoln Center Jazz Orchestra are the only remaining big bands (aside from "ghost bands" or reunion bands, such as the Glenn Miller and Woody Herman bands, respectively) that continue regular touring schedules. Consequently, the steady flow of qualified, young jazz musicians, groomed by an increasing number of university jazz programs, has very few outlets for apprenticeships, as had been the case in earlier decades. The supply of highly qualified musicians is greater than ever, but there is very little work to sustain them.

Although Congress may have designated jazz a "national treasure," since 1996 it has forbidden the National Endowment for the Arts to give grants to individuals, aside from a select few senior artists awarded prestigious American Jazz Masters Fellowships. Fortunately, the MacArthur Foundation has, in recent years, begun to recognize gifted emerging artists with its "genius" grants, which are actually substantial, no-strings-attached fellowship awards. However, emerging artists have very few avenues to turn to for assistance. Clearly, we must do a better job at supporting these artists. A society without its art would certainly make for a drab and meaningless existence, and, in many ways, art helps to define a culture and its society; we are what we make, and art is one of the most significant, lasting things left behind by a culture.

The digital revolution continued to flourish through much of the 1990s and into this century, with exploding markets and innovations in desktop computing, personal digital assistants, wireless networks (WiFi), cellular phones, DVD and Blu-ray players and recorders, digital cameras, MP3 audio players, and global positioning systems—all helping to serve what appears to be a common theme—improved communication and content sharing. Social and professional networking websites, along with digital music sharing, have proliferated on the Internet to satisfy this demand. This rapidly changing landscape has affected the way music is recorded, marketed, distributed, and even, in some cases, conceived. Although major record labels have faltered, diminishing in numbers and in their support of jazz, an abundance of new, independent labels have emerged—so many to make tracking nearly impossible. Nearly every month, reviews of self-released CDs appear in major magazines such as *Down Beat* and *Jazz Times*, a phenomenon created by the decline of major labels, an increase in Internet downloading as a means for distribution, and the decreasing cost of technology to produce high-quality recordings. Young, emerging artists have found that they have no choice but to self-produce their recordings. Even major artists such as Branford and Wynton Marsalis, Dave Holland, Dave Douglas, Maria Schneider, and others have abandoned major labels to release and control their own products. However, the world had already been introduced to these seasoned artists by the major labels, which is not the case for young, lesser-known emerging artists. A consequence of these new circumstances is that, according to *Jazz Times* magazine, there are about 400 CDs a month submitted for review, probably more than, or at least as many as, were produced in an entire year 40 years ago! Although it is easier than ever to release a recording, the burden of promotion and marketing falls more and more to the musicians, who now must find the time to acquire entrepreneurial savvy along with pursuing their ongoing evolution as an artist. Much of this work that used to be handled by the record labels now falls to the artists. The All About Jazz website lists 452 publicists available for hire by musicians who can afford them, and, without them, their new CD release may never be discovered by anyone outside their immediate, local fan base. Despite these challenges, a young generation of musicians, born between the mid 1960s and 1980s and with a newfound entrepreneurial savvy, continues to emerge, challenging audiences and themselves to move jazz forward.

Musicians were not the only ones doing their best to advance the art form at the close of the 20th century. Scholarship in jazz had, for years, lagged behind research and writing about other forms of music, especially Western classical styles. The new generation of jazz scholars looks more carefully at the music, those who created it, the times in which it was created, and other factors that may have exercised influence on the musicians and their products. For the first time, jazz archives became important additions to existing, non-jazz collections. Well-established institutions such as the Rutgers Institute of Jazz Studies, the Smithsonian Institute, and the Library of Congress have done much to acquire, cultivate, curate, and display their holdings, while giving scholars access to treasure troves of material. Grants from various foundations to support historical research, video documentaries, aural history projects, and exhibits helped to raise Americans' awareness of jazz to heights not experienced since the Swing Era. A good example is *Jazz*, the 10-episode series produced for PBS television by Ken Burns, watched by millions of Americans. Although all of these accomplishments seem to indicate a promising future for the art form and its practitioners, the future isn't all rosy. Record sales plunged to new lows, with jazz representing less than 2% of the market share, a low position it shares with classical music—quite a dismaying situation, as jazz was once America's pop music.

Although record sales gradually declined during the 1990s, the still fairly new CD format and a new listener base encouraged major labels to reissue vast numbers of out-of-print LPs. Reissue packages required very low production overheads and offered new and old collectors an exceptional opportunity to enhance their libraries. A survey of those CDs awarded five stars in *Down Beat* throughout the 1990s shows that slightly more than 30% were not new recordings but reissues. The percentages are a bit better in the four and a half-star category, which shows that only 25% were actually reissues. There has been no better time in the history of jazz to build a collection and gain easy access to even the most obscure artists' materials, recorded many years earlier.

TRENDS IN CONTEMPORARY JAZZ

The eclecticism prevalent throughout the 1980s and the absence of any prevailing jazz style forecast the future, as the 1990s and the first decade of the new century are even more difficult to grasp, in terms of pinpointing developments in jazz that will have a lasting significance. We are too close to enjoy a good perspective, and recent trends in jazz have not had sufficient time for their outcomes to be fully realized. Although jazz is certainly not dead, it seems that we can no longer expect a single trend, as had been the case in the early decades.

Although categorization is always risky, particularly in recent years, Figure 15.1 summarizes recent trends in jazz with example artists. It is quite a list, especially when we realize that the same four-letter word we started out with in Chapter 1 is used to describe all that is listed. It is clear that there is a strong tendency toward straight-ahead jazz, as so many musicians and record labels seem concerned with the re-evaluation and re-invention of past traditions. Some jazz practitioners are doing their best to renew the music by retreading older styles, rebuilding audiences that appreciate and understand them, but, in doing so, some feel the music is in danger of homogenization (in part owing to the jazz education movement), which puts at risk the very spirit of individuality that has always been a cornerstone of jazz. However, the diversity seen in Figure 15.1 should dispel such concerns.

Although no one has a crystal ball, the discussions that follow address music and a few of the artists who best represent 21st-century jazz. Through their innovative work, they are more likely to have a long-lasting impact and influence on the future and have already gained traction with critics and public.

- *Tribute bands and artists*—The Mingus Big Band, Marcus Roberts
- *Contemporary big bands and composition for larger forms*—Lincoln Center Jazz Orchestra, Maria Schneider Orchestra, John Hollenbeck Large Ensemble, Vanguard Jazz Orchestra
- *Reissue campaigns of earlier recordings*—The Complete Herbie Nichols
- *Repertoire ensembles specializing in historic works*—Lincoln Center Jazz Orchestra and Smithsonian Masterworks Orchestra
- *Well-established and rediscovery artists who emerged in the '60s and '70s*—Joe Henderson, Andrew Hill, Miles Davis alumni including Herbie Hancock, Chick Corea, Keith Jarrett, Wayne Shorter and Dave Holland
- *Music by the not so "Young Lions" performing a mix of neoclassic jazz and new music*—Wynton and Branford Marsalis, Terrance Blanchard, Chris Potter
- *Experimental jazz concerned with innovation*—Ornette Coleman, John Zorn, Don Byron, Anthony Braxton, Tim Berne, Anthony Davis, David Murray
- *Pop influenced jazz such as "smooth jazz," "jam jazz," "acid jazz," "groove music" and "bass 'n' drums"*—Kenny G, Chris Botti, Tim Hagans, Madeski Martin and Wood, Roy Hargrove
- *Renaissance for new and established vocal artists*—Cassandra Wilson, Diana Krall, Nora Jones
- *Women instrumentalists, composers and bandleaders emerging as innovators*—Maria Schneider, Esperanza Spalding, Anat Cohen
- *Jazz becomes a truly global language through cross-cultural influences*—Vijay Iyer, Rudresh Mahanthappa
- *Afro-Cuban and Afro-Latin Jazz*—Eddie Palmieri, Conrad Herwig, Danielo Perez, Chucho Valdez, Bobby Sanabria
- *New Generation of Emerging artists*—Jason Moran, Ambrose Akinmusire, Robert Glasper, Anat Cohen

FIGURE 15.1 Late 20th- and early 21st-century trends and artists in jazz

ESTABLISHED ARTISTS OFFER SEASONED JAZZ

Some of the highly acclaimed jazz during the 1990s seems to defy any clear categorization and was created by a group of musicians who, unlike a new wave of young musicians just beginning their careers, found themselves on the second or third leg of their journey. These artists reached a point in their careers where they transcended virtuosity for its own sake and had surpassed their earlier phases of obsession with building technique and mastering the tradition. Their newfound freedom, through complete instrumental control, empowered them, in the 1990s, to use what they had learned to create new work that was not bound or overly encumbered by tradition, but rather grew from it, while at the same time reflecting their contemporary society. In every case, these artists have found reward in exploring numerous styles throughout their careers, much like those many sidemen who had worked with Miles Davis, years before. Among these still prolific artists are Davis alumni—Herbie Hancock, Chick Corea, Keith Jarrett, Wayne Shorter, and Dave Holland. Suggested recent recordings by the jazz masters are cited at the end of this chapter.

John Scofield (1951–) and Joe Lovano (1952–)

John Scofield (1951–) provides additional proof of the power that Miles Davis exerted, even after his death. Scofield, who performed with Davis in the final stage of his career, has proven to be one of the most influential guitarists since John McLaughlin, and certainly one of the most important jazz artists in the new millennium. He is comfortable in quiet chamber ensembles, free-form experiments, loud, rock-influenced bands, progressive-bop contexts, Latin grooves, soulful settings, and postmodern techno styles of jazz, and there is clear evidence of this diversity throughout his discography.

Joe Lovano (1952–), his partner on the accompanying recording, exemplifies one of two new schools of tenor saxophone playing and, along with Michael Brecker, has become one of the most sought after and widely impersonated artists in today's jazz scene. Imitation in jazz is considered the highest form of flattery and, although it discourages individuality, is a strong measure of an artist's impact on a future generation of performers. Lovano is somewhat steeped in what could be considered a modern-day, Lester Young school of playing, while Brecker is the contemporary equivalent of a Coleman Hawkins-style player. "Some Nerve," included in the companion media, serves as an excellent example, combining new and old aspects of the tradition. The drum groove is inspired by the funky, second-line, early New Orleans parade bands. The overall tenor of the piece is bluesy, with both soloists reaching deeply into this rich tradition during their solos. Drummer Bill Stewart eventually moves to a modern, straight-ahead, hard-bop-inspired approach during the tenor and guitar solos. Using the latest technology to modify his guitar sound, Scofield enables the instrument to sound like an organ while comping for Lovano. During the "head" and guitar solo, Scofield uses distortion devices to add a "grungy" element to the guitar sound.

Michael Brecker (1949–2007) and Pat Metheny (1954–)

Saxophonist Michael Brecker (1949–2007) is another musician who reached the pinnacle of his career at the close of the 20th century and in the opening years of this new millennium. He was on the scene for many years, pioneering fusion almost before anyone was ready to listen. Along with his trumpet-playing brother Randy, Michael also performed as a sideman with Horace Silver, toured with bass phenomenon Jaco Pastorius and drummer Billy Cobham, co-led, with his brother, the successful Brecker Brothers fusion-style band in the mid 1970s, and served as

LISTENING GUIDE 🔊

John Scofield and Joe Lovano

"Some Nerve" (Scofield) 5:12

Recorded December 1990

John Scofield Quartet, *Meant To Be*, Blue Note CDP 0777 7 95479–2

Personnel: John Scofield, guitar; Joe Lovano, tenor saxophone; Marc Johnson, acoustic bass; Bill Stewart, drums

Form and **key**: Repeated 16-bar choruses (AB, 8 + 8) 2/4 meter, New Orleans-style second-line groove

0:00–0:07	Introduction—8 bars, drum solo sets up New Orleans-style second-line groove
0:07–0:21	First chorus—16 bars, guitar and tenor sax play theme in unison, with bass and drum second-line accompaniment
0:22–0:36	Second chorus—16 bars, guitar and tenor sax repeat theme as in first chorus
0:37–0:51	Third chorus—16 bars, guitar solo over song chord changes, with continuing bass and drum accompaniment
0:52–1:06	Fourth chorus—16 bars, guitar and tenor sax repeat theme as in first chorus
1:07–2:07	Fifth–eighth choruses—16 bars each, tenor sax solo over song chord changes, with continuing bass and drum second-line-style accompaniment
2:07–2:53	Ninth–eleventh choruses—16 bars each, sax solo continues, drums changing to swinging jazz feel, bass changing from second-line style to walking pattern
2:54–3:53	12th–15th choruses—16 bars each, guitar solo over song chord changes, bass and drums return to second-line–pattern accompaniment
3:53–4:38	16th–18th choruses—16 bars each, guitar solo continues, drums changing to swinging jazz feel, bass changing from second-line style to walking pattern
4:38–4:53	19th chorus—16 bars, guitar and tenor sax play theme in unison, with bass and drum accompaniment, as in first chorus
4:53–5:12	20th chorus—16 bars, guitar and sax repeat theme as in second chorus, with abrupt ending

founding member of the exceptional neo-bop Steps Ahead (Steps) band. Much like other musicians from his generation, Brecker was at home in virtually any style of music. Consequently, he graced recordings by many jazz and pop musicians, including James Taylor, John Lennon, Joni Mitchell, and Paul Simon. Brecker pioneered the use of the electronic wind instrument, which allows wind players to control synthesizers, applying their own technique and breath control to electronic tone generators, and, as volumes escalated, enabled saxophonists to compete with keyboard synthesizers, electric guitars, and other amplified instruments. He developed greater control of the saxophone than any who came before, and many feel he was the next most important player to hit the scene since John Coltrane. His technical mastery of the instrument, including the ability to play far beyond the normal upper-range limit, and use of harmonics in a musical fashion were unparalleled. His sound and very identifiable phrasing (like a distinct accent or speech pattern) on the tenor saxophone became the model for many young players in the last two decades of the 20th century. He played in NBC's *Saturday Night Live* band and won *Down Beat* polls in the late 1980s. His untimely death in 2007, from a rare form of leukemia, nearly coincided with the release of his Grammy Award-winning final recording, made while in pain but still in total command of the instrument.

It would be difficult to assemble a more impressive group of all stars than the personnel Brecker included on his *Tales from the Hudson* recording, his fourth album as a leader after years as a much-in-demand sideman and co-leader of the Brecker Brothers fusion-style band. Hailed as the most important tenor saxophonist since John Coltrane, the appearance of Coltrane's pianist McCoy Tyner on several tracks seems only appropriate. The rhythm section is filled out with two of the most visible and prolific artists in contemporary jazz—bassist Dave Holland and drummer Jack DeJohnette (both of whom performed with Miles Davis)—and guitarist Pat Metheny (1954–), who doubles on the guitar synthesizer, an instrument he has helped to develop.

Metheny's debut album, *Bright Size Life*, is now legendary and helped to launch the German ECM label. Jazz journalist Bob Blumenthal wrote that: "Metheny . . . emerged in the '80s as the rare artistic/ commercial success who could boldly rub shoulders with Ornette Coleman's circle after providing feel-good grooves for his larger audience."[3] Metheny has introduced a fresh, sophisticated approach to composition, conception, and production, presenting a group sound concerned with improvisation, but draped in lush, contemporary, electronic, orchestral-like textures and Latin American-influenced grooves. His typical use of Latin American percussionists and indigenous instruments adds an element of authenticity to his music. Borrowing from Chick Corea, Metheny also made use of vocalists, often imitating an instrument by using wordless syllables. Other world-music styles, such as Indian and Cambodian, also serve to influence his music. His music is always graceful, lyrical, and often tranquil, qualities that have became the recognizable Metheny trademark. As a composer, Metheny has also enjoyed inventing music with complex rhythms, odd time signatures, and less than predictable multi-thematic forms. As a guitarist, he is a master technician, known to spin out clean, very long, improvised phrases before pausing for a breath. Metheny is known for his approachable, listener-friendly tunes, but is comfortable in many jazz styles, performing with musicians representing a wide range of preferences. He and his own band continue to be a major force in the 21st century, contributing to film scores such as *Map of the World* and *The Falcon and the Snowman*, as well as collaborations with choreographers and dance companies.

Michael Brecker performing with the Brecker Brothers at the New Orleans Jazz & Heritage Festival

Contemporary guitarist Pat Metheny

The listening guide that follows tracks the Metheny original "Song For Bilbao," a straight-forward tune—aside from the B section, which comes as a surprise—that provides a driving foundation for improvisations by Brecker, Tyner, and Metheny.

LISTENING GUIDE

Pat Metheny

"Song For Bilbao" (Pat Metheny) 5:44

From *Tales from the Hudson*

Recorded 1996, New York

Impulse IMPD-191

Personnel: Michael Brecker, tenor saxophone; Pat Metheny, guitar and guitar synthesizer; McCoy Tyner, piano; Dave Holland, bass; Jack DeJohnette, drums

Form: 28-bar form AABA; A section in 4/4 meter, 4-bar B section shifts to 3/4 meter, before returning to 4/4 in final A section of form

0:00–0:35	First chorus—rhythm section plays through entire AABA form without tune
0:36–0:55	Second chorus—guitar synthesizer and tenor sax enter with tune
0:56–0:59	B section (bridge) in 3/4 meter
1:00–1:10	A section returns along with 4/4 meter
1:11–1:20	Third chorus—tenor sax solos on first A section
1:21–1:31	Sax solo on second A of form
1:32–1:35	Sax solo on B section in 3/4 meter
1:36–1:45	Sax solo on last A of chorus
1:46–2:06	Fourth chorus—sax solos on A sections
2:07–2:10	Sax solo on B section (bridge)
2:11–2:20	Sax solo on final A section
2:21–2:55	Fifth chorus—piano solo on AABA form
2:56–3:29	Sixth chorus—piano continues for second solo chorus on AABA
3:30–4:05	Seventh chorus—guitar solo on AABA form
4:06–4:39	Eighth chorus—guitar continues for a second chorus on form
4:40–4:50	Ninth chorus—return to A section of tune stated by guitar synthesizer and tenor sax
4:51–5:00	Second A section played in harmony by sax and guitar synthesizer
5:01–5:05	B section of tune
5:06–end	Final A section slows down for dramatic ending with final drum flourish

 Additional listening guides for Pat Metheny's "Better Days Ahead" and Michael Brecker's "Suspone" can be found in the corresponding chapter on the website.

POPULAR MUSIC INFLUENCES

Saxophonist Kenny G became both a controversial performer and popular success story in the 1990s. G's overwhelming success justifiably branded him as the leader of the 1990s "smooth-jazz" movement and gave rise to a host of other instrumentalists who sought to promote an easy-listening style of jazz that would be accepted by the masses. Also described as contemporary jazz, this popular style was promoted by Boney James, Rick Braun, Shadowfax, Dave Koz, Larry Carlton, Acoustic Alchemy, Lee Ritenour, Walter Beasley, David Benoit, Richard Elliot, Marc Antoine, and Chris Botti. Their melodically memorable music (almost like pop vocals, without the lyrics) is typically derived from simple harmonic progressions, with easy, danceable grooves and an

Popular smooth-jazz artist Chris Botti

unobtrusive sound that was popular with AM radio stations, which had all but banned jazz from their play lists. Critics of smooth jazz point out the absence of any real challenge or controversy presented to the listener, and the absence of any apparent jazz roots in most of the performers. They cannot find in it the range of emotion that is a cornerstone of more traditionally rooted jazz. It cannot be denied, however, that this style has gained more momentum than initially anticipated and attracts many new listeners to instrumental jazz, sometimes leading them to broaden their listening habits, exploring even more challenging music.

"Acid jazz," another 1990s variation on a pop-jazz theme, was a term coined by London DJ Gilles Peterson. Acid jazz grew out of London dance clubs, where groovy, electronic remakes of funky 1960s jazz were popular. Its success encouraged a new music that was the result of a bond between soul and funk music, hip-hop dance rhythms, aspects of the jazz tradition, and Latin percussion. Bands known for this new hybrid style include Buckshot LeFonque (once associated with Branford Marsalis), Us3, Incognito, and Jamiroquai. Jazz artists such as trumpeter Russell Gunn and vocalist Cassandra Wilson, who are known for their work in more mainstream contexts, have also explored this direction, which makes some sense, as acid jazz relies heavily on important aspects of the jazz tradition—strong emotional content, along with improvisation. Much like "smooth jazz," this style of music provides an easy entry point for the uninitiated to become acquainted with jazz, without wading in too deeply at first with bebop or classic-jazz styles. These modern bands are providing an experience not dissimilar to that offered to 1920s music lovers who were drawn to jazz first through Paul Whiteman's music, or the dance crowd who found jazz during the Swing Era, later to discover bebop and cool jazz. Acid jazz has become very popular in Japan, parts of Europe, and Latin America. It is a brand of jazz that is known by many names, including "street soul," "electro jazz," "hip-bop" (check out Miles Davis's final recording *Doo-Bop*), and so forth, but the styles essentially have the same salient features:

* heavy bass lines that are often repetitive;
* lots of electronically processed sounds;
* danceable tempos and rhythms;
* strong drum beats (played by drummers or electronic drum machines), sometimes featuring back-beat accents (emphasis on beats 2 and 4);
* repetitive rhythms;
* melodies and harmonies informed by the blues.

Tim Hagans (1954–)

Trumpeter/composer Tim Hagans at the 2008 IAJE Conference in Toronto, Canada

The popular rap, DJ mix, bass 'n drums, hip-hop, and urban electronic styles have exerted influences on 21st-century jazz musicians, just as Sly Stone and Jimi Hendrix provided new motivation to an earlier generation of jazz musicians. Trumpeter Tim Hagans (1954–) and composer/arranger/saxophonist Bob Belden teamed up to record *Animation/Imagination* and *Re-Animation Live*, which offered unique fusions of the latest esoteric electronic pop and a full dose of improvisation à la Miles Davis post 1970s. Hagans's imaginative live band adds splashes of freely improvised bass, drums, and keyboard to electronic samples, DJ mixes, drum loops, funky electronic dance grooves, and various other soundscapes. Hagans and Belden improvise in a very free, unencumbered style on top of these shifting aural landscapes. In some ways, "Trumpet Sandwich" could be considered a sophisticated, experimental brand of acid jazz. There is absolutely no commercial compromise about either recording, and both represent the finest in cutting-edge, 21st-century jazz. Tim Hagans discusses his work on "Trumpet Sandwich," which is included on the companion audio anthology.

Trumpet Sandwich is a through-improvised composition. Each phrase is 16 bars containing smaller subdivisions of 4 bars each. The first 3 subdivisions present improvised melodic material that builds and weaves, as do traditional melodies. The last segment, usually simpler, is the summation of the 16 bar phrase.

The piece stresses the importance of meaningful melodic construction whether supported by traditional harmony or not. One can improvise over the chords of a tune or, on a deeper level one can improvise over the emotions generated by those chords. Here, I am improvising over the emotions of a nonexistent chord progression with the emphasis on a standard melodic form.

The original version, on *Animation/Imagination*, was an improvised jam with Billy Kilson (drums) and David Dyson (bass) during a session lunch break, hence the title. With no plan in advance, we turned the lights out, Dave started playing the bass line and the rest is . . . [open to chance].

In order to keep my mind totally free, I avoided figuring out the key Dave was playing in. That prevented me from assigning scale numbers and traditional emotions to the notes I used.

After the initial studio recording, the tune's basic concept was established but with this group of freethinkers, the direction and vibe was new and fresh every time. This version closed our set at the Montreal Jazz Festival in 1999.[4]

 An excerpt of "Trumpet Sandwich" is included on the companion audio anthology.

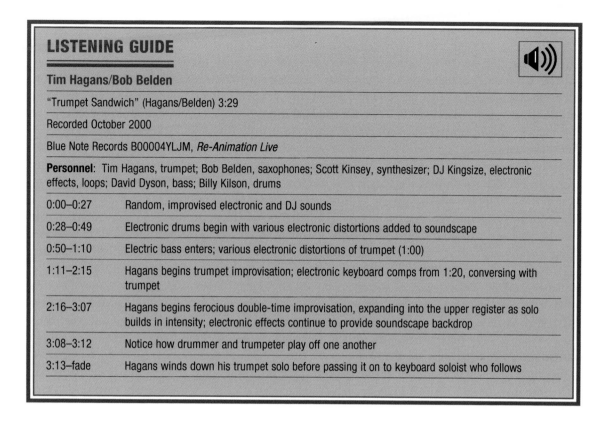

LISTENING GUIDE

Tim Hagans/Bob Belden

"Trumpet Sandwich" (Hagans/Belden) 3:29

Recorded October 2000

Blue Note Records B00004YLJM, *Re-Animation Live*

Personnel: Tim Hagans, trumpet; Bob Belden, saxophones; Scott Kinsey, synthesizer; DJ Kingsize, electronic effects, loops; David Dyson, bass; Billy Kilson, drums

0:00–0:27	Random, improvised electronic and DJ sounds
0:28–0:49	Electronic drums begin with various electronic distortions added to soundscape
0:50–1:10	Electric bass enters; various electronic distortions of trumpet (1:00)
1:11–2:15	Hagans begins trumpet improvisation; electronic keyboard comps from 1:20, conversing with trumpet
2:16–3:07	Hagans begins ferocious double-time improvisation, expanding into the upper register as solo builds in intensity; electronic effects continue to provide soundscape backdrop
3:08–3:12	Notice how drummer and trumpeter play off one another
3:13–fade	Hagans winds down his trumpet solo before passing it on to keyboard soloist who follows

The website offers interviews with Tim Hagans discussing his work in the US and abroad. The interview is found in the corresponding chapter.

"Groove music," "jam jazz," or "bass 'n' drums" all essentially describe the same style, something quite similar to acid jazz. This "groove music" often shows the following characteristics:

- catchy rhythm grooves;
- rhythmically earthy and sometimes simplistic;
- reliance on strong, repetitive bass lines;
- funky drum beats emphasizing numerous subdivisions of the basic beat;
- resemblance to the R & B tradition;
- simple harmonic form involving only a few chords.

Artists who participate in this style are often the same performers who are dedicated to many other styles of jazz and enjoy the challenge of diversity. Many of these groups feature organ and guitar, much like the organ groups in the late 1950s and 1960s. Groups or artists that have pioneered this style are Medeski Martin & Wood and guitarist John Scofield. It is often difficult to separate hip-hop influenced jazz from acid jazz and this bass 'n' drums jam style, as they all share similar characteristics.

VOCAL RENAISSANCE

The 1990s and the early years of this century have been kind to the jazz vocalist. There has not only been a rise in popularity of new vocalists singing music that is informed by the jazz tradition, but a rebirth of several older artists, including Tony Bennett and Jon Hendricks. Hendricks sang an important role in Marsalis's *Blood on the Fields*, as did newcomer Cassandra Wilson. An eclectic vocalist who has been involved with projects that range from fringe to traditional, Wilson believes that: "jazz has to be a current music for its survival. It has to be grounded in our lives as they are today."[5] Perhaps the biggest box-office draw in recent years has been Canadian singer/pianist Diana Krall. Her romantic ballad style is in stark contrast to those female artists such as Diane Schuur who helped pave the way a decade earlier for renewed interest in jazz singers. Schuur, who continues to enjoy modest popularity, is a more robust singer, in the Ella Fitzgerald tradition, than Krall. Karrin Allyson, Tierney Sutton, Patricia Barber, and Jane Monheit are newcomers, along with Nora Jones and Esperanza Spalding, whose careers were suddenly launched by Grammy Awards. Jones has created quite a stir as a new young singer, but, despite her Blue Note label affiliation, many question her classification as a jazz singer. Barber and Monheit, on the other hand, are more reverent, clearly showing their roots in the jazz vocal tradition. More seasoned artists such as Dee Dee Bridgewater, Patti Austin, Roseanna Vitro, and Natalie Cole paid their dues for some time before enjoying greater exposure in recent years. Just as jazz labels sought out talented "Young Lions" in the image of Wynton Marsalis, they now are rushing to sign new young male and female vocalists in time to capitalize on the success of Krall and Jones. Who can blame these corporate efforts? They are no doubt made in an effort to energize record sales that have dropped 20% or more in recent years.

Diana Krall performing in 2004 at the Mountain Winery, in Saratoga, California

Esperanza Spalding (1984–)

Singer/bassist Esperanza Spalding (1984–) is the most recent example of this phenomenon, representing the new breed of jazz musician who refuses to commit to one brand of jazz—nor does she want to. Her only concern, like that of her comrades, is that her music is honest and of the highest caliber. *Jazz Times* called her a "Bop-trained Beyoncé." She replied that: "If they want to put us in the pop rack or market us with Beyoncé, I don't care, because I'm pretty sure that sincere music will cut through any setting."[6] Some critics and journalists have branded her as a crossover artist, but, whatever the label, this young performer is one of a kind and an extraordinary musician. Not yet 30, the Portland, Oregon native was raised by a single parent in a multilingual household. Her musical influences are wide-ranging, including R & B, pop, Brazilian, and classical styles. She is clearly a prodigy on the bass and as a vocalist, a rare and unusual combination.

Spalding began her fascination and love affair with music at age 5, learning the violin on her own after being inspired by cellist Yo Yo Ma's appearance on *Mister Rogers' Neighborhood*, the children's TV show. Within a year, the Oregon Chamber Music Society community orchestra accepted her, and Esperanza became the orchestra's concertmaster at age 15. Somewhere along the way, though, she discovered the bass and its stylistic versatility. She soon began performing with local bands and writing her own music and lyrics. Largely home schooled by her mother, Spalding earned her GED at 16

Esperanza Spalding performs at the 4th Annual Roots Picnic at the Festival Pier, in Philadelphia, Pennsylvania, June 4, 2011

and was accepted to the music program at Portland State as a bass major. She transferred to Boston's Berklee College of Music, which is responsible for grooming many prominent jazz artists, including Toshiko Akiyoshi, Anat Cohen, and vocalist Diana Krall. Three years later she graduated and, in 2005, she became Berklee's youngest assistant professor, while performing with seasoned artists Joe Lovano and Pat Metheny. Her first major recording as a solo artist, in 2008, titled *Esperanza*, launched the career of this charismatic dynamo. Since then she has appeared on the *Late Show* with David Letterman, the *Tavis Smiley Show*, *Jimmy Kimmel Live!*, *Austin City Limits*, Jay Leno's *Tonight Show*, and even at the White House. Her uncanny, ambidextrous ability to simultaneously scat sing and improvise on the double bass is spellbinding and unusual, to say the least. She is a captivating, radioactive performer who exudes the confidence of a musician who is at one with her instrument and completely devoted to her music.

"Body and Soul," from her first solo recording, is included in the companion audio collection and for discussion as it serves as an interesting comparison to the earlier versions by Coleman Hawkins (Chapter 7) and Billie Holiday (Chapter 8). It also illustrates that this new generation of young artists has not turned their backs on the jazz tradition, but tend to reinterpret the past rather than recreate it. Listen again to the first few phrases of the Billie Holiday recording and you will hear how Spalding has obviously absorbed aspects of Holiday's phrasing in her own,

LISTENING GUIDE 🔊

Esperanza Spalding

"Cuerpo y Alma" (Body and Soul) (Green–Sour–Heyman–Eyton) 8:02

From *Esperanza*

2008 Heads Up International

Recorded 2008

Personnel: Esperanza Spalding, acoustic bass and vocals; Leo Genovese, piano; Otis Brown, drums

Form: A interlude A interlude B interlude A—essentially song form with added interludes

0:00–0:07	Intro—ostinato bass line introduced outlining 5/4 meter
0:08–0:21	Piano and drums join bass on intro
0:22–0:51	First chorus—A section: vocal begins, sung in Spanish
0:52–1:05	Interlude—separating A sections; bass playing ostinato
1:06–1:35	Second A section—vocal returns
1:36–2:05	B Section—rhythm section changes to walking
2:06–2:21	Interlude—8-bar vamp with bass ostinato-like intro
2:21–2:49	Last A—completes first chorus with vocal
2:50–3:47	Second chorus—A sections: piano solos, walking bass and swing feel
3:48–4:16	B section or bridge—piano solo continues
4:17–4:45	Last A section to complete second chorus
4:46–5:43	Third chorus—A sections: Spalding solos, scats simultaneously with improvised bass lines
5:44–6:12	B Section—return to vocal lyric
6:13–6:28	Interlude—bass ostinato vamp-like intro
6:29–6:54	A section—vocal concludes third chorus
6:55–7:14	Coda—extension of form serves as ending
7:15–end	Bass ostinato vamp returns and fades to end

unique version of this jazz classic. Spalding's version is based on an infectious introduction featuring an ostinato bass line that outlines 5/4 meter and is repeated as a transition between A and B sections sung in Spanish. The 5/4 meter is maintained through both verses and through the solos for Spalding and the pianist. Listen to her impressive scat vocal and unison bass solo on the A section of the tune, before the vocal lyric returns.

In a nearly unprecedented move, the National Academy of Recording Arts and Sciences awarded a Grammy for Best New Artist of 2011 to Spalding, a distinction nearly always achieved by pop artists. She was 26 at the time! The award has existed since 1959, and, previously, only one other jazz artist has won—crossover singer Nora Jones, whose first CD sold over 25 million copies.

On the male side, Kurt Elling, Mark Murphy, Jamie Cullum, Kevin Mahogany, and Harry Connick Jr. have all made contributions as relative newcomers to the contemporary jazz scene. Kurt Elling is best described as the kind of singer instrumentalists love, as he bases his impressive vocal technique on the best horn soloists, scatting and reinterpreting tunes like veteran jazz instrumentalists. Bobby McFerrin, the singer turned orchestral conductor, may have been responsible for the renewed and widespread interest in the jazz vocalist, although much of his repertoire in the 1990s was more about improvisation than it was specifically about jazz. He is an amazing talent nevertheless, whose roots are unmistakably from the jazz and African traditions.

It is perhaps more difficult for vocalists than for instrumentalists to bring anything significantly new to the tradition, but many of the newcomers are enjoying popularity by recasting exceptional, forgotten repertoire from the archives, or by introducing newly penned songs. It remains to be seen if any of these artists will have the same lasting influence as Billie Holiday, Sarah Vaughan, Ella Fitzgerald, Frank Sinatra, or Joe Williams. At the moment, they are enjoying good press and have helped to rejuvenate sagging jazz-label record sales.

CONTEMPORARY WOMEN EMERGING AS INNOVATORS

Much has already been said about the vocal renaissance in recent years, but a more astonishing recent trend is that women instrumentalists, bandleaders, and composers are gaining a much stronger foothold, now showing significant presence and exerting major influences in this new century. Never before have so many women instrumentalists enjoyed a position of prominence and influence in the world of jazz. Some historic perspective is important to understanding of this recent phenomenon.

You will recall from reading Chapter 8 and the discussion surrounding Mary Lou Williams that women in jazz, with the exception of vocalists, have been anomalies in an otherwise male-dominated art form. In the early years, they were looked upon more as novelties and window dressing. With only a few examples to serve as exceptions, including Williams and, before her, Lilian Hardin (both pianists), women were relegated to applying their musical talents, skills, and education to church, community, and classroom service. The very education system they served discouraged women from playing certain instruments, and societal mores frowned on women engaging with the environments associated with jazz. Men did not believe women, the "fairer sex," had the stamina to tour or play the physically demanding wind instruments associated with jazz. A long process of women's rights movements, over many years, has been instrumental in encouraging women to pursue careers in jazz, and not just as singers and pianists. Most attribute this success, especially in the last 10 years, to the growth of high-school and university jazz programs, with enlightened educators who have encouraged female participation. It is easy also to recognize a parallel in the general concerted effort toward women's equality as professionals in the workplace, including fields such as medicine, politics, engineering, law, journalism, film, and many other professions that had been dominated by men. The climate for women in jazz began to noticeably change in the 1970s and 1980s, when role models for 21st-century women became noticed by the emerging younger generation. These important role models include such artists as soprano saxophonist/composer Jane Ira Bloom, composer/pianist/big bandleader and Grammy winner Toshiko Akiyoshi, composer/bandleader Carla Bley, and pianists Marian McPartland, Joanne Brackeen, and Geri Allen. These women are pioneers, like the few others who, generations before them, stood out as exceptions in a male-dominated crowd. However, the work of these modern women was recognized, whereas the earlier generations' work often went unrecognized until years later.

Not only has their work been recognized by fans, they have also been singled out by critics in annual polls.

An analysis of readers' and critics' polls in *Down Beat* and *Jazz Times* magazines from 1998 to 2011 offers further evidence of the impact women are having on the jazz scene:

- In 1998, *Jazz Times* readers voted for 12 women among all categories, and there were no winners.
- In 2010, there were 25 women receiving votes, and 5 won their category. Only five instruments went unrepresented by women contenders, and it is clear that they were making significant contributions as composers and arrangers, a trend started in the latter years of the previous century.
- *Down Beat* critics voted for 21 women in 2002, with one category winner.
- In 2009, *Down Beat* critics nearly doubled that number by voting for 41 women, with 4 winning a category.
- In 2008, polls in the same magazine showed that two out of four performers in the Best New Artist category were women (one a non-native American). That same year, 11 of the 50 best jazz recordings cited by *Jazz Times* were produced by female artists.
- Drummer Terri Lyne Carrington's *Mosaic* recording won a Grammy in 2012 and features an exclusively female cast of 19 prominent instrumentalists and vocalists.

Artists consistently cited in these polls are soprano saxophonists Jane Ira Bloom and Jane Bunnett, violinist and recent MacArthur Fellow Regina Carter, drummer extraordinaire Terri Lyne Carrington, composer/bandleader Maria Schneider, and newcomers clarinet/saxophonist Anat Cohen and, recently, bassist/vocalist Esperanza Spalding.

MARIA SCHNEIDER (1960–)

These artists are not the only ones at the forefront of accomplishments of women in jazz in the early years of this young century. For example, Maria Schneider (1960–), the renowned composer/arranger/bandleader and multiple poll winner, won a Grammy in 2005 for a recording that could only be purchased on the Internet. Although it is true that she began to generate a following for her earlier recordings, released in the traditional fashion by the German ENJA label, the fan-funded concept that is central to the strictly online ArtistShare label was, and still is, a revolutionary concept. This concept was first proven to be a successful new model by Maria Schneider's Jazz Orchestra recording entitled *Concert In the Garden*. Schneider serves as an example and role model of what is possible for women in jazz. She was raised in a small, rural, Minnesota town, where she studied piano before pursuing two degrees, a Bachelor of Music at the University of Minnesota and a Master of Music from the Eastman School of Music. She risked moving to New York following graduation and was waiting tables until she was fortunate to become an apprentice to the renowned composer and Miles Davis collaborator Gil Evans. She also studied with influential composer Bob Brookmeyer. "Evocative," "majestic," "magical," "heart-stoppingly gorgeous," and "beyond categorization" are words and phrases that critics have used to describe her music. Her first recording, supported in part by the Herb Alpert Commission, awarded by the National Association of Jazz Educators, was released in 1994 (*Evanessence*). Since that recording, she has worked to develop a unique, contemporary composing and arranging style that sometimes incorporates Latin American dance rhythms and other non-American styles. What distinguishes her from many other large-ensemble leaders, including Toshiko Akiyoshi, is that she does not play an instrument in her band, choosing only to conduct. Her work as a composer, conductor, and bandleader has taken her to some 30 countries, spanning Europe, South America, Australia, Asia, and North

Maria Schneider conducts the Maria Schneider Orchestra on stage during the *Festival Internacional de Jazz de Barcelona* at Palau De La Musica, in Barcelona, Spain, 2011

America. As with many 21st-century jazz artists, her work crosses boundaries and blurs lines. She finds inspiration from her world travels, the musicians who surround her, and her earlier work with artists such as Sting, Evans, and Brookmeyer. She has composed for the dance company Pilobolus, the cutting-edge, crossover Kronos String Quartet, and chamber orchestras featuring the sensational soprano soloist Dawn Upshaw. Schneider and her orchestra have been recognized with nine Grammy nominations, two Grammy Awards, as well as countless critics', readers' poll, and jazz journalists top honors. To quote *Time Magazine*: "To call Schneider the most important woman in jazz is missing the point . . . She is a major composer—period."[7] Schneider has not been without some criticism from jazz purists, although they are in the minority, suggesting that her music is too orchestral and doesn't have enough of the typical elements that define jazz, but improvised solos are plentiful throughout her music.

Much of Maria Schneider's work is lengthy, episodic, programmatic at times, and multi-movement in nature, which precludes including a discussion of one of her entire pieces. Providing an excerpt, however, seemed more than appropriate and will hopefully whet your appetite to investigate more of her music on your own. The selection provided on the companion audio collection is Part 3 of her *Three Romances* suite included on *Concert in the Garden*, the acclaimed Grammy-winning recording and first release by the online ArtistShare label. Highly motivated by dance and influenced in her youth by Gene Kelly and Fred Astaire movies featuring dance, Maria writes that this last movement is "my imaginary foxtrot. I gave it a Portuguese title because while a foxtrot is as American as can be, the harmony I've used here owes much more to Brazil."[8] The Portuguese title, "Dança Ilusória," means illusionary dance. The piece shows she is a masterful orchestrator, mixing orchestral wind instruments such as clarinets and flutes with brass. Schneider constantly reinvents her melodies through varied orchestration and other subtle changes. The thematic material is a combination of striking, romantic, melodic lines, juxtaposed with syncopated rhythms, together creating an overall, tension-ridden Brazilian character. See if you can find the subtle sigh-like gestures used sporadically in the woodwinds and brass, even at the final chord.

Based on earlier accomplishments by women who crashed the male jazz world, it's not terribly new or surprising to hear fabulous 21st-century jazz pianists, such as first-generation Chinese–American Helen Sung, who now occupies the bench in the Mingus Big Band, or flutists such as Jamie Baum, or even composers such as Maria Schneider or Anat Cohen, equally well known for her clarinet and soprano sax work. What are quite amazing and new to this century are emerging talents on instruments such as the bass (Spalding), drums (Carrington) and trumpet—Canadian Ingrid Jensen, who is a frequently featured soloist in Schneider's orchestra. Ingrid is one of two women in Schneider's ensemble, with trumpeter Laurie Frink. Jensen's younger sister, saxophonist Christine Jensen, is just now emerging as a composer/arranger/bandleader, following in the footsteps of Maria Schneider with her first CD *Treelines*. Diva and Maiden Voyage, although they don't work regularly, are both contemporary big bands with all-female casts and serve as incubators for outstanding female jazz instrumentalists. Many musicians in these ensembles are working in their own small groups outside the big band, producing high-quality live music and recordings.

What all of these musicians have in common has been access to an educational system open to, and encouraging of, their pursuit of jazz, regardless of their instrument. The jazz-education movement has embraced women, and the results are now bearing fruit. They have been encouraged and respected as peers by the still male-dominated profession. However, as Figure 15.2 shows, there are growing numbers of women instrumentalists and composers making a difference, and this trend continues to tick upwards.

Unfortunately, these women, and those who have no doubt been inadvertently omitted, are still in a minority. Surveys conducted in 2000 showed that an average of only 20% of the working jazz musicians were women, compared with their 47% share of the overall U.S. workforce. However, times are changing, and I suspect that at the time of writing, 10 years after the previous data were posted, this percentage has increased based on the previous study of jazz critics' and readers' polls. It will be exciting to watch this trend continue.

Saxophonists
Jane Ira Bloom
Jane Bunnett
Anat Cohen*
Clare Daily
Candy Dulfer*
Tia Fuller
Christine Jensen*
Grace Kelly*
Anne Peterson
Tineke Postma*

Trombone
Janice Robinson

Trumpet
Laurie Frink
Ingrid Jensen*
Carol Morgan

Arranger/Composer
Toshiko Akiyoshi*
Carla Bley
Christine Jensen*
Maria Schneider

Pianists
Toshiko Akiyoshi*
Geri Allen
Joanne Brackeen
Eliane Ellias*
Hiromi*
Reneé Rosnes*
Patrice Rushen
Helen Sung*

Percussion
Cindy Blackman
Sue Evans
Marilyn Mazur

Drums
Terri Lyne Carrington
Sheila E
Sheri Maricle
Kim Thompson
Rachael Z

Flute
Jaime Baum
Jane Bunnett
Nicole Mitchell

Bass
Anne Mette Iversen*
Linda Oh*
Esperanza Spalding*

FIGURE 15.2 21st-century women in jazz

* Indicates non-native American or first-generation American

LISTENING GUIDE

Maria Schneider

Three Romances Part 3 "Dança Ilusória" (Maria Schneider) 9:06

From *Concert in the Garden*

ArtitShare 0001

Recorded 3/8–11/2004

Personnel: Tim Ries, alto/soprano/clarinet/flute/alto flute/bass flute; Charles Pillow, alto/soprano/clarinet/flute/alto flute/oboe/English horn; Rich Perry, tenor sax and flute; Andy Middleton, tenor; Donny McCaslin, tenor/soprano/clarinet/flute; Scott Robinson, baritone/flute/bass clarinet/clarinet/contrabass clarinet; Tony Kadleck, trumpet and flugelhorn; Greg Gisbert, trumpet and flugelhorn; Laurie Frink, trumpet and flugelhorn; Ingrid Jensen, trumpet and flugelhorn; Keith O'Quinn. trombone; Larry Farrell, trombone; Pete McGuinness, trombone; Rock Ciccarone, trombone; George Flynn, bass trombone and contrabass trombone; Ben Monder, guitar; Frank Kimbrough, piano; Jay Anderson, bass; Clarence Penn, drums

Soloists: Frank Kimbrough, piano; Larry Farrell, trombone

Form: Rubato introduction followed by AABA thematic form, with each section stitched together with a reoccurring, descending, scale-like gesture described here as the interlude.

0:00–0:58	Rubato piano solo that hints at thematic material
0:59–1:15	First appearance of melodic phrase referred to as "interlude," which connects main themes reoccurring throughout the piece in varied forms
1:16–1:37	A theme melodic material
1:38–1:44	Interlude reappears, now with counterpoint
1:45–2:07	A theme repeats with variation and different orchestration
2:08–2:14	Interlude reappears
2:15–2:39	B theme shows new material
2:40–3:00	A theme repeated
3:01–3:08	Interlude
3:08–3:28	Improvised piano solo begins over form; band background material derived from A theme
3:29–3:30	Brief appearance of the interlude material
3:31–4:19	Piano solo continues featuring nice interplay with bass
4:20–4:40	Piano solo continues with low sustained backgrounds based on A theme
4:41–5:11	Interlude material to end piano solo
5:12–6:19	Trombone solo continues, with sustained woodwind backgrounds
6:20–2:29	Interlude material brings dynamic level up to conclude solo and introduce full ensemble
6:30–6:49	Full ensemble in counterpoint with brass and saxophones builds to first climax
7:04–7:11	Builds to penultimate climax, winding down to what appears to be the end
7:12–8:00	Ensemble builds again to final climax at 7:51
8:01–8:13	Interlude serves to bring piece to a close
8:14–end	Coda with piano stating final interlude material

JAZZ AS A GLOBAL MUSIC

Afro-Cuban and Latin Jazz

Afro-Cuban and Afro-Latin influences on jazz have been well documented throughout this book, and examples of these external influences have been plentiful even since the beginnings of jazz. Nothing has significantly changed over the past 20 years or so, and musicians on both sides of the aisle continue to embrace the marriage of jazz and Afro-Cuban-Latin elements. Afro-Latin and Afro-Caribbean music continues to bring rhythmic vitality and spontaneity to jazz, and the nature of jazz and its harmonic complexity will interest Latin and Caribbean musicians.

Contemporary jazz musicians such as Paquito D'Rivera, Eddie Palmieri, Clare Fischer, Jerry Gonzalez, Claudio Roditi, Michel Camilo, Hilton Ruiz, Gonzalo Rubalcaba, the Caribbean Jazz Project, Bobby Sanabria, Bobby Carcassés, Chucho Valdés, Luciana Souza, Ruben Blades, Danilo Pérez, and Arturo Sandoval, among others, continue to bring new focus to the Afro-Latin and Afro-Cuban jazz connection, each offering new, exciting blends of these styles and featuring Latin musicians alongside American jazz artists. In some cases, Latino musicians play their own brand of Latin-influenced jazz. For example, the Cuban band Irakere nurtured several prominent Afro-Cuban jazz musicians, including Valdés, Sandoval, and D'Rivera. One by one, each of them sought exile in the US, where they were free to travel and explore, through collaborations, the improvised music that to them represented freedom. In 2005, D'Rivera was awarded the distinguished NEA Jazz Masters award for his contributions to American music. Rubalcaba, like Valdés, is from Havana, and both demonstrate a macho, fiery style of Afro-Cuban piano playing. The Dallas, Texas-born "Young Lion" Roy Hargrove took his trumpet to Cuba to learn first hand about this invigorating music. Here, he came into contact with Valdés and a number of other Cuban musicians. The result of their collaboration produced Hargrove's Crisol band, and its recording, *Habana*, offers an electrifying mix of jazz and Cuban music.

For many years, jazz artists have looked outside the Western world for inspiration, and it is certainly well known that improvisation plays a central role in the music of many other cultures, and so the marriage is logical. More recent trends toward drawing on world-music styles may actually have been sparked by Paul Simon's successful Afro-pop recording, *Graceland* (1986), and the energized Afro-Cuban salsa style from the 1960s and 1970s. This long-established trend, based on the fusion of jazz characteristics and Afro-Cuban and Afro-Latin music, can be traced back to Jelly Roll Morton and W.C. Handy, who incorporated Latin rhythms into their 1920s music, and will no doubt continue throughout this century.

Danilo Pérez (1965–)

Pianist Danilo Pérez (1965–) is a young, contemporary artist who, because of his Panamanian heritage and American education, offers an excellent case study in which to more closely evaluate the potential for jazz drawing on numerous world-music sources. The track from his CD *Motherland* included on the companion audio anthology was released at the dawn of this century and embraces a diverse worldview. He successfully molds elements of Caribbean, African, Andalucian, Moorish, and of course American jazz into something entirely new. The ethnicity of his group is as diverse as the music, featuring African-American, Brazilian, Anglo-American, and other Latin-tinged musicians. Pérez, like many of his contemporaries, also has a penchant for exploring odd time signatures, striving to make them sound as normal and comfortable as a 4/4 march or 3/4 waltz. Part 1 of his "Suite For The Americas" is reminiscent of Corea's earlier work in the 1970s, in that it is multi-thematic and through composed in its organization and structure. **Through composed** is a compositional approach that resembles stream-of-consciousness writing, in that typically there are no reoccurring themes, links from one to another, or character development to provide a more traditional, discernible form or shape. One idea moves on to the next and is followed by yet another idea, and so on. In this case, Pérez does finally return, briefly, to the initial 'A' theme and makes use of Arabic and Latin rhythms and bass ostinatos to provide adhesive to help hold the various fragments together. This piece is a composition and not merely a tune that serves as the basis for improvised solos. In fact, there is very little improvisation in this entire piece. If you try to tap your toe and count along as you listen to this track, you will be challenged by the odd and changing meters, but the piece is primarily in 7/4 meter. Saxophonist Chris Potter, vocalist Luciana Souza, violinist Regina Carter, and, of course, pianist/composer Pérez are some of the most promising musicians of this young century.

Jazz has always been known for absorbing the cultural influences of its surroundings and spawning new hybrids. There is little doubt that the Latin–jazz marriage will continue to offer spicy new outcomes.

Pianist Danilo Pérez

LISTENING GUIDE

Danilo Pérez

"Suite For The Americas, Part 1" (Pérez) 2:54

Recorded February–March 2000, New York City

Motherland

Verve 3145439042

Personnel: Danilo Pérez, piano, electronic piano; Carlos Henriquez, acoustic bass; Antonio Sanchez, drums; Regina Carter, violin; Luciana Souza, vocals; Chris Potter, soprano saxophone; Luisito Quintero, congas, small percussion, caja, tambora, chimes, durban drums; Ricuarte Villereal, tambor repicador

Form: Sectional, through-composed form using several different melodic elements, sometimes repeated and in several key centers; overall Latin rhythmic feel in 7/4, 5/4 meters

0:00–0:17	Introduction—8 bars of 7/4, Latin groove in D minor, created by bass, drums, piano 2 bars: bass enters with 7/4 ostinato pattern 2 bars: drums and percussion join bass 4 bars: piano enters with chord, then sparse Latin comping
0:18–0:55	A-theme section: 17 bars of 7/4, A theme, in D minor, played twice by piano, sax, and violin, with continuing rhythm-section accompaniment
0:18–0:35	Part 1: 8 bars, A theme 4 bars: piano plays first phrase of A theme (2 + 2)

	2 bars: violin, sax, and piano play in unison answering second phrase of A theme 2 bars: piano plays ad-lib solo, with rhythm-section accompaniment
0:35–0:55	Part 2: 9 bars, A theme repeated 4 bars: violin, sax, and piano play unison 4 bars of A theme (2 + 2) 2 bars: violin, sax, and piano play unison answering 2 bars of A theme 2 bars: piano and electronic piano ad-lib solo with rhythm-section accompaniment 1 bar (7/4): Closing idea performed in unison by violin, sax, and piano, used as transition to B-theme section
0:55–1:19	B-theme section—10 bars of 7/4, new key, performed twice by voice, piano and saxophone, with continuing rhythm-section accompaniment B theme repeat is varied
0:55–1:06	Part 1—5 bars: B theme performed by voice, piano, violin, and sax 3 bars: first phrase of B theme 2 bars: second "answering" phrase of B theme
1:07–1:19	Part 2—5 bars: B theme repeated by voice, piano, violin, and sax with variation at end 3 bars: first phrase of B theme 2 bars: altered second phrase of B theme, with dramatic, held C-sharp vocal note, violin, sax, and piano "break," and loud ensemble line that crescendos to climactic chord
1:19–1:42	C section—10 bars of 7/4, long D-major melodies, performed by voice, violin, sax, and piano, with frequent rhythm-section breaks
1:43–2:02	D section—8 bars of 7/4, modal "Arabic" melodies, performed by piano, voice, sax, and violin 2 bars: piano, bass, drums, and percussion (tambourine) set up highly syncopated groove 2 bars: 1-bar vocal phrase answered by voice, sax, and violin 4 bars: voice elaborates 1-bar vocal phrase, with continued overlapping "answers" in sax and violin
2:03–2:24	E section—9 bars of 7/4, vocal and saxophone solos, with funky rhythm section led by electric piano, alternating between D major and B minor, with 1-bar closing acoustic piano break
2:25–2:34	F section—4 bars in 7/4, ensemble "shout" theme, in C-sharp minor, performed twice by voice, sax, violin, and piano, with rhythm-section accompaniment
2:35–2:54	A-theme section: 8 bars in 5/4, A theme paraphrased in C-sharp minor, performed twice by voice, sax, violin, and piano; first theme statement is unison, repeat is harmonized; with 1-bar (7/4) tag: Closing idea in new key, from end of A-theme section

JAZZ AS AN INTERNATIONAL LANGUAGE

It is only fitting that jazz and pop musicians have been drawn to African music, as the American styles are rooted in its music, but now a more global mix, a worldwide two-way street, encouraging jazz to be spoken, borrowed, and altered in new ways, has taken shape. The international jazz scene became increasingly active in the latter years of the 20th century and gave even more credence to American experimental efforts to take jazz in directions that sometimes bear little resemblance to the earlier roots of jazz. European artists have learned to bring their own cultural traditions to be reconciled with the roots of jazz. For example, saxophonist Jan Garbarek improvises with an a cappella vocal ensemble singing somber, Renaissance music in a grand European cathedral. Although this music could certainly not be considered avant-garde, or even jazz by usual definitions, what an exciting way to combine two Western music traditions in order to realize something altogether new.

Almost from its inception, musicians and audiences outside the US have been curious about jazz. A brief glimpse of how jazz gained exposure outside the US will enlighten our view of what is happening on the jazz scene today, outside and inside the US. This overview will also explain why jazz has become so popular worldwide, and how it has gained its status as a celebrated, international language.

The first phase coincides nearly with the beginnings of jazz in the US, when the first American jazz artists began to tour Europe. You will remember that the Original Dixieland Jazz Band was well received during its tour of the UK in 1919. Even before that, James Reese Europe's "Negro" regimental military band performed in Paris, to the amazement of French musicians. Early jazz clarinetist/soprano saxophonist Sidney Bechet spent years in Europe in the 1920s, when he traveled as far as Russia playing jazz. Louis Armstrong, who eventually became an international star, performing often as an American cultural ambassador, made his first impression on European audiences in 1932. In that same decade, Duke Ellington's Orchestra performed abroad, as did Swing Era tenor saxophonist Coleman Hawkins, who took up residency in Europe from 1934 to 1939. This long list of American international jazz travelers in the first half of the 20th century also includes Dizzy Gillespie and his big band, Miles Davis, Charlie Parker, and many, many others. Important artists who have been discussed throughout this book took refuge in Europe as expatriates at some point in their careers. The African-American artists found Europeans to be more respectful of their profession and racial discrimination to be nearly non-existent. Ironically, these Americans played music that represented freedom, but racial discrimination was still ever present at home in the US.

By the mid 1930s, European musicians began forging their own approaches to jazz. Take, for example, guitarist Django Reinhardt, who was raised outside of Paris in a gypsy community and later teamed with swing violinist Stéphane Grappelli. Both artists became the first generation of important, internationally recognized, non-American jazz artists. Simultaneously, swing-style dance bands and rhythm or hot clubs sprang up throughout the UK and France. The first publications devoted to jazz were also created by European writers in the 1930s.

Although traditional New Orleans jazz was embraced for years throughout much of Europe, more modern trends in bebop attracted the younger generation. UK saxophonist John Dankworth's band, in the 1950s and 1960s, for example, served as an incubator for British musicians such as bassist Dave Holland and trumpeter Kenny Wheeler, who were developing their own brand of jazz. As European musicians had not experienced, first hand, traditions such as the blues or other influences from the African diaspora fundamental to jazz, they were forced to look elsewhere for inspiration, using music that they could identify with and was part of their heritage. Certainly, improvisation had been a key ingredient of much European classical and folk music for centuries, and indigenous folk music, particularly in the Nordic countries, provided the same nationalistic spirit that the blues provided to American jazz. Free-jazz movements that, to a great extent, rely on improvisation also found traction across Europe. A steady influx of American artists performing in clubs abroad, conducting workshops, composing for and performing with government-sponsored radio orchestras, and even taking up residency, helped to advance this process of assimilation and reinvention. Although radio, recordings, and personal appearances by American jazz artists were important to shaping new forms of jazz outside its native land, European musicians were not bound by a tradition they did not create, and they explored new directions based on their own traditions. They could borrow jazz elements they chose, without the near-religious commitment to the American jazz tradition students in the US are often bound to. This gradual process has led, logically, to worldwide exportation of their own homegrown talent, e.g. British pianists George Shearing and Marian McPartland (host of NPR *Piano Jazz* until 2012), Japanese pianist Toshiko Akiyoshi, Scottish saxophonist Joe Temperley (Lincoln Center Jazz Orchestra), French violinist Jean-Luc Ponty and composer/pianist Michel Legrand, Polish jazz-fusion artist

Michael Urbaniak, and a number of musicians who performed over time with Miles Davis, including British musicians Victor Feldman, John McLaughlin, and Dave Holland and Austrian Joe Zawinul (co-founder of Weather Report). These musicians represent the second wave of talent exported from abroad.

Only the communist bloc countries of the USSR, Czechoslovakia, Poland, and Romania lagged in the cultivation of jazz, and, even there, through black-market recordings and America's Radio Free Europe, jazz was quietly and secretly cultivated. Jazz around the world, and particularly in communist-ruled countries, became a symbol of individuality, freedom, and tolerance. In these countries, jazz recordings were traded like contraband. All that changed following glasnost in the 1980s. Today, very experimental, free jazz is cultivated in many of these countries, an irony as, for many years, their peoples were anything but "free."

The German ECM label, discussed in detail in Chapter 14, did much to advance a new European jazz sound and also helped support American artists who chose not to follow the loud, electric fusion-jazz path popularized in the US in the late 1960s and 1970s. The jazz that began to emerge from Europe at this time and in the decades since illustrates that European musicians have not only learned aspects of the improvised jazz tradition, they had also found numerous other influences to bring to their own new music. For example, the Scandinavian countries, as well as Italy and the former communist bloc countries, have become hotbeds for what many refer to as "improvisational music," rather than jazz. It borrows from minimalism, native folk music, electronica, and pop music (even hip-hop), using improvisation and instrumentations associated with jazz and pop. Contemporary classical-music experimentalists have also provided inspiration for this new breed of European jazz musician. For them, no tradition is sacred or off limits, and all present possibilities for inspiring a new dialect within the language, based on improvisation. Audiences abroad seem inherently more curious about adventuresome new musics and support artists who take risks.

> Europe has not produced a stylistic innovator along the lines of an Armstrong, Parker or Coltrane to call their own and establish an historical continuum, but once they learned that they did not have to be slaves to the American jazz canon all things have been possible through artists' innovations.[9]

 See the corresponding chapter on the website to listen to interviews with Tim Hagans and Alex Coke, who speak about their extensive experience working in Europe.

The growing number of jazz clubs and festivals throughout Europe has helped to develop larger audiences and new record labels, and to inspire pre-college institutions and universities to provide comprehensive curricula to train future generations of jazz-informed musicians. For example, in Italy, there are 600–700 schools that embrace jazz instruction. Sweden alone has at least six universities offering jazz curricula and approximately 100 jazz clubs. France boasts 150 record labels and 300 festivals that promote jazz. Radio stations in Portugal and Chile have produced weekly jazz radio programming since the 1940s. Jazz India was established as a non-profit trust in 1975 to encourage the cultural exchange of jazz and Indian music. Appreciation for jazz in Japan began in the 1950s. Even today, during difficult financial times, governments across Europe provide support for jazz orchestras, often referred to as radio orchestras, as they regularly broadcast performances across the continent. Many of the musical directors for these jazz orchestras, as well as guest soloists and commissioned composers, are Americans!

Jazz has truly become the language of a global village. Musicians in many other countries outside Europe have embraced it. Young people have come to associate it with independence of thought and freedom of expression. Jazz is now practiced and taught in places such as Turkey, Chile, and many other countries throughout South America, Israel, Australia, South Africa, Cuba, Puerto Rico, New Zealand, Japan, Korea, and even India. These countries are not only supporting their own local styles of jazz, they also continue to export performers and students seeking to improve their musicianship at American music schools. However, schooling in America, which was once essential, is now less so, as many countries have developed their own jazz-education infrastructure.

Jazz is now being practiced and taught around the globe. The world has become a smaller place, with improved communication and travel, especially over the past 20 years. Consequently, the world is far more globally aware and ethnically diverse than it was when jazz was born. America still ranks as one of the world's most multicultural populations, and so it is no surprise that young, multinational jazz musicians, first- or second-generation sons and daughters of non-American parents, are leaving their mark on the continuing evolution of jazz, in many cases bringing to bear on jazz certain non-American musical traditions from their homelands. Musicians from Israel, for example, have become quite visible on the U.S. jazz scene in recent years, including Anat Cohen, Avashi Cohen (both the bass player and trumpet player), and Yuval Cohen. West African guitarist Lionel Louke, Puerto Rican saxophonist/composer Miguel Zenón, pianists Hiromi (Japanese) and Helen Sung (Chinese–American), French pianist Jean-Michel Pilc, Virgin Islands saxophonist Jean Toussaint, and Cuban percussionist/composer Dafnis Prieto are all members of this vibrant global community. Each artist, in their own way, brings new ideas and new cultural points of view to the always-evolving jazz tradition.

Rudresh Mahanthappa and Vijay Iyer

One of the enduring qualities of jazz, and a defining characteristic, has been its ability to change, chameleon-like in nature, while absorbing and transforming every style it encounters, resulting in a new by-product. Two examples of young artists who exemplify this attribute, pushing jazz boundaries by injecting elements of their own cultural heritage, are pianist Vijay Iyer and alto saxophonist Rudresh Mahanthappa. Both are poll winners, recipients of other forms of recognition, and first-generation Indian–Americans who have been educated in American, absorbing the Western jazz and pop traditions that are reflected in their music. However, they often also look to their ethnic cultural roots for inspiration, as illustrated in the audio track included in the accompanying anthology. "The Shape of Things" illustrates how world music has exerted such strong influences on jazz that the result bears little resemblance to a classic definition of jazz, giving some credibility to the argument that using the term "improvisational music" rather than "jazz" might be a more appropriate label. This issue is likely to sort itself out in the course of debates throughout this new century, but for now it will still be considered as jazz, or perhaps better termed "world jazz."

LISTENING GUIDE

Rudresh Mahanthappa and Vijay Iyer

"The Shape of Things" (R. Mahanthappa and V. Iyer) 3:25

From *Raw Materials*

Savoy Jazz

Recorded 5/23/2006

Personnel: Rudresh Mahanthappa, alto saxophone; Vijay Iyer, piano

This performance might best be described as an incantation or prayer and is an example of pure improvisation by this duo. The only consistent anchor point is the drone or pedal point, played by Iyer's left hand in the extremely low register of the piano. In contrast to this drone, Iyer's right hand improvises in the piano's high register, providing shifting textures and in dialogue with Mahanthappa's alto sax improvisations. The saxophonist suggests a Middle-Eastern flavor by improvising around the drone using an exotic, non-Western scale (Indian Bhairiv scale) as source material. He also alters his saxophone's tone quality to take on a more non-Western character. Keeping to the non-Western musical traditions, Mahanthappa occasionally plays quarter-tones, or micro-tones (most obvious from 2:10 to 2:13). Quarter-tones, or micro-tones, defy the Western system by breaking the octave into 24 equal parts, rather than the 12 half-steps that form the octave in Western music. Imagine a piano keyboard with its black and white keys representing half-steps and whole steps. In the quarter-tone system, it would be necessary to add keys between each of these existing black and white keys to create an octave (C to C) with 24 pitches rather than 12. In other words, following the example below, it would be necessary to add additional notes in the quarter-tone system between C and C sharp, C sharp and D, D and D sharp, and so on. This track exemplifies the exciting new possibilities that are being explored by young, 21st-century jazz musicians who are introducing aspects of the improvised jazz tradition while exploring their non-Western ethnic heritages.

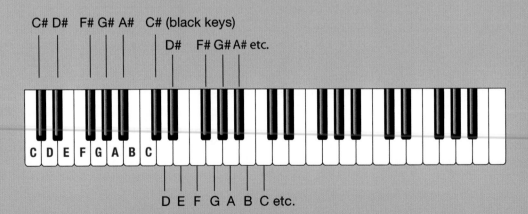

EXAMPLE 15.1 Piano keyboard based on Western music system with half-steps. Imagine 12 more keys (notes) added between C and C on this traditional Western keyboard

THE NEW INNOVATORS: 21ST-CENTURY EMERGING ARTISTS

In the first decade of this new millennium, a new generation of "lions," which we might refer to as "leopards," show similarities to the earlier generation of "lions" in that they are daring performers with complete command of their instruments, steadfastly focused on shedding clichés associated with earlier jazz styles. Like their forebears, they are risk-takers, looking to build on the tradition but refusing to be tethered by it. Born between the 1960s and early 1980s, these artists have been students of a well-defined century of jazz, no doubt studying in school rather than on the street like their forefathers. Not much has significantly revolutionized the music in their lifetime, at least not on the scale of Bird's bebop, Miles's and Coltrane's modal jazz, or Coleman's experimental free jazz. What they have grown up with as young apprentices is the multiplicity of stylistic activity practiced by mature artists such as Hancock, Metheny, Corea, Dave Douglas, and others, who regularly move freely between different styles, consistently producing the highest-quality music. They were also born of a generation where change for the sake of innovation has been commonplace, an everyday fact of life often brought about by rapidly changing technology. This emerging generation has learned they can do anything they want, including breaking away from established traditions. They are fearless, determined, committed, collaborative, highly accomplished on their instruments, versatile, and very much aware of the jazz legacy, but not at all bound by it. They are products of their time, when no single style prevails. The public debates between the neoclassic jazz purists and the pioneers of new jazz seem to have subsided, making it easier for this new generation to move in all directions without criticism. Crossing over genres and combining forms, styles, and even other art forms seem to be this new generation's mantra, as they draw on a wide range of styles, including hip-hop, rap, pop, electronica, gospel, classical music, Afro-Cuban, free experimental, and anything else that might intrigue them, including poetry, dance, visual art, and world-music styles. Above all, it is improvisation that lies at the heart of their new mixes and hybrids.

Composers and pianists seem to stand out in this new wave of innovative jazz artists, but all instruments are represented, and small groups seem to be the most assessable medium, germinating experimental, cutting-edge jazz. The members of this new generation all seem to have been influenced by past generations of adventuresome artists, including Thelonious Monk, Ornette Coleman, Cecil Taylor, Muhal Richard Abrams, Andrew Hill, Anthony Braxton, Keith Jarrett, and Steve Coleman. At the risk of omitting names, Figure 15.3 points to many of these pianists, as well as other emerging instrumentalists worth watching in the years ahead.

Pianists	Bassist	Saxophonists	Trumpet
Mathew Shipp	Ben Allison	Miguel Zeñon	Avishai Cohen
Jason Moran	Esperanza Spalding	Rudresh Mahanthappa	Christian Scott
Brad Mehldau,	Avishai Cohen	Seamus Blake	Ambrose Akinmusire
Robert Glasper		Eric Alexander	Jeremy Pelt
Vijay Iyer	**Drums**	Walter Smith III	
Jason Lindner	Dafnis Prieto	Ron Blake	**Guitar**
Matt Mitchell	John Hollenbeck	Joel Frahm	Ben Monder
Edward Simon		Anat Cohen	Lionel Loueke
Craig Taborn	**Composers**	Chris Potter	
Hiromi	John Hollenbeck	Jaleel Shaw	
	Darcy James Argue		

FIGURE 15.3 21st-century emerging innovators

JASON MORAN (1975–)

Jason Moran (1975–) stands as a totem, an example of this new breed of adventuresome, postmodern leopards. As a pianist and composer, he is an artist who, through collaborations and commission projects, has ensured that he is never forced into any one box. He draws on a wide range of styles, including classical music, hip-hop, R & B and gospel, electronica, spoken word, visual art, and jazz, including the stride piano stylings of James P. Johnson and Fats Waller. However, when he interprets these early jazz classics, they are first deconstructed and then reassembled in his own unique style. In a recent interview, Moran told *Down Beat* that, "I don't want to be defined solely by what I do as a jazz musician at a club or festival." He has worked hard to "avoid being stuck in a genre or discipline. I don't want any of my records to sound like one style throughout."[10]

His daring and adventuresome exploits often stray far from the jazz tradition and have won praise and rewards from critics, grant agencies, and audiences. For example, in 2006, *Down Beat* critics recognized him as the most outstanding artist in four "rising-star" categories—Jazz Artist of the Year, Pianist, Acoustic Group, and Composer. He was awarded the prestigious MacArthur Fellowship in 2010, and, in 2011, *Down Beat* critics returned to award him Artist of the Year, Best Pianist, and Album of the Year for his CD *Ten*.

Moran's earlier work with saxophonists Greg Osby and Steve Coleman was an important step toward forging his style and gaining exposure. Osby now calls him a "musical chef. You get an amalgam of Monk, Bud Powell and Keith Jarrett plus stride and hip-hop fused with Third Stream."[11] His eclectic performances and compositions have already left an indelible mark on jazz and suggest what numerous shapes this music might take in the future.

It was not an easy task to select one Moran track that, not only best represents his diverse body of work and the work of this new generation of artists, but also adds a fitting final statement to this book. The track "Artists Ought to Be Writing" seemed to be the best choice, showcasing his solo piano artistry and interest in collaboration, stepping outside the boundaries of more mainstream jazz. The work is one excerpt of four pieces comprising *Milestone*, commissioned by the Walker Art Center. The pieces all blend jazz and improvised music with work by multidisciplinary conceptual artist and philosopher Adrian Piper, whose creations take the form of a variety of media and often focus on racism, stereotyping, and other such deep pathologies. In "Artists Ought to Be Writing," Moran performs along with a Piper narration recorded to mini-disc, sometimes accompanying the spoken words and at other times closely mimicking them, guided by the rhythm and phrasing of the narration. In this way, Moran uses a process similar to the way lyrics are written to a song or a poem is set to music; however, here he is working with narration. The words themselves are also important, as they express what many contemporary artists are trying to do to bring their work and creative processes closer to their audience, just as this book has sought to draw new listeners to jazz, with a closer examination and understanding of the artists and their musical processes.

Jason Moran performs at the Thelonious Monk Town Hall 50th Anniversary Celebration, 2009

LISTENING GUIDE

Jason Moran

*"Artists Ought to Be Writing" (3:51) Jason Moran, piano, with Adrian Piper, narrator

From *Artist in Residence*

Recorded 1/6 and 2/16/2006

Blue Note Records 0946 3 62711 2 5

Form: Through composed

Like several other highly improvised recordings discussed throughout this book, this particular piece defies the usual time-based listening guide. Highlights of this performance, however, are provided as follows and should help guide your listening experience.

00:00–0:24	Moran plays in a more supportive, accompanying role, as if accompanying a singer and not duplicating or mimicking the narration
0:25	The first obvious coordinated pianistic gesture occurs on the important central word "break down" (the title of another movement from *Milestone* included on this CD)
0:29–0:31	Piano statements more closely mimic and follow the narration motivated by the rhythm and contour of the text
0:39–1:16	Piano becomes more closely intwined with the rhythm of the narration, following the rhythm of the text
1:17–end	Moran improvises, gradually building and departing from thematic material and gestures that were inspired earlier by the narration

* Track not available for streaming on website.

CLOSING THOUGHTS

On an optimistic note, America has proven to be an amazingly resilient society, recovering from severe economic downturns, civil wars at home and world wars abroad, graft and corruption, divisive racial turmoil, terrorism, political controversy, social and moral revolutions, and every other imaginable trial. Just as American society has always recovered, jazz too has rebounded, and musicians have more than once resuscitated it, often in unanticipated ways, and at times when it had been declared all but dead. However, for jazz to remain ever present and a significant fiber in the American cultural fabric, it needs new audiences. These new listeners must embrace innovation, nurture preservation, encourage experimentation, and respect established technique. There is no need to debate the value of one style or trend over another, and, in fact, this form of divisiveness does more to harm the music than help its advancement. New audiences must be receptive to having their minds challenged, values tested, and tastes expanded. They must learn to welcome the unfamiliar. Learning to appreciate art can be compared to acquiring a taste for new foods—you often have to be willing to take the risk and try something new on the menu. New listeners will have to learn to appreciate, or at least give equal opportunity to, what they don't understand and be curious enough to reconcile new experiences with old familiar ones. New audiences are needed to be proactive in supporting the most engaging artists, although they may be the most daring and obscure, operating against the grain in terms of what trends are dictated by popular culture. The power of the most unknown artist should not be underestimated, even though they often attract the least promotion for their work. Local clubs that feature the best area talent, as well as nationally established performers, should be patronized. Above all, don't accept at face value what someone else says is good. Individuals should form their own aesthetics and values, based at least in part on sources such as *Experiencing Jazz*. The jazz art form needs to be experienced first hand as much and as often as possible, for the personal enrichment will be well worth the effort.

MILESTONES

Chronicle of Historic Events

The timeline that follows will put the developments of jazz discussed in this chapter into a larger historical context, providing you with a better sense of how landmark musical events may relate to others that match your personal areas of interest.

1990
- Russian leader Michael Gorbachev wins a Nobel Peace Prize.
- Germany is reunited under President Helmut Kohl.
- Civil liberties and political activist Nelson Mandela is freed from imprisonment.
- Kuwait is invaded by Iraq.
- John Scofield and Joe Lovano record "Some Nerve."

1991
- Gorbachev resigns as the last president of the USSR.
- The Soviet Union is dissolved, leaving 15 republics.
- President de Klerk of South Africa abolishes the apartheid laws.
- The U.S. attack of Iraq to liberate Kuwait is labeled Operation Desert Storm.

1992
- Bill Clinton is elected U.S. president.
- Riots in Los Angeles over the Rodney King verdict draw attention to racial profiling.
- South Africa bestows equal legal rights on blacks.
- An Earth Summit is held in an effort to protect habitat and the environment.

1993
- Steven Spielberg's popular film *Schindler's List* draws new attention to Nazi Germany and the persecution of Jews.
- The unified European market begins.
- Islamic terrorists' bomb rocks the World Trade Center in New York City.
- Waco, Texas is the site of a 51-day stand-off between U.S. officials and a right-wing religious sect.
- The Palestinian leader Arafat and Israeli Prime Minister Rabin sign a peace agreement in the United States.

1994
- Los Angeles experiences a significant earthquake.
- 30,000-year-old paintings are found in a French cave.
- 16 million black voters elect Nelson Mandela president of South Africa.
- Sports legend O.J. Simpson is tried for murder.

1995
- The Oklahoma federal building is destroyed by a car bomb.
- A peace agreement is reached between the leaders of Bosnia, Serbia, and Croatia.
- Israel's Prime Minister Rabin is assassinated.
- O.J. Simpson is acquitted on murder charges.
- For the first time in 40 years, the Republican Party controls Congress.

1996
- Mad cow disease forces a ban on beef by the European Union.
- There is a $10 million tobacco company settlement for the treatment of smokers.
- Bill Clinton is reelected U.S. president.
- The Taliban takes over Afghanistan.

- Church burnings in the US are fueled by racial hostilities.

- Michael Brecker records "Song For Bilbao" with Pat Metheny, McCoy Tyner, and other important late-20th-century jazz artists.

1997
- A lamb is cloned by a Scottish DNA researcher.

- Wynton Marsalis becomes the first jazz artist to win a Pulitzer Prize for *Blood on the Fields*.

- The NASA space probe Sojourner sends back images of Mars.

1998
- Internet and email see widespread use, revolutionizing commerce and the exchange of information.

- Iraq bans UN weapons inspectors; the US launches an offensive.

- President Clinton is impeached.

- Singer Frank Sinatra dies.

- The technology boom sparks Internet commerce and start-up industries.

- Google is founded.

1999
- Clinton is acquitted by the Senate of impeachment charges.

- The world awaits the consequences, particularly for computers, of Y2K (year 2000).

- A Columbine, Colorado, high-school shoot out leaves 15 dead.

- *Star Wars Episode I* breaks box-office records.

- The number of Internet users reaches 150 million, with over half in the US.

- Pat Metheny, Chick Corea, Herbie Hancock, Gary Burton, and the Count Basie Orchestra win Grammy Awards.

2000
- The stock market falters with the decline of dot.com businesses and high-tech industries.

- The International Space Station is placed in orbit.

- G.W. Bush wins the close, controversial election over Democratic candidate Al Gore.

- Middle East tensions continue to rise, but North and South Korea sign a peace accord.

- Terrorists attack the Navy ship USS Cole.

- Author Stephen King is the first to offer a novella as an online digital download.

- Danilo Peréz records "Suite For The Americas."

- Tim Hagans and Bob Belden record "Trumpet Sandwich."

2001
- A power crisis causes sporadic blackouts in California.

- The Enron Corp. scandal shocks the US.

- US and NATO forces invade Afghanistan to defeat the Al-Qaeda-supportive Taliban government.

- 9/11: Al Qaeda terrorists use commercial airliners to destroy the World Trade Center, killing 3,000 Americans, and attack the Pentagon.

- President Bush vows revenge against the terrorist attacks, eventually leading to the invasion of Iraq and capture of President Saddam Hussein.

- PBS airs Ken Burns's 10-episode series *Jazz*.

2002
- There is growing unrest throughout the Middle East.

- President Bush establishes the cabinet-level Homeland Security Office.

- African-American actors Halle Berry and Denzel Washington win Oscars.

- Crossover jazz singer Nora Jones scores a hit with her first recording, *Come Away With Me*.

	• Jazz vibraphonist Lionel Hampton and singer Rosemary Clooney pass away.
2003	• The US launches war against Iraq and seeks the removal of Saddam Hussein.
	• Hussein is captured, and President Bush declares victory, and yet the occupation and war with insurgents continues for years.
	• The space shuttle Columbia explodes, killing all seven astronauts.
	• Nora Jones wins five Grammy Awards.
	• The recording industry attempts to crack down on illegal file sharing; Apple launches iTunes as a legal means of purchasing and downloading digital music files.
	• Dan Brown's *The Da Vinci Code* is a bestseller.
2004	• NASA's rover lands on Mars.
	• George Bush is reelected to his second term as U.S. president, defeating the Kerry/Edwards Democratic ticket.
	• A tragic 9.0 earthquake and tsunami push Southeast Asian death toll to around 100,000.
	• Michael Moore's controversial, highest-grossing, and award-winning documentary *Fahrenheit 9/11* harshly criticizes President Bush and his administration's handling of the Iraq war.
	• The legal sale of digital albums and songs continues to escalate.
	• *American Idol* is the top-rated TV show.
	• Facebook, the social-networking website, is founded.
2005	• Hurricane Katrina devastates the gulf coast, especially New Orleans.
	• The *Harry Potter* books and movies continue to top the charts.
	• Political and moral controversy surrounds scientists' ability to produce human stem-cell lines from a cloned human embryo.
	• George W. Bush is sworn in for a second term as U.S. president.
	• The government and American people continue their preoccupation with the war on terrorism.
	• Corruption in government officials takes down Delay, Libby, and Cunningham.
	• YouTube is founded as a video-sharing website.
2006	• Astronomers reclassify Pluto as a dwarf planet.
	• 33 are killed by a gunman at Virginia Tech, causing shockwaves about preparedness throughout U.S. universities.
	• Nora Jones and Ray Charles (posthumously) win Grammy Awards.
	• The Maria Schneider Jazz Orchestra and ArtistShare label receive the first Grammy for recording never made available in retail stores and only online.
	• There is ongoing unrest in the Middle East and Africa.
	• Herbie Hancock's crossover album *River: The Joni Letters* is the first jazz Grammy Album of the Year since 1965 for Getz/Gilberto.
	• Michael Brecker wins a Grammy Award for his final recording.
	• *Jersey Boys* and *The History* Boys capture Tony Awards.
	• President Bush renews the Patriot Act.
	• Prisoner abuse at Abu Ghraib prison draws worldwide attention.
	• Twitter is established as a mini-social-networking/blogging website.

- The jazz community loses Michael Brecker, Andrew Hill, Max Roach, and Joe Zawinul.

- Jazz artists Regina Carter and John Zorn win the MacArthur Foundation Genius Grant.

- Rudresh Mahanthappa and Vijay Iyer record *Raw Materials*.

2007
- Mortgage concerns hit U.S. markets.

- There is ongoing unrest in the Middle East.

- California Democrat Nancy Pelosi becomes the first woman Speaker of the House.

- There is ongoing U.S. involvement in wars in Iraq and Afghanistan.

- A study on global warming is released.

- Chick Corea and the Brecker Brothers win jazz category Grammy Awards.

- *The Sopranos* TV series captures Emmy Awards.

- Ornette Coleman wins a Pulitzer Prize.

2008
- The US elects Barack Obama as the nation's first African-American president.

- This is the year that the DVD replaces the VCR.

- The Great Recession in the US spreads throughout the world and extends through 2011, with record levels of unemployment and bank and mortgage failures.

- The U.S. government attempts to bail out the U.S. financial sector and auto industry.

- Gay rights to marry under the law are defended in some states.

- The space shuttle Atlantis delivers a lab to the International Space Station.

- The International Association for Jazz Education, founded in 1968, files for bankruptcy under Chapter 7.

- Herbie Hancock's *River: The Joni Letters* wins a Grammy Award for Album of the Year—the first time in 43 years that a jazz album has won.

- Esperanza Spalding records "Body and Soul" on her first major album.

2009
- *Avatar* is a box-office 3D movie success.

- The International Monetary Fund declares the global economy is shrinking for the first time in 60 years.

- GM enters bankruptcy protection—the economy and job growth are stagnant.

- Pop singer and icon Michael Jackson dies.

- Water is discovered on the Moon.

- Bernie Madoff admits to the massive Ponzi scheme.

2010
- The BP gulf oil spill causes millions of dollars of damage to the environment.

- A devastating earthquake hits Haiti.

- The US continues its military efforts in Afghanistan.

- The U.S. budget deficit continues to soar, while the unemployment rate drops slightly to 9.7%; data show the worst economic picture since the Great Depression.

- President Obama and the House pass a controversial health-care plan.

- Immigration laws become the center of controversy.

- Six top movies (*Toy Story 3, Alice In Wonderland, Harry Potter and the Deathly Hallows, Shrek Forever After, The Karate Kid*, and *How to Train Your Dragon*) show the US is looking for fantasy to escape from reality.

- The US withdraws all troops from Iraq.

2011	• U.S. special forces kill terrorist Al-Qaeda leader Osama bin Laden, responsible for masterminding the 9/11 terrorist actions.
	• The Occupy Wallstreet movement unifies protestors nationwide against social and economic inequity, high unemployment, greed, and corruption.
	• Congresswomen Gifford is among 17 shot in an assassination attempt—this increases conversation about gun control and terrorism.
	• Protests in Lebanon and Tunisia topple the governments.
	• Apple pioneer, entrepreneur, and inventor Steve Jobs dies.
	• Japan is devastated by an earthquake and tsunami.

CHAPTER SUMMARY

Jazz in the 1990s and recent years continued to include many diverse substyles. Other than the fact that women will continue to have more of an impact in jazz, one can only blindly predict the lasting effects of the many new trends. It would seem, though, with the shrinking of the world via advances in communication, including the Internet, that jazz will continue to have an important, world-music aspect. Pat Metheny, Indians Rudresh Mahanthappa and Vijay Iyer, and Panamanian pianist Danilo Pérez are a few of the many who have very successfully fused elements of world music with jazz.

Although not as popular as in the 1930s and 1940s, new big bands (and a few existing ones) came to the forefront, fueled by great soloists and outstanding composer/arrangers. The 2005 Grammy Award winner Maria Schneider, one of the most original in this new group, leads an excellent band far different than 1940s swing bands. A notable aspect of Schneider's band is the fact that its recordings and arrangements are not available from the usual retail outlets, but only via her website. The Mingus Big Band and Lincoln Center Jazz Orchestra continue to keep big-band music alive, through both new compositions and the replication of classic arrangements.

A number of performers from previous jazz styles were "rediscovered" in the 1990s, giving their careers a second life. Tenor saxophonist Joe Henderson probably benefited from this trend the most, receiving multiple Grammy Awards in the 1990s. The popularity of the CD format encouraged companies to reissue long-out-of-print LPs, a trend that probably helped the older players considerably. The downside of this, however, is that consumers use a large portion of their budgets purchasing reissues, leaving less money available to support new, emerging artists. Veteran jazz performers still active through the 1990s include Miles Davis alumni Herbie Hancock, Wayne Shorter, Dave Holland, Keith Jarrett, and Chick Corea. Others stand out, not only for their artistry, but also for their influence on young players. Guitarists Pat Metheny and John Scofield and tenor saxophonists Michael Brecker and Joe Lovano fit this category. Brecker and Lovano represent the two current schools of jazz tenor sax, much as Coleman Hawkins and Lester Young did years earlier. Scofield and Metheny are the most influential jazz guitarists since John McLaughlin.

Many other styles of jazz, including free/experimental jazz, jazz vocal styles, smooth jazz, and jam bands are also a part of the present-day jazz fabric. Experimental jazz performers, Ornette Coleman still among them, continue their journey. Many new artists have learned to include elements of rap or other popular styles in their music.

At the other end of the spectrum, performers such as Kenny G perform a more easy-listening, simplistic, "smooth jazz," aimed at the mass market and frequently used as background or mood music in stores, restaurants, doctors' offices, and elevators. Jam bands such as Medeski Martin & Wood have drawn sizable audiences with their repetitive, infectious grooves. Although jazz vocal styles have changed less over the years than their instrumental counterparts, the popularity of Diana Krall, Nora Jones, and multi-talented Esperanza Spalding has helped to boost sagging jazz record sales. A new generation of adventuresome postmodernists, some who bring non-Western and European influences, are reinventing jazz as a collaborative, improvised music, not bound by well-established traditions but informed by them. It is anyone's guess what tomorrow will bring, and only one thing can be certain—jazz will continue to be renewed, becoming even more surprising, global, and different than it was yesterday.

KEY TERMS

Important terms, people, and bands:

Terms		Bands
Through composed	Kurt Elling	Kronos Quartet
	Joe Henderson	Lincoln Center Jazz Orchestra
	Andrew Hill	Mingus Big Band
People	Nora Jones	Steps Ahead
Toshiko Akiyoshi	Diana Krall	Turtle Island Quartet
Geri Allen	Bobby McFerrin	World Saxophone Quartet
Jane Ira Bloom	Pat Metheny	
Joanne Brackeen	Danilo Pérez	
Jane Bunnett	Maria Schneider	
Terri Lyne Carrington	Esperanza Spalding	
Regina Carter		

STUDY QUESTIONS

1. Jazz was perhaps more fractured stylistically than ever before at the close of the 20th century. Name the various styles and subcategories of jazz popular at this time.

2. Can you name the bandleader/composers who have sought to sustain the big band as a viable jazz medium over the past 20 years?

3. The advent of CDs has encouraged major record labels to reissue older artists' material. Can you name some of these living rediscovery figures who have profited from this new recording format?

4. Following Wynton Marsalis's lead, a number of young artists emerged, capitalizing on the preservationist trend established in the 1980s by Marsalis and other Young Lions. Name some of these new young artists.

5. European artists begin to emerge, offering their own, new view of jazz by the late 20th and early 21st centuries. Name a few of these important artists.

6. How would you describe some of the new styles of jazz, including acid, smooth, bass 'n drums and jam jazz?

7. Record labels have capitalized on the increased popularity of the jazz vocal stylist. Name a few of these singers who have brought significant attention to their jazz-inspired music.

8. Music from around the world has always exerted influences on jazz, and, in recent years, this trend has intensified. Name one of the world influences that seems to have made an impact on jazz in the late 20th and early 21st centuries.

9. Why is Pat Metheny's music so popular?

10. Name two guitarists who have exerted significant influences on jazz in recent years.

11. Many contemporary artists, such as Michael Brecker, Pat Metheny, Dave Holland, Joe Lovano, Danilo Pérez, John Scofield, and others are very eclectic in their approach to jazz, displaying numerous interests and influences. When did this trend begin, and with what artists who preceded them?

12. Women have finally established themselves in jazz, receiving significant attention for their contributions, not just as singers, but also as instrumentalists and composers. Name several in each category.

13. What seem to be the most significant problems facing jazz artists in the 21st century?

14. How has technology, at the start of this century, had an effect on jazz music and performers?

15. Who is the most significant saxophonist of the late 20th and early 21st centuries, following John Coltrane?

Glossary of Terms

accelerando—gradually to get faster

accent—emphasis on a note or notes

accompaniment—the musical background for a solo performer or performers (e.g., a piano accompanying a trumpet solo)

acculturation—the modification of a primitive culture by contact with an advanced culture

ad lib—to improvise or create on the spur of the moment. The term can relate to the work of musicians, comedians, actors, and visual artists, although all do not improvise

aharmonic—see **atonal**

aleatoric—describes a style of music based on improvisations where all elements of music are based on chance and total spontaneity and without premeditation.

altissimo—notes played an octave or more above the top of the treble clef staff; the term often is used to describe notes above the accepted top range of an instrument like the saxophone

antiphonal—a form of musical response, as of one singer, choir, or instrument answering another

arco—a manner of playing the double bass (or violin, viola, or cello) using a bow

arpeggio—playing the notes of a chord consecutively, one note at a time (**arpeggiate, arpeggiated**)

arrangement—a reconstruction/adaptation of a musical composition for a specific ensemble of instruments. In a written arrangement, the arranger has written down the specific notes he wants each instrument to play. A particular setting or interpretation of a pre-composed piece of music

arranger—the individual who constructs a new interpretation of pre-composed works. Composers often serve as their own arrangers

articulation—a general term to describe the length of notes in a performance, i.e., short or long, or somewhere in between

attack—the manner of beginning a tone

atonal—without a specific key or tonal center

avant-garde—a group (writers, musicians, artists, etc.) regarded as preeminent in the invention and application of new techniques

backbeat rhythm—a strong emphasis on the 2 and 4 beats of a measure by the drummer

ballad—a slow-to-very-slow song, often with romantic overtones, that uses the same melody for each verse

bass line—the lowest musical line; usually played by the tuba, string bass, or electric bass guitar

black and tans—cabarets and saloons that catered to a mixed black and white clientele in the 1920s and 1930s

blue notes—the third, fifth, and seventh notes of a chord that are altered by lowering the pitch to create blues inflections. These alterations, which don't necessarily conform to precise semitones, are often created through improvisatory interpretations rather than dictated by the printed, pre-composed page

blues—a musical term often misused to describe an African-American style of music that gradually evolved through the cross influences of African and American musical practices. It originated as a vocal practice adopted by instrumentalists. The blues form is most often 12 measures long, repeated. **Blue notes**, or lowered third and fifth scale degrees, characterize the blues style

boogie-woogie—rhythmically charged, blues-inspired solo piano style that emerged in the mid 1920s. The style featured a repetitive left-hand pattern

bossa nova—Brazilian dance style made popular in the United States in the 1960s

brass section—a section of an ensemble that includes trumpets, trombones, French horns, and tubas; in jazz ensembles, the brass section includes trumpets and trombones (bones)

break—a point in an arrangement at which all instruments suddenly stop playing for about 2–4 measures, while the soloist/improviser continues to play

bridge—middle section of a popular song, also described formally as the B section. This second section is typically surrounded by the A section and appears in a different key

cadenza—a solo by one instrument, often played without regard for strict tempo

cakewalk—Black folk dance style derived from European traditions and also referred to as clog dancing. Cakewalks, also described as two-steps, were popular in the late 19th and early 20th centuries

call and response—an African-originated pattern used in jazz and some religious music, in which a call (by a solo vocalist or instrumentalist) is answered by another vocalist or instrumentalist, or by an ensemble of vocalists/instruments

changes—the entire sequence of chords used in a composition

Chopin (1810–1849)—a composer of Romantic music, particularly for the piano

chart—musician's slang for arrangement

chékere—a percussion instrument of African origin, made from a hollow gourd covered with a loose mesh of beads

chords—the simultaneous sounding of three or more notes. Also described as **harmony**

chord progressions—a series of successive chords. Also known as the "changes"

chord voicing—see **voicing**

chorus—the main body, refrain, or harmonic outline, as distinct from the verse (which comes first)

chromatic—half-step intervals of a scale or melody

clavé—an Afro-Caribbean rhythm pattern based on the organization of subgroupings 3 + 2 or 2 + 3 and derived from the Spanish habanera or Cuban rhythm. The clavé pattern serves as the foundation of many Afro-Caribbean music styles

clavés—a pair of round, polished, hard-wood dowels that are struck together to create the clavé pattern

cluster—a group of notes very closely organized to form a dense chord cluster. Clusters can be consonant or dissonant

coda—a passage at the end of a composition that may or may not contain material that was presented earlier in the composition

collective improvisation—a situation where all performers improvise simultaneously, as was the case in early jazz and in much free, avant-garde jazz

comp(ing)—a performance practice used to describe improvised harmonic accompaniment typically governed by those chords set forth in a prescribed chord progression. Any instrument capable of playing chords can "comp"

conga—a Latin dance form; also a Latin or Afro-Cuban drum (see below)

conga drums—long, round-bodied, single headed Afro-Caribbean drums of varying sizes and pitches. The name is derived from an African line dance called the "conga"

Congo Square—park-like place in New Orleans (now Louis Armstrong Park) where blacks were permitted to congregate and participate in various ceremonies and rituals, both secular and sacred. Such gatherings often featured music and dance, improvisational in nature

consonance and dissonance—the very foundation of tonal music; consonance is created by the relationship of pitches that produce an agreeable effect, whereas dissonance is the result of disturbing musical relationships that create tension and often displeasure

contrafact—new melodies composed over chord progressions borrowed from other songs. This was a popular approach during the bebop period

contrapuntal—describes music that features counterpoint or simultaneously occurring melodies.

countermelody—a secondary melody accompanying a primary voice or musical idea

counterpoint—a form of musical composition that is based on two or more intertwined melodic lines. The different melodic lines are said to be moving in counterpoint (literally note against note) to one another

creole—the result of intermarriage, created by merging any combination of French, Spanish, and African-American descent. This race is associated with the New Orleans Delta area

cubop—a jazz style from the late 1940s and early 1950s that merged bebop and Afro-Cuban styles

diatonic—notes within a given scale key and without alteration

dissonance—see **consonance**

double-time—doubling a tempo, or implying such, so that the music becomes twice as fast in comparison to the initial tempo

drone—a sustained or repeated note, often in the bass or lowest part, sounded while upper musical structures change

drum kit—another term for drum set consisting of snare, bass and tom-toms and an array of cymbals including the pedal operated sock (hit-hat) cymbal

dynamics—the degree of volume of sound. The most common dynamic markings and definitions of relative volume are as follows:

pianissimo	pp	—	very soft
piano	p	—	soft
mezzo piano	mp	—	medium soft
mezzo forte	mf	—	medium loud
forte	f	—	loud
fortissimo	ff	—	very loud
crescendo	<	—	gradually becoming louder
decrescendo or diminuendo	>	—	gradually becoming softer

extension tones—notes added to a four-note seventh chord and designed to enrich the harmony—usually the ninth, eleventh, and thirteenth

field hollers—improvised African-American vocal singing practice closely related to work songs and serving the same purpose but with less structure

fill—term used to describe a drummer's or horn player's brief, improvised passage

flat—to lower a pitch

form—describes the architecture and overall organization of a piece of music and as defined by key melodic/harmonic components

front line—refers to the principal wind instruments associated with early New Orleans jazz and street bands, including cornet or trumpet, clarinet, and trombone. The percussion occupied the "second line," marching behind the wind instruments

functional harmony—used to describe the tendency in much Western music harmony of one chord naturally to lead to another chord—often moving away from, and back to, the tonic chord that defines the key or tonal center of a composition

funk (funky)—originally a blues influenced African-American jazz style that emerged in the mid-1950s and was popular through the 1960s. It showed roots in black church music and African musical traditions such as call and response and was often deeply influenced by the blues.

fusion—the stylistic term first used in the late 1960s and 1970s to describe music that drew on influences from rock and jazz.

gig—a musical engagement

glissando (gliss)—to slide from note to note in a very smooth, legato fashion

gospel—secular songs were created by blacks and white Americans and originated in late 19th and early 20th century as vocal style. The style developed some years after the spiritual. These songs were designed to be sung in harmony and without accompaniment by instruments

ground rhythm (ground pattern)—a fundamental, reoccurring pattern that serves as the foundation on top of which other changing rhythms, melodies, and/or chords are layered

guiro—Afro-Caribbean percussion instrument fashioned from a long, cylindrical, serrated, hollow gourd and played with a stick in a scraping motion

habanera—Spanish rhythm also associated with Cuba and serving as the heart of many Afro-Caribbean and Latin American folk styles and dance rhythms

Harlem—an area in New York City that served as a hot house for the germination of black intellectualism, cultural development and community pride during the 1920s

Harlem Pianists—a group of New York City pianists known for their contributions to the development of the stride piano style

harmolodics—a term coined by Ornette Coleman describing ever-shifting relationships that can occur when freely improvised melodies interact with one another implying different accidental harmonies and tonalities

harmonic rhythm—describes the pace at which chords change from one to another

harmonics—overtones (notes occurring above a fundamental tone or frequency) that result from the division of a vibrating string or air column

harmony—a collection of two or more notes played simultaneously (see **chords** and **chord progression**)

head—the main theme (composed melody) as stated in jazz performance. The "head" is usually played first, before improvised solos

head charts (arrangements)—impromptu arrangements that are improvised by members of a band and often performed from memory rather than notated scores

high-hat (hi-hat)—a synonym for the sock cymbal, which is an integral part of the drum set. This pair of inverted cymbals is caused to clap together by a foot pedal

homophonic—describes music that consists of only one predominant melodic line, accompanied by chords defining harmony

improvisation—a musical practice of impromptu, extemporaneous performance where the performer spontaneously invents new musical ideas; often based on a chord progression or derived in part from the original melody but not always

interval—the distance separating two different pitches

intonation—the degree of accuracy, based on a particular agreement concerning the matching of two pitches, in a musical performance

jubilee—a high-spirited song of praise and celebration. Some jubilees were the early predecessors to Dixieland instrumental pieces like "When the Saints Go Marching In"

key—defines the tonality and tonal center of a piece of music and serves to further describe the key signature

key center—central pitch that defines the tonal center of a composition

key signature—refers to sharps and flats that regulate the tonality and tonal center of a piece of music. The key signature instructs the performer to alter certain notes by raising or lowering them one half-step, i.e., one flat in the key signature implies either F major or D minor and requires the performer to flat (lower by one half-step) the note B

kit—an abbreviation for drum set or drum kit

lay out—an abbreviation instructing the performer to rest or not play (also tacet)

lay back—a style of performing where musicians play slightly behind a consistent beat or tempo, creating a slight tension

lead player—the principal or first player in a group. In a big band, this often refers to the first trumpet player, who sets the standard for interpretation for all of the wind players to follow

legato—very smooth and connected playing, without noticeable tonguing and often without emphasis on any particular note

lick—a melodic phrase that has become an accepted part of the jazz language, often, but not always, associated with a specific musician who first created it

locked hands—refers to a piano style in which chords are voiced closely in both left and right hands, and all voices move in parallel motion. A style of solo piano playing using chords rather than single-note lines accompanied by chords

mainstream jazz—a term often used to describe jazz form the 1950s and '60s that embraced key elements of the tradition including traditional harmonic progressions, driving swing and blues

major—the further clarification of tonality (key) and used to further define chords and scales

measure/bar—the space between vertical lines (bar lines) in written music; a means of division of music that groups beats together in specific, consistent numbers (see **time signature**)

melody—a succession of single tones varying in pitch and rhythm and having a recognizable shape

merengue—A fast, Latin or Afro-Cuban, 2-beat dance rhythm originating from the Dominican Republic

meter—a division of beats or pulses into unaccented and accented groupings of two beats, three beats, etc.

MIDI (musical instrument digital interface)—a way for musical instruments to be controlled and information distributed using a simple binary computer code

minor—the further clarification of tonality and used to further define chords and scales

modality—the use of harmonic and melodic formations based on the church modes, as opposed to those based on the major and minor modes. Also refers to a particularly "tonality"

mode—used synonymously with the term "scale," as the seven Greek-labeled "church modes" are contrived by rearranging the occurrence of notes found within the fundamental or parent major scale

modulate—to change key or tone center

moldy figs—term used to describe fans who supported traditional jazz (New Orleans Dixieland and Chicago jazz) during the more modern swing and bebop movements

monophonic—describes a single melodic line without accompaniment

monorhythm—one rhythm

montuno—refers to a reoccurring, vamp-like piano accompaniment that often serves at the heart of much Afro-Cuban music

motif—a short, melodic fragment of a few notes that recurs through a composition or a section as a unifying element; distinguished from a theme or subject by being shorter; often derived from themes (analogues to riffs)

motive—smallest recognizable musical idea (see **motif**)

multiphonic—two or more notes sounded simultaneously by a wind instrument

mute—a device for softening, muffling, and altering the tones of a musical instrument, particularly brass instruments

neo-classicism—a movement of 20th-century music characterized by the inclusion of 17th- and 18th-century musical features into contemporary-style music

obligato—an accompanying but important melody that is less prominent and plays a secondary role to the main melody of a composition. These melodies are often improvised

octave—the distance that is defined in music between two notes with the same name separated by 12 half steps

oral tradition—all spoken or sung testimonies about the past and the process by which traditions are passed on through generations

orchestration—the ways in which instruments are assigned to play certain roles in a musical arrangement. Orchestrate is the act of orchestration, or assigning instruments to certain notes and musical lines in a score

ostinato—a persistently repeated rhythmic and/or melodic phrase, and sometimes an accompaniment phrase, that is repeated over and over again in a composition

outside playing—refers to a performance practice in which musicians elect to purposely draw attention to dissonant relationships by playing musical ideas that run contrary to traditional notions of consonance in music. A term often associated with free and postmodern jazz styles

overtones—see **harmonics**

pedal point—see **drone**

pentatonic—implies five notes, as in **pentatonic scale**

percussive—to play in a strongly emphasized manner; to strike

phrase—a small unit or subdivision of a melody; can also refer to a particular manner in which a musician interprets a melody, as compared to how an individual enunciates a sentence usually termed **phrase** or how something is **phrased**

pizzicato—a manner of playing the double bass (or other string instrument) using only the fingers to pluck the strings

polymeters—simultaneous use or implication of several meters

polyphony—music that combines several simultaneous melodies

polyrhythms—simultaneous use of several rhythms

postmodern—art that expresses a mixture of historical styles and new approaches, warped through various forms of reinterpretation and purposeful misrepresentation. The result is considered unconventional and sometimes a parody. Process is often considered as more important than product which is not judged or analyzed by conventional standards

Prohibition Act—a United Sates law, also known as the Volstead Act, passed January 16, 1920, declaring the importation, exportation, transportation, sale, and manufacturing of alcoholic beverages as illegal activities punishable by law

quartet—ensemble of four musicians

quintet—ensemble of five musicians

race records—records marketed in the 1920s for black listeners, featuring largely black, female blues singers who were often accompanied by jazz instrumentalists

ragtime—originally a solo piano style popular in the US from1895 to 1915, this European-derived form followed a rondo scheme also featured in marches along with 2/4-meter, simple right-hand syncopations with very regular, oompah-like left-hand chord accompaniment. Ragtime was initially a composed, not improvised style. It is considered the first style of American music to enjoy widespread popularity and demonstrate that a music highly influenced by black performers and composers could be the basis of commercial success

range—the distance between the lowest and highest notes capable of being played on an instrument or sung. Can also refer to the highest and lowest pitches in a song

reed—a thin, elongated piece of cane wood or other material that is fixed at one end but free to vibrate at the other end. In clarinets and saxophones, a column of air passed rapidly between the reed and mouthpiece causes the reed to vibrate, creating a sound

reed (or **woodwind**) **section**—a group of saxophones, clarinets, flutes, and, occasionally, oboes that performs together in a jazz ensemble

reharmonization—to embellish, enhance or alter in some way the original chord progression of a song

rhythm—the whole feeling of forward movement in music, as defined by the speed at which the melody moves and the different durations of those notes comprising a melody

rhythm and blues (R & B)—a popular music style that uses African-American musical elements, such as the 12-bar-blues progression, blue notes, repetitious chords over heavily emphasized rhythms, heavy, gutsy vocals, and lyrics that often communicate a sense of melancholy, disappointment, or other such emotions

rhythm changes—refers to the harmonic progression of chords in an AABA form that was the basis of George and Ira Gershwin's song "I've Got Rhythm" from their musical *Crazy Girl*. It has served as the basis for many new jazz melodies

rhythm section—refers to standard instrumentation including piano, bass, drums, and sometimes guitar

ride—a synonym often used in early jazz styles to indicate improvise—i.e., "take a ride" means to improvise a solo

ride cymbal—generally the larger cymbal in a drum kit on which a steady, somewhat repetitive pattern is played, usually by the right hand, helping to establish the tempo

riff—a short, repeated musical phrase played by a soloist or a group

ritardondo (ritard)—gradually to slow down the tempo or pace of music

rondo—a classical form in origin, where one section of a musical composition (A) reoccurs, with contrasting sections (B,C,D) that are juxtaposed (such as ABACADA, etc.)

rubato—flexible, free, inconsistent tempo permitting interpretation by the performer

samba—Brazilian folk-music style closely associated with dance and the Carnaval celebration

salsa—a broad term that evolved in the 1960s to describe music of Afro-Cuban descent. Now the term can imply elements of Son, rock 'n' roll, jazz, and other Afro-Caribbean influences

scale—a precise progression of notes upwards or downwards, in stepwise motion

scat—an improvised jazz solo by a singer, using meaningless syllables

sequence—an architecturally or geometrically equal musical restatement of a series of pitches, without repeating the same notes; a reoccurring shape or gesture, but with different notes at a different pitch level—either higher or lower

seventh chord—a chord consisting of four different pitches and arranged with a major or minor third between each. Seventh chords serve as the foundation of jazz and popular music harmony

sharp—to raise a pitch

sheets of sound—term used to describe John Coltrane's practice of playing rapidly ascending, harp-like gestures of notes that together represent the sound of an entire harmony

shout chorus—a chorus or section of an arrangement (usually big band) that involves the entire ensemble, uses new material, and serves to bring the piece to a climax. The shout chorus usually appears near the end of the composition

shuffle—a medium-tempo style using the boogie-woogie rhythm as the basis

sideman—a musician who is not the leader of a band

soli—the section of a composition where a group of instruments, usually from the same family such as the saxophones, play a passage of music together. Each member of the section is playing a different note while rhythmically following the lead melodic voice

solo break—a point in a piece of music, lasting usually 2–4 measures, when everyone in the ensemble stops playing except the soloist

Son—a popular dance style of Spanish and African origins that served as the foundation for later styles, including "salsa"

song form—term used to define the architecture of the classic American popular song following a symmetrical ABA or AABA structure

spiritual—vocal music from the late 19th and early part of the 20th century that typically features long, sustained melodies and communicate sadness and were often associated with and influenced by the blues. Lyrics were usually of a sacred nature

staccato—played short and crisply

stock or **stock arrangement**—a standard rendition or arrangement, usually referring to a popular dance-band arrangement from the Swing Era

stomp—a style of music in which the band plays certain heavily accented rhythmic patterns over and over again in riff fashion, providing momentum and excitement through syncopation and repetition

stop time—a series of short notes played by the band in tempo and on certain major beats (often 1, 2, and 3) that usually serves as accompaniment to solo improvisations

Storyville—a district in New Orleans prior to 1917 where night life in all forms including prostitution was permitted

stride—a type of piano playing derived from ragtime; it often has no prescribed form, is frequently improvised, can be blues-influenced, and is faster and more intense than rag

style—the characteristic manner in which something is performed

swing—rhythmic phenomenon associated with jazz performance practice and referring to the rhythmic buoyancy created by the uneven, skipping rhythms that anticipate primary beats and are sometimes a consequence of syncopated rhythms

syncopation—a music rhythm that emphasizes a weak or normally unaccented beat or portion of a beat

tacet—be silent—an indication in printed music instructing the performer not to play a particular passage

tag—a short addition to the end of a musical composition, often based on the repetition of ingredients of the main melody

tailgate—refers to a New Orleans style of trombone playing in which the musician smears notes together using the instrument's slide to perform glissandos. This technique was forced by limited space on flatbed, horse-drawn wagons that forced trombonists to sit on the "tailgate" as the band paraded through the streets

tangana—Argentinean folk dance form that served as the predecessor of the "tango"

tango—Argentinean dance form

tempo—the rate or speed of a musical composition; the speed at which the melody is performed

territory bands—bands that limited tours to specific geographic regions and were well known in these areas. Some territory bands eventually made a national impact through recordings and touring

texture—the character of the musical fabric of a composition, determined by the arrangement of musical elements; the density, selection, organization, and range of instruments all contribute to the "texture"

theme—a melody forming the basis for variations or improvisation in composition

32-bar structure—a musical form that takes 32 bars to complete; can be used for a popular **song form**

through composed—a compositional approach that resembles stream-of-consciousness writing in that, typically, there are no reoccurring themes that provide a more traditional, discernible form or shape. Musical ideas seem to evolve organically, each moving freely from one to the next

timbales—Afro-Caribbean percussion drums made of resonant metal shell and single, tightly stretched head (plastic or calf-skin membrane), hit with sticks

timbre—the quality of a sound that distinguishes it from other sounds and is dictated by the number of overtones (harmonics) present in the sound. By comparison, a pure sine wave has no overtones. Each instrument has its own unique set of overtones and "timbre"

time signature—the numbers at the beginning of a composition indicating the groupings of beats for each measure (for example, in 3/4 time, the "3" indicates the number of beats to each measure, and the "4" indicates the note value that receives one beat

tonality—tonal character as determined by the relationship of the tones to the keynote or key center. Tonality is defined by a series of chords dictated by **functional harmony** or modality

tonic—the fundamental pitch or keynote (first note of a scale) that defines the key center of a piece of music

trading fours—two solo instrumentalists or instrument groups alternately playing four measures each; a typical jazz solo practice, where instrumentalists exchange solos with drummer

trap set—a synonym for drum set usually consisting of a bass drum, snare drum, sock cymbal, ride cymbal, and one or more tom toms

tremolo—a rapid alternation between two notes

triad—a three-note chord or sonority described as either major, minor, diminished, or augmented in quality

trill—a rapid alternation of two, immediately adjacent tones (whole or half-step apart)

trio—three performers playing as a group

tumbao—a reoccurring bass pattern associated with Afro-Cuban music that creates a sense of syncopation and tension, as it rarely emphasizes the first beat of the measure

12-tone technique—relating to, consisting of, or based on, an atonal arrangement of the 12 chromatic tones

two-beat—a jazz rhythmic style from the Swing Era defined by bass and drums emphasizing only two beats per measure (1 and 3) in a 4/4 meter. This gives the illusion of a slower 2/4 meter rather than the faster 4/4 meter of the piece

vamp—a repeated chord or rhythmic progression of indefinite length, used as filler until the soloist is ready to start or as accompaniment to a solo, or as a filler to delay the next section of a piece; this repetition can also occur at the beginning or end of a song

variation—a melody that has been altered

vibraharp/vibraphone/vibes—a musical instrument that has metal bars and rotating disks in the resonators to produce a vibrato

vibrato—the regulated fluctuation of a tone; used to add warmth and expression to a tone created by a singer or instrumentalist, except piano

voicing—the manner of organizing, doubling, omitting, or adding to the notes of a chord, and the assignment of notes to each particular instrument in the case of an arrangement for an ensemble

walking bass—a bass line that moves like a scale, four (or more) notes per bar

whole step—a musical interval comprising two half-steps. For example, from C to D is a whole step; from C to C sharp is a half-step

    Chromatic scale starting on C:
    whole   step
    C   (C sharp)   D
             half-step

woodshed or shed—jazz slang term to mean diligent, self-disciplined practice on an instrument in an effort to improve one's performance abilities

woodwind doubler—a musician who is a proficient performer on more than one woodwind instrument, e.g., saxophone, clarinet, and flute

work song—spontaneous, often improvised music associated with menial labor; often sung by prison workforces, chain gangs and slaves performing field labor

WPA—President Franklin D. Roosevelt's Works Progress Administration: a federal relief program and aspect of his "New Deal" that was designed to create employment and improve unemployment following the Depression

APPENDIX II

Suggested Jazz DVDs and Videos

For those readers who have become real aficionados and want, not only to hear, but also to see their favorite performers, there is a plethora of readily available resources. The home-video explosion that began in the late 1970s with videotape and moved to DVD in recent years has contributed to an entirely new industry, supporting fans, educators, and students of jazz. Instructional, documentary, and full-length films featuring musical scores by jazz artists or starring jazz performers are now plentiful. The following list is a brief selection of recommended videos, many of which have been aired by Arts and Entertainment, Bravo!, and PBS TV stations. Sources for acquiring these jazz videos, aside from libraries and local rental establishments, can be easily found on the Internet. A "must-have" resource for jazz film and video collectors is David Meeker's *Jazz in the Movies*, published in 1981 by Da Capo Press. Meeker's book is a filmography, supplying detailed information about when films were produced, who produced them, and a listing of jazz artists associated with each film. Another such reference source is *Jazz on Film*, by Scott Yanow, published in 2004 by Back Beat Books.

BIOGRAPHICAL

The Billie Holiday Story
But Then She's Betty Carter
Women in Jazz: The Instrumentalists
A Duke Named Ellington
Reminiscing in Tempo (Ellington)
Biography: Legendary Entertainers Series—*Ella Fitzgerald*
The Miles Davis Story
Thelonious Monk—American Composer
Thelonious Monk—Straight, No Chaser
Jazz Masters Series: *Charlie Parker*
Celebrating the Bird (Charlie Parker)
American Masters:*Charlie Parker*
American Masters: *John Hammond*
American Masters: *Sarah Vaughan: The Divine One*
American Masters: *Dizzy Gillespie*
American Masters: *Ella Fitzgerald, Something to Live For*
American Masters: *Duke Ellington*
American Masters: *Benny Goodman*

American Masters: *Billie Holiday*
Lady Day, The Many Faces of Billie Holiday
Time is All You've Got (Artie Shaw)
The Coltrane Legacy
The World According to John Coltrane
Satchmo: Louis Armstrong
Toshiko Akiyoshi: Jazz is My Native Language
Oscar Peterson, Life of a Legend
40 Years of the Modern Jazz Quartet
Charlie Christian: Solo Flight
Charles Mingus: Mingus in Greenwich Village
Charles Mingus—Triumph of the Underdog
Let's Get Lost (Chet Baker)

HISTORICAL DOCUMENTARIES

Duke Ellington's Washington
The Story of Jazz
Trumpet Kings (history of jazz trumpet players)
Reed Royalty (history of jazz saxophonists)
On the Road With Duke Ellington
Minnie the Moocher and Many, Many More (features Cab Calloway, with Louis Armstrong, Count Basie, Nat "King" Cole, Fats Waller, Duke Ellington, and Lena Horne)
Jazz (10-part, 19-hour series by Ken Burns)
Adventures in the Kingdom of Swing (Benny Goodman)
Swingin' The Blues (Count Basie)
Legends of Jazz Drumming Parts I & II
Piano Legends (hosted by Chick Corea)
The Last of the Blues Devils: The Kansas City Jazz Story
Phil Woods—A Life in E Flat

PERFORMANCE/INSTRUCTIONAL

The Universal Mind (Bill Evans)
Women in Jazz, The Vocalists: Scatting—Carmen McRae host
Jivin' in Bebop (1947, Dizzy Gillespie Big Band)
The Sound of Jazz (1957, CBS TV broadcast featuring Count Basie Band, Gerry Mulligan, Billie Holiday, Lester Young, Coleman Hawkins, and Thelonious Monk)
Blue Note: A Story of Modern Jazz
Born to Swing (Count Basie)
Jazz Life Volume 2—Mike Mainieri Group and Art Blakey & The Jazz Messengers (with Marsalis brothers)
Jazz at the Smithsonian: Art Blakey and the Jazz Messengers (with Wynton Marsalis)
Jazz Casual—Cannonball Adderley
Charles Mingus Sextet
Ornette Coleman Trio
Wes Montgomery—Belgium, 1965

Eric Dolphy—Last Date
Chick Corea—A Very Special Concert
Herbie Hancock and the Rocket Band
Brecker Brothers: Return of the Brecker Brothers
Steps Ahead—Copenhagen Live
Grover Washington, Jr. in Concert
Keith Jarrett: Standards
Keith Jarrett: Last Solo
Keith Jarrett/Gary Peacock/Jack DeJohnette: Tokyo 1996
Dexter Gordon: More Than You Know
Sonny Rollins and Dexter Gordon
Dexter Gordon: Live at the Maintenance Shop
Wynton Marsalis: Blues and Swing
Branford Marsalis: The Music Tells You
Jazz Casual—Thad Jones/Mel Lewis and Woody Herman
Cecil Taylor: Burning Poles
Sun Ra: Space is the Place
Sun Ra—Make a Joyful Noise
Branford Marsalis: The Music Tells You
Jam Miami—A Celebration of Latin Jazz
Antonio Carlos Jobim: An All-Star Tribute

IMPORTANT FEATURE FILMS

St. Louis Blues (1929, Bessie Smith, James P. Johnson, W.C. Handy Choir)
King of Jazz (1930 Paul Whiteman film)
Minnie the Moocher (1932 Betty Boop cartoon with music by Cab Calloway)
I Heard (1933 Betty Boop cartoon featuring music by Don Redman)
Stormy Weather (1943, Cab Calloway, Fats Waller, Lena Horne, and others)
The Fabulous Dorseys (1947 Tommy and Jimmy Dorsey feature with Art Tatum, Paul Whiteman,
    Charlie Barnet, Helen O'Connell, Ziggy Elman)
I Want to Live (1958, music by Mundell Lowe, Gerry Mulligan, Art Farmer, etc.)
Asphalt Jungle (1959, Duke Ellington score)
Anatomy of a Murder (1959, Duke Ellington score)
Paris Blues (1961, score by Duke Ellington)
Mickey One (1965, music by Stan Getz)
Alfie (1966, with music by Sonny Rollins, Oliver Nelson, Kenny Burrell, etc.)
Round Midnight (1986, featuring Herbie Hancock, Dexter Gordon, etc.)
The Color of Money (1986, with music by Gil Evans)
Bird (1988 film by Clint Eastwood about Charlie Parker)

Chapter Notes and Additional Sources

1 THE NATURE OF JAZZ

Notes

1. Pat Metheny, Keynote Address at 2001 International Association For Jazz Education Conference.
2. Bill Crow, *Jazz Anecdotes* (New York: Oxford University Press, 1990), p. 19.
3. Alan P. Merriam and Fradley H. Garner, "Jazz—The Word," in *The Jazz Cadence of American Culture*, edited by Robert G. O'Meally (New York: Columbia University Press, 1998), pp. 7–31.
4. Ibid., p.20.
5. Ibid., p. 20.
6. Ibid., p. 19.
7. Ibid., p. 20.
8. Ibid., pp. 7–31.
9. *Down Beat*, "New Word for Jazz Worth $1000," Vol. 16, No. 10, July 15, 1949. *Down Beat*, "Judges Named in 'Word' Contest—Prizes Pile Up," Vol. 16, No. 1, August 26, 1949. Don Read, "All That Crewcut," *Jazz Journal International*, Vol. 50, No. 5, May 1997, p. 10.

Additional Sources

Dom Cerulli, Burt Korall, and Mort Nasatir (editors), *The Jazz Word* (New York: Da Capo Press, 1960).

Bill Crow, *Jazz Anecdotes* (New York: Oxford University Press, 1990), pp. 19–22.

James Reese Europe, "A Negro Explains Jazz," *Literary Digest*, April 26, 1919, pp. 28–29.

Sidney Finkelstein, *Jazz: A People's Music* (New York: The Citadel Press, 1948).

Ted Gioia, *The Imperfect Art* (New York: Oxford University Press, 1988).

Robert Goffin, *Jazz From the Congo to the Metropolitan* (New York: Doubleday and Co., 1946), pp. 1–22.

Wilder Hobson, *American Jazz Music* (New York: W.W. Norton and Co., 1939).

Barry Kernfeld, *The New Grove Dictionary of Jazz* (New York: St. Martins Press, 1995).

Henry O. Osgood, *So This Is Jazz* (Boston: Little Brown and Co., 1926).

Leroy Ostransky, *The Anatomy of Jazz* (Seattle: University of Washington Press, 1960), pp. 14–21.

Leroy Ostransky, *Understanding Jazz* (Englewood Cliffs: Prentice-Hall, 1977), pp. 3–43.

Lewis Porter, *Jazz: A Century of Change, Readings and New Essays* (New York: Schirmer Books, 1997), pp. 1–38.

Winthrop Sargeant, *Jazz, Hot and Hybrid* (London: Jazz Book Club, 1946).

Tony Sherman, "What Is Jazz, An Interview With Wynton Marsalis," *American Heritage*, October 1995, pp. 67–85.

Smithsonian Collection of Classic Jazz, Notes by Martin Williams and Ira Gitler (Washington: The Smithsonian Collection of Recordings, Smithsonian Institution, 1997).

Marshall W. Stearns, *The Story of Jazz* (New York: Oxford University Press, 1956), pp. 275–282.

Robert Walser (editor), *Keeping Time Readings in Jazz History* (New York: Oxford University Press, 1999).

Paul Whiteman and Mary Margaret McBride, *Jazz* (New York: J.H. Sears, 1926).

2   THE ELEMENTS OF JAZZ

Notes

1. Martin Williams, *The Jazz Tradition* (New York: Oxford University Press, 1970), p. 11.
2. Gunther Schuller, *Early Jazz* (New York: Oxford University Press, 1968), p. 16.
3. Count Basie, CBS Television *60 Minutes*, Interview 1981.
4. Robert Walser (editor), *Keeping Time Readings in Jazz History* (New York: Oxford University Press, 1999), pp. 73–76.
5. Nat Hentoff, *Jazz Is* (New York: Limelight Editions, 1991), pp. 18–19.
6. Robert Walser (editor), *Keeping Time Readings in Jazz History* (New York: Oxford University Press, 1999), p. 109.
7. André Hodeir, *Jazz: Its Evolution and Essence* (New York: Grove Press, 1956), p. 240.
8. Ibid., p. 195.
9. Leroy Ostransky, *Understanding Jazz* (Englewood Cliffs: Prentice-Hall, 1977), p. 93.
10. James Lincoln Collier, *Jazz: The American Theme Song* (New York: Oxford University Press, 1993), p. 25.
11. Michael Neal Jacobson, *A Comparison of the Improvisational Performance Practices of Jazz Saxophonists Charlie Parker, and Julian Adderley with the Embellishments Found in the Methodical Sonatas of Georg Philipp Teleman*, D.M.A. Treatise, The University of Texas, 1999.
12. "Improvisation," in *The New Gove Dictionary of Music and Musicians*, Volume 9, edited by Stanley Sadie (London: Macmillan Publishers Limited), 1980, p. 43.
13. Ibid., p. 49.
14. Leroy Ostransky, *Understanding Jazz* (Englewood Cliffs: Prentice-Hall, 1977), p. 80.
15. Nat Shapiro and Nat Hentoff (editors), *Hear Me Talkin' To Ya* (New York: Reinhart and Co., 1955), p. 19.
16. Leroy, Ostransky, *The Anatomy of Jazz* (Seattle: University of Washington Press, 1960), p. 69.
17. Duke Ellington, *The Future of Jazz*, 1958.
18. Whitney Balliett, "Tom and Jeru," *New Yorker*, March 15, 1990, pp. 93–95.
19. Dan Morganstern, "The Art of Playing," *Down Beat*, December 1994, pp. 46–47 (reprinted from *Down Beat*, October 22, 1964).
20. Pat Harris, "Pres Talks About Himself, Copycats," *Down Beat*, May 6, 1949.
21. McCoy Tyner, from a presentation made at the University of the Arts, Philadelphia, PA, April 8, 2005.

Additional Resources

James Lincoln Collier, *Jazz the American Theme Song* (New York: Oxford University Press, 1993), pp. 25–70.
Sidney Finkelstein, *Jazz: A People's Music* (New York: The Citadel Press, 1948).
Samuel A. Floyd, Jr., "African Roots of Jazz," in *The Oxford Companion to Jazz*, edited by Bill Kirchner (New York: Oxford University Press, 2000) pp. 7–16.
Wilder Hobson, *American Jazz Music* (New York: W.W. Norton, 1939), pp. 40–73.
André Hodeir, *Jazz: Its Evolution and Essence* (New York: Grove Press, 1956), pp. 195–241.
Roger Kamien, *Music And Appreciation* (New York: McGraw-Hill, 1988), pp. 1–88.
Barry Kernfeld, *The New Grove Dictionary of Jazz* (New York: St. Martins Press, 1995).
Henry O. Osgood, *So This Is Jazz* (Boston: Little Brown and Co., 1926).
Leroy Ostransky, *Understanding Jazz* (Englewood Cliffs: Prentice-Hall, 1977), pp. 47–93.
Winthrop Sargeant, *Jazz, Hot and Hybrid* (London: Jazz Book Club, 1946).
Smithsonian Collection of Classic Jazz, Notes by Martin Williams and Ira Gitler (Washington: The Smithsonian Collection of Recordings, Smithsonian Institution, 1997).
Marshall W. Stearns, *The Story of Jazz* (New York: Oxford University Press, 1956), pp. 275–282.
Jeff Taylor, "The Early Origins of Jazz," in *The Oxford Companion to Jazz*, edited by Bill Kirchner (New York: Oxford University Press, 2000), pp. 39–52.
William H. Youngren, "European Roots of Jazz," in *The Oxford Companion to Jazz*, edited by Bill Kirchner (New York: Oxford University Press, 2000), pp. 17–28.

3   LISTENING TO JAZZ

Notes

1. Paul Tanner, David Megill, and Maurice Gerow, *Jazz* (New York: McGraw-Hill, 2005), p. 6.
2. Stanley Dance and Freddie Green, *The World of Swing* (New York: Da Capo Press, 1974), pp. 13–17.

3. Ted Gioia, *The Imperfect Art, Reflections on Jazz and Modern Culture* (New York: Oxford University Press, 1988), 50–69.

Additional Sources

Scott DeVeaux, *The Birth of Bebop* (Los Angeles: University of California Press, 1997), pp. 202–235.

Leroy Ostransky, *Understanding Jazz* (Englewood Cliffs: Prentice-Hall, 1977), pp. 73–115.

Lewis Porter and Michael Ullman, *Jazz: From its Origins to the Present* (Englewood Cliffs: Prentice-Hall, 1993), pp. 449–459.

Paul Tanner, David Megill, and Maurice Gerow, *Jazz* (New York: McGraw-Hill, 2005), pp. 1–13.

4   THE ROOTS OF JAZZ

Notes

1. John Miller Chernoff, *African rhythm and African sensibility: Aesthetics and Social Action in African Musical Idioms* (Chicago: University of Chicago Press, 1979), p. 30.
2. Gene Santoro, "Latin Jazz," in *The Oxford Companion to Jazz*, edited by Bill Kirchner (New York: Oxford University Press, 2000), pp. 522–533.
3. Lawrence W. Levine, "Jazz and American Culture," in *The Jazz Cadence of American Culture*, edited by Robert G. O'Meally (New York: Columbia University Press, 1998), p. 435.
4. David A. Jansen and Gene Jones, *Spreadin' Rhythm Around: Black Popular Song Writers 1880–1930* (New York: Schirmer Books, 1998), p. 236.
5. Ibid., p. 237.
6. Ibid., p. 25.
7. Porter, *Jazz: A Century of Change* (New York: Schirmer Books, 1997), p. 127. (James Reese Europe, "A Negro Explains Jazz," originally published in *Literary Digest*, 1919.)

Additional Sources

Edward A. Berlin, *Ragtime: A Musical and Cultural History* (Berkley: University of California Press, 1980), pp. 5–20.

Ken Burns, *The Story of America's Music*, Columbia/Legacy CSK 61432.

Clifton Daniels (editor), *Chronicle of America* (Mont Kisco: Chronicle Publications, 1990).

James Reese Europe's 369th U.S. Infantry "Hellfighter" Band, Memphis Archives, 1996, MA7020.

Ted Gioia, *The History of Jazz* (New York: Oxford University Press, 1997), pp. 3–28.

W.C. Handy Memphis Blues Band, Memphis Archives, 1994, MA7006.

André Hodeir, *Jazz, Its Evolution and Essence* (New York: Grove Press, 1956).

Anne Lemon, "Robert Johnson Biography," from the *The Robert Johnson Notebooks*, edited by Courtney Danforth and Adriana Rissetto, 1997; http://xroads.virginia.edu/~music/rjhome.html (7 July, 1997).

Marshall Stearns, *The Story of Jazz* (New York: Oxford University Press, 1956), pp. 3–150.

Richard Marshall (editor), *Great Events of the 20th Century* (Pleasantville: The Reader's Digest Association, 1977).

William J. Schafer, with assistance from Richard B. Allen, *Brass Bands and New Orleans Jazz* (Baton Rouge: Louisiana State University Press, 1977).

Gunther Schuller, *Early Jazz* (New York: Oxford University Press, 1968), pp. 3–88.

The Smithsonian Collection of Classic jazz, Notes by Martin Williams and Ira Gitler (Washington: Smithsonian Institute, 1997).

Jim Steinblatt, "The Handy Man Can," ASCAP, *Playback*, Summer, 1996; www.deltahaze.com/dhcrj.html

5   JAZZ TAKES ROOT

Notes

1. Frank Paterson, *Musical Courier* (May 11, 1922), p.6, cited in James Lincoln Collier, *The Reception of Jazz in America: A New View* (New York: Institute for Studies in American Music, 1988), p. 14.
2. "Jazz and Jassism," *The Times–Picayune* (New Orleans: June 20, 1918), p. 4.
3. "Jazzing Away Prejudice," *Chicago Defender* (Chicago: May 10, 1919), p. 20.
4. H.O. Brunn, *The Story of the Original Dixieland Jazz Band* (London: Sidgwick and Jackson, 1963), p. 107.

5. John R. McMahon, "Unspeakable Jazz Must Go," *The Ladies' Home Journal*, December 1921, pp. 34, 115–116.

6. "Does Jazz Put the Sin in Syncopation?," *The Ladies' Home Journal*, August 1921, pp. 16, 34.

7. Ibid.

8. Ibid.

9. Robert Walser, *Keeping Time Readings in Jazz History* (New York: Oxford University Press, 1999), p.42. (Excerpts reprinted from "Where the Etude Stands on Jazz," *The Etude*, August 1924.)

10. Ibid., pp. 43–44.

11. Ibid., p. 50.

12. Ibid., p. 52.

13. James Lincoln Collier, *The Reception of Jazz in America: A New View* (New York: Institute for Studies in American Music, 1988), p. 11.

14. Ibid., p. 14.

15. Ibid.

16. John Chilton, *Sidney Bechet: The Wizard of Jazz* (New York: Oxford University Press, 1987), p. 15.

17. H.O. Brunn, *The Story of the Original Dixieland Jazz Band* (London: Sidgwick and Jackson, 1963), pp. 108–109.

18. Ibid., p. 135.

19. Ibid., pp. 68–69.

20. Louis Armstrong, *The Complete Hot Five and Hot Seven Recordings*, Columbia/Legacy C4K 63527, New York, 2000.

21. William Howland Kenney, *Chicago Jazz: A Cultural History, 1904–1930* (New York: Oxford University Press, 1993), p. 46.

22. Martin Williams, *The Smithsonian Collection of Classic Jazz* (Washington: Smithsonian Institution, 1997), p. 36.

Additional Sources

Louis Armstrong: The Complete Hot Five and Hot Seven Recordings, liner notes by Phil Schaap and Robert G.O'Meally (Columbia/Legacy C4K 63527).

H. O. Brunn, *The Story of the Original Dixieland Jazz Band* (London: Sidgwick and Jackson, 1963).

James Lincoln Collier, *Jazz The American Theme Song* (New York: Oxford University Press, 1993).

James Lincoln Collier, *The Reception of Jazz in America a New View* (New York: Institute for Studies in American Music, 1988).

James Lincoln Collier, "Sidney Bechet," in *The New Grove Dictionary of Jazz*, Barry Kernfeld (editor) (New York: St. Martins Press, 1995), pp. 88–90.

Clifton Daniel (editor), *Chronicle of America* (Mount Kisco: Chronicle Publications, 1990).

Ted Gioia, *The History of Jazz* (New York: Oxford University Press, 1997), pp. 29–54.

Lawrence Gushee, "Joe 'King' Oliver," in *The New Grove Dictionary of Jazz*, Barry Kernfeld (editor) (New York: St. Martins Press, 1995), pp. 935–936.

Wilder Hobson, *American Jazz Music* (New York: W.W. Norton and Co., 1939).

André Hodeir, *Jazz: Its Evolution and Essence* (New York: Grove Press, 1956).

José Hosiasson, "Kid Ory," in *The New Grove Dictionary of Jazz*, Barry Kernfeld (editor) (New York: St. Martins Press, 1995), p. 945.

Richard Marshall (editor), *Great Events of the 20th Century* (Pleasantville: The Reader's Digest Association, Inc., 1977).

John McDonough, "Jass Record #1, Original Dixieland Jazz Band," *Down Beat*, February 1992.

Burton Perretti, *Jazz in American Culture* (Chicago: Ivan R. Dee, 1997), pp. 10–60.

Lewis Porter, *Jazz: A Century of Change* (New York: Schirmer Books, 1997), pp. 121–158.

Lewis Porter and Michael Ullman, *Jazz From Its Origins to the Present* (Englewood Cliffs: Prentice-Hall, 1992), pp. 7–73.

Willa Rouder, "James P. Johnson," in *The New Grove Dictionary of Jazz*, Barry Kernfeld (editor) (New York: St. Martins Press, 1995), pp. 619–621.

Gunther Schuller, *Early Jazz* (New York: Oxford University Press, 1968), pp. 89–241.

Gunther Schuller, "Jelly Roll Morton," in *The New Grove Dictionary of Jazz*, Barry Kernfeld (editor) (New York: St. Martins Press, 1995), pp. 804–806.

The Complete Original Dixieland Jazz Band, 1917–1936, Jazz Tribune No. 70, RCA/BMG, 1992.

6   THE JAZZ AGE: FROM CHICAGO TO NEW YORK

Notes

1. Hoagy Carmichael, *Stardust Road* (New York: Reinhart, 1946), pp. 7–8.
2. William Howland Kenney, *Chicago Jazz: A Cultural History, 1904–1930* (New York: Oxford University Press, 1993), p. 14.
3. Ibid., p. 30.
4. Ibid., p. 24.
5. H.O. Brunn, *The Original Dixieland Jazz Band* (London: Sedgwick and Jackson, 1963), p. 173.
6. Neil Leonard, *Jazz and the White Americans* (Chicago: The University of Chicago Press, 1962), p. 37.
7. Ibid., p. 83.
8. James Lincoln Collier, *The Reception of Jazz in America: A New View* (New York: Institute for Studies in American Music, 1988), p. 18.
9. William Howland Kenney, *Chicago Jazz: A Cultural History, 1904–1930* (New York: Oxford University Press, 1993), p. 71.
10. Ibid., p. 45.
11. Ibid., p. 97.
12. James Lincoln Collier, *Jazz the American Theme Song* (New York: Oxford University Press, 1993), p. 201.
13. Wilder Hobson, *American Jazz Music* (New York: W.W. Norton, 1939), p. 126.
14. Richard M. Sudhalter, *Lost Chords: White Musicians and Their Contribution to Jazz* (New York: Oxford University Press, 1999), p. 450.
15. Ibid., p. 450.
16. Marshall Stearns, *The Story of Jazz* (New York: Oxford University Press, 1956), p. 165.
17. Henry Osgood, *So This is Jazz* (Boston: Little Brown and Co., 1926), p. 136.
18. Robert Goffin, *Jazz From the Congo to the Metropolitan* (Garden City: Doubleday, 1946), p. 145.
19. James Lincoln Collier, *The Reception of Jazz in America: A New View* (New York: Institute for Studies in American Music, 1988) pp. 16–17.
20. William Howland Kenney, *Chicago Jazz: A Cultural History, 1904–1930* (New York: Oxford University Press, 1993), p. 30.
21. Ibid., p. 155.
22. Wilder Hobson, *American Jazz Music* (New York: W.W. Norton, 1939), p. 129.
23. Ibid., p. 127.
24. William Howland Kenney, *Chicago Jazz: A Cultural History, 1904–1930* (New York: Oxford University Press, 1993), pp. 167–168.
25. Ibid., p. 168.
26. Ibid., p. 168.
27. William Howland Kenney, *Chicago Jazz: A Cultural History, 1904–1930* (New York: Oxford University Press, 1993), p. 71.
28. Neil Leonard, *Jazz and the White Americans* (Chicago: The University of Chicago Press, 1962), p. 92.
29. James Lincoln Collier, *The Reception of Jazz in America: A New View* (Brooklyn: Institute for Studies in American Music, 1988), p. 18. (From *Bill Board*, February 14, 1925, p. 20.)
30. Neil Leonard, *Jazz and the White Americans* (Chicago: The University of Chicago Press, 1962), p. 74.
31. Paul Whiteman and Mary Margaret McBride, *Jazz* (New York: J.H. Sears and Co., 1926), p. 130.
32. The Recording Industry Association of America (RIAA) established gold-record (created in 1958) and platinum-record awards (created in 1976) to recognize recordings with sales of 500,000 or more and 1 million or more, respectively. In the case of Whiteman's 1922 recording, had the award been available, he would have received a platinum award for "Whispering." In comparison, Elvis Presley's first three albums in the 1950s won only gold status. Michael Jackson won platinum-record awards for *Bad* and *Thriller*.

Additional Sources

Clifton Daniel (editor), *Chronicle of America* (Mount Kisco: Chronicle Publications, 1990).
Ted Gioia, *The History of Jazz* (New York: Oxford University Press, 1997), pp. 70–91.
William Howland Kenney, *Chicago Jazz: A Cultural History, 1904–1930* (New York: Oxford University Press, 1993).
William Howland Kenney, "Historical Context and the Definition of Jazz: Putting More of the History in 'Jazz History'," in *Jazz Among the Discourses*, edited by Krin Gabbard (Durham, NC: Duke University Press, 1995), pp. 100–116.

Neil Leonard, *Jazz and the White Americans* (Chicago: The University of Chicago Press, 1962), pp. 29–107.

Richard Marshall (editor), *Great Events of the 20th Century* (Pleasantville, NY: The Reader's Digest Association, 1977).

Ronald L. Morris, *Wait Until Dark: Jazz and the Underworld, 1880–1940* (Bowling Green, KY: Bowling Green University Popular Press, 1980).

Burton Peretti, *Jazz in American Culture* (Chicago: Ivan R. Dee, 1997), pp. 31–60.

Burton Peretti, *The Creation of Jazz: Music, Race and Culture in Urban America* (Urbana: University of Illinois Press, 1992).

Lewis Porter, *Jazz: A Century of Change* (New York: Schirmer Books, 1997), pp. 121–158.

Marshall Stearns, *The Story of Jazz* (New York: Oxford University Press, 1956), pp. 151–194.

Richard M. Sudhalter, *Lost Chords: White Musicians and Their Contribution to Jazz* (New York: Oxford University Press, 1999).

7   THE SWING ERA: JAZZ AT ITS PEAK

Notes

1. Duke Ellington, *Down Beat*, February 1939, pp. 2, 16, 17.
2. Burton Peretti, *Jazz in American Culture* (Chicago: Ivan R. Dee, 1997), p. 67.
3. John Edward Hasse (editor), *Jazz: The First Century* (New York: Harper Collins, 1999), p. 73.
4. Burton Peretti, *Jazz in American Culture* (Chicago: Ivan R. Dee, 1997), pp. 61–75.
5. Scott DeVaux, *The Birth of Bebop: A Social and Musical History* (Berkley and Los Angeles: University of California Press, 1997), pp. 99–100.
6. John Edward Hasse, *Beyond Category: The Life and Genius of Duke Ellington* (New York: Simon and Schuster, 1993), pp. 14–19.
7. Robert Goffin, *Jazz From the Congo to Swing* (London: Musicians Press, 1946), pp. 262–263.
8. Martin Williams, *The Smithsonian Collection of Classic Jazz* (Washington, DC: Smithsonian Institution, 1997), p. 65.
9. Gunther Schuller, *The Swing Era: The Development of Jazz 1930–1945* (New York: Oxford University Press, 1989), pp. 11, 23, 44.
10. Gunther Schuller, *The Swing Era: the Development of Jazz 1930–1945* (New York: Oxford University Press, 1989), p. 567.

Additional Sources

James Lincoln Collier, *Duke Ellington* (New York: Oxford University Press, 1987).

James Lincoln Collier, "Fletcher Henderson," in *The New Grove Dictionary of Jazz*, edited by Barry Kernfeld (New York: St. Martin's Press, 1995), pp. 514–516.

Clifton Daniel (editor), *Chronicle of America* (Mount Kisco: Chronicle Publications, 1989).

Scott DeVaux, *The Birth of Bebop: A Social and Musical History* (Berkley and London: University of California Press, 1997), pp. 1–31, 35–269.

Ted Gioia, *The History of Jazz* (New York: Oxford University Press, 1997), pp. 93–197.

Fletcher Henderson, A Study in Frustration, Notes by Frank Driggs and John Hammond, Columbia/Legacy 557596.

Richard Marshall (editor), *Great Events of the 20th Century* (Pleasantville, KY: The Reader's Digest Association, 1977).

Dave McAleer (compiler), *The Book of Hit Singles* (San Francisco: Miller Freeman Books, 1999) pp. 10–85.

Burton Peretti, *Jazz in American Culture* (Chicago: Ivan R. Dee, 1997), pp. 61–84.

Lewis Porter, "Coleman Hawkins," in *The New Grove Dictionary of Jazz*, edited by Barry Kernfeld (New York: St. Martin's Press, 1995), pp. 505–507.

Brian Priestley, *Jazz on Record* (New York: Billboard Books, 1991), pp. 43–87.

Ken Rattenbury, *Duke Ellington Jazz Composer* (New Haven: Yale University Press, 1990).

Gunther Schuller, *Early Jazz* (New York: Oxford University Press, 1968), pp. 242–357.

Gunther Schuller, *The Swing Era* (New York: Oxford University Press, 1989), pp. 3–157, 323–325, 426–449.

George T. Simon, *The Big Bands* (New York: Macmillan Publishing Co., 1974), pp. 33–39.

Mark Tucker, *Ellington: The Early Years* (Urbana: University of Illinois Press, 1991), pp. 3–118.

Robert Walser, *Keeping Time Readings in Jazz History* (New York: Oxford University Press, 1999), pp. 71–150.

8 SWINGING ACROSS THE COUNTRY: THE BANDS, SINGERS, AND PIANISTS

Notes

1. Bernard Gendron, "Moldy Figs and Modernists: Jazz at War (1942–1946)," in *Jazz Among the Discourses*, edited by Krin Garrard (Durham, NC: Duke University Press, 1995), p. 17.
2. Cited from an interview with Art Vincent on the radio show *Art of Jazz*, December 1, 1973.
3. Ross Russell, *Jazz Style in Kansas City and the Southwest* (Berkley: University of California Press, 1971), p. 3.
4. Cited from an interview with the author, Richard Lawn, Austin, Texas, Fall 1982.
5. Ross Russell, *Jazz Style in Kansas City and the Southwest* (Berkley: University of California Press, 1971), pp. 104–105.
6. www.audio-play.com/toodead/calif40.htm (website no longer available)
7. Robert Walser, *Keeping Time, Readings in Jazz History* (New York: Oxford University Press, 1999), p. 112.
8. Ibid., pp. 111–120.
9. John Edward Hasse, editor, *Jazz: The First Century* (New York: HarperCollins, 2000), p. 56.
10. "Billie Holiday: A Portrait in Testimony," compiled by Christopher Porter, *Jazz Times* (May 2005), p. 67.
11. Cited from an interview with the author, Richard Lawn, Austin, Texas, Fall 1982.
12. John Edward Hasse (editor), *Jazz: The First Century* (New York: HarperCollins, 2000), p. 56.
13. George T. Simon, *The Big Bands* (New York: Macmillan, 1997), p. 4.
14. Robert S. Gold, *Jazz Talk* (Indianapolis: The Bobbs-Merrill Company, 1975), pp. 61, 47, 30, 128, 104.
15. Cited from an interview with the author, Richard Lawn, Austin, Texas, Fall 1982.
16. Ibid.
17. John Edward Hasse (editor), *Jazz: The First Century* (New York: HarperCollins, 2000), p. 82.
18. Leonard Feather, "A Survey of Jazz Today," in *Esquire's 1945 Jazz Book*, edited by Paul Eduard Miller (New York: A.S. Barnes & Company, 1945), pp. 15–27.
19. Wilder Hobson, *American Jazz Music* (New York: W.W. Norton, 1939), pp. 154–155.
20. Ibid., p. 156.

Additional Sources

James Lincoln Collier, "Billie Holiday," in *The New Grove Dictionary of Jazz*, edited by Barry Kernfeld (New York: St. Martin's Press, 1995), pp. 533–534.

Clifton Daniel (editor), *Chronicle of America* (Mount Kisco: Chronicle Publications, 1989).

Bernard Gendron, "Moldy Figs and Modernists: Jazz at War (1942–1946)," in *Jazz Among the Discourses*, edited by Krin Gabbard (Durham: Duke University Press, 1995), pp. 31–51.

John Edward Hasse, *Jazz: The First Century* (New York: HarperCollins, 1999), pp. 53–85.

Felicity Howlett and J. Bradford Robinson, "Art Tatum," in *The New Grove Dictionary of Jazz*, edited by Barry Kernfeld (New York: St. Martin's Press, 1995), pp. 1187–1188.

Richard Marshall (editor), *Great Events of the 20th Century* (Pleasantville, NY: The Reader's Digest Association, 1977).

Lewis Porter, "Lester Young," in *The New Grove Dictionary of Jazz*, edited by Barry Kernfeld (New York: St. Martin's Press, 1995), pp. 1317–1319.

Fredric Ramsey, Jr. and Charles Edward Smith (editors), *Jazzmen* (New York: Harcourt Brace Jovanovich, 1939).

J. Bradford Robinson, "Ella Fitzgerald," in *The New Grove Dictionary of Jazz*, edited by Barry Kernfeld (New York: St. Martin's Press, 1995), pp. 388–389.

J. Bradford Robinson, "Mary Lou Williams," in *The New Grove Dictionary of Jazz*, edited by Barry Kernfeld (New York: St. Martin's Press, 1995), pp. 1294–1295.

Ross Russell, *Jazz Style in Kansas City and the Southwest* (Berkley: University of California Press, 1971).

Gunther Schuller, *The Swing Era* (New York: Oxford University Press, 1989), pp. 222–262.

Gunther Schuller and Martin Williams, liner notes from *Big Band Jazz From the Beginnings to the Fifties* (Washington: Smithsonian Collection of Recordings).

George T. Simon, *The Big Bands* (New York: Macmillan, 1967), pp. 3–72.

9 THE BEBOP REVOLUTION

Notes

1. Gunther Schuller, *The Swing Era, The Development of Jazz 1930–1945* (New York: Oxford University Press, 1989), p. 23.
2. Scott DeVaux, *The Birth of Bebop, A Social and Cultural History* (Berkley: University of California Press, 1997), pp. 243–244.

3. "The Petrillo Years," *International Musician*, Vol. 95, No. 4, October 1996.

4. Roger Pryor Dodge, *Hot Jazz and Jazz Dance* (New York: Oxford University Press, 1995), p. 148.

5. Terry Gross interview of Stan Getz, for NPR station WHYY, June 14, 1990.

6. Ira Gitler, *Jazz Masters of the '40s* (New York: Da Capo Press, 1966), p. 79 (quoted from Norman Granz, *Down Beat*, 1945).

7. Robert Walser, *Keeping Time* (New York: Oxford University Press, 1999), p. 153. (Reprint of "Bop Will Kill Business Unless it Kills ItselfFirst," *Down Beat*, April 7, 1948, pp. 2–3.)

8. Burton Peretti, *Jazz in American Culture* (Chicago: Ivan R. Dee, 1997), p. 103.

9. Ibid.

10. Marshall Stearns, *The Story of Jazz* (New York: Oxford University Press, 1956), p. 222.

11. *Down Beat*, 1955. (Reprinted in Vol. 56, No. 9, September 1989, p. 39.)

12. Joe Goldberg, *Jazz Masters of the 50s* (New York: Da Capo Press, 1965), p. 44.

13. John Birks Gillespie and Al Fraser, *To Be or Not to Bop, Memoirs of Dizzy Gillespie* (New York: Da Capo Press, 1979), p. 193.

14. Ibid., p. 350.

Additional Sources

Clifton Daniel (editor), *Chronicle of America* (Mount Kisco: Chronicle Publications, 1989).

Scott DeVaux, *The Birth of Bebop: A Social and Musical History* (Berkley: University of California Press, 1997), pp. 1–31, 202–317.

Scott DeVaux, "The Advent of Bebop," in *The Oxford Companion to Jazz*, edited by Bill Kirchner (New York: Oxford University Press, 2000), pp. 292–304.

Ira Gitler, *Jazz Masters of the 40s* (New York: Da Capo Press, 1966).

Max Harrison, "Tadd Dameron," in *The New Grove Dictionary of Jazz*, edited by Barry Kernfeld (New York: St. Martin's Press, 1995), p. 264.

Barry Kernfeld, "Sonny Rollins," in *The New Grove Dictionary of Jazz*, edited by Barry Kernfeld (New York: St. Martin's Press, 1995), pp. 1058–1060.

Barry Kernfeld, "Sarah Vaughan," in *The New Grove Dictionary of Jazz*, edited by Barry Kernfeld (New York: St. Martin's Press, 1995), pp. 1241–1242.

Richard Marshall (editor), *Great Events of the 20th Century* (Pleasantville, NY: The Reader's Digest Association, Inc., 1977).

Thomas Owens, "Fats Navarro," in *The New Grove Dictionary of Jazz*, edited by Barry Kernfeld (New York: St. Martin's Press, 1995), pp. 830–831.

Burton W. Peretti, *Jazz in American Culture* (Chicago: Ivan R. Dee, 1997), pp. 83–108.

Lewis Porter, "Dexter Gordon," in *The New Grove Dictionary of Jazz*, edited by Barry Kernfeld (New York: St. Martin's Press, 1995), p. 442.

Lewis Porter, "J.J. Johnson," in *The New Grove Dictionary of Jazz*, edited by Barry Kernfeld (New York: St. Martin's Press, 1995), pp. 621–622.

Brian Priestly, *Jazz on Record* (New York: Billboard Books, 1991), pp. 86–106.

J. Bradford Robinson, "Oscar Pettiford," in *The New Grove Dictionary of Jazz*, edited by Barry Kernfeld (New York: St. Martin's Press, 1995), pp. 974–975.

J. Bradford Robinson, "Bud Powell," in *The New Grove Dictionary of Jazz*, edited by Barry Kernfeld (New York: St. Martin's Press, 1995), pp. 995–996.

Geoffrey C. Ward, "Bird on a Wire," *Vanity Fair*, November 2000.

Ollie Wilson and J. Bradford Robinson, "Kenny Clarke," in *The New Grove Dictionary of Jazz*, edited by Barry Kernfeld (New York: St. Martin's Press, 1995), pp. 218–219.

Ollie Wilson and J. Bradford Robinson, "Max Roach," in *The New Grove Dictionary of Jazz*, edited by Barry Kernfeld (New York: St. Martin's Press, 1995), pp. 1045–1050.

Martin Williams, *The Jazz Tradition* (New York: Oxford University Press, 1970), pp. 103–130.

10 THE 1950s AND EARLY 1960s: COOL, INTELLECTUAL, AND ABSTRACT JAZZ

Notes

1. Ted Gioia, *West Coast Jazz, Modern Jazz in California 1945–1960* (Berkley: University of California Press, 1992), p. 187.

2. Robert Walser (editor), *Keeping Time, Readings in Jazz History* (New York: Oxford University Press, 1999), p. 247.

3. Joe Goldberg, *Jazz Masters of the 50s* (New York: Da Capo Press, 1965), p. 117.

4. Joe Goldberg, *Jazz Masters of the 50s* (New York: Da Capo Press, 1965), p. 12.

5. "Pipe and Slippers Jazz is For Me: Gerry Mulligan," *Down Beat*, September 1989, p. 42.

6. Ted Gioia, *West Coast Jazz, Modern Jazz in California 1945–1960* (Berkley: University of California Press, 1992), p. 68.

7. Joe Goldberg, *Jazz Masters of the 50s* (New York: Da Capo Press, 1965), p. 154; http://vancouverjazz.com/forums/archive/index.php/t-98.html

8. Ted Gioia, *West Coast Jazz, Modern Jazz in California 1945–1960* (Berkley: University of California Press, 1992), p. 77.

9. As told to the author, Richard Lawn, in an interview in Austin, Texas, September 2000.

10. Terry Gross interview of Stan Getz for WHYY and NPR, June 1, 1990.

11. *The Birth of Third Stream*, liner notes by Gunther Schuller (p. 19–20), Columbia/Legacy, CK 64 929, 1996.

12. Ibid.

13. Lennie Tristano, "Why Don't They Leave Me Alone?" *Down Beat*, July 10, 1969, p. 28.

Additional Sources

David Adler, "Give the Drummer Some," *Jazz Times*, June 2004, pp. 68–74.

Larry Blumenfeld, "The Good Reverend Caine," *Jazziz*, January 2001, pp. 38–42.

Bob Blumenthal, "When Worlds Collide," *Jazz Times*, January/February 2001, pp. 51–53.

Michael J. Budds, *Jazz in the Sixties: The Expansion of Musical Resources and Techniques* (Iowa: University of Iowa Press, 1978), pp. 85–90.

Wayne Delacoma, "Stravinsky Dug Jazz," *Jazziz*, January 2001, pp. 43–45.

Clifton Daniel (editor), *Chronicle of America* (Mount Kisco: Chronicle Publications, 1989).

Scott DeVaux, "Harmonic Convergence," *Jazziz*, January 2001, p. 36.

Joe Goldberg, *Jazz Masters of the 50s* (New York: Da Capo Press, 1965), pp. 9–23, 113–131, 154–167.

Ted Gioia, "Cool Jazz and West Coast Jazz," in *The Oxford Companion to Jazz*, edited by Bill Kirchner (New York: Oxford University Press, 2000), pp. 332–342.

Ted Gioia, *The History of Jazz* (New York: Oxford University Press, 1997), pp. 277–313.

Ted Gioia, *West Coast Jazz, Modern Jazz in California 1945–1960* (Berkley: University of California Press, 1992), pp. 60–99, 167–199.

Ira Gitler, *Jazz Masters of the 40s* (New York: Da Capo Press, 1966) pp. 226–261.

Charlotte Greig, *100 Best Selling Albums of the '50s*, New York: Barnes and Noble Books, 2004)

Richard Marshall (editor), *Great Events of the 20th Century* (Pleasantville, NY: The Reader's Digest Association, Inc., 1977).

Brad Mehldau, "Brahms, Interpretation and Improvisation," *Jazz Times*, January/February 2001, pp. 55–56, 180–181.

Burton Peretti, *Jazz in American Culture* (Chicago: Ivan R. Dee, 1997), pp. 109–133.

Brian Priestley, *Jazz on Record* (New York: Billboard Books, 1991), pp. 94–121.

J. Bradford Robinson, "Lennie Tristano," in *The New Grove Dictionary of Jazz*, edited by Barry Kernfeld (New York: St. Martin's Press, 1995), pp. 1218–1219.

Bill Shoemaker, "Third Stream From the Source: Gunther Schuller," *Jazz Times*, January/February 2001, p. 54.

Lucy Tauss, "When Worlds Collide," *Jazziz*, January 2001, pp. 48–49.

Terry Teachout, "Jazz and Classical Music: The Third Stream and Beyond," in *The Oxford Companion to Jazz*, edited by Bill Kirchner (New York: Oxford University Press, 2000), pp. 343–356.

Robert Walser (editor), *Keeping Time, Readings in Jazz History* (New York: Oxford University Press, 1999), pp. 195–249.

Martin Williams, *Jazz Masters in Transition* (New York: Da Capo Press, 1970), pp. 112–119.

11 TRADITION MEETS THE AVANT-GARDE: MODERNS AND EARLY POSTMODERNS COEXIST

Notes

1. David H. Rosenthal, *Hard Bop: Jazz and Black Music 1955–1965* (New York: Oxford University Press, 1992), p. 73.

2. Isaac Newton, *Compton's Interactive Encyclopedia* (West Sussex: The Learning Company, 1998).

3. Burton W. Peretti, *Jazz in American Culture* (Chicago: Ivan R. Dee, 1997), p. 107.

4. David H. Rosenthal, *Hard Bop: Jazz and Black Music 1955–1965* (New York: Oxford University Press, 1992), pp. 118, 163.

5. Ibid., p. 36.

6. Brian Priestly, *Jazz on Record* (New York: Billboard Books, 1991), p. 137.

7. David H. Rosenthal, *Hard Bop: Jazz and Black Music 1955–1965* (New York: Oxford University Press, 1992), pp. 62–73.

8. Ibid., pp. 117–129.

9. Ibid., p. 73.

10. Ibid., p. 129.

11. Don DeMicheal, "Cannonball Adderley The Responsibilities of Success," *Down Beat*, June 21, 1962 (reprint January 1996), pp. 34–35.

12. David H. Rosenthal, *Hard Bop: Jazz and Black Music 1955–1965* (New York: Oxford University Press, 1992), p. 111.

13. Mary Klages, "Postmodernism"; www.colorado.edu/English/ENGL2012Klages/pomo.html

14. A.B. Spellman, *Black Music: Four Lives* (New York: Schocken Books, 1971), p. 119.

15. John Litweiler, *Ornette Coleman: A Harmolodic Life* (New York: Da Capo, 1994), p. 46.

16. Peter Niklas Wilson, *Ornette Colemann, His Life and Music* (Berkley: Berkley Hills Books, 1999), p. 35.

17. John Litweiler, *Ornette Coleman: A Harmolodic Life* (New York: Da Cappo Press, 1994), p. 75.

18. Don Cherry, *Mind and Time*, liner notes, Contemporary 7569, reissued on OJC OJCCD-342-2.

19. Pete Welding, review of *Free Jazz, Down Beat*, January, 1962, in *Keeping Time Readings in Jazz History*, edited by Robert Walser (New York: Oxford, 1999), pp. 253–255.

20. Ibid.

21. John A. Tynan, "Double View of a Double Quartet," *Down Beat*, January 18, 1962, p. 28.

22. Charles Mingus, *Beneath the Underdog* (New York: Alfred A. Knopf, 1971), in *Keeping Time, Readings in Jazz History*, edited by Robert Walser (New York: Oxford University Press, 1999), p. 225.

23. David H. Rosenthal, *Hard Bop: Jazz and Black Music 1955–1965* (New York: Oxford University Press, 1992), p. 152.

24. Ted Gioia, *The History of Jazz* (New York: Oxford University Press, 1997), p. 330.

25. David H. Rosenthal, *Hard Bop: Jazz and Black Music 1955–1965* (New York: Oxford University Press, 1992), p. 83.

26. Ibid.

27. Oscar Peterson, *A Jazz Odyssey* (New York: Continuum, 2002), p. 328.

28. David H. Rosenthal, *Hard Bop: Jazz and Black Music 1955–1965* (New York: Oxford University Press, 1992), p. 130.

29. Ibid., p. 84.

Additional Sources

Julian Cannonball Adderley, "Cannonball Looks at Ornette Coleman," *Down Beat*, May 26, 1960, pp. 20–21.

John Chilton, "Jimmy Smith," in *The New Grove Dictionary of Jazz*, edited by Barry Kernfeld (New York: St. Martin's Press, 1995), pp. 1138–1139.

Clifton Daniel (editor), *Chronicle of America* (Mount Kisco: Chronicle Publications, 1989).

Ted Gioia, *West Coast Jazz, Modern Jazz in California 1945–1960* (Berkley: University of California Press, 1992), pp. 331–359.

Don Heckman, "Inside Ornette Coleman Pt. I," *Down Beat*, September 9, 1965, pp. 13–15.

Don Heckman, "Inside Ornette Coleman Pt. II," *Down Beat*, December 16, 1965, pp. 20–21.

Richard Marshall (editor), *Great Events of the 20th Century* (Pleasantville, NY: The Reader's Digest Association, Inc., 1977).

Charles Mingus, "Mingus on Ornette Coleman," *Down Beat*, May 26, 1960, p. 21.

John Litweiler, *Ornette Coleman, A Harmolodic Life* (New York: Da Capo Press, 1994).

John Litweiler, *The Freedom Principle, Jazz After 1958* (New York: William Morrow and Co., 1984), pp. 31–58.

Burton Peretti, *Jazz in American Culture* (Chicago: Ivan R. Dee, 1997), pp. 109–133.

Lewis Porter, "Wes Montgomery," in *The New Grove Dictionary of Jazz*, edited by Barry Kernfeld (New York: St. Martin's Press, 1995), pp. 792–793.

Brian Priestley, *Jazz on Record* (New York: Billboard Books, 1991), pp. 122–145.

David H. Rosenthal, *Hard Bop: Jazz and Black Music 1955–1965* (New York: Oxford University Press, 1992).

Gene Seymour, "Hard Bop," in *The Oxford Companion to Jazz*, edited by Bill Kirchner (New York: Oxford University Press), pp. 373–388.

A.B. Spellman, *Black Music: Four Lives* (New York: Schocken Books, 1971), pp. 71–150.

Robert Walser (editor), *Keeling Time, Readings in Jazz History* (New York: Oxford University Press, 1999), pp. 253–293.

Martin Williams, *The Jazz Tradition* (New York: Oxford University Press, 1970), pp. 172–182.

Martin Williams, "Ornette Coleman 10 Years After," *Down Beat*, December 1969, pp. 24–25.

Ollie Wilson, "Clifford Brown," in *The New Grove Dictionary of Jazz*, edited Barry Kernfeld (New York: St. Martin's Press, 1995), pp. 156–157.

Peter Niklas Wilson, *Ornette Coleman: His Life and Music* (Berkley: Berkley Hills Books, 1999).

12 MILES AND MILES OF MILES: MILES DAVIS AND HIS SIDEMEN REDEFINE POSTMODERN JAZZ

Notes

1. Miles Davis and Quincy Troupe, "Miles Davis Speaks His Mind," in *Keeping Time, Readings in Jazz History*, edited by Robert Walser (New York: Oxford University Press, 1999), p. 367.
2. Burton Peretti, *Jazz in American Culture* (Chicago: Ivan R. Dee, 1997), pp. 146–154.
3. Martin Williams, *The Jazz Tradition* (New York: Oxford University Press, 1970 reprint), p. 156.
4. Miles Davis and Quincy Troupe, *Miles, The Autobiography* (New York: Simon and Schuster, 1989), p. 119.
5. Miles Davis and Quincy Troupe, "Miles Davis Speaks His Mind," in *Keeping Time, Readings in Jazz History*, edited by Robert Walser (New York: Oxford University Press, 1999), p. 367.
6. Ibid., p. 366.
7. Miles Davis and Quincy Troupe, *Miles, The Autobiography* (New York: Simon and Schuster, 1989), p. 220.
8. Ibid., p. 104.
9. Ibid., p. 116.
10. Stephanie Stein Crease, *Gil Evans: Out of the Cool, His Life and Music* (Chicago: A Cappella Books, 2002), p. 197.
11. Ibid., p. 199.
12. Todd Coolman, *The Quintet*, liner notes on *Miles Davis Quintet 1965–1968*, Columbia/Legacy.
13. Miles Davis and Quincy Troupe, *Miles, The Autobiography* (New York: Simon and Schuster, 1989), p. 271.
14. Ibid., p. 272
15. Ibid., p. 297.
16. Ibid., p. 298.
17. Ibid.
18. Ibid., p. 299.
19. Ibid., p. 200.
20. Ibid., p. 352.
21. Ibid., p. 322.
22. Ibid., p. 205.
23. David H. Rosenthal, *Hard Bop Jazz and Black Music 1955–1965* (New York: Oxford University Press, 1992), p. 147.
24. Ted Gioia, *The History of Jazz* (New York: Oxford University Press, 1997), p. 245.
25. David H. Rosenthal, *Hard Bop Jazz and Black Music 1955–1965* (New York: Oxford University Press, 1992), p. 197.
26. Bill Shoemaker, "John Coltrane, Giant Steps," *Down Beat*, September 1989, p. 57.
27. Brian Priestley, *Jazz on Record* (New York: Billboard Books, 1991), p. 128.
28. Peter Watrous, "John Coltrane, A Life Supreme," *Musician*, July 12, 1987, p. 106.
29. Don DeMicheal, "John Coltrane and Eric Dolphy Answer the Critics," *Down Beat*, April 12, 1962 (in reprint July 12, 1979), pp. 16, 52, 53.
30. Don De Michael, "John Coltrane and Eric Dolphy Answer the Jazz Critics," *Down Beat*, July 1994 (reprint from November 23, 1961 by John Tynan), p. 72.
31. Ibid., p. 73.
32. Don DeMicheal, "John Coltrane and Eric Dolphy Answer the Critics," *Down Beat*, April 12, 1962 (in reprint July 12, 1979), pp. 16, 52, 53.
33. Lewis Porter, *John Coltrane His Life and Music* (Ann Arbor: The University of Michigan Press, 1999), p. 204.
34. Howard Mandel, *Down Beat*, July 12, 1979, p. 15.
35. *Down Beat*, December 1966.
36. Harvey Pekar, "Miles Davis: 1964–1969 Recordings," in *A Miles Davis Reader*, edited by Bill Kirchner (Washington: Smithsonian Institution Press, 1997), p. 166.
37. Miles Davis and Quincy Troupe, *Miles, The Autobiography* (New York: Simon and Schuster, 1989), p. 273.
38. Ibid., pp. 273–274.
39. Don Heckman and Wayne Shorter, liner notes, *Speak No Evil*, 1964, Blue Note CDP7 46509 2.

Additional Sources

Bob Belden, "Miles Davis," in *The Oxford Companion to Jazz*, edited by Bill Kirchner (New York: Oxford University Press, 2000), pp. 389–402.

Bob Belden and John Ephland, "Miles Davis, What Was That Note?" *Down Beat*, December 1995, pp. 16–22.

Joachim Berendt, *The Jazz Book, From New Orleans to Rock and Free Jazz* (New York: Lawrence Hill and Co., 1973), pp. 92–117.

Bitches Brew, liner notes by Carlos Santana, Michael Cuscuna, Ralph J. Gleason, Qunicy Troupe, and Bob Belden, Columbia/Legacy, 1998.

Marc Crawford, "Miles Davis and Gil Evans, Portrait of a Friendship," *Down Beat*, February 1994 (reprint from February 12, 1961), pp. 28–29.

Clifton Daniel (editor), *Chronicle of America* (Mount Kisco: Chronicle Publications, 1989).

Down Beat, September 1989, pp. 74–92.

Down Beat, "Louder Than Words," June 1998, pp. 20–27.

Leonard Feather, "Miles Davis: Miles and the Fifties," *Down Beat*, March 1995 (reprint from July 2, 1964), pp. 36–39.

Pat Harris, "Nothing But Bop? 'Stupid,' Says Miles," *Down Beat*, July 1994 (reprint from January 27, 1950).

Bill Kirchner (editor), *A Miles Davis Reader* (Washington: Smithsonian Institution Press, 1997).

John Litweiler, *The Freedom Principle, Jazz After 1958* (New York: William Morrow and Co., Inc., 1984), pp. 59–128.

Richard Marshall (editor), *Great Events of the 20th Century* (Pleasantville: The Reader's Digest Association, 1977).

Dan Ouellette, "*Bitches Brew*, The Making of the Most Revolutionary Jazz Album in History," *Down Beat*, December 1999, pp. 32–37.

Dan Ouellette, "Dark Prince in Twilight, Band Members and Associates Discuss the Last Years of Miles Davis' Life," *Down Beat*, May 2001, pp. 25–29.

Burton Peretti, *Jazz in American Culture* (Chicago: Ivan R. Dee, 1997), pp. 134–176.

Gene Santoro, "Miles Davis, the Enabler Pt. II," *Down Beat*, November 1988, pp. 16–19.

Greg Tate, "The Electric Miles Pt. I," *Down Beat*, July 1983, pp. 16–18.

Peter Watrous, "John Coltrane: A Life Supreme," *Musician*, July 1987, pp. 103–112, 136–138.

13 THE ELECTRIC 1970s AND 1980s

Notes

1. Carlos Santana, "Remembering Miles and *Bitches Brew*," *Miles Davis the Complete Bitches Brew Sessions*, liner notes, 1989, p. 8, Columbia/Legacy.
2. Bill Milkowski, "Jazz Plugs In," *Down Beat*, July 1994, p. 58.
3. Pat Metheny, *Down Beat*, January 1985.
4. Stuart Nicholson, *Jazz–Rock: A History* (New York: Schirmer Books, 1998), pp. 166–181.
5. Larry Birnbaum, "Weather Report Answers Its Critics," *Down Beat*, July 1994, p. 60 (reprinted from February 8, 1979).
6. Stuart Nicholson, *Jazz–Rock: A History* (New York: Schirmer Books, 1998), p. 165.
7. Ibid., p. 186.
8. Josef Woodward, "Storm Surge, The Rise and Fall of Weather Report, The Best Jazz Band of the Past 30 Years," *Down Beat*, January 2001, p. 24.
9. Stuart Nicholson, *Jazz–Rock: A History* (New York: Schirmer Books, 1998), p. 176.
10. Elaine Guregian, "Weather Report," *Down Beat*, September 1989, p. 86.
11. Stuart Nicholson, *Jazz–Rock: A History* (New York: Schirmer Books, 1998), p. 184.
12. Ibid., p. 186.
13. Ibid.
14. *Down Beat*, August 21, 1971, p. 15.
15. Herbie Hancock, *Head Hunters*, liner notes, Columbia/Legacy CK65123, 1996.
16. Scott Thompson, *Head Hunters*, liner notes, p. 9, Columbia/Legacy CK65123, 1996.
17. Stuart Nicholson, *Jazz–Rock: A History* (New York: Schirmer Books, 1998), p. 136.
18. Ibid., p. 149.
19. Ibid., p. 200.
20. Ibid., p. 202.
21. John Toner, "Chick Corea: Return To Forever," *Down Beat*, July 1994, p. 66 (reprinted from March 28, 1974).
22. Robin Tolleson, "David Sanborn: The Voice of Emotion," *Down Beat*, July 1994, p. 64 (reprint from March 1983).

23. Zan Stewart, "Chuck Mangione," *Music America Magazine*, Vol. 1, No. 4, January 1977, pp. 19–20.
24. John McDonough, "The Feelings Back," review in *Down Beat*, June 1999, p. 56.

Additional Sources

Christopher Collins, "Joe Zawinul," *Jazz Education Journal*, May/June 2002, pp. 45–50.
Clifton Daniel (editor), *Chronicle of America* (Mount Kisco: Chronicle Publications, 1989).
Ted Gioia, *The History of Jazz* (New York: Oxford University Press, 1997), pp. 64–374.
Richard Marshall (editor), *Great Events of the 20th Century* (Pleasantville: The Reader's Digest Association, 1977).
Barry Kernfeld, "Grover Washington, Jr.," in *The New Grove Dictionary of Jazz*, edited by Barry Kernfeld (New York: St. Martin's Press, 1995), p. 1265.
Stuart Nicholson, *Jazz–Rock: A History* (New York: Schirmer Books, 1998).
Burton Peretti, *Jazz In American Culture* (Chicago: Ivan R. Dee, 1997), pp. 155–176.
Brian Priestley, *Jazz on Record* (New York: Billboard Books, 1991) p. 158.
Zan Stewart, "Chuck Mangione," *Music America Magazine*, Vol. 1, No. IV, January 1977, pp. 16–20.
Patrick T. Will, "Steps Ahead," in *The New Grove Dictionary of Jazz*, edited by Barry Kernfeld (New York: St. Martin's Press, 1995), p. 1159.

14 The Unplugged, Eclectic 1970s and 1980s

Notes

1. Pat Metheny, *Down Beat*, September 1989, p. 78 (reprint from 1978).
2. Bob Suter, "How ECM Records Has Made Jazz Work For It," *Jazz*, Vol. 4, No. 1, Winter 1979, p. 65.
3. Ibid.
4. Ibid., p. 67.
5. Ibid., p. 68.
6. Robert Walser, *Keeping Time, Readings in Jazz History* (New York: Oxford University Press, 1999), p. 414.
7. Ibid., p. 412.
8. Ibid., p. 414.
9. Robert L. Doerschuk, "Keith Jarrett, Provocative Reflections on Creativity and the Crisis in Modern Music," *Keyboard*, March 1993, p. 83.
10. Lewis Porter, *Jazz: A Century of Change, Readings and New Essays* (New York: Schirmer Books, 1997), p. 269.
11. Bill Dobbins, "Cecil Taylor," in *The New Grove Dictionary of Jazz,* edited by Barry Kernfeld (New York: St. Martin's Press, 1995), p. 1190.
12. A.B. Spellman, *Black Music: Four Lives* (New York: Schocken Books, 1971), p. 29.
13. Bill Dobbins, "Cecil Taylor," in *The New Grove Dictionary of Jazz*, edited by Barry Kernfeld (New York: St. Martin's Press, 1995), p. 1190.
14. *Long Yellow Road Toshiko Akiyoshi—Lew Tabackin Big Band*, liner notes by Leonard Feather, RCA, 1976.
15. Ibid.
16. Art Lange, "The 80's," *Down Beat*, September 1989, p. 88.
17. Robert Walser (editor), *Keeping Time, Readings in Jazz History* (New York: Oxford University Press, 1999), p. 333.

Additional Sources

Clifton Daniel (editor), *Chronicle of America* (Mount Kisco: Chronicle Publications, 1989).
Ted Gioia, *The History of Jazz* (New York: Oxford University Press, 1997), pp. 377–395.
Nat Hentoff, *Jazz Is* (New York: Limelight Editions, 1991), pp. 225–233.
Peter Keepnews, "Jazz Since 1968," in *The Oxford Companion to Jazz*, edited by Bill Kirchner (New York: Oxford University Press, 2000), pp. 488–501.
Barry Kernfeld, "Grover Washington, Jr.," in *The New Grove Dictionary of Jazz*, edited by Barry Kernfeld (New York: St. Martin's Press, 1995), p. 1265.
John Litweiler, *The Freedom Principle: Jazz After 1958* (New York: William Morrow and Co., 1984), pp. 200–221.
Richard Marshall (editor), *Great Events of the 20th Century* (Pleasantville, NY: The Reader's Digest Association, 1977).
Tom Moon, "Keith Jarrett," *Jazz Times*, May 1999, pp. 38–46.
Stuart Nicholson, *Jazz–Rock, A History* (New York: Schirmer Books, 1998).

Burton Peretti, *Jazz in American Culture* (Chicago: Ivan R. Dee, 1997), pp. 155–176.

Lewis Porter, *Jazz: A Century of Change, Readings and New Essays* (New York: Schirmer Books, 1997), pp. 219–273.

Brian Priestley, *Jazz On Record* (New York: Billboard Books, 1991), pp. 150–151, 167, 172–194.

Zan Stewart, "Chuck Mangione," *Music America Magazine*, Vol. 1, No. IV, January 1977, pp. 16–20.

The Complete Solid State Recordings of the Thad Jones/Mel Lewis Orchestra, liner notes by Bill Kirchner, Mosaic Records.

Patrick T. Will, "Steps Ahead," in *The New Grove Dictionary of Jazz*, edited by Barry Kernfeld (New York: St. Martin's Press, 1995), p. 1159.

15 JAZZ FOR A NEW CENTURY

Notes

1. Rafi Zabor and Vic Garbaini, "Wynton Vs. Herbie: The Purist and the Crossbreeder Duke it Out," *Musician* (March 1985) in *Keeping Time, Readings in Jazz History*, edited by Robert Walser (New York: Oxford University Press, 1999), p. 342.
2. Robert L. Doerschuk, "Keith Jarrett: Provocative Reflections on Creativity and the Crisis in Modern Music," *Keyboard*, March 1993, p. 89.
3. Bob Blumenthal, "The Eighties," *Jazz Times*, September 2000, p. 47.
4. Tim Hagans (2004)—used by permission.
5. "Cassandra Wilson—Eclectic Vocalist," *New Yorker*, December 2002.
6. *Jazz Times*, Vol. 38, No. 7, September 2008, p. 43.
7. *Time* magazine, as quoted at: www.mariaschneider.com/about.aspx
8. Maria Schneider, *Concert in the Garden* (CD notes), (New York: ArtistShare 0001, 2004).
9. Stuart Nicholson, "British Jazz," *Jazz Education Journal*, January 2008, p. C8.
10. Dan Ouellette, "Jason Moran Adventurous Soul," *Down Beat*, August 2011, p. 22.
11. Ibid., p. 25.

Additional Sources

Whitney Balliett, "Young Guns," *New Yorker*, Vol. 71, June 5, 1955, pp. 97–99.

Bob Blumenthal, "Survival of the Biggest," *Jazz Times*, September 1998, pp. 28–31, 35, 50.

Bourne, Michael, "Global Jazz Boosters Demand More U.S. Music," *Down Beat*, January 1980, pp. 25–27, 60–63.

Clifton Daniel (editor), *Chronicle of America* (Mount Kisco: Chronicle Publications, 1989).

Francis Davis, "Like Young," *Atlantic Monthly*, July 1996, pp. 92–98.

Ted Gioia, *The History of Jazz* (New York: Oxford University Press, 2011), pp. 369–388.

Down Beat, October 2006, p. 22.

Down Beat, August 2007, p. 24.

Down Beat, February 2007, p. 20.

Down Beat, February 2009, p. 19.

Alex Dutilh, "France, USA—A Jazz Life," *Jazz Education Journal*, January 2007, pp. C2–C8.

"Year in Review 2008," *Jazz Times*, February 2009.

"Year in Review 2007," *Jazz Times*, February 2008.

"Year in Review 2006," *Jazz Times*, February 2007.

"Year in Review 2004," *Jazz Times*, February 2005.

Jazz Times, September 2008, pp. 43–44.

Martin Johnson, "Acid Jazz: Where the Past & Future Collid," *Down Beat*, April 1997, pp. 16–21.

Richard Marshall (editor), *Great Events of the 20th Century* (Pleasantville, NY: The Reader's Digest Association, 1977).

Bill Milkowski, "Wynton Marsalis and John Zorn," *Jazz Times*, March 2000, pp. 28–39, 118–121.

Stuart Nicholson, "British Jazz," *Jazz Education Journal*, January 2008, pp. C2–C8.

Bobby Reed, "Famous Jazz Families," *Down Beat*, January 2012, p. 8.

Johan Scherwin, "Nordic Jazz," *Jazz Education Journal*, February 2006, pp. C2–C7.

Robert Walser, *Keeping Time, Readings in Jazz History* (New York: Oxford University Press, 1999), pp. 389–424.

Peter Watrous, "The Nineties," *Jazz Times*, September 2000, pp. 51–55.

Andrew Solomon, "The Jazz Martyr," *New York Times Magazine*, February 9, 1997, pp. 32–35.

Index

Within strings of page references, major discussions of topics are given in **bold**. Album, track, and publication titles are filed under the first significant word, thus *Love Supreme, A*, "Shape of Things, The," and "Fiesta, La." Track titles are followed by the composer(s) in brackets, and album titles by the main artist(s).

abstract art 227
accents 18, 37, 116
"acid jazz" 265, 313, 325, 329, 371, 372–373; "groove music" 373
acoustic jazz rebirth 330, **343–344**, 357–358; big bands 356–357; ECM sound **344–345**, 346, 369, 386; innovators 345–355
Adderley, Julian Cannonball 264, 265, 289, 290, 292
aesthetics *see* art(s)
African influences 6, **6–8**, 16–17, 34–35, **45–49**, 292, 329; blue notes 24–25; work songs/field hollers 24, 54–55; *see also* Afro-Latin/Caribbean influences; blues
"Afro Blue" (Santamaria) 308
Afro-Latin/Caribbean influences **49–54**, 61, 294, 333–334, **382–384**; bossa nova 241–245; "Spanish tinge" 89, **155**; *see also* "Cubop"
"Airmail Special" (Goodman–Mundy–Christian) 150
Akiyoshi, Toshiko (b. 1929) **356–357**, 377
"Alabama" (Coltrane) 309
aleatoric ("chance") music 272, 273
"All-American Rhythm Section", Basie **163–164**, 165–166
All Rise (Marsalis) 247, 351
Almeida, Laurindo 242
"altissimo" notes 38
American Federation of Musicians (AFofM) 190–191

Ammons, Albert 111
amplification 129, 149
Animation/Imagination (Hagans) 372
"Anthropology" (Parker) 204
Armstrong, Lilian Hardin 86–87, 100
Armstrong, Louis (1901–1971) 18, 27, 37, 39, 63, 81, 86–88, **91–94**, 100, 105, 117, 127, 130, 133, 194, 226
arpeggios 82; arpeggiated/linear styles 136, 165
arrangements (charts) 36–37; bebop 196, **197–199**; cool jazz 231; hard bop 257; head charts, blues-riff style 131, 162–163; Swing Era 130, **131–132**, 133
Arshawsky, Arthur *see* Shaw, Artie
art and literature: **46–47**, 77, 227, 256
Art Ensemble 274, 353
articulation 37, 135–136
"Artists Ought to Be Writing" (Moran) 390–391
Ascension (Coltrane) 310–311
Association for the Advancement of Creative Music (AACM) 274
atonality 19
aural tradition 36
Austin High Gang 103, 147
avant-garde jazz 210, 256; free-jazz experimentalists, 1970s 352–355

Babbit, Milton 245–246
backgrounds 163

Baker, Chet (1929–1988) **233–235**, 248
banjos 68, 82
Baroque music 23
bars *see* measures/bars
Basie, William "Count" (1904–1984) 18, 128, 142, 161, **162–164**, 165–166
bass instruments 82, 197; fretless electric bass 326–327; walking bass lines 91, 129, 142–143, 144, 164, 239
Bauza, Mario 155, 213, 214
beat generation 227
Beatlemania 286–287
beats 15; *see also* rhythm sections
bebop (bop/rebop) 10, 29, 135–136, 150, 192, 198, **217**, 230, 287–288, 337, 385; and acoustic rebirth 350–352; and Afro-Latin/Cuban music ("Cubop") 213, **213–217**, 268–270; lifestyle/characteristics/instrumentation **192–193**, **196–199**, 230; main innovators 199–206; New York clubs 194–196; rhythm section innovators 207–210; singers 211–212; *see also* hard bop
Bechet, Sidney (1897–1959) 67, 80, **94**, 309
Beiderbecke, Bix (1903–1931) 103, **105–106**, 107–108
Belden, Bob 372, **373**
bend 38
Berlin, Irving 79, 131

big bands 39, 109, 117, 127–128,
    189–192; all-female 380; of the 1950s
    268–270; of the 1970s and 1980s
    356–357; *see also* Swing Era
Birdland, New York 195, 202
"Birdland" (Zawinul) 328
Birds of Fire (Mahavishnu Orchestra) 332
Birth of the Cool (Davis–Evans) **231–232**,
    247, 294
Bitches Brew (Davis) 301–302
"black and tans" 77, 100
"Black Bottom Stomp" (Morton) **89–90**,
    91
Blakey, Art (1919–1990) 255, **258–260**,
    297, 345, 350
Blanton, Jimmy 142–143, 144, 197
Blesh, Rudi 113
Blood on the Fields (Marsalis) 351
Blood, Sweat and Tears (BS&T) 300,
    323–324
Bloom, Jane Ira 377, 378
Blue Devils 161, 164
Blue Train (Coltrane) 306–307, 308
blues 8, 22, 39, **56–57**, 88, 89; blue
    notes/blues scale 24–25; blues-riff style
    162–163; 12-bar blues form 42, **57**,
    62, 63
"Body and Soul"
    (Green–Sour–Heyman–Eyton) 23, 37,
    135, **137**, **171**, 199, **375–376**
Bolden, Buddy 67, 80, 81
"Boogie Stop Shuffle" (Mingus) 278, **277**
boogie-woogie piano style 10, 110–111
bop *see* bebop; hard bop
bossa nova dance form 241–245
Botti, Chris 371
brass bands 67–68
brass instruments 34, 37, **38**, 80–81, 82,
    128–129, 228–229, 246, 337, 338
Braxton, Anthony 210, 333, 353
Brazilian bossa nova 241–245
Brecker, Michael (1949–2007) and
    Randy **336**, **367–369**, 370
bridges/channels 22
Brookmeyer, Bob 234
Brown Brothers 106
Brown, Clifford (1930–1956) 210, 258,
    261–262, 263
Brubeck, Dave (b. 1920) **235–237**, 248,
    279

cakewalk dance form 64
California *see* West Coast
call and response format **48–49**, 55–56,
    57, 62, 63, 131, 143–144, 163, 292
Calloway, Cab 155, 199
"Camptown Races" (Foster) 64, 65

Capone, Al 112
Captain Marvel (Getz) 333
Caribbean *see* Afro-Latin/Caribbean
    influences
Carmichael, Hoagy 99, 106, 132
Carnegie Hall, New York 169, 177
Carney, Harry 143, 144
"Carolina Shout" (Johnson) 115–116
Carpenter, John Alden 79
Carrington, Terri Lyne 378
Carter, Regina 378, 383–384
Carter, Ron 296–300
Cascales, John *see* Richards, Johnny
Chambers, Paul 289
"Chameleon" (Hancock) 329, **331**
"chance" (aleatoric) music 272, 273
channels/bridges 22
Charleston dance form 52, 53
charts *see* arrangements
Chernoff, John Miller 45
Cherry, Don 271, 272
Chicago (band) 300, 323
Chicago (city) 10, 89, 99, 118, 147, 177,
    352–353; "jazz age" and the Chicago
    sound 100–113
chord tones, dissonant/consonant 136,
    139
chord voicings 143
chords/chord progressions **20**, 22, 27, 37,
    39, 57, 136, 196, 307 ; blue
    notes/blues scale 24–25
choruses/refrains 22, 27, 39
Christian, Charlie 148, **149–150**, 194
Circle 333
civil rights movement 127, 210, 225, 226,
    255, 257, **264–265**, 286, 322, 352
clarinets *see* woodwind instruments
Clark Monroe's Uptown House, New
    York 194–196, 210, 217
Clarke, Kenny (1914–1985) 195, 197,
    209–210
Clarke, Stanley 333, 335
classical influences **23–24**, 148, 233,
    235–236, 290, 351, 386; aleatoric
    ("chance") music 272, 273; the ECM
    sound 334–345; third-stream jazz
    245–248
clavé rhythm 53–54
Clef Club Band 3
Clinton, Bill 363
clubs and cabarets 76, 77–78, 112; bebop,
    New York 77, 117, 138, **194–196**,
    217; *see also* dance halls
codas/tags 39
Cole, Nat "King" 153, 197
Coleman, Ornette (b. 1930) 19, 256,
    270, **271–274**, 278, 310

Collier, James Lincoln 23, 109, 279
Coltrane, John (1926–1967) 205, 289,
    290, 292, **306–311**
"common man" theme 127
communication, music as 49
communism 226
comping, piano 130, 164, 197, 203,
    208
computers *see* digital revolution
Concert in the Garden (Schneider) 378,
    379–380, 381
conga dance form 52, 155
Congo Square, New Orleans 54, 143
consonant chord tones 27, 136
contrafacts, bebop 196
contrapuntal music *see* counterpoint
Conversations with Myself (Evans) 239
Cook, Will Marion 68, 94
cool jazz 10, 227, 230, 256; bossa nova
    241–245; characteristics 228–230;
    East/West Coast innovators **231–241**,
    248; third-stream jazz 245–248
coon songs 62
Cooper, Jack 42
"copy cats" 29
Corea, Chick (b. 1941) 289, 300, 332,
    333–335, 345
cornets *see* brass instruments
Cotton Club, New York 77, 117,
    138
"Countdown" (Coltrane) 307
counterpoint 21–22, 235
Creative Orchestra Music 1976 (Braxton)
    353
Creole Jazz Band 86–88
"Creole Rhapsody" (Ellington) 141
Creoles 6, 51, 80
criticism of jazz **78–80**, 100, 273–274
Crossings (Hancock) 329
Cuban Fire Suite (Kenton) 268–269
Cuban influences 53, **382**; *see also*
    Afro-Latin/Caribbean influences
"Cubop" 213, **213–217**, 268–270
"Cuerpo y Alma" *see* "Body and Soul"
Cugat, Xavier 155
"cutting contests" 115, 178
cymbals, drum **34–35**, 130, 297

Dameron, Tadd (1917–1965) **205–206**,
    258
"Dança Illusória" (Schneider) 379–380,
    381
dance bands: "sweet" 102, 127, 153;
    see also big bands; Swing Era
dance forms 15, 20, 22, 47–48, 50, 61,
    294, 379–380; bossa nova 241–245;
    clavé rhythm 53–54; and "Cubop"

213–217; habanera 51–52, 53, 89, 241; and ragtime 52, 64; "Spanish tinge" 89, **155**; tango craze 52–53

dance halls 101, 102, 117, 118–119, 126, 127, 190

Davis, Miles 20, 195, 201, 217, 226, 238, 245, 246, 279, 285, 287, 312, 345–346; *Birth of the Cool* **231–232**, 247, 288, 294; early career 287–289; electronic jazz–rock fusion 300–305; and Gil Evans 294–296; first great quintet and modal jazz 289–293; innovations 305; second great quintet 296–300; sidemen 301, **305–313**, **325–335**

deconstructionism 353–354

DeJohnette, Jack 289, 345, 369, 370

"Delfeayo's Dilemma" (Marsalis) 16, **352**

Depression era 111–112, 117, 126

Desmond, Paul (1924–1977) **236–237**, 248

Di Meola, Al 333, 335

digital revolution 325, 338, 364

"Digression" (Tristano) 247, 251

"Dippermouth Blues" (Oliver–Armstrong) 86, **88**, 131, **134**

dissonance 136, 139

Diva 380

"Dixie Jass Band One-Step" (Jordan–ODJB) 85

Dixieland jazz 10, **81–82**, 177; *see also* "hot" jazz

Dodds, Johnny 92

doit 38

Dolphy, Eric 310

Doo Bop (Davis) 304

Dorsey, Tommy 151

double-time phrases/solo breaks 92, 93, 135

doublers, woodwind **94**, 128

Down Beat magazine 6, 29, 168, 177–178, 194, 273–274, 310, 378, 390

drones (pedal points) 300, 307, 388

drop 38

drug use **193–194**, **279**, 286–287

drum sets/kits **34–36**, 130, 197, 209, 297; *see also* rhythm sections

Durham, Eddie 162–163

Eagle Band 80, 81

East Coast 68; cool jazz innovators 231–233, 238–241; Swing Era innovators 132–150; *see also* New York

"Easy Living" (Robin–Rainger) 212

Eckstine, Billy 194, 199, 211

eclecticism 343–344, 365–366, 374, 375; the ECM sound **334–345**, 346, 369, 386; European musicians 386; free-jazz experimentalists, 1970s 352–355; 21st-century innovators 389–391

ECM (Editions of Contemporary Music) **344–345**, 346, 369, 386

education *see* jazz-education movement

Eicher, Manfred 344–345, 346

"eight to the bar" rhythm 111, 266

"81" (Carter) 300

"El Barrio," New York 50–51

Eldridge, Roy 172, 173–174

electric pianos 333

electronic jazz–rock fusion: Miles Davis 300–305; 1970s 323–335

electronic instruments: keyboards 266, 300, 326, 330; wind 368

Elling, Kurt 377

Ellington, Edward Kennedy "Duke" (1899–1974) 18, 19, 28, 66, 114, 115, 117, 228, 233, 245–246; Swing Era 125, 127, 131–132, **137–146**, 181, 189

emotional content 50

entertainment industry **76–78**, 111–112, **118–119**, 126, 364

"Epistrophy" (Monk) 208

E.S.P. (Davis) 298

Europe, James Reese 3, 6, 51, 68

European influences **23–24**, 50, 64, 108

European musicians 344–345, 347, **384–386**

Evans, Bill (1929–1980) xxiii, 19, 28–29, 229, **238–241**, 289, 290, 292

Evans, Gil 248, **294–296**; *Birth of the Cool* **231–232**, 247, 288, 294

"Every Tub" (Basie–Durham) 16, 18, **165–166**

"Experiment in American Music" 108–109

fall-off 38

fan-funded music 378

"Far East Suite" (Ellington–Strayhorn) 144, 146

Ferguson, Maynard (1928–2006) 142, 270, 356

field hollers 24, 54–55

"Fiesta, La" (Corea) 16, **334**

52nd Street, New York xxiii, xxiv, 196, 217

Filles de Kilimanjaro (Davis) 300, 301

fills 130

Fisk Jubilee Singers 55, 56

Fitzgerald, Ella (1918–1996) **172–174**, 248

flamenco dance form 50

flugelhorns 246, 337, 338

folk songs, racist 62

folklore, music as 50

"For No Reason At All in C" (Beiderbecke–Trumbauer) 107

Ford, Henry and Edsel 99

form 22–23

"Fortune of Fools" *see* "Suerte de los Tontos, La"

free jazz 10, 247, **271–274**, 275, 301–302, 310–311; the ECM sound **344–345**, 346, 369, 386; European musicians 385–386; experimentalists of the 1970s 352–355

Free Jazz (Coleman) 273–274

"Freedom Jazz Dance" (Harris) 300

Freeman, Bud 103

French influences 6, 51, 80

Friars Society Club Orchestra *see* New Orleans Rhythm Kings (NORK)

"From Spirituals to Swing" (1938) 177

functional harmony 20, 291

funeral music 46

funky jazz (soul jazz) **264–265**, 313, 329, 336; guitar and organ trios 265–267

fusion 10, 322–323; jazz–rock 300–305, 323–335; soul/R & B/pop-influenced jazz 336–338

gangsters 4, 77, 112, 117, 160

Garland, Red 289

Garrison, Jimmy 309

Georgia Jazz Band 13, 25

Gershwin, George 115, 131, 196, 294–295

Getz, Stan (1927–1991) 23, 192–194, 229, 242–243, **243–245**, 248, 333

Giant Steps (Coltrane) 306–307

Gilberto, João and Astrud 242, 243, 244–245

Gillespie, John Birks "Dizzy" (1917–1993) 155, 194, 194–195, 199, **199–200**, 288; and "Cubop" 213–217

gliss(ando)/slide 38, 82

Goldkette, Jean 105

"Good Enough to Keep" (Goodman–Mundy–Christian) 150

Goodman, Benny (1909–1986) 103, 104, 118, 128, 132, 145, **147–150**, 151, 177, 178, 194

Gordon, Dexter (1923–1990) **205–206**, 349

gospels 55–56, 336

Granz, Norman 172, 194, 228

Great Depression 111, 112, 117, 126

Great Recession 364

Green, Freddie 35, 163, 164
Grillo, Frank Raul *see* Machito
Grimes, Tiny 174, 175
Grofé, Ferde 108
"groove music" 267, 373
ground rhythms/patterns 34–35, 48
"Guest of Honor, A" (Joplin) 66
guitars 34, 129, 164, 196, 242–243, 303,
    325, 333; guitar and organ trios
    265–267

habanera dance form 51–52, 53, 89,
    241
Hagans, Tim (b. 1954) 372–373
Haitian influences 50–51
"half-valve" effect 38
Hammond, John 59, 147, 148–149, 162,
    177
Hampton, Lionel 148–149, 265
Hancock, Herbie (b. 1940) 175, 264,
    289, 296–300, **313**, **329–331**
Handy, W.C. (1873–1958) 61–62, 63
"Happy Birthday" (Hill) 14, 22
hard bop 10, 210, 256, **278–279**, 307,
    349; characteristics and artists
    256–264; *see also* funky jazz (soul jazz)
Hardin, Lilian 86–87, 100
Hargrove, Roy 382
Harlem, New York **114–117**, 125,
    194–196
"harmolodics" 272
harmonics 138–139; fingerings 306;
    rhythms 20, 130
harmony 19, **20**, 27, 291, 306; *see also*
    chords/chord progressions
Hawkins, Coleman (1904–1969) 37, 117,
    134, **135–137**, 164–165, 194, 199
Haynes, Roy (b. 1925) 204
head charts, blues-riff style 131, 162–163
Head Hunters 329–331
Heavy Weather (Weather Report)
    327–328
"Heebie Jeebies" (Atkins) 39, 93
Henderson, Fletcher (1897–1952) 66,
    117, 127, **133–134**, 147–148
Henderson, Joe 362
Herman, Woody (1913–1987) 142, 153,
    154, 181, 194, 243, 356
"He's Funny That Way" (Holiday) 172
hi-hat (sock) cymbals 34–35, 297
Hines, Earl 93–94, 100, 112, 211
hip-hop 329, 373
Hobson, Wilder 113, 180–181
Hodeir, André 18, 227
Hodges, Johnny 144
Holiday, Billie (1915–1959) 23, 37, 147,
    165, **170–172**

Holland, Dave 369, 370
homophonic textures 19, **21–22**
"Honeysuckle Rose" (Waller–Razaf)
    173–174
Horace-Scope (Silver) 261
Hot Five/Hot Seven bands **91–94**, 105,
    127
"hot" jazz 102, 117, 128, 177; *see also*
    Dixieland jazz
Hubbard, Freddie 297
Hughes, Langston 77, 226

improvisation 7, 19, 20, 22–23, **26–29**,
    41, 49, 57, 84, 208, 247–248, 301,
    385; aleatoric ("chance") music 272,
    273; and bebop 135–136, 196; blue
    notes 24–25; European classical
    influences 23–24; scat singing 39,
    92–93, 173, 211
"improvisational music" 386, **387–388**
In a Silent Way (Davis) 300, 301
"Index" (Gordon) 205, **206**
Indian musicians 387–388
Inner Mounting Flame (Mahavishnu
    Orchestra) 332
instrumental effects/techniques 6–7,
    37–38
instrumentation **36–37**, 104, 198, 229,
    257, 275, 294, 295; bebop 197–199;
    Dixieland jazz 81–82; Swing Era
    128–130
instruments 34; *see also* brass instruments;
    rhythm sections; string instruments;
    woodwind instruments
international musicians 384–388
intervals 24
"Intuition" (Tristano) 16, 247, **248**, 251
"Isfahan" (Ellington–Strayhorn) 144, 146
Iyer, Vijay 387–388

Jack Johnson (Davis) 303
Jackson, Milt 233
"James and Wes" (Smith) 23, **267**
Jarrett, Keith (b. 1945) 17, 22, 289, 345,
    345–348, 363
"jazz": defining 6–8; origins of the word
    4–6
"jazz age" 76–78; Chicago 100–113;
    entertainment industry 118–119;
    Harlem, New York 114–117; *see also*
    Dixieland jazz
Jazz at the Philharmonic series 172, 228
"jazz cannon" *see* repertoire
jazz-education movement 270, 358, 365,
    366, 377, 380, 386, 387
Jazz Messengers **258–260**, 297, 345,
    350

jazz performance 39, 41–43, 275; bebop
    197–199
jazz styles, elements/features/timeline 8,
    10
Jazz Times magazine 378
"Jean Pierre" (Davis) 303–304
Jensen, Ingrid and Christine 380
"Jitney No. 2" (Taylor) 354–355
Jobim, Antonio Carlos 242, 244–245
Johnson, Bunk (1889–1949) 67, 80
Johnson, J.J. (1924–2001) 22, **206**, 245,
    246–247, 248
Johnson, James P. 61, 66, 114, **115–116**
Johnson, Robert (1911–1938) 57–59
Jones, Elvin 309
Jones, Jo 163, 164
Jones, Nora 374
Jones, Philly Joe 289
Jones, Thad (1923–1986) 356
Joplin, Scott (1868–1917) 22, 64, 65,
    66–67
jubilees 55–56
jukeboxes 118, 180, 191

Kansas City 160, **161–166**, 201
Kenton, Stan (1911–1979) 142, 153, 154,
    181, 194, 227, 248, **268–270**, 356
Keppard, Freddie (1889–1933) 80, 81,
    100
keyboard diagrams 19, 24, 290, 388
keyboard instruments 34, 266, 300, 326,
    330, 333
keys/key changes 19, 22, 64
Kind of Blue (Davis) 279, 290, 292–293,
    306
King, Dr. Martin Luther Jr. (1929–1968)
    226, 255, 286
Kirk, Andy 168, **169**
"Klook-mop music" 209
"Ko-Ko" (Ellington) 19, 139, **143–144**,
    145
Konitz, Lee 231–232
Krall, Diana 374
Krupa, Gene 147, 148, 152

LaFaro, Scott 239
LaMothe, Ferdinand Joseph *see* Morton,
    Jelly Roll
Lang, Eddie (1902–1933) 107
language: jazz slang 178, 264; origins of
    word "jazz" 4–6
LaRocca, Nick 83
Latin jazz 10, 53, 155, 214, **382–384**; *see
    also* Afro-Latin/Caribbean influences
laying back 16
"Lazy Bird" (Coltrane) 307, **308**
legato 135–136

Leprechaun (Corea) 335
Lewis, John 209, **233**, 245–246
Lewis, Meade "Lux" 111
Lewis, Mel (1929–1990) 356
"licks" (pre-learned phrases) **27–29**, 231
Lincoln Center Jazz Orchestra 351
"Line for Lyons" (Mulligan) 22, **234**, 235
linear/arpeggiated styles 136, 165
literature *see* art and literature
locked hands piano style 238
loft scene, New York 352
"Lost Your Head Blues" (Smith) 59–60
Louis Armstrong Park, New Orleans 54
Lovano, Joe (b. 1952) 367, 368
Love Supreme, A (Coltrane) 309
Lunceford, Jimmy 126, 128
lyrics 18–19, 39, 191; narration 390–391

McCarthyism 226
McFerrin, Bobby 377
Machito 213, 214
McLaughlin, John (b. 1942) 289, 303, **331–332**
McPartland, Jimmy 103
McShann, Jay 128, 179, 201
magazines *see* press and publishing
Mahanthappa, Rudresh 387–388
Mahavishnu Orchestra 331–332
Maiden Voyage 380
"mainstream" jazz 275; *see also* hard bop
major/minor tonality 19, 24
Malcolm X 286
Mandel, Johnny 213
Mangione, Chuck (b. 1940) 337–338
"Manteca" (Gillespie–Fuller–Pozo) 213, 214–215, **216**
"Maple Leaf Rag" (Joplin) 22, 65, **66–67**
Marable, Fate 91
marches/marching bands 15, 20, 22, 48, 64, **67–68**, 81–82, 84–85
Marsalis, Branford 263, 350, 350–351
Marsalis, Wynton 16, 247, 330, 344, 350, **350–352**, 363
Marsh, Warne 247, 248
"Mary's Idea" (Williams) 169
measures/bars 15, 35, 47–48, 139–140; clavé rhythm 53–54; 12-bar blues form 42, **57**, 62
medieval music 23, 290
melody **18–19**, 27, 48
"Memphis Blues" (Handy) 61
merengue dance form 52
meter 15–16
Metheny, Pat (b. 1954) 3, 325, 343, 345, **369–370**
metronomes 15
"mickey (mouse)" bands 153

micro-tones (quarter-tones) 388
Midwest 66; *see also* Chicago, Illinois
Miles Ahead (Davis–Evans) 294, 295
"Miles Runs the Voodoo Down" (Davis) 301–302
Miles Smiles (Davis) 298–299
Milestone (Moran) 390
Milestones (Davis) 290, 292, 306
military bands 67–68
Miller, Glenn 127–128, 178, 190
Miller, Marcus 304
Milt Jackson Quartet *see* Modern Jazz Quartet (MJQ)
"Mind and Time" (Coleman) 19, 273, **274**
Mingus, Charles (1922–1979) 203, 245, **276–278**, 287
minimalism 303
minor/major tonality 19, 24
minstrel shows 61, 62, 64
Minton's Playhouse, New York 150, 194–196, 203, 207, 209, 210, 217
Mississippi Delta 6, 50, 57–59; *see also* New Orleans
"Mississippi Mud" (Barris–Cavanaugh) 109–110
"Moanin'" (Timmons) 38, 259, **260**, 292
mobsters *see* gangsters
modal jazz **290–291**, 300, 306, 307, 309–310
modern jazz 275, **278–279**; *see also* bebop; cool jazz
Modern Jazz Quartet (MJQ) 209, **233**, 236, 248
moldy figs 177, 194, 231
Monk, Thelonious Sphere (1917–1982) 115, 135, 195, 203, **207–208**, 287, 306
monophonic textures 21–22
Monroe's *see* Clark Monroe's Uptown House
Montgomery, Wes (1923–1968) 265–267
Moody, James 215
"Moon Dreams" (MacGregor–Mercer) 16, 20, **232**
moral values 76, 77, **78–80**, 100; drug/alcohol use **193–194**, **279**, 286–287
Moran, Jason (b. 1975) 390–391
Morello, Joe 236
Morgan, Lee 38, 258, 259–260
Morton, Jelly Roll (1890–1941) 7, 65, **89–91**, 100, 104
Moten, Benny **161**, 162
Motherland (Pérez) 382–384
Motian, Paul 239

motives 48, 163
Motown 300, 301, 324, 336
movie industry 77, 118, 126
Mulligan, Gerry (1927–1996) 231–232, **233–235**, 248
multiculturalism 51, 322, 387
multiphonics 306
music publishers 76
Musical Instrument Digital Interface (MIDI) 325
musicians' unions 190–191
mutes 34, 38, 88, 138
Mwandishi (Hancock) 329
"My Favorite Things" (Coltrane) 309

"Naima" (Coltrane) 307
Navarro, Fats (1923–1950) **205–206**, 217
"New Deal" 127
New Orleans 51, 54, 67, 77–78, **80–81**, 86, 177; *see also* Dixieland jazz
New Orleans Rhythm Kings (NORK) 104–105
"new thing" 273, 278, 310
New York xxiii, xxiv, 50–51, 76, 77, 99, 111, 112, 119, 352, 356; and bebop 193, **194–196**, 217; "jazz age" and Harlem **114–117**, 118, 125; Minton's Playhouse 150, 194–196, 203, 207, 209, 210, 217; Swing Era 132, 133, 138, 139, 141, 148
Newport Jazz Festival 228, 289
Niehaus, Lennie 269
"Night in Tunisia, A" (Gillespie) 214
No Mystery (Return to Forever) 333
Noone, Jimmie/Jimmy 67, 100
notation 68
nuclear age 226
"nut" music 83

O'Farrill, Chico 215, 217
obligato 85
octaves 19
Oliver, Joe "King" (1885–1938) 67, 80, 81, **86–88**, 100
Olympia Brass Band 68
On the Corner (Davis) 303
Onyx, New York 193, 194–196, 217
oral tradition 36
"Orbits" (Shorter) **298–299**, 312
orchestration **36–37**, 132, 138
organ trios 265, **266–267**
Original Dixieland Jazz/Jass Band (ODJB) 5, 77, **83–85**
Ory, Edward "Kid" (1890–1973) 80, **86**, 92, 100
Osgood, Henry 108, 119
ostinato rhythm 111, 266

Ostransky, Leroy 23, 24, 28
"outside" jazz 271, 310
overdubbing 295, 301

Page, Walter 161, 163, 164, 197
"Palladium" (Shorter) **327**, 328
Panassié, Hugo 113
Paris, France 203, 209–210
Parker, Charlie "Bird" (1920–1955) 28, 194, 199, 200, **201–203**, 287–288
Pastorius, Jaco 326–327, 341
peace protests 286, 321
pedal points (drones) 300, 307, 388
Pendergast, Tom 160
pendulum theory 256
"Pent Up House" (Rollins) 16, 39, **263**, 264
percussion instruments *see* rhythm sections; rhythm(s)
Pérez, Danilo (b. 1965) 382–384
performance *see* jazz performance
Peterson, Oscar 175, 279
Petrillo, James 190–191
Pettiford, Oscar (1922–1960) 194, **209**
phrases/phrasing 18, 22, 27, 37, 92, 135, 139–140; pre-learned "licks" **27–29**, 231
piano styles 89, 93, 94; boogie-woogie 110–111; comping 130, 164, 197, 203, 208; ragtime 10, 15, 22, 48, 52, **62**, **64–67**, 68, 84, 89, 90; stride 67, 89, **114–116**
pianos *see* keyboard instruments
Piper, Adrian 390–391
pitch 14, 48
Poem/Suite For Brass (Johnson) 16, 22, **246**, 247
polyphonic textures 19, **21–22**
polyrhythms 16, 17, **47–48**, **53–54**
Ponty, Jean-Luc 332
popular music 19, 22, 140, 191, 227–228, 264–265, **371–373**; Swing Era white bands **151–154**, 178; *see also* fusion
Porgy and Bess (Gershwin) 294–295
Porter, Cole 131
postmodernism 256, **270**, 286–287, 321–323, 343–344, 357–358, 364–366
Potter, Chris 383–384
Powell, Earl "Bud" (1924–1966) 175, **203–204**
Pozo, Chano 213, 214, 215, 217
"Prelude to a Kiss" (Ellington) 140
press and publishing 78–80, 100–101, 119, 177–178, 180
progressions *see* chord progressions
"progressive" jazz 298

Prohibition 77, 117, 127
Puerto Rican influences 50–51

quarter-tones (micro-tones) 388

Ra, Sun 353
race records 118
racial discrimination 62, 126, 127, 226, 309, 385; *see also* civil rights movement
radio broadcasts 26–27, 77, 118–119, 178, 191
ragtime 10, 15, 22, 48, 52, **62**, **64–67**, 68, 84, 89, 90
Rainey, Gertrude "Ma" 13, 25
"Ramblin' on My Mind" (Johnson) 58
Ramey, Gene 35, 160, 161, 170, 174–175, 178, 179–180
Re-Animation Live (Hagans–Belden) 372
rebop *see* bebop
Recession, Great 364
recording industry 26–27, 77, 82, 83, 111, 118, 126, 191, 279; the ECM sound **344–345**, 346, 369, 386; fan-funded music 378; overdubbing 295, 301; Swing Era 180, **220–223**; technological developments 325, 338, 364–365; traditional jazz revival 177
Red Hot Peppers 89–91
Redman, Don 117, 127, 133–134
reharmonization 37
reissue campaigns and CDs 338, 365
religious songs **55–56**, 336
Renaissance music 23
repertoire 196, **131–132**, 275
rests 14
Return to Forever (RTF) 333, 335
"Rhapsody in Blue" (Gershwin) 108–109
rhythm and blues (R & B) 10, 300; soul/R & B–jazz fusion 336–338
"rhythm changes" model 131, 196, 298
rhythm sections 16, 27, 37, 82, 128, 129–130, 142–143, 297; Basie's 163–164, 165–166; bebop innovators 197, **207–210**; drum sets/kits **34–36**, 130, 197, 209, 297
rhythm(s) 7, **14–18**, 20, **47–48**, 68, 111, 129–130, 238–239, 266; Afro-Latin and Caribbean 50, 51–52, 213; bossa nova 241–243; clavé rhythm 53–54; ragtime 64–65; stride piano 115–116; *see also* dance forms
Rich, Buddy (1917–1987) 142, 356
Richards, Johnny 268–270
ride cymbals 34–35
riffs 131, 162–163

Roach, Max (1924–2007) 197, 209, **210**, 261–262, 263
rock–jazz fusion 300–305, 323–335
rock 'n' roll 227–228, 286–287, 300–301
"Rockit" (Hancock) 330
Rollins, Sonny "Newk" (b. 1930) 205, **262–264**
rondo form 22, 64
Roosevelt, Franklin D. 127
Roseland Ballroom, New York 118, 132
Royal Canadians 102, 127
Rubalcalba, Gonzalo 382
rubato 15, 39
rural blues 10
Russell, George 227, 238, 245–246

St. Cyr, Johnny 92
"St. Louis Blues" (Handy) **61–62**, 63, 131
"St. Thomas" (Rollins) 264
samba dance form 155, 241, 242
Sanborn, David (b. 1945) 336
Sandoval, Arturo 382
Savoy Ballroom, New York 117, 118
saxophones *see* woodwind instruments
scales 19, 24–25, 290, 388
scat singing 39, 92–93, 173, 211
Schneider, Maria (b. 1960) 378–380, 381
Schuller, Gunther 16–17, 113, 245–246, 278
Schuur, Diane 374
Scofield, John (b. 1951) 304, **367**, **368**
scoop 38
Seven Steps to Heaven (Davis) 296
shake 38
"Shape of Things, The" (Mahanthappa–Iyer) 387–388
Shaw, Artie (1910–2005) 128, 151, **151–152**, 171, 178
Shaw, Woody 349
"sheets of sound" 306
Shepp, Archie 210
Shorter, Wayne (b. 1933) 258, 289, 297–300, **312–313**, 325–328
shout choruses 39
show tunes 19
sidemen: Davis's 301, **305–313**, **325–335**; Ellington's 142–144; Herman's 154; Jazz Messengers' and Horace Silver's 259; Kenton's 154
Silent Tongues (Taylor) 354–355
Silver, Horace (b. 1928) **258–259**, **260–261**, 264
Sinatra, Frank 191, 248
"Singin' the Blues" (McHugh–Fields) 107–108

singing/singers 109, 153–155, 179, 191, 248; religious songs **55–56**, 336; scat singing 39, 92–93, 173, 211; vocal renaissance, 1990s–2000s 374–377; work songs/field hollers 54–55

Sketches of Spain (Davis–Evans) 294, 295

slang expressions 178, 264

slave-trade routes 51

slide/glissando 38, 82

Smith, Bessie (1894–1937) **59–60**, 61, **63**

Smith, Jimmy 264, **266–267**

Smith, Joe 59–60

Smith, Pine Top 111

"smooth jazz" 337–338, 371; *see also* "acid jazz"

"So Danço Samba" (de Moraes–Jobim) 23, **244–245**

"So What" (Davis) 292, **293**

society bands 68

sock cymbals *see* hi-hat cymbals

soli sections 39, 133

solos/soloists 129, 135–136, 191; and improvisation 27–29; solo breaks 85, 92, 93; *see also* sidemen; singing/singers

"Some Nerve" (Scofield) 367, **368**

"Song for Bilbao" (Metheny) 370

"Sonnet for Brass" (Johnson) 246

song forms/patterns **22–23**, 39, 62, 63, 292

"Sophisticated Lady" (Ellington) 140

soul jazz *see* funky jazz

soul/R & B/pop–jazz fusion 336–338

sound recordings *see* recording industry

Sousa, John Phillip 64, 79

Souza, Luciana 383–384

space race 226, 285, 286

Spalding, Esperanza (b. 1984) 37, 374, **375–376**, 378

Spanish music *see* Afro-Latin/Caribbean influences; Latin jazz

Speak No Evil (Shorter) 312

special effects 37–38

spirituals 55–56

Standards Trio 347

Stearns, Marshall 227

Stein's Dixie Jass Band 83

Stewart, Bill 367, 368

Stewart, Slam 174, 175, 197

Stokowski, Leopold 79

Storyville, New Orleans 77–78, 86

Strayhorn, Billy 143, 144

stride piano style 10, 67, 89, **114–116**

string instruments 34, 68, 82, 129; *see also* guitars

Stringham, Edwin J. 101

"Strollin'" (Silver) 260, **261**

"sub-tone" technique 38

"Suerte de los Tontos, La" (Richards) **269**, 270

suffragettes 75

"Sugar Foot Stomp" *see* "Dippermouth Blues"

"Suite For The Americas, Part 1" (Pérez) 382–384

Suite/Poem for Brass (Johnson) **246**, 247

"Summertime" (Gershwin) 16, 295, **296**

Sunshine Orchestra 86

"sweet" dance bands 102, 127, 153

Swing Era **127–128**, **155**, 160, **177–181**, 198; bestselling albums 220–223; East Coast innovators 132–150; instrumentation 128–130; Kansas City innovators 161–166; popular white bands **151–154**, 178; repertoire and arrangement **131–132**, 133; singers and pianists **170–176**, 179; territory bands 167–169

"Swing Street" (52nd Street), New York xxiii, xxiv, 196, 217

swing style 7, 10, 17, **18**, **34–36**, 37, 52, 91–92, 198, 385; *see also* Swing Era

symphonic jazz **108–110**, 141–142, 144

syncopation **16–17**, 52, 53, 241, 243; ragtime 10, 15, 22, 48, 52, **62**, **64–67**, 68, 84, 89, 90

synthesizers/keyboards, electronic 266, 300, 326, 330

Tabackin, Lew (b. 1940) 356–357

tags/codas 39

"tailgate" technique 82

"Take Five" (Desmond) 16, 22, 23, 39, 236, **237**

"Take the 'A' Train" (Strayhorn) 143

Tales from the Hudson (Brecker) 369, 370

tangana dance form 61

tango dance form 52–53

Tanno, Vinnie 269

Tatum, Art (1909–1956) 114, **174–176**

Taylor, Cecil (b. 1929) 210, 353, **354–355**

"Tea For Two" (Caesar–Youmans) 176

Teagarden, Jack and Charlie 107, 147

"Tears" (Armstrong–Hardin) 86

technological developments 77, 118, 325, 338, 364

television 228, 279

tempo **15–16**, 35

"Terraplane Blues" (Johnson) 59

territory bands, Swing Era 167–169

Teschemacher, Frankie 103

textures 19, **21–22**, 291

thematic variation 26

theme songs, swing bands 132

third-stream jazz 10, **245–248**

Thornhill, Claude 231, 294

Three Romances (Schneider) 379–380, **381**

Three T's 107

through-composed form 382–383

"Tiger Rag" (ODJB) 83, 131

timbre, harmonic fingerings 306

Timmons, Bobby 259–260

Tin Pan Alley, New York 76

Tizol, Juan 155

tonality 19, 24, 291

Tough, Dave 103

"Tout de Suite" (Davis) 300, 301

Touzet, Rene 213

trading phrases 39, 49; *see also* call–response format

"Traffic Jam" (Shaw–McRae) 151, **152**

transportation 78, 190

"Treemonisha" (Joplin) 66

triads 20

triplet patterns 238–239

Tristano, Lennie (1919–1978) 175, **247–248**

trombones *see* brass instruments

Trumbauer, Frankie "Tram" (1901–1956) 105, **106–108**

"Trumpet Sandwich" (Hagans–Belden) 372–373

trumpets *see* brass instruments

12-bar blues form 42, **57**, 62

12 Clouds of Joy 168, **169**

2-beat swing style 104, 114–115, 261

2001: A Space Odyssey (movie) 286

Tynan, John 273–274

Tyner, McCoy 29, 309, 369, 370

urban blues 10

V-Discs 191

Valdés, Chucho 382

"Valse Hot" (Rollins) 264

vamps 237, 302, 329

variations 49

Vaughan, Sarah (1924–1990) 211–212

"verse" sections 39

vibraphones 149

vibrato 92, 135, 228

Video Blues (Cooper) 42

Vietnam War 286, 321

vocalists *see* singing/singers

"Walking" (Davis) 289

walking bass lines 91, 129, 142–143, 144, 164, 239

Waller, Fats 66, 112, 114, 115

waltz dance form 15

Washington, Grover, Jr.
(1943–1999) 337
Washingtonians 117, 138
Watts, Jeff "Tain" 350, 351
We Insist—Freedom Now (Roach)
210
We Want Miles (Davis) 303–304
Weather Report 325–328
Welding, Pete 273
West Africa *see* African influences
West Coast 147–148, 177, 227,
229, 271; cool jazz innovators
233–237, 248
"West End Blues"
(Oliver/Williams) 93–94
Wheeler, Kenny 344–345
"Whispering" (Schonberger) 77,
108
"Witchcraft" (Leigh–Coleman) 19,
240
Whiteman, Paul (1890–1967) 77,
102, 105–106, 107, **108–110**,
119, 127
Wiedoeft, Rudy 106

Williams, Joe 7
Williams, Mary Lou (1910–1981)
168–169
Williams, Tony 289, 296–300
Wilson, Cassandra 374
Wilson, Teddy 131, 148–149, 171
wind *see* brass instruments;
woodwind instruments
Winding, Kai 206
"Windup, The" (Jarrett) 17, 22,
347, **348**
Wolverines 103, 105
women in jazz 86–87;
contemporary innovators
356–357, 377–381; Swing Era
168–169, 170–174; vocalists,
1990s–2000s 374–376
women's liberation movement 75,
76, 286
woodwind doublers **94**, 128
woodwind instruments 34, 37, **38**,
82, 128–129, 142, 196, 368;
C-melody sax 106; soprano sax
94, 307, 309

work songs 24, 54–55
world-music influences 10, 309,
382–384; international musicians
384–388; "world jazz" 387–388;
see also Afro-Latin/Caribbean
influences
World Saxophone Quartet (WSQ)
9, 353
World Wars I and II 77, 159, 189,
190
Wright, Eugene 236

Yancey, Jimmy 111
Young, Lester "Prez" (1909–1959)
29, 107, **164–165**, 170–171,
243
"Young Lions" 344, 350, **350–352**,
382

Zawinul, Joe (1932–2007) 289, 300,
325–328
"Zodiac Suite" (Williams) 169
"zone," the 28–29

SPORT FACILITY AND EVENT MANAGEMENT

Second Edition

Thomas J. Aicher, PhD
Assistant Professor of Sport
Management
College of Business
University of Colorado – Colorado
Springs
Colorado Springs, Colorado

Brianna L. Newland, EdD
Academic Director and Clinical
Associate Professor
Preston Robert Tisch Institute for
Global Sport
New York University
New York City, New York

Amanda L. Paule-Koba, PhD
Associate Professor of Sport
Management
College of Education and Human
Development
Bowling Green State University
Bowling Green, Ohio

JONES & BARTLETT
LEARNING

World Headquarters
Jones & Bartlett Learning
5 Wall Street
Burlington, MA 01803
978-443-5000
info@jblearning.com
www.jblearning.com

Jones & Bartlett Learning books and products are available through most bookstores and online booksellers. To contact Jones & Bartlett Learning directly, call 800-832-0034, fax 978-443-8000, or visit our website, www.jblearning.com.

Substantial discounts on bulk quantities of Jones & Bartlett Learning publications are available to corporations, professional associations, and other qualified organizations. For details and specific discount information, contact the special sales department at Jones & Bartlett Learning via the above contact information or send an email to specialsales@jblearning.com.

16296-7

Production Credits

VP, Product Management: Amanda Martin
Director of Product Management: Cathy L. Esperti
Product Manager: Sean Fabery
Product Assistant: Andrew LaBelle
Project Specialist: Kelly Sylvester
Digital Products Manager: Jordan McKenzie
Digital Project Specialist: Angela Dooley
VP, Manufacturing and Inventory Control: Therese Connell
Composition: Exela Technologies

Project Management: Exela Technologies
Cover Design: Michael O'Donnell
Text Design: Michael O'Donnell
Rights & Media Specialist: John Rusk
Media Development Editor: Troy Liston
Cover Image: © Levi Bianco/Getty Images
Printing and Binding: LSC Communications
Cover Printing: LSC Communications

Library of Congress Cataloging-in-Publication Data

Names: Aicher, Thomas J., author. | Newland, Brianna L., author. | Paule-Koba, Amanda L., author.
Title: Sport facility and event management / Thomas J. Aicher, Brianna L. Newland, and Amanda L. Paule-Koba.
Description: 2nd edition. | Burlington, MA : Jones & Bartlett Learning, [2019] | Includes index.
Identifiers: LCCN 2018047257 | ISBN 9781284152944 (pbk. : alk. paper)
Subjects: LCSH: Sports facilities--Management. | Special events–Management.
Classification: LCC GV401 .A35 2019 | DDC 796.06/9–dc23
LC record available at https://lccn.loc.gov/2018047257

6048

Printed in the United States of America
23 22 21 20 19   10 9 8 7 6 5 4 3 2

CHAPTER 1   Introduction and History   1

CHAPTER 2   Project Management and Event Planning   17

CHAPTER 3   Facility Design and Construction   37

CHAPTER 4   Risk Management   61

CHAPTER 5   Finance and Budgeting   81

CHAPTER 6   Bidding and Planning for Different Events   105

CHAPTER 7   Designing the Event Experience   125

CHAPTER 8   Marketing the Facility and Events   147

CHAPTER 9   Consumer Behavior   169

CHAPTER 10   Managing People in Facilities and Events   191

CHAPTER 11   Customer Service   213

CHAPTER 12   Sponsorship   235

CHAPTER 13   **Traditional Revenue Generation
in Sport and Recreation**   259

CHAPTER 14   **Sustainability and Legacy**   287

CHAPTER 15   **Measurement and Evaluation**   309

Glossary   333
Index   347

CONTENTS

Preface   xiii

Acknowledgments   xxi

About the Authors   xxiii

Contributors   xxv

Reviewers   xxix

CHAPTER 1   **Introduction and History**   **1**
             Thomas J. Aicher and Amanda L. Paule-Koba

             Introduction   3
             Evolution of Facilities   5
             Trends in Sport Facilities   7
             Trends in Local Sport Facilities and Events   10
             Scale of the Sport Event Industry   12
             Who Manages Sport Events?   12
             Summary   13
             Discussion Questions   13
             References   15

CHAPTER 2   **Project Management and Event Planning**   **17**
             Brianna L. Newland

             Introduction   19
             Project Management   20
             Phases of Project Management   23
             The Processes   23
             The Phases   24
             The Domains   30

Tools of Project Management   33
Summary   34
Discussion Questions   34
References   36

CHAPTER 3   Facility Design and Construction   37
Michael Newland and Brianna L. Newland

Introduction   40
The Construction Project   41
Feasibility   41
Estimating Costs and Budgeting   43
Estimating Construction Costs   45
Site Selection   46
Finding the Site   47
Design Process   48
Construction Process   51
Insurance   54
Green Construction and LEED Certification   55
Summary   58
Discussion Questions   58
References   59

CHAPTER 4   Risk Management   61
Thomas J. Aicher and Amanda L. Paule-Koba

Introduction   63
What Is Risk?   64
Types of Risk   64
Terrorism and Sport   65
What Is Risk Management?   68
What Are the Benefits of Good Risk Management?   68
Steps in the Risk Management Process   69
Summary   78
Discussion Questions   78
Case References   80
References   80

CHAPTER 5   **Finance and Budgeting**   **81**
Emily Sparvero and Deane Swanson

Introduction	83
Capital Projects	84
Equity Finance	86
Debt Finance	89
Operational Revenues	95
Budgeting for Facilities and Events	96
Budgeting Approaches	97
Common Expenses in Facility and Event Budgets	100
Summary	101
Discussion Questions	101
References	103

CHAPTER 6   **Bidding and Planning for Different Events**   **105**
Amanda L. Paule-Koba

Introduction	108
Executing Events	108
Identifying Reasons for Creating, Bidding, or Hosting an Event	108
Event Feasibility	110
SWOT Analysis	112
The Bidding Process	114
Types of Events	116
Timelines for Events	120
Summary	123
Discussion Questions	123
References	124

CHAPTER 7   **Designing the Event Experience**   **125**
Brianna L. Newland

Introduction	127
Creating the Sport Event Experience	129
Characteristics of Experiences	131

Experience Dimensions   133
Designing Experiences   135
Co-creating Experiences   140
Meanings Attached   141
Summary   142
Discussion Questions   142
References   144

CHAPTER 8   Marketing the Facility and Events   147
Brianna L. Newland

Introduction   151
Feasibility   152
Developing the Marketing Strategy and Plan   154
Segmentation   155
Building the Relationship   156
Positioning   158
Price   159
Place   160
Promotion   161
Communicating the Message   161
Summary   164
Discussion Questions   164
References   166

CHAPTER 9   Consumer Behavior   169
Brianna L. Newland and Thomas J. Aicher

Introduction   171
Consumption Factors   171
Motivating Factors   174
The Decision-Making Process   182
Summary   186
Discussion Questions   186
References   187

CHAPTER 10   **Managing People in Facilities and Events**   **191**
Michael Odio and Dale Sheptak

Introduction   193
Event Organizations   193
Managing the Staff   196
Managing Volunteers   201
Summary   208
Discussion Questions   208
References   210

CHAPTER 11   **Customer Service**   **213**
Kevin P. Cattani

Introduction   216
The Customer Service Plan   221
Ways to Measure Customer Service and Service Quality   223
Outcomes of Service Encounters   226
A Damaged Reputation   226
A Loss of Good Employees   227
Satisfaction   227
Loyalty and Repatronage   228
Summary   230
Discussion Questions   230
References   232

CHAPTER 12   **Sponsorship**   **235**
Amanda L. Paule-Koba

Sponsorship Defined   237
Defining Each Level   237
Interconnectivity of Levels   239
Sponsorship Inventory   240
Finding and Acquiring Sponsors   244
Writing a Sponsorship Proposal Letter   247

How to Sell Your Event to Potential Sponsors   248
Determining Objectives   249
The Sponsorship Agreement   249
Activation   252
Summary   253
Discussion Questions   253
References   256

**CHAPTER 13   Traditional Revenue Generation
in Sport and Recreation   259**
Brian Menaker

Introduction   261
Why Is It Important to Identify Sources of Revenue?   262
Venue Revenue   262
Ticket Sales Strategies   263
Promotions   270
Loyalty Programs   270
Ancillary Revenue   271
Event Revenue   274
Multipurpose Sport Facilities   277
Event Packaging   280
Summary   282
Discussion Questions   282
References   284

CHAPTER 14   Sustainability and Legacy   287
Kostas Karadakis, Trevor Bopp, and Thomas J. Aicher

Introduction   290
What Are Legacies?   290
Growth in Sport Tourism   291
Sport Event Sizes   292
Medium- and Small-Scale Events   293
Why Is Legacy Important?   294
Components of Legacy Impacts   296
Legacy Event Structures   297

	Measuring Legacies	301
	Summary	303
	Discussion Questions	305
	References	306

CHAPTER 15 **Measurement and Evaluation**   **309**
Thomas J. Aicher

	Introduction	311
	Why Are Measurement and Evaluation Important?	311
	What Are Performance Measurements Used For?	312
	How and When to Measure Performance	313
	What to Measure	314
	Economic Impact Analysis	320
	Environmental Impact Analysis	323
	Summary	329
	Discussion Questions	329
	References	330

| | **Glossary** | **333** |
| | **Index** | **347** |

Sport Facility and Event Management, Second Edition focuses on the major components of both facility and event management: Planning, financing, marketing, implementation, and evaluation. The text integrates timely theoretical insights with real-world practicality and application to afford the reader a strong foundation in facility and event management. It focuses on a broad range of facilities and events to demonstrate the diversity of the industry, touching on various topics relating to recreation, leisure, health, and fitness.

The objective of this text is to provide a working knowledge of how to manage sport facilities and how to plan, manage, implement, and evaluate sport events. As such, the chapters are designed to focus on various components of the sport facility and event management structures to provide a primer for effectively managing sport, recreation, and leisure facilities and events.

Each chapter begins with an Industry Voice feature, in which a person from the sport industry describes how the chapter topic impacts his or her daily routines. This glimpse into the everyday operations of the sport industry orients readers to the content that follows. As the chapter proceeds, both theoretical and practical considerations relating to the topic are explored. Discussions are backed by current research, and real-world examples and tips are provided to engage readers. The chapter concludes with a Case Study and Discussion Questions to help students apply the content and to assess their comprehension.

Chapter Overview

Each chapter contains various features intended to enhance student learning, including Chapter Objectives, Industry Voices, Vignettes, Case Studies,

Discussion Questions, and Tips. A major selling point of this text is that it includes actual examples from the industries covered in the text. No other text on the market successfully employs this strategy.

Chapter 1, *Introduction and History,* provides an overview of the industry and reviews its history. From this foundation, readers will build an understanding of facility and event management as they read the chapters that follow.

Chapter 2, *Project Management and Event Planning,* explores the elements of staging and implementing a sport event. This chapter introduces the five phases of project management (initiation, planning, implementation, monitoring, and shutdown) and the concepts and tools to assist the sport event manager in planning and implementing the event. Concepts such as the work breakdown structure, Gantt charts, and other project management tools will be introduced.

Chapter 3, *Facility Design and Construction,* starts with a blueprint, which is a set of plans to develop a facility, and progresses through a series of interrelated steps until the product is completed and the ribbon is cut in the grand opening ceremony. The importance of site selection and evaluation, planning and design, construction costs, and the bidding process is discussed. Furthermore, an examination about green building and how it has increased over the past 10 years is included in the chapter.

Chapter 4, *Risk Management,* discusses the process of examining the uncertainty or chance of loss—usually accidental loss, which is sudden, unusual, or unforeseen—and creating a plan to attempt to reduce any risks to all involved in the event. Implementing a comprehensive risk management plan is vital to a facility and/or event. In today's litigious society, understanding how to mitigate financial loss and negligence should be front and center in minimizing risk and potential lawsuits. The growth of new and renovated sport facilities and the creation of diverse events has made this area of the industry much more difficult for managers.

Chapter 5, *Finance and Budgeting,* discusses the basic concepts of financing sport facilities. A capital project is a long-term investment that will increase the organization's assets. If an organization wants to build a new facility (or renovate an existing facility), there are many upfront costs, including costs associated with land acquisition, construction, and infrastructure development. Thus, it is important that the project manager(s) understands financial statements and how they can be utilized to develop a budget as a forecasting measure.

Chapter 6, *Bidding and Planning for Different Events,* explains the five main types of events: Mega-events, recurring events, traveling events, ancillary events, and community events. When creating an event, the managers need to identify goals and objectives. These will guide all of the forthcoming decisions. When setting goals, the managers should follow the SMART (specific, measurable, attainable, relevant, and time-based) principle. It is important to remember that when creating a new event, in addition to your goals for the event, you must assess where it fits in the current marketplace. Being unique is crucial to attracting sponsors, event participants, spectators, and/or media.

If you are submitting a bid to run an event for a national or international sporting event, you need to follow the bid process provided by the event's rights holder. The criteria of the bid will vary depending on the event, but, in most cases, it is not a solitary process. A multitude of individuals (the organizing committee) will need to come together to gather and present the required information in the most cohesive manner possible.

Chapter 7, *Designing the Event Experience,* outlines the elements of designing the event experience, such as understanding experience characteristics, designing the event concept, co-creating event experiences, and attaching meaning. This process will include identifying unique elements of events; developing a concept, theme, and subsequent experience; and finding ways to tie these elements together to create meaning at the event. Experiences are highly subjective in that two people can have completely different experiences at the same event. Thus, it is imperative that event managers create an event experience that will appeal to a wide range of individuals.

Chapter 8, *Marketing the Facility and Events,* discusses the elements of a marketing plan. The discussion starts with conducting a feasibility study to determine if the facility has the capacity to host the event and that market demands are well matched. Next it reviews developing a marketing strategy and plan. It outlines the value, mission, vision, and goals of the event as offered in the marketing plan and explains how these considerations can help identify the ancillary opportunities associated with the event. These aspects provide sport facility and event managers the information they need to conduct proper segmentation.

The chapter introduces the four common ways that segmentation occurs: Demographics, psychographics, media preferences, and purchasing behaviors. It examines the value of relationship marketing and the use of customer relationships and data-based management systems to improve customer relations. The chapter then outlines how events can utilize the marketing mix (price, product, place, and promotion) to position themselves in the marketplace. Finally, the chapter covers the different strategies that events may pursue to communicate their message to consumers. These strategies include traditional marketing techniques as well as some innovative methods (e.g., guerilla and viral marketing).

Chapter 9, *Consumer Behavior,* outlines three major components of how and why people attend or participate in sport events. First, it develops how people are socialized into sport from three different levels: Socialization, involvement, and commitment. Next, it provides several motivational forces that act upon individuals as they select the types of events they would like to either spectate or in which they would like to participate. Finally, it outlines the seven steps in the decision-making process and highlights how both event owners and participants make their purchase decisions.

Chapter 10, *Managing People in Facilities and Events,* discusses the management of people in sport by looking at some unique characteristics of the people and organizations involved in facility and event management. The chapter will explain that event managers must be cognizant of the need to create an attractive work environment and create systems that will allow them to respond effectively to the needs of a diverse workforce in terms of motivation and expectations.

Chapter 11, *Customer Service,* reviews the various aspects involved with customer service in the sport marketplace. Customer service is a sequence of activities designed to enhance the level of customer satisfaction. Understanding why customers attend events provides information that allows for the tailoring of an experience to best suit the customers' needs and wants. Being familiar with alternative ways of measuring service quality will not only set an organization apart from competition but it will also save the organization valuable resources in targeting external firms to provide those services. This chapter also discusses various ways to measure and better understand how an organization is attending to customer service. It examines the consequences of customer service and why they are so vital in maintaining a competitive edge in an already saturated marketplace.

Chapter 12, *Sponsorship,* describes an incredibly important and often necessary part of creating an event. The importance of sponsorship in producing successful events and providing revenue for a facility cannot be ignored. This chapter discusses ways in which an event manager can find potential sponsors, the process for creating a sponsorship agreement, and the sponsorship agreement itself. The event manager must understand the process of identifying and targeting potential sponsors and ways of proposing the sponsorship relationship to the company.

Chapter 13, *Traditional Revenue Generation in Sport and Recreation,* reviews the various techniques used to generate revenue through sport and recreation organizations and facilities. Sport facilities and associated events provide owners, operators, managers, and other connected stakeholders with the opportunity to generate revenue through numerous forms of creative planning. Techniques and principles of revenue generation from sport, participatory, and recreation facilities and events are categorized and summarized. Furthermore, categories of sources of revenue include venue-related revenue such as ticket sales, concessions, merchandise, event fees, and participatory event monies, such as exposition-related income and registration fees.

Chapter 14, *Sustainability and Legacy,* outlines the strategies and techniques that organizations employ to create sustainable facilities and events that have a positive impact on the facility, event, and community. It discusses the economic, environmental, and social impacts that facilities and events generate in their host community, the common methodologies utilized to measure each, and strategies to enhance the positive while minimizing the negative impacts. Positive impacts of hosting events can include new and updated roads, entertainment venues, and other infrastructures, as well as increased tourism revenue, media exposure, commercial appeal, and civic pride. Negative impacts can include overcrowding and increased travel concerns, disruption to the local environment, the building or renovating of uneconomical and unsustainable infrastructures, and unfavorable perceptions of the host community. Further, facilities often are left empty or are underutilized, and events sometimes do not make it past the inaugural year.

Chapter 15, *Measurement and Evaluation,* reviews the various techniques to measure the performance of the event or facility from a multi-stakeholder perspective. The facility and event industry faces many challenges and serves a variety of stakeholders who each play a significant role in the success of the organization. It is, therefore, very important that facility and event organizations measure success based on the organization objectives they have put into place. First, the chapter establishes the importance of continuous evaluation of the organization and its performance from pre-event to post-event to ensure that all stakeholder expectations were met. The chapter then outlines the major components of SERVQUAL, economic, environmental, and social, among other, methods of evaluating the organization's performance.

New to the *Second Edition*

In crafting the *Second Edition*, each chapter has been revised to reflect the latest developments and research impacting sport facility and event management. This includes updated Industry Voice features in every chapter that spotlight new people from the sport industry, as well as updated references throughout the text. Chapter-specific updates are detailed below.

Chapter 1 includes updated examples and highlights new trends in facilities and events.

Chapter 2 now features information on managing the planning process, as well as a discussion of developing new events and how to create an event plan.

Chapter 3 includes a discussion of conducting feasibility studies, including SWOT, PEST, and Porters. The green design section has been enhanced.

Chapter 4 now reviews emerging trends in security and safety, and the chapter boasts updated examples.

Chapter 5 includes more event and facility examples.

Chapter 6 now discusses the importance of a bid committee, as well as the role of tourism in bid selection. This chapter includes an example of an evaluation form.

Chapter 7 includes a focus on how event design is impacted by the experience. The liminal and liminoid zone sections have been increased.

Chapter 8 considers emerging trends in marketing and now includes a section on social media.

Chapter 9 features an updated section on motivation and discusses constraints on participation.

Chapter 10 incorporates a brief overview of the functions of management within facility and event organizations. This chapter also discusses volunteer recruitment and management.

Chapter 11 considers how to train people in order to activate the customer service plan, as well as how to manage game-day employees to ensure customer satisfaction. The consumer behavior section was eliminated as this content is covered elsewhere in the text.

Chapter 12 details how to create a sponsorship agreement for new and smaller events, and it includes examples of sponsorship agreements. It also discusses activation strategies for events and facilities, and it provides unique sponsorship examples.

Chapter 13 discusses packaging of events and includes reward-based ticketing.

Chapter 14 includes discussions about leveraging events and sustainability, and its examples are focused on local outcomes.

Chapter 15 outlines emerging methodologies for measurement and evaluation, and it also features updated examples.

Instructor Resources

Several resources have been developed to help the instructor organize the course's content and assess student learning. They include the following:

- Test Bank, containing more than 450 questions
- Slides in PowerPoint format, valuable for use as lecture talking points or student study guides
- Image Bank, including the photographs and illustrations featured in this text
- Sample syllabus, demonstrating how this text can be deployed in a course

ACKNOWLEDGMENTS

First, I would like to thank the world's best coeditors, Bri and Amanda, for continuing to work with me to produce a high-quality product. I could not have asked for a better pair of colleagues to continue on this literary journey. To our contributors, new and old, your expertise and time are greatly appreciated. It is truly you who helped us make this a much stronger edition. Finally, I would like to thank my friends and family, especially my parents, who supported me through the years and who have always encouraged me to accomplish great things.

Thomas J. Aicher

I find myself lucky to have had the opportunity to work so closely with my two coeditors, Tommy and Amanda. Your considerate feedback and support were so welcomed and appreciated through the entire process. I would also like to thank both the chapter authors and the industry contacts for your valuable time and effort. The strength and success of this textbook are due to your fantastic experience and expertise. We all greatly appreciate the giving of your valuable time. Finally, I'd like to thank our Jones & Bartlett Learning team for your insight and suggestions as this book came to fruition.

Brianna L. Newland

I would first like to thank my coeditors, Tommy and Bri, for being such great colleagues to work with on this book. This book would not have been possible without our fantastic contributors. Thank you all for the time and expertise you brought to each of your chapters. Thank you to our team at Jones & Bartlett Learning for your patience, insight, and thoughtful suggestions as we completed the second edition of this book. We could not have completed this book without your encouragement and deadline reminders. Finally, thank you to my family for understanding and encouraging my professional pursuits.

Amanda L. Paule-Koba

Thomas J. Aicher is an Assistant Professor of Sport Management at the University of Colorado—Colorado Springs, where he teaches Sport Facility and Event Management, Sport Selling and Analytics, and College Sport Admin-istration. Dr. Aicher has been an active scholar, examining the motivations and meanings that people associate with participation in events, as well as the impacts associated with those events in the host communities. He has been published in leading academic journals, including the *International Journal of Event and Festival Management, Journal of Travel Tourism and Marketing, Journal of Sport and Tourism, International Journal of Sport Management and Marketing, International Journal of Sport Management,* and several others.

Dr. Aicher earned his PhD in sport management from Texas A&M University in 2009. He holds a master's degree in sport management from Texas A&M and a bachelor's degree in marketing management from Virginia Tech. Prior to entering academia, Dr. Aicher worked for several sport organizations, including the Salem Avalanche, the Durham Bulls, and First and 10 Marketing. With the latter two organizations, he managed several sport- and nonsport-related events. He has continued his endeavors in event planning throughout his academic career.

Brianna L. Newland is the Academic Director for Undergraduate Programs and Clinical Associate Professor of Sport Management at New York Univer-sity, where she teaches Applied Research in Sport. Dr. Newland has been an active scholar, exploring how sport events can be leveraged to develop sport and community, how sport organizations sustain their future by attract-ing and nurturing participation within the organization and via events, and how particular factors may foster or hinder adult participation in sport. Dr. Newland has been published in leading academic journals, including the

Journal of Sport Management, Sport Management Review, Managing Leisure, and *Sport Marketing Quarterly.*

Dr. Newland earned her doctorate in sport management from the United States Sports Academy in 2006 and completed a postdoctoral fellowship at the University of Texas at Austin in 2007. She holds a master's degree in exercise physiology and nutrition and a bachelor's degree in exercise science from the University of Nebraska—Lincoln. Dr. Newland has also served as a race director for endurance sports for over 10 years, which is where she gained her real-life experience in event management.

Amanda L. Paule-Koba is an Associate Professor of Sport Management at Bowling Green State University, where she teaches Sport and Event Management, Sport and Gender, Contemporary Issues, and Sport in Higher Education. Dr. Paule-Koba has been an active scholar, examining issues in intercollegiate sport (such as the recruitment process, academic clustering, and athlete development), gender equity policies, and Title IX. Dr. Paule-Koba has been published in leading academic journals, including the *Journal of Sport Management, International Journal of Sport Management, Sport Management Review, Research Quarterly for Exercise and Sport, Journal of Intercollegiate Sport, Journal of Issues in Intercollegiate Athletics,* and *Women in Sport and Physical Activity Journal.* She is also the cofounder and coeditor of the *Journal of Athlete Development and Experience.*

Dr. Paule-Koba earned her PhD in sport sociology from Michigan State University in 2008. She holds a master's degree in sport studies and a bachelor's degree in sport organization from Miami University. Prior to entering academia, Dr. Paule-Koba worked for a company that ran professional athletes' summer youth sporting camps all over the United States, which is where she gained her real-life experience in event management.

Chapter Authors

Trevor Bopp, PhD
Lecturer and Program Coordinator
Department of Tourism, Recreation, and Sport Management
College of Health and Human Performance
University of Florida
Gainesville, Florida

Kevin P. Cattani, PhD
Associate Professor of Sport Marketing and Management
Department of Health, Wellness, and Sport Marketing and Management
University of Dubuque
Dubuque, Iowa

Kostas Karadakis, PhD
Assistant Professor of Sport Management
Sport Management Department
Southern New Hampshire University
Manchester, New Hampshire

Brian Menaker, PhD
Assistant Professor of Sport Management
School of Education and Professional Studies
Lake Erie College
Painesville, Ohio

Michael Odio, PhD
Assistant Professor of Sport Administration
School of Human Services
University of Cincinnati
Cincinnati, Ohio

Michael Newland, LEED AP
Project Manager
Meltech Corporation, Inc.

Dale Sheptak, DSSc
Associate Professor of Sport Management
School of Health, Physical Education, & Sport Sciences
Baldwin Wallace University
Berea, Ohio

Emily Sparvero, PhD
Clinical Assistant Professor
Department of Kinesiology and Health Education
College of Education
The University of Texas at Austin
Austin, Texas

Deane Swanson, MEd
Lecturer
Department of Kinesiology and Health Education
College of Education
The University of Texas at Austin
Austin, Texas

Industry Voice Authors

Omar Banks
Executive Associate Athletics Director & Chief Financial Officer
Virginia Tech Athletics

James A. DeMeo, MS, CEO
Founder
Unified Sports & Entertainment Security Consulting (USESC)

Matt Futterman
Associate Manager Referee Operations
National Basketball Association

Becky Griesmer
Programming and Event Manager
Greater Cleveland Sports Commission

Ignacio Gutierrez
Senior Manager, Match Day, Events and Hospitality
Sydney Swans Football Club

Jen Jorgensen
Director of Quant
Egg Strategy

Alexandra (Alexx) Klein
Senior Studio Production Coordinator
Big Ten Network

Franzter LeBlanc
Director of Events and Operations
University of Maryland Baltimore County (UMBC) Event Center

Nick Michaels
Account Executive, Corporate Partnerships
Philadelphia Eagles

Lisa Murray
Global Chief Marketing Officer
Octagon Sports and Entertainment Network

C.J. O'Leary
Special Event and Game Day Presentation Coordinator
Toledo Mud Hens and Toledo Walleye

Chris Pierce
Senior Director—Fan Commerce
New York Jets

Brad Timberlake
Vice President, Event Marketing and Sales Southeast
Feld Entertainment

Maxilis Triantafyllidis
Owner/Operator
Triantafyllidis Beach Arena

Rachel Wright
Championship Volunteer Operations Specialist
PGA of America

Beth Birky, PhD
Assistant Professor
Department of Health and Physical Education
College of Education and Technology
Eastern New Mexico University
Portales, New Mexico

Dexter J. Davis, EdD
Associate Professor and Program Coordinator
Department of Management, Marketing, and Information Systems
College of Business and Global Affairs
University of Tennessee at Martin
Martin, Tennessee

Courtney L. Flowers, PhD
Assistant Professor
Department of Health, Kinesiology, and Sport Studies
College of Education
Texas Southern University
Houston, Texas

Paul Hogan, MEd
Professor
Sport, Recreation, and Tourism Studies Program
NHTI, Concord's Community College
Concord, New Hampshire

Brad King, MEd
Associate Professor
Department of Natural, Health, and Mathematical Sciences
MidAmerica Nazarene University
Olathe, Kansas

Gary Polk, MS
Lecturer
California State University Dominguez Hills
Carson, California

Thomas A. Raunig, EdD
Professor
Department of Health and Physical Education
University of Providence
Great Falls, Montana

Timothy Rice, DSM
Lead Faculty
Sport and Performance Psychology Program
University of the Rockies
Denver, Colorado

Gregg Rich, PhD
Assistant Professor
Department of Health Sciences and Kinesiology
Georgia Southern University
Statesboro, Georgia

Scott A. Sproat
Adjunct Faculty
School of Business and Entrepreneurial Leadership
University of Saint Francis
Fort Wayne, Indiana

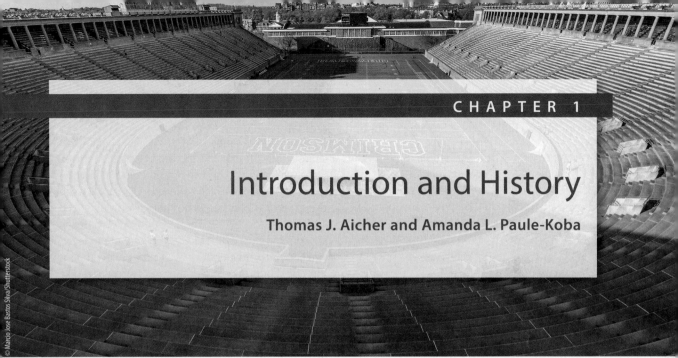

CHAPTER 1

Introduction and History

Thomas J. Aicher and Amanda L. Paule-Koba

CHAPTER OBJECTIVES

Upon completion of this chapter, the reader will be able to:

1. Outline the origins of sport facilities and events.
2. Explain the evolution of facilities in terms of design, financing, and use.
3. Define the main components of the sport facility and event management and main content areas discussed in detail throughout this text.

CHAPTER OVERVIEW

This chapter will outline the evolution of facilities and events from the Greek and Roman eras to modern day. It will outline the trends in facility construction, financing, and design over the past few centuries to develop a strong understanding of the evolution to modern facilities. Finally, it will give a brief outline of the entire text to establish an understanding of how to properly navigate the text.

IndustryVOICE

Alexandra (Alexx) Klein, Senior Studio Production Coordinator—Big Ten Network

As the studio production coordinator, it is my responsibility to be the conduit between the network and 1) the universities' public relations departments, 2) the universities' video services departments, 3) the conference, and 4) bowl games and major tournaments. To prepare for this role, I advanced my education by obtaining a master's degree in Sport Administration. While completing this degree, I worked as a Sports Information Director dealing with facility operations and event managers on a day-to-day basis, through public relations (PR) and communications. When I was hired at Big Ten Network (BTN) after graduation, I was able to combine my experiences with PR and event management and used those skills as a foundation for success.

The biggest challenge that I believe is facing this segment of the sport industry is "cord cutting." This is when an individual chooses to drop his or her cable TV subscription in favor of streaming over the Internet. The biggest reason that people seem to be making this switch is rising cable bills. Over the past few years, streaming video services have skyrocketed in popularity; however, there is one major flaw with the model: No live programming, which is great news for the staff of BTN because live events are such a major part of the day-to-day operation. The goal is maintaining the current cable TV model, while appeasing the cord cutters and getting the fans to become content through over-the-top (OTT) platforms.

In the future, I believe that there will be an increase on the emphasis of digital media. Specifically, real-time interactions with fans through digital platforms. The success of these interactions affect distribution strategy, advertising, and the broadcasts themselves. Social media is also becoming more and more integrated into the overall fan experience. To capitalize on these trends, BTN created a position called Multi-Video Platform Editor (MVPE). There is one MVPE on each school's campus, which allows the network to leverage access to create new ways to connect with fans through school-specific content. Fans want to feel like they're getting to know their favorite teams and athletes, so this position allows us to accomplish that. An increased presence on digital media platforms leads to better sponsorship opportunities, which ultimately helps offset monetary losses from cord cutting.

When hiring someone for an entry-level position, I look for someone with skills that will contribute to the company, along with the confidence to know that they can. We seek individuals who are eager to learn, are curious, and are team players. These characteristics make for a successful entry-level employee. There are also skills commonly missing among new graduates. The two most significant missing skills that I've seen are an understanding of how organizations work and how to navigate complexity, as well as a struggle to deal with ambiguity. To be better prepared for the workforce, I recommend that students get field experience outside of the classroom. The combination of a good education plus outside experience will set a candidate apart from a student who only focused on one of those things. For example, my current position is unique in that it involves multiple departments. Because of this, it requires an employee to come into the company with previous experience in multiple fields. Students should participate in, and volunteer for, a variety of opportunities throughout their undergraduate careers in order to be best prepared for the workforce.

Introduction

Throughout history, sport, sport events, and sport facilities have been a major cultural component of our societies. Dating as far back as 30,000 years, there is evidence to suggest the enjoyment of sport and sport for leisure, as supported by the prehistoric cave art found in France, Africa, and Australia (Masterman, 2009). The common sports displayed in these renderings are wrestling, running, swimming, and archery. While these renderings do not truly depict sport in a manner in which it is consumed and participated in today, cave paintings in Mongolia dating back to 7000 BC display wrestling matches with crowds of spectators. Combined, these portrayals demonstrate the continued importance of sport participation and consumption within our societies.

This rich history of sport events was largely associated with ceremonies created to honor either religious gods or leaders of the civilization. For example, drawings found on pharaonic monuments depicted individuals participating in various sporting activities (e.g., swimming, boxing, wrestling, running, handball), believed to be designed and governed by ancient kings, princes, and statesmen. In addition, some argue that these events were the first in which basic rules, officials, and uniforms were used during the sport events. While some argue that England is the birthplace of football (commonly known as soccer in the United States), the ancient game of Cuju was played from 206 BC to 220 AD in China, Korea, Japan, and Vietnam. This game was very similar to football: Players were not allowed to use their hands, points were scored when the ball was passed into a net, and two teams would compete against one another. The games were designed as a method of military training in which the two teams would strive to control the ball to demonstrate their dominance over their opponent. In the United States, lacrosse is considered the country's oldest sporting activity on record. According to records, the game was designed and participated in by Native American men located in the western Great Lakes region. Rules during that time are very similar to the rules of the current version of the sport.

The modern Olympic Games are also rooted in a rich tradition. Originating sometime in the tenth or ninth century BC, the events that would become the Olympic Games were a component of a much larger religious ceremony to honor Zeus, the god of the sky and ruler of the Olympic gods. These ceremonies were held every 4 years, similar to today's Olympics, and included the discus and javelin throws, a foot race, and the long jump. Along with the Olympic Games, these events included the Hera Games, Pythian Games, Isthmian Games, and Nemea Games (Toohey & Veal, 2000), and they are largely considered the first instance of mega-events in which multiple regions participated in and spectated the event. In 393 AD, these events were discontinued by Theodosius I, a Christian Roman Emperor, because of their affiliation with the Greek god. They were revitalized in 1896 AD.

The stadiums that hosted the ancient events were located in the Peloponnese region of southern Greece and were combined with religious facilities. It is widely believed that the first Olympic Games were held in 776 BC; however, recent archeological evidence suggests that the original Olympic stadium and hippodrome were constructed after 700 BC. The stadium held an estimated 40,000 people, and the design was not very different from the U-shaped style commonly used today. The hippodrome, which originally hosted chariot and horse racing events, could host hundreds, or even thousands, of spectators, depending on the event. The Roman Empire continued to follow a similar design and style of the facilities constructed during the Greek Empire.

> **TIP**
>
> The History Channel provides several videos discussing the construction of the ancient and modern Olympic Games. Visit https://www.history.com/topics /olympic-games to learn more about the Olympic movement.

The Roman Colosseum, originally named the Flavian Amphitheater after the Flavian Dynasty, was constructed in 80 AD under the order of Emperor Vespasian as a gift to the people of Rome. For those who have seen the movie *Gladiator*, the truth behind the story is that Titus, the son of Vespasian, did, in fact, host 100 days of games, including the gladiatorial contests; however, it was to celebrate the opening of the Colosseum. Other events that took place during this time included venationes, or wild beast hunts, which placed humans and animals in the Colosseum in a fight to the death, and naumachiae, also called sea battles, in which the arena was flooded and two fleets of ships fought in a portrayal of previous naval battles. The Romans during this time provided us with some of the same tools we use today to build stadiums. For example, they used one of the first known cranes, consisting of rope, wooden wheels, and a long wooden arm that would lift items to the higher levels. The Colosseum was one of the first structures made from a concrete-type material, and the arched design is still modeled in many modern stadiums. Archeological evidence also shows that the Romans used tickets, numbered gates, and reserved seating during their events. Finally, one of the most impressive features of the Roman Colosseum was that the design allowed for 50,000-plus people to exit the stadium in less than 5 minutes—something most modern facilities are unable to achieve.

Evolution of Facilities

The revival of the Olympic Games in 1896, the addition of collegiate sports in the United States, and the early growth of professional baseball fueled the development of sport facilities in the modern era. From an international perspective, the revival of the Olympic movement facilitated the construction of facilities in Greece, London, and Los Angeles, as these cities hosted the first three editions of the modern Olympic Games. The Panathenaic Stadium was constructed from the remains of an ancient Greek stadium and is the only stadium in the world constructed of white marble. Recently, the Panathenaic Stadium was renovated to host various events associated with the Olympic Games in 2004, and it is still in use for national and regional events. The White City Stadium in London was constructed to host the 1900 Olympic Games and went through several renovations until it was demolished in 1985. During its time, it housed varying sporting events but was most recently known for greyhound and auto racing. Los Angeles Memorial Coliseum is the only stadium to host two Olympic Games (1932 and 1984). It has also hosted two National Football League Super Bowls (I and VII) and a Major League Baseball World Series (1959, when the Dodgers hosted three home games). In addition, the Coliseum holds attendance records in international soccer (92,650 spectators during

TIP

You can view photos of the transformation of these two facilities. For a timeline and photos of Fenway Park, visit mlb.mlb.com/bos/fenwaypark100/timeline.jsp. For Wrigley Field, visit www.chicagotribune.com/videogallery/76640826/.

a Chivas vs. Barcelona match in 2006), baseball (115,300 spectators during a Dodgers vs. Red Sox exhibition game in 2008), and special events (134,254 spectators during a Billy Graham event in 1963). In 1984, the Coliseum became a registered landmark, and recently, the University of Southern California signed a lease agreement through 2054, which should guarantee its maintenance and upkeep.

Within intercollegiate athletics, Franklin Field in Philadelphia, Pennsylvania is recognized by the National Collegiate Athletic Association as the oldest university stadium used to host an intercollegiate event. Originally constructed in 1895 for $100,000, the facility hosted the first Penn Relays (the oldest and largest track and field competition in the United States) and

VIGNETTE 1-1

Practice Facilities Are the New Arms Race in Intercollegiate Athletics

The facility arms race is not a new phenomenon in intercollegiate athletics; however, the stadium and arena build has slowed to give way to other capital spending. For example, the University of Illinois recently announced plans to spend more than $200 million for a newly constructed football performance center; upgrades to the basketball practice facility, soccer facility, and track facilities; and an indoor practice space for baseball and softball. This is in addition to a multisport facility being constructed to host hockey, volleyball, wrestling, and gymnastics. Not to be outdone, the University of Notre Dame announced that it is constructing a 114,000 square foot, indoor practice facility, price tag unknown, to house the football, men's soccer, and women's soccer teams. Even lower level conferences at schools such as University of Nevada, Las Vegas (UNLV) are joining in the race. UNLV recently announced that it will spend $22.5 million on a football training complex complete with a 9,000-square-foot, weight-lifting area, a full kitchen, study areas, coaches' offices, locker rooms, and a barbershop. Columbia University of the Ivy League is also adding a bubble to the soccer facility on campus to create an indoor facility for training and practice during the winter months.

© Marcio Jose Bastos Silva/Shutterstock.

the University of Pennsylvania (Penn) football team, with a capacity of approximately 30,000 seats. Since then, the facility has gone through several renovations and has been home to other Penn intercollegiate teams and even the Philadelphia Eagles. Currently, Franklin Field is the home of Penn's football and lacrosse teams, with a capacity of more than 50,000 seats. Even in the early years of intercollegiate athletics, universities participated in what is known as the **arms race**, in which they compete with one another to have the biggest or best facilities and amenities associated with their athletic programs. Review the vignette for more information about the arms races as well as early and modern examples.

The oldest Major League Baseball (MLB) facility still in use in the United States is Fenway Park (1912), home of the Boston Red Sox, followed closely by Wrigley Field (1914), home of the Chicago Cubs. These two facilities are staples in the sport facility landscape but have gone through several renovations since their inception. Both facilities followed what is known as the jewel box design, which is characterized by the two-tier grandstand; steel, wood, or concrete support beams left exposed and incorporated into the design; seats that are traditionally green; and an unconventionally shaped outfield, as most stadiums in this era were built to fit within one square city block. During this early era of baseball, several facilities were constructed across the country to host teams. In fact, between 1880 and 1920, the MLB lists more than 60 stadiums that were built. The growth in the number of teams and stadiums became a part of the American landscape during this era and was part of the great migration toward the city centers and away from the farmlands during that time.

arms race As it relates to the sport event industry, the competition among sport organizations to have the best facilities, resources, revenue-generating amenities, and other event features to ensure an advantage in the marketplace.

Trends in Sport Facilities

From this early part of the modern era until the early 1990s, stadiums were constructed and continuously maintained and renovated to remain competitive on the sport facility landscape. However, with changes in the way stadiums were funded, an increase in demand for suites and luxury seating and a rise in sport-specific stadiums, an estimated 84 percent of professional sport facilities underwent either major renovations or brand new construction since 1980 (Fried, 2010). The recent construction of Levi's Stadium in Santa Clara, California, the home of the San Francisco 49ers, may be the best example of the various reasons for the changes in sport facilities and will be used as an example throughout the following discussion to highlight these changes.

Brown, Rascher, Nagel, and McEvoy (2017) outlined the five phases of facility financing and the evolution of funding over time. Phase one was the original construction era (1880s–1910s) and all stadiums were 100 percent financed by the ownership of the sport team. Wrigley Field is the only remaining structure from this era. The transition occurred when the previously mentioned LA Coliseum was constructed in 1923. This marked the transition in which stadiums were financed with less than 1/3 of the funds coming from public financing with the balance left to the ownership group. In the 1960s, the shift to more public financing occurred with more than 80 percent of the funding for the majority of the stadiums coming from public funds, which is representative of the second phase of stadium financing (Brown et al., 2017). The beginning of the 1980s marked a quiet period for stadium construction until Miami built Joe Robbie Stadium in 1987. This development marked a bomb in sport facility development with more than 90 new facilities being constructed through the 1990s. The 2000s continued this trend of major renovations and new constructions and the majority used some public monies. Brown et al. (2017) reported of the $21 billion spent on facility projects, public monies were responsible for $12 billion of the costs. Currently, citizens are beginning to call into question the use of public funds for these facilities and are voting down **referendums** to increase taxes to fund their construction. For example, the city of Arlington, Texas, agreed to use a half-cent sales tax, 2 percent hotel occupancy tax, 5 percent rental vehicle tax, and $2 million in rent per year to fund $500 million of the proposed $1.1 billion needed for the stadium. Alternatively, the city of San Diego selected to not fund a new stadium for the San Diego Chargers, leading to the subsequent departure of the Chargers to Los Angeles.

referendum A direct vote in which an entire electorate (i.e., voting public) is asked to accept or reject a proposal put forward by the community leadership.

Sport facilities are moving further away from the "seat 'em and feed 'em" mentality. Stadiums and arenas alike are being filled with seating zones, play areas, and vendors to enhance the fans' entertainment. Seating zones include the move of the luxury box seats to indoor club areas, which are complete with a bar, restaurant, and numerous televisions to keep up with the action. Another type of seating zone is the standing-room-only seats in which individuals have access to high-top tables and a full-service concession stand to use as their private space. Another alternative to traditional seating are social zones. For example, the Oriole Park at Camden Yards in Baltimore features a rooftop deck and bar. This section is behind the centerfield wall and features a great view and open seating to allow people to mingle with their "new friends." This new social space is also occurring more and more in soccer. Football Club Cincinnati currently plays in Nippert Stadium on the campus of the University of Cincinnati. During a recent renovation of the facility, two bump-outs were created behind the end line. This space now features an open-seating area complete with food and beverage service for individuals to host larger groups of people. The sideline experience can be found courtside as well.

As the demographics and needs of sports fans continue to evolve, stadium managers and professional sport organizations are beginning to respond to the need for connectivity. The younger generation of sport fans consider Internet connectivity equally important to basic needs of life (i.e., water, food, and shelter) and removing the ability to share their experience via their social media platform of choice limits their desire to attend sport events. Additionally, the increase in size and quality of televisions has forced sport stadiums to consider the quality of the in-stadium experience, especially when the costs are tremendously high. This has led many sport venues to increase their connectivity via wifi or cell service to allow sport fans the ability to remain connected while in stadium. In doing so, they are also developing ways to enhance revenues in the stadium, as well as collect more data on sport fans via in-stadium purchases. For instance, when you arrive at a game that is not sold out, the ticket app you used to purchase the ticket may alert you to a $25 seat upgrade to the lower level sections. Or you may order your favorite drink and hotdog to have it delivered to your seat so that you do not miss a minute of the action. And rather than standing in a long line at the restroom, you could check the stadium app to see which

VIGNETTE 1-2

Changes to Parking and Transportation Services

Parking has been a point of contention for many fans over the years. The high costs associated with parking and the traffic into and out of the stadium has led many facility managers to search for new ways to improve this experience. The challenge has moved beyond having the correct number of spaces within a close distance and helping individuals to get in and out of the area quickly, however. With services such as Uber and Lyft gaining popularity, facility managers are now faced with the challenge of cars attempting to enter the stadium area while everyone else is trying to exit. For example, MetLife Stadium introduced a partnership with Uber to create the "Uber Zone" in one of its parking lots. Complete with instructions on their website, MetLife officials outline the steps and directions to meeting the Uber driver. The relationship has also led to a sponsorship for the facility and Uber recoups some of that expense by charging individuals an extra $5 fee for the ride.

bathroom closest to you has the shortest lines. The best change is when your favorite player scores a goal and you will be able to view the replay on the team app and share the video with your friends on social media. The challenge of all of this is creating and maintaining the infrastructure needed to ensure that the fans have the fastest and best access to the Internet. Most stadiums have turned to their communication partners (e.g., AT&T) to help them develop the infrastructure needed to maintain the level of speed needed to keep the fans entertained and engaged.

Trends in Local Sport Facilities and Events

The arms race is not only a college sport issue. Municipalities are continuing to invest millions of dollars in developing their parks and recreation spaces to increase their capacity to host sport events. The youth sport market is the driver of this growth as countless national and international events promise large economic impact within the host community. This has led to the development and construction of mega sport complexes complete with entertainment and accommodations within the location. For example, Spooky Nook is opening its second location in Hamilton, Ohio, a city located just north of Cincinnati. This facility will feature indoor soccer fields, basketball courts, a workout facility, outdoor fields, and a hotel with restaurants. Other facilities are outlined throughout the textbook which highlights the growth in this sector.

The role of emerging sports such as eSports, drone racing, Quidditch, and others has led local organizations to turn to developing their own events and tournaments rather than focusing on winning the bid for national or international events. In doing so, this creates new collaborations in the sport marketplace. For example, universities are now housing sport commissions that are used to develop events to host in the varsity and intramural facilities during the periods in which there is limited use. Destination marketing organizations (e.g., Visitors' Bureau, Chamber of Commerce, Sport Commission) are partnering with local sport clubs and groups to assist them with the development of new events and tournaments to drive tourism to the local community. The destination marketing organizations are also becoming more savvy and including performance clauses and incentive programs to ensure that the event owners deliver on the promises made during the bid selection process.

Another major factor facing local sport events and facilities are issues with volunteers and what volunteering means to the events. A current lawsuit, Liebeman v. Competitor Group, Inc. (management company of the rock and roll marathon series) challenges the use of volunteers for charity-related events as the competitor group obscured its for-profit status. This lawsuit may alter the definition of who should be considered an employee and who should be considered a volunteer.

While spending tax money on professional stadiums is lessening, there has been an increase of tax monies used to construct and renovate local facilities. For example, the Paco Tourism Development Council was able to pass a 2 percent increase (up to 4 percent) in hotel taxes to pay to market the county as a tourism destination and construct a new sportsplex.

Recreation Management recently reported that more than half of the community centers in their survey expected to engage in new construction projects within the next 3 years. The top planned features for all facility types include: Splash pads, synthetic turf fields, fitness trails and outdoor fitness equipment, fitness centers, walking and hiking trails, playgrounds, park shelters, dog parks, exercise studios, and disc golf courses. In addition to the changes in their facilities, centers also plan to add new programming such as nutrition and diet counseling, mind–body programs, sport clubs (e.g., running, swimming, cycling), and sport tournaments and races.

VIGNETTE 1-3

If You Lower Prices, They Will Come and Spend Money

In 2017, the Atlanta Falcons opened their new stadium, Mercedes-Benz Stadium. Along with state-of-the-art facilities, the Falcons made the news when they announced their concession prices. A soda, which includes free, unlimited refills, cost $2. Additionally, bottled water, popcorn, and a soft pretzel also cost $2. A slice of pizza, peanuts, nachos with cheese, and French fries were $3; $5 for a cheeseburger; and a chicken tenders basket was $6. In order to expedite the concession process, the Falcons installed 65 percent more point-of-sale checkout registers than the previous facility. There were also self-serve soda machines installed around the stadium so patrons would not have to stand in a long line for their free refill.

The gamble to lower prices paid off since fans spent 16 percent more at concessions than they did the previous season. Each home game also saw an increase of 6,000 additional fans coming into the stadium two hours before kickoff. However, the biggest change may be how the fans viewed the team. After the 2016 season, the Falcons were ranked 18th for food and beverage satisfaction. Once they launched their new concession plan, the fans ranked the Falcons 1st in food and beverage customer satisfaction in the league.

The Atlanta Falcons proved that departing from the standard way of doing concession operations was not only profitable but created a better atmosphere for fans and improved customer satisfaction. And, at the end of the day, a happy customer is a return customer.

Scale of the Sport Event Industry

The sport event industry may be one of the most challenging industries to define because of the volume and variety of sport-event opportunities that could be included in industry estimates. For example, the sport-event industry could include something as small as a 50-person 5K (5-kilometer) fun run to raise money for a local charity or something as large as the FIFA World Cup, an event that draws more than 3 million spectators, with another 250 million watching via various international broadcasts. This example highlights two different kinds of events that will be commonly discussed throughout this text: Participant-led and spectator-led. In the first example, the 5K race is considered a participant-led event because the majority of the revenue is generated from those who are participating in the event. In contrast, spectator-led events either derive the revenue directly (e.g., tickets) or indirectly (e.g., sponsorship) from those who are watching the event.

In 2018, the Plunkett Report, a market research organization that provides annual industry reports, estimated that the international sport industry is a $1.3 trillion industry, with annual spending of more than $38 billion on sport-related products or services. In the United States alone, the sport industry employs approximately 5 million people in the broad categories of interscholastic and intercollegiate athletics; professional, community, recreation, and sport organizations; health and fitness organizations; and sporting goods manufacturers. Additionally, the U.S. Bureau of Labor Statistics has reported that 130,570 people work in the spectator sport industry, a small segment of the overall sport industry, with a 9.8 percent growth rate from 2002.

Who Manages Sport Events?

Sport event management is vastly spreading from the normal professional, collegiate, and parks and recreation governing structures. For instance, chambers of commerce and visitors' bureaus have begun to invest in staff and infrastructure associated with hosting sport events to attract tourists to their communities. The National Association of Sports Commissions (www.sportscommissions.org) was developed in 1992 to provide a communication network between event owners and facility owners to increase access to event information and education to best practices. Currently, the membership is at an all-time high, with more than 650 member organizations and

1,600 event owners. With this level of growth in the sport event and facility management industry, there is an increased need for individuals who can manage multiple sport events throughout the year and a need for a better understanding of the event management discipline. For instance, sport event and facility managers need a strong foundation in risk management, finance, human resource management, marketing, customer service, and project management, which leads us to the contents that you will find throughout this text.

SUMMARY

For more than 30,000 years, organized sport has been a component of human civilization. As humans and communities have evolved during this time, so have the sport events in which we participate and spectate, as have the facilities that we use to host those events. While the designs of our facilities have not changed much in terms of structure, the ancillary items we place inside of them and the events they host have changed considerably. The remainder of this text will outline the major components of both facility and event management as they pertain to recreational, leisure, and competitive sport events.

DISCUSSION QUESTIONS

1. Explain the relationship between religion and sport in the development of sport events.
2. What is the foundation of sport facilities and how have the designs and funding changed over time?
3. What role has the "arms race" played in the development of facilities in the United States?
4. Which organizations are involved in the management of sport events in your local community? University community?

Case STUDY

Is it Time to Renovate or Rebuild Cameron Indoor Stadium?

Duke University is a private institution located in Durham, North Carolina. With an enrollment of 6,600 undergraduate and 6,000 graduate students, it is one of the most prestigious universities in the country. Tuition runs about $40,000 a year, making it one of the most affluent schools in the country. Located in what is known as the Research Triangle area of North Carolina, the Raleigh–Durham area has a metropolitan population of 1.5 million people and hosts several headquarters for major corporations.

(continues)

Case STUDY (continued)

The Duke University men's and women's basketball teams play their home games in Cameron Indoor Stadium, the crown jewel of college basketball. The stadium was originally built in 1935 and was remodeled in the late 1980s.

Sports Illustrated ranked the stadium fourth on the list of the country's greatest sporting venues of the twentieth century, ahead of Pebble Beach, Wrigley Field, and Fenway Park. The stadium offers little room for concessions and no room for corporate sponsorships. Stadium capacity is 9,314, with 3,500 of those seats being bleacher seats reserved for students. To say that the stadium is antiquated is an understatement. The Board of Regents thinks a new facility needs to be on par with the other schools in the area; however, they are aware of the public sentiment for Cameron Indoor Stadium. Keep in mind that the University of North Carolina, Wake Forest, and North Carolina State all play in new, modern facilities.

Things to Consider

Take into account that the University of North Carolina sits 8 miles away from the Duke campus, and North Carolina State is about 22 miles away. Wake Forest University is located about 80 miles away. The Raleigh–Durham area is full of graduates and fans from these and other Atlantic Coast Conference schools who would love to buy tickets and watch their school play against Duke but have been unable to do so because of Cameron's low seating capacity. Thus, in addition to the opportunity to sell more tickets to its own fans, Duke has the opportunity to sell lots of tickets to visiting teams' fans.

Questions That Need to be Addressed

In determining the fate of the Cameron Indoor Stadium, the following questions must be addressed:

- Who pays?
- Who should pay?
- Who benefits?
- How do you finance this project?

As an agency hired by the Duke athletic department, the athletic director of the university has asked you to evaluate building a new basketball arena or a complete remodeling of the current facility. The athletic director wants you to take into account the number of seats the arena will hold and the added revenue from corporate sponsorship as well as a possible naming rights deal. In theory, a new arena would have many new areas for corporate advertising and hospitality. However, this is debatable because donors might want the new arena to have more of a "campus field house" feel (such as that found in the University of Maryland or Indiana Pacers facilities).

You will have a chance to present your proposal to the Board of Regents. The Board is split on this proposal, and it is a very touchy subject. Some feel that the success of Duke teams in the last 20 years makes this the perfect time to build an arena, while others disagree. Choose whether you would like to renovate or rebuild the arena, and answer the following questions:

1. Which part will the Iron Dukes (the athletic department's fundraising/donor group) play in the financial process?
2. What is the Basketball Legacy Fund?
3. Does the Raleigh–Durham area have the corporate infrastructure to support suite/club seat sales?
4. Would a surcharge on student fees work at Duke?
5. How many suites and club seats would you include in a new arena?
6. How would you position a capital campaign for a new stadium?
7. How many seats would this arena hold?
8. Who will own and manage the arena, the athletic department, or the school?
9. If remodeling, where does Duke play in the meantime?
10. Would the women's team continue to play in Cameron? Consider this decision from a financial standpoint.
11. Will a new facility be a recruiting advantage or disadvantage?

REFERENCES

Brown, M. T., Rascher, D. A., Nagel, M. S., & McEvoy, C. D. (2017). *Financial management in sport industry.* New York, NY: Routelege.

Fried, G. (2010). *Managing sport facilities* (2nd ed.). Champaign, IL: Human Kinetics.

Masterman, G. (2009). *Strategic sports event management.* Oxford, UK: Butterworth-Heinemann.

Plunkett, J. W., Plunkett, M. B., Steinberg, J. S., Faulk, J., & Snider, I. J. (2018). Introduction to the sports industry. *Sports Industry.* Retrieved from http://www.plunkettresearchonline.com.

Toohey, K., & Veal, A. J. (2000). *The Olympic Games: A social perspective.* Cambridge, MA: CABI Publishing.

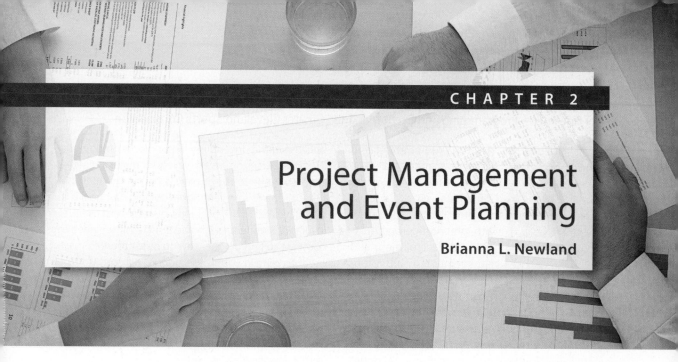

CHAPTER 2

Project Management and Event Planning

Brianna L. Newland

CHAPTER OBJECTIVES

Upon completion of this chapter, the reader will be able to:

1. Describe the necessity of project management in the management of sport events.
2. Use project management tools to plan a successful event.
3. Outline the phases of project management and planning.

CHAPTER OVERVIEW

This chapter introduces project management concepts and tools to assist the sport event manager in planning and implementing the event. Concepts such as the work breakdown structure, Gantt charts, and other project management tools will be introduced.

IndustryVOICE

Becky Griesmer—Programming and Event Manager, Greater Cleveland Sports Commission

As the Programming and Event Manager for the Greater Cleveland Sports Commission (GCSC), I focus on our Youth Education Through Sports program, as well as the recruitment and management of all volunteers, supporting our mid-career professionals on the Associate Board and working with local hotels and housing for GCSC events. My interest in the sporting industry began in 2010 when I interned with GCSC and was the lead student liaison for the World School Games. I continued my path in this field through internships with the Anthony Muñoz Foundation, Greater Cincinnati Sports Corporation, Greater Cincinnati Independent Business Alliance and Xavier University Athletics Department. After graduating from Xavier University with a degree in Sports Management, I accepted a contracted role with GCSC. The position was supposed to only be for one year, but two months into the Fellowship, a new position was created, and I was hired full time in my current role.

Since 2000, GCSC has been responsible for attracting over 190 sporting events, which have contributed over $570 million in economic activity to Northeast Ohio. Our mission is to positively impact the economy, image, and quality of life in Cleveland by hosting and managing amateur sporting events. We are a non-profit organization and a full-service sports commission with 12 full-time staff members focusing on a variety of tasks, including sponsorships, event logistics, event attraction, community outreach, marketing, communications, and funding.

Two current challenges in this area of the industry include changes in current state legislation and the increased costs it takes to run an event. As state legislation is reformed, our organization is impacted because of the uncertainty that it places on potential funding sources on which we rely for major events. As costs continue to rise, it plays a part in the bids that GCSC prepares for event rights holders. Our goal is to put Cleveland in the best light possible, but as hotel, insurance, venue, and labor fees increase, we need to continue to find unique ways to offset these items in order to remain within the budget set forth for the event. GCSC has been able to do this by offering other resources or services that would benefit the client and offset these potential costs. For example, if labor costs are higher than normal at a venue, we would explore the possibility of utilizing staff and volunteers to work in that specific area instead.

The event industry must continue to find a way to stay current with the increased use of technology and the desire that clients have to experience unique venues. A typical ballroom may not do the trick any longer for a conference, but clients would rather look for more interactive, exclusive setups in a space that is a bit different and out of the box. Technology will continue to play a key role in the success of events, due to the inevitable change that is to come for registration processes, ticket sales, or special effects offered. GCSC has continued to stay current with these trends because we know the success of our events and industry rely on it. From a staff management standpoint, the system that we use to gather sign-ups will come out with updates that help enhance the seasonal staff member's experience. We have the option of implementing this technology, such as text message reminders or user-friendly screens, to help our team recruit, communicate, and manage the season staff's experience from start to finish. In addition, our team continues to maintain a close relationship with unique venues and settings around the Cleveland area, so that we might be able to utilize that partnership if the need comes up. We must always keep the customer in the front of our mind and continue to highlight our area in a fun and diverse way to all visitors. Our goal is to change the mindset that people have about Cleveland, and offer groups services and the extra effort that they can't get anywhere else.

When hiring someone for an entry-level position, our organization must first establish if that person aligns well with our core values. The passion that someone displays in an interview helps highlight whether they will fit with the culture of the organization. I like to look for someone who asks thoughtful questions, can multitask, has a strong work ethic, and is determined to make a difference. I think that fresh college graduates have the tendency to think too seriously about their dream job and miss the moment that is in front of them. I believe that the skills you learn during an internship or first job are often transferable and can be carried from one role to the next. College graduates often overlook and take for granted the skills that they will learn through volunteer work or informational interviews with professionals already in the field. Many positions within my organization require one to possess the ability to think creatively, work hard, and have the team-first mentality. A winning attitude and scrappy, entrepreneurial spirit are a few of the guiding principles that help lead the team to success.

I would encourage students to become familiar with the many different types of tools that help you to plan and assign roles to various staff members. Depending on the event, we have general volunteers who sign up for a shift or two to assist; volunteer captains, who are more of a higher-end volunteer and looked at as the liaisons between general volunteers and our staff; event crew, who are often individuals who are an extension of our staff and work the event full time; additionally, there are ticket takers, venue staff, union workers, and more. Managing all of these people takes communication and a coordinated effort among all parties (venue, event logistics, event rights holder) in order to pull off a successful event. And to do this, you need to really plan to determine how the staff will impact the overall project—the event. Therefore, it is important not only to plan for the main logistics of the event but also to know how you will assign people during the planning, initiation, execution, and breakdown of the event.

Introduction

"The devil is in the details" expresses the idea that whatever one does, he or she should do it thoroughly—meaning that the details are important. This is an important concept to remember when planning and staging events because there is high pressure and often only one opportunity to "get it right." Therefore, sport event managers must incorporate techniques that offer advantages and support for managing events. Project management techniques offer the sport event manager this advantage by integrating the various objectives from the event units (i.e., marketing, sponsorship, operations, and logistics) into one workable plan for the entire project—the sport event. This chapter examines how project management tools can assist the manager in the planning, staging, and implementation of a sporting event.

Project Management

WHAT IS PROJECT MANAGEMENT?

project management
The dynamic process of organizing and managing appropriate resources in a controlled and structured manner to deliver the clearly defined work required to complete a project within the given scope, time, and, often, cost constraints.

project A temporary and one-time venture undertaken to create a unique product with specific outcomes and benefits.

project triple constraint The cost, time, and scope constraints that impact the final quality of an event.

Project management is the dynamic process of organizing and managing appropriate resources in a controlled and structured manner to deliver the clearly defined work required to complete a project within the given scope, time, and, often, cost constraints (Patel, 2008; Young, 2007). Sport events, whether they are one-off, annual, or weekly, are projects. A **project** is a temporary and one-time venture undertaken to create a unique product with specific outcomes and benefits (Patel, 2008)—in this case, the sport event. An important aspect to keep in mind is that the event is a deliverable of the project management process (Allen, O'Toole, Harris, & McDonnell, 2011). The event itself might occur over a few hours, days, or even weeks, but the project management process may take place over many months, or, as in the case of the Olympic Games, many years. A misunderstanding of project management leads individuals to believe that it is merely a scheduling process. However, this is not accurate. Project management integrates all of the management tasks necessary to oversee the work before, during, and after the event has occurred. In other words, it is the planning and controlling of scarce resources to ensure a successful event (Lewis, 1998).

There are two main challenges of project management. The first challenge is to ensure that the event can be delivered within the defined constraints (i.e., time, cost, quality, and scope). Known as the **project triple constraint** (Allen et al., 2011), each constraint cannot be altered without impacting the other sides of the triangle and, in the process, the *quality* of the event (see **Figure 2-1**).

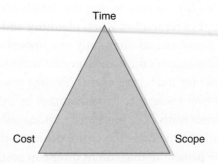

Figure 2-1   The Project Triple Constraint

The *scope* of the project includes **project outputs** necessary to produce the final product (the event). The *time* constraint refers to the amount of time allotted to complete the project. Since sport events are bound by a specific date, when the project runs behind schedule, cost and scope are (often negatively) impacted. The *cost* constraint refers to the amount of money budgeted to complete the project. If the scope of the project falls behind schedule and a sport event manager does not want to affect the event quality in any way, costs will go up considerably. Most sport events are greatly bound by costs, especially in the initial planning stages. This challenge impacts participation sport events that rely on registration fees to finance the event, which can be inconsistent and delayed. Events cannot rely on teams and/or individuals to sign up for the event a year, or even months, in advance. The reality is that many register for events as they draw closer.

Take, for example, a softball tournament. Much of the planning and coordination begins many months (and even a year) before the team registration fees begin trickling in. Therefore, sport event managers must carefully forecast a budget that takes into consideration not only the project outputs but also *when* the money will be accessible. Marketing expenses are frequently required early in the implementation stage. By building relationships with key vendors, event managers can defer payment until after the event in order to avoid up-front expenses. The ability to delay payment is key when the money is not immediately accessible. It requires the building of trust between the event manager and vendor to ensure delayed payment.

Changes to the other two sides of the triangle could be very detrimental to the costs associated with the event. If an event falls behind schedule and containing costs is a concern, scope—and the quality—will be compromised. The scope involves the planning, coordination and implementation of the sport event. Project management tools help to prevent delays that can be costly and impact the quality of the event. Let us return to our softball tournament example. Perhaps in the planning stage the event manager had planned to hire a DJ to entertain the spectators and players in the common area between games. However, the event planning has fallen behind schedule and costs have gone up. The event manager can no longer pay the $1,500 to have the professional DJ perform on the weekend of the tournament.

project outputs The transformation of resources (human, financial, physical) into new assets through a defined deliverable.

TIP

First-year and one-off event budgets are very difficult to forecast. Do your research early! Call multiple vendors and suppliers of your event equipment and ask for detailed bids. Not only will this provide you with a picture of your expenses but it will also give you an opportunity to negotiate better prices.

© iStockphoto.com/hocus-focus

However, with a little creativity, the event manager is able to secure a university student and amateur DJ for a fraction of the price, $600. This quick thinking allows the event to still provide entertainment, but the quality will be compromised, if we assume that the amateur does not have the skills and expertise of the professional DJ.

The second (and perhaps more ambitious) challenge is the proper allocation and assimilation of the inputs (e.g., people, money, time) needed to meet the objectives of the event (Patel, 2008). Project management tools help the event manager to systematically define the tasks necessary to meet overall objectives, delegate those tasks to the right people, allocate financial resources appropriately, and coordinate when the tasks must be completed. Project management accounts for elements that are not usually found in ongoing management of typical organizations. Events have a specific end date, budget, and deliverable (the event itself) that cannot be improved upon (Allen et al., 2011). While conventional products are continuously updated and improved based on consumer feedback, events do not have that same luxury. An event must produce its best product the first time, especially if it's a one-off sport event.

VIGNETTE 2-1

The 2016 Rio de Janeiro Olympic Games

The 2016 Rio Olympic Games were beset with a number of expensive obstacles throughout the planning and staging phases that nearly compromised the event to the point that the state government of Rio declared a "state of public calamity" just 50 days from the start of the Olympics (Bowater, 2016). Besieged by a fall in oil prices, the country suffered from a major decline in public revenue that threatened Brazil's ability to honor its Olympic commitments. Suffering from severe construction delays, delays in the depollution of competition venues, the failure to secure proper environmental licenses, a rise in tourist crime, disputes between drug traffickers, and a collapsed bicycle path that killed two people, it is a wonder that the Games occurred at all. These delays and complications did come at a price; the state owes the Brazilian government $21 billion and another $10 billion to public banks and international lenders (Barbara, 2016).

Phases of Project Management

A main aim of project management is to control risk and potential failure by providing a clear direction that aligns with the strategic goals and objectives for the event. The management of the sport event will pass through a number of phases, each of which will include a number of tasks that yield a deliverable that sparks the next phase. The number of phases varies by industry, but most disciplines that utilize project management tools agree on five core phases: Initiation, planning, implementation, monitoring, and shutdown (Patel, 2008; Young, 2007). Additionally, the International Event Management Body of Knowledge (EMBOK) [2006] has conceptualized a four-dimensional depiction of the phases, processes, and core values that feed into the domains necessary to create and deliver sport events. This conceptualization is adapted in **Figure 2-2**.

The Processes

The processes are sequential and iterative systems that recognize the dynamic nature of events. The first of the processes is **assessment**, which includes *identifying* and *analyzing*. As an event manager begins to assess the needs for the event, he or she must identify all of the elements in each phase and domain. The analysis of these elements facilitates the prioritizing of an element and supports predictive capabilities when forecasting (Rutherford Silvers, 2004).

     The next of the processes is **selection**, which is the decision-making point. An event manager must not only choose the tactics necessary to complete the task or goal but he or she must also assign the resources to carry out the task. Assigning key staff to specific tasks, determining the financial cost to complete the event outcomes, and giving authority to carry out the work are all part of the selection process. The third process is **monitoring** (not to be confused with the monitoring element of the phases), which is the systematic tracking of the progress of a task. The monitoring process is iterative and might require a team to reassess and select new tactics.

     Documentation is the fourth process, which involves recording, reporting, and maintaining assessments; analyses, monitoring reports, and other records that provide valuable data to build upon during the current event; and future improvements for the next event. Finally, **communication** is final and the most vital component of the processes because it requires

assessment Identifying and analyzing the environment to assess the needs of the event.

selection The decision point of the planning process.

monitoring The systematic tracking of the progress of a task.

documentation Recording, reporting, and maintaining assessments of progress in order to collect valuable data for current and future event processes.

communication The open and transparent channels of discussion about the processes.

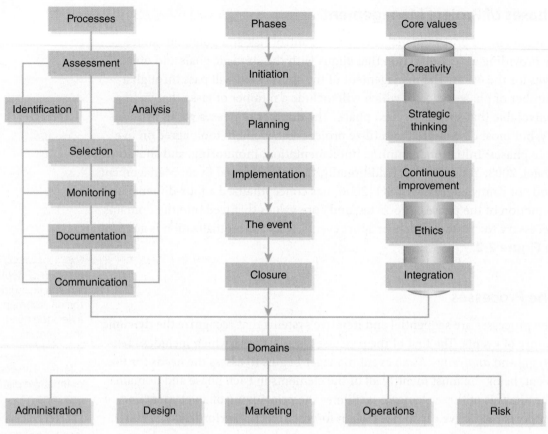

Figure 2-2   EMBOK Model for Event Management

Modified from International EMBOK Executive (www.embok.org), 2006.

timely acquisition and distribution of information for decision-making and execution of tasks required to achieve event product outcomes (Rutherford Silvers, 2004).

The Phases

initiation phase The stage in event planning that allows sport event organizers to define the event, set objectives, and determine the sport event's feasibility.

The phases highlight the critical nature of time in the event project. First and foremost, the sport event requires direction. The **initiation phase** allows sport event organizers to define the event, set objectives, and determine the sport event's feasibility. Many events are unsuccessful because inadequate information collection in the initiation phase leads to unclear goals and objectives, unrealistic resource and time estimates, and changes to objectives midproject (Zarndt, 2011). Furthermore, if you are seeking financial assistance for the sport event with a bank loan, a bank will most likely require a detailed feasibility study before granting funds (Lock, 2013). In the initiation stage, a feasibility study will detail the viability of a sport event and the managerial requirements necessary to deliver it. This report may also detail date and venue suggestions, an assessment of competing events operating within the host location, potential sponsors, market research identifying potential customers and sponsors, a draft budget, identification of key stakeholders, and, in some cases, the potential social, political, and environmental impacts (Allen et al., 2011). A thorough feasibility study will include alternative configurations of the sport event to enable a variety of options prior to the planning phase. The end of the initiation phase is often marked by a red or green light to continue to the planning stages. **Table 2-1** identifies the areas by domain to explore feasibility of a sport event.

One very important area on which to focus the feasibility study is the financial concerns, under the risk domain. A good event manager should know whether an event is financially feasible prior to green-lighting the event. To determine what financial risk exists, a breakeven analysis should be conducted using the breakeven equation, EBIT = Fixed Costs / (Registration Fee − Variable Costs). This equation is an incredibly useful way to examine the number of attendees (or registered participants, if you are running a tournament, for example) required for the event to break even. The key to a strong analysis is to accurately predict all of the operational expenses involved, both variable and fixed.

> **TIP**
>
> Event Registration Fee: $150.00
> Variable costs per competitor: $95.00
>
> Total Fixed Costs: $15,000
>
> 15,000 / (150 − 95) = 272.7
>
> You need 273 participants to register for the event to break even.

Table 2-1   Feasibility Areas by Domain

Administration	Design	Marketing	Operations	Risk
• Expertise of staff • Resource viability: Draft budget, staff requirements • Identification of key stakeholders • Timeline for project completion	• Event date and venue • Location accessibility • Program and production viability • Environment capability	• Competing events • Market research • Customer identification • Sponsor identification • Promotion, public relations, sponsor capability	• Managerial requirements • Venue/ infrastructure capability • Social, environmental, political impacts • Technical capability	• Social, environmental, political impacts • Financial concerns • Operational concerns • Legal concerns, insurance • Security

planning phase
The proactive and dynamic stage in event planning in which the various suggested options suggestion in the initiation phase are reviewed for the best course of action and preparation of the event.

This can be very difficult for a first-time event that does not have a financial history. In this case, strong budget forecasting and obtaining accurate bids for the event expenses are critical. When considering event revenue streams, an event manager should not only consider direct event revenues (such as participation registrations) but also the supplemental revenue-generating options such as concessions, auxiliary event ticket sales, sponsorship, memorabilia, etc. The revenues will be projected based on a per-unit average.

In the **planning phase**, the various options suggested in the initiation stage are reviewed to determine the best ones, and the planning begins. Planning is straightforward and can be considered a process of asking questions (Young, 2007), such as:

- What actions need to be taken?
- When will these actions occur?
- Who is going to take on these actions?
- What resources (including human, financial, and supplies/equipment) are required for these actions?
- Is there a bid submission requirement?
- Is there demand for such an event?
- How many staff and volunteers are needed to execute the event?

The answers to these questions can be used to develop a project form that is completed in order to reduce risks and uncertainty, establish standards of performance, provide a structure and procedures for executing work, and serve as a means to obtain required outcomes (Young, 2007). **Figure 2-3** is a sample work plan form that can be used in the planning and implementation stages. A different form can be used for various stages throughout the preparation process.

The planning stage is dynamic and continuous, and sport event managers must remain proactive and diligent. It is wise not to plan all the details at the outset to avoid reworking the plan and wasting valuable time. Furthermore, it is important to identify the key workers who will be involved in the planning process. The planning team should cover all of the previously mentioned domains to ensure well-balanced skills and expertise. Additionally, there are a number of factors, both internal and external, that can have a massive impact on the outcome of the project.

External factors lie outside of the organization's and sport event manager's control but can have a profound impact on the event—including

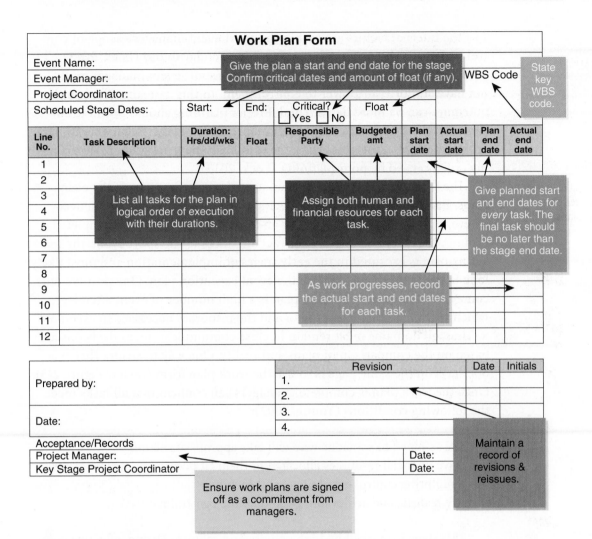

Figure 2-3   Example Work Plan

cancellation. *Acts of God* include extreme weather (e.g., hurricanes, devastating storms, heavy snow/blizzards), and earthquakes. *Fiscal policy* can impact an event when the national government modifies or enacts policy changes on taxation and other financial measures, such as choosing to abandon a government-funded event. An event can be impacted by *statutory regulations* when national or local government imposes new legislation. Such regulations can be particularly important for events that occur in foreign countries, which can be impacted by international, foreign, and local law.

The internal factors are within the sport event manager's scope of control and are likely to affect the staff and project day to day (Lock, 2013). While these factors are internal, at times, the sport event manager might not have authority or power to control them. In this case, the effect on the outcomes can be more detrimental. Proper planning should promote efficient work and maintain the project management triangle elements (time, scope, and costs), thereby saving the staff from the frustration of overcoming crises caused by poor planning (Lock, 2013).

The third phase is the execution, or **implementation phase**, of the event plans. Each domain will have a specific plan that contributes to the overall event plan that must detail how and when the work will be completed (Young, 2007). For example, to attract attendees to the sport event, the marketing plan is executed in the early stages of implementation and most likely long before other plans, such as the event execution plan. One positive outcome of a successful marketing plan is a high number of event attendees, which will affect the logistics plan and the resources necessary to execute it. Thus, all domains must remain in close communication, as decisions are based on the comparison of plans and reality. One way to ensure that everyone stays on the same page is to use the work plan form (review Figure 2-3). Once the work plan is complete, managers can confirm that all tasks meet the following conditions (Young, 2007):

- Are assigned to someone who will take appropriate action
- Have financial resources allocated to them (if necessary), which allows for monitoring control over budget and spending
- Are realistic and achievable given the time constraints

This stage is marked by high activity and requires strong, effective communication among the event team members. There is the possibility that managers will need to revisit the planning stage in light of major problems or changes to the event program (Allen et al., 2011). Poor communication during this stage can lead to a major source of conflict and work slippages.

Monitoring and control systems are implemented to ensure that performance standards are achieved as the sport event is executed. According to Young (2007, 2013), there are three operating modes:

- Measuring, which determines progress through formal and informal reporting

implementation phase The execution of the event plans.

monitoring and control system The controls that are implemented to ensure that performance standards are achieved as the sport event is executed.

- Evaluating, which determines the cause of deviations from the plan and how to react
- Correcting, which involves taking actions to correct the deviations from the plan

The overall event plan and schedule will dictate how and what objectives are to be met. The job of the sport event manager, then, is to regulate the activities and resources to achieve the results defined by the plan (Young, 2007). Because the event environment is dynamic, a great deal of flexibility is necessary in the planning stages, but the execution and monitoring of the event should be systematic in order to achieve goals (Van der Wagen & White, 2010). There are a number of reasons why events fail, including failure to plan, external factors, incompetent staff, poor control of costs or lack of income, and lack of leadership. Monitoring and controls can help safeguard the organization and assist in achieving a successful event.

The best controls are simple and provide risk prevention and feedback on progress (Van der Wagen & White, 2010; Young, 2013). Preventive controls are established in the planning stages and continue into execution. For example, requiring that only key staff be authorized to sign purchase orders or requiring that all purchase orders be signed by a superior prior to purchase can help to curtail unauthorized spending. Also designing a checklist for event setup would serve as a preventive control *and* a feedback control. As the checklist is completed on event day, it can serve as a way to document missing activities and/or other information. Feedback controls can assist with decision making during an event by allowing an event worker to evaluate a situation and make a decision. For example, perhaps during a warm-up session, the athletes relay an issue with the equipment. The event staff can implement a preventive measure to alleviate the problem prior to competition starting.

The last stage of the project is the **closure or shutdown** of the event, and it, too, must be carefully planned. Management of attendees' departure,

closure/shutdown
The final stage of event planning to ensure that nothing is lost, equipment is returned properly, and the flow of those involved occurs seamlessly.

domain As used by the International Event Management Body of Knowledge, a division of the labor required at an event.

administration domain The event management domain that includes the finance, human resources, information, procurement, stakeholders, systems, and time elements of an event.

design domain The event management domain that contains the event's content, theme, program, environment, and production, entertainment, and catering needs.

removal of equipment, and event cleanup can take a great deal of time and effort. Shutdown requires proper planning and execution to ensure that nothing is lost, equipment is returned properly, and the flow of those involved occurs seamlessly. Shutdown is the most forgotten element of the project (Allen et al., 2011). Like the planning and execution stages, shutdown should include a work breakdown structure, task and responsibility checklists, and a schedule, which is subject to risk analysis (Allen et al., 2011). Items and equipment should be inventoried as they are packed up (especially small items like walkie-talkies) both to ensure that nothing is lost and in preparation for the next event. Proper coding and organization of equipment will not only ensure that the details are organized for the next event but they can also help with the closeout of contracts and bills to vendors and suppliers.

The Domains

According to EMBOK (2006), the **domains** can be further divided to provide greater detail for the management of the event. For example, the **administration domain** includes the management of finance, human resources, information, procurement, stakeholders, systems, and time. The **design domain** contains the event's content, theme, program, environment, and production; entertainment; and catering needs. The **marketing domain** is composed of the event marketing plan, marketing materials, merchandise, promotion, public relations, sales, and sponsorship. The **operations domain** consists of communications, event infrastructure, logistics, the venue, technical needs, participants, and attendees. Finally, the **risk domain** involves compliance issues, emergency plans, health and safety plans, insurance needs, legal concerns, security needs, and any risk-related decisions. These domains could easily represent the departments that are developed to manage the sport event and provide an organizational structure. However, because smaller events do not have the financial or human resources to cordon off these domains into departments, typically, a small number of staff members must work within all of these domains. Therefore, it is important to organize the work by domain to ensure that the tasks necessary to complete the project and deliver the event are completed.

Each domain will have tasks specifically associated with the particular phase at hand. Some domains may depend on the other domain in order to begin or complete work. For example, it is important that the event stakeholders are clearly defined by the administration domain prior to the marketing domain developing the materials directed to stakeholders. Another possibility is that one domain could potentially move through one phase faster than another domain, which can create chaos if not properly managed. Going back to the stakeholder example, developing the marketing materials before the stakeholders are properly defined could lead to the costly consequence of having to revise or redo materials. Project management tools provide useful communication tools and processes to ensure that each domain communicates openly at each stage, while keeping the domains on track to deliver a successful event. Planning by stage will also keep the tasks organized for each domain. The stages of event planning are initiation, planning, implementation, monitoring, and closure/shutdown.

WORK BREAKDOWN STRUCTURE

The **work breakdown structure (WBS)** is simply the project tasks broken down into manageable parts. Once the scope of the event has been defined, the WBS allows the work required to deliver the event to be visually categorized and communicated to the staff (Allen et al., 2011). The WBS allows the numerous tasks to be aggregated under specific categories in order to better manage the large scope of work. For example, the tasks related specifically to the marketing plan would be grouped and presented on the WBS as "Marketing." Once completed, the WBS resembles a hierarchical chart, with the event itself at the top and the major activity flowing down the chart (Shone & Parry, 2010).

GANTT CHART

A **Gantt chart** is a bar chart that illustrates the various tasks that must be completed in a time-sequence order (Shone & Parry, 2010). The Gantt chart

marketing domain The event management domain composed of the event's marketing plan, marketing materials, merchandize, promotions, public relations, sales, and sponsorship.

operations domain The event management domain that consists of communications, event infrastructure, logistics, the venue, technical needs, participants, and attendees.

risk domain The event management domain that consists of compliance issues, emergency plans, health and safety plans, insurance needs, legal concerns, security needs, and any risk-related decisions.

work breakdown structure (WBS) Project tasks broken down into manageable parts.

gantt chart A bar chart that illustrates the various tasks that must be completed for the event in a time-sequence order.

displays the details of the work to be completed for the WBS and can be created using the following components (Allen et al., 2011):

- *Tasks* break down the work involved into manageable activities
- *Timelines* set the time scale for each task. Factors to consider are the start and end time and the availability of the assigned resources (both human and financial)
- *Priorities* set the order of important items and identify what tasks must be completed prior to the current task starting
- *Milestones* assist in monitoring the event. Tasks that are of particular importance are designated as milestones

The benefit of this chart is that the tasks are displayed interdependently. One can easily see when a task is to start and end, the progress to date, and which tasks are dependent on one finishing prior to another beginning. A limitation is the inability to visually track resource (staff) workload. While some software programs do allow the event manager to assign resources to tasks, these resources do not appear on the Gantt chart. Therefore, it is difficult to gauge the workload of each resource visually. More sophisticated programs will have a means for monitoring workload, but they will not appear in this chart.

PROGRAM EVALUATION AND REVIEW TECHNIQUE CHART AND CRITICAL PATH

program evaluation and review technique (PERT) chart An illustration of the tasks, duration, and dependency information, which can be useful in defining the critical path for the project.

The **program evaluation and review technique (PERT) chart** illustrates the tasks, duration, and dependency information, which can be useful in defining the **critical path** for the project (Van der Wagen & White, 2010). The PERT chart allows for a series of subtasks to be analyzed to find the most efficient scheduling, or the critical path (Allen et al., 2011).

critical path An analysis of the most efficient scheduling of tasks and subtasks.

RUN SHEETS

run sheet A detailed schedule of the sequencing and timing for each element of the event.

The **run sheet** is vital for the execution of the event, as it is for the program, or schedule, of events (Van der Wagen & White, 2010). The run sheet will detail the timing for each element of the event schedule and provides correct sequencing and timing of those elements. Sequencing in the run sheet will specify the order of actions, while timing will identify when the action will commence (Van der Wagen & White, 2010).

CHECKLISTS

The **checklist** is an indispensable control tool that the sport event manager uses to ensure that each individual is performing all tasks essential to the success of the event. Checklists serve as preventive control during the planning process to account for the specific tasks prior to the event. Additionally, they are feedback control during the event as a recordkeeping process in order to prevent problems and serve to reduce risk, should plans go awry (Van der Wagen & White, 2010).

FLOOR PLANS AND FLOW DIAGRAMS

Floor plans illustrate where equipment or items are to be placed within the event venue. These plans are integral in the proper ordering of equipment based on attendee numbers and in determining whether the venue has the space to accommodate the event design and occupants. **Flow diagrams** are a graphic representation of how attendees will move through your event and venue. These diagrams ensure that queues are held to a minimum, thereby avoiding line backups; display how attendees will enter and exit the venue or event areas; and can determine and mitigate potential areas of risk due to an emergency or other problem. Flow diagrams are especially important for high-traffic areas, such as routes from the parking locations, areas where high numbers will congregate (such as registration or ticket queues), and regions where space is limited or dense.

Tools of Project Management

SOFTWARE

Make good use of technology. There are a number of project management programs that offer free online software. Furthermore, there are a number of computer software programs that provide a link to a mobile phone application so the sport event manager can easily navigate from computer to tablet to smart-phone, depending on location and accessibility. Much of the current software and web/mobile applications are excellent for planning a sport event; however, due to the dynamic nature of an event, some programs are limited in their usefulness. While there are a number of options available on the Internet, only a few examples and their functionality will be discussed here.

Smartsheet. Smartsheet is a cloud-based tool that allows teams to interface on complex projects in a simple and easy format. Managing projects with the use of Gantt charts, automated workflows, and resource management.

checklist A preventive control tool that ensures that each individual is performing all tasks essential for to the success of the event.

floor plan An illustration of where equipment or items are to be placed within the event venue.

flow diagram A graphical representation as toof how attendees will move through the event and venue.

Teams can work in real-time, accessing their tasks, files, and calendars from any device. While this tool is not free, it does offer more functionality than other tools in its category. For more information, visit www.smartsheet.com.

Wrike. Wrike is a project management tool that enables teams to collaborate the platform. The tool offers live editing and file management so teams can see changes in real-time. It also enables Gantt charts to visualize the project schedule as well as resource management allocations and time/budget tracking. Unlike other tools on the market, Wrike offers a free individual tool for teams of five or fewer. More information on this tool can be found at www.wrike.com.

monday. monday is a visually driven project management tool that enables teams to simplify how the team works by managing workload in a more visual platform. This tool requires that you create a board (i.e., project) for the team to track workload. Projects, tasks, missions, and simple to-dos can be easily assigned to team members, where the exact status can be tracked easily and clearly. Like the other programs, monday allows for the creation of Gantt charts and other visuals. More information can be found at www.monday.com.

These are just three examples of many. A quick search of project management tools reveals hundreds of free and paid options. Other popular options include Microsoft Project, Asana, Slack, Trello, Basecamp, and Teamwork Projects. These are just a few examples and there might be a better option for your event management team.

SUMMARY

Because the sport event contains the characteristics of a project, the traditional tools of project management prove incredibly useful to the sport event manager. Project management can offer structure to the sport event and allow for detailed planning, monitoring, and evaluation. Event managers can benefit by using tools such as the WBS and Gantt charts to analyze, categorize, assign, and implement the sport event plan.

DISCUSSION QUESTIONS

1. Discuss why project management is vital for a successful event. Provide a brief overview of three different technological tools for project management. What tool would be the best for your team, if you were an event director. Why did you choose this tool?
2. Discuss the stages of event planning and describe how resources might be assigned for the development of a three-day, three-on-three basketball tournament.
3. Describe the domains of event management and the main duties of each area. Why is it important that each domain be designated for an event?

Case STUDY

Staging Events with Multiple Venues

The logistics of planning and staging a multivenue sport event is no easy task. There will be a number of elements that are compounded by the additional venues, including, but not limited to, scheduling, human resources, equipment resources, communication between venues, security within and between venues, and additional traffic/parking challenges (especially if athletes/patrons require shuttling between venues). The following case introduces the challenges faced when staging a multivenue sport event.

You are the new event director for the inaugural State Games in [the city and state of your choice]. As the newly appointed director, you are tasked with organizing the venues and equipment as well as the schedule for the week-long event. As the schedule is developed, consider the following.

A total of 25 sports have been included in the program. These include:

Archery	Flag football	Tennis
Badminton	Golf	Track and field
Baseball	Racquetball	Triathlon
Basketball	Rowing	Volleyball
BMX racing	Skateboarding	Weightlifting
Bowling	Softball	Wheelchair basketball
CrossFit	Sport skydiving	Wrestling
Diving	Swimming: Indoor	
Fencing	Swimming: Open water	

Note: These listed sports do not include all of the available events. For example, swimming offers a number of sprint- and long-distance, as well as relay, events. Take this into consideration when developing your schedule and staging plan.

- The games are inclusive of all ages and ability. You must decide the age divisions as part of the scheduling process. The games allow any athletes from 12 to 100 years of age to compete.
- The games offer three competitive levels: Novice, intermediate, and advanced.

You may find it helpful to review the Cornhusker State Games website as a resource as you work through this case: www.cornhuskerstategames.com. Using what you have just learned in the chapter about staging and implementing events, develop a plan and schedule for the State Games. Be sure to include the following:

1. The city and state chosen to host the games.
2. A list of venues and the sports they each will host. This list must be realistic and based on the venues available in the city you chose in Question 1. The venues should also be illustrated on a map, along with parking availability and shuttle transport pickup/drop-off points (if relevant).

(continues)

Case STUDY (continued)

3. The complete schedule for each venue over the weeklong event, detailing the following specifically:
   a. The type of competition for each sport (e.g., tournament vs. head-to-head) [All sports will have different competition needs.]
   b. The schedule breakdown by age group and level
   c. The resources needed at each venue (e.g., numbers of officials, volunteers, staff)
4. Your overall plan for the staging implementation of the event:

   a. Operations and logistics   d. Financial resources
   b. Equipment needs   e. Other
   c. Human resources

REFERENCES

Allen, J., O'Toole, W., Harris, R., & McDonnell, I. (2011). *Festival and special event management* (5th ed.). Brisbane, Australia: John Wiley & Sons.

Barbara, V. (2016, July). *Brazil's Olympic Catastrophe.* New York Times. Retrieved from https://www.nytimes.com/2016/07/03/opinion/sunday/brazils-olympic -catastrophe.html

Bowater, D. (2016, June 17). *Rio declares 'state of calamity' amid cash crisis that could threaten Olympics as city hospital forced to close doors.* The Telegraph. Retrieved from https://www.telegraph.co.uk/news/2016/06/17/rio-declares-state-of -calamity-amid-cash-crisis-ahead-of-olympic/

International Event Management Body of Knowledge. (2006). *Event management body of knowledge: An introduction.* Retrieved from http://www.embok.org.

Lewis, J. P. (1998). *Team-based Project Management.* New York: AMACOM.

Lock, D. (2013). *Project management* (10th ed.). Burlington, VT: Gower Publishing.

Patel, V. (2008). *Project management.* Jaipur, India: Oxford Book Company.

Rutherford Silvers, J. (2004, December). *Updated EMBOK structure as a risk management framework for events.* Retrieved from http://www.juliasilvers.com/embok /EMBOK_structure_update.htm

Shone, A., & Parry, B. (2010). *Successful event management: A practical handbook* (3rd ed.). Hampshire, UK: Cengage Learning.

Van der Wagen, L., & White, L. (2010). *Events management: For tourism, cultural, business, and sporting events* (4th ed.). New South Wales, Australia: Pearson Publishing.

Young, T. (2007). *The handbook of project management: A practical guide to effective policies, techniques, and processes.* London, UK: Kogan Page.

Young, T. (2013). *Successful project management* (4th ed.). London, UK: Kogan Page.

Zarndt, F. (2011). Project management 101: Plan well, communicate a lot, and don't forget acceptance criteria. *OCLC Systems and Services, 27*(3), 170–174.

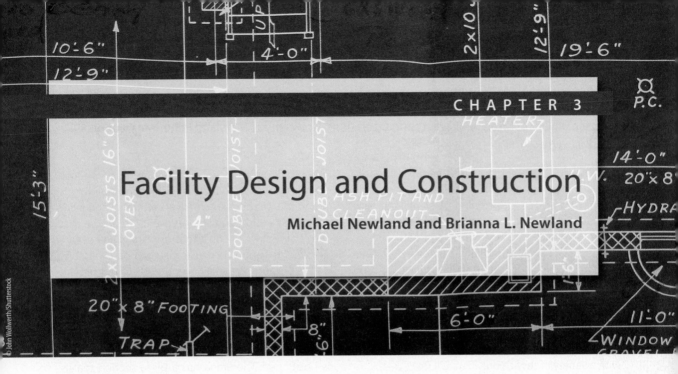

CHAPTER 3

Facility Design and Construction

Michael Newland and Brianna L. Newland

CHAPTER OBJECTIVES

Upon completion of this chapter, the reader will be able to:

1. Describe the process of facility design and construction.
2. Demonstrate proficiency in the interrelated steps involved in planning, programming, site selection, and designing.
3. Discuss the estimating and bidding processes and the construction of the facility.

CHAPTER OVERVIEW

This chapter will explore the elements of sport facility design and construction. Facility development starts with a plan, which creates a program that defines the site selection, develops the drawings, constructs the facility, and progresses through a set of interrelated steps until the product is completed. This chapter will outline the main components of this process, including feasibility studies, site selection and evaluation, planning and design, the estimation of construction costs, the bidding of the work, and the construction process. Green construction, design, and issues will also be addressed in this chapter.

IndustryVOICE

Franzter LeBlanc—Director of Events and Operations, University of Maryland Baltimore County (UMBC) Event Center

As the Director of Events at UMBC, I oversee all planning of events, the daily operations of the arena, event estimates and settlements, facilities maintenance, as well as supervising the negotiation and execution of service contracts. I manages four full-time employees—an event manager, operations manager, building engineer, and AV manager—and I am also responsible for building and maintaining relationships with a variety of service providers.

I started my career at American University; first as an intern and then as the facilities and operations coordinator. After one year, I left American University for Wagner College, where I pursued and earned an MBA in Management. At Wagner, I worked as a facilities and operations intern and was quickly promoted to Director of Outside Facilities and Game Operations. After two years at Wagner College, Hofstra University hired me as an Assistant Director of Facilities and Operations. At Hofstra, my main responsibility was to run the day-to-day operations of the football stadium and adjacent fieldhouse. It was here that I first gained experience managing concerts and shows. After eight years at Hofstra, University of Delaware hired me—first, to serve as the Assistant Athletic Director for Facilities and later as an Assistant Athletic Director for Bob Carpenter Center Operations and Events. After three years at Delaware, I found myself in my current role as UMBC where I have had the opportunity to open a brand new sport arena.

My job at UMBC is unique in that, while I work at the university, the arena is privately run by Pinnacle Venue Services (PVS). PVS helps make the UMBC arena more profitable, efficient, and safer for its customers and employees. With that being said, PVS is a for-profit organization and, as such, the venue must continually find ways to limit the days that the building is not in use. To do this, I creatively attract events with rental deals and I sign smaller events to ensure that the facility stays in consistent use. The small events are very important because they can be profitable! This is because the small event tends to not require high expenses, so we are able to capitalize on that. Other challenges I face are those related to safety and security. While the standard practices of metal detectors and bag checks are used to ensure safety, I must also consider security issues due to how the venue is positioned. The arena has a plaza section that is highly accessible and, in fact, is connected to a campus street. This could pose a danger to pedestrians and patrons if a car should enter this space. Therefore, I must ensure that police vehicles block the car access directly to the arena.

When I consider new trends in the industry, three major areas immediately come to mind: (1) the fan experience, (2) safety and security, and (3) technology.

FAN EXPERIENCE

Throughout this industry, I have found that venues and organizations constantly seek ways to improve the fan experience to attract more customers in this ultra-competitive business. Unlike 20 to 30 years ago—when patrons based their entertainment decisions on loyalty to a brand, venue, or team—event attendees are more concerned with how far that entertainment dollar will stretch. They also tend to choose experiences over brand loyalty. Most decisions for new constructions and renovations focus on enhancing the game experience. The best example of this is the Jacksonville Jaguars and University of Central Florida. In an effort to create new experiences for their guests, both of these organizations actually *removed seats* from their respective football stadia during their renovation projects. EverBank Stadium (Jaguars) built cabanas and two swimming pools. And now, the poolside experience has become the most sought-after ticket for the Jags and quickly sells out for each game. At UCF, the football stadium renovations replaced the bleachers with mid-level cabanas. This project was so successful, UCF recently removed *more* seats and created additional mid-level cabanas to meet the demand for this new in-stadium experience. These are just a couple of examples of how decision making has changed to enhance the fan experience in sport. There are so many innovative ideas being implemented across the country from improved courtside experiences, end-line suites at college basketball games, programmable LED lights, and so much more.

SAFETY AND SECURITY

Unfortunately, at this time, we have to protect our venues and guests from the threat of terrorism. In the last two to three years, sports and entertainment venues and events have become potential targets for terrorist activity. As a result, security measures continue to change each year. Every major sport venue has walk-through metal detectors at the doors and has a clear bag or no bag policy. Additionally, there are social media security teams that review mentions of the sport event or venue as a way to track threats. At most outdoor stadia, there are no-fly zones due to the increased sales of commercial drones. Some venues have installed software that enables the security team to take over drones entering the no-fly space and send them back home. Many of the Power Five conferences have installed the same measures to avoid becoming a soft target for a terrorist threat. I imagine that within the next five years, most colleges and universities across the country will have the same security standard at their events.

TECHNOLOGY

Most of the new facilities on the market now provide a venue app that patrons can download. These apps provide directions to the facility and, once arrived, the seats. They have a concessions tool that allows the customer to order food that is delivered to the seats and provides game-day information. Venues also spend a significant amount of money on the wireless systems throughout the venue to ensure that each guest can connect to his or her favorite social media apps. Technology is dynamic and ever-changing, and it is added and updated regularly to ensure that the customer receives an unforgettable experience.

I need good people who have diverse skillsets. When I hire an entry level position, I look for the following traits: (1) Experience—not work experience per se, but your overall experience. I want to see if this person was serious enough during his or her time at school to pursue any experience and learning prior graduation. This shows me that the candidate is serious about the field and is invested; (2) Ambition—I hire based on potential. I want to know if this person has a plan for his or her career. I want an entry level employee to see this job as a jump start to their career and not the last step. Why is this important? Because entry level positions are hard work with low pay. I want someone who maximizes that opportunity to prepare them for the next step; (3) Sponge mentality—I look for people who want to learn about their job but who are also curious about other positions and want to discover the overall picture. This is the time when this person can start to identify his or her own leadership styles based on what he or she sees and start to understand his or her strengths and weaknesses. To do this, the person must have the mentality to soak up everything good and bad about the organization; and (4) Cultural fit—I hire people who are humble. People who pitch in to help regardless of their position. I look for team players who want to get the job done. Most importantly, I want people on my team who will treat the general manager (GM) and the custodians with the same respect and not view themselves as being better than anyone else.

I have two major concerns about new graduates. The first is a lack of diverse experiences on their resume.

(continues)

Again, I do not mean full-time job experience. I see college students attempting to gain work experience in their senior year of school only. It's rare to see students taking advantage of volunteer hours to build a resume during college. Get involved early! Go volunteer as a freshman; value those experiences—they matter! Try different things. So, you want to be in professional sports? Ok, but try other areas of sport. It will broaden your knowledge and understanding. The second concern is attitude. I think that this has more to do with the culture in which we now live. No one wants to start at the bottom. Everyone has a dream to become the next GM, but they fail to realize the value that comes with starting at the bottom and moving up. Make connections and find mentors in the field who can help you build your career. Learn from their successes and, more importantly, from their mistakes. Ask them questions about how they got to their positions and use them as a resource so that when you are about to graduate, these individuals can become advocates for you as you are trying to get your first job.

Learn as much about the business as possible. A person in my position needs to have at least an overview if not direct knowledge of custodial management, mechanical designs and maintenance, event operations, collegiate athletic rules and regulations, basketball court designs and maintenance, budget oversight, negotiation tactics, contract negotiation, construction design, audio-visual management, IT, lighting and sound design, communication, rigging, capital project management, box office, marketing, leadership strategies, and overall problem solving skills. I can say I use every one of those skills every week in my position.

Finally, with regard to construction and capital projects—remember, the project you start with is never the finished project. There will be numerous changes throughout the process, depending on the budget. Always have a contingency plan and fight for what you need in the design. And, be sure to get the end-user involved. You don't know everything, so you need to get advice from the people who are actually going to operate and use the facility. The next best thing is have a consultant involved in the project that has the interest of the finished project in mind. You need to pay attention to the future trends and build for the future, not the present. A clear example of this is wireless technology. Wireless access is now an expectation when people come to the venue. So, if you are upgrading or building a new building and do not include wireless as a big part of your building, you made a major mistake. Avoid that and good luck!

Introduction

capital projects A project that maintains or improves upon an asset, like a sport facility.

owner The party, whether public or private, responsible for getting the project financed, designed, and built.

There are two important key elements for **capital projects**. The first key element to the successful construction of a sport facility is controlling costs; the second is keeping the project on schedule. That responsibility falls on the **owner**, who is the responsible party for getting the project financed, designed, and built (Sears et al., 2015). The owner typically works closely with the construction team and the future facility operations manager. While it is the owner's responsibility to ensure that the project is financed and built, it is imperative that the facility operations manager not only understand the aspects of facility design and build but also how to properly plan for the future operational

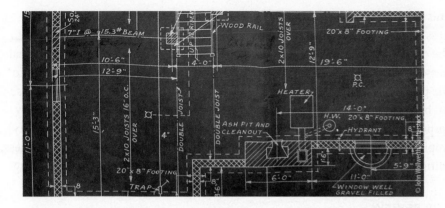

costs to maintain the facility once it is built. This entails working closely with the owner to develop a strong feasibility study prior to building and durable construction and use plans for the future facility operations. This chapter will begin to develop a foundation of knowledge by focusing on the key segments of the capital project.

The Construction Project

Construction projects are complex, elaborate undertakings that require careful planning in numerous project stages. The first stage is determining the feasibility of the project, which involves determining the practicality of the project, as well as estimating costs and budgeting. Defining the broad project requirements will enable the team to delineate budgetary constraints (Sears et al., 2015). Once these are determined, the project moves to the design phase, in which the architectural and engineering design begins. Finally, **procurement** and construction begins. Aspects of each phase are discussed below.

procurement The ordering, expediting, and delivering of key equipment and materials required for the construction project.

Feasibility

Feasibility is to determine realistic and practical solutions. For capital projects, it is to determine need, achievability of funding for construction, and viability of the project for future use. There are a few options to determine project feasibility, but this chapter will discuss three—a SWOT (strengths, weaknesses, opportunities, and threats) analyses, PEST (political, economic, social, and technological) analysis, and Porters 5 Forces. The strength and weakness reviews the internal elements of the project—what is happening within the capital project that can be capitalized on (strengths) and mitigated (weaknesses). The opportunities and threats review what is happening external to the project that can be capitalized on and mitigated. SWOT analyses are useful because they can help decision-makers to use resources more efficiently (especially if you have to make a decision to renovate or build a new facility), improve operations, discover opportunities that help grow the sport business, mitigate risks (especially of project failure), and set competitive positioning.

FOR REVIEW

Suppose you are the operations manager for a parks and recreation organization in a small rural town about 50 miles from a larger metropolis. Your town mayor has asked that you research the feasibility of renovating the current softball and baseball diamonds in town. The mayor wants to start attracting more youth and adult tournaments to the town as a means of increasing tourism. She asks you to conduct a SWOT analysis to determine whether she should earmark funds for such a capital project. What information would you need to begin a SWOT analysis?

A PEST analysis is a planning tool that allows you to evaluate the *political, economic, social, and technological* factors of a capital project. According to Haughey (2018), the political factors can include tax law or policy, employment laws, construction regulations, green/environmental policies and regulations, and general political stability. Economic factors include the current status of the economy, interest rates, and inflation rates—as these can really influence the cost of a construction project. The social factors include the growth of the population, trends in job and leisure opportunities, and age distributions. These rates are important to note because they can really influence current support of building a project, as well as future use of the facility. And finally, technological factors include automation, technology incentives, and rate of technological change.

Porter (2008) is a framework for understanding the competitive forces at work in an industry and allows one to assess industry attractiveness and how future trends will affect competition, which can help the organization position itself for success. The first force is supplier power—how easy is it for suppliers to drive up prices? When this is low, there are a higher number of suppliers or the product/service is not very unique. The second force is buyer power—how easy is it for buyers to drive prices down? This is driven by the number of buyers on the market and their power. If there are a few powerful buyers, they can often determine the terms. The third force is competitive rivalry—what is the number and capability of the competitors in the market? Many competitors with undifferentiated products will reduce the attractiveness on the market. The forth force is the threat of substitution—are there close substitute products/services on the market? If so, customers may switch to alternatives in response to any price increases. And, finally, the fifth force is the threat of a new entry—is this market profitable? If so, it can attract new entrants, which erode the profitability. Porter's 5 forces are rated from low to high and each is key to helping the sport organization understand the factors that could affect the future profitability of the facility.

Estimating Costs and Budgeting

Once the feasibility study is completed and the capital project is green lighted (can move ahead), the owner must acquire capital funds for the project. To attain the necessary capital, the owner must estimate the costs to maintain the completed venue. Preparing a budget for a proposed project begins with the basics of weighing the potential expenses against the projected revenue to determine the feasibility of a profitable sporting facility. During the design phase, costs are approximated and reviewed as each design change occurs in a working budget. These preliminary estimates can be difficult as they are compiled before the project is completely defined, so it really is an art (Sears et al., 2015). To calculate the initial costs of a project, all of the estimated costs, including fixed and variable costs, are prepared in a document called a **pro forma** (**Figure 3-1**). Pro forma statements summarize the projected future status of a company and are the foundation for financial planning for an organization or project (Ross, Westerfield, & Jordan, 2008). They are vital for determining valuation and are required by the bank to secure funding for the project when there is no financial history. The **fixed costs** are expenses that do not change as a function of the business activity and include such items as the rent, operations, advertising, and insurance. The **variable costs** are volume-related and include labor, cost of goods sold, and raw materials, which are typically managed payouts based on use of the facility and the number of part-time staff and/or subcontractors required at any one time. The pro forma can help managers evaluate new ventures or new strategic initiatives, such as the design and build of a new sporting facility.

pro forma A statement that summarizes the projected future status of a company and that is used as the foundation for financial planning for an organization or project.

fixed cost An expense that does not change as a function of the business activity.

variable cost An expense that changes based on the volume of business activity.

SAMPLE PROFORMA

Project Name:

USES	Budget		Actual	SOURCES	Budget		Actual
Construction							
Demolition	$ 150,000	$	135,750	TRF Loan	$ 3,500,000	$	3,500,000
Environmental Clearances	17,000	$	18,400	Other: Investment	250,000	$	250,000
Hard Costs	3,000,000	$	3,027,500	Other	-	$	-
Contractor Fee	50,000	$	50,000	Other	-	$	-
Construction Contingency	100,000	$	125,000	Developer Equity During Construction	600,000	$	600,000
Construction Management	90,000	$	90,825	**TOTAL PROJECT SOURCES**	**4,350,000**	**$**	**4,350,000**
Other	-	$	-				
Subtotal: Construction	$ 3,407,000	$	3,447,475				
				Developer Equity During Construction:			
Professional Fees				Construction Deferrals (Attorney, Marketing/Advertising, Developer Fee):	$600,000		$600,000
Appraisal	$ 15,000	$	16,025	Cash needed:	$92,000		$89,750
Architect	240,000	$	242,200				
Attorney	10,000	$	10,000	Interest (assume 50% of loan outstanding during the construction term):	$ 508,000	$	510,250
Cost Cert/Audit	7,500	$	7,500	*Requested Interest Rate (insert a rate 5.5%):*			
Engineer	240,000	$	242,200		$ 38,500.00	$	38,500.00
Environmental Consultant	5,000	$	5,000				
Soil Investigation	8,000	$	7,500				
Surveyor	4,000	$	4,000				
Marketing/Advertising	10,000	$	9,750				
Other	-	$	2,000				
Subtotal: Professional Fees	$ 539,500	$	546,175				
Carrying Costs & Other Project Fees							
Application Fees	$ 350	$	500				
Inspections	7,500	$	7,500				
Interest Costs	210,000	$	192,500				
Bank Fees	5,000	$	4,300				
Property Insurance	2,500	$	2,650				
Real Estate Taxes	27,000	$	21,358				
Title Insurance & Recording	800	$	900				
Other	-	$	-				
Subtotal: Carrying Costs & Other Project Fees	$ 253,150	$	229,708				
Developer Fee	$ 72,000	$	70,000				
TOTAL PROJECT COST	$ 4,271,650	$	4,293,358				

Figure 3-1 Example of a Pro Forma

The potential revenue streams for the sport facility include monthly rental fees from sport teams and venue rental fees for entertainment events, concession and merchandise sales, and other additional revenue, such as venue tours. Most commonly, private organizations own and build a sport venue and lease it to sport organizations or event promoters. For example, the Barclays Center in Brooklyn, New York is owned by the real estate developer Forest City Ratner Companies (FCRC); it is leased by the Brooklyn Nets (basketball) and the New York Islanders (hockey) and has an event calendar that is packed solid with boxing, conference (ACC) basketball tournaments, UFC fights, World Wrestling Entertainment (WWE), concerts, comedians, food festivals, and conferences. While the Barclays is an example of what an established venue can schedule, it is important to begin to determine what the new venue could attract. The estimation of revenue streams should be conservative at the outset, as it is common to fall short of reaching goals. This consideration is important if sport managers are also responsible for managing stakeholder expectations for the construction project and future use revenue streams.

Estimating Construction Costs

Once the budget for the facility has been estimated and the preliminary pro forma developed, the construction costs can be estimated. Soft and hard costs are common construction terms used to describe the expenses specifically associated with the construction project; they should not be confused with the fixed and variable costs that the completed facility will incur, as described previously. The **soft costs**, often referred to as indirect costs, are not directly related to the physical construction of the project and commonly occur prior to the project. These costs can include legal fees, permits, real estate commissions and fees, financing fees, insurance, loans, design fees, and equipment rental fees. The **hard costs**, in contrast, are direct costs specifically related to construction, including land cost, labor, materials, equipment, basic building services, and mechanical and electrical services. These costs are directly affected by the decisions made by the contractor and design team working on the project, so it is very important to closely supervise this process to maintain construction costs overall. A real challenge for estimating costs is determining labor expenditures, which vary greatly. For example, a project manager must complete a thorough job analysis as well as think about how construction operations will be managed. Will direct and indirect costs be

soft cost A cost that is not directly related to the physical construction of the project and commonly occurs prior to the project; also called indirect cost.

hard cost A direct cost specifically related to the project.

determined separately or will that be wrapped into the hourly rate? (Sears, et al., 2015). Furthermore, subcontractors can be unreliable, thereby creating work stoppages or delays. That delay costs time and money, thus driving up the hard costs of your project.

To determine the costs of the proposed construction project, research must be conducted on the costs of available sites (land), building design, building per square foot, materials, labor, and utilities. Due diligence is of the utmost importance! It is wise to investigate the costs of similar sites and buildings by visiting other facilities, asking questions, and seeking professional advice from seasoned contractors. A very detailed and accurate assessment of the costs is imperative for an appropriate project budget estimate. Once the pricing of each component is complete and the pro forma presents a profitable project, financing can be acquired to proceed (if necessary).

Site Selection

Site selection is important because a good site location will contribute to attracting future patrons to the sport facility. Therefore, a dedicated site search for land and location that has potential to produce anticipated revenues is key to future success.

schematic drawing A drawing that exhibits the size of the facility and assists in defining the maximum capacity of land needed to build.

The planning phase for the facility involves defining the components that the facility will offer. Once the facility requirements have been established, a space planner can produce **schematic drawings** that depict the proposed building layout. These schematics exhibit the size of the facility, which then defines maximum capacity and parking requirements. If the facility is not properly planned with defined capacities, it will be impossible to determine the amount of land required to build. For example, the parking lot supporting a building is based on the capacity of patrons permitted in the building. If you do not calculate capacity properly and provide sufficient parking spaces, the amount of patrons who are able to access the building will be reduced. Having to access off-site parking will inhibit customer service and potentially lead to dissatisfaction from future patrons. Local government agencies provide resources and codes that delineate parking specifications based on capacity for a proposed building. A sound plan and schematics that define the facility's requirements are vital to properly determine the size of your site.

Finding ways to minimize initial building costs is also key in planning. One tactic is to build a smaller building first that can be expanded or added to in phases so that, eventually, the size of the facility reaches full capacity. By having sufficient parking for the final build-out of the facility, the project manager can ensure the ability to park your new patrons appropriately.

Another consideration, especially in urban areas, is the utilization of existing facilities. These areas have sites or buildings available that can be repositioned and reapportioned. The key here is to fully vet the building structures and existing materials to ensure that the building can be converted to the facility you envision. Many cities allow for less parking ratios for existing facilities to attract potential users and buyers. Reappropriating or renovating an existing structure can reduce the overall building costs substantially, especially if the building does not require many updates or structural changes.

It could prove useful to hire a realtor to assist in the search for existing buildings and sites. **Realtors** are not only familiar with the zoning requirements for the proposed facility but they can also provide the area demographics and traffic volumes around the site location. Accessibility to the site is paramount; a facility that patrons cannot see or easily access can hinder future success!

realtor An expert in real estate who can assist in identifying land options, demographics, and traffic volumes of an area, as well as zoning requirements for specific areas.

Finding the Site

It is likely that numerous sites are available but are not conducive to building large facilities. The most important function of a site is that it has the capacity to house the building with appropriate parking and the open space that will be designated by local and state regulations. Another important consideration is patron (and construction, while building) access to the site and traffic flow in and out of the area (Ganaway, 2006). Some questions to consider include the following:

- Is the site near or off major interstates or highways?
- Can the site be accessed from all directions or at least from two opposing directions?
- Can the surrounding infrastructure handle heavy traffic?

Furthermore, considering site factors such as multiple entry and exit points, traffic lights, and dedicated turn lanes (or the capability to add them during the construction phase) is extremely important.

TIP

It can be very costly to add traffic lights if they are not present and there are code stipulations that require them at the entry/exit points. This cost can be a detriment to the budget if not accounted for in the estimating phase.

topographical report
A survey of the land that identifies any existing buildings, site surface evaluations, and availability of electrical, sewer, water, and gas services.

There are a few important reports that should be reviewed prior to acquiring the land. First is a **topographical report**, which will show the lot corners, any existing buildings, site surface elevations, finished floor elevations, manholes, storm and sanitary pipes, utility poles, fire hydrants, trees, and any other important objects affecting the site (Ganaway, 2006). The availability of electrical, sewer, water, and gas connections on the site is crucial, as adding them can be a substantial cost. The topographical survey can be compared with the proposed schematics of the proposed site to better understand construction needs.

geotechnical report A report of the soil conditions that dictate what materials are necessary to support the foundation for the proposed building as well as provisions for drainage of surface and runoff water that can affect the drying time of certain materials.

Second, a **geotechnical report** should also be generated to ensure that the site can support the sport facility foundation. The geotechnical report will indicate soil conditions that dictate which materials are necessary to support the foundation for the proposed building. In addition to the soil conditions, the geotechnical report will provide provisions for drainage of surface and runoff water that can affect the drying time of certain materials (Ganaway, 2006). Nonporous soils may require several days to dry before work can continue (in the case of poor weather), and soft/unsuitable soils will incur a greater expense for additional support materials. Knowing the site conditions and/or constraints can provide necessary information to better assess the construction budget estimates, which can help determine if the site is worth the financial risk.

Once the information is collected, the total value of the site can be assessed to determine if the purchase not only satisfies the needs for the project but also matches the estimates that were presented in the pro forma.

TIP

Today, storm water (rain water) is required to be held on-site, so building a retention system is a necessary expense that must be built into the project budget. A designer will be able to provide the requirements when laying out the site. A retention system can be bio-retention tanks, storm water management tanks, or an area that holds water in a lake or along the roadways via the construction of a ditch.

Design Process

By defining the components for the site schematics, a framework is established for the design elements to start. Once a site that can support the build requirements by accommodating the size of the facility is found, a design firm can be approached to begin the next phase of the project.

Hiring a design firm that is adept at designing sport facilities is essential. A worldwide leader in the field of sport facility design is Populous. Founded in 1983, Populous has built a reputation for designing innovative sport facilities. A few examples of sites/events on which Populous has worked include the

Paris 2024 Olympic Bid, T-Mobile Arena in Las Vegas (2016), 2014 Sochi Olympic Games, the 2012 London Olympic Games, Texas A&M's Kyle Field (redevelopment), the Melbourne Cricket Ground in Australia, and Yankee Stadium (2009). It is recommended that you visit the Populous website (www.populous.com) for an extensive (and impressive) list of their projects. Referrals and recommendations from various sources for design firms are helpful, but it is crucial that the firm of choice meets the needs of the sport organization, listens closely, and provides economical services. It is beneficial to interview up to four firms to determine fit and to secure a proposal that includes concept designs and total fees prior to making an informed decision. Reviewing a portfolio of recent and past projects can build confidence that the firm will deliver the right solutions for the project. The pro forma will designate the amount allocated to design the facility. The contract with the design firm must stipulate that the facility will be designed based on the established budget. The designer's contract should include the following:

- Design costs for schematic, design development, and contract drawings
- Costs for the civil engineer and the topographical and geotechnical reports
- Landscape design costs for landscaping, parking, walks, and retention systems
- Mechanical, plumbing, electrical, and fire protection drawings
- Details regarding acquirement of proper permit issuance
- Details regarding construction administration (i.e., answer contractor questions and provide field verification to ensure that the contractor is constructing the building according to the drawings)
- Details regarding closeout of the project and final punch list for final repairs prior to acceptance

Once the design firm has been retained, work can begin on the schematic drawings, which determine the function of the building and the layouts, showing the proposed components and required spaces per code. Buildings grow in size as patron counts are established, which then determines the number of elements, such as bathroom fixtures, shower facility sizes (such as for locker rooms), and ancillary spaces, such as mechanical and electrical rooms (which are required). As the building grows in size, costs will also increase. It is important to stay true to the pro forma in order to contain costs and keep the project on track.

After the planning/schematic drawings have been developed and a site has been selected, the architecture and engineering firm can finalize the drawings based on the information attained from the finalized site. This information includes, but is not limited to, the allowable footage distances from the roadway to the front of the property, the side yards, and the rear of the site. Many local codes enforce distances from the road to the building. The added space outside of the building footprint is typically used for parking and open space requirements dictated by the local government and community. A good design group will set the building where parking is efficient and allows for easy access to the building, as well as in and out of the property.

The design for an existing building conversion to a sports facility requires less planning, but more scrutiny in the foundation, existing column layouts, and utilities (e.g., water, sewer, storm, and electric) to ensure that required loads are available for the intended purpose. Raising a roof to allow for basketball, digging a foundation for a swimming pool or removing columns to allow for more open space are all obstacles that need to be researched during the design phase to minimize costs.

As the drawings are finalized, the design firm will confirm and review the components and adjacencies to ensure compliance with the original design plans. Material selections, paint colors, and flooring materials are confirmed and implemented into the drawings. This typically occurs when modifications are discussed and agreed upon by both parties. Disagreements are often encountered in the design of the exterior of the facility, with the designers possibly wanting to introduce innovative elements and expensive materials to achieve a certain look. Many design firms receive awards for exterior design. While creativity can win awards, it comes at a price. Therefore, it is beneficial to be thorough during the exterior design phase to ensure that the original design is created according to specifications to avoid running over budget and delaying construction.

It can take 8 to 12 months to produce a set of drawings and obtain permits before construction can start. Acquiring the construction permits varies by local code officials, which can greatly impact the project start date *and* can cause delays if changes have to be made once construction begins. Construction permits generally include a site layout plan that specifically designates the locations of temporary fencing, temporary electrical feeds, temporary toilets, and silt fencing. **Silt fencing** is used to keep any debris from passing from the site to any areas beyond the construction zone. The site layout plan is submitted early in the design process so that site work can begin before the final construction permits are obtained. Building permits

silt fencing Temporary fencing used to keep any debris from passing from the site to any areas beyond the construction zone.

involves an understanding of the local building codes (as determined by the governing entity) and a full review by local officials on all aspects of the design, including the foundations, superstructure (the building itself), façade materials, mechanical elements, plumbing elements, electrical elements, and fire protection. The drawings are checked for compliance with local building codes, and permits are granted once all standards are met. In most cases, the mechanical, electrical, and plumbing elements, as well as fire protection, are often delegated to subcontractors who submit and receive their own permits for the project. This task is typically done by the subcontractors because they are required to demonstrate licensure to complete the work as part of the permitting process. Therefore, it is important to build contingency plans and delays into the overall timeline of the project because a number of delays can occur when relying on multiple parties to obtain permits. Keep in mind that any delay or modification to the original plans will cost not only time but also money.

Construction Process

As the design phase commences, the search should begin for the **contractor** who will build the facility. As with the design groups, conduct interviews with local contractors who have been recommended or have built a strong reputation for constructing similar projects in the area. It is wise to choose three to four potential contractors to provide a project estimate based on the uncompleted drawings provided by the designer. By requesting this proposal, one can begin to approximate the cost to build as well as management fees and overhead expenses. The fees and allowances for unknown costs not shown on the drawings are generally negotiable with the contractor. A contractor should be selected prior to the finalization of the design to provide recommendations that identify cost reduction, enhance constructability, streamline the construction processes, and improve quality (Arsht, 2003).

A review of the contractor's pricing proposal can highlight when it is appropriate (or necessary) to use higher-quality materials and/or when savings can be recouped using lower-grade elements. Engineering reviews can provide valuable information on materials if follow-up is necessary. For a high-use venue, like a sport facility, the choice of materials is paramount as they must endure the daily wear and tear and high volume of traffic. The installation of a ceramic tile or stone entry guarantees a greater number of years of use, whereas a vinyl tile or carpet (that will provide an initial

contractor A firm that contracts directly with the owner for the construction of a project.

clean look) will deteriorate quickly. Therefore, spending more at the outset on materials that can withstand greater wear and tear will provide cost savings in the long term. More durable materials are recommended for locker rooms, showers, sport-specific training areas, swimming pool areas, and other high-use, high-traffic areas within the sport facility. Longevity is key, requiring more costly materials. However, it might be more costly to install new materials earlier than anticipated, so it is important to choose materials wisely. It is advisable to have the architect select the appropriate materials for the project, as this individual will be most educated on the durability and cost of materials.

For the construction of large facilities, it is common to receive a minimum of four contractor bids, with the lowest bid typically winning the project. Often, when the contractor is involved in the final design phase, the outcome is a better project at a lower cost. The contractor can provide valuable insight and address problematic areas as the drawings are finalized, which tends to support the project in four main ways (Arsht, 2003) by:

change order A document used to record an amendment to the original scope of construction work.

1. Minimizing the need for redesign.
2. Reducing the need for **change orders** during construction.
3. Addressing questionable areas or issues early on in the project.
4. Allowing for collaboration among professionals at the start of project.

As with the design phase, a construction phase is also established in accordance with the terms of a contract that will contain provisions defining the costs and protecting the owner from potential issues that can arise throughout the project (Rounds, 2011). The contract should clearly define that the facility will be constructed according to the drawings for a specific cost over the duration of a set timeline, with agreed-upon materials and high-quality workmanship, all while providing a safe site for workers. Full compliance with the contract terms will lead to a successful project. The drawings for construction typically include the interior layouts for equipment and furniture, but these items are usually not provided by the contractor—which will be noted in the contract. Therefore, during the construction phase, the owner must meet with equipment and furniture vendors to finalize deliveries for installation.

The timeline for the construction of a facility not only depends on the size of the facility but also on the availability and delivery of supplies, equipment, and materials. Unique building materials can delay the project,

VIGNETTE 3-1

Qatar World Cup 2022

© Henry Makushin/iStock/Thinkstock

Many were skeptical when the decision to award the 2022 World Cup to Qatar was made. Not only did the country not have the required infrastructure but it is also not known to have any soccer tradition. Debate as to how Qatar was able to continue preparing for and hosting the Cup was intensified as a report of vote-buying was made public (BBC, 2017). This was closely followed by rumors that Qatar would be stripped of its World Cup hosting rights and given to the UK or United States (Harwood, 2018). With past reports of allegations by the International Trade Union Confederation (ITUC) of more than 1,200 migrant worker deaths (Manfred, 2014), the ITUC now predicts that at least 4,000 worker will perish by the time the 2022 World Cup begins (Foster, 2017). In addition to the corruption and humanitarian crisis plaguing Qatar through the construction phase, it is estimated that over $200 billion will be spent to build the 12 stadiums and supporting infrastructure, which includes complete cities, not just hotels, restaurants, medical facilities, and other necessary structures. Furthermore, the futuristic and innovative designs that won them the bid are not possible, according to the design firm Populous (Associated Press, 2011). Avoiding such problems is precisely why feasibility studies are conducted and well-developed pro formas are necessary before any bids are conducted and building begins! However, this example also begs the question—are sport events, like the World Cup, more important than human life? At what point should FIFA or human rights groups step in to protect those dying from extreme conditions?

so one must consider the lead time for materials and components when reviewing and setting the construction schedule. Smaller construction projects typically take 8 to 12 months to complete and larger construction projects take from 12 to 18 months, so this time frame, like the design time, must be carefully planned for in the overall schedule in order to meet the deadline for the grand opening of the facility.

As construction begins, there will be a number of meetings on a weekly basis with both the designer and the contractor to review any questions that arise. The owner will be expected to make decisions on how to proceed based on the professional advice and guidance offered by the designer. It is important that any questions be addressed in a timely manner to avoid construction delays. Therefore, it is extremely important to attend project meetings to address these questions and also modify the construction schedule based on the progress (or lack thereof) of the contractor. If the project is lagging, the contractor should produce tactics to restore the timeline without affecting quality, cost, and worker safety. These meetings are also a means for the designer to review completed work to verify that construction complies with the design plans within the scope of the local codes. On a monthly basis, the owner should conduct a review of the contractor's pay requests with the designer to verify that the work billed has been completed. The designer should approve the invoices with an accurate account of completed work prior to dispensing pay. Many owners hire construction managers to oversee the project, especially if he or she is not sufficiently adept at handling unfamiliar issues. A construction manager is the owner's agent. This means that he or she will provide direction to the contractor and will ensure compliance with the contract, timelines, quality, and costs.

operation and maintenance manuals (O&M manuals) A collection of documents that contain pertinent information to maintain the building by providing detailed information on the management of the new systems in addition to the maintenance and repair of equipment.

As construction reaches completion, the contractor will begin to develop the **operation and maintenance manuals (O&M manuals)**, which will contain pertinent information for the facility manager to maintain the building. These manuals provide detailed information on the management of the new systems in addition to the maintenance and repair of equipment. Additionally, all warranties on materials and components built into the facility will be provided.

The designer and owner should approve of the final construction site. Once approval is obtained, the designer approves the documents that provide the contractor clearance for final payment. At this time, a final lien waver is issued to ensure that the contractor pays all of the subcontractors and suppliers on the project. This is a required document needed to release final payment.

Insurance

Insurance is a necessity to build. The designer and contractor must carry the appropriate insurances when designing and building a project, which can be easily verified in the vetting stages. A design firm is required to have sufficient

errors and omissions insurance (E&O) to guarantee against failure of the architecture and engineering of the building in the event that it collapses after construction. Architects and engineers carry E&O insurance to guard against perilous events for which they are at fault. It is in the owner's best interest to have an attorney review these details to ensure that there is no liability of the owner prior to, during, and after construction. In addition to liability, contractors also carry insurance, such as workmen's compensation insurance, that protects against accidents or injuries that may occur during construction for which the contractor is at fault. With this insurance, the owner and the contractor are protected from liabilities related to workman injuries and, thus, are not responsible for any and all costs related to their medical care.

The owner must acquire insurance immediately upon purchasing the site. The two critical types of insurance include general liability insurance and builder's risk insurance. These two insurance policies protect the owner during construction against theft of materials on the site, fire, and destruction of the constructed building by an **act of God** (which is typically a coverage not provided by the general contractor). This insurance also protects the owner from injuries at the site not associated with the actual construction of the project. The general contractor is also required to carry insurance to protect the owner from any liability of any construction-related injuries of the contracted or subcontracted workers. These insurance policies protect the owner from injuries incurred on site prior to, during, and after construction. Reducing the risk by keeping the site free from debris and anything that can harm a person is important. The contractor, in most cases, will fence the site as soon as construction begins to alleviate any potential issues from outside parties. Greater detail on risk management is provided in the "Risk Management" chapter.

Green Construction and LEED Certification

The design, construction, building, and maintenance of facilities involve a great deal of energy, water, and other resources that create considerable waste and impact the environment and ecosystem (Environmental Protection Agency [EPA], 2017). The **US Green Building Council (USGBC)** has implemented green building requisites leading to a legacy of sustainable practices. The USGBC is now a primary aspect of the design and construction program and they have developed a range of certifications that teach sustainable practices in construction, known as **LEED Certifications**. LEED stands for Leadership

errors & omissions insurance A form of liability insurance that protects the service-providing companies from claims made by clients for inadequate work or negligent action.

act of God An instance of uncontrollable natural forces (often used in insurance claims).

USGBC (United States Green Building Council) An organization that promotes Green Building through Leadership in Energy & Environmental Designs (LEED) certifications.

LEED certification A green building certification program that recognizes best-in-class building strategies and practices. LEED stands for Leadership in Energy and Environmental Design.

in Energy and Environmental Design, which is a certification now required in most states in order to build. The architect will most likely manage the LEED certification requirements for a project. Today, there are five separate LEED-accredited professional certifications:

1. LEED—Building Design and Construction—New Buildings.
2. LEED—Building Operations and Maintenance—Existing Buildings.
3. LEED—Interior Design and Construction—Interiors.
4. LEED—Neighborhood Development—Outdoor Green Spaces.
5. LEED—Homes—Residences.

LEED certification ensures construction professionals have knowledge to build healthier, more productive places that reduce stress on the envi-

ronment by encouraging energy and resource-efficient buildings (USGBC, 2018). In doing so, owners should observe savings for increased building value, higher lease rates, and decreased utility costs. A typical green design–build design tends to carefully select sites to minimize the impact on the surrounding environment, uses renewable and/or energy conservation techniques and natural resources, conserves water, incorporates proper storm water management, limits disruption of natural watershed functions, and uses low-volatile organic compound products and proper ventilation practices to improve indoor environment quality (EPA, 2017).

Designers today have a host of specified materials and techniques that are renewable and reusable and often take care to install mechanical and electrical systems that reduce the carbon footprint and are energy efficient. For example, the design of light-colored roofing materials and use of **pervious materials** on the site are common actions meant to address a green building program. The light-colored roofing materials allow for less heat

pervious material A material that allows water to soak naturally into the ground.

transfer on the building, which reduces air-conditioning costs. The pervious materials allow water to escape from the building or site, which allows the water to soak naturally into the ground. **Impervious surfaces**, such as cement pavement prevent precipitation from naturally soaking into the ground, causing water to run rapidly into storm drains, sewer systems, and drainage ditches (EPA, 2017). According to the **Environmental Protection Agency (EPA)**, this can cause a number of problems, including:

- Downstream flooding
- Stream bank erosion
- Increased turbidity (muddiness created by stirred-up sediment) from erosion
- Habitat destruction
- Changes in the stream flow hydrograph (a graph that displays the flow rate of a stream over a period of time)
- Combined sewer overflows
- Infrastructure damage
- Contaminated streams, rivers, and coastal water

Most construction sites also use some type of **waste diversion**, which is the prevention or reduction of generated waste through recycling, reuse, or composting (EPA, 2017). Waste from a construction project is typically divided and parceled into separate containers designated for immediate reuse, potential reuse, and landfill disposal. Waste diversion generates a number of environmental, financial, and social benefits to the owner of the construction site as well as to the community, including energy conservation, reduced disposal costs, and a reduced burden on landfills.

Choosing to purchase recycled materials is also a way to incorporate green elements. For example, rubber products and carpeting typically have recycled content. Choosing to buy products and materials within a close proximity of your project reduces the carbon footprint by limiting emissions released through transportation. There are numerous ways to insert green building elements into a project in order to lessen the impact on the environment while developing a strong and economical building program. As noted above, LEED certification is a great way of making sure construction projects maintain environmentally ethical building and waste disposal standards.

impervious surface A surface, such as cement pavement, that prevents precipitation from naturally soaking into the ground, causing water to run rapidly into storm drains, sewer systems, and drainage ditches.

environmental protection agency (EPA) The U.S. federal agency responsible for protecting the environment and human health as it relates to the environment.

waste diversion The prevention/reduction of generated waste through recycling, reuse, or composting.

SUMMARY

This chapter has discussed the importance of proper planning and management of a design–build project. Successful execution of the design–build plan will occur through careful research of contractors who can bid on and deliver the best project based on the owner's pro forma. Considering ways to incorporate green materials and design elements is critical and often required in the building of new facilities. A good sport manager will choose a design firm and contractors who are well versed in these requirements.

DISCUSSION QUESTIONS

1. Your city council has decided to build a new indoor sport facility specifically for basketball, tennis, and soccer. What are the first three steps to consider in the process?
2. A number of green design–build elements were discussed in this chapter. Compare and contrast the green components needed for a skate park and a baseball field. How are they similar? Different?
3. There are a number of green aspects to consider when building a new facility. Discuss three main issues that can lead to problems if not considered early in the design–build phase.
4. A number of insurance policy suggestions were made in this chapter. In which specific ways are they important? Which do you think is most critical as you begin a new build project? Why?

Case STUDY

Building a Sport Facility to Enhance Tourism

You are the mayor of a rural town (population 10,000) just 30 minutes outside of a small city (population 200,000). You, along with the city council, have devised a new vision for sport in the community, based largely on sport tourism. After some brief research, you learned that youth sport travel teams are on the rise. You think that you can attract adult sport tournaments as well. The primary goal of the new vision for sport in your community is to attract new money. By building the new sport infrastructure, you believe that you can attract new tourists who will spend money in shops, restaurants, and your (limited) hotels as they attend sport tournaments. The new sport fields will also serve the community. The new vision includes developing a new outdoor sport facility that includes softball and baseball fields, soccer fields, basketball courts, and tennis courts. There are a number of objectives that the city council hopes to meet with this new sport facility. First, the community leaders want to provide more access and opportunity for sport for children, adults, and seniors in the community. The council wants active leagues for all ages for the sports that could be offered in the new facility. Second, the council wants to attract visitors to the community by using the space for competition and tournament play. Finally, when the facility is not in use by the events and/or league play or practice, the space is to be open for general public use to support the council's efforts in creating and sustaining a healthy and active community. As the mayor, and the one who will be responsible for securing funding for the project, you must determine the feasibility of such a project:

1. Pick one of the feasibility analysis tools described above and determine the feasibility of such a project.
2. Research the available lots for sale within a rural community that is in close proximity to a small city to determine if there is a site with the acreage to develop the outdoor sport facility.
3. Once a few sites have been determined, begin to develop a pro forma to detail the costs to build such a facility.
4. Research the possible green elements that could be incorporated into the design and build of the project.
5. Does your town have the capacity to host tournaments? Is this vision to expand the sport infrastructure beyond the community smart? If no one comes to the tournaments, will this facility be too large for the community, leading to disuse?

REFERENCES

Arsht, S. (2003). Construction management: Planning ahead. *American School & University, 75*(11), 1–18.

Associated Press. (2011, November 8). Qatar urged to scrap air conditioning in stadium. *ESPN Soccer*. Retrieved from http://sports.espn.go.com/espn/wire?section=soccer&id=7206958

British Broadcasting Company (BBC). (2017, June 27). World Cup 2022: Claims of corruption in Qatar bid published in Germany. *BBC Sport*. Retrieved from http://www.bbc.com/sport/football/40412928

Environmental Protection Agency. (2017). Greening EPA. Retrieved from http://www.epa.gov/oaintrnt/index.htm

Foster, A. (2017, September 29). Death toll rises in the lead up to the 2022 World Cup. *News.com.au.* Retrieved from http://www.news.com.au/world/asia/death-toll-rises-in-the-lead-up-to-the-2022-world-cup/news-story/43896b31023dd6ab6ed213637fe4d3e7

Ganaway, N. B. (2006). *Construction business management: What every construction contractor, builder, and subcontractor needs to know.* Hoboken, NJ: Wiley & Sons.

Harwood, A. (2018, February 28). FIFA respond to reports Qatar could be stripped of 2022 World Cup after England are tipped to host tournament. *The Mirror.* Retrieved from https://www.mirror.co.uk/sport/football/news/fifa-respond-reports-qatar-could-12099278

Haughey, D. (2018). PEST Analysis. *Project Smart.* Retrieved from https://www
.projectsmart.co.uk/pest-analysis.php

Manfred, T. (2014, March 18). The Qatar World Cup is a disaster: 1,200 workers
dead, new bribery investigation. *Business Insider.* Retrieved from http://www
.businessinsider.com/qatar-world-cup-workers-dead-2014-3

Porter, M. E. (2008). The five competitive forces that shape strategy. *Harvard Business
Review, 86*(1), 25–40.

Ross, S. A., Westerfield, R., & Jordan, B. D. (2008). Fundamentals of corporate
finance. New York, NY: McGraw-Hill Education.

Rounds, J. L. (2011). *Construction supervision.* Hoboken, NJ: Wiley & Sons.

Sears, S. K., Sears, G. A., Clough, R. H., Rounds, J. L., & Segner, R. O. (2015).
*Construction project management: A practical guild to field construction
management.* Hoboken, NJ: Wiley & Sons.

USGBC (2018). Better buildings are our legacy. *USGBC about us.* Retrieved from
https://new.usgbc.org/about Sears

CHAPTER 4

Risk Management

Thomas J. Aicher and Amanda L. Paule-Koba

CHAPTER OBJECTIVES

Upon completion of this chapter, the reader will be able to:

1. Define risk and risk management.
2. Outline key risk issues and types of risk.
3. Identify concrete methods for minimizing risk.
4. Apply risk reduction techniques elucidated in this chapter.

CHAPTER OVERVIEW

Implementing a comprehensive risk management plan is vital to a facility and/or event. In today's litigious society, understanding how to mitigate financial loss and negligence should be front and center in minimizing risk and potential lawsuits. The growth of new and renovated sport facilities and the creation of diverse events has made this area of the industry much more difficult for managers.

IndustryVOICE

James A. DeMeo, M.S., CEO—Unified Sports & Entertainment Security Consulting (USESC)

I am the Founder, President, and CEO of USESC, an event security consulting company based in Raleigh, North Carolina. I have 28 years of security industry experience, 21 of which were spent during my public service career with the Nassau County Police Department on Long Island, New York. After retiring from law enforcement in 2011, I earned a master's degree from Adelphi University in Sport Management. I have been able to carve out a specialized niche as a thought leader and subject matter expert in the sport event security space. Fortunately, I have been able to combine my public service background with my passion for sports. I also wrote a best-selling book, *What's Your Plan? A Step-by-Step Guide to Keep Your Family Safe During Emergency Situations*, to help support family safety and preparedness during these most difficult times. I am extremely proud of this project.

USESC's philosophy is client-focused, employee-centric, and geared toward today's event security staff. The purpose is to create tailored training modules and career development resources for event staff, the gatekeepers to today's stadiums, venues, and arenas. The world of event security is evolving and ever-changing and the challenges continue to mount for those entrusted with duty of care responsibilities. USESC's overall mission is to create value for stadium ownership groups looking to safeguard sport fans, brands, and organizational assets. The vision is to impact the world and create meaningful, positive change. I visualize this on a daily basis.

This industry faces many challenges. First, competition in the marketplace. It's without question a very crowded field. To combat this, I build trusting relationships with other subject matter experts trying to pursue similar opportunities. A sign of true leadership is realizing that you don't have to be the smartest person in the room. Surrounding yourself with additional experts enables you to provide a force multiplier effect when approaching potential clients/organizations. To me, that's confidence. If you want people to find you highly credible, you have to believe in your talents, skill set, and abilities. It's that simple.

The next big challenge is educating organizations to not have a reactionary security mindset, but one that is more proactive in nature. Security is not viewed as a revenue producer, so it can be a challenge to get sport entities to understand that security should be viewed holistically, from multiple angles. While I am not an attorney, my work helps to shield organizations from potential lawsuits by changing the reactionary mindset. This starts by working diligently to educate CEOs, CSOs, CTOs, CIOs, the C-Suites—the key stakeholders in the organization—about the intrinsic value that security has in the overall operations. I address such issues as business continuity, resiliency, fan and brand protection, duty of care, and all essential aspects to an organization's bottom line, i.e., profits vs. loss.

After the Las Vegas mass shooting, the need to safeguard confined spaces and densely populated areas of people visiting stadiums, venues, and arenas cannot be underscored. The need to educate and train staff, law enforcement, security, guest services, operations, facilities, box office, conversion crew, parking attendants, maintenance, housekeeping, volunteers—all those working events—about the importance of personal situational awareness, threat, and behavioral analysis; verbal de-escalation techniques, active shooter, bomb scares, errant drones, suicide bomber, workplace violence, inclement/severe weather preparedness, IED, vehicles used as weapons, responsible social media monitoring, command center controls, access control, effective screening measures, cyber threats, and workplace violence is paramount for protecting the sport organization and/or event.

For those interested in working in sport security, if I were to hire a potential candidate, I would look for individuals who are willing to work hard, put in *very* long hours, and who have strong potential to become an asset to the organization. Trust, transparency, commitment, perseverance, interpersonal communications, time management, computer skills, and emotional intelligence are all traits that I look for in a potential applicant. Ex-military, retired law enforcement is often preferred, but not necessarily required experience as I look to build my team. Students really need to create their own personal brand on such social media platforms like LinkedIn, Twitter, Facebook, Instagram, etc. Furthermore, it is paramount that students find experienced, highly credible mentors to assist with the transitional role of the post-college to job market. I encourage students to write blogs, publish articles, white papers, and join professional organizations such as IAVM, NCS4, and ASIS, to name a few. Attend conferences and networking events in your local area, whenever possible. Internships are also a great way to get your foot in the door. Finally, continuing education is the key to lifelong success—don't forget to keep learning!

Risk Management is a key component for an overall effective and efficient security program. For example, marathons are especially challenging to safeguard due to complexity and length. There is so much open space, multiple ingress/egress checkpoints, potential severe weather, errant drones, mass transportation hubs, entertainment zones, etc., that are present when organizing such an event. The Boston Marathon bombing was a real game changer in the sports security space. Duty of care, lessons learned, and sharing best practices is now the prevailing industry theme. Conducting thorough site visits, threats and vulnerability assessments, and computer simulations are key risk management/mitigation strategies for industry leaders to implement. Our work continues on a daily basis and we must remain diligent.

Introduction

Facility and event managers must be mindful of the need to mitigate negligence insofar as spectators and participants are protected under the law. They have a duty to act reasonably and prudently in situations involving their spectators and participants. Having knowledge and training in what constitutes duty, breach of duty, proximate causes of injuries, and the injury itself is critical in determining the liability for a facility or event. Since the enactment of the Tort Claims Act, persons engaging in activities involving personal risk have had increasingly greater expectations concerning their safety and are litigating in increasing numbers (Pyles & Pyles, 1992).

Litigation resulting from personal injury or financial loss is at an all-time high. Lawsuits have increased, especially since 2008, when the U.S. recession began. In a struggling economy, sport managers should expect that even the smallest incident may result in a lawsuit (Cunningham, 2010). Facility and event managers should have a heightened sense of responsibility and employ the appropriate checks and balances to help ensure a safe and successful result for their respective organizations. Consequently, it is important to develop a strong understanding of the different types of risk and the best strategies for minimizing the impact of the risk. One thing that is certain and important to realize is that eliminating risk completely is extremely difficult, even under the best circumstances. Reduction of the likelihood of an occurrence, however, can be achieved with proper training, supervision, and action plans.

What Is Risk?

risk The probability that a hazard will lead to a loss.

The challenge of defining **risk** is that individuals subjectively categorize different behaviors and actions as risk. For example, one skier may deviate from the standard courses at the slope and head into unmarked terrain for a unique and fun experience, while another may find such action too dangerous and elect to remain on course. For facility and event managers, the same differences in perception are at work; thus, we have evaluated broader definitions to capture the different levels of risk. Van der Smissen (1990) defines risk as an uncertainty or chance of loss, usually accidental loss, which is sudden, unusual, or unforeseen. Giddens (1988) defines risk as "dangers that we seek to actively identify, confront, and control" (p. 23). Finally, Griffith (2011) states that risk is "the probability that a hazard will lead to a loss" (p. 1), which is the definition we consider most applicable to sport facility and event management. The broadness of the term allows it to apply to any component of the facility or event that could engender a loss or negative outcome for the managers. Moreover, the term implies that there are varying degrees of both hazards and losses, which, in the subsequent sections of this chapter, should become clear.

Types of Risk

Given the various types of facilities and events, it is nearly impossible to generate a complete list of the types of risks that facility and event managers may face. Rushing and Miller (2009) outline four broad categories of risk: Public liability caused by negligence, public liability excluding negligence, business operations, and property exposures. Public liability caused by negligence occurs when the facility or event manager fails to provide a reasonably safe environment for individuals to work, spectate, or participate in the sporting

Table 4-1   Broad Categories of Risk

Human Risks	Facility Risks	Environmental Risks
Sport participation	Accreditation	Legal issues
Spectators	Facility/equipment/property	Economic circumstances
Terrorism	Storage	Political circumstances
Athlete protection	Transportation	Loss prevention
Management activities/ controls	Safety/security	Weather
Employment/training		

activity. Ensuring a safe environment may include providing proper warning signs, supervision, security, equipment, facilities, medical/emergency care, and travel/transportation (Rushing & Miller, 2009). Public liability excluding negligence occurs when individuals are affected by the practices of the personnel within the facility. For example, claims may include discrimination, sexual harassment, wrongful termination, invasion of privacy, or false imprisonment (Rushing & Miller, 2009). Risk associated with business operations includes business interruptions, property loss, contractual issues, or employee health. Finally, natural disasters, fire, vandalism/terrorism, and theft comprise property exposure risks.

Facility and event managers tend to focus primarily on the risk associated with bodily injury to the spectators and/or participants. These risks can include slips and falls, injuries during participation, or altercations between spectators. However, risk may also include inadequate waivers of responsibility forms, lack of appropriate insurance, incomplete training or supervision of employees and participants, weather-related risks, and others, as outlined in **Table 4-1**.

Terrorism and Sport

A more recent risk development in sport event and facility management has been the threat or the occurrence of terrorist activity. The attacks on the World Trade Center in 2001 impacted the sport industry in terms of how facility and event managers perceived terrorist threats on their facilities and events. Most individuals recognize only the 1972 Munich Olympic Games terrorist attack and the 1996 Centennial Olympic Park bombing in Atlanta, Georgia, and the bombing at the 2013 Boston Marathon as occurrences of terrorist activity at sporting events. However, as Toohey (2008) points out, there were 168 sport-related terrorist attacks in the world between 1972 and 2004, with no signs of abatement. To underline the growing concerns for risk at various venues, Toohey (2008) also notes that sport is a platform where many spectators and participants are aggregated in one place with numerous opportunities and methods of potential attack. The bombing during the Boston Marathon in 2013 highlighted the challenge of policing such large areas, especially when crowds enter and exit from a variety of points, as highlighted in Vignette 4-1.

Following the bombings in Boston, other marathons changed their security procedures. For instance, the Chicago Marathon now limits runners to entering through four distinct checkpoints. Additionally, each runner must collect his or her own bib and timing chip at the exposition. Previously, friends or family members were allowed to pick up these items for others. Runners are also restricted to using a race-issued clear plastic bag for gear check. One of the final changes involves family members and/or friends congregating at the start and finish lines. For the first time, spectators who want to meet their friends or family members who participated in the marathon are required to go through one of two security checkpoints. In addition to these protocols for the marathon industry, many

> **TIP**
>
> For those unfamiliar with the 1996 Atlanta Olympic bombing, *Judging Jewel* by ESPN Films is an excellent portrayal of those tragic events.

VIGNETTE 4-1

Boston Marathon Tragedy Changes Risk Management Strategies

On April 15, 2013, the bombings at the Boston Marathon, which killed three individuals and wounded 264 others, brought the need for risk management and security to the forefront of event managers' minds. This was the largest mass-casualty attack on U.S. soil since September 11, 2001.

This attack marked changes to security at the Boston Marathon and marathons across the country. The Boston Athletic Association has decided that runners cannot have backpacks or bags at or near the start or finish lines or along the course. Bags are also not allowed on the buses that run between the start and finish lines. Runners are allowed to bring a change of clothing and shoes in designated clear plastic bags and leave them in Boston Common, which is approximately a half mile from the finish area, prior to the race.

Additional security measures for the Boston Marathon include an increase in uniformed and plainclothes police officers and additional bomb-sniffing dogs. There are additional security procedures in place that the marathon director and security personnel are reluctant to disclose.

spectator- and participant-driven events schedule regular meetings with local, state, and national law enforcement groups, including Homeland Security, leading up to and during the event as a measure of risk management.

The changes in the marathon have impacted event management more broadly as concerts, festivals, and other large population events are incorporating similar strategies.

Similarly, venues and closed events (i.e., confined areas with few points of entry) have made several adjustments over the years to deal with the potential threat of terrorist activity. For instance, it is commonplace for facility and event managers to search backpacks and purses upon entry to the facility, ask spectators to walk through metal detectors, or use the metal detecting wands to ensure that no weapons are being brought onto the site; and disallow hazards such as bottles or solid trash that can be thrown and cause injury or potentially contain explosive material. The National Football League has implemented a policy stating that only clear or see-through bags are allowed into the stadium in order to ensure safety and expedite fan entry into the stadium. Major League Baseball instructed the teams in the league to install and use metal detectors in their stadiums; however, some are calling into question the viability of these devices.

Facilities have also invested millions of dollars in surveillance equipment to increase the security of their stadiums (Carey, 2011). For instance, they have installed security cameras that can zoom in on any seat in the stadium, as well as video equipment to record for later review. The two serve both as a method of monitoring spectator activity and as a deterrent for much lower forms of crime. Some major events have utilized dirty bomb detectors, while others sample the air quality to identify any potential contaminants in the air designed for a terrorist attack. In the case of Super Bowl XLV, hosted in Dallas, Texas, a drone was used to patrol the airfield above the facility to ensure that it was safe from attack and could retaliate if needed. These strategies to reduce the likelihood of a terrorist attack begin to highlight how organizations may manage their risk.

What Is Risk Management?

To overcome the potential problems associated with risks, sport facilities and events should establish a sound framework to minimize the potential and severity of the risk, a process known as **risk management**. Risk management has been defined as "systematically identifying threats (risks) to your organization and developing ways to minimize them from occurring" (Office of Sport and Recreation, 2009, p. 2–1). Taylor and Booty (2006) state that a risk management strategy "provides a framework for determining an individual company's response to risk, including who would undertake the work involved at a tactical level" (p. 232). A simple way to define risk management is the identification, assessment, and prioritization of risk. This means that facility and event managers should develop a standard set of policies, procedures, and processes so that employees, volunteers, and other stakeholders know how to best minimize the various risks associated with hosting the event.

To create a strong risk management plan, facility and event managers should include what may be "foreseeable." The broad range of concerns requires one to be a forward thinker, crisis manager, and problem solver in order to provide the protections and enjoyment fans, spectators, and participants have come to expect.

risk management
A sound framework to minimize the potential and severity of the risk.

What Are the Benefits of Good Risk Management?

The value of a good risk management plan cannot be understated as it brings considerable value to facility or event owners. Proper risk management can reduce the likelihood of undesirable and costly impacts, increase the safety of the patrons, and improve financial issues more generally (Sawyer & Smith, 1999). For example, there are standard railing heights for sport facilities to have if the seating is above a large drop-off. In an incident in 2011 at a Texas Rangers baseball game, a 39-year-old fan fell over a railing 20 feet to his death while trying to catch a ball for his son thrown by Josh Hamilton. Even though Rangers Ballpark in Arlington (now called Globe Life Park) exceeded the building code for railing height at the park, management has decided to raise the rails in front of the seating areas; to post new signs reminding fans not to lean on, sit on, or stand by the rails; and to make a verbal warning through a public address announcement at the beginning of all games.

A quality risk-management program may also reduce costs associated with insurance premiums (Viney, 1999). Similar to driver's insurance, the longer a facility or event demonstrates a quality safety record, the less the insurance premium costs. Risk management may also improve the quality of the sporting experience that the event offers (Viney, 1999). In the large events with a large number of spectators, security presence and measures (e.g., metal detectors, bomb sniffing dogs) provide a greater sense of safety, which leads to greater levels of satisfaction. The measures facility and event managers take to ensure the safety of the participants and spectators will likely enhance the visibility and image of the organization as individuals learn about the quality of service that the organization provides. Finally, risk management will enhance the managers', employees', and volunteers' level of confidence in their abilities, which will lead to better strategic outcomes for the organization (Viney, 1999).

Steps in the Risk Management Process

The idea of managing risk is imperative both for hallmark and mega-events and for small-scale events on either a global or local level. Many of the elements to consider are similar but will differ when considering the size and scope of an organization's objective. As previously highlighted, the numerous types of events inherently create a limitless number of risks because they vary in size, structure, operation, sport, and countless other aspects.

RISK IDENTIFICATION

Properly identifying risks associated with the facility or event requires a mix of knowledge, experience, and critical thinking. At this stage, facility and event managers should evaluate the environment, structures, and marketplace to determine the sources of risk associated with the previously described areas. When managers lack experience or knowledge, there are several resources they can use to assist with **risk identification**. First, the local, state, or national sporting organization may be able to provide them with the typical risks associated with the event they are planning to host. For example, if an event manager is working with the local sports commission to host her first skateboard competition, it would be important to meet with the local- and state-level clubs to determine the various risks associated with participation. Additionally, the event manager may seek counsel from event organizations that have hosted similar events. Their knowledge and expertise in the area will likely be invaluable to identifying areas of risk that are not

risk identification
Evaluation of the environment, structures, and marketplace to determine the sources of risk associated with the sport facility or event.

VIGNETTE 4-2

Tragedy Leads to Change in Facility Management

On April 15, 1989, one of the worst tragedies in sport occurred in Hillsborough football stadium in Sheffield, England. The football (or soccer) match was the semi-final game between Liverpool and Nottingham Forrest for the Football Association Challenge Cup (FA Cup). In two different measures for both fan and player safety from hooligans, the crowds from the opposing teams were segregated, and to keep hooligans from entering the pitch, high steel fencing was placed at the bottom of the stands. As individuals attempted to enter the stadium through their respective supporter gates, several issues occurred. Some were at the wrong gate but unable to return to another gate because of the number of people behind them; trains and construction issues delayed many of the fans' arrival times, leading them all to arrive at once, and the decision to not delay the match led to panic for those who were issued tickets. This led to the decision to open an exit gate, allowing the people to enter the stadium all at once and into only two sections, pens 3 and 4 of the stadium. As the number of fans entering those pens was far greater than the number the sections could hold, the crowd began to push forward, creating a crush of those in the front of the section against the metal fence. Fans began climbing over the fence in an attempt to escape the crush, which initially was viewed as a field invasion by security personnel. As the action on the field heightened with a shot on goal, the crush worsened, resulting in the match being discontinued. Those remaining in the stands died mostly from compressive asphyxia while others were trampled or injured severely. In total, 96 people died that day and another 766 were injured. After several inquiries, investigations, and inquests, it was most recently (2016) determined that the supporters were unlawfully killed due to gross negligent failures by emergency and security personnel in response to the incident, as well as the design of the stadium. In 2017, six people were charged with various offenses based on their roles in response to the incident.

audit A systematic critical examination of the facility or event to identify key risks or safety issues.

as obvious. Finally, some national governing organizations provide audits or checklists associated with hosting sport events. An **audit** is a systematic critical examination of the facility or event to identify key risk (related to organizational risks) or safety issues (related to injury risks).

RISK ANALYSIS

risk analysis Categorization of the levels of risks based on the severity and likelihood of occurrence.

Once facility and event managers identify the sources of risk that can impact either the facility or event, the next step in the process is to categorize the levels of risks, a process known as **risk analysis**. Most facility and event managers categorize risk using two questions: How likely is the risk to occur, and what are the consequences associated with the risk? **Figure 4-1** provides a matrix to assist with the categorization process.

The risk matrix gives a visual representation of what could happen, how serious the incident could be, and the frequency of a potential occurrence. The likelihood of an occurrence is shown in relation to the consequences

Simple Risk Matrix

Likelihood	Consequences		
	Minor	Moderate	Major
Likely			
Possible			
Unlikely			

Risk Treatment Key

Intolerable Risk Level Immediate action required.
Tolerable Risk Level Risks must be reduced so far as is practicable.
Broadly Acceptable Risk Level Monitor and further reduce where practicable.

Figure 4-1   Risk Assessment Matrix

of the occurrence. Analyzing the risks developed in the first stage enables facility and event managers to begin to determine which risks need further evaluation. **Figure 4-2** provides an example of a completed matrix. While the list of risks is not exhaustive for a high school football game, it does illustrate the types of risks associated with events and the level of frequency and impact associated with them.

RISK EVALUATION

Once the risk analysis is completed, the next step is to determine whether the risk is acceptable or not, a process known as **risk evaluation**. To answer this question, the organization should evaluate the mission and vision of the organization and the risk matrix to indicate whether the risk is worth the costs associated with minimizing it. Using a financial term, facility and event owners would evaluate the risk using a cost–benefit analysis. For instance, the addition of alcohol to an event may improve overall sales and possibly atmosphere; however, it will also increase the level of insurance required and additional security and permits to be able to sell alcohol. In this event, the increase in sales volume may not be worth the additional expenses incurred, and therefore, the event or facility manager may choose not to have alcohol at the event.

risk evaluation A process of determining the acceptability of the risk through a cost–benefit analysis.

TIP

To avoid the additional permitting, insurance, and other costs associated with alcohol sales, facility and event organizers partner with local bottling companies or breweries to manage the alcohol sales. This transfers the liability from the facility or event owner to the distributor.

Consequences			
Likelihood	Minor	Moderate	Major/Catastrophic
Likely	Kids sneak in without paying	Injury from unruly fans throwing debris	None
Possible	Slip and fall on wet bleachers or ice	Hypo- or hyperthermia from severe weather temperatures	Player suffers severe life-threatening injury from tackle
Unlikely	Food poisoning from concession stand due to improper refrigeration	Camera and speakers are stolen after game	Spectator has fatal cardiac arrest Bomb threat

Figure 4-2   Example of a Risk Matrix Chart for a High School Football Game. Orange Text Indicates Intolerable Risk Level, Purple Text Indicates Tolerable Risk Level, and Green Text Indicates Broadly Acceptable Risk Level

RISK TREATMENT

risk treatment
A method of managing risk that involves minimizing the impact and/or occurrence of the risk.

risk avoidance
A method of managing risk that involves discontinuing the component of the activity considered to be a risk.

Once the risks for a particular event are identified and the risk matrix is considered, facility and event managers must decide how they should handle the potential risks or which method of **risk treatment** they will use. Within the sport event context, there are five common strategies facility and event owners use to minimize the impact of risk: Avoidance, acceptance and financing, reduction through proactive measures, transfer, and retention.

Risk avoidance occurs when managers establish the risk as both a major risk and nonessential to the mission of the organization and, therefore, discontinue the component of the activity considered to be a risk (Rushing & Miller, 2009). The avoidance strategy is used when the likelihood of injury is high and happens fairly frequently. For example, Florida has the highest incidence of lightning strikes and frequent storms. School administrators and managers should postpone, reschedule, or cancel outdoor games and events for the safety of everyone involved when the threat of severe weather has moved into the area. At times, risks associated with sport event participants and spectators are unavoidable. As a result, facility and event managers must implement one of the following strategies.

Preparing for the risk through budgeting or establishing deductibles or self-insurance is considered acceptance and financing, or **risk acceptance**. In this scenario, the facility or event managers absorb all of the liability and financial responsibility for anything that might happen regarding the participants, stakeholders, and facility. The operating budget of the event and venue should include provisions for possible injuries and damage in the unlikely event of an occurrence. When accepting the risk, the sport manager is assuming the risk and potential need to pay small settlements, as in the case of injury or repairs if fans or participants damage equipment. The manager may also be absorbing the expense of small medical bills, emergency personnel, and sports medicine clinicians because the calculations for risk frequency and severity are low.

When the risk is unavoidable and greater than an acceptable level, facility and event owners may employ **risk reduction through proactive measures** by establishing a series of controls to reduce either the likelihood of occurrence or the consequences associated with the risk. One method of control is to establish a set of standardized practices for employees and volunteers to follow, or a standard operating procedure (SOP) manual. The importance of practicing the protocols in the SOP manual, as well as continued training and updates for employees and volunteers as new potential risks are identified, cannot be underestimated. Clearly, one cannot predict everything that could possibly happen during an event, and thus the SOP manual provides employees with a series of guidelines to use as a method to deal with various issues. Employee manuals may also be helpful for delineating some specific guidelines that have been identified as critical, such as weather-related emergency protocols, communication procedures, and injury or illness strategies. Training and practice scenarios should be required of all staff and conducted on a regular basis. First aid, cardiopulmonary resuscitation (CPR), and automated external defibrillator (AED) training and certification should be provided and encouraged in light of new legislation in many states requiring these safety measures to be in place at facilities and venues.

Risk transfer consists of moving the risk to another entity. There are two commonly used methods to transfer risk: Insurance and waiver of liability. The use of insurance or an insurance policy covers the potential monetary

risk acceptance
A method of managing risk that involves preparing for the risk through budgeting, deductibles, or self-insurance.

risk reduction through proactive measures
A method of managing risk that involves establishing a series of controls to reduce either the likelihood of occurrence or the consequences associated with the risk.

risk transfer
A method of managing risk that involves moving the risk to another entity.

or financial losses considered too large for the facility or event managers to handle independently. By taking out insurance, facility and event managers opt to pay a premium or dollar amount to have these losses covered in the event of a lawsuit due to injury, a financial loss due to unexpected low attendance, a contract violation, and other developments. Similar to personal auto coverage, amounts may depend on the inherent or obvious risks identified, the level of the liability limits, the amount of the deductible, and the safety record. Limited-liability coverage is the total amount of coverage available to the facility or event for general claims against the organization. Amounts vary based on the event as well as the location of the event. The laws vary from state to state in terms of the minimum liability coverage that facility and events owners should possess. Deductibles are the amount of money paid when a claim is made. Typically, the larger the deductible, the smaller the premium. A high deductible may be a wise decision for the organization in terms of the upfront costs to host the event; however, the deductible costs should be built into the operating budget. See **Table 4-2** for commonly used insurance coverages.

Table 4-2   Common Types of Insurance Coverage for Events

Insurance	Description
Accidental medical	Covers medical expenses incurred as a result of an injury while participating in an insured activity
Accidental death and dismemberment	Covers accidental death or the loss of limb or limbs as a result of participation
Blanket coverage	Insures property under a single amount applying to several different pieces of property
Business income/interruption	Covers loss of income in case the insured's business is shut down by a covered loss
Causality/liability insurance	Is primarily concerned with the legal liability for losses caused by injury to persons or damage to property of others
Event cancellation insurance	Protects against loss due to rain, hail, snow, or sleet, which causes cancellation or reduced earnings of an outdoor event
General liability insurance	Covers professional and commercial risks; broad term meaning liability insurance other than automobile liability or employer's liability
Liquor liability	Provides coverage for bodily injury or property damage for which you may be held liable by reason of alcohol consumption
Umbrella coverage	Provides coverage over a single underlying policy, or several different underlying policies

The second common form of transferring risk is the waiver of liability. Many facility and event managers will require participants, and potentially spectators, to sign a waiver that limits or eliminates liability in the event of an injury (see **Figure 4-3**). These waivers of liability typically require participants to comply with the rules and behaviors expected in order to participate. For example, a waiver may indicate that the event is not responsible for injuries that occur if the participant violates a written rule set forth by the event or facility. Many spectator events have disclaimers written on the

---

In consideration of being allowed to participate in any way in the [Organization Name] athletic sports program, related events, and activities, the undersigned acknowledges, appreciates, and agrees that:

1. The risk of injury from the activities involved in this program is significant, including the potential for permanent paralysis and death, and while particular rules, equipment, and personal discipline may reduce this risk, the risk of serious injury does exist; and,
2. I KNOWINGLY AND FREELY ASSUME ALL SUCH RISKS, both known and unknown, EVEN IF ARISING FROM THE NEGLIGENCE OF THE RELEASEES or others, and assume full responsibility for my participation; and,
3. I willingly agree to comply with the stated and customary terms and conditions for participation. If, however, I observe any unusual significant hazard during my presence or participation, I will remove myself from participation and bring such to the attention of the nearest official immediately; and,
4. I, for myself and on behalf of my heirs, assignees, personal representatives, and next of kin, HEREBY RELEASE AND HOLD HARMLESS [Organization Name], their officers, officials, agents, and/or employees, other participants, sponsoring agencies, sponsors, advertisers, and if applicable, owners and lessors of premises used to conduct the event ("RELEASEES"), WITH RESPECT TO ANY AND ALL INJURY, DISABILITY, DEATH, or loss or damage to person or property, WHETHER ARISING FROM THE NEGLIGENCE OF THE RELEASEES OR OTHERWISE, to the fullest extent permitted by law.

I HAVE READ THIS RELEASE OF LIABILITY AND ASSUMPTION OF RISK AGREEMENT, FULLY UNDERSTAND ITS TERMS, UNDERSTAND THAT I HAVE GIVEN UP SUBSTANTIAL RIGHTS BY SIGNING IT, AND SIGN IT FREELY AND VOLUNTARILY WITHOUT ANY INDUCEMENT.

_____DATE

SIGNED:_____ (participant's signature)

Figure 4-3 Example of a Waiver Release Form

backs of tickets that they purchase, as well as posted signs and announcements of warnings or rules for behaviors.

As with insurance, the laws vary from state to state; thus, it is important to understand the laws within your facility's or event's state. In most cases, if the event or facility provides the participant with a safe environment with proper medical personnel present, the waiver will hold up. All events and facilities are required to provide a standard of reasonable care to their participants and spectators, but accidents do happen, and these measures may demonstrate reasonable care by the facility and event managers.

The final method for managing risk occurs when the organization does not employ any of the preceding strategies. Rather, the facility or event manager has adopted **risk retention** because the likelihood of occurrence is extremely low and/or one of the treatment strategies would compromise the objectives of the event. For example, an event organizer hosting a sand volleyball tournament may list a tornado as a possible risk; however, because the likelihood of severe weather is minimal at that time of year, the event owner would decide not to take out various forms of insurance or include management strategies in the SOP manual. Frequently, it is not the case that treating the risk impacts the objectives of the event, and; therefore, some form of planning to manage the risk should occur.

RISK MONITORING

The last step in the risk management process should not be viewed as a final step, but rather as a continuous assessment of the risk associated with hosting the event, as well as the management strategies to reduce the risks (Westerbeek et al., 2005). **Risk monitoring** occurs throughout the entire planning, implementation, and evaluation stages of the event process; however, most view it as a component of the evaluation stage. It is important to review the procedures and policies set in place during each stage of the event to ensure that they are well designed to minimize the level of risk associated with hosting the various events.

During the event implementation stage, for instance, facility and event managers would monitor the activities associated with the various risks that they have identified, such as the communication of risk, the occurrence of risk, and the overall response to the risks that occur. Monitoring the risk at the implementation stage may allow for facility and event managers to make adjustments to the policies and procedures designed during the

risk retention
A method of managing risk in which the organization does not employ any risk management strategies.

risk monitoring The continuous assessment of the risk associated with facilities and events, as well as the management strategies to reduce those risks.

planning stage. For example, a local facility is hosting an upcoming soccer tournament featuring children 12 to 18 years old. Initially, the field surface was sound, so they planned for the minimal amount of injury risk associated with typical soccer play. However, the night before the tournament, a heavy rainstorm moved through the area, which caused significant wear to the field. The additional stress on the fields may increase the chance of risk because of the unevenness created from use on the wet surface. Therefore, the tournament director and facility manager determine a method to rotate the fields throughout the day so that the facility manager may level the field surface after each use.

Tracking the performance of and evaluating your risk management plan will allow for better training of employees, identification of gaps within your SOP manual, and further development of proper reporting systems. Common monitoring strategies at the evaluation stage of the event include the following:

- Documenting occurrences and updating the risk management plan as necessary
- Reviewing the occurrences of incidents and the consequences associated with them
- Reviewing unexpected occurrences and developing a plan to mitigate or manage them in the future
- Gathering information from managers, employees, and volunteers to determine any other risk management issues (Sport New Zealand, 2014)

In addition to these activities, it is important to gather information from other stakeholders associated with the event. For instance, participants and spectators may have identified areas of risk associated with their own or others' behavior on the field of play or in the audience. Other stakeholders with information pertaining to the facility or event may include city officials, media, sponsors, and contractors, all of whom may have perceived differing levels of risk associated with the facility or event.

A final strategy to monitor risk would be to employ a risk manager. This is a very important hiring decision because the risk manager should possess excellent organizational and follow-up skills. The risk manager will develop and maintain the facility and employee policy manual, provide training and practice for any certifications, educate in the areas of communication and procedures, and, ultimately, be responsible for running a first-rate facility and/or event. It may also be necessary for the risk manager to develop a facility maintenance schedule, update insurance requirements, communicate with all stakeholders' current status reports, and retain legal counsel to review contracts, potential lawsuits or settlements, and changes in negligence and premises liability laws.

SUMMARY

As competition for additional participants and spectators increases, so does the responsibility for running facilities and events in which everyone takes pride. Employees should be invested as much as possible in the desire to produce the best events in safe, well-maintained facilities that are managed by a strong and motivated sport manager.

While not every risk or accident can be predicted, evaluating the risk management plan in view of occurrences at other facilities as well as one's own can help prevent liability and negligence from happening. A good rule of thumb is to critically think about worst-case scenarios and what can be done to prevent them. The sport manager is responsible for identifying potential risks and then eliminating or reducing these risks.

DISCUSSION QUESTIONS

1. Define risk and risk management, and explain the importance of a good risk management program for a facility or event.
2. What role have terrorism and other attacks had on risk management and sport events?
3. Define and differentiate the strategies associated with treating risk.
4. Outline and explain the strategies a facility or event manager can use to monitor risk management policies and procedures.
5. Identify a sport event or facility and use the steps in the risk management process to explain how this event/facility manages risk.

Case STUDY

Warrior Dash Tragedy

The Warrior Dash is a 5k obstacle course that was established in 2009. The Warrior Dash website boasts that their event is a "get-dirty race anyone can start and everyone can finish" (n.d. b, ¶ 1). They go on to claim that "Warrior Nation is the diverse crew of athletes and couch potatoes, families and weekend warriors, run-for-a-cause-ers and veteran racers all united by the Warrior Creed and the love of a good time" (Warrior Dash, n.d. b, ¶ 2). In essence, the Warrior Dash organizers are inviting all types of people—both those in shape and those who are out of shape—to partake in their race, which could pose a problem. How do you create a race that is challenging to athletes and not intimidating to individuals who are new to racing or are out of shape?

Warrior Dash races are held in cities across the United States and each race features various obstacles meant to challenge you in several ways. The obstacles in a Warrior Dash are based on the elements of earth, air, fire, and water. For example, Under the Wire, has participants crawling under 100 feet of barbed wire in the mud. In Warrior Roast, participants must jump over a row of real fire. The website tells you to "plan your leap accordingly: You'll most likely want to make this photo op your new profile picture" (n.d. a, ¶ 1). Another obstacle that was a part of the Warrior Dash is the Diesel Dome. This event was a 30-by-50-foot wooden dome that was intended to ignite a sense of vertigo in each participant.

On October 8, 2016, in St. Francisville, Louisiana, a Warrior Dash event was taking place. Everything was going as the event organizers had planned until the Diesel Dome obstacle collapsed with 20–30 people on it. According to witnesses at the event, the Diesel Dome started swaying back and forth and then fell to the ground. Once the structure collapsed, it took between 10 and 15 minutes for those who were injured to receive treatment. This delay was due to the safety monitors who were in charge of watching this structure being only 13 and 14 years old. There was also a question about the training they received regarding how many people to allow on the structure at a time and what to do in the event of an emergency.

Ultimately, three people were airlifted to the hospital, seven individuals were taken by ambulance to the hospital, and 10 to 15 others drove themselves to seek treatment for their injuries at the hospital. The participants' injuries included broken bones, cuts, and head injuries.

An investigation into the incident resulted in five arrest warrants being issued that accused contractors of poor construction work and event staffers of failing to follow written safety procedures. There were also charges of failing to get a contractor's license in Louisiana. Due to the negligence by the construction company and event staff, it is a wonder additional structures did not collapse.

1. Research the risk management procedures for Warrior Dash and other extreme sport events. What are the protocols in place if an emergency arises?
2. How would you have handled the situation?
3. Do you think there is an element of personal responsibility that racers must assume when they participate in these traveling races? Why or why not?
4. Create an emergency management/risk management plan for the Warrior Dash to ensure that another structural collapse or serious issue does not occur. Be thorough in this plan. You must discuss how you would specifically deal with the event overall and five specific obstacles.

CASE REFERENCES

Warrior Dash. (n.d. a). Warrior Roast. Retrieved from https://warriordash.com/obstacle/warrior-roast/.

Warrior Dash. (n.d. b). What is warrior dash. Retrieved from https://warriordash.com/info/what-is-warrior-dash/.

REFERENCES

Carey, B. (2011). Stadium security continues to evolve ten years after 9/11. *Sports Illustrated.* Retrieved from http://www.si.com/more-sports/2011/09/09/stadium-securitychangessince911

Cunningham, G. (2010). Sports centers, recreational facilities facing more risks in tough economy. Retrieved from http://www.propertycasualty360.com/2010/04/12/sports-centers-recreational-facilities-facing-more-risks-in-tough-economy

Giddens, A. (1988). Risk society: The context of British politics. In J. Franklin (Ed.), *The politics of risk society* (pp. 23–24). Cambridge, UK: Polity Press.

Griffith, M. D. (2011). The uncertainty of risk management: Kneejerk reactions do more harm than good. Retrieved from http://www.sportrisk.com/2011/11/the-uncertainty-factor-in-risk-management/

Office of Sport and Recreation. (2009). *Risk management resource for recreation and sport organisations.* Retrieved from http://ors.sa.gov.au/__data/assets/pdf_file/0006/255309/Risk_Management_Booklet_20164_2.pdf

Pyles, C. D., & Pyles, R. B. (1992). Risk management of sports facilities. *Journal of Legal Aspects of Sport, 2*(1), 53–64.

Rushing, G., & Miller, J. J. (2009). Facility and event risk management. In T. H. Sawyer (Ed.), *Facility management for physical activity and sport.* Champaign, IL: Sagamore Publishing.

Sawyer, T. H., & Smith, O. (1999). *The management of clubs, recreation, and sport: Concepts and applications.* Champaign, IL: Sagamore Publishing.

Sport New Zealand. (2014). Risk management for event organizers. Retrieved from http://www.sportnz.org.nz/

Taylor, C., & Booty, F. (2006). Risk management. In F. Booty (Ed.), *Facilities management handbook* (2nd ed.). Burlington, MA: Elsevier/Butterworth-Heinemann.

Toohey, K. (2008). Terrorism, sport and public policy in the risk society. *Sport in Society, 11*(4), 429–442.

van der Smissen, B. (1990). *Legal liability and risk management for public and private entities, volume 2.* Cincinnati: W. H. Anderson.

Viney, C. (1999). *A sporting chance: A risk management framework for the sport and recreation industry,* Tasmania, Australia: Office Sport & Recreation.

Westerbeek, H., Smith, A., Turner, P., Emery, P., Green, C., & van Leeuwen, L. (2005). *Managing sport facilities and major events.* New York, NY: Routledge.

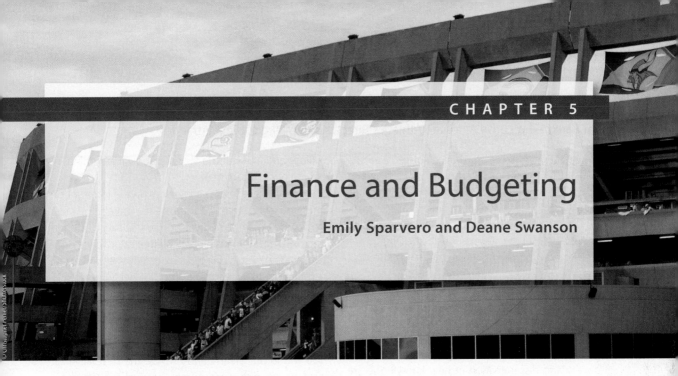

CHAPTER 5

Finance and Budgeting

Emily Sparvero and Deane Swanson

CHAPTER OBJECTIVES

Upon completion of this chapter, the reader will be able to:

1. Define capital projects and explain why both for-profit and nonprofit organizations undertake them.
2. Identify equity and debt funding sources available for a sport organization's capital projects.
3. Distinguish between general obligation, revenue, and special tax bonds.
4. Compare line-item and program budgets.
5. Discuss advantages and disadvantages of zero-based versus incremental budgeting.
6. Explain what variance analysis is and how it is used by managers.

CHAPTER OVERVIEW

This chapter will outline the basic concepts of financing sport facilities. First, it will describe the basic components of financial statements and how they can be utilized to develop a budget as a forecasting measure. Second, it will discuss the means of financing the construction or renovation of a new facility. Finally, it will review budgeting practices for facilities and events and identify common expenses.

IndustryVOICE

Omar Banks—Executive Associate Athletics Director & CFO, Virginia Tech Athletics

I am the Executive Associate Director of Athletics and CFO for Virginia Polytechnic Institute and State University (Virginia Tech) Athletics. My responsibilities include all financial matters that impact our department, including capital project financing, debt payments, and all other items related to facility maintenance and enhancements. Virginia Tech is a public land-grant university serving the Commonwealth of Virginia, the nation, and the world community. The discovery and dissemination of new knowledge are central to its mission. Through its focus on teaching and learning, research and discovery, and outreach and engagement, the university creates, conveys, and applies knowledge to expand personal growth and opportunity, advance social and community development, foster economic competitiveness, and improve quality of life.

The specific mission of the Athletics Department is the commitment to excellence, both academically and athletically, and to the personal development of our student athletes. In the spirit of Ut Prosim, we stand together to serve and represent our university and community with integrity and respect.

Before arriving at Virginia Tech, I had a successful career outside of the sport industry. I worked for IBM, FedEx, and Fidelity Investments, all of which played different roles in my personal and professional development. I mostly worked in accounting and financial roles, taking on special projects that others did not want. I gained a reputation as a problem solver during my time in corporate America. When I made the transition into college athletics, I worked mostly on the financial side, having experiences in fundraising, ticket sales, and business. I decided to focus on the business side of athletics because it aligned very well with my skillset and allowed me to learn about everything in an athletics department.

Financial challenges are always on the forefront of intercollegiate athletic departments. There is the race to have the newest, biggest, and best facility to attract recruits. The focus has recently shifted to providing top notch amenities for fans to really enjoy the game-day experience to prevent the trend of declining attendance at our sport events. Emergency action plans are big, as most institutions of higher education tend to be risk-averse, and we are no different. To manage these challenges, we try to "control the controllables," … live within our means, and provide the best facilities that we can with the resources that we have. We try to ensure that the needs of each sport are met, taking a careful eye to mitigate any risk issues, while providing the best aesthetics and visuals for our fans, recruits, visitors, and campus community.

Similar to one of the challenges, a big trend that I see happening is related to enhancing the fan experience to retain the current fan base and to attract the new generation of sports fans. I believe that you will see more college and professional venues lowering concession product pricing to drive sales profits through volume, and more venues will renovate their venues to create premium suites and luxury spaces to attract and retain fans and to provide enhanced services. All of these changes will focus on providing fans with unique and memorable experiences. We are currently constructing plans to reduce concession pricing and are looking to implement concession vouchers that fans can pre-purchase at a discount and use them in all of our venues over the course of the entire season. We are also working to enhance the fan experience by creating memorable pregame, in-game, and postgame experiences. From parking lot to stadium and back home, everything is about the fan experience and making sure that they leave with the impression that we not only care but that we also do things the right way to keep them interested.

Athletics is a unique industry that rewards drive, hard work, perseverance, and individuals who have a great attitude. I find that characteristics of self-motivation, ability to communicate, ability to listen, willingness to learn, positive attitude, adaptability, creativity, and organizational skills are some of the qualities of candidates who become successful. It is not an easy industry to get into, and it is very relational, so those qualities that make you stand out are the ones that others had to exhibit in order to get in themselves. I can teach new hires the technical skills to learn a job, but with all of the qualities listed above, this would ensure that the person has the ability to leave the job in a better position than when he or she started. First, I teach them to identify their own

personal core values. Understanding them will provide a road map, which should guide them to the right opportunities. Second, I would teach them about the business of athletics. Understanding revenues and expenses of an organization offers a perspective on the total organization, since 90 percent to 95 percent of all decisions have some sort of financial impact. From there, you can begin to understand how all of the pieces of the organization fit together.

In order to be successful as an executive within Athletics, you should know and understand your personal core values. This provides the roadmap for decision-making, how you conduct business, and how to operate within the "gray" areas. You also need to know how to manage people and coaches, keep emotions out of your decisions, and look at the facts and circumstances to help guide the process.

Introduction

Financial issues related to facilities and events are often key to the success or failure of a project. If an organization fails to secure the capital funding necessary for a project, or if the organization's budget does not reflect its priorities, the ability of the project to meet organizational goals is in jeopardy. This chapter begins with a discussion of capital funding and the various sources of capital available to different types of organizations. The next section of the chapter provides an overview of facility budgeting, including different budgeting approaches and variance analyses. The chapter concludes with a discussion on common expenses in event and facility operation.

In April of 2018, Northwestern University opened the Walter Athletics Center and Ryan Fieldhouse, a $270 million athletic department project that ushered in a new era of spending in the world of big time college sport. The facility was financed as part of Northwestern's capital campaign and it includes an indoor practice facility for football, the department's administrative offices, academic services, and space for five other varsity sports. The facility has all the bells and

TIP

When the capital funding source requires a referendum, proponents of a bond issue should be willing and have the financial resources necessary to fund a public information campaign to persuade voters to vote for the proposal.

whistles that have become common-place in the major athletic department facilities—amenities like an in-house barber, hot tub, and elaborate meeting rooms for the football team. However, the real "wow factor" comes from the panoramic views of Lake Michigan, the campus, and Chicago, through the facility's 44-foot windows. On a recent visit, the father of a recruit called the facility "The Infinity Pool of Indoors" (Thamel, 2018), a comment that suggests that this new facility may finally give Northwestern an advantage that its peers in the Big Ten may find hard to match.

Northwestern's athletic complex is only one example of the facilities arms race currently underway. From 2016 to 2018, close to $17 billion were spent on new or substantially renovated facilities (Broughton, 2018). A listing of professional sport projects that opened in 2018 is provided in **Table 5-1**. This construction boom provides spectators with new and/or substantially renovated facilities in which to view sport events at the high school, college, and professional levels. The facility expenditures are not limited to venues for sport spectatorship. Facilities for sport participation are flourishing, and organizations, including campus recreation departments; public parks and recreation departments; and private, for-profit sport clubs; are renovating or building new facilities. Given the magnitude of facility spending, it is important to understand the mechanisms through which these facilities are funded and the budgeting processes that are applicable to sport facilities.

Capital Projects

capital project
A long-term investment project that will increase the organization's assets.

Sport facilities are common capital projects that sport organizations undertake. Capital refers to the funds needed to finance an organization's assets. A **capital project** is a long-term investment project that will increase the organization's assets. If an organization wants to build a new facility (or renovate

Table 5-1   Professional and College Sport Projects Completed in 2018

Facility	Location	Team(s) Hosted	Cost
Entertainment and Sports Center	Milwaukee, WI	Milwaukee Bucks, Marquette University men's basketball	$524 million
Louis Armstrong Stadium	New York, NY	USTA US Open	$450 million
Banc of California Stadium	Los Angeles, CA	Los Angeles Football Club	$350 million
Audi Field	Washington, DC	DC United	$300 million
Phillips Arena	Atlanta, GA	Atlanta Hawks	$192.5 million
ISM Raceway	Avondale, AZ	Motorsports	$178 million
M&T Bank Stadium	Baltimore, MD	Baltimore Ravens	$144 million
Richmond Raceway	Richmond, VA	Motorsports	$30 million
Spectrum Center	Charlotte, NC	Charlotte Hornets	$27.5 million
New Era Field	Orchard Park, NY	Buffalo Bills	$15 million
Target Field	Minneapolis, MN	Minnesota Twins	$13 million
Coors Field	Denver, CO	Colorado Rockies	$8.5 million

an existing facility), there are many upfront costs, including costs associated with land acquisition, construction, and infrastructure development. In order to begin construction, the sport organization needs to have cash available to cover these expenses. Thus, a capital project typically requires large, up-front cash outlays. The projects continue to have both cash inflows and outflows over the course of the useful life of the project. In order to determine whether an organization should pursue a capital project, managers need to determine whether the project will increase the value of the organization.

In for-profit sport organizations, this determination is fairly straightforward. Managers can estimate the present value of all revenues that are expected to be generated by the facility (cash inflows) and the present value of all expenses expected to be incurred by the facility (cash outflows). As a simple decision rule, if the present value of the cash inflow is greater than the present value of the cash outflow, undertaking the facility project will increase the value of the firm. This rule is well illustrated by looking at the values of professional sport team franchises. In 2016, the Minnesota Vikings realized a 38 percent increase in franchise value, which was largely due to their construction of a new stadium. Once the stadium opened in 2017, the value of the Vikings increased by an additional 9 percent. In 2017, the Atlanta Falcons were worth $2.48 billion, an increase of 19 percent over the previous year. This increase in value was driven by the opening of Mercedes-Benz Stadium.

In nonprofit and public-sector sport organizations, decision making about capital projects is complicated by the public service orientation of these organizations. Public-sector organizations include federal, state, and local governmental agencies that serve the public good. Nonprofit organizations provide programs and services that the for-profit and public sectors either cannot or are not willing to provide. Public-sector and nonprofit organizations do not have shareholders to whom they are accountable. However, they are accountable to their stakeholders (e.g., clients, elected officials, community residents) and, as such, should consider the financial feasibility and sustainability of projects. Specifically, managers should still estimate the present value of the project's revenues and expenses, but the decision of whether to proceed might not be made solely for financial reasons. For example, decisions made by a parks and recreation department might be influenced by the department's commitment to providing a diversity of recreational opportunities to users at all socioeconomic levels. This guiding principle might cause the department to build a new recreation center in an underserved neighborhood, even if the cash inflow from the facility (i.e., membership and program fees) are not sufficient to cover the cost of the facility.

With an understanding of what defines a capital project and why a sport organization would choose to undertake such a project, we can now turn our attention to how sport organizations obtain capital needed for these projects. The acquisition, construction, or renovation of a facility will increase the assets of an organization. The increase in the organization's assets is made possible by an equivalent increase in the organization's liabilities, equity, or some combination of the two. We will examine specific ways in which sport organizations can raise the funds necessary to pay for facility projects.

Equity Finance

Equity is ownership interest in an organization, and sport facilities may pursue several different forms of equity financing for capital projects, including sale of stock, retained earnings, and gifts (Brown, Rascher, Nagel, & McEvoy, 2017).

SALE OF STOCK

The first form of equity financing available to sport organizations is the sale of stock shares. When the shares of stock are sold, the stockholder becomes a part owner of the organization. Each stockholder has specific rights, and these typically include the right to any dividends that are paid by the organization and the right to vote on organizational issues. While the sale of stock is commonly used by corporations to generate funds, there are limitations to a sport organization's ability to issue stocks to fund facility development.

The Green Bay Packers are the only publicly owned team in the four primary North American professional sport leagues (NFL, National Basketball Association [NBA], Major League Baseball [MLB], and National Hockey League [NHL]). The Packers have sold stock to the public on five occasions in the team's history, with the most recent stock sales in 1997 and 2011. The 1997 stock offering raised $24 million, and the 2011 stock offering raised approximately $67 million for Lambeau Field renovations (Cheffins, 1999; Spofford, 2012). Other North American teams, including the Cleveland Indians, Boston Celtics, and Florida Panthers, have also issued stock during their history, but these stock issues were not directly linked to facility development. The NFL, NBA, MLB, and NHL currently have policies in place that either discourage or prohibit the sale of stock. A public offering of stock requires extensive disclosure of a company's business practices. In order to protect its competitive advantage, a team may be reluctant to pursue a process that would make its business practices public. In addition to reluctance on the part of team owners to pursue this type of equity financing, there is also reluctance on the part of potential shareholders to invest in sport stocks. The North American sport stocks have underperformed the market in each instance. For example, Cleveland Indians stock showed a 50 percent return on investment for shareholders who bought the stock through the team's initial public offering and sold the stock when the team went private. However, other stocks that were traded on NASDAQ during this time produced a 123 percent return on investment for their shareholders (Smith, 2012). The sale of sport team stocks is more likely to be viewed as a souvenir for the diehard fan than a serious personal financial investment.

The sale of stock is not limited to professional sports, although instances of sale of stock for recreational or amateur sport are less common. At the recreational level, a stockholder system can be used for recreation centers and swimming pools. For example, the Hidenwood Recreation Association in Newport News, Virginia, offers a stockholder membership. This membership includes as $250 stock fee (in addition to the member's annual dues). In return, the stockholder is a voting member, can hold a position on the Association Board of Directors, and is exempt from the fee associated with reserving the swimming pool. The revenue raised through this type of stock issue is commonly, although not necessarily, used for capital projects. Other examples of stockholder programs at local recreation centers include the Shadow Oaks Recreation Association in the Spring Branch neighborhood of Houston, Texas, and the Ken Grill Recreation Center in Berks County, Pennsylvania.

RETAINED EARNINGS

retained earnings
Revenues generated by the sport organization that are reinvested to finance improvements and additions.

Sport organizations may also use retained earnings to fund facility development. **Retained earnings** are funds that are reinvested in the sport organization. In a for-profit organization, profit can either be distributed to shareholders in the form of dividends, or the profit can be reinvested in the company (i.e., retained earnings). Nonprofit organizations do not distribute earnings through dividend payments. Rather, any excess income is reinvested in the organization in order to expand its capacity to support the organization's mission. The advantage to using retained earnings to finance facility development is that the organization maintains control of how the funds are used (Stewart, 2007).

GIFTS

gift A donation provided to an organization to finance a project that is tax deductible.

Another form of equity financing that is available to nonprofit sport organizations is **gifts** or donations. Under the U.S. federal tax code, individuals who make gifts to nonprofit organizations receive a tax deduction equal to their donations. A gift to an eligible nonprofit organization will reduce the donor's adjusted gross income when he or she files his or her federal income tax. Since federal income tax is calculated as a percentage of an individual's adjusted gross income, the tax benefit associated with a donation will reduce the amount of federal income tax that the donor owes the Internal Revenue Service.

When gifts are solicited specifically for facility development, or "brick-and-mortar" projects, they are part of the organization's capital campaign. Capital campaigns can support different types of organizations, with different missions, different aims, and different levels of capital needed. The common thread among these capital campaigns is that they are focused on acquisition, development, or renovation of facilities, as illustrated by the following examples. The Philadelphia Girls' Rowing Club (PGRC) promotes rowing among women with an interest in amateur rowing, and the organization's house is the oldest structure on Philadelphia's historic Boat House Row. "Shore Her Up!" is the PGRC's capital campaign to raise funds for preservation of the boathouse. In 2015, the PGRC completed the first phase of the project, which raised $600,000 and allowed for the structural stabilization and reconstruction of its piers and docks. Subsequent phases of the campaign were planned to restore the historic exterior and renovate the interior. In 2017, Duke University concluded Duke Forward, a multi-year capital campaign that raised $3.85 billion for improvements across campus. This included several athletic department projects, including improvements to the football field, an expansion of Cameron Indoor Stadium, and the creation of a track and field stadium.

Debt Finance

As mentioned previously, in order to procure the capital necessary for facility projects, an organization will increase either its liabilities or its equity. This section will examine what happens when an organization increases its liabilities (i.e., debt financing).

LOANS

Sport organizations commonly borrow money in the form of a loan. The important features of a loan are its interest rate, maturity, and prepayment provisions (Brown et al., 2017). Interest is the amount charged by a lender in exchange for loaning the organization funds. The interest rate, or the percentage of principal charged as interest, reflects the risk inherent in the transaction. The riskier the sport organization is perceived to be, the higher the interest rate it will be charged. Maturity is the date that a loan is paid in full, including both principal and interest. Finally, a prepayment provision establishes what penalties, if any, will be charged should the recipient of the loan funds pay off the amount of the loan earlier than the date of maturity. Any sport organization can pursue loan financing from a financial institution.

Professional sport teams have special loan options available to them through their respective leagues instead of individual banks. In 2015, the NFL increased the amount a team could borrow from its Stadium Construction Support, or G-4, program to $250 million (Kaplan, 2017). Teams that have benefited from the G-4 program in recent years include the Green Bay Packers, San Francisco 49ers, Los Angeles Chargers, Minnesota Vikings, and Atlanta Falcons. The NBA has a $3.5 billion league-wide credit facility, and two-thirds of the teams in the league have borrowed funds (Kaplan & Lombardo, 2017). MLB has a $1.5 billion league-wide credit facility, and the NHL established its $1.4 billion facility in 2015. Whereas the funds borrowed through the NFL G-4 program must be used for stadium projects, the NBA, MLB, and NHL do not specify how the funds borrowed through their credit facilities are to be used. The benefit to the league is that these league-wide loan programs may support franchise stability and improve the fan experience. The benefit to the team (or loan recipient) is access to capital needed for facility projects at a low interest rate. The league's assets (e.g., national media contracts, franchise values, stable underlying league economics) secure the loan, which reduces the risk for the lenders. Remember that the interest rate charged reflects the risk of the investment. In the case of the NFL, teams that borrow through the league's loan pool can secure rates as low as 1.5 percent (Kaplan, 2012).

BONDS

bonds A debt security in which the issuer owes the bondholder a designated amount; payment, interest, and maturity date details are provided.

Bonds are another form of debt financing available to a sport organization. Whereas the loan process depends on a financial institution to provide capital to the sport organization, the funds from a bond issue come from a range of investors active in the bond market. A bond represents a promise to pay back the amount borrowed (principal) plus the interest rate. The investor, or bondholder, holds the bond until the date of maturity, at which time the principal is due.

MUNICIPAL BONDS

municipal bonds Tax-exempt bonds issued by the local or state government to support capital projects.

Municipal bonds are a special type of bond that may be available for sport organizations that need to raise funds. Municipal bonds can be issued only by state and local government, and they are usually issued for the purpose of financing capital projects. Municipal bonds are an attractive means of debt finance because they are tax exempt. This means that when municipal bonds are issued, the bondholder does not have to pay federal income tax on the interest received. Because of the investor's tax exemption, municipal bond rates are typically offered at a lower interest rate than nonmunicipal bond rates. This lower interest rate reduces the total cost of the project.

The rationale for tax exemption of municipal bonds is that the state and local governments issued these bonds for the benefit of the public and the federal government offers an implicit subsidy. Municipal bonds may be issued by state and local governments on their own behalf, as in the case of a local parks and recreation department issuing bonds to finance a new swimming pool. The local parks and recreation department is a division of local government, and it is consistent with the purpose of municipal bonds that they be issued for this type of project.

Municipal bonds are also frequently issued by state and local governments for the purpose of constructing or renovating facilities for professional sport teams. The public benefits from a professional sport stadium are not as immediately obvious. Still, a Brookings Institution report estimates that the use of municipal debt for professional sport facilities has cost the US taxpayers $3.7 billion in foregone revenue since 2000 (Gayer, Drucker, & Gold, 2016). Presumably, the owners of sport teams have access to well-developed capital markets, including those mentioned previously in this chapter. Still, we see state and local governments embarking on joint ventures with sport teams and issuing municipal bonds on their behalf. In addition to agreeing to provide a specific amount of construction costs (typically funded through the municipal bond process described later in the chapter), state and local governments also provide a variety of noncash support for sport facilities. Governments frequently offer favorable lease terms to professional sport teams that are housed in government-owned facilities. For example, the Dallas Cowboys pay the City of Arlington $2 million per year for the use of the AT&T Stadium complex. According to Badenhausen (2017), the Dallas Cowboys were valued at $4.8 billion, making them the most valuable NFL franchise. The Cowboys have an operating income of $350 million, which makes the team's lease payment equal to 0.6 percent of its revenues. In addition to the $2 million per year in lease payments that the city of Arlington receives, it receives a maximum of $500,000 from any future naming rights deals; in turn, it has to cover the debt service on the $325 million in municipal bonds that were issued for stadium construction.

Local governments may also provide land and infrastructure improvements, which can double the real cost of a stadium project.

The advantages to the team are clear. When the team enters into a public–private partnership, each party agrees to contribute a specified dollar amount or percentage of construction costs as well as additional resources. By partnering with a state or local government, the team's share of costs is reduced. Additionally, when the government issues a municipal bond, the total cost of the project is effectively lowered because (as we have already learned) municipal bonds carry a lower interest rate than bank loans or corporate bonds. Finally, while the costs of facility construction are typically shared, the facility's revenues are not. The sport team is able to maximize new revenue streams in a new facility, and these revenues (e.g., naming rights, premium seating, sponsorship) are captured almost exclusively by the team's owners.

There are also advantages, or perceived advantages, for the local governments of the communities that host professional sport facilities. Common justifications for public subsidies for professional sport facility projects include both economic and noneconomic benefits. The specific economic benefits claimed include job creation, higher wages, and increased tax revenues. These benefits can be realized through (1) the construction and operation of the facility and (2) the economic development that is enabled by the presence of the facility. The construction of a new stadium creates jobs in the construction sector, which benefits the host city if the team hires local residents. The operation of a new stadium also creates jobs, although they are for the most part temporary, seasonal, and low-paying jobs. Sport facilities also attract visitors to the area surrounding the facility. Visitors spend money in hotels, restaurants, bars, and shops, which generate tax revenues through the local sales tax and any special taxes, such as a hotel/motel tax.

Economic benefits are frequently promoted by local leaders and special-interest groups that want to secure public financing for a stadium project. However, there is a general consensus that the economic benefits of sport facilities are often overstated (c.f., Siegfried & Zimbalist, 2000). While local governments are predisposed to accept that sport facilities are "magic bullets" for economic activity and development, the federal government has not accepted these claims. In 2007, the House Committee on Oversight and Government Affairs held separate hearings to examine (1) whether local governments realize the benefits promised by leaders who promote public funding of sport projects and (2) whether public funding of sport projects diverted necessary funding from other government infrastructure projects. Additionally, in 2009, when U.S. Congress was debating the American Recovery and Reinvestment Act (i.e., the stimulus bill), an amendment was offered to prohibit the use of stimulus funds for stadiums. While this amendment was not included in the final passage of the bill, it highlights the skepticism with which some lawmakers treat claims of economic benefits.

In addition to economic claims, public support for professional sport facilities may be justified on social and quality-of-life (i.e., noneconomic) grounds. A facility that allows a city to host a professional team can improve the image of the city. The presence of a professional sport team can confer status as a "major league" city. The image enhancement attributable to a sport team can help to attract tourists as well as potentially attracting new businesses. The presence of a professional sport team can also provide residents with a point of connection to or commonality with other residents. Finally, the presence of a sport team can increase community self-esteem, or the symbolic importance of how residents view their community (Eckstein & Delaney, 2002). While these benefits are largely associated with the sport team or event hosted by the community, it is often the facility that allows the attraction or retention of the team or event.

SECURITY FOR MUNICIPAL BONDS

Once the bond is issued, the sport organization must raise sufficient funds to cover the amount owed to the bondholder. While there are numerous municipal bond arrangements, we will focus on three types of municipal bonds commonly used for sport facility projects: (1) general obligation bonds, (2) revenue bonds, and (3) special tax bonds.

General obligation bonds, or GO bonds, are bonds that are secured by state and local governments' authority to levy income, property, or sales taxes. GO bonds are backed by the faith and credit of the government, which means that the revenues from these tax collections will be used to cover the debt service on the bonds. In general, anyone who purchases a taxable good or service in a government's jurisdiction must pay sales tax. Similarly, anyone who earns income within a government's jurisdiction must pay income tax, if a state or local income tax exists. Finally, anyone who owns taxable property within a government's jurisdiction must pay property taxes. Even if an individual

general obligation bonds Bonds that are secured by state and local governments' authority to levy income, property, or sales taxes.

rents a property, it is quite likely that the property taxes that the owner owes the government are reflected in the rent that is charged. Because the state and local governments can compel residents to pay these taxes, GO bonds have a very low chance of default and are generally deemed safe investments. However, GO bonds frequently require voter approval of proposed tax increases.

GO bonds are frequently used for public sport and recreation projects. Local recreation and sport capital projects (e.g., swimming pools, marinas, golf courses, parks) are widely believed to enhance the quality of life of a community. Additionally, some recreation projects increase the assessed value of nearby properties, which increases the tax revenues collected by local taxing authorities.

In 2012, voters in Austin, Texas, approved Proposition 14, a $77.7 million bond issue for parks and recreation projects. The bond package included renovation or replacement of swimming pools, playscapes, and basketball courts. The city's plan was to issue GO bonds for these projects and then repay the bond with property tax revenue. In addition to the quality of life and property value benefits, supporters of the Austin bond issue insisted in public information campaigns that the project would not increase property taxes. This claim was technically true, as the property tax rate would remain the same. However, if the bond issue had not been approved by voters, the property tax rate in Austin would have *decreased* from 12 cents per $100 of assessed value to 10 cents per $100 of assessed value (Coppola, 2012). The framing provided by supporters was effective in persuading voters that they could have improved sport and recreation assets in the community without an increased tax burden, and the measure passed with 58 percent of the vote (Travis County Clerk, 2012). As of July 2018, the parks and recreation department had only spent 1/3 of the $77 million approved by voters. Still, the city went back to the voters in 2018 to secure an additional $120 million.

revenue bonds Issued for a specific project and are secured through the project's revenues.

Another option for bond financing is the use of **revenue bonds**. Revenue bonds are issued for a specific project and are secured through the project's revenues. One advantage of revenue bonds is that they do not typically require voter approval. Also, revenue bonds adhere to the benefit principle of taxation. According to the benefit principle, those who derive the benefit from a project should bear the burden of tax payments. A disadvantage to the use of revenue bonds is that it can be difficult to accurately forecast a project's revenue streams. The funded project must be capable of generating sufficient revenue to cover the debt service. If revenue from the project does not meet or exceed estimated revenues, the sport organization could default on its payments to bondholders. Consequently, revenue bonds are riskier than GO bonds and investors demand a higher interest rate.

Special tax bonds, like GO bonds, are secured by taxes. However, constituents are not legally obligated to engage in the activities or use the services that are taxed in the case of special tax bonds. Common examples of special tax bonds are visitor taxes, such as hotel/motel taxes and rental car taxes, as well as sin taxes, such as taxes on alcohol or cigarettes. The burden for the payment of visitor taxes falls primarily on individuals who are not local residents. This makes visitor taxes popular among residents and voters, but they may have negative effects on a community's tourism industry. In 2004, Dallas was in contention for the new Cowboys stadium. The team's proposal called for a 6 percent rental car tax and a 3 percent hotel/motel tax, which would have given Dallas the highest hotel/motel tax rate in the country. One of the most vocal critics of this proposal was Mary Kay, the Dallas-based cosmetics company. Mary Kay officials said that this tax plan would prevent them from holding their annual conference in Dallas. Mary Kay was joined by other companies involved in travel and tourism in lobbying against the proposed tax increase.

Sin taxes, in contrast to visitor taxes, are borne primarily by local residents. In May of 2014, by a margin of 56 percent to 44 percent, voters in Cuyahoga County, Ohio, passed a ballot issue to extend the county's sin tax until 2035. The tax extension on alcohol and cigarettes will be used to cover the costs of "constructing, renovating, improving, or repairing sports facilities and reimbursing a county for costs incurred by the county in the construction of sports facilities" (Coalition Against the Sin Tax, n.d.). As of 2018, the sin tax generates between $13 and $15 million per year, but more than half of this amount is committed to payments on bonds that were already issued for capital projects. The remaining funds are insufficient to cover basic maintenance, let alone the cost of the team's desired capital projects (Allard, 2018). If Cuyahoga County officials are unwilling to find new sources of public funds for the teams, it is possible that they may consider relocation in order to access new funds from voters in new locations.

Operational Revenues

The revenues generated by operations can also be used to finance a facility and cover debt service. This is typically done through **securitization**, where sport organizations use contractually obligated income as collateral for debt.

special tax bonds
Bonds that are secured by local taxes. Typically in the form of bed, car rental, or sin tax.

securitization When sport organizations use contractually obligated income as collateral for debt.

Contractually obligated income includes future revenues that the sport organization is guaranteed to receive, such as revenue from media contracts, naming rights, and other sponsorship agreements; and multiyear premium seating contracts. The guaranteed nature of the contractually obligated income makes this method of financing less risky than depending on more volatile operational revenues, such as ticket sales.

Budgeting for Facilities and Events

The first section of this chapter examined how sport organizations access capital needed to finance a facility project. This section presents the basics of budgeting for a facility or events.

operating budget
Authorizes the funds necessary for the day-to-day operations of the facility or event.

line-item budget
Revenues and expenses are estimated and grouped together into categories.

An organization's budget is a key component of its financial management. The **operating budget** refers to "those activities that are ongoing and necessary to maintain the *current capabilities* of the organization to produce, sell, and service its core products and services provided to the customer base" (Lalli, 2012). An operational budget authorizes the funds that are necessary for the day-to-day operations of the facility or event. The specific categories of expenses vary, depending on the type of facility or event.

The financial information included in an operating budget can be formatted in two different ways. The first option is a **line-item budget**. In a line-item budget, revenues and expenses are broken down into specific categories. Revenues are estimated for each category, and expense limits are established for each category. The advantage of a line-item budget is that it is simple to prepare. However, it does not provide information with regard to how spending in the designated categories contributes to the efficient and effective delivery of programs. This makes it difficult for an organization to evaluate the extent to which its budget aligns with its strategic

© Christopher Penler/Shutterstock

priorities. The second format for an operating budget is a **program budget**. In a program budget, funds are allocated for specific programs or projects. Whereas the operating budget is focused on what the organization buys, the program budget is focused on programs that meet the organization's strategic goals.

Take the operating budget for Qualcomm Stadium, the home of the NFL's San Diego Chargers. Qualcomm Stadium is owned by the city of San Diego, and the Chargers lease the facility from the city. The revenues and expenses included in the facility's operating budget include only revenues and expenses for the stadium, and not for any team or event that leases the facility. Qualcomm's budget includes both a line-item budget and a program budget. When you compare the total expenses in the line-item budget with the total expenditures in the program budget, you find that the totals are the same ($16,467,691 in fiscal year 2014), regardless of budget format. The information from Qualcomm's operating budget can be used to develop a revenue and expense statement for the facility. The **revenue and expense statement** is a financial statement commonly used by governments. For nonprofit and for-profit organizations, the budget can be used to create an income statement.

Budgeting Approaches

An organization's budget should be aligned with the company's strategic plan. Budgeting decisions can be made using a variety of budgeting approaches, of which the most commonly used are incremental budgeting and zero-based budgeting.

INCREMENTAL BUDGETING

Incremental budgeting is the budgeting approach that has traditionally been used. In incremental budgeting, management makes an allocation decision based on the previous year's allocation. The previous year's budget allocation is treated as a given, and adjustments are made from the status quo. Managers may choose to hold funding constant, increase funding, or decrease funding, but any change is consistent across expense categories and only the proposed incremental change is typically scrutinized. The benefits of incremental budgeting are (1) it has the same impact on programs and projects across the budget, (2) it is quick and easy, and (3) the budget remains stable from year to year. There are also several disadvantages to using incremental

---

program budget
Funds are allocated for specific programs or projects.

revenue and expense statement Financial statement that presents budgeted and actual revenues and expenses in summary form for a given period of time.

incremental budgeting Budgeting system that makes slight changes to the previous period's actual revenues and expenses.

budgeting. First, incremental budgeting does not allow for a thorough examination of expenses to determine the extent to which they are in alignment with the organization's strategic goals. Second, if managers know that their future budget will be based on the current year, there is pressure to spend any money that is currently allocated. This practice may result in frivolous spending, especially near the end of the organization's fiscal year. Finally, there is no incentive to cut costs in the current year or to propose alternative ways to accomplish program objectives in the future. Nevertheless, when a facility or event faces budget cutbacks, the default approach is incremental budgeting.

ZERO-BASED BUDGETING

zero-based budgeting (ZBB) Requires that each line item from a previous budget be reviewed and approved and starts from a zero amount.

An alternative to incremental budgeting is **zero-based budgeting (ZBB)**. In ZBB, managers must evaluate all spending decisions on a regular basis, with the intent of adapting to a changing business environment and maximizing efficiency. In ZBB, managers start from scratch each year, and the starting budget is zero. Each expenditure is carefully considered and must be justified through cost–benefit analysis. According to Lalli (2012), there are five key elements to ZBB: (1) identification of objectives, (2) evaluation of alternative means of accomplishing each activity, (3) evaluation of alternative funding levels, (4) evaluation of workload and performance measures, and (5) establishment of priorities. The advantages to ZBB are that (1) it forces managers to question every expenditure (which will presumably lead to more effective and efficient budgeting decisions), (2) it prevents budget creep, and (3) it allows managers to link budget expenditures to performance goals. The time required is a major disadvantage and is one of the primary reasons that we rarely see true ZBB implemented. In most cases, it would be impractical for an organization to "zero" out every program and expenditure category. Rather, when practically implemented, ZBB requires strict scrutiny of spending so that all activities are evaluated to determine whether they should be eliminated altogether (i.e., a $0 budget allocation) or whether funding should be increased, decreased, or held constant compared with the previous fiscal period. In contrast to incremental budgeting, this modified form of ZBB does not require consistent budget increases or cuts for each budgetary unit.

Many sport organizations are classified as nonprofit organizations, and as such, have special budgeting considerations. However, according to Shim, Siegel, and Allison (2011), the estimated revenues for nonprofit organizations differ from for-profit organizations in two important ways. First, the estimated revenues for many nonprofit organizations are not directly related to the provision of services. Second, the objective of a nonprofit is to have equality of revenues and expenses so that any excess revenues from one period should be available in the subsequent period. Whereas for-profit organizations use revenue estimation to establish their budgets, nonprofit organizations may instead estimate program expenditures to determine the budget and raise funds accordingly.

VARIANCE ANALYSIS

An organization's budget is set at the beginning of the fiscal year and is based on estimates of revenues and expenses. An organization may realize unexpected savings or encounter unexpected increases in expenses. Because estimates are likely to deviate from actual revenues and expenses, it is important that organizations periodically compare budgeted figures with actual figures. Variance analysis is an ex-post examination of budgeted and actual figures, and the variance can be either favorable or unfavorable for the organization (Stewart, 2007).

Variance analysis for PETCO Park is shown in **Table 5-2**. The amount that the organization is over or under budget is calculated by subtracting the year-end projection from the adopted budget. The variance is expressed as a percentage. In this case, revenues exceeded their budgeted levels. Year-end expenses were also greater than anticipated, in large part due to increased variable costs associated with increased attendance. According to the adopted budget, the city of San Diego expected to lose $1,145,696 in 2016. The real year-end figures showed a slightly greater loss of $1,310,218. Variance analysis can act as an early warning sign by identifying revenues that fail to meet established goals and expenses that exceed estimates. If revenue and expense variance is minimal, managers may choose to monitor the situation closely. If variance falls outside of an acceptable range, managers should reevaluate the situation and take remedial action as necessary.

Table 5-2   PETCO Park Fund FY 2016

	FY 2016 Adopted Budget	FY 2016 Actual Budget	Over Budget (Under Budget)	Variance
Revenues	$15,207,773	$17,181,691	$1,973,918	12.98 percent
Expenses	$16,353,469	$18,491,909	$2,138,440	13.08 percent

Data from The City of San Diego Fiscal Year 2017 Adopted Budget Volume II: Department Detail, https://www.sandiego.gov/sites/default/files/petco_park.pdf.

Common Expenses in Facility and Event Budgets

In this section, we will examine common expenses in facility and event budgets. There is a symbiotic relationship between sport facilities and events. Almost all events require some type of physical structure in which the sport event can be conducted, and most facilities face pressure to fill their facility calendar with events in order to maximize profitability. If an entity is the owner of both the event and the facility in which it is held, facility and event costs may be combined in a single budget. For example, the Washington NFL Franchise owns Fed Ex Field, the stadium in which the team plays. As a result, the organization does not have an annual rent payment, but rather, the organization is not only responsible for both the facility operations costs but also the cost of putting on the team's home games (i.e., the event).

It is much more common for the event owner and facility owner to be separate entities. In the case of separate owners, the event owner enters into a lease agreement with the facility owner. A portion or all of the facility owner's costs, including staffing, utilities, maintenance, and even debt service, are passed on to the event owner and reflected in the lease amount. For example, the Round Rock Sports Center (RRSC) is an 82,800 square foot multipurpose center located in Round Rock, Texas. The RRSC is owned by the city and regularly hosts youth sport tournaments. Tournament organizers who wish to hold their events at the RRSC pay an hourly rate based on the number of participants, number of spectators, and time of the events. Additionally, event owners must use the athletic training staff provided by the RRSC and must also comply with RRSC policies with regard to the number of police officers for security, crowd control, and traffic control.

If a facility is owned by a local government, there may be less pressure to fully recoup costs through revenues from lease payments. In the case of small-scale events hosted in facilities like the RRSC, the city may experience an increase in economic activity (and the subsequent increase in tax collections) from visitor spending that compensates for a failure to break even. The same rationale is also commonly used to justify the low rents that professional sport teams pay to the local governments that own their facilities.

In addition to facility rental or management costs, other common expenses are associated with staffing, operations, marketing, and volunteer management. All events, regardless of their size, should also include a contingency fee. This fee is typically 8 percent to 10 percent of the total budget and ensures that the event has sufficient reserves to cover unexpected expenses.

The range of an event's expenses varies based on the type and scale of the events. It is possible for an event to incur almost no expenses. For example, a public park in Georgetown, Texas, is the site of Vern's No-Frills 5K, a small local event held each month that has a budget to match its name. The event offers only day-of registration, one water stop on the course, and one water stop after the race. The race is produced by a small running company and the main costs are those associated with promotion of the event, the water stops, legal advice related to waivers, and liability issues. Any proceeds from the event are donated to the city parks department for maintenance and improvement projects. Larger events necessarily require larger budgets, and the cost of producing mega-events can reach into the billions. The estimated budget for the 2024 Olympic Games in Los Angeles is $5.3 billion, which includes a $491.9 million contingency (Wharton, 2016).

SUMMARY

In this chapter, the major financial and budgeting considerations related to facilities and events were presented. First, special financial issues related to capital budgeting were presented with examples of both debt and equity funding used for such projects. Operational budgets were discussed next, including incremental and zero-based approaches to budgeting. Financial issues are also important to events, even if the event does not require funding and operation of a facility by the organization. Thus, the final section of this chapter discussed common expenses in facility and event management.

DISCUSSION QUESTIONS

1. Identify a professional sport team near you and research how the team secured funding for its facility. How was the facility financed (i.e., debt or equity financing)? To what extent was the financing method used by the team consistent with the benefit principle?

2. You are the parks and recreation director, and your city council recently announced that all city departments, including the parks and recreation department, will have to implement a mandatory 10 percent across-the-board cut during the next fiscal year. Do you agree with the incremental approach proposed by the city council? In what ways could zero-based budgeting improve your financial outcomes? You may wish to locate the annual budget for a local parks and recreation department to consider specific impacts and make recommendations.

3. Identify a sport event in your community that is currently run on a shoestring, or no-frills, budget. Which event characteristics make this type of budget appropriate for your event? What enhancements would you make to the event if you could double or triple the budget?

Case STUDY

Special Olympics Texas

Events play an important role in the ability of nonprofit organizations to carry out their missions. Events can be central to a nonprofit organization's programming, and they can also be used to raise funds to support programs. The case of Special Olympics Texas (SOTX) illustrates the challenges created when an organization's ability to conduct events is threatened.

SOTX provides year-round sports training and competitions for children and adults with intellectual disabilities. Its mission is "to provide continuing opportunities to develop physical fitness, demonstrate courage, experience joy, and participate in the sharing of gifts, skills, and friendship with their families, other Special Olympians, and the community." Over 300 events are held each year across the state, culminating in the Summer, Winter, and Fall Classic Games. In 2016, SOTX served 58,884 individuals with disabilities, managed over 40,000 volunteers, and raised funds from over 68,000 donors. SOTX hosts over 300 competitions annually. In 2016 alone, it cost SOTX over $2 million to stage the state and area games. This was the organization's second largest expense (behind wages and salaries) and was 23 percent of the total annual budget. Events were also a major source of revenue. SOTX had net special event revenues of $3.1 million, which represents 40 percent of their total revenues.

While SOTX is viewed positively by stakeholders, it consistently operated at a financial loss from 2014 to 2016. Over three years, SOTX had cumulative revenues of $24.1 million and cumulative expenses of 26.8 million, resulting in a loss of $2.6 million over this period.

A few weeks before SOTX was to host the 2017 Fall Games in Bryan/College Station, Hurricane Harvey made landfall as a Category 4 storm. Hurricane Harvey devastated Houston and the Coastal Bend region in South Texas. SOTX was able to hold its Fall Games as planned, but the effect on fundraising was profound. Several fundraising events were canceled because venues were flooded, and donors and sponsors redirected their spending toward hurricane relief efforts. Additionally, the organization had difficulty recruiting volunteers, as many past and potential volunteers redirected their efforts toward hurricane relief.

On September 27, Richard Brown, the vice president of resource development, stated, "Our organization is doing everything it can to reduce expenses, but for us to be able to put on the high-quality service that we provide for our athletes, we need help more than ever." Suzanne Anderson, the interim CEO of SOTX, outlined specific cuts that the organization was making to address its $1.1 million shortfall: "We are definitely making a ton of expense cuts. We still want to make sure our events are going in every way possible, but the tent that used to be there is no longer there, the stage that used to be there is no longer there" (Rapaport, 2017, ¶ 11). The spokesperson for SOTX did acknowledge that there was a possibility that it would have to cancel some of its competitions (Betts, 2017).

SOTX launched #SOTXStrong, a dedicated social media and online fundraising campaign. The goal of the campaign was to raise $100,000 in 30 days to make up their budget shortfall. The campaign fell far short of its goal, raising less than $35,000.

1. Common categories of expenses for SOTX events include: (1) facility rental, including table/chairs, security, and sound system; (2) signage, lighting, and decorations;

(3) medals and awards; (4) food and beverage; (5) entertainment, including appearance fees, travel, and accommodations; (6) printing; (7) uniforms and credentials for staff and volunteers; (8) volunteer training; and (9) sponsor hospitality. Given SOTX's budget shortfall, to which categories would you make cuts? How would you defend them to event stakeholders?

2. Events are also an important source of revenue for SOTX. In addition to the budget cuts you were asked to make in Question 1, you also need to find ways to drive new revenues. What recommendations would you make to SOTX, keeping in mind the impact that Hurricane Harvey had on sponsor and donor priorities?

The information in this case study is drawn from Special Olympics Texas public documents, available at http://www.sotx.org.

REFERENCES

Allard, S. (2018, July 3). Sin tax funds will be gone soon, yet stadiums continue to heedlessly seek major upgrades. *Cleveland Scene.* Retrieved from https://www.clevescene.com/scene-and-heard/archives/2018/07/03/sin-tax-funds-will-be-gone-soon-yet-stadiums-continue-to-heedlessly-seek-major-upgrades

Badenhausen, K. (2017, September 18). The Dallas Cowboys head the NFL's most valuable teams at $4.8 billion. *Forbes.* Retrieved from https://www.forbes.com/sites/kurtbadenhausen/2017/09/18/the-dallas-cowboys-head-the-nfls-most-valuable-teams-at-4-8-billion/#719d1b34243f

Betts, K. (2017, October 1). Special Olympics Texas facing massive funding deficit after Harvey. Retrieved from KVUE's website: https://www.kvue.com/article/news/local/special-olympics-texas-facing-massive-funding-deficit-after-harvey/479728856

Broughton, D. (2018, January 8). A reset, then reboot: Record run ends, but construction spending to take off again in '19. *Sports Business Journal.* Retrieved from https://www.sportsbusinessdaily.com/Journal/Issues/2018/01/08/Facilities/New-facilities.aspx

Brown, M. T., Rascher, D. A., Nagel, M. S., & McEvoy, C. D. (2017). *Financial management in the sport industry* (2nd edition). Scottsdale, AZ: Holcomb Hathaway.

Cheffins, B. R. (1999). Playing the stock market: "Going public" and professional team sports. *Journal of Corporation Law, 24,* 641, 643–646.

Coalition Against the Sin Tax. (n.d.). Issue 7 ballot language. Retrieved from http://www.noclevelandsintax.com/

Coppola, S. (2012, October 19). Austin voters to weigh $78.3 million in bonds for affordable housing. Retrieved from http://www.statesman.com/news/news/local-govt-politics/austin-voters-to-weigh-783-million-in-bonds-for-af/nSg2C/

Eckstein, R., & Delaney, K. (2002). New sports stadiums, community self-esteem, and collective conscience. *Journal of Sport and Social Issues, 26*(3), 235–247.

Gayer, T., Drukker, A. J., & Gold, A. K. (2016, September 8). Tax-exempt municipal bonds and the financing of professional sports stadiums. Retrieved from Brookings Institution website: https://www.brookings.edu/wp-content/uploads/2016/09/gayerdrukkergold_stadiumsubsidies_090816.pdf

Kaplan, D. (2012, June 25). NFL seeks to double loan pool by borrowing $600M. *Street & Smith's Sports Business Journal.* Retrieved from http://www.sportsbusinessdaily.com/Journal/Issues/2012/06/25/Leagues-and-Governing-Bodies/NFL-finance.aspx?hl=Daniel%20Kaplan&sc=0

Kaplan, D. (2017, September 4). NFL ups loan-pool financing to $2.7B. *Sports Business Journal.* Retrieved from https://www.sportsbusinessdaily.com/Journal/Issues/2017/09/04/Leagues-and-Governing-Bodies/NFL-finance.aspx

Kaplan, D., & Lombardo, J. (2017, January 30). Strong outlook cuts borrowing cost for NBA. *Sports Business Journal.* Retrieved from https://www.sportsbusinessdaily.com/Journal/Issues/2017/01/30/Leagues-and-Governing-Bodies/NBA-borrowing.aspx

Lalli, W. R. (2012). *Handbook of budgeting.* Hoboken, NJ: John Wiley & Sons.

Rapaport, W. (2017, September 27). *A third of Texas special Olympians held back by Harvey.* Retrieved from KXAN's website: https://www.kxan.com/news/a-third-of-texas-special-olympians-held-back-by-harvey/994800054

Shim, J. K., Siegel, J. G., & Allison, I. (2011). *Budgeting basics and beyond.* Hoboken, NJ: Wiley & Sons.

Siegfried, J. J., & Zimbalist, A. (2000). The economics of sports facilities and their communities. *Journal of Economic Perspectives, 14*(3), 95–114.

Smith, C. (2012, August 10). Manchester United IPO: History says don't buy. Retrieved from https://www.forbes.com/sites/chrissmith/2012/08/10/manchester-united-ipo-history-says-dont-buy/#10aeb64148fb

Spofford, M. (2012, March 1). Stock sale closes; shares top 268,000. Retrieved from http://www.packers.com/news-and-events/article_spofford/article-1/Stock-sale-closes-shares-top-268000/19d9b0a8-f4ce-497b-b5ae-73f6c72fd973

Stewart, B. (2007). *Sport funding and finance.* Burlington, MA: Elsevier.

Thamel, P. (2018, May 23). Move over Clemson, Oregon and Alabama…Northwestern's ridiculous new practice facility is on another level. *Yahoo Sports.* Retrieved from https://sports.yahoo.com/move-clemson-oregon-alabama-northwesterns-ridiculous-new-practice-facility-unparalleled-college-football-220858185.html

Travis County Clerk. (2012, November 18). Travis County official results: Joint general and special elections. Retrieved from http://www.traviscountyclerk.org/eclerk/content/images/election_results/2012.11.06/20121106tccume.pdf

Wharton, D. (2016, December 2). LA 2024 releases revised budget for Olympics, revenue to equal $5.3 billion in costs. *Los Angeles Times.* Retrieved from http://www.latimes.com/sports/olympics/la-sp-olympics-la-2024-story.html

CHAPTER 6

Bidding and Planning for Different Events

Amanda L. Paule-Koba

CHAPTER OBJECTIVES

Upon completion of this chapter, the reader will be able to:

1. Write a mission statement that articulates the purpose of the event.
2. Define and write SMART goals.
3. Assess whether it is feasible to execute an event.
4. Explain the event bid process.
5. Provide examples of the different types of events.

CHAPTER OVERVIEW

This chapter will outline the process of bidding and planning for a variety of different events. A discussion of the different categories of events, the bid process, and how to assess the feasibility of an event will be presented. Additionally, a SWOT analysis will be reviewed.

IndustryVOICE

C.J. O'Leary—Special Event & Game Day Presentation Coordinator, Toledo Mud Hens and Toledo Walleye

As Special Event and Game Day Presentation Coordinator, my main responsibility is scripting all of our pregame, postgame, and in-game entertainment for about one-third of our home games. Each game has sponsored elements that occur as part of corporate contracts, and it is my job to ensure that they occur as scheduled and are presented in the best possible way. Our intern staff, the Swamp Squad, is responsible for actually executing these promotions on the field and in the stands as I have scripted and directed them from our video room. In the video room during games, I will direct our interns, PA announcer, stadium host, DJ, and video board staff. Most of my day-to-day activities consist of working with our sponsorship and ticket departments to make sure that everything they sell for a certain game is executed as directed in the contract. For instance, our ticket department is responsible for selling many things other than just tickets. They book most of our national anthem groups, youth baseball parades, boy and girl scout sleepovers, first pitches, etc. It is extremely detail oriented so communication is key.

I was first exposed to the sport industry when I took a sport and leisure studies survey class that introduces you to the major. In the class, I conducted a job shadow with one of the Assistant Directors of Fan Experience in the Ohio State athletic department. That led me to my first internship on their game day staff, in which I helped execute all of the in-game activities during my sophomore year. My supervisors at Ohio State were able to get me in contact with the Director of Marketing on the Columbus Crew. That connection presented me with the opportunity to join the Crew's game day staff, executing in-game promotions and other special events around Columbus. From there, I was able

to move up in both organizations; I was given more responsibilities during games and some office duties.

I continued to work with the Crew and OSU for the next 2 years until I graduated with an undergraduate degree. I then went to Bowling Green State University to get my master's in Sport Administration. While there, I landed an internship with the Toledo Mud Hens and Walleye. That internship lasted about 2 years until I finished grad school. My first full-time job was at the University of North Carolina at Greensboro, a small NCAA D1 school down in Greensboro, North Carolina. I moved to North Carolina about 3 months after graduation. There, I basically did what I do here. However, in college athletics, you have multiple sports you are responsible for each season. I was responsible for men's and women's soccer in the fall, women's basketball in the winter, and baseball in the Spring. We all had a hand in working men's basketball games as well since that is UNCG's biggest revenue generator. I was there for a little over a year before my current position opened and I moved back to Toledo.

Our stated promise is "To deliver a Grand Slam in Affordable Family Entertainment by covering all the bases: Fun, Family, Fabulous Food, and Affordability." Our goal is to provide the city of Toledo and its surrounding areas with affordable, year-round entertainment at Fifth Third Field, the Huntington Center, and the Hensville Entertainment District, which includes Hensville Park, Holy Toledo! Tavern, and Fleetwood's Taproom. We believe that in accomplishing this, we can be a catalyst in the continued revitalization of downtown Toledo.

This past year, we have reanalyzed our structure and tried to find areas in which certain departments may overlap in order to increase efficiency as well as cut some of our costs. One of the solutions that we have been testing is the merging of our Operations and Promotions departments. It makes sense since our two departments are the most responsible for day-of-event execution. One example of how we've become more efficient is in the utilization of part-time staff during games. By adding in game operations tasks to our promotions interns' responsibilities, we have been able to greatly cut down on part-time labor costs. For example, interns will have a couple of innings off between their promotion responsibilities. We now use that downtime to finish certain operation tasks, e.g., concourse table breakdown, manning our Guest Services HQ, etc. Essentially, we are getting more done with fewer people than in previous seasons. Not only has this helped our budget but we also feel that it makes the internship more attractive to applicants because it exposes them to multiple areas of event execution as opposed to promotions only.

In minor league baseball and hockey, there are often league-wide promotions and collaborations that involve multiple teams. For example, the ECHL has a contract with Marvel so every team in the league does a Super Hero/Comic Book night and has jerseys based on a Marvel superhero. It's definitely a lot of fun getting your opponent to participate because it just adds another level to the night. For example, doing a Superhero night in which the home team's jersey is based on the hero and the visiting team's jersey is based on the villain. The fans have a lot more fun with it.

We always reach out to opposing teams to see if they'll participate in a theme night that we are hosting. I feel that in minor league sports, it is far more common for teams to work together and share ideas. The answer is almost always yes that teams will participate in the theme night as long as we agree to return the favor at one of their games.

When I look for prospective employees, I think that experience in any internship or job that centers around running events provides extremely valuable experience that would be transferable to the sport industry, including charity events, concerts, marathons, 5ks, etc. These events allow you to work in a fast-paced environment that requires attention to detail and communicating with both staff and customers; skills that you definitely need in the sport industry. Try to find *any* opportunity working in live events.

Outside of relevant experience, I think the most important thing that we look for is an ability to communicate effectively. There is nothing worse than getting a radio call during an event and not being able to understand the person on the other end of the call. Problems can pop up quickly and need to be addressed quickly. Effective communication expedites the problem-solving process. Effective communication ahead of time can eliminate problems altogether.

My advice to students who want to be involved in the sport industry is to get involved in as much as you can outside of class. The university setting provides so many opportunities to volunteer in such a wide variety of organizations and events. Take advantage of it. In doing so, you are both gaining experience as well as making contacts that may open up other opportunities down the road.

In terms of planning for different events, one of the things that my first internship really opened my eyes to is just how many different moving parts and how much collaboration it takes to execute an event. In no particular order: Promotions, operations, communications, ticket sales, merchandising, food and beverage, catering, audio/video, security, and first aid. I think it would be beneficial to mock up an event and then map out all of the different responsibilities that these departments cover. Is your event ticketed? You need someone to sell and process payments. Do you want them to have food? You need someone to order the product, cook it, and serve it. Do you want them to be able to sit down when they eat? You need to account for tables and chairs when mapping out your event space. Where is the event occurring? You need to make sure it is large enough to accommodate your guests and the other needs of your event. Where are people parking when they arrive? Will streets need to be closed to make sure that people are able to walk to and from your event safely? How are you advertising your event and communicating details to the public? It can be a little overwhelming, but the key is having processes in place for each of these tasks so when the time comes, you are essentially just filling in the blanks, e.g., we rented X event space with a capacity of Y so we need Z amount of tables. It makes the whole process a lot simpler.

Introduction

Bidding and planning for events is a crucial part of the management process. What is the process of planning an event from idea to completion? How does an event manager know if an event if feasible? How do you bid for an event that you do not own the rights to? All of these questions will be answered in this chapter.

Executing Events

Events, by their very nature, are not permanent. They occur at different times and in different locations. They also may occur for different reasons. One of the challenges of running events is that there are many types of events, both sport and non-sport related, that event managers and facility managers might have to execute. The variety of events that an event or facility manager may have to deal with is vast and can be challenging if one is not prepared for the realities of the different types of events.

The five main types of events that an event or facility manager may have to deal with are:

- Mega events
- Recurring events
- Traveling events
- Ancillary events
- Community events

In order to successfully manage an event, the manager needs to assess the resources that the organization has at its disposal, the objectives of the event, and the goals of the event and the event manager. During this assessment, the manager needs to ensure that the resources that the organization has are enough to produce a high-quality event.

Identifying Reasons for Creating, Bidding, or Hosting an Event

Some events are created to help a local economy, generate buzz about a new product or sport, or deliver benefits to sponsors/stakeholders. Other events may be run in order to raise money for a charity or philanthropic organization. Another possibility is that an event is created for the purpose of generating revenue for the organization. All of these goals are perfectly acceptable reasons for creating an event. However, the event manager must assess whether the goals for the event are feasible while evaluating multiple factors (time, resources, staffing, the economy, and so forth).

Of course, there is the possibility that an event is created with multiple goals in mind. For instance, a company may partner with a professional soccer player to create a youth soccer camp. The initial goals of this youth camp could possibly be to:

1. Increase the skills of the young athletes.
2. Raise money for the professional soccer player's Foundation or charity that he/she supports.
3. Generate a profit for the organization running the event or the event owner.

All of these are examples of realistic goals for such an event. Ideally, the youth soccer camp would be able to obtain each of these goals. However, the goals are not as detailed as they could be. How would the director of the event be able to assess whether the goals were achieved or not? When creating goals, an event manager should follow the SMART principle. While there are variations of what each letter stands for, **SMART goals** are Specific, Measurable, Attainable, Relevant, and Time-Based (Doran, 1981; Farrelly, 2010; Meyer, 2006).

SMART goals An acronym used to describe the goals of an event; stands for specific, measurable, attainable, relevant, and time-based.

Specific stands for goals that are well defined. They do not leave any room for confusion and are clear to everyone involved in the execution of the event. For instance, if you were running the youth soccer camp mentioned earlier, you could change the first goal of the event to "increase the shooting accuracy of all participants by 10 percent." This would be assessed by having a shooting drill on the first day of the camp to measure accuracy and then complete the same drill on the final day of the camp to see if there was a 10 percent increase in accuracy.

Measurable goals provide enough detail so the event manager can determine if the goal was achieved. For example, the second goal could be adapted to state "to raise $2,500 for the professional soccer players Foundation." This goal could be assessed by tallying the final numbers at the end of the camp. If the camp generated at least $2,500 for the professional athlete's charity, the goal was reached.

Attainable means that the goals listed are actually capable of being achieved. An example of a goal that is not attainable would be thinking and stating that the youth soccer camp would raise $1,000,000 for charity. While this is a fantastic goal, it is not very realistic or attainable. The goal stated previously regarding generating $2,500 for the athlete's charity is much more attainable, especially in the first year of an event.

Relevant goals make sense given the event that is being produced and resources available to the organizing team. Furthermore, these goals correlate well with the event with which they are associated. For example, the new first goal of increasing "shooting accuracy of all participants by 10 percent" would be a relevant goal for this specific camp. Ideally, each young soccer player's skill development would be enhanced during this camp session so increase in the shooting accuracy goal is relevant for this event.

Time-based goals have a time limit placed on them. This time limit allows enough time for the goal to be completed but has a specific end time or due date that will identify whether the goal was achieved. An example of a time-based goal is one that would be achieved if we added to the first goal, which would now read, "to increase the shooting accuracy of all participants by 10 percent by the last day of the camp." By putting the time element of the last day of camp into this goal, we have satisfied this part of the SMART goals principle.

It is important to remember that when creating a new event, in addition to your goals for the event, you must assess where it fits in the current marketplace. If you are going to create a youth soccer camp for a professional athlete, is this event unique to the area or are there other soccer camps that are held in your geographic region that also feature prominent athletes? Being unique is crucial to attracting sponsors, event participants, spectators, and/or media.

Furthermore, you must also assess whether there is a demand for that type of event. In the youth soccer camp example, you need to assess if there are enough young soccer players in the area to fill the camp. The event manager would do this by researching the number of youth soccer teams and leagues within a given geographic area. If soccer were not a popular sport with young athletes in the region, it would be best to not create this event. Or if you still wanted to create the event in order to increase awareness and interest in the sport, the goals of the event would need to be altered in order to be in line with the new purpose of creating the event. The event manager, in essence, is attempting to assess whether the event is feasible or not.

Event Feasibility

Event feasibility The likelihood that an event can be executed at the desired level given the resources at the event organizer's disposal.

Once you have an idea for an event, it is important to investigate whether this event is feasible. **Event feasibility** examines whether or not the event can be executed at the desired level given the resources at your disposal (Torkildsen, 1999;

Watt, 1998). Examining the feasibility will also help the manager determine a budget for the event. When assessing all of the direct and indirect costs, the manager has a better understanding of exactly what it will take to run this event.

The manager would want to conduct a feasibility study, which is the analysis of the potential event and assessment of the strengths and weaknesses of the event. When conducting a feasibility study, the manager needs to hire the staff necessary to complete the study, plan how the study will be executed, implement the study, record the results, and distribute the study.

The first step after receiving a Request for Proposal (RFP) to potentially host an event is to read the proposal and request any documents from the requesting organization that may not be readily available on their website or in the RFP. Next, the individual in charge of the bidding process should read through the RFP to ensure that he or she understands everything that is required to host this event. The larger the financial commitment to host the event, the more comprehensive the feasibility study should be in order to ensure that you have the financial resources to execute the event if you are awarded the event after putting together a successful bid.

In the feasibility study portion of deciding whether or not to bid for an event, it is important to take an unbiased and realistic look at the assets, accommodations, transportation, etc., that you have at your disposal for this event? You may have a state-of-the art facility but do you have hotels to house all of the participants and spectators? These are things that need to be considered before really diving into writing the bid.

During the feasibility study, some of the questions the manager may ask to decide whether the event can be successfully produced are:

- Is there a bid submission?
- Does this event fit within our mission and objectives?
- What are the benefits to hosting this event?
- Where would we hold the event?
- How many staff members are necessary to execute the event?
- How many volunteers are necessary to execute the event and where would we find the volunteers?
- Is there interest in this geographic region for the event?
- What else is taking place in our region that would compete with the event?
- Where would we find participants for the event?
- Are there sponsors who would be interested in partnering with this event to offset costs?

- What is the best strategy to market this event?
- What are the costs associated with the event?
- What equipment do we already own? What could we borrow? What do we have to buy?
- What potential barriers might this event face and do we have the resources to overcome those challenges?
- Are there any other events that occur in our area that would compete with this event?
- Do we have enough time to produce this event?
- What are our strengths?
- What are our weaknesses and how can these be diminished?
- What opportunities exist?
- What are the threats that exist that could ruin this event?
- What are our chances of winning the bid?

The person conducting the feasibility study needs to be unbiased in his or her evaluation of whether this event should be produced. If after examining the event, the manager decides to proceed, the next step is to go forward with the bid process (if there is one). Generally, the process to determine event feasibility will look like **Figure 6-1**.

SWOT Analysis

SWOT analysis A tool an organization can utilize to identify the internal strengths and weaknesses, and assess the opportunities and threats facing the organization.

A **SWOT analysis** is a way to assess the strengths, weaknesses, opportunities, and threats of an organization, venture, or proposal. A SWOT analysis can be conducted for individuals as well. A SWOT analysis can be an incredibly useful tool in any decision-making process.

When conducting a SWOT analysis, it is important to remember that strengths and weaknesses are internal to an organization, while opportunities and threats are external to the organization. This means that the internal features (strengths and weaknesses) are things over which the organization has control. In contrast, the external features (opportunities and threats) are areas over which the organization has little or no control.

When assessing an organization's or event's strengths, it is important to look at what you do better than other individuals in the market. What gives you an advantage over others? You need to identify strengths both from your perspective as a stakeholder in the organization and from

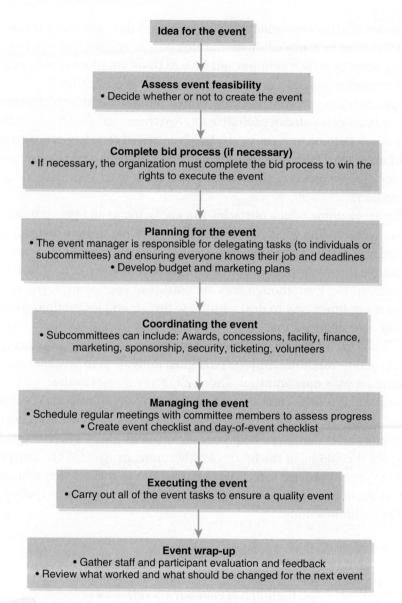

Figure 6-1   The Process of Determining Event Feasibility

your customer's perspective. It does not matter if you view something as a strength if your customer views it as a weakness.

Weaknesses are taking a hard look at what you can improve within your organization. It is important to remember that every organization has weaknesses. Stating that something is a weakness does not mean it completely needs to be replaced. Instead, think of it as an area that you can improve upon. Again, it is important here to think about what your customer or market view as weaknesses within your organization.

Opportunities involve examining which trends, technological advances, and new prospects you can capitalize on. Are there changes in government policy or regulations that you can take advantage of to help your organization? Have there been changes to population profiles, new or reinvigorated social movements, or local events that can impact your success as an organization?

Threats examine which obstacles you are facing as an organization. They also involve assessing what your competition is doing or how that can negatively impact you. Further, there are areas completely outside of your control that are threats to your organization, such as weather, acts of terrorism, the economy, etc. Even though they are outside of your control, you still need to try to find a way to deal with these threats and lessen their potential effect on your organization.

Conducting a detailed, realistic examination of your organization can help you to capitalize on your strengths, mitigate your weaknesses, capitalize on your opportunities, and combat any threats to the organization. It is important to remember that a SWOT analysis is subjective and should be specific to avoid gray areas. A benefit of conducting a SWOT analysis is that it can help your organization show where it is today and where it could be in the future. Furthermore, using a SWOT analysis as part of the bid process can allow organizations to make a well-educated decision about whether to continue with the bidding process or ending it with the feasibility study.

The Bidding Process

bid It is a competitive process in which the objective is to win the right to organize a specific sporting event.

Each national and international sporting event, run by a national or international governing body, has its own unique bidding process. A **bid** "represents a collection of interests and skills (sports federations, local authorities, economic partners, the media, etc.) that have to be focused on the single objective of winning" (Chappelet, 2005, p. 19).

Event owners, or rights holders, are the individuals or governing body that control the event. Sport governance refers to "the exercise of power and authority in sport organizations, including policy making, to determine the organization's mission, membership, eligibility, and regulatory power, with the organization's appropriate local, national, or international scope" (Hums and MacLean, 2008, p. 4). The rights holders are the individuals or groups of people who will ultimately make the decision about who has successfully won the bid (the right to produce the event). In addition to deciding who has won the event bid, these rights holders are also charged with sanctioning events on a variety of different scales from youth to professional sports. Examples of governing bodies at all levels include the Amateur Athletic Union (AAU), high school athletic associations (such as the Ohio High School Athletic Association); the National Collegiate Athletic Association, the National Football League, Major League Baseball, or USA Track and Field; and other national governing bodies.

Sport mega events, such as the Olympic Games or the FIFA World Cup, or, on a smaller scale, NCAA regional events, attract competing bids from nations or cities. Pomfret, Wilson, and Lobmayr (2009) argue that these bids are "mostly made at tax-payers expense and spending is often large and nontransparent" (p. 2). That means that it is the city, state, and/or nation's residents who have to pay for these events through taxes. The researchers also state that the "benefits from bidding are equal to the net benefits from hosting the event multiplied by the probability of a successful bid, minus the cost of the bidding process. Losing bids incur costs for little, if any, ex post benefit" (p. 2).

Important areas in the event bid are often an explanation of the target market or consumer profile of the area. The target market refers to the segment of the community you intend to pursue to attend your event. In addition to demographic information, the committee that evaluates all of the submitted bids will want to know how many youth sport teams are in that area, the disposable income of people in the region, how reachable your target market is, and how sizable the target market is. It is important to understand that you can have multiple target markets. However, they all need to be reachable and selected based on the belief that they will attend and enhance the event. Keep in mind that the largest target market may not be the best for your event. For example, if you are bidding to host the NCAA Women's Soccer Championship, the largest target market in your area might be college students. However, they may not be the best fit for your event. Instead, you may choose to use local soccer clubs and high school teams.

These are people with an interest in soccer and are potentially more likely to want to go to the game than a college student who has never attended a soccer game in his or her life.

It is important to keep in mind that not all bid processes are the same. The criteria will be different depending on the event; however, there are some similarities that exist across the bidding process. Completing a bidding process is, in most cases, not a solitary event. A multitude of individuals (the organizing committee) will need to come together in order to gather and present the required information in the most cohesive manner possible.

The organizing committee may be composed of members of the local convention and visitors' bureaus, sports commissions, and other interested parties (which may include local politicians, media, business leaders, and/or notable athletes). Local convention and visitors' bureaus and sports commissions both exist to attract outside businesses or events to the area. Therefore, the individuals who work at these organizations will be crucial in helping the individual in charge of the organizing committee to gather facts and figures about the local area, demographics, and key information about area facilities, such as restaurants, hotels, local attractions, etc., that may be important when completing the bid. The importance of the individuals who compose the bid committee cannot be stressed enough. These are the people who understand the region, the strengths of the city, and are in the best position to "sell" the city and/or venue to the bid committee. Among the individuals on the bid committee is the bid team leader who is tasked with steering the team through the entire process. Again, this process will include a feasibility study, putting together the bid proposal and submitting the bid to the organizing committee.

Types of Events

MEGA EVENTS

mega event The most complicated type of event to execute because it is often international in nature and requires years of planning to implement.

A **mega event** is the most complicated type of event to execute. Based on the fact that they are often international in nature, mega events often require years of planning to implement and a bid process to earn the right to host the event. Due to the scope and visibility of mega events, they are often easily identifiable to the general public. Thus, it is important that the planning committee or event manager consider all aspects of the event in order to not damage the brand.

VIGNETTE 6-1

Bid Process to Host the Final Four of the NCAA Women's Basketball Tournament

Putting together a bid to be the Final Four host for the NCAA women's basketball tournament is a complex process. The bid must be perfect because each host city is competing against a wide variety of other equally great cities that want to host this event. The bid should begin with an overview of your infrastructure. You should describe your facility thoroughly, including locker rooms, number of seats, number of suites, etc.

The type of facility alone will not win a city the bid to host. The bid must include a description of the city's demographics, lodging, transportation, and restaurants. The city's visitor's bureau or similar organization should be brought in to help with this portion of the bid. The organizing committee should also include a discussion of its marketing plan, security plan, media, and ticketing plan. The NCAA bid selection committee will want to see the plan of action on how the potential host city will sell out the arena during the two semifinal games and the championship game. This is where showing a history of community support for women's basketball will be crucial.

Ancillary events will add a nice touch to the bid package. Where and when will the fan fest be? What other events will go on in conjunction with the Final Four games? How will the host city engage youth? All of these details need to be thought out and included in the bid. It is important to be creative and unique and to offer an array of different events to make this a celebration and not just a basketball game.

Once the bids are submitted, the NCAA bid selection committee will review each bid. The bids will be narrowed down, and site visits will be made to each finalist city. Members of each city's bid committee will make in-person presentations to the committee. When assessing potential hosts, the NCAA committee will review each city's competition venue, transportation and lodging options, and the region's overall commitment to the event. A huge factor in determining whether a city is a viable candidate to host the Final Four is the venue. Venues must hold a minimum of 18,000 fans, including suite seats.

Due to the nature of mega events, there is often a bidding process involved in securing the right to present the event. As discussed earlier, bidding for the right to hold an event involves competing against other potential host cities or sites and presenting the potential city's plan for that event.

Examples of mega events at the highest level include the Olympic Games or the World Cup. These events often have full-time staffs devoted to something that occurs once every 4 years. When a city prepares its bid to attempt to win the Olympic Games, it must address eighteen different themes, which include:

- National, regional, and candidate city characteristics
- Legal aspects
- Customs and immigration formalities
- Environmental protection and meteorology
- Finance

- Marketing
- General sports concept
- Sports
- Paralympic games
- Olympic village
- Medical and health services
- Security
- Accommodations
- Transport
- Technology
- Communications and media services
- Olympism and culture
- Guarantees

Furthermore, the Olympics announce in which city the Games will be held years in advance, which ensures that the city's planning committee has a great deal of time to produce a memorable Olympic Games event and address each of the eighteen themes that have been mentioned in the bid.

RECURRING EVENTS

recurring event An event that happens on a regular basis; it is the "easiest" type of event to execute because it occurs consistently.

Recurring events happen on a regular basis. They are the "easiest" type of event to execute because they occur consistently. Due to the regularity of these events, the staff is able to understand all of the details of executing the event. The benefit of recurring events is that the event managers know how much food to order for the concession stand, the appropriate number of staff and volunteers needed, the amount of security, timing of the event, and where the signage should be placed.

Examples of recurring events can include Friday night football games at a local high school, a college rivalry game such as the Ohio State versus Michigan football game, North Carolina versus Duke basketball game, or New York City marathon. All of these events may differ in size and the amount of planning that goes into the event, but the one thing that they have in common is that they are all recurring events.

TRAVELING EVENTS

traveling event An event that occurs on a regular basis but in various locations.

Traveling events are events that occur on a regular basis but in a different location each year. While they occur on a regular basis, the fact that the location varies year-to-year presents a challenge. The individual or group of individuals who is charged with executing the event is rarely the same. This presents a challenge for the organizing committee. However, the nice thing is that since the event is done on a regular basis, the organizers are able to contact the previous host sites to identify what worked well for them, what they would do differently, and what, if any, challenges were present at the event.

An example of a traveling event is any of the NCAA championships. These championships often involve many regional sites in the early rounds of the championship and eventually culminate in the top teams arriving in one city to compete for the National Championship.

ANCILLARY EVENTS

Ancillary events occur in conjunction with another type of event. These events may require as much planning as another type of event but the major difference is that they are paired with a larger event. These events can provide additional revenue for the event organizers through ticket sales, merchandise, additional opportunities to sell or increase the price of sponsorships, and a way to involve different target markets.

For example, a Fan Fest at the Super Bowl would be an ancillary event. The Fan Fest requires marketing to attract spectators, sponsors to offset the costs, volunteers to help run the games and exhibits, security to keep everyone safe, and so forth. While this event could stand alone, having it in conjunction with the Super Bowl is beneficial because it captures the excitement of many football fans who are in town for the game but may or may not have a ticket to go to the actual Super Bowl. It allows fans to be a part of the Super Bowl experience without having to pay hundreds or thousands of dollars for the game ticket.

ancillary event An event that occurs in conjunction with another type of event.

COMMUNITY EVENTS

Community events are smaller in scale and appeal to a specific geographic region. While these types of events may not require the resources that a large traveling event would, they still require planning and forethought before they can be implemented. Local YMCAs or parks and recreation centers are organizations that often hold community-sporting events for the people who reside within the town. When planning an event for the community, the event manager sometimes has the freedom to be a little more creative or to try different things because it is not occurring on such a large scale.

Community event A relatively small-scale event that appeals to a specific geographic region.

Examples of community events could be a holiday 5k race, a mini-triathlon for young children to expose them to the sport, or a youth swim meet. Even though these events may be considered small to some people, they all still require planning and the planning process.

HOSTING EXTERNAL EVENTS IN A SPORT FACILITY

Between 2008 and 2011, $8.137 billion was invested in new, major facility renovation expenses across the NFL, NBA, MLB, and NHL (Baade & Matheson, 2011). Those figures do not account for the number of new facilities that colleges, universities, or local communities constructed. These facility costs need to be recouped somehow so organizations often look to bring in outside entities to generate revenue.

When you are in charge of a sport facility, there are times when you may have to host non-sporting events in your facility. These events could vary from a bridal show to a concert to the circus to a business meeting. Since these events are not what the facility manager is generally in charge of executing, it is necessary to ensure that there is adequate up-front planning to account for all of the details. Some of these details may include proper training of the staff, bringing in additional equipment, setting down false floors to cover the basketball court, removing seats, hanging decorations, and so forth.

Timelines for Events

It is crucial that event managers have timelines when running events. These timelines will help keep all of the employees on track and ensure that all tasks are completed in advance. Timelines also help the event manager to make sure that each area is accounted for and nothing slips through the cracks.

There are different types of timelines that are useful for event managers to employ during the event management process. The first is an event timeline. This timeline is useful for all of the planning that is required leading up to the event. This timeline will list who is in charge of each event planning area and the deadlines for when the event must be completed. See **Figure 6-2** for an example of an event timeline.

The event manager should list the appropriate information at the top of the spreadsheet being used on the event timeline. Days-Out refers to how

Event: Youth Soccer Camp

Date: July 15-18, 2014

Days Out	Task	Task Due Date	Responsible Party	Date Completed
−270	Secure soccer fields	10/17/2013		
−120	Create registration forms	3/16/2014		
−120	Secure event sponsors	3/16/2014		
−60	Start airing commercials for camp	5/15/2014		
−45	Finalize coaches for camp	5/30/2014		
−30	Obtain lunch for campers	6/14/2014		
−21	Plan drills for each day of camp	6/23/2014		
−14	Order camp t-shirts	6/30/2014		
−14	Purchase all equipment not obtained through sponsorship	6/30/2014		
−1	Print registration lists	7/14/2014		
5	Process all camp evaluation forms	7/23/2014		

Figure 6-2   Event Planning Timeline

many days before the event the task must be completed. Task indicates what must be finished prior to the event. Task Due Date refers to the exact date the task must be finalized. Responsible Party is the staff member who is in charge of completing the task. Date Completed marks the actual date the task was finalized.

The second type of timeline is a day of event timeline. This timeline is necessary to guarantee that all details that need to be completed on the day of the event are done. This timeline will also list who is in charge of executing each of the details listed. **Figure 6-3** lists an example of a day of event timeline.

For the day-of timeline, Time refers to when the task is to begin. Task indicates what is to be done during the time period listed. Responsible Party is the staff member who is in charge of completing the task. Finally, the notes section is for anything the event manager needs to highlight or remind the responsible party to do during that task.

Event: Youth Soccer Camp

Date: July 15-18, 2014

Day 1: July 15, 2014

Time	Task	Responsible Party	Notes
6:00 AM	Staff arrives at camp		
6:30 AM	Set up registration/check-in station		
6:30 AM	Check soccer fields for safety		
7:00 AM	Staff meeting		
8:00 AM	Registration open		
9:00 AM	Camp begins		
9:15 AM	Drill #1		
9:55 AM	Water break		
10:00 AM	Drill #2		
10:30 AM	Ensure water coolers are full		
10:55 AM	Water break		
11:00 AM	Drill #3		
11:00 AM	Begin set-up for lunch		
12:00 PM	Lunch		
1:00 PM	Tactics session		
1:30 PM	Drill #4		
2:00 PM	Ensure water coolers are full		
2:25 PM	Water break		
2:30 PM	Scrimmage		
4:00 PM	Camp dismissal		
4:30 PM	Inventory equipment		
5:00 PM	End of day staff meeting		
5:30 PM	Pack up for the day		

Figure 6-3   Example of Day-of-Event Timeline

SUMMARY

Creating events, whether they are mega events, recurring events, traveling events, ancillary events, or community events, requires much up-front planning. The event managers must set goals and find a way to differentiate themselves from other events currently in the marketplace. Much of the event's success will be determined in early planning meetings when the key decisions, such as sponsor acquisition, participant recruitment, marketing strategies, and sales, are made. If you are submitting a bid for an event, it is important to work with other stakeholders to ensure that you are putting together the most thorough bid possible for the event's rights holder. Regardless of the type of event and whether a bid is required, it is critical that the manager and his or her team think through each decision in the planning process to maximize their success. Timelines can help the manager stay organized. These tools will keep the whole team on track and ensure that each task is completed by the due date.

DISCUSSION QUESTIONS

1. What is the point of having a mission statement for an event? How does this contribute to the event?
2. What are SMART goals? Why is goal setting important to the overall success of an event?
3. How would you conduct a feasibility study for the event?
4. What types of events require an event bid? How long before an event should you prepare a bid? Who should you include in the process to help you put together the best bid possible?
5. What are three examples of each type of event?

Case STUDY

Bidding to Host a NCAA Championship

You are working for a Division I athletic department and are a part of the committee working to put together a bid to be a host site for the second and third rounds of the men's NCAA basketball championship. You have been nominated to write the section of the bid that examines and discusses your bid city (including infrastructure, hotels, things to do, restaurants, demographics, and access/proximity to airports).

This bid is an incredibly serious and important undertaking for your athletic department. The athletic department has never hosted an event of this size so you do not have any previous documents to use as a guide.

Furthermore, some previous host cities have had difficulty selling out their arena. The mistake that some previous sites have made was to assume that these tickets would

(continues)

Case STUDY (continued)

sell themselves because it is a NCAA men's basketball tournament event. You are determined not to let this happen. Therefore, it is important to identify multiple target markets that you can go after to sell tickets.

Your job is to:

1. Write up your section of the bid (see above for requirements).
2. What makes your host site unique and different?
3. Identify five target markets that you and your colleagues in the athletic department can target to sell tickets.
4. How are you going to persuade these target markets to buy tickets?
5. How do you involve the surrounding community in the bid and the event?

REFERENCES

Baade, R., & Matheson, V. (2011). Financing professional sports facilities. In Z. Kotvel & S. White (Eds.) *Financing for Local Economic Development* (2nd ed). New York, NY: Sharpe Publishers.

Chappelet, J. L. (ed.) (2005). *From initial idea to success: A guide to bidding for sports events for politicians and administrators.* Chavannes-Lausanne, Switzerland: Sports Event Network for Tourism and Economic Development of the Alpine Space.

Doran, G. T. (1981). There's a S.M.A.R.T. way to write management's goals and objectives. *Management Review, 70*(11), 35.

Farrelly, F. (2010). Not playing the game: Why sport sponsorship relationships break down. *Journal of Sport Management, 24*(3), 319–337.

Hums, M. A., & MacLean, J. C. (2008). *Governance and policy in sport organizations.* Phoenix, AZ: Holcomb-Hathaway Publishing.

Meyer, P. J. (2006). What would you do if you knew you couldn't fail? Creating S.M.A.R.T. Goals. *Attitude is everything: If you want to succeed above and beyond.* Merced, CA: The Leading Edge Publishing Co.

Pomfret, R., Wilson, J. K., & Lobmayr, B. (2009). *Bidding for sport mega-events.* Paper to be presented at the First European Conference in Sports Economics at University Paris 1 (Panthéon Sorbonne) on 14–15 September 2009.

Torkildsen, G. (1999). Organisation of major events. In G Torkildsen, *Leisure and Recreation Management,* (4th Ed.). New York, NY: Routledge.

Watt, D. C. (1998). *Event management in leisure and tourism.* Harlow, Essex: Addison Wesley Longman Ltd.

CHAPTER 7

Designing the Event Experience

Brianna L. Newland

CHAPTER OBJECTIVES

Upon completion of this chapter, the reader will be able to:

1. Clearly define the characteristics of the event experience.
2. Recognize the importance of designing an event experience that creates meaning.
3. Understand how to develop an event experience.
4. Appreciate that stakeholders will have varied experiences.
5. Identify how the unique elements of an event impact the experience.

CHAPTER OVERVIEW

This chapter will outline the elements of designing the event experience, such as understanding experience characteristics, designing the event concept, co-creating event experiences, and attaching meaning. Designing the event involves identifying the unique elements of events; developing a concept, theme, and subsequent experience; and understanding how these elements tie together to create meaning at the event.

IndustryVOICE

Ignacio Gutierrez—Senior Manager, Match Day, Events & Hospitality, Sydney Swans Football Club

As the Match Day Senior Manager, I lead a team of five to project manage and deliver match-day operations, events, sponsor activations, and corporate hospitality for New South Wales, Australia's largest sporting team.

From a match-day operations perspective, I oversee:

- Holistic administration operations for all matches played at the SCG, relationship management including stadium operations teams and key suppliers

- Overarching staff and budgetary requirements for Match-Day execution including sports presentation, entertainment, medical and emergency, and casual staff

- That the stadium is match ready ahead of each game spanning football management, in-stadia entertainment, corporate hospitality & functions, catering, security, internal and external corporate activation, big screen content, and LED/static signage

- The delivery of a safe, efficient, and effective operation of the match day including the critical incident and emergency management program, risk assessments, and mitigation strategies spanning integrity, crowd safety, and counter-terrorism

- All corporate hospitality at match is delivered to the highest possible standard, including food & beverage service, RSA, security, and guest experience

From a corporate partner activation perspective, I manage:

- Partner activations both inside and outside of the stadium

- Concept ideation, activation execution, and managing partner's external agencies to bring their brands to life

- Building bespoke leverage plans that meet the partner's individual objectives but, importantly, still deliver on fan experience

From an events perspective, I oversee:

- The project management of the club's largest events

- The budgetary management, which includes operational savings and maximizing commercial opportunities

- The integration across the business spanning football, membership, fan engagement, and corporate to ensure that the events meet the Club's objectives and are executed to the highest possible standard

My background before this role was in Marketing Agencies for 4 years. I executed brand experience events across Australia. I worked on some large accounts including Coca-Cola, Moet Hennessy, and Samsung. I currently work for the Sydney Swans Football Club. The Club is a team that plays within the Australian Football League (AFL). Our main goal is to grow our membership-based football club so that it is capable of not only winning AFL premierships but it is also consistently recognized as one of the leading football clubs, both on and off the field in Australia. In pursuit of our goal, key measures of success will be:

- On-field performance
- Stakeholder satisfaction
- Reputation and image
- Financial strength and independence
- Legitimate self-belief

We face various challenges. First, the Sydney Cricket Ground is an old stadium with only one new concession stand, which was refurbished in 2013. The other stands are all quite old and the facilities (amenities, F&B outlets, etc.) that are available in these stands reflect this. We work closely with the SCG Trust to constantly improve facilities where possible to provide a better experience for our members and fans. Our second challenge is our corporate partner. All of our corporate partners want different things for events and match days and trying to balance this is difficult. We work closely with our corporate partnership team to best manage expectations and try to make all parties happy. It is a fine art to balance sponsor content and club content.

Technology is a trend that is ever-growing and one that will continue to evolve. Whether technology is used to show interesting content or used to provide a better experience, it is ever-changing in the way that it is used and it is difficult to keep up. The way I see it, you have to pick and choose and select the things that are effectively and efficiently going to change a fan's experience. The experience can be from the couch at home, or at the stadium, but the investment has to be justified in both.

When hiring for entry-level positions, I look for the following characteristics:

- Work experience in a volunteer or internship capacity. This shows that the candidate is motivated and is self-driven.

- Education—this is a must.

- Culture fit. One of the key things we look for in our candidates is ensuring they fit the culture and values of the club.

The key skill and qualification commonly missing among new graduates is the experience. While I understand that gaining experience while earning a degree is difficult, where there is a will, there is a way. People undervalue the amount of experience you gain from volunteering and doing internships. It is the best way to get invaluable experience that will help your career a lot in the long run. The sport industry is a very fast-paced environment that pushes you to think on your feet—this is a valuable skill. Be prepared to work long hours and pay attention to detail. Every single thing matters and will affect the end execution of a game/event. Volunteer and do internships; these will pay dividends in the future and introduce you to people who may one day offer you a job. Finally, be persistent and stand out from the crowd—many people want to work in sport and only a few get the chance to do it. Working in sport exposes you to some amazing people and some amazing stories. Soak it all in.

We work closely with our sponsor to ensure that the activations are relevant to the product that we "sell" our match days. When I first started at the Swans, there were some partners whose activations weren't relevant to our organization. In other words, they were trying to sell their own product rather than leverage the partnership to enhance brand image and, in turn, convert this to sales. For all activations, we ensure that not only are they relevant to the Sydney Swans but they also have to add value to our fans' and members' experience. We also work closely with our partners on the type of activation. We act as an internal agency and execute their activations from ideation through to execution. Everything we do needs to add to and enhance the event experience. There is no point in investing, or getting partners to invest, in things that won't make our product better and the fan's experience more meaningful and fun.

Introduction

When managing a sport event, good planning and implementation are effective only if the event is attractive and compels an audience to attend (Morgan, 2009). When people attend a sport event, it is often for more than just the sport competition itself; they will perceive the competition, the atmosphere,

the food, the entertainment, etc., and attach meaning. That meaning then creates an **experience** for the attendee. A central concern of every sport event manager is the experience, both positive and negative, that the individual had. Therefore, to ensure a positive experience, the sport event manager must understand how the design features will influence the experience and what meaning will be attached to the event by the attendees (Getz, 2012). Since the advent of the **experience economy**, whereby consumers desire occurrences beyond the goods or services alone (Pine & Gilmore, 1998), there has been recognition that the experience is an important foundational element of an event (Berridge, 2012; Getz, 2012; Morgan, 2009; Petterson & Getz, 2009). In the past, experiences were not seen as a distinct core offering; rather, they were combined as an aspect of services (Pine & Gilmore, 1998).

However, there is more to an experience than just the delivery of a service or the purchase of a good. If the design is conceptualized and implemented correctly, the services will set the stage and the goods will become the props to engage and create a memorable event for the individual (Berridge, 2012; Pine & Gilmore, 1998). For example, a guide at a sport museum provides a service as he or she conducts a tour of the History of Baseball section. This tour becomes an experience when the guide is dressed in accordance with a specific era, such as a uniform from the past, with others acting out the scene using props that would have been commonplace at that time. The guide is providing a service, but the tour becomes an experience as the patron is dispatched back in time through the recreation of the event. Much of the sport experience is now offered by the sponsor through sponsorship activations. Experience activations allow the sponsor to engage with consumers in a way that creates a meaningful experience that is associated with the sport event. For example, Reebok set up a lifesize interactive display where attendees at all six of the Reebok CrossFit Regional Competitions could test their skills against the top CrossFit athletes. Reebok filmed athletes in a 60-second athletic contest and displayed the results

experience In the sport event industry, the meaning attached to the event through the perception of the competition, atmosphere, social interactions, food, and entertainment, among other factors.

experience economy The consumer's reaction to an event beyond the goods or services of the event alone.

on a 72-inch LCD screen. Athletes received a video of their performance for sharing on social media (O'Loughlin, 2016).

Designing a sport event is a predictive skill; an event manager needs to anticipate what the attendee will want and then design around that desire (Berridge, 2012). In the case of sport events, sport itself is the main purpose, but watching or participating in the sport is only a piece of what the attendee expects to experience. To create such a memorable event, one must understand the context in which an event is to take place, beyond the sport itself. Therefore, a sport event manager must have a clear understanding of the event's purpose, the key players (i.e., the stakeholders who are most likely to be affected by the event), the overall event objectives, and the setting and/or environment in which the sport takes place. Once these elements are clearly understood and delineated, the creative elements can be introduced.

Creating the Sport Event Experience

WHAT IS EXPERIENCE?

Above all, experiences are meant to be memorable and to engage in a personal way. However, defining *experience* is challenging because it is highly personal, inherent, and difficult to evaluate (Petterson & Getz, 2009). Experiences are highly **subjective** and **heterogeneous**. Experience is subjective in that two people can have completely different experiences at the same event (Ooi, 2005). For example, consider two marathon runners crossing the finish line at the exact time of 3:59.8. One runner might be ecstatic to finish in under 4 hours and has perhaps set a personal record, thereby positively influencing the runner's overall race experience. For the other, this time might be considered disappointing and frustrating, thereby negatively impacting the overall experience. As a race director, you must consider how the elements you have design control over, such as the challenge of the course or how well the aid stations are stocked and spaced, can impact the performance, and therefore, the experience of the participants. If the other design elements are done exceptionally well, one can mitigate the challenge of a poor performance and heighten the impact of a positive one.

Experiences are also heterogeneous in that no two people will have the same experience, even with the same event features. Consider the same two runners from the marathon example attending the prerace exposition

subjective A unique and personal venture undertaken by an individual, who attaches his or her own meaning.

heterogeneous Relating to perceptions of an experience that are widely dissimilar.

(or "expo") to pick up their registration packet. The expo serves as a registration site for the thousands of runners who must attend to pick up their race number and event-related materials and provides a variety of run-related vendors with products to showcase. Perhaps the expo is packed with people, lights, sounds, and vendors, creating an electrified and busy atmosphere. Runner A might love the excitement created by the people and atmosphere, which might positively impact his or her overall experience of the event. Meanwhile, runner B might not be at all interested in what the vendors have to offer and could become annoyed by having to sift through the crowd to get his or her registration packet. Therefore, as an event director, it is important to consider that not all of the registered runners will enjoy an expo or care to engage with vendors. As such, traffic flow might be designed to allow for quick pickup of registration packets by those who would prefer to get their information and immediately leave, while enabling other runners to engage with the vendors if they wish to do so. The director can thereby create an optimal experience for the majority of runners.

CONSIDERING STAKEHOLDER EXPERIENCES

stakeholder A person or entity that has a vested interest in the event.

Sport event design is meant for the guests (usually considered to be the fans and other spectators), but a number of other key **stakeholders** whose experiences matter greatly (e.g., volunteers, sponsors, media, residents near the venue, *the athlete*) are often overlooked (Petterson & Getz, 2009). Most often overlooked is the athlete. Event managers and researchers are often concerned with athletes' event-related motives or satisfaction with participation, but rarely are the athletes' event experiences considered (Petterson & Getz, 2009). For example, sport marketers are quick to research the satisfaction and experience of a spectator at the college football national championship game. And feedback from this key stakeholder group certainly is vital. However, rarely (if ever) are the teams and/or individuals competing ever asked about their participation experience. The participants are the *reason* for the event; it is not staged only for the spectator. The experiences of the athletes are assumed because it is the pinnacle of competition, but the sport event manager should be warned! Disregarding this important stakeholder is risky and can have a negative influence on the experiences of the other stakeholders.

For participation in sport events, it is important to understand the athletes' motives as they can vary based on the sport, the level of the competitor, and the interest in the event and/or the host destination (Aicher & Newland, 2017; Newland & Aicher, 2018). Furthermore, the athletes' travel companions (Buning & Gibson, 2016a) and how immersed the participant is in that sport will also influence their experience (Buning & Gibson, 2016b). Therefore, it is a necessity for the event director to understand that the participants' experience will vary greatly based on the type of sport, the athletes' competitive level (ie., novice vs. advanced), how immersed they are in the sport, and whom they choose to travel with to compete.

From the fan's perspective, the overall experience of the event is closely tied to the performance of the athlete or team. While we know that fans' experiences are often tied to expectations, superior experiences were often the result of positive game outcomes (Petterson & Getz, 2009). For a more casual spectator, perhaps the entertainment or elements beyond the competition impact the experience (Getz, 2012). The volunteers' and officials' experiences are linked to professional development and networking, which are similar to the experiences of the sponsors and vendors, who have interests in the business development experience. Different stakeholders will be directly or indirectly affected, depending on their role, so it is important to understand all angles of the expectations that people bring to sport events (Getz, 2012).

Characteristics of Experiences

As discussed, experiences cannot be designed and delivered like products due to the subjectivity and heterogeneity of the individual (Petterson & Getz, 2009). To make matters even more challenging, the term experience can be used as either a noun or a verb and is often used as such to describe the event. Take, for example, a student describing her experience at the 2016 Rio Olympic Games: "My experience at the Olympics was amazing! Even though I worked long, exhausting hours, I learned so much about running an event and I got to meet so many people! The networking opportunities were beyond what I expected. I also had an opportunity to explore Rio de Janeiro (the safer parts). I was amazed by the cultural differences and learned that the people are similar to me in a lot of ways despite the

TIP

The event setting and the surrounding environment will shape the visitor's experience (Petterson & Getz, 2009). As such, coordinate the setting and environment into your event design plan! How? Work with destination marketers to design packages that connect people to the destination through excursions that can be added on to the event offerings.

generic experience An experience that is commonly found at every event.

specific expectation An expectation or belief that one holds about an event.

intensity The strength of the experience.

duration The length that the experience stays present for the individual.

memorability: The ability of an experience to remain an intense and enduring memory.

interesting differences we share. I was also blown away by the level of poverty outside the Olympic center. It opened my eyes in so many ways; it was such a cool experience." In this one quote, the student touches upon a range of experiences that involve intellectual, physical, emotional, cultural, and social dynamics, all of which lead to her overall "amazing experience." Considering how the multifaceted nature of an experience influences the design elements can be quite daunting for a sport event manager. Fortunately, there are characteristics that can be defined and principles that can be followed to support sport event managers in creating the experience.

All events share **generic experiences**. When people attend sport events, they generally expect the opportunity to relax, socialize with others, and have fun. Because generic experiences can occur at any event, they relate more to the individual's state of mind and expectations for the event than the event's theme, concept, or setting (Petterson & Getz, 2009). These generic experiences can be staged to meet the more customary expectations. However, sport event attendees are often there for a *specific* purpose and will have **specific expectations** related to that event. For example, the specific expectations that one has for a roller-derby event will be far different from those for a fencing event, although, *generally*, you would perhaps expect to have fun and be entertained at both. Another vital consideration for the sport event design is to note that different stakeholders (e.g., spectators, sponsors, media, volunteers, athletes) will all have varied, but also specific expectations at the same sport event. Therefore, it is important to consider how the needs of the attendee will affect his or her individual experience. The anatomy of an experience, therefore, can be understood by exploring overall event satisfaction as measured in terms of intensity, duration, memorability, and meaning (Petterson & Getz, 2009) for each stakeholder group.

Intensity is the strength of the experience. For example, the intensity of an experience to which an individual is directly related, such as watching your favorite team at the World Series, would escalate based on those related expectations. **Duration** is the length that experience stays present in the attendee's mind. **Memorability** relates to the ability of the experience to be memorable. The more intense and enduring the experience, the more likely one is to remember and cherish the experience. Finally, the experience must hold **meaning** for the attendee. Meaning is shaped by the memories and interests of the individual attending the event and is highly dependent on how that person interprets the event theme (Morgan, 2009).

Experience Dimensions

Mannell and Kleiber (1997) posit three dimensions of experience: Conative, cognitive, and affective. The **conative dimension** describes experience as actual behavior. This dimension describes the things people do physically; an individual's attitudes are manifested in their behaviors. This behavior can be observed through the purchasing of memorabilia, photos with athletes or event signage/landmarks, or the framing of artifacts as a reminder of the event. For example, an athlete might frame a photo of herself crossing the finish line with her finisher's certificate and medal as a reminder of completing her first marathon. This experience, and the associated memories, might then drive this person to compete in future marathons or other running events. And, if this person is a "one and done" participant (only doing the distance one time), the memorabilia from the event can serve as the reminder of the time that person achieved a feat never imagined.

meaning The perception and interpretation of the event elements that make the event significant.

conative dimension The behavior, or physical responses, of event attendees.

© Matursports/Shutterstock

cognitive dimension
Making sense of an experience through awareness, perception, memory, learning, and judgment.

affective dimension The emotional response to the experience.

The **cognitive dimension** relates to making sense of the experience through awareness, perception, memory, learning, and judgment. It is difficult, as sport event managers, to assess what spectators or participants are thinking or imagining during a sport event experience, but it can be done. For example, participants of a sport skills event will experience the cognitive dimension when mastering new skills and learning from experts in the sport. Observations or surveys of participants after an event can assist the sport event manager in understanding how the cognitive dimension influenced the experience.

The **affective dimension** defines the emotions associated with the experience. A sport event can greatly affect emotions or moods. As a spectator, moods can vary along a positive–negative spectrum, depending on how well the team or athlete is performing. Likewise, the teams' and athletes' personal moods can be influenced by the sport event outcome. Due to the spontaneity of sport events, a number of emotions from elation to anxiety or frustration can change from one moment to the next, taking the attendee on a roller-coaster ride of emotion throughout the event. Experiencing the highs and lows of a sport event is not unique to just the spectator; the competing athlete feels dynamics as well. The response from the crowd can help fuel the competition unfolding between the participants, creating a unique, affective experience for all involved.

In the 1999 article "Welcome to the Experience Economy," Pine and Gilmore discuss two dimensions of experience: *Customer participation* and *connection*. One end of the customer participation spectrum is anchored by passive participation, which mainly involves spectating. The participants have no direct interaction with the athletes involved in the competition. Such participants would include cycling spectators attending a road race event and watching from the side of the road. At the other end of the spectrum lies active participation, which allows the participants to play a direct role in creating the event. These participants would include athletes running in a marathon or the cyclists described in the first example.

The second dimension described by Pine and Gilmore (1998) is the relationship of the experience through connection. *Absorption* anchors one end of the connection spectrum and describes how participants "drink in" the event around them. The participant sitting in the stands watching the basketball game absorbs the action unfolding on the court. At the other end of the spectrum lies *immersion*, which involves a drowning of the senses. The participant is completely immersed in the sights, sounds, and smells infused into the environment. A spectator would be immersed at the same basketball game if he or she were invited onto the court to participate in leading the team into the arena. The fan would experience firsthand the fog that rolls out as lights flash and the music drowns the roar of the crowd.

By incorporating the two dimensions, four broad categories of experiences can be illustrated according to where they fall in the spectra. These broad categories create the four realms of experience—entertainment, educational, escapist, and aesthetic—that can be used to describe different experiences.

The *entertainment realm* tends to include more passive forms of participation that are more likely to absorb the participant than to immerse the participant in the experience. An example would be a fan watching the broadcast of a NCAA National Championship game on ESPN in the comfort of home or a local pub. The *educational realm* includes experiences that involve greater immersion and active participation. For example, perhaps an event expo for sport participants includes experts offering short seminars or workshops related to skill mastery or nutritional tips. The participating athletes might have their sport skills and/or diets assessed, allowing an individual to learn from the experts. The *escapist realm* includes experiences that enable the participant to be fully immersed in the active participation. An example of this experience involves an athlete competing in the Olympics. These athletes are fully immersed in the ritual, ceremony, and atmosphere of the Games. Finally, the *aesthetic realm* includes experiences that are similar to the escapist experiences without the active participation. In this realm, the spectator in the stands watching the Olympic Games would be absorbed in the same ritual, ceremony, and atmosphere but, as a spectator, would be a passive participant.

Designing Experiences

THEMING

Once the context and stakeholders of the event are determined, the first design task is to establish the concept and theme of the experience. **Theming** an event involves more than just decorations; it should alter the attendees' sense of time and reality through tangible and memorable **cues** that leave

theming Alteration of the attendees' sense of time and reality through tangible and memorable cues that leave lasting impressions.

cues A feature or element of the event that is perceived and interpreted by the attendee with the intended outcome of a lasting (hopefully positive) impression or memory.

Noosa Surfing Festival

The Noosa Surfing Festival is held at Noosa Heads on the Sunshine Coast in Queensland, Australia. While the event itself is one of the most popular international longboard surfing events, what is of greatest interest to some visitors is how the area is themed. Although many are not an official part of the event, the businesses in Noosa Heads have chosen to theme their stores to align with the event. Surf-themed elements like longboards, surfing posters, and board shorts are displayed in storefront windows and within the stores, which not only bolsters visitor spending, but also provides further local support and enthusiasm around the event (O'Brien, 2008).

lasting impressions (Getz, 2012). To create impressions that foster meaning, the theme should convey a story using symbolic elements like logos, flags, color schemes, and displays. These elements should be layered throughout the event spaces and places in which the attendees gather.

It is the sport event manager's job to maximize the use of positive cues while minimizing the negative cues (Pine & Gilmore, 1998). Positive cues fulfill the theme through impressions, or takeaways, of the experience, such as exceptional customer service, design elements, entertainment, food and beverage (Getz, 2012), and elements of surprise (Petterson & Getz, 2009). Therefore, incorporating serendipitous moments of surprise for the attendee is a good way to exceed customer expectations and create positive experience outcomes (Chalip, 2006; Getz, 2012; Petterson & Getz, 2009). To stage a customer surprise, one must facilitate what the customer actually gets from what the customer expects to get. **Figure 7-1** illustrates this formula with an example. Positive cues must affirm the nature of the experience by supporting the theme with design elements and memorabilia. However, it is not only the positive cues the event manager should manage to ensure a good experience. The event manager must also eliminate anything that

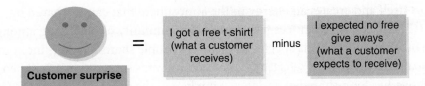

Figure 7-1   Staging customer surprise

Modified from Pine & Gilmore, 1999.

could diminish or detract from the theme. For example, spectator experiences can become an immediate negative cue when other fans are drunk and unruly and require security staff to eject them from the event. It is important to mitigate these negative cues by setting clear alcohol policies and training staff to detect potential problems and handle them discretely. These proactive steps can help create a more pleasurable experience.

Memorabilia can support cues with the tangible goods available for purchase or free takeaways. For example, the event experience can begin with the event registration process. Consider, as a race director, the positive cues and memorabilia you could incorporate into the registration process for an Ironman triathlon (2.4-mile swim, 112-mile bike ride, and 26.2-mile run that must be completed in under 17 hours). For those brave enough to participate, the event elicits a range of emotions from trepidation to ecstasy, and the experience begins the moment the athlete decides to register. To achieve Ironman status by completing this endurance event is of great importance in the triathlon community, so as an event director, you can facilitate that status with cues in the registration process. Allowing athletes to personalize their bib number can provide a personal cue of the experience (and add a piece of memorabilia). When finalizing the registration, the system could provide written or audio cues saying, "Congratulations! Your registration is complete. Only 102 days until . . . You. Are. An. IRONMAN!" Even the smallest cue and piece of memorabilia, such as in this example, can aid in the creation of a unique event experience.

memorabilia Tangible goods that support theme cues and that are available for purchase or as free takeaways.

CREATING LIMINALITY

There's no denying that sporting outcomes will impact the experience. Experiences are tied closely to the expectations that sport fans have about their team's performance and competition (Petterson & Getz, 2009). Still, a sport event tends to elicit a sense of something more important that transcends sport itself and creates an energy in the atmosphere that can be shared by all (Chalip, 2006). Attendees feel a sense of community or belonging among the other attendees. This special place where people share very specific commonalities is known as **communitas**. The communitas serves to bring all people together for a shared experience. Simply put, the spirit of communitas is to create a space that allows for a sense of fellowship and belonging. A sport event can create such atmosphere by finding ways to bring people together through a shared, heightened experience (Chalip, 2006). Often, this is created by the excitement of a team doing well or winning. For example, the fans of Mexico celebrated so much over Mexico's win over Germany in the 2018 World Cup that very minor seismographic readings detected the "massive jumps" of the fans celebrating the win in Mexico City (Park, 2018). The exhileration of this win served to bring the Mexican community together and create a sense of belonging.

With roots in anthropology, the sense of community has been discussed in the sport context (Green & Chalip, 1998). At the core of an experience is a zone that creates meaning that transcends the person and creates meaning outside of normal everyday life. For a ritualistic or sacred event, this special, transcended space is known as the **liminal zone**. Liminality is the condition that occurs during rites of passage that are performed to transfer a person from one stage of life to another (Thomassen, 2009). This unfolds in a number of ways in society from weddings, funerals, and bar mitzvahs, for example. Turner (1974) noted that others were practicing a transcendence through secular (unsacred) rites of passages doing leisure activity, like sport. Turner coined this the *liminoid genres*. For sport events, this special transcended space is known as the **liminoid zone**. In both cases, people experience a phenomenon that takes the individual beyond an average day, creating a feeling that the individual belongs to something bigger and this zone provides an escape or freedom from set social structures. Here, people are liberated to create meaning and live in a nearly utopian space (Turner, 1974). This zone, which is defined by spatial and temporal terms, can be engendered through the event design and programming (Chalip, 2006; Petterson & Getz, 2009). Sport event managers can create a space where fans, participants, or other key stakeholders can feel like they have stepped away from everyday life or have accomplished a feat that has moved them to a new stage of life. For example, sport offers stages that athletes pass through. In the United States, for example, athletes pass from youth sport, to school sport and club, to intercollegiate athletics, to professional sport. At each

communitas A special place where event attendees share a heightened sense of community and belonging.

liminal zone A zone within a sacred, ritualistic event that creates meaning that transcends the person and creates meaning outside of normal everyday life.

liminoid zone A zone within an unsacred, secular event that creates meaning that transcends the person and creates meaning outside of normal everyday life.

stage, there is a rite of passage that occurs. Signing a scholarship, getting drafted by a professional team—these provide a ceremony or ritual that welcomes that athlete to the next level.

Certainly, sport events—many of which are steeped in ritual, ceremony, and tradition—have the means to enable liminality to render social value. To many sport event managers, this social value is an important event impact to be leveraged. Liminal events require two key elements: A sense of celebration and social camaraderie (Chalip, 2006). To foster these two elements, the event design must enable points of sociability where people can share the experience. Chalip (2006) suggests five strategies to promote celebration and camaraderie (see **Figure 7-2**).

Together, these techniques provide sport event managers with tools that can allow them to use celebration and social interaction to build social capital and enhance a sense of community. Creating a liminoid zone for sport events enables communication and brings together groups that might otherwise not come together (Chalip, 2006). For example, at the Australian Open event in Melbourne, Australia, there is a specific area in the heart of the various staged courts known as Garden Square, which features tennis on the big screen, roving entertainers, and a Fan Zone where sponsors and partners can engage with attendees. The area also has the Heinekin Live

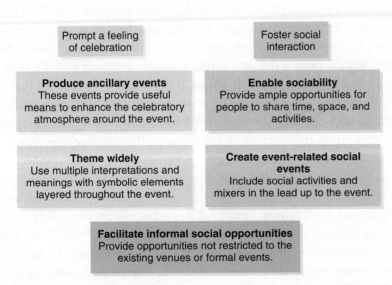

Figure 7-2   Creating the Liminoid Zone

Data from Chalip, L. (2006). Towards social leverage of sport events. *Journal of Sport & Tourism, 11*(2), 109–127.

Stage featuring a range of music genres and top performers to create a social and entertaining zone for people to come together to share the experience, socialize, and enjoy entertainment beyond tennis.

ENGAGING THE SENSES

In addition to the symbolic elements used to create the liminoid zone, the theme can be enhanced by stimulating the senses. Some of the cues can heighten an experience by just affecting one sense, like the smell of popcorn or hot dogs at a baseball game. Engaging the senses is a balancing act, and the event design should immerse the attendees in the experience, thereby drawing them in, but, at the same time, avoiding sensory overload. Lights and sounds that are overpowering and limit interaction can not only create sensory overload but they can also negate the effect of engagement and socialization that is sought in the liminoid zone. Therefore, when creating areas for socializing, music and other sounds should not be set to a volume that disallows conversation.

Co-creating Experiences

There are a number of events competing for the attendees' valued leisure time. On any given weekday or weekend, an attendee can go to a music festival, a performing-arts show, the local shopping center, or a baseball game. Sport events must compete within a very saturated marketplace where people have a multitude of leisure events at which they may spend their valuable time. Co-creation is the interaction between the event and the attendee to create value together (Lusch & Vargo, 2006) and is a design tool that provides additional value to an event by allowing the attendee high-quality interactions with the event (Prahalad & Ramaswamy, 2004; Van Limburg, 2008). Often in sport events, there is a focus on the attendee experience, but it is often a passive one. Furthermore, opportunities for value creation are enhanced when an event provides personalized co-creation as a unique experience (Prahalad & Ramaswamy, 2004). For co-creation to occur, the attendee and event must work jointly. **Table 7-1** describes the concept of co-creation.

Interaction is a key driver for the co-creation experience (Van Limburg, 2008). Communitas engendered through the liminoid zone at a sport event is an important tool to create the interaction. The goal of co-creation is to move the attendee from passive–absorbed participant to active–immersed participant within the four realms of experience (Pine & Gilmore, 1998).

Table 7-1   The Concept of Co-creation

What Co-creation Is Not	What Co-creation Is
Focus on the attendee	Joint creation of experience
Enablement of the "attendee is always right" viewpoint	Creation of a relationship with attendee, not mass market
Pampering the attendee with lavish customer service	Opportunity for the attendee to co-construct the service
Mass customization of offerings	Creation of an experience with the environment
Transfer of activities from the event to the customer	Shared creation of activities
Attendee as product manager or co-designer	Co-construction of personalized experiences
Product variety	Experience variety
Staging experiences	Innovative experience environments

Reprinted from *Journal of Interactive Marketing, 18*(3), C.K. Prahalad, Venkat Ramaswamy, Co-creation experiences: The next practice in value creation, pages 5–14, Copyright 2004, with permission from Elsevier.

Meanings Attached

What is an experience without meaning? In sport, meaning is conveyed through the symbolic elements used to create the liminoid zone: Ceremony, ritual, logos, flags, banners, and color schemes (Chalip, 2006; Getz, 2012). Memories and interests of the attendee shape the meaning attached to an experience; it is highly dependent on the interaction between the event theme and the interpretations by the attendee (Morgan, 2009). To be competitive through experience design, sport event managers must address attendees' need for meaning by understanding the role of meaning in their lives and

VIGNETTE 7-2

Co-creation Using Technology!

There are few examples in the sport event world that enable co-creation, but there are plenty of opportunities for growth in this area. One example is the use of event-specific application technology (or "app"). The creation of an event-specific app that allows users to not only interact with the event but also to interact socially with friends can add to the experience. The ability to set a schedule, check in to various areas of the event, and make and receive updates in real time allows attendees to stay in touch, plan their event experience, and stay up to date on the latest information from you, the sport event director, through texts, posts, Tweets, or other social networking technologies.

Table 7-2   Meanings Attached to Sport Events

Personal	Sociocultural	Political	Economic
Belonging	Sense of community	Community development programs	Increased tourism
Self-esteem	Community pride		New jobs
Mastery	Sharing of customs/values	Improved infrastructure	New business
Health/well-being		National identity building	
Accomplishment	Shared celebration		
Self-discovery	Social interaction	International awareness	
Nostalgia			

how to evoke meaning through the event (Diller, Shedroff, & Rhea, 2005). Sport events induce a number of meanings, including personal, social, cultural, economic, political, and nostalgic (see **Table 7-2**). Sport event experiences range from unimportant entertainment to a profoundly transforming experience. Creating the liminoid zone and theming the sport event using symbolism, ritual, and ceremony can deepen the meaning that one attaches to the experience, thereby enhancing the memory of the event.

SUMMARY

As this chapter illustrates, creating the event experience involves much more than just offering an event. There are a number of key elements to consider and carefully plan in order to elicit a positive response from event attendees. It is important to remember that the attendees' experiences will be subjective and heterogeneous. Therefore, an event manager cannot control every specific aspect. Rather, the event manager should consider how theming, creating communities, and allowing for attendees to create their own experience could impact the overall success of the event.

DISCUSSION QUESTIONS

1. Define the *experience economy* and discuss how you could incorporate it into a spectator sport event. How might this differ from a sport participation event?
2. Co-creation is an innovative method for involving your patrons in helping you shape their experiences. Discuss how you might incorporate co-creation elements into a spectator sport event.
3. The liminoid zone is that area that transcends normal space and time. How might you create this for participants *and* spectators at a sport event?
4. Develop a theme for a sport event and discuss how you would engage the senses through this theme.

Case STUDY

Creating an Experience: A Glance at the Red Bull 400

The Red Bull brand has both sponsored and created sport events, from Formula 1, surfing, surf and rescue, archery, and skateboarding to soapbox race, standup paddling, and mountain running. The Red Bull 400 Park City is an annual event where athletes run 400m up a 134m hill, climbing 2,126m in altitude. With an incline of 35 degrees, this challenge is not for the faint-hearted. In 2018, the event was in its fourth year and gaining in popularity. The work record for the men stands at 3m 59s and for the women at 4m 39s.

As an event director, you have just won a bid to host a new Red Bull 400 event on Keystone Mountain in Silverthorne, Colorado. For this inaugural event, your main goal is to create an experience that your key stakeholders will never forget. You have three main objectives for this event: (1) to create a sense of celebration with multiple points for socialization among the event patrons, (2) to create a memorable experience that encourages event attendees to return annually for the event, and (3) to increase the length of stay in Silverthorne. The local government in Silverthorne is interested in offsetting the effects of seasonality during the summer, so they are encouraged by your proposal to extend the amount of time that visitors stay in the area. You should assume that you found a point on the mountain that equals that of the course in Park City, UT.

Using what you have just learned in the chapter about designing events that inspire memorable experiences, develop a design plan for your event. Be sure to consider the following:

1. What is your event concept, keeping in mind Red Bull's brand image?
    a. How do you use this concept to theme your event?
    b. How do you create an atmosphere that leaves a meaningful experience?

2. Who are the key stakeholders?
    a. How might their needs differ in a way that could affect their experience?
    b. Will these needs influence your concept/theme as described in Question 1?

3. What aspects of the setting and environment could be incorporated into your theme and design concept?

4. How would you create your liminoid zone?

5. When there are multiple races in one event, how do you tie these races together over the multiday event to drive interest, spending, and length of stay among your attendees?

Resources for Case Study: http://www.silverthorne.org; https://www.redbull.com/us-en/events/rb400-park-city.

Readings for Case Study: Petterson, R., & Getz, D. (2009). Event experiences in time and space: A study of visitors to the 2007 World Alpine Ski Championships in Åre, Sweden. *Scandinavian Journal of Hospitality and Tourism, 9*, 308–326.

REFERENCES

Aicher, T. J., & Newland, B. L. (2017). To explore or race? Examining endurance athletes' destination event choices. *Journal of Vacation Marketing*, 1–15. doi.org/10.1177/1356766717736364

Berridge, G. (2012). *Events design and experience*. Oxford, UK: Taylor and Francis.

Buning, R. J., & Gibson, H. J. (2016a). The role of travel conditions in cycling tourism: Implications for destination and event management. *Journal of Sport & Tourism*, 1–19.

Buning, R. J., & Gibson, H. J. (2016b). Exploring the trajectory of active-sport-event travel careers: A social worlds perspective. *Journal of Sport Management*, 30, 265–281.

Chalip, L. (2006). Towards social leverage of sport events. *Journal of Sport & Tourism*, *11*(2), 109–127.

Diller, S., Shedroff, N., & Rhea, D. (2005). *Making meaning: How successful businesses deliver meaningful customer experiences*. San Francisco, CA: Pearson Education.

Getz, D. (2012). *Event studies. Theory, research and policy for planned events*. New York, NY: Routledge.

Green, B. C., & Chalip, L. (1998). Sport tourism as celebration of subculture. *Annals of Tourism*, *25*(2), 275–291.

Lusch, R. F., Vargo, S. L., & Malter, A. (2006). Marketing as service-exchange: Taking a leadership role in global marketing management. *Organizational Dynamics*, *35*(3), 264–278.

Mannell, R. C., & Kleiber, D. A. (1997). *A social psychology of leisure*. State College, PA: Venture Publishing.

Morgan, M. (2009). What makes a good festival? Understanding the event experience. *Event Management*, *12*(2), 81–93.

Newland, B. L., & Aicher, T. J. (2018). Exploring sport participants' event and destination choices. *Journal of Sport & Tourism*, *22*(2), 131–149.

O'Brien, D. (2008). Points of leverage: Maximizing host community benefit from a regional surfing festival. *European Sport Management Quarterly*, *7*(2), 141–165.

O'Loughlin, S. (2016, December). *Inside 10 of the industry's best digital sports sponsorship activations*. Retrieved from http://www.eventmarketer.com/inside-10-of-the-industrys-best-digital-sports-sponsorship-activations/

Ooi, C. (2005). A theory of tourism experiences. In: T. O'Dell & P. Billing (Eds.), *Experience-scapes: Tourism, culture, and economy* (pp. 51–68). Copenhagen: Copenhagen Business School Press.

Park, M. (2018, June). *Did World Cup goal celebration trigger an 'artificial earthquake' in Mexico?* CNN Americas. Retrieved from https://www.cnn.com/2018/06/18/americas/mexico-earthquake-world-cup-goal-celebration/index.html

Petterson, R., & Getz, D. (2009). Event experiences in time and space: A study of visitors to the 2007 World Alpine Ski Championships in Åre, Sweden. *Scandinavian Journal of Hospitality and Tourism*, *9(2–3)*, 308–326.

Pine, J. B., & Gilmore, J. H. (1998). Welcome to the experience economy. *Harvard Business Review, July–August* 97–105 (Reprint: # 98407).

Prahalad, C. K., & Ramaswamy, V. (2004). Co-creation experiences: The next practice in value creation. *Journal of Interactive Marketing, 18*(3), 5–14.

Thomassen, B. (2009). The uses and meanings of liminality. *International Political Anthropology, 2*(1), 5–28.

Turner, V. W. (1974). Liminal to liminoid, in play, flow, and ritual: An essay in comparative symbology. *Rice University Studies.* Retrieved from https://scholarship.rice.edu/bitstream/handle/1911/63159/article_RIP603_part4.pdf

Van Limburg, B. (2008). Innovation in pop festivals by cocreation. *Event Management, 12*(2), 105–117.

CHAPTER 8

Marketing the Facility and Events

Brianna L. Newland

CHAPTER OBJECTIVES

Upon completion of this chapter, the reader will be able to:

1. Clearly understand the elements of a marketing plan.
2. Recognize the importance of a well-developed marketing strategy and plan.
3. Develop an integrated marketing communications plan.
4. Realize the importance of knowing and building a relationship with the consumer.
5. Identify how the unique marketing elements can influence an event.

CHAPTER OVERVIEW

This chapter will discuss the importance of properly marketing the facility and/or event. It will discuss marketing elements, such as understanding the consumers, building the relationship, and communicating the message. This chapter will highlight the use of social networking and other digital methods within the marketing plan.

IndustryVOICE

Nick Michaels—Account Executive, Corporate Partnerships, Philadelphia Eagles

As an account executive for corporate partnerships, it is my job to connect brands to the Eagles in a way that translates a fan's passion for the team into support for the products and/or services offered by the corporate partner. The overarching goal is to help regional, national, and global companies achieve their marketing and business objectives through Eagles assets. Depending on the brand's marketing strategy, a partnership can consist of a variety of benefits including custom digital content, social posts, TV spots, radio units, VIP experiences, hospitality opportunities, etc. At the core, my role is a sales/revenue generation position, helping brands achieve their marketing and business objectives through the development of custom Eagles marketing platforms.

My first internship in the sport industry was with the University of Delaware athletic operations department. From there, I became a football operations intern at UD, then I served as a game day operations intern for the Philadelphia Soul and Philadelphia Union. These internships enabled me to intern with the Eagles, where I completed ticket operations, mascot events, and corporate sales and service internships. In August of 2013, the Eagles hired me full-time as a service coordinator in the corporate partnerships department. In September of 2015, I transitioned to the sales side and continue to serve in this current revenue-generating role.

The mission of the Eagles is to inspire and serve the city of Philadelphia. Beyond the on-field performance, the Eagles organization is uniquely positioned to positively influence the city of Philadelphia

and social responsibility is a top priority for the organization. For example, we were one of the first NFL teams to launch a "Go Green" platform to reduce our environmental footprint. Now, 99 percent of waste generated in the stadium is diverted from landfills and 100 percent of the team's operations are powered by the sun and wind. While winning football games is undoubtedly an important part of the equation, the organization focuses on how we can use our unique platform to inspire and serve the city of Philadelphia.

The two biggest challenges that I face with the Eagles are both internal. First, cross communication among all of the internal departments poses a challenge. For example, if we were to host an Eagles cruise where fans could purchase vacation trips to travel with their favorite players, alumni and team personalities, everyone from executive leadership to the marketing department to the digital/social department is involved. Balancing internal opinions, while trying to satisfy the prospective client's (aka, cruise lines) needs, and then selling the prospective client on the idea, investment level and term length, etc., can be challenging. The second challenge, also internal, relates to how a corporate partner is managed and renewed. The service coordinator is responsible for the day-to-day execution of the partnership. At the end of the partnership, it is sales' responsibility to renew the account. The sales person must remain in contact with the account and continually foster a professional relationship so that when it comes time for renewal there is an established relationship. The service coordinators' performance on the account can greatly influence the outcome of the renewal for which the sales person is responsible. Striking a balance of motivating, helping, and being involved while not overstepping and micromanaging is difficult. To combat both of these challenges, I rely heavily on frequent communication. It has been my experience that if I'm constantly communicating, and in some cases overcommunicating, it seems to help. People like to be kept in the loop and updated even if the update is "no answers yet but still working on this."

A unique trend that I see within my segment of the industry is that brands are focusing more on custom digital and social content—especially custom content that can be consumed on mobile devices. In the early days of sports marketing, brands were focused on in-stadium signage and traditional media assets like TV and radio. Digital and social content used to be perceived as "added value" but now custom content is a top priority. It has flipped the sponsorship structure upside down. As brand marketing becomes more sophisticated, we are also seeing a growing focus on ROI, metrics, reporting, engagement, etc. It is no longer enough to measure "impressions" and "reach." We need to take the reporting a step further and explain to brands how their investment in the Philadelphia Eagles is engaging fans and encouraging them to use our partners' products and services.

To capitalize on these trends, the Eagles organization invested significant resources to build a large digital/social department. We have one of the largest digital/social departments in the NFL, which allows us to produce unprecedented amounts of contents and stay ahead of trends. For measurement and reporting, we hire outside companies to help us track, evaluate, and report. For example, we hired an independent 3rd party to help us quantify the impact of the Eagles trademarks on our partners' marketing materials.

I do no hiring in my current role. However, there are three main characteristics that I look for in a new hire: Emotional intelligence (EQ), drive, and a growth mindset. EQ is the presence of social skills, communication skills, and self-awareness. Due to the rise in technology, it is my personal belief that EQ is more important now than ever before. TalentSmart, a company used by more than 75 percent of Fortune 500 companies, conducted a research study of over 1 million people and found that EQ is responsible for 58 percent of job performance, 90 percent of top performers have high EQs, and people with high EQs make $29,000 more annually than their low EQ counterparts—it matters! The second set of characteristics that I look for in a candidate are drive and persistence. In the words of Thomas Edison, "genius is often really just persistence in disguise." If a student has the work ethic, drive, and willingness to prepare, all of the technical job skills can be taught easily. Finally, the third characteristic that is important, but often overlooked, is a growth mindset. When someone has a growth mindset, they believe that their abilities can be developed through dedication and hard work; they are in a constant state of learning. It is being able to say, "I don't know" or "I made a mistake" and learning from those experiences. A growth mindset means that you are a sponge, soaking up as much knowledge as possible.

Two of the biggest skills or qualifications commonly missing among new graduates are interpersonal skills and lack of continued self-development. When communicating a message, it is important to focus on what you say and how you say it. According to UCLA professor Albert Mehrabian, the way a message is received is 7 percent based on word selection, 38 percent tone of voice, and 55 percent body language. A Carnegie Mellon study identified confidence as more important than a professional's skill set, reputation, or history (i.e., the way you present yourself (verbal language and non-verbal body language)) is more important than your professional experience. It is important to take a step back and clarify that confidence must manifest itself as presence without

(continues)

arrogance. If arrogance is a part of confidence, the above statements won't hold true. With the rise of texting, social media, emails, etc., it seems that younger students hide behind digital platforms. Rather than having an in-person conversation with someone sitting three desks down, they will send an email. Or, they are afraid to speak on the phone with someone but will text them back immediately. Since technology will only become more integrated into our daily lives, it is my belief that the successful leaders of tomorrow will be able to embrace technology while still developing the requisite interpersonal communication skills. The second qualification commonly missing is a lack of continued personal development and learning. In my experience, it seems that recent graduates no longer feel a need to learn once they have earned their degree. Consider Warren Buffett and Charlie Munger—even at their advanced ages, and being widely regarded as the best in their field, they continue to emphasize continued learning and growth. Learning can be through reading, watching training videos, attending conferences, or listening to podcasts. Find a way (or preferably, multiple ways) that you enjoy to continue to learn.

In the words of bestselling author, Harvey Mackay, "dig your well before you're thirsty." In a world of instant gratification, it can be difficult to lay the groundwork now for something that won't materialize for years, but it is important to start as soon as possible. To provide students with actionable strategies that can be implemented, I'd recommend the following:

- Cut out (or drastically reduce) TV consumption— 1 hour of TV a day for 365 days = over two weeks of wasted time over the course of the year. Think about the progress you could make toward your dream job if you gained two weeks per year.

- Download an app that tracks the time spent on your phone (e.g., Moment). Use the app to track time spent on other phone apps (Snapchat, Twitter, etc.) and cut out unproductive time spent on the phone. Ninety-nine times out of 100, people will find that they spend entirely too much time on their phones mindlessly scrolling through different apps and not being productive.

- Schedule one informational interview per week. Currently, professionals are more than willing to help students who take initiative and show an interest in learning about their profession. If you have a LinkedIn profile, use it to identify and ask industry professionals if they'd be willing to schedule 15 minutes for a brief informational interview. Show that you respect their time and keep it to the time you promised (in this case 15 minutes). Those 15 minutes not only gained you an industry contact but someone you can go back to when you are looking for a job. Now, you have a pre-established relationship vs. simply reaching out in search of a job (aka, digging your well before you're thirsty).

- Begin acquiring work experience immediately! At first, it doesn't matter what you do, just get started by taking immediate action. One open door leads to the next. Don't think one internship qualifies you to land your dream job in sport. It took me seven internships to land my first full-time position in sports.

- Be open to the idea of a sales position. A sales position has the potential to act as rocket fuel for your career trajectory. This is one item that I wish I could go back and convince myself of at an earlier age. All through college, I said that I would never be in sales. It wasn't until I was in the industry and saw the opportunity for growth on the sales side that I opened up to the idea and eventually made the switch. Generating revenue is the life blood of a company. If you are successful on the sales side and generate money for the company, it is the quickest way to jumpstart your career.

Introduction

Marketing a product involves knowing the customer well and communicating how a product meets needs. But, it is much more than that. Organizations, including sport events and facilities, need customers to survive. To attract and retain those customers while building demand for a brand, an organization must do the following:

- Develop a brand that will stick in the mind of the consumer
- Create awareness about the products and/or services offered
- Generate a perception in the mind of the consumer that leads to brand equity and loyalty
- Differentiate the organization and products/services from the competitor
- Integrate marketing communications across a range of platforms to ensure that consumers receive the brand message

These are not easy tasks and require coordination of a well thought-out strategy and plan.

Sport is even more unique than other business fields and industries for a number of reasons, as demarcated by Mullin, Hardy, and Sutton (2007):

- *Sport is consumed as it is produced.* Unfortunately, sport cannot be created and shelved to purchase when the moment suits us. While it is possible to watch the event again, if it is recorded and/or rebroadcast, it will never inspire the same effect as the live event.
- *Sport is intangible.* While we would all enjoy bringing LeBron James home and placing him on our mantle or playing a pickup game with him in our backyard, this is not possible. To make sport more tangible, organizations sell merchandise related to the game or event. However, this is not the same as taking the athlete home as you would a new pair of shoes.
- *Sport is emotional, subjective, and* **heterogeneous**. Fans and sport participants experience sport very differently. For some, the experience can elicit myriad emotions that ebb and flow throughout the sport event. Many can be deeply affected by the team's performance, which can influence their everyday life. Others might enjoy the game but feel no further effect. Furthermore, no two people will have the same sport experiences. While one person might be drawn to the strategy of play, another may enjoy the fanfare and atmosphere, and still another may be completely bored and wish that he had gone to the movies. Sport is deeply personal, which is challenging for sport marketers.

heterogeneous Relating to perceptions of an experience that are widely dissimilar.

- *Sport is inconsistent and unpredictable.* It is much easier to sell tickets to sporting events when the team is winning. But when the team is in a multiseason slump, even the most loyal fans can get discouraged. Furthermore, weather can threaten performance, lineups can change, and momentum and injuries can be game changers.
- *The core product is uncontrollable.* Adding to the unpredictability and inconsistency, this game itself is out of the control of the sport marketer. Marketers cannot set rosters, acquire players, or make decisions that can influence the outcome of the game. To counter this, marketers sell merchandise and mementos and develop **product extensions** that create an experience and atmosphere around the event.
- *Sport organizations cooperate and compete simultaneously.* The sport industry is unique in that it requires other organizations in order to be competitive. Those teams must have strong talent in order to create an atmosphere that is both competitive and entertaining. If one team consistently dominates, this would impact interest in the sport. Therefore, teams agree to cooperate on certain levels to preserve the competitive environment.

product extension
An additional event component that creates an atmosphere and experience for an event.

As one can see, sport is a unique enterprise and marketers must promote products and services that are inconsistent and unpredictable, intangible, perishable, subjective, and open to interpretation (Mullin et al., 2007). Furthermore, the environment is highly competitive and requires strong research on the consumer and environment before a viable strategy can be developed.

Feasibility

To develop a strong marketing strategy, a facility and/or event must determine what is feasible. As discussed in Chapter 2, a **feasibility study** is typically conducted in the initiation stage of planning and provides information for event directors to do the following:

feasibility study An assessment that is conducted to determine key market characteristics.

1. Provide quality information to support decision making.
2. Identify reasons *not* to proceed (such as risk, cost, lack of resources, etc.).
3. Develop a strong marketing strategy, if the event is a "go."
4. Help establish a vision, mission, and concept for the event.
5. Assist in securing funding or other support.

This study should also be completed by facilities, although the focus is slightly different. The marketing director for a facility must determine the feasibility and capacity to host events, which events to attract, and any reasons to not proceed. While the focus is slightly different for the event marketer than for the facility marketer, both use feasibility results to devise the best course of action.

A feasibility study conducted by the marketer should consider three key elements. First, one must determine the market characteristics. What is the demand for such an event? Or, in the case of the facility, what is the demand for events to use this venue? Is the market currently saturated with similar events or other facilities that could potentially host? Is the barrier to entry difficult? That is, to host such an event, will it require substantial human, financial, and operational resources? A good event marketer will determine if such an event can not only be implemented but can also be sustained over a specific period while remaining competitive. Second, one must consider the geographic factors that could potentially influence the viability of the event. Is the venue difficult to access? What are the amenities near the venue? Can the community hotels and restaurants support the influx of people? Will the environment be easily damaged by the event? What infrastructure does the location provide? That is, will the event require additional equipment and/or structures? And finally, one must carefully analyze all financial aspects, including projected revenue and operating costs. It is wise to develop a pro forma (as discussed in the "Facility Design and Construction" chapter) and conduct a breakeven analysis (as discussed in the "Project Management" chapter) very early in the process. A **breakeven analysis** is used to determine at what point the event can cover all of the expenses and begin to make a profit. It is important to be as accurate as possible when determining the startup costs, as these numbers will help determine the sales revenue needed to pay ongoing operational expenses.

While all types of feasibility are important to the event manager in deciding to move forward with event implementation, the climate is of the utmost importance to the marketer. In addition to determining whether the event can move forward, the marketer will also consider the internal and external strengths of the event through a **SWOT analysis**. The acronym SWOT stands for strengths, weaknesses, opportunities, and threats. A SWOT analysis allows a marketer to capitalize on strengths and opportunities while mitigating the potentially negative effects of weaknesses and threats. Take, for example, a SWOT conducted on a potential youth triathlon event. As you review the

breakeven analysis An assessment used to determine at what point the event can cover all of the expenses and begin to make a profit.

SWOT analysis A tool used to assess the internal and external strengths and weaknesses of an event; SWOT stands for strengths, weaknesses, opportunities, and threats.

Table 8-1 SWOT of a Youth Triathlon Event

Internal	External
Strengths	**Opportunities**
✓ Event staff has over 5 years of experience hosting triathlons. ✓ The facility is financially stable and capable of an event addition. ✓ Current events have grown consistently.	✓ Outreach to a local organization that promotes physical activity and health could enable access to children. ✓ A strong relationship with governing officials could lead to potential funding sources.
Weaknesses	**Threats**
– The staff has never done a youth-specific event. – The event location is in a high-traffic area, so additional support will be necessary.	– Weather could cancel the event unexpectedly. – The environment is very saturated for youth sport in general and triathlon specifically.

table, notice how the strengths and weaknesses focus on the internal environment of the organization while the opportunities and threats target the external climate (**Table 8-1**).

Once a feasibility study and SWOT analysis have been conducted and the decision makers have decided to implement the event, the next step for the marketer is to determine the strategy and lay out the plan.

Developing the Marketing Strategy and Plan

Before a strong marketing plan and campaign can be developed, a marketer must determine the purpose of the event and the main goals. To begin, the mission and vision of the event must be determined. A **mission statement** defines the purpose of the organization (or event). It identifies why the organization exists for the consumer and allows for the development of organizational goals. The **vision statement** is what the organization would like to accomplish. This statement describes what the organization aspires to be and/or do as it grows and evolves.

As described previously, sport marketing is unique, which creates a number of marketing challenges. To add to these challenges, consider that the sport product itself is complex and dynamic. From a sport event perspective, the core product is the competition itself, which includes the type of sport played, the participants (athletes, coaches, and officials), and the

mission statement A statement defining the purpose of the organization (or event).

vision statement A statement of what the organization would like to achieve or accomplish.

environment (e.g., the challenge of a triathlon race course or the weather conditions at a golf tournament; Pedersen et al., 2014). Additionally, sport events typically include product extensions that create an atmosphere around the event. These extensions can include a music festival that accompanies the sport event, halftime shows, games for children and families, and other non-competition-related activities. For example, The Mountain Sports Festival is a weekend of sports and music that celebrates community, outdoor sports, and the local businesses that support the event (Mountain Sports Festival, 2018). The event is held annually on Memorial Day weekend in Asheville, North Carolina, and features a range of sporting events like rock climbing, a river dash, a beer mile, SUP yoga, a 5k and 1 mile fun run, disc golf, a BMX Street Jam, a 20K mountain trail relay, and culminates with a bike criterium known as the *Rumble on the River*. The festival was developed to bring together outdoor enthusiasts, outdoor equipment creators, and adventure companies in an atmosphere filled with food, music, and celebration. The festival and event board of directors created the fun-filled weekend event to encourage fun and participation on all levels (Mountain Sports Festival, 2018).

© TK Kurikawa/Shutterstock

Segmentation

Once an organization has defined its purpose and identified future aspirations, marketers must consider which consumers would be most interested in the products or services offered by the organization. Because consumers are so heterogeneous, considering incredibly large consumer bases can be a daunting task. Therefore, marketers break consumers into smaller clusters or groups identified by certain characteristics rather than attempting to sell to everyone. This process is known as **segmentation**. Typically, these categorizations are determined through demographic, psychographic, media preference and use, and purchasing behavior characteristics. **Demographics**

segmentation The breaking of consumers into smaller clusters or groups identified by certain characteristics rather than attempting to sell to everyone.

demographics The categorization of consumers based on age, gender, ethnicity, education, income, socioeconomic status, profession, geographic location, religion, type of sport played, and other such identifiers.

psychographics The categorization of consumers based on the consumers' interests, beliefs, and attitudes.

media preference and use The categorization of consumers based on the type of media consumed and how it is consumed.

purchasing behavior The frequency with which individuals consume a product and the manner in which they use the products and services.

target market The consumer most likely to purchase the product or service.

categorize consumers based on age, gender, ethnicity, education, income, socioeconomic status, profession, geographic location, religion, type of sport played, and other such identifiers. **Psychographics** categorize based on the consumers' interests, beliefs, and attitudes. Also, the motives that drive consumers to participate and watch sport would be considered here. Greater detail and discussion on this topic can be found in the "Consumer Behavior" chapter.

Considering the increased adoption and use of technology, it is important for marketers to know consumers' **media preference and use**. Not only is it important to understand how they consume sport (e.g., TV, Internet, radio) but also what they use to access information (e.g., smartphones, computers, newspaper, TV, radio) and the preference for various media (e.g., organization applications, Snapchat, Instagram, Twitter, Facebook, email, print). Knowledge of this information can help marketers to streamline communication more effectively in ways that suit the audience best. For example, if 20- to 29-year-old men get their information through social media, putting an ad in a newspaper is not a wise marketing decision. Tweeting information would target this group better.

Finally, **purchasing behavior** describes the frequency and use of products and services. Knowing what individuals buy and when and how they buy it can help you understand purchasing trends better. For example, perhaps you notice that Bob Smith purchases baseball tickets on family promotional nights and only on these nights. A marketer could target Bob with family-themed offerings to attract him to additional events. Armed with such information, marketers can target those most likely to consume the product or service. The **target market** is the consumer most likely to purchase the product. An example of segmenting a sport event is provided in **Table 8-2**.

TIP

Take the time to understand your consumers and learn how to attract them. If you plan to use social media, like Facebook or Twitter, to reach your consumer, they actually need to follow you! Creating content that is easily shared by others is one way of attracting attention. People are attracted to videos and photos. Use that to engage them and then remind them to follow you on your social media platforms.

Building the Relationship

Once the customer characteristics have been identified, a customer profile can be developed. A **customer profile** is a description of the customer or set of customers based on their demographic, psychographic, media preferences, and purchasing behavior. The profile gives you the information you need to further develop relationships and increase spending with existing customers, while using information gathered

Table 8-2   Segmentation Elements: Local Youth Triathlon

Demographics	Psychographics	Media Preferences	Purchasing Habits
Boys and girls 7 to 12 years old, middle- to upper-middle class families, located in the central Texas area.	Active families with swimming, biking, or running backgrounds, interested in new sports, adventurous, look for family-oriented activities.	Consumption methods: Social networks (Facebook, Twitter), moderate to heavy Internet, TV, and smartphone use.	Frequently purchase/use fitness and sport goods/services, active gym or sport recreation memberships.

from them to attract new customers. This process is known as **relationship marketing**, which is "the marketing activities directed toward establishing, developing, and maintaining relational exchanges" with customers (Morgan & Hunt, 1994, p. 22). The strategy of relationship marketing is to invest in the development of long-term relationships with customers and other key stakeholders in order to garner a better understanding of one another's expectations and concerns (Pressey & Tzokas, 2006). Competitive advantage is gained when the organization properly aligns its products and services with customer demand, allowing for stronger bonds to develop between organization and consumer—yet another competitive advantage (Pressey & Tzokas, 2006). Customers are likely to see direct benefits from products and services that better align with their individual wants and needs (Morgan & Hunt, 1994).

To build a relationship, organizations require a means of maintaining vital information about customers. **Data-based marketing (DBM)** software is a comprehensive system that captures critical demographic, psychographic, media use, and purchasing behavior information on customers and potential customers in order to enable direct marketing strategies (Mullin et al., 2007). However, when organizations are trying to build a relationship with a customer, more information is required. Customer relationship management (CRM) systems expand on the information gathered in the DBM to include information such as the following (Mullin et al., 2007):

- Purchase transactions, including what was purchased, amount purchased, and frequency of purchase
- Key relationships, such as family, friends, and coworkers
- Frequency of attendance, key dates attended, popular reasons for attending (e.g., birthday celebrations, work incentives)

customer profile A description of the customer or set of customers based on their demographics, psychographics, media preferences, and purchasing behavior.

relationship marketing A marketing strategy that seeks to develop and maintain relationships with customers, while using information gathered from them to attract new customers; the client–consumer relationship is emphasized over a more purely transactional behavior.

data-based marketing (DBM) A comprehensive system that captures critical demographics, psychographics, media use, and purchasing behavior information on customers and potential customers in order to enable direct marketing strategies.

- Brief notes on any interactions with the customer (e.g., unsatisfactory experience)
- Personal information such as favorite teams or sports, birthday, anniversary, the company they work for and their business contact information
- Results of customer surveys, feedback about services or products, and email preferences
- Information on direct mail, email blasts, wellness calls, or other marketing campaign touches

While appealing, a CRM system can be difficult to implement. Organizations must integrate the DBM and CRM into every facet of the organization to ensure that the optimum level of information is collected. Every opportunity to capture and properly code and categorize information must be capitalized. According to Gordon, Perrey, and Spellecke (2013), organizations that use data at the foci of marketing decisions (through the use of DBM and CRM) can improve their marketing return on investment by 15 to 20 percent. However, the data in and of themselves are not the reason for success. According to Gordon et al. (2013), organizations that successfully use DBM and CRM can identify valuable opportunities and use the data-derived information to communicate specific and relevant messages.

Positioning

Understanding customer needs and delivering a product that is perceived as more valuable than *and* distinctly different from other products is the key to winning and keeping customers (Moore & Pareek, 2010). Sport organizations position their products in ways that make them stand out from the competitors. **Differentiation** entails **positioning** the product in the minds of the consumer by highlighting the important attributes and benefits. For example, Nike and Under Armour sell similar products. When you think about the two brands; however, they are different. Think about the attributes you assign to each. What makes them different in your mind? To stand out in a highly cluttered sport marketplace, organizations use a number of strategies to stand out, including the following (Moore & Pareek, 2010):

- *Contrasting their product* or *service*'s key features and benefits against the shortcomings of the competition. This is often seen in advertisements in

differentiation The positioning of a product in the minds of the consumer by highlighting the important attributes and benefits.

positioning Developing and delivering a product that is perceived as more valuable than and distinctly different from other products.

which the company will note the superiority of the product in relation to the "other guys." This is most obvious with mobile phone carriers, like Verizon and AT&T.

- *Grabbing the unoccupied* by filling a gap that the competition has not yet secured. For example, Tough Mudder roared into the running marketplace by offering a unique alternative to the "boredom of marathoning." "Why run miles on pavement," Tough Mudder asks, "when you can do this?" (Tough Mudder, 2014).
- *Repositioning* the product. While repositioning can require a large investment, doing so can change or enhance the perception of a product and produce positive financial rewards for the organization. Consider the Tampa Bay Buccaneers of the National Football League. In the late 1990s, under new ownership, the Buccaneers repositioned themselves with a new logo, stadium, coaching staff, and team philosophy. While this was an incredibly hefty investment, the changes paid off with a Super Bowl win in 2002.
- *Creating exclusivity* is another strategy to position a product. This can be difficult to do. Finding ways to include elements in your event that do not exist in other products can make your event more exclusive and unique.

All organizations seek a competitive advantage over the scarce resources in a marketplace. By identifying potential sources of competitive advantage, marketers can determine which will be promoted as a means to differentiate their product from the competition (Moore & Pareek, 2010).

Price

Determining how to price a product or service is no easy task. There are a number of philosophies on what constitutes a fair price, but all agree that price must cover the cost of the product and the return to the producer to compensate for the risk incurred (Moore & Pareek, 2010). Where the debate lies is in determining how high the realized profit should be in regard to said risk. It is clear that consumers can be very **price sensitive**, so marketers should be cautious when setting a pricing strategy. Customers equate price with value and quality. **Table 8-3** illustrates the four Cs (customer, competitor, company, and climate) that should be considered when setting a pricing strategy.

price sensitive
Susceptibility to variations in price.

Table 8-3 Pricing Factors—The Four Cs

Factor	Description
Customer	Analyze the customer profile characteristics to determine how characteristics would impact certain pricing strategies and/or how specific segments will respond to pricing.
Competitor	Analyze how the consumer perceives the value of the product compared with competing products. Also, analyze the competitors' pricing schemes.
Company	Analyze the production costs and the minimum price necessary to cover these costs.
Climate	Analyze the external factors that can impact cost of production and consumers' ability to spend.

place The location of the sport product where the product is distributed; the geographic location of the target market and other channels that might be relevant to the sport product.

As price relates to sport events and the facility, consumers will consider much more than just the price of entry. The cost to the consumer includes travel to the venue, parking, concessions, and other costs related to the event. Thus, the consumer must feel that the overall value of the sport event experience exceeds (not matches) the price of admission.

© Martin Good/Shutterstock

Place

As discussed earlier, sport is unique from other industries because it is simultaneously consumed and produced. Therefore, how the sport product is distributed is also unique. In sport, **place** refers to the location of the sport product (e.g., stadium, park), where the product is distributed (e.g., online event registration, event admission sales at the venue), the geographic dynamics of the target market (e.g., international, national, local), and other channels that might be relevant to the sport product (e.g., media distribution, availability of the product by season, broadcast). Furthermore, the accessibility of the facility can impact the sport product greatly. Easy access to the venue from major roadways, the flow of traffic in and out of the venue space, and the environment at the venue can all have an impact on the perception of the facility and the event hosted there.

Promotion

Promotion is the most visible aspect of the marketing plan, and, in fact, many people confuse the two terms. *Marketing* is the overall, broad strategy for a sport product, whereas *promotion* is a specific tactic used as part of the marketing plan to attain goals. These two terms are not interchangeable. **Promotion** is the communication of the marketing message. It is not only used to communicate the overall message of the organization but also to further position the sport product in the mind of the consumer. The **promotion mix** is the varied use of a number of promotional methods, such as advertising (print, TV, radio, electronic); personal selling; public, community, and media relations; direct and online marketing; public service announcements; publicity; and sponsorship. The promotional mix is used to communicate the desired message and image about the product, create awareness, and educate the consumer about the product and persuade the consumer to buy the product (Moore & Pareek, 2010).

promotion The communication of the marketing message.

promotion mix The varied use of a number of promotional methods to create a message.

Communicating the Message

As the most visible aspect of the marketing plan, promotion involves the dissemination of information about the organization and product in ways that build strong equity with the brand and ensure good publicity for the firm (Moore & Pareek, 2010). Understanding how marketing decisions are made and how they impact the long-term strategy of the event or facility is important. In the case of a sport event, a strong marketing communications plan must be developed to create awareness and promote the event, but it should be remembered that the event itself is a strategic marketing tool. Therefore, marketing communications, or the promotional mix, must be designed not only to present the event and/or facility in the most appropriate manner but it should also capitalize on the event itself as a way to interact with customers. An important strategy to harness the synergy across various tactics to achieve marketing outcomes is known as **integrated marketing communication (IMC)**. IMC uses a consistent delivery strategy through which brand positioning, personality, and key messaging are delivered synergistically across every element of communication (Smith, Berry, & Pulford, 1999). With IMC, all sources of contact that a stakeholder has with the event are potential delivery channels (Shimp, 2003). Because opinions are formed based on marketing messages and interaction with the business (Belch & Belch, 2004), it is important to coordinate all messages and points of contact between

integrated marketing communication (IMC) A delivery strategy that ensures that brand positioning, personality, and key messages are delivered synergistically across every element of communication.

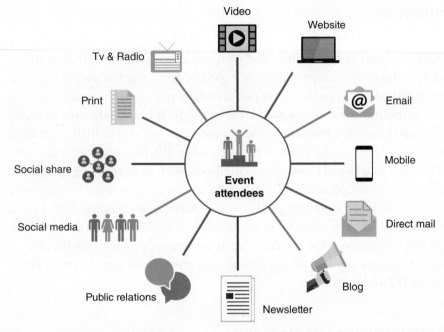

Figure 8-1 Marketing Channels

the marketer and the consumer. IMC consists of various tactics that work best when they are integrated to achieve the overall marketing goals (Raj, Walters, & Rashid, 2009). **Figure 8-1** illustrates the various channels that a marketer must consider when disseminating event messaging. For example, suppose you are the managing supervisor for a recreation center with regular adult basketball leagues. You decide to host a 3-on-3 basketball tournament with goals to attract teams from the region. As you think about your promotional plan and how you will attract athletes to your tournament, consider how the message will be conveyed for each channel presented in Figure 8-1. If you were the event director for this tournament, how would you use each of these channels?

Traditional marketing has its place, but it can be costly and might not help marketers reach their target markets. Integrating the message into a number of tactics ensures greater opportunity to achieve marketing goals (Raj et al., 2009). With the average consumer exposed to over 3,000 advertisements daily (Kimmel, 2005), consumers are worn out by familiar/repeated messages. Marketers aggressively promote messages that can stand out and grab the attention of the consumer in a cluttered marketplace (Hutter & Hoffman, 2011). However, there is a cost. These additional activities produce a higher marketing budget and prompt even stronger avoidance and worn-out behavior from consumers. There has been a trend in recent years toward more digital marketing tactics and use of social media. This can be a very cost-effective tactic if the target market's media preferences align.

Social media is an effective and efficient way to reach target markets and it is important to understand how the different demographic groups engage with the various platforms. According to Smith and Anderson (2018), the majority of Americans use Facebook (68 percent) and YouTube (73 percent) followed by Instagram (35 percent), Pinterest (29 percent), Snapchat (27 percent), LinkedIn (25 percent), and Twitter (24 percent). Youth, aged 18 to 24 years, are more likely to use Instagram, Snapchat, and Twitter. More than 78 percent of 18 to 24 year olds use Snapchat, but this falls drastically to 54 percent for those 24 to 29 years of age (Smith & Anderson 2018). Women are more likely than men to use Facebook (74/62 percent), Pinterest (41/16 percent), Instagram (39/30 percent), and Snapchat (31/23 percent), while men are more likely to use YouTube (75/72 percent). While it is easy and cost-effective to post information on social media platforms, for it to be effective, the organization or event must have followers! To get followers, creating content that is interesting and engaging is critical. Creating short, engaging videos or posting interesting photos that capture people's attention and inspire them to share with others is the best way to attract new followers. If the newly reached individual likes the content you post, he or she is more likely to follow you for more.

Guerrilla and viral marketing tactics have grown in an effort to creatively capture new audiences through innovation and surprise (Hutter & Hoffman, 2011). The objective of **guerrilla marketing** is to gain large effects at low expenses (Baltes & Leibing, 2008), while **viral marketing** uses social networks to increase brand awareness through self-replicating processes (Raj et al., 2009). Guerrilla marketing certainly has viral tendencies, but it does not necessarily depend on social networks to increase awareness. While past efforts of guerrilla marketing were considered "below the line," as the focus was to weaken competitors and level the playing field (Levinson, 1984), recent efforts are customer focused, specifically to win customers (Solomon et al., 2009). Rather than sabotaging a brand, which could have a potentially negative effect on the saboteur, organizations are using guerrilla tactics to

guerrilla marketing
A marketing strategy that uses unique methods to gain large effects at low expenses.

viral marketing The use of social networks to increase brand awareness through self-replicating processes.

surprise their target markets. For example, Adidas set up a giant shoebox at an event and as customers walked by, a secret door would open and free shoes would be given to the passerby. This tactic introduced the audience to a new product line in a surprising and innovative way, thereby creating a buzz around the new shoe offering.

The objective of both of these approaches is to create a buzz around a product to inspire word-of-mouth advertising at a low cost. The advent of social networking has facilitated further word-of-mouth through viral marketing and has become a crucial strategy for marketers. Social networking sites have enabled organizations to connect with consumers on an individual level that traditional methods have been unable to do. Information can spread more readily by word-of-mouth among social networks, which organizations can capitalize on to generate a significant increase in sales while reducing promotion costs (Li, Lai, & Chen, 2011).

SUMMARY

Marketing for facility and sport events requires a very complex plan actualized through a clear and well-developed overall strategy. Successful execution of the plan will occur through careful research of internal and external factors that influence the sport product, the consumer and competitors, the ability to capitalize on opportunities that this information provides, the execution of the plan, and careful assessment of the results. Considering ways in which several marketing tactics can be integrated into the promotional mix to ensure multiple opportunities to engage with customers is critical.

DISCUSSION QUESTIONS

1. Describe why feasibility studies are necessary. How is a SWOT analysis used to develop a marketing plan?
2. Explain why it is necessary to segment. What are the elements that make up segmentation? How might this information be used to create a consumer profile?
3. What is relationship marketing? Describe how this might be implemented for a sport event.
4. Discuss the importance of a pricing strategy. Explain the four Cs and describe how they impact pricing.
5. What is integrated marketing communication? Describe the various tactics and how you might incorporate them into a promotional mix for a sport facility.

Case STUDY

If You Build It, Will They Come?

Contrary to popular belief, "they" do not come simply because you've built a facility and/ or created a new event. It takes a strong feasibility study, informative market research, and a well-developed marketing strategy and plan to get "them" to the facility and/or event. One area communities see as potential growth for the community is investing in the youth sport tourism sector. In 2014, Westfield, Indiana, a small community with the population of 30,000 opened a 400-acre, $49 million sports complex in the hopes of improving tourism. It worked. In 2016, the facility brought in 1.5 million visitors and $162.6 million to local businesses. However, many warn that the pace of development across the United States is so high that many in the industry fear that there will be an excess of facilities and oversaturation of events (US News, 2017). The Vadnais Sports Center in the Twin Cities, Minnesota, area is a classic example of the if we build it, they will come mentality that utterly failed. The facility was built in 2010 through the support of $26 million in revenue bonds issued by Vadnais Heights on behalf of the nonprofit group Community Facility Partners (Anderson, 2014). After poor revenue projections and growth through rentals, the city found itself covering shortfalls of hundreds of thousands of dollars (PRWeb.com, 2014). In 2013, the facility was put up for sale after Community Facility Partners defaulted on the bonds when the city stopped financial support (Anderson, 2014). In the spring of 2014, Ramsay County signed a letter of intent to buy the facility for $10.5 million.

(continues)

Case STUDY (continued)

Some communities have pushed back and the residents have voted down referendums that would require their tax dollars be spent on multi-million dollar venues for children. Many do not agree that public funds should support the development of venues that might not directly benefit the rest of the community; especially if the venue fails to produce the projected economic benefits.

Suppose your community has decided to build a multi-million dollar facility for youth sport tournaments. The first order of business for your organization is to develop a strong feasibility plan and then a marketing strategy to ensure that this facility is profitable over time. Before you can do this, however, you need information in order to develop the strongest plan possible. Answer the following questions:

1. What is the mission and vision for this facility? How will your mission and vision differ from other youth sport venues? What will set your facility apart from the competition?
2. Conduct a feasibility study. Based on what you've learned in other chapters, what resources will be necessary? What information do you need before you can even break ground on this project? What will be the deciding factors to "green light" the project? What might you still need to know in order to ensure that this facility will be profitable?
3. What goals and objectives would you set for years 1, 2, and 3, respectively?
4. What is your overall strategy for the facility?
5. Develop a marketing plan based on the information that you have collected in questions 1 to 4.

REFERENCES

Anderson, J. (2014, April). Ramsey County signs on to buy Vadnais Sports Center for $10.5 million. *Star Tribune, East Metro*. Retrieved from http://www.startribune.com/local/east/253303441.html

Baltes, G., & Leibing, I. (2008). Guerrilla marketing for information services. *New Library World, 109*, 46–55.

Belch, G. E., & Belch, M. A. (2004). *Introduction to advertising and promotion* (5th ed.). New York, NY: McGraw-Hill.

Gordon, J. W., Perrey, J., & Spellecke, D. (2013, July). Big data, analytics and the future of marketing and sales. *Forbes.com*. Retrieved from http://www.forbes.com/sites/mckinsey/2013/07/22/big-data-analytics-and-the-future-of-marketing-sales/

Hutter, K., & Hoffman, S. (2011). Guerilla marketing: The nature of the concept and propositions for further research. *Asian Journal of Marketing, 5*(2), 39–54.

Kimmel, A. J. (2005). Introduction: Marketing communication in the new millennium. In A. J. Kimmel (Ed.), *Marketing communication: New approaches, technologies and styles* (pp. 1–6). Oxford, United Kingdom: Oxford University Press.

Levinson, J. C. (1984). *Guerrilla marketing: Secrets of making big profit form your small business.* Boston, MA: Houghton Mifflin.

Li, Y-M., Lai, C-Y., & Chen, C-W. (2011). Discovering influencers for marketing in the blogosphere. *Information Sciences, 181,* 5143–5157.

Moore, K., & Pareek, N. (2010). *Marketing: The basics* (2nd ed.). New York, NY: Routledge.

Morgan, R. M., & Hunt, S. D. (1994). The commitment-trust theory of relationship marketing. *Journal of Marketing, 58,* 20–38.

Mountain Sports Festival (2018). *Festival details.* Retrieved from https://mountainsportsfestival.com

Mullin, B. J., Hardy, S., & Sutton, W. A. (2007). *Sport marketing* (3rd ed.). Champaign, IL: Human Kinetics.

Pedersen, P. M., & Thibault, L. (Eds.). (2014). *Contemporary sport management* (5th ed.). Champaign, IL: Human Kinetics.

Pressey, A., & Tzokas, N. (2006). Relationship marketing: Theory, applications and future research directions. *Journal of Marketing Management, 22*(1–2), 1–4.

PRWeb.com. (2014, June). Underperforming sports complexes: The Sports Facilities Advisory says poor planning and management to blame. *prweb.com.* Retrieved from http://www.prweb.com/releases/2014/02/prweb11552781.htm

Raj, R., Walters, P., & Rashid, T. (2009). *Event management: An integrated and practical approach.* London, United Kingdom: Sage.

Shimp, T. A. (2003). *Advertising, promotion, and supplemental aspects of integrated marketing communications* (6th ed.). Mason, OH: South-Western Publishing.

Smith, A., & Anderson, M. (2018, March). *Social media use in 2018.* Retrieved from http://www.pewinternet.org/2018/03/01/social-media-use-in-2018/

Smith, P. R., Berry, C., & Pulford, A. (1999). *Strategic marketing management.* London, United Kingdom: Kogan Page.

Solomon, M. R., Marshall, G. W., Stuart, E. W., Barnes, B., & Mitchell, V. W. (2009). *Marketing: Real people, real decisions* (5th ed.). England: Pearson Education, Ltd.

Tough Mudder. (2014). About the events. *toughmudder.com.* Retrieved from https://toughmudder.com/events/what-is-tough-mudder

US News, (2017, July). Communities banking on mega youth sports complexes. Retrieved from, https://www.usnews.com/news/best-states/articles/2017-07-31/communities-banking-on-mega-youth-sports-complexes

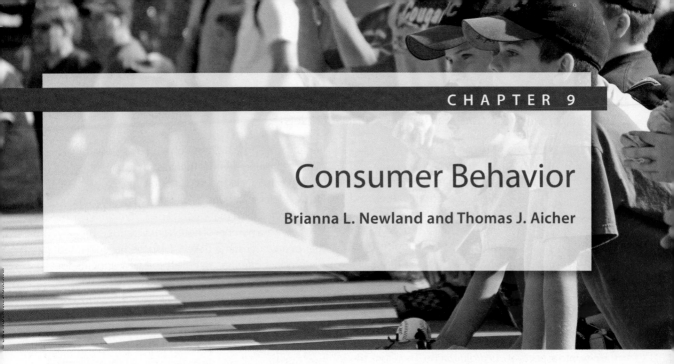

CHAPTER 9

Consumer Behavior

Brianna L. Newland and Thomas J. Aicher

CHAPTER OBJECTIVES

Upon completion of this chapter, the reader will be able to:

1. Describe the concepts of socialization, involvement, and commitment.
2. Define motivation and apply it to sport participation and spectating.
3. Explain the different motivation factors.
4. Outline the decision-making process in the purchasing decision by sport participants and spectators.

CHAPTER OVERVIEW

This chapter will discuss the motivations to participate in and spectate sport events. It will discuss communication, persuasion, and decision making by the consumer.

IndustryVOICE

Chris Pierce, Senior Director—Fan Commerce, New York Jets

I began my career in retail as a Buyer at Lord & Taylor and held positions with Calvin Klein, Joe Boxer, Diesel, and J. Crew prior to joining the Jets. The Jets acquired me to run their Merchandise business, but my responsibilities grew to other fan experience elements including all Merchandise, Food and Beverage, Fan Engagement, and the Jets Legends Alumni Network.

Working for the Jets in New York City is an incredible experience, and we try to bring the elements of the city into aspects of our organization. Therefore, the New York Jets mission is to be:

ELECTRIC: Like the nonstop pulse of our city, our team and our fans always bring unrelenting energy—under the brightest lights and on the biggest stage.

RELENTLESS: As a team, we constantly forge ahead, creating and controlling our own destiny. Channeling the power and tenacity of every individual, we stand united no matter what comes our way.

COMMITTED: Our commitment to our team and to our fans is unwavering. We know our goals and we have a vision for how we want to get there. We will share in this journey together.

One of the challenges facing me in my role is to ensure that game-day is a compelling and a can't-miss experience that delivers value to each and every fan. To ensure that we deliver the best possible fan experience, this has become an organizational priority in every way. We not only listen to fans but watch and analyze their behavior to provide engagement elements that resonate with them on a granular level. Examples are constant open dialogue with a dedicated service team, increasing the consumer touchpoints, surveys post-event, Fan Advisory Boards, and constant communication opportunities.

Another challenge is standing out in an incredibly crowded marketplace. We are competing for attention and people's limited leisure time. We are living in a world that gives us so much choice and distraction at our fingertips; being heard through all of that noise poses a difficult challenge. Rather than resist, we have adapted by embracing social media platforms, engaging emerging technologies around ticketing and finding a unique voice and position that sets us apart from others.

There are a number of noteworthy trends in the way that people consume tickets. First, we have adapted our product offerings to reflect the new appetite for ticket options as well as reimagining the experience as people look for more social interactions. The growth of data analytics has helped us build a better customer portrait, so we can understand and serve our fans better. We want to know as much as possible about our fans and their behavior in order to provide experiences that leave them feeling valued.

What do you need to know about working for the Jets in my area? Well, when hiring an entry-level candidate, I look for someone who is bright, thoughtful, hardworking, and who will be a good fit culturally. I often see new graduates who lack real-world experience. I cannot stress enough how important it is to intern or volunteer while in college. Many times, new graduates are missing trust in their decision-making, humility, and in the ability to listen in order to learn. By gaining valuable real-world experiences, these skills can be improved. What is most important to understand as a new graduate is that your first position is not your last. In your first position at an organization, you have an opportunity to contribute and foster strong relationships in that company that can and will lead to growth opportunities. Also, don't be afraid to use those critical thinking skills. Don't be afraid to be a respectful disruptor.

One thing to remember about consumer behavior—it is akin to a cloud. It is constantly in motion and changing in shape and size. At times, fans also articulate one thought, but their behavior indicates something else entirely. Data helps us understand these sometimes very perplexing behaviors. Game-day can be one enormous laboratory where we test our hypothesis and get instant and immediate feedback from thousands of fans. I love that part of my job!

Introduction

In sport, there are a number of key consumers to consider. Understanding how
and why these key consumers behave
as they do is critical for the success of
a sport facility and/or event. But, more
importantly, how an individual is introduced to sport can have a long-term
impact on how involved and committed
the person becomes as a consumer. For
example, perhaps your parents took you
to the Preakness Stake at Pimlico as a
child. In all likelihood, the meaning you
attached to the experience of watching
the spectacle of the event and the overall experience and atmosphere that
the event staff created at the stadium deeply influenced how you consume
horse racing to this day.

Future success is contingent on understanding how and why an individual or group comes to consume sport. Building on the motivations and
factors that drive consumer decision-making processes prompts more
effective marketing strategies, streamlined communications, enhanced
consumer experiences and, as a result, more loyal consumers. This deeper
understanding of the consumer can also help facility and event managers to design event experiences that better meet the needs of their patrons.
In other words, understanding the wants and needs of the consumer will
help ensure that you are delivering a better sport product or service. Within
this chapter, the concepts of socialization, involvement, and commitment
and the motivating factors that drive consumer behavior will be explored.
Having established this foundation, the decision-making processes that
individuals utilize to make their selections will be outlined.

Consumption Factors

SOCIALIZATION

Socialization has been defined as "the process whereby individuals learn skills,
traits, values, attitudes, norms, and knowledge associated with the performance of present or anticipated social roles" (McPherson & Brown, 1988,
p. 267). How an individual is introduced to sport can influence his or her
future involvement in and commitment to sport and sport events. There are

socialization The
process whereby
individuals learn
skills, traits, values,
attitudes, norms,
and knowledge
associated with the
performance of pres-
ent or anticipated
social roles.

Table 9-1   Sport Socialization

	Socialization *into* Sport	Socialization *via* Sport	Socialization *out of* Sport
Description	The social and psychological influences that shape an individual's initial attraction to sport.	The acquisition of attitudes, values, and knowledge as a consequence of sport involvement.	The influences that contribute to an individual discontinuing his or her sport participation.
Source of Influence	The prevalent attitudes and values within the family or peer group.	The prevalent attitudes and values of teams, coaches, and clubs.	The prevalent attitudes and values of family, peers, and sport.

three components to how an individual can be socialized into sport (Brustad, 1992): Socialization *into* sport, socialization *via* sport, and socialization *out of* sport (see **Table 9-1**).

How you are socialized into sport shapes your attitude toward it. For example, if you were raised to believe that sport should only exist if it is highly competitive, you might have a negative attitude toward sport for all programming that allows for individuals to play at all possible levels of sport—not just high performance levels. The attitudes and values you carry based on coaching philosophy and/or team and/or club values are how you are socialized via sport. For example, if you were trained by a coach who was highly autocratic (i.e., "it's my way or the highway" mentality), you too might believe that this is the best way to be coached or to coach others. Finally, you are also influenced by others to continue (or not) your participation in sport. This happened to me when my father asked me why I still participate in Ironman triathlons in my forties. Because of the value I place on lifelong sport participation, and the influence of my other peer groups, my father's influence did not impact my sport participation. However, this is not always the case for others whose families play a big role in decision-making.

INVOLVEMENT

consumer involvement A blend of the individual's interest in sport and the degree of importance that sport has in his or her life.

Socialization into sport assumes some type of involvement. **Consumer involvement** is a blend of the individual's interest in sport and the degree of importance that sport has in his or her life (Wakefield, 2007). Many sport spectators and participants become highly involved with their sports, so much so that it consumes their lives. For example, a highly involved fan will purchase season tickets (or attend as many games as possible), will spend money on merchandise, and will travel to sporting events specifically for the team. And in the case of some soccer fans, they may join a pride group and spend the match chanting and singing on their team.

Typically, individuals can be involved in sport in one of three ways: *Cognitively, emotionally*, or *behaviorally*. **Cognitive involvement** is the acquisition of information/knowledge about a sport. Seeking information through print, electronic, and digital media as well as attending seminars and trade shows would be considered cognitive involvement. For example, a volleyball player who watches different instructional videos online to improve his or her hitting ability. **Emotional involvement** is the individual's affective response to the sport. It includes the attitudes, feelings, and emotions that the individual associates with sport. For example, a baseball fan who becomes so emotionally invested in her team that she feels despair when the team loses or elation when they win. Finally, **behavioral involvement** is the action one takes in sport, through participating and/or spectating. This individual acts as part of his involvement. For example, following his team to the National Championship game demonstrates an involved behavior to the team. Individuals who are highly involved tend to feel more deeply about sport and are more likely to devote more time and money to sport.

cognitive involvement
The acquisition of information/knowledge about a sport.

emotional involvement
The effect that a sport event produces in the individual.

behavioral involvement The action one takes in sport, whether as a participant or a spectator.

COMMITMENT

The more an individual becomes involved in sport, the greater the individual's **commitment** and, thus, the intensity of his or her attachment is to his or her sport. Willingness to expend money, time, and energy increases as the sport becomes more ingrained in a person's identity (Wakefield, 2007). The more highly identified the person (as a participant or fan), the more central that identity becomes to the individual (Shamir, 1992). An individual who closely identifies with a sport typically makes statements like "I am a triathlete" (sport identification) and "I am a Reds fan" (team identification). Consumers who are highly involved in and committed to their sport or team are less price sensitive and are likely to remain loyal to the sport product. This means that they will spend more on equipment and event registration (participant) or memorabilia and tickets (spectator) and they will continue to support the sport product, even if the event is poor or the team hits a losing streak.

commitment The frequency, duration, and intensity of attachment to sport.

VIGNETTE 9-1

Understanding the Millennial Runner

The health of any industry is the ability to continue to develop new customers. In 2014, Running USA began to evaluate the second largest generation since the baby boomers; the Millennial Generation (those born between 1980 and 2000). This group of individuals was perceived as more active than their previous generations, developed a significant amount of purchasing power, is the most technologically advanced, and appears to consume sport and fitness differently. In a two-part study, Running USA was able to decipher some interesting and valuable insights to those managing running events. For example, in terms of demographics, this generation has an over-representation of women (72 percent) compared with the overall average (57 percent), more racially diverse (79 percent of Millennials report being white while 90 percent of all runners report the same), but are similar in terms of being well educated and affluent. According to the study, the three main motivations for this group of runners was to improve physical health, maintain physical health, and run in a unique or new environment,

and most importantly, reported being highly committed to the sport (Running USA, 2015). Interestingly, while the focus of something new and unique was important, the focus of the Millennial runner is more on competitive events than those considered "fun runs." In terms of being able to market events, the report indicated that social media is the best way to reach this group with 64 percent reporting that they learned about events via various social platforms, with Facebook leading the way. While the Millennial generation is known for its focus on "doing good," they do not select runs for the charity that the event supports and are unlikely to engage in fundraising to participate in an event. This information led to a few different recommendations for event organizers to better reach this demographic of runners: Cultivate relationships (e.g., specific e-mails based on the distance rather than mass e-mails); incorporate elements of mental and emotional health; diversify the markets targeted; add in elements identified as important (e.g., swag, cost, distances); and focus on a well-organized event.

Motivating Factors

ORGANIZATIONAL FACTORS

organizational factor
An element that differentiates one event from another and influences a participant's motivation to attend an event.

There are a number of **organizational factors** that differentiate one event from another and influence a participant's motivation to attend an event. How the organizational factors are perceived by the attendee, such as how well the organization is prepared to stage the event, can influence participation choices. The organizational components of the facility and/or the infrastructure and interstructure of the event can also impact these perceptions. Hallmann, Kaplanidou, and Breuer (2010) outlined several organizational components that event managers should include in the production (e.g., marketing, logistics, security, and sponsorship) to enhance the event's image. Aicher and Newland (2017) found that the event reputation was an important factor for selecting that event by athlete type (skill level and amount of consumption), as well as the sport type (i.e., runners,

VIGNETTE 9-2

Having a "Blast"

Beginning in 2001, the Hyde Park Blast has hosted running, cycling, and chariot racing events. Originally organized by Cheryl Koopman and Chad Simms to raise money in the fight against cancer, while providing the community with an opportunity to have fun and be active. With more than 2,000 runners completing the run each year, the event starts with a four-mile run through the neighborhood; starting and ending in the town's trademark square. Next, the kids compete in their own foot races of various distances (.2 mile to 1 mile) based on their age or ability. The late morning begins the criterium cycling races featuring men's and women's category 1 to 5 races. The highlight of the event is the chariot race in which teams of three compete for either speed or costume design. The competitive race features two runners pulling a homemade chariot with a rider on board. The race is approximately a .5 mile loop, and at times, the construction of the chariots does not hold up, leading to many spills and crashes. The crowd builds throughout the event and remains to cheer on the category 1 men's criterium cycling race. The event ends with a block party, complete with food and beer trucks and local musicians performing on stage. In its 18 years of existence, the event has raised more than $500,000 for the *Cure Starts Now* and the *Karen Weddington Foundation*.

cyclists, triathletes). Thus, failure in any production elements that can hinder the event's reputation may impact how or why consumers are attracted or return to an event. Furthermore, word of mouth about the event's reputation can influence how the event's customer service is perceived. These factors can negatively impact future attendance as well as word-of-mouth marketing and advertising for the event.

Several studies have explored event participants' evaluation of organizational factors and the impact on the event's image. For example, Getz and McConnell (2011) found that sport participants' desire for events to be well organized, to provide a challenging course or scenic route, and to offer a user-friendly website factored more heavily into their opinion of the event than more common factors such as cost, prizes, or exclusivity. Furthermore, sport event managers should pay particular attention to signage, competent officiating, and efficiency throughout the entire event (Ryan & Lockyer, 2002). Participants have also reported that they want to be treated as serious athletes who expect accuracy in timing, measurement, and performance recording by the event officials regardless of the event's competitive level (Trauer, Ryan, & Lockyer, 2003). Finally, Buning and Gibson (2016) determined that the competitiveness of the field within an event, prize money available, registration costs, and reputation all play important roles in event selection.

Similar organizational factors may impact individuals who attend sport fantasy camps or events. For instance, Gammons (2002) outlined five motivational factors to attend a sport fantasy camp, three of which relate directly to organizational factors: (1) desire to be associated with a famous event, (2) opportunity to train in a famous or meaningful facility, (3) increased identification with the organizing group (e.g., club or team), (4) enhanced association with sport heroes, and (5) development of personal skills. Similar elements may play a part in other types of events. For instance, both the Boston Marathon and the Ironman World Championships in Kona, Hawaii, require individuals to qualify or to be chosen through a lottery process in order to register and participate. The prestige and pride that participants associate with these events is highly motivational. Many of the individuals who participate in such highly touted marathon or triathlon events tend to discuss them as career goals or events they *have* to finish.

ENVIRONMENTAL/DESTINATION FACTORS

**environmental/
destination factor**
The attractiveness of a destination or the environment in which an event is hosted that can impact individuals' motivations to attend or participate in an event.

The attractiveness of a destination or the environment in which an event is hosted may impact the individual's motivation to attend or participate in an event. Kaplanidou and Vogt (2010) define these **environmental/destination factors** as beautiful scenery, new and/or exotic places, new or unique cultural experiences, locale prestige, and other factors directly related to the host destination. The destination's attractiveness may enhance individuals' motivation to travel to a destination and selection of the events in which individuals participate (Snelgrove & Wood, 2010). The location of sites and itineraries are often contingent upon the diverse natural conditions, which do not readily lend themselves to the satisfaction (accessibility), demographic, or economic needs of the traveler (Bourdeau, Corneloup, & Mao, 2002). Aicher and Newland (2017) demonstrated how destination attributes could be utilized to create consumer segments, which would enhance the effectiveness of destination marketing. For example, the researchers found that runners were more likely to explore the destination through group tours and other destination-supported activities, whereas triathletes were more interested in relaxing activities or self-exploration of the natural environment.

Further environmental/destination factors may impact individuals' decisions to travel to a location or facility. First, accessibility, or the ease with which an individual can reach the location through standard transportation, is important. Take, for example, rock climbers. These individuals are motivated by the physical and mental requirements of the route, the outdoor setting, and the remoteness of the site provided by the destination (Attarian, 2002; Bourdeau et al., 2002). However, in order for these athletes to enjoy the challenge of their sport, they need access to the environment they intend to climb (both natural and artificial). The creation and improvement of rock climbing walls have led to an increase in participation rates within the sport by enhancing accessibility for more people (Mittelstaedt, 1997). On a much larger scale, spectators at the Lillehammer Olympic Games reported that the availability and ease of transportation to the event impacted their purchase decisions (Teigland, 1999). Finally, accommodation and entertainment quality, perceived value, friendliness of the host community, and the physical environment can affect the motivation levels to participate in a sport event (Shonk & Chelladurai, 2008).

The topography of the location or the challenge created by the destination may also provide a source of motivation. For example, snow skiers are drawn to the technical difficulty of the various courses, which depends largely on the destination's topography (Richards, 1996). Individuals who participate in sport fishing and scuba diving are drawn to locations based on the quality of the sporting experience (Roehl, Ditton, Holland, & Perdue, 1993; Tabata, 1992). Similarly, marathon runners may select a specific event based on whether the topography provides a challenging or easy course (Shipway & Jones, 2007).

Research suggests that timing impacts the influence of destination factors. For instance, Snelgrove and Wood (2010) suggest that destination motivations may be limited to first-time visitors, while repeat visitors may be motivated by other factors. This finding is further supported by several other research studies demonstrating the role of novelty in event choices (Bello & Etzel, 1985; Kaplanidou & Gibson, 2010; Lee & Crompton, 1992; Wahlers & Etzel, 1985). Walker, Hinch, and Higham (2010) have found that some participants had a moderate place motivation while others did not indicate the same motivation, further supporting the mixed results of destination as a source of motivation.

SOCIAL/GROUP FACTORS

Social identities provide individuals with a sense of belonging or membership to a wider social group, a place within that environment, and the subsequent opportunity to use membership of that group (Green & Jones, 2005). Traditionally, individuals are identified with specific social groups such as gender, race, religion, and work; however, as previously noted, as a person becomes more involved and committed to sport, leisure, and recreation, these contexts may form stronger, more valued social identities for the individuals (Green & Jones, 2005). Additionally, the membership in this new group drives individuals to select events to both participate and spectate (Aicher & Brenner, 2015). As athletes join a sport and become more involved in a sport, they become more immersed in the social world of the sport, moving from strangers to tourists to regulars, and finally, to insiders (Unruh, 1980). **Table 9-2** provides an overview of each social world category. It is important that event managers understand how social world categories can influence consumer behavior. For example, as Buning and Gibson (2016) noted, strangers are

Table 9-2 Social World Categories

Category	Stranger	Tourist	Regular	Insider
Definition	Marginally involved; exist outside of the central concerns of the social world.	More involved than strangers, but only generically involved through curiosity and have little to no commitment to the social world.	Characterized through habitual participation, significant commitment, and integration into the ongoing activities of a social world.	Differentiated from the other types by involvement that encompasses nearly their entire life; focused on creating and maintaining activities for others in the social world.
Example	A new runner completing his or her first 5k.	A runner entering races inconsistently and/or dabbling with different distances.	A runner who trains for events, competes in multiple races annually, and begins to interact with other runners outside of the sport.	A highly immersed runner who trains hard, focuses on performance, organizes life around the sport, and interacts mostly with other runners outside of the sport.

Modified from Unruh (1980) and Buning & Gibson (2016).

often motivated to participate due to physical activity and improved skill. So, marketing to these motives for the novice runner is key. As the athlete progresses through the categories, motives change and other elements become more important—such as a more challenging course, novel event experiences, and how well the event is organized (Buning & Gibson, 2016).

Several researchers support social identity as a potential source of motivation to select certain events. Most participants and spectators in large sporting events engage in their sport with someone else rather than alone so that they may share intense or unique moments. For example, Newland and Aicher (2018) found that the motivation for social interaction among sport participants was an important push motivation, or intrinsic factor that drives a person to an event, for both event and destination selection. This means that an athlete travels to participate in order to improve his or her skills or set a new best time rather than external factors like the award for winning. Ko, Park, and Claussen (2008) suggest that event managers capitalize on this behavior by creating a fun environment in which individuals can socialize with others rather than focusing too much on the competition itself.

competitive factor
A rivalry or event meant to measure ability in relation to another.

COMPETITIVE FACTORS

Competitive factors can be described as the factors that motivate a person to enter into a rivalry or event in order to measure ability in relation to another person or a standard (McDonald, Milne, & Hong, 2002). This motivation is linked to the individuals' ability to challenge themselves (Getz & McConnell, 2011). The challenge may come in the form of competing against other athletes (Cassidy & Pegg, 2008; Kurtzman & Zauhar, 2005) or against the course or event (Gillett & Kelly, 2006). In either case, a successful outcome can enhance self-esteem (Ogles & Masters, 2003). Selecting events based on the level of competition is a consistent motivating factor for individuals.

These factors have led to numerous changes in the sport facility and event industries. For instance, Richards (1996) outlined how facility owners have enhanced their golf courses, ski slopes, and tennis courts to provide consumers with the same quality and challenge enjoyed by their professional idols.

TIP

Due to the importance of competitive factors, the tourism industry has begun to provide more sport and physical activities as additional marketing dimensions for travelers (Gibson, 1998). In doing so, these organizations have developed new and intriguing opportunities for individuals to challenge themselves while on vacation. One example is the Caribbean Running Cruise, an event in which runners cruise the islands of the Caribbean and run the islands when the boat docks. For more information, visit www.cimcruise.com.

MASTERY FACTORS

mastery factor A factor relating to the skill, learning, and personal challenge of participating in sport.

Mastery factors are tied to, and even enhanced by, competitive factors and refer to an individual's autonomous motivation to gain mastery of skills. Individuals who are driven by skill development, learning, and personal challenge are more interested in the intrinsic factors associated with sport participation. Certainly, those driven by competition factors cannot win without strong mastery of skills, but the individual driven by mastery is typically interested in self-competition, not winning. The final outcome is about the personal challenge and accomplishment, not the external rewards.

EMOTIONAL FACTORS

emotional factor The excitement, enjoyment, and self-fulfillment individuals gain from participating in sport.

Kaplanidou and Vogt (2010) define **emotional factors**, as they relate to motivation, as the excitement, enjoyment, and self-fulfillment individuals gain from participating in sport tourism. They explain that individuals find it important to have fun when participating at an event. Emotional factors can be further subdivided into escapism, nostalgia, and enjoyment.

Escapism has long been considered a source of motivation for travel (Crompton, 1979) and is defined as participating in an event or traveling to a facility to get away from the routines and stresses of everyday life, but not necessarily away from people (Yfantidou, Costa, & Michalopoulos, 2008). Individuals who travel to compete in or spectate events do so to escape from their home lives. Fans travel to support their teams to enjoy a release from everyday life, camaraderie, and a sense of belonging (Stewart, 2001). Likewise, event participants believe that events are pleasurable and integral to their lifestyle; they engage in them as an opportunity to have fun and for the thrill of it (Getz & McConnell, 2011). Interestingly, this motivation to escape is stronger among older sport participants than younger participants—at least in endurance sports like running, cycling, and triathlon (Aicher & Newland, 2017).

Traveling for sport can spark feelings of nostalgia and yearning to relive previous life experiences, thereby providing spectators and participants with a different type of reality (Fairly, 2003). Nostalgia can range from an attachment to physical places, such as museums, stadiums, or halls of fame; to actual experiences of participating or watching a sport in which an individual once participated. For instance, one may choose to visit the Major League Baseball Hall of Fame to remember the players of their youth, or a lover of horse racing may visit Pimlico Race Course and reflect on the important events that took place there in the past.

People will choose to attend or participate in events because of the excitement or enjoyment that being a part of the event provides. People who are considered thrill seekers desire novel and adventurous experiences associated with events (Wahlers & Etzel, 1985). For example, younger participants select events for the entertainment and nightlife provided by the destination compared with older participants (Aicher & Newland, 2017). Regardless of age, gender, or class rank, students tend to participate in intramural sports because of interest in the activity or for the enjoyment derived from simply engaging in play (Cooper, Scheutt, & Phillips, 2012).

LEARNING FACTORS

Learning factors refer to the individual's desire to learn about or explore the facility or destination. These factors may enhance an individual's motivation to select an event (Ryan & Glendon, 1998; Snelgrove, Taks, Chalip, & Green, 2008). Individuals who attended the 2002 Federation of Association Football (FIFA) World Cup in South Korea did so because they wanted to take the opportunity to learn more about the local culture (Kim & Chalip, 2004). International sport tourists, including the event participants, typically want to learn about the culture of the host country when they attend these mega-events (Funk & Bruun, 2007). Participants in the Gold Coast Marathon held in Queensland, Australia, selected the event specifically because they wanted to learn more about Australian culture (Funk, Toohey, & Bruun, 2007).

Individuals who participate in charity sport events may also be driven by a desire to acquire knowledge and information about the charity organization. For instance, participants in some local charity events (e.g., 5K fun runs) selected these events because they want to learn more about the cause associated with the event (Filo, Funk, & O'Brien, 2008; Wharf Higgins, & Lauzon, 2003). It is important to note that having a charity does not guarantee an increase in participation. For example, Snelgrove and Wood (2010) found that cyclists participating in events to raise money for the National Multiple Sclerosis Society were not particularly concerned about learning more about the organization. In fact, they found some of the other factors (e.g., socialization, cycling identity) to be much more compelling reasons for selection.

learning factor The desire to learn about or explore the facility or destination of a sport event.

The Decision-Making Process

decision-making process The process of weighing the factors to determine the best option for purchase.

The **decision-making process** can be as complex or as simple as the product, good, or service that the person is purchasing (Blythe, 2013). The amount of time that it takes an individual to complete the decision-making process will fluctuate depending on the complexity of factors. For example, it may take an event director several months or even a year to select the perfect venue for a sporting event, while it may take only moments for a person to decide to participate in that same event. In the example of venue selection, the event director may put out a request for proposal and receive several bids to host the events at certain venues. It may take weeks or months to narrow down the pool of potential locations and to conduct site visits. Once completed, the event director will continue to evaluate alternatives and ultimately make a decision. In contrast, a person intending to play in a basketball tournament may simply research a few events online, discuss the options with his or her teammates, and make a selection. Despite the complexity of the first example and the simplicity of the second, both people have followed similar steps to reach the decision.

Blackwell, Mianiard, and Engel (2006) outline seven stages in the consumer decision process (CDP) model: Need recognition, search for information, prepurchase evaluation of alternatives, purchase, consumption, postconsumption evaluation, and divestment (see **Figure 9-1**). While described as stages, the process is not strictly linear; individuals may return to or skip various stages based on the information they receive during the process.

NEED RECOGNITION

need A state of perceived deprivation.

want The form taken by human needs as they are shaped by culture and individual personality.

The first stage of the CDP model is need recognition. Kotler, Brown, Adam, and Armstrong (2004) define **needs** as "states of felt deprivation" and **wants** as "the form taken by human needs as they are shaped by culture and individual personality" (p. 4). To explain this further, people *need* to live a healthy lifestyle and *want* to participate in a sport event to do so. In terms of the decision-making process, a need recognition occurs when individuals perceive that something is missing from their lives. In the case of sport facilities and events, the two earlier examples highlight this stage: The event owner recognizes that he or she needs a facility to host the event, and the participant feels a need to reconnect with his or her friends and believes that playing in a basketball tournament is the perfect way to do so.

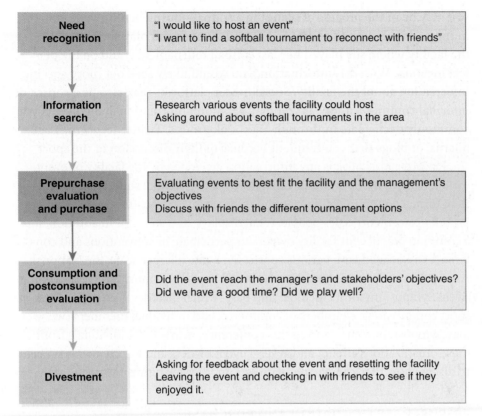

Need recognition	"I would like to host an event" "I want to find a softball tournament to reconnect with friends"
Information search	Research various events the facility could host Asking around about softball tournaments in the area
Prepurchase evaluation and purchase	Evaluating events to best fit the facility and the management's objectives Discuss with friends the different tournament options
Consumption and postconsumption evaluation	Did the event reach the manager's and stakeholders' objectives? Did we have a good time? Did we play well?
Divestment	Asking for feedback about the event and resetting the facility Leaving the event and checking in with friends to see if they enjoyed it.

Figure 9-1   Model Representing The Decision-Making Process

SEARCH FOR INFORMATION

The information search can be one of the most time-consuming stages of the CDP. Individuals can search for information from a variety of sources, which may be broadly categorized as internal (from memory) and external (from outside sources). Internal searches occur when individuals reflect on their past experiences with the sport product and information they already know about it. The amount of this experience or information may be limited. Therefore, the bulk of the information evaluated is collected from outside sources, which may be broken down into formal and informal communication (Middleton, Fyall, & Morgan, 2009).

Informal communication is the information that we receive from our friends, family, or groups of people we interact with socially. Word-of-mouth communication is the most common form of informal communication. For example,

informal communication The information we receive from our friends, family, or groups of people we interact with socially.

you may be in the process of planning a softball tournament in your community and mention the event to a friend. Your friend may suggest that the facility where she played her last softball tournament could be the perfect location. With this information, you would likely seek out more specific information about the facility. Social media platforms may also be a source of informal communication, as you may get more information about events you commonly participate in through Facebook groups, Twitter feeds, message boards, or blogs that you frequent because of their discussion of the sport.

formal communication
Information generated by the facility or sport event owner.

Formal communication is any information generated by the facility or event owner. Although this is not an exhaustive list of potential sources of information, formal communication is found in the form of brochures, advertisements, product placements, sales people, retail displays, and so forth. In addition, it is a common practice for facility owners to participate in conventions and conferences associated with various sports. On a much larger scale, the National Association of Sport Commissions (NASC) hosts the annual NASC Sports Event Symposium for its membership base, which includes visitors' bureaus, sport commissions, chambers of commerce, and individual members (www .nascsymposium.com). During this conference, nearly 800 individuals from these organizations attend, and several event owners and facility owners meet to discuss how they can partner with one another for future events.

PREPURCHASE EVALUATION AND PURCHASE

During this stage, the individual considers the different alternatives and makes a selection. As outlined previously, the individual's selection will depend on the motivational factors for hosting, spectating, or participating in the event. Using the event owner example from before, event owners may want to host their events in a unique destination to attract individuals who may not normally participate; thus, they will consider destination or environmental factors to select their event. In the participant example, the player is hoping to reconnect with friends by playing in this basketball tournament. Therefore, the athlete is drawn to an event that meets the social factors she is seeking. During this stage, the consumer will develop a set of alternatives and evaluate all of the information gathered during the information search.

Individuals at this stage establish a set of criteria or rules by which they can judge the alternatives so they know which selection will meet their needs. Blythe (2013) suggests that there are three broad categories of decision rules. Noncompensatory decision rules are absolute and will not be deviated. They are of greater importance than other factors. For example, someone searching for a softball league to participate in may not want to drive more than 20 minutes to games or practices. This person would be willing to select only softball leagues within that driving distance. Alternatively, compensatory rules allow for concessions and negotiations. Using the same example, the person may wish to pay only a certain amount for the season but will concede to a higher amount because of the convenience of the driving time. Finally, conjunctive rules are the rules by which individuals judge the final alternatives in the consideration set. These rules are similar to noncompensatory rules in that they must be met for the alternative to be selected. Ultimately, these are the rules by which the final decision is made. This act of making a final selection is known as **purchase**.

purchase The act of making a final selection.

CONSUMPTION AND POSTCONSUMPTION EVALUATION

Once individuals have purchased the product, they transition into the **consumption** phase, in which they use the product, good, or service. Once the event is over, event owners or consumers evaluate their experience with the facility or event. To do so, they evaluate the various experiences that they had to determine whether using that facility or attending that event satisfied their needs. They may also evaluate any issues, challenges, or problems that occurred during consumption that led to dissatisfaction. The major difference between an event owner and a consumer at this stage is that the event owner should evaluate the event and facility far more formally to ensure that the goals and objectives for hosting the event were reached and that the facility provided the proper service, amenities, and location. In contrast, participants or spectators would evaluate their experience informally based on the enjoyment of the event, or how well the event met their expectations. For example, after participating in a half marathon, runners may evaluate the exposition, crowd support, volunteer support, and other event structures to determine how much they enjoyed the event and whether they would consider participating in the event a second time.

consumption The active use of a product or service.

DIVESTMENT

There are two major components of **divestment**. First is the disposal or removal of remaining items associated with consuming the product that has little to no value to the consumer (Blythe, 2013). Second is the termination

divestment The disposal/removal of the items associated with consuming a product or service and/or the ceasing of the relationship with the organization altogether.

of the relationship and the return of postevent evaluations and other information. For instance, after hosting a beach volleyball tournament at a resort in Florida, the facility owner may ask for feedback of their performance. The event owner would provide this evaluation and return any items they may have used while implementing the event (e.g., keys, tables, chairs). The goal of the facility owner will likely be to maintain this relationship if the event was successful for their organization; even if this was not the case, they could use the event owner's feedback to improve the quality of their services and amenities to host future events.

SUMMARY

Within this chapter, we outlined the decision-making process that an event owner uses when selecting a host facility and that a participant or spectator uses when selecting an event. The consumption factors help to define participants' and consumers' association with a sport and can be utilized to develop strong customer relationships. Motivational factors of participants and spectators were also outlined and may impact the design of your event or facility. Depending on your consumers' motivations, you may change your event's design.

DISCUSSION QUESTIONS

1. Define and provide examples of the three consumption factors.
2. Utilizing an event in which you have participated in the past, describe why you attended the event. Use one of the motivational factors outlined to explain your motivation for participating. How might your motivations change as you age?
3. You would like to host a small community event of your choosing. Using the seven steps in the decision-making process, provide an example of how you would select a facility to host your event.

Case STUDY

Creating a Consumer Profile

Marketers understand that ingrained consumer behavior cannot be changed overnight, but niches can be created and developed to drive change. One such example is the Mud and Chocolate half marathon (www.mudandchocolate.com), in which the motto is, "if you love running and you love chocolate, these races are for you." Based in Seattle, the event takes athletes on a muddy trail running course with aid stations stocked with chocolate. All finishers receive a chocolate medal, Seattle Chocolate bar, and enjoy treats at our chocolate finisher's table, CHOCOMANIA!

© Thomas Barwick/Getty Images

You have just been hired as the new marketing director for Mud & Chocolate, and you have been tasked with developing more events across the United States as part of an expansion effort. To do so, you were instructed to develop a consumer profile for your supervisor. Specifically, she asked you to research and document the demographics and psychographics for trail runners and other runners who might be interested in longer distance "fun runs." To help guide you through the process, answer the following questions:

1. Based on the profiles that you have developed for each of these runner types, how do these running consumers differ? How are they similar?
2. How might you attract an athlete who identifies with and is highly involved in other running or endurance events to try this event?
3. Develop a brief plan that details the data you collected and recommendations to attract new athletes to the sport.

Case resource: Mud and Chocolate Half Marathon and 4.5 Mile Run—https://www.mudandchocolate.com/

REFERENCES

Aicher, T. J., & Brenner, J. (2015). A conceptual framework to determine an individual's motivation to participate in an event. *International Journal of Sport Management, Recreation, & Tourism, 18*(d), 57–81.

Aicher, T. J., & Newland, B. L. (2017). To explore or race? Examining endurance athletes' destination event choices. *Journal of Vacation Marketing*, 1–15.

Attarian, A. (2002). Rock climbers' self-perceptions of first aid, safety, and rescue skills. *Wilderness and Environmental Medicine, 13*(4), 238–244.

Bello, D., & Etzel, M. (1985). The role of novelty in the pleasure travel experience. *Journal of Travel Research, 24*(1), 20–26.

Blackwell, R. D., Mianiard, P. W., & Engel J. F. (2006). Consumer behavior (10th ed.). Mason, OH: Thomson Southwest.

Blythe, J. (2013). *Consumer behavior.* Thousand Oaks, CA: Sage Publishers.

Bourdeau, P., Corneloup, J., & Mao, P. (2002). Adventure sports and tourism in the French mountains: Dynamics of change and challenges for sustainable development. *Current Issues in Tourism, 5*(1), 22–32.

Brustad, R. J. (1992). Integrating socialization influences into the study of children's motivation in sport. *Journal of Sport & Exercise Psychology, 14*(1), 59–77.

Buning, R. J., & Gibson, H. J. (2016). Exploring the Trajectory of Active-Sport-Event Travel Careers: A Social Worlds Perspective. *Journal of Sport Management, 30*(3), 265–281.

Cassidy, F., & Pegg, S. (2008). Exploring the motivations for engagement in sport tourism. Retrieved from https://www.researchgate.net/publication/43496741 _Exploring_the_motivations_for_engagement_in_sport_tourism

Cooper, N., Schuett, P. A., & Phillips, H. M. (2012). Examining intrinsic motivations in campus intramural sports. *Recreational Sports Journal, 36*(1), 25–36.

Crompton, H. (1979). Motivations for pleasure vacation. *Annals of Tourism, 6*(4), 408–424.

Fairly, S. (2003). In search of relived social experience: Group-based nostalgia sport tourism. *Journal of Sport Management, 17*(3), 284–304.

Filo, K. R., Funk, D. C., & O' Brien, D. (2008). It's really not about the bike: Exploring attraction and attachment to the events of the Lance Armstrong Foundation. *Journal of Sport Management, 22*(5), 501–525.

Funk, D. C., & Bruun, T. (2007). The role of socio-psychological and culture-education motives in marketing international sport tourism: A cross-cultural perspective. *Tourism Management, 28*(3), 806–819.

Funk, D. C., Toohey, K., & Bruun, T. (2007). International sport event participation: Prior sport involvement; destination image; and travel motives. *European Sport Management Quarterly, 7*(3), 227–248.

Gammons, S. (2002). Fantasy, nostalgia and the pursuit of what never was. In S. Gammon & J. Kurtzman (Eds.), *Sport tourism: Principles and practice* (pp. 61–72). Eastbourne, UK: Leisure Studies Association Publications.

Getz, D., & McConnell, A. (2011). Serious sport tourism and event travel careers. *Journal of Sport Management, 25*(4), 326–338.

Gibson, H. J. (1998). Active sport tourism: Who participates? *Leisure Studies, 17*(2), 155–170.

Gillett, P., & Kelly, S. (2006). 'Non-local' masters games participants: An investigation of competitive active sport tourist motives. *Journal of Sport Tourism, 11*(3–4), 239–257.

Green, B., & Jones, I. (2005). Serious leisure, social identity and sport tourism. *Sport in Society, 8*(2), 164–181.

Hallmann, K., Kaplanidou, K., & Breuer, C. (2010). Event image perceptions among active and passive sport tourists at marathon races. *International Journal of Sport Marketing & Sponsorship, 12*(1), 37–52.

Kaplanidou, K., & Gibson, H. J. (2010). Predicting behavioral intentions of active event sport tourists: The case of a small-scale recurring sports event. *Journal of Sport & Tourism, 15*(2), 163–179.

Kaplanidou, K., & Vogt, C. (2010). The meaning and measurement of a sport event experience among active sport tourists. *Journal of Sport Management, 24*(5), 544–566.

Kim, N. S., & Chalip, L. (2004). Why travel to the FIFA World Cup? Effects of motives, background, interest, and constraints. *Tourism Management, 25*(6), 695–707.

Ko, Y. J., Park, H., & Claussen, C. L. (2008). Action sports participation: Consumer motivation. *International Journal of Sports Marketing and Sponsorship, 9*(2), 111–124.

Kotler, P., Brown, L., Adam, S., & Armstrong, G. (2004). *Marketing* (6th ed.). Sydney, Australia: Prentice Hall.

Kurtzman, J., & Zauhar, J. (2005). Sports tourism consumer motivation. *Journal of Sport & Tourism, 10*(1), 21–31.

Lee, T., & Crompton, J. (1992). Measuring novelty seeking in tourism. *Annals of Tourism Research, 19*, 732–751.

McDonald, M., Milne, G. R., & Hong, J. (2002). Motivational factors for evaluating sport spectator and participant markets. *Sport Marketing Quarterly, 11*(2), 100–113.

McPherson, B. D., & Brown, B. A. (1988). The structure, processes, and consequences of sport for children. *Children in Sport, 3*, 265–286.

Middleton, V. T. C., Fyall, A., & Morgan, M. (2009). *Marketing in travel and tourism*. London, UK: Routledge.

Mittelstaedt, R. (1997). Indoor climbing walls: The sport of the nineties. *Journal of Physical Education, Recreation, & Dance, 68*(9), 26–29.

Newland, B. L., & Aicher, T. J. (2018). Exploring sport participants' event and destination choices. *Journal of Sport & Tourism, 22*(2), 131–149.

Ogles, B. M., & Masters, K. S. (2003). A typology of marathon runners based on cluster analysis of motivations. *Journal of Sport Behavior, 26*(1), 69–85.

Richards, G. (1996). Skilled consumption and UK ski holidays. *Tourism Management, 17*(1), 25–34.

Roehl, W., Ditton, R., Holland, S., & Perdue, R. (1993). Developing new tourism products: Sport fishing in the south-east United States. *Tourism Management, 14*, 279–288.

Running USA (2015). *2015 State of the Sport—U.S.Race Trends*. Available at: http://www.runningusa.org/2015-state-of-sport-us-trends?returnTo.annual-reports (accessed 1 March 2017).

Ryan, C., & Glendon, I. (1998). Applications in leisure motivation scale to tourism. *Annals of Tourism Research, 24*, 301–323.

Ryan, C., & Lockyer, T. (2002). Masters' games—The nature of competitor's involvement and requirements. *Event Management, 7*(4), 259–270.

Shamir, B. (1992). Some correlates of leisure identity salience: Three exploratory studies. *Journal of Leisure Research, 24*(4), 301–323.

Shipway, R., & Jones, I. (2007). Running away from home: Understanding visitor experiences and behaviour at sport tourism events. *International Journal of Tourism Research, 9*(5), 373–383.

Shonk, D. J., & Chelladurai, P. (2008). Service quality, satisfaction, and intent to return in event sport tourism. *Journal of Sport Management, 22*(5), 587–602.

Snelgrove, R., Taks, M., Chalip, L., & Green, B. C. (2008). How visitors and locals at a sport event differ in their motives and identity. *Journal of Sport & Tourism, 13*(3), 165–180.

Snelgrove, R., & Wood, L. (2010). Attracting and leveraging visitors at a charity cycling event. *Journal of Sport & Tourism, 15*(4), 269–285.

Stewart, B. (2001). Fan club. *Australia Leisure Management,* (Oct/Nov), 16–19.

Tabata, R. (1992). Scuba diving holidays. In B. Weiler & C. M. Hall (Eds.), *Special interest tourism* (pp. 171–184). London, UK: Bellhaven Press.

Teigland, J. (1999). Mega-events and impacts on tourism: The predictions and realities of the Lillehammer Olympics. *Impact Assessment and Project Appraisal, 17*(4), 305–317.

Trauer, B. B., Ryan, C. C., & Lockyer, T. T. (2003). The South Pacific Masters' Games—competitor involvement and games development: Implications for management and tourism. *Journal of Sport & Tourism, 8*(4), 240–259.

Unruh, D. R. (1980). The nature of social worlds. *Pacific Sociological Review, 23*(3), 271–296.

Wahlers, R. G., & Etzel, M. J. (1985). Vacation preference as a manifestation of optimal simulation and lifestyle experience. *Journal of Leisure Research, 17*(4), 283–295.

Wakefield, K. (2007). *Team sports marketing.* Burlington, MA: Butterworth-Heinemann.

Walker, G. J., Hinch, T., & Higham, J. (2010). Athletes as tourists: The roles of mode of experience and achievement orientation. *Journal of Sport & Tourism, 15*(4), 287–305.

Wharf Higgins, J., & Lauzon, L. (2003). Finding the funds in fun runs: Exploring physical activity events as fundraising tools in the nonprofit sector. *International Journal of Nonprofit and Voluntary Sector Marketing, 8*(4), 363–377.

Yfantidou, G., Costa, G., & Michalopoulos, M. (2008). Tourist roles, gender and age: A study of tourists in Greece. *International Journal of Sport Management, Recreation, and Tourism, 1,* 14–30.

CHAPTER 10

Managing People in Facilities and Events

Michael Odio and Dale Sheptak

CHAPTER OBJECTIVES

Upon completion of this chapter, the reader will be able to:

1. Discuss the unique managerial issues associated with the facility and events workplace.

2. Identify the diverse populations and roles involved with producing and operating events and facilities.

3. Explain the factors that impact the motivation, management, and retention of volunteers.

CHAPTER OVERVIEW

This chapter will discuss the management of people in sport by looking at some unique characteristics of the people and organizations involved in facility and event management.

IndustryVOICE

Matt Futterman, Associate Manager Referee Operations, National Basketball Association (NBA)

My career in sports started in my senior year of high school when I was a ball boy for the NBA's New Jersey Nets during the 2008–2009 season. It was then that I learned to love basketball and decided I wanted to stay connected to the game as closely as possible. I saw firsthand the behind-the-scenes work that goes into a sport that I had previously only watched on TV—and I was hooked! After high school, I attended the University of Delaware, where I majored in sports management and was a manager for the men's basketball team. I learned valuable time management and networking skills as I traveled the country meeting others in the sports industry. Following graduation, I joined the NBA as the Chief Video Logger. In my new league role, I was responsible for 15 game loggers each night and would aggregate reports that were forwarded to senior management. This was a great entry-level position as it allowed me to interact with multiple areas of the organization and truly learn the business of the NBA.

I was promoted to my current role of Associate Manager in the Referee Operations department, where I work closely with the Referee Managers to analyze and track overall referee performance. I also lead our technology and innovation initiatives that focus on developing and improving referee training. This job has taken me all over the world, where I have met and interacted with some incredible people. I look forward to what is to come!

At the NBA, our calling is to compete with intensity, lead with integrity, and inspire play. As it relates to Referee Operations and the officials, we look to serve as stewards of the game. Our purpose is to develop the best professional officials who will lead with integrity and meet every moment with strength and grace. That

can be difficult with the ever-changing landscape of the sport industry. Keeping up with the latest trends in the sport and the growing influence that social media plays as it relates to officiating is a big challenge. We have taken a fresh approach to how we build curricula to continue to develop the best referees. This involves continuing to grow the candidate pool globally to garner more overall interest in officiating as a profession. We also invest in educating the public on officiating to showcase how challenging it is to make it to the NBA and how well prepared our officials must be to work the games. Through all of this, we have definitely felt the impact of technology. At the NBA, we are focused on recent technological advancements to ensure that our referees are provided with the best tools to perform at the highest level. This is especially true when it comes to instant replay and how we share video for training and development. For example, with the state-of-the-art NBA Replay Center in Secaucus, New Jersey, we can enhance the performance of NBA referees by the acceleration of the replay review process.

Are you interested in working for the NBA some day? In such a competitive and broad industry as sports, it is important to educate yourself about all of the different areas of opportunities that exist. When considering candidates for entry-level positions, I look for someone who is eager to learn and grow. The candidate should be passionate about the industry and the opportunities that come with the role. It is imperative that students understand the importance of patience. Often, candidates enter new roles and immediately try to advance, but there is value in becoming an expert in your position before looking to branch out and advance upward. Students should learn to form meaningful connections and relationships as their career progresses and invest in mutual relationships—it is just as important to give back and help others as it is to ask for favors or advice.

Throughout my career, I have found it important to stay connected not only to the basketball world but also to the entire sports industry. It is very beneficial to look to other leagues and organizations to learn best practices. Personally, I stay connected to the *Sports Business Journal* and the *Wall Street Journal* for general business and sports information. I have also had the opportunity to attend conferences and seminars such as the MIT Sloan Sports Analytics Conferences and have enjoyed listening to different speakers and panel discussions on the business of sport. Through these events, I am able to meet others in my industry and create connections that lead to new business opportunities for our organization.

In my career with the league, I have learned the immense responsibilities of our officials and their passion and dedication to their craft. Being able to sit in classroom sessions with some of the best referee minds in the world has been an amazing experience. These men and women show courage and humility night in and night out—and I have great respect for what we do. As we manage officials, we are tasked with the challenge to use the innovations in technology and communications to improve the training and feedback methods of our officials.

Introduction

Events are only made possible by the people who work to plan and execute them. Coordinating the efforts of everyone from high-level executives to the part-time parking lot attendants requires special skills and knowledge. Factors such as time, stress, and motivation all coalesce to make the event management context unique. In this chapter, we will take a look at the unique issues faced by event organizations, including how all of the different people work together to make the event happen.

Event Organizations

The organizations that bring together the resources needed for planning and executing an event can differ drastically based on the nature of the event. Two uncommon organizational forms are found in this context: Those where the event occurs regularly in the same location and "one off" events that either move around or are never repeated. These different types of event organizations face some unique challenges relating to how people are managed, which are not seen in traditional organizations.

ORGANIZATIONAL FORMS

As you can imagine, when hosting an annual event in the same site, like a city marathon or state softball championship, the operations can become routine and many people will continue to work on the event year after year. On the other hand, events that move around like the Olympics of the Final Four usually require the formation of an organizing or host committee to plan the entire event. These local organizing committees are temporary organizations created for the sole purpose of planning and carrying out the conditions of the bid documents. In both of these cases, the functioning of these event organizations differ greatly from more traditional organizations that are permanent and stable. The following is a discussion of the unique aspects of these two organizations.

One-off Event Organizing Committees

Parent (2008) outlined the three major phases of one-off organizing major sports events, which include the planning, implementation, and wrap-up phases. An example of this type of organization is the host committees associated with the NFL's annual Super Bowl, a mega-event held in a different host city each year. Host cities for the Super Bowl are announced four years in advance in order to allow the formation of a host committee, which follows the evolutionary pattern described by Parent (2008).

Each Super Bowl host committee is a temporary organization that is staffed by people who are recruited to work in areas such as community relations, marketing, and volunteer management. At each phase of development, new staff are brought in with the knowledge and skills needed for that phase of the event. The staff grows astronomically as the event nears, but once the event ends and the host committee dissolves, all of the staff members move on or become unemployed.

Pulsating Organizations

pulsating organization
An organization that creates a cycle where they radically expand their labor force and operations around the time of the event and then contract to a more modest core staff.

The organizations that produce the same recurring event are known as **pulsating organizations** as they create a cycle in which they radically expand their labor force and operations around the time of the event and then contract to a more modest core staff (Hanlon & Cuskelly, 2002). Examples of events that are operated by pulsating organizations are college football bowl games and major tennis tournaments held at the same site each year. Such organizations follow a similar pattern of planning, implementation, and wrap-up, but then repeat the process each time the event is held. Sports facilities and public assembly venues of any type that hold multiple events in a year also fall into this category. They experience multiple small pulses instead of one major pulse, but they nevertheless have a flexible labor force and go through similar organizational phases. For example, a multipurpose event facility has to organize a different approach for its staff based on whether it is hosting a concert, circus, monster truck rally, or a sporting event, as these events require different levels of security and types of services for the different number of patrons, type of patron, and expectations of patrons.

ORGANIZATIONAL CULTURE

How people interact with each other in these unconventional organizations can influence the ultimate success of the organization. Famed psychologist Edgar Schein described **organizational culture** as a set of shared values, beliefs, and assumptions that guide behavior (Schein, 1985). Organizational culture is important because it helps to integrate and teach new people the proper way to behave in the organization and provides everyone in the organization with guidance on how to handle a new situation. Both of these functions are critically important to events, where new people are being hired at various stages of event development, and new and unexpected scenarios arise that would benefit from the guidance that a strong culture provides.

organizational culture
Set of shared values, beliefs, and assumptions that guide behavior.

For One-off Organizing Committees

The organizing committees for one-off events are in the unusual position in that they must create an organizational culture for an organization that will continue to grow and add people until the event is complete. The people in the organization will have limited history to draw from and limited time to create a culture. Parent and MacIntosh (2013) studied the culture of the organizing committee for the 2010 Vancouver Olympics, and found that, at the outset, the committee based much of its culture on aspects of the Olympic Movement. However, as the organizing committee grew, middle managers facilitated the development of

therefore, creating increased competition in the recruitment and retention of volunteers. According to the US Bureau of Labor Statistics (2016), the national volunteer rate decreased by .4 percent in the 2015 period. Although accurate data are not available for the rate of volunteerism in the sport industry, it is prudent for human resource managers and volunteer coordinators to heed national trends and plan accordingly.

According to the Independent Sectors 2017 Study, 63 million Americans volunteer and give approximately 8 billion hours of their time to various organizations. The study calculates the value of a volunteer hour to be $24.14, which means that volunteers are contributing approximately $193 billion to the national economy with the average volunteer working approximately 127 hours per year (the equivalent of 3.9 million full-time workers). Although data regarding volunteer participation in sport as a separate sector are not readily available, if we follow Chelladurai's (2006) lead and use Tedrick and Henderson's (1989) estimate that 21 percent of all volunteers do so in a sport setting, we can calculate that 13.2 million Americans volunteer in sport for an approximate economic value of $40 billion (the equivalent of 797,000 full time workers). As impressive as these economic contributions are, experts in the field contend that the focus of volunteers' impact should be on the service and knowledge that they deliver, as in many cases, they are the "core component of the sport delivery service" (Green and Chalip, 1998, p.14) and offer a non-economic benefit that is tied to their ability to give direct and candid feedback to the organization (Chelladurai, 2006).

DEFINING VOLUNTEERS

While there exists wide consensus regarding the importance of volunteer workers in the delivery of both sport and non-profit services, less clarity exists with regard to a clear and universally applicable definition of volunteerism. Issues of motivation, satisfaction, and reward seem to complicate both understanding and application of the word.

Ilsley (1990) defines volunteerism as commitment to a cause or to other people in the deliberate spirit of service in response to perceived social needs. Often, these actions occur within a formal organizational environment and are carried out in return for **intrinsic rewards**. Morris (1969, p. 23) defined volunteers as "people who undertake unpaid work for the community as a whole or for individual members of it." Henderson (1984, p. 55)

intrinsic rewards
Internal drive to perform tasks within the organization.

simply suggests that a "volunteer is someone who freely chooses to give his/her time and effort for no monetary gain."

As you can see, the definitions above provide an overarching definition of a volunteer as someone who, generally speaking, freely chooses to act in fulfillment of a need, with a recognition toward social responsibility, without concern for monetary gain. In other words, volunteerism is an altruistic act. In the United States, the Volunteer Protection act of 1997 states that a volunteer is someone who performs services for a non-profit organization or government entity without compensation or does not receive anything in lieu of compensation in excess of $500 per year.

However, from a management perspective, it is important to view volunteers as more than altruistic actors. Indeed, issues of egoistic-based motivation and **extrinsic rewards** should be considered. Hence, volunteers cannot be understood from a singular or unidimensional view. For example, at a community-based sports facility in Northeast Ohio, the management staff has to deal with a wide range of volunteer types. Some of the volunteer population gives their time just to give back to the community, whereas others are looking to gain experience and hopefully further their career in the sports industry.

extrinsic rewards
External drive to perform tasks within the organization.

VOLUNTEER CHARACTERISTICS

The wide range of activities in which volunteers engage, the motivational factors, and the personal characteristics of the volunteer further complicate defining volunteerism. Often, volunteers utilize their leisure time in pursuit of the endeavor to which they have committed themselves (Stebbins, 2002). Volunteers also represent different socio-demographic segments of society ranging across age, gender, economic status, political ideology, geographic constraints, and ethnic background. Stebbins (2004) separates volunteerism into three main forms of leisure: *Serious, casual, and project based.*

Volunteering as Serious Leisure

Volunteering as serious leisure is defined as a methodical and deliberate pursuit of a voluntary activity, which gives the participant an adequate challenge in which they can acquire, develop, and express special skills, knowledge, and experience. Volunteering as serious leisure is also referred to as career volunteering, which often occurs at the pulsating organization outlined earlier in the chapter. Examples of career volunteering could be working with people with disabilities, serving on the board of a non-profit sports

specialist volunteer
Volunteers who could fill technical roles or bring specific skill sets to the event or organization.

organization, working with children in literacy and reading programs, or coaching youth sports. Career volunteers often fill the role of a **specialist volunteer**. Specialist volunteers are volunteers who could fill technical roles or bring specific skill sets to the event or organization (Costa et al., 2006). Volunteers within the specialist group tend to be repeat volunteers and have high levels of retention.

Volunteering as Casual Leisure

In contrast, volunteering as casual leisure or episodic volunteering does not require the acquisition or attainment of any special skills or knowledge (Stebbins, 2004). Casual volunteer (or **episodic volunteer**) activities are usually short term, require lower levels of commitment, and are non-specialist in nature. They include activities such as taking tickets at a community sports event, ushering, distributing information, or emptying garbage cans at community events. Stebbins (2004) describes project-based leisure volunteering as a short-term, yet reasonably complicated, one-off or occasional activity.

episodic volunteer
Short-term volunteers who require lower levels of commitment and are non-specialist in nature.

Project-based Volunteering

Project-based leisure volunteering, like serious leisure, will require skill, knowledge, and careful planning. However, it does not turn into a long-term ongoing commitment. Examples of project-based volunteering would be preparation for a one-time civic event, a sports tournament, a political rally, or a victory celebration.

VOLUNTEER DEMOGRAPHICS

Research has also taken the demographic characteristics of age, gender, and marital status into account when comparing the volunteer's reasons for engagement in volunteer activity. Age has been found to impact the motivation of older volunteers, citing "contribution to the community" as a motive more often than for younger respondents. Younger respondents, on the other hand, cited the "ability to obtain relevant job skills" as a motive to volunteer more than older respondents (Sheptak and Menaker, 2016).

The idea that engaging in volunteer activity is used by individuals to gain experience, enhance one's own skill set and develop career opportunities presents another challenge to volunteer managers in sports organizations. In an environment in which retaining volunteer talent is essential, it becomes important to have systems in place to track volunteer motivation and satisfaction.

VOLUNTEER MOTIVATION

Studying motivational theories builds a foundation upon which volunteer motivation can be better understood and is, therefore, important to volunteer managers in sport. Volunteers are driven to action by many factors, whether it be the organization itself, the event, personal ties, or fulfillment of personal needs. **Egoism** and **altruism** are two major factors that come up in research on volunteer motivation. Egoism focuses on fulfillment of personal needs as the primary motivating factor, and altruism focuses on helping others. Another popular approach applied to volunteer motivation includes three components: Altruistic motives, egoistic motives, and social motives (AES Motives) (Snyder and Cantor, 1998).

egoism Fulfillment of personal needs as the primary motivating factor.

altruism Individual's selfless desire to help improve others' welfare.

Altruistic Motives

Altruistic motives include the individual's selfless desire to help improve others' welfare. For example, volunteers' work includes coaching children in need, staffing a local community center, or working in child literacy programs such as America Scores.

Egoistic Motives

Egoistic motives focus on the individual's self-driven needs and rewards that could improve his or her own status. Gaining career-related experience and gaining greater social acceptance are common egoistic motivations. For example, volunteers serve as coaches or managers in youth sports so that their children can experience the benefits of participation; volunteers serve on boards of organizations to improve their status; volunteers engage in volunteer activities in organizations to help improve their chances of securing permanent employment or learning the skills to help them do so.

Social Motives

Social motive refers to the building of relationships with others or paying back or offsetting a debt to society. For example, an individual volunteering in an organization that had served them in some way gives their time as a sense of duty or reciprocation; volunteers participate in services with the idea that they will meet new people and build social relationships.

AES Motives Applied

To illustrate the application of AES motives, we use the findings of a study conducted at the Twin-Cities Marathon in 2004. In this study, Bang and Ross (2004) found seven factors that affect volunteer motivation. Those factors were: Expression of values; community involvement; intrapersonal contacts; career orientation; personal growth; extrinsic rewards; and love of sport. As you can see, each of these factors holds an altruistic, egoistic, or social motive (and sometimes more than one). For example, the motivation factor, "intrapersonal contacts" could be an egoistic motive in that the volunteer could be networking to make future professional contacts but could also be a social motive in that the volunteer is looking to network to make personal connections. The "love of sport" factor could be seen as both altruistic and social. Whereas a factor such as "career orientation" would be purely egoistic. To be clear, there is no value judgment placed on any of the altruistic, egoistic, or social motives. One is not better than the other. However, as has already been stated, it is important that the volunteer manager be cognizant of why his or her volunteer workers are giving their time. In doing so, the organization or event can benefit from higher volunteer satisfaction and retention rates.

VOLUNTEER SATISFACTION

In the context of paid work, job satisfaction can be seen as an emotional reaction based on previous experiences, expectations, and viable alternatives (Balzer, Kihm, Smith, Irwin, Bachiochi, Robie, Sinar, & Parra, 1997). Furthermore, job satisfaction is driven by someone's affective state or attitude toward the work that he or she does based on his or her own perceptions about the job that is done, management styles, organizational climate (internal and external), co-worker relations, benefits, and financial compensation.

There is a common misconception that human resource models developed within the context of paid work will translate equally well to a volunteer environment. Although it should be recognized that there is value to be had from traditional human resource models, they do not account for the fact that volunteerism in sport is often a leisure choice and not a work choice.

Therefore, the needs and values that prompt satisfaction from volunteering may not be fully represented by measurement items related to paid work.

Research found that volunteer satisfaction is a complex concept that can change as the volunteer experiences the event. Therefore, the event (or volunteer episode) itself can influence satisfaction. Green and Chalip's (2004) research at the 2000 Summer Olympics in Sydney, Australia, found that a volunteer's satisfaction with his or her experience drives eventual commitment and that satisfaction is driven by benefits that are obtained by participating in the voluntary experience. The question that should be asked at this point is "how can a volunteer manager control the experiential outcome of an event?" The obvious answer is that managers in a volunteer setting cannot possibly control the experiential outcome for one, let alone hundreds of volunteers. To this point, numerous researchers and practitioners alike have argued that a number of the factors that influence volunteers' satisfaction are outside of the direct control of the volunteer organization and suggest that managers in a volunteer setting need to focus on areas where they can have an impact (Sheptak & Menaker, 2016).

One of the areas that fall under the volunteer manager's control is managing motivations and expectations. Drawing from self-regulation theory, which states that satisfying individual needs promotes increased motivation; volunteer satisfaction could be within the control of the management practices within the volunteer organization. First, volunteer managers need to understand what motivates people to volunteer in a sports organization and how they can help volunteers to achieve satisfaction by identifying different motivational factors. Second, volunteer managers need to understand the volunteer's expectations from an outcome-based point of view. Finally, organizations that successfully identify volunteers' motivating factors can assign appropriate tasks to specific volunteers, thereby enhancing the volunteers' experience, increasing the level of satisfaction, and enhancing the retention of volunteer services (Sheptak & Menaker, 2016).

It is important to note that diminished volunteer satisfaction can hinder the overall success of the organization or event. Meeting volunteer expectations and maintaining a high level of satisfaction may be one of the most significant challenges for managers in voluntary sport organizations and events. Volunteer satisfaction ultimately affects the ability of the organization to retain a trained and competent workforce, which can help the organization meet long-term strategic goals.

SUMMARY

In summary, this chapter discusses the unique organizational challenges and human capital components of running a sports event. The two major types of sporting event are those that occur in the same place on a recurring basis and those that occupy a unique space every time the event occurs. From an organizational standpoint, recurring events, which have similar patterns every year, require a more consistent organizational framework (pulsating), which will expand and contract (from a workload and labor-management standpoint) in a predictable fashion. In contrast, one-off events present particular challenges due to the temporary nature of the organization and the labor force.

It is also important for organizations running sporting events to understand the different sources of labor that will be essential to their success. Unlike most traditional workplaces, running events requires the engagement of paid full-time, part-time, temporary, and outsourced labor. Each of these labor types will present the event-management team with a diverse array of issues regarding worker motivation, commitment, and satisfaction. Added to this already-complex mix of workers is the set of challenges presented by the use of volunteer workers, who, in and of themselves, present a unique set of management issues.

Sport event success is inextricably linked to the performance of the people who work in the trenches to make sure that things happen on time, get people to where they need to be, and ensure that patrons have the information they need to enjoy the experience. Therefore, it is essential that event managers be cognizant of the need to create an attractive work environment and create systems that will allow them to respond effectively to the needs of a diverse workforce in terms of motivation and expectations.

DISCUSSION QUESTIONS

1. What are three unique managerial challenges associated with running events?
2. How does role ambiguity play a role in employee burnout? How can an event manager avoid burnout among employees or volunteers?
3. Research shows that fewer people are volunteering than in previous years. As an event manager, how would you obtain volunteers?
4. What factors motivate volunteers and how can managers address each of these motivations?

Case STUDY

Volunteer Expectations

Sarah is the volunteer coordinator for a large, non-profit, multi-purpose sport facility called VOLSports, which hosts local, regional, and national sports events. The facility is very dependent on volunteer workers for both its day-to-day operations and for

the running of events. In order to manage this dependence on volunteers, VOLSports recruits its volunteers from a wide range of sources. Within the volunteer pool are local residents with professional backgrounds who see the facility as a tool for economic development and want to help it to be successful, local retirees who see the volunteering opportunity as an avenue to socialize and meet new people, students from local colleges and universities who volunteer at VOLSports to gain experience and network, and volunteers who want to give back to the sport that they played in their youth. Most VOLSports' volunteers have been there for numerous years. As a facility/organization that is dependent on the contribution of volunteers, it is Sarah's job, as the volunteer coordinator, to understand volunteer motivations and try to manage their expectations and satisfaction. One of the policies that Sarah has put in place is a seniority-based job selection process. In other words, the longer serving volunteers have first choice at the jobs they do. The introduction of the seniority-based selection system was put in place to address previously low levels of volunteer satisfaction and was welcomed by the senior volunteers at VOLSports. In fact, a recent satisfaction survey that Sarah sent to volunteers showed that volunteers with over one year of service to VOLSports felt that the policy demonstrated appreciation of service. This perceived appreciation gave senior volunteers a higher level of commitment to VOLSports.

During events, one of the important tasks that volunteers fulfill is working in the parking lot, taking fees, and directing traffic. Overall, the parking system works but tends to get congested and unruly at times. Stuart is a new volunteer who has worked at VOLSports three times. Stuart is a Police Captain in the neighboring town and has over 20 years' experience and extensive training in traffic management. However, even though Stuart has requested to work parking lot duty, Sarah is yet to place him there because all of the parking lot jobs are taken. She places Stuart at the information desk. After his second shift at the information desk, Stuart becomes frustrated and lets Sarah know that they are not using his skills to improve the facility and that he feels like he is wasting his time sitting at the information desk. He has ideas to make the parking lot flow better and wants to be part of the "parking lot crew." He states that if he continues to be placed at the information desk, he will stop volunteering.

As the volunteer coordinator, Sarah is faced with a dilemma. If she does not address Stuart's concerns, she not only risks losing him as a volunteer but he, as a local volunteer, may have had a negative experience. If she circumvents the seniority system and allows Stuart to work in the parking lot, she risks upsetting numerous volunteers and unsettling the job selection process. The result of the latter could be catastrophic from a volunteer management and retention standpoint.

1. What suggestions would you give to Sarah when it comes to dealing with Stuart?
2. Where do you think the flaw in the VOLSports volunteer job selection system is? How would you change it?
3. Why is understanding volunteer motivations and expectations so important to volunteer coordinators?

REFERENCES

Balzer, W. K., Kihm, J. A., Smith, P. C., Irwin, J. L., Bachiochi, P. D., Robie, C., Sinar, E. F., & Parra, L. F. (1997). *Users' manual for the Job Descriptive Index (JDI; 1997 Revision) and the Job In General scales.* Bowling Green, OH: Bowling Green State University.

Bang, H., & Ross, S. (2004). *Volunteer motivation and satisfaction,* retrieved from http://www.hrsm.sc.edu/JVEM/Vol1No1/VolunteerMotivation.pdf on May 12, 2010

Bureau of Labor Statistics. (2016). *Volunteering in the United States - 2015,* retrieved from https://www.bls.gov/news.release/volun.nr0.htm.

Chelladurai, P. (2006). *Human resource management in sport and recreation* (2nd ed.). Champaign, IL: Human Kinetics.

Costa, C., Chalip, L., Green, B. C., & Simes, C. (2006). Reconsidering the role of training in event volunteers' satisfaction. *Sport Management Review, 9,* 165–182.

Deery, M. (2010). Employee retention strategies for event management. In T. Baum, M. Deery, C. Hanlon, L. Lockstone, & K. Smith (Eds.), *People and work in events and conventions: A research perspective* (127–137). London: CAB International.

Green, B. C., & Chalip, L. (1998). Sport volunteers: Research agenda and application. *Sport Marketing Quarterly, 7*(2), 14–23.

Green, B. C., & Chalip, L. (2004). Paths to volunteer commitment: Lessons from the Sydney Olympic Games. In R. A. Stebbins, & M. Graham (Eds.), *Volunteering as leisure/leisure as volunteering: An international assessment* (pp. 49–67). Cambridge, MA: CABI Publishing.

Hanlon, C., & Cuskelly, G. (2002). Pulsating major sport event organizations: A framework for inducting managerial personnel. *Event Management, 7*(4), 231–243.

Hanlon, C., & Jago, L. (2004). The challenge of retaining personnel in major sport event organizations. *Event Management, 9*(1/2), 39–49.

Henderson, K. A. (1984). Volunteerism as leisure. *Journal of Voluntary Action Research, 13,* 55–63.

Ilsley, P. J. (1990). *Enhancing the volunteer experience: New insights on strengthening volunteer participation, learning, and commitment.* San Francisco: Jossey-Bass.

Kalleberg, A. L. (2000). Nonstandard employment relations: Part-time, temporary and contract work. *Annual Review of Sociology, 26,* 341–365.

Morris, D. (1969). Voluntary work in the welfare state. London: Routledge.

Odio, M. A., Walker, M., & Kim, M. (2013). Examining the stress and coping process of mega-event employees. *International Journal of Event and Festival Management, 4*(2), 140–155.

Odio, M. A., Wells, J., & Kerwin, S. (2014). Full-time student, part-time employee: Capturing the effects of socialization influence on affective commitment for student employees. *Event Management, 18*(3), 325–336.

Parent, M. M. (2008). Evolution and issue patterns for major-sport-event organizing committees and their stakeholders. *Journal of Sport Management, 22*(2), 135–164.

Parent, M. M. (2010). Decision making in major sports events over time: Parameters, drivers, and strategies. *Journal of Sport Management, 24*(3), 291–318.

Parent, M. M., & MacIntosh, E. W. (2013). Organizational culture evolution in temporary organizations: The case of the 2010 Olympic Winter Games. *Canadian Journal of Administrative Sciences, 30*(4), 223–237.

Schein, E. H. (1985). Organizational culture and leadership. San Francisco, CA: Jossey Bass.

Sheptak Jr, R. D., & Menaker, B. E. (2016). The frustration factor: Volunteer perspectives of frustration in a sport setting. *Voluntas: International Journal of Voluntary and Non-Profit Organizations, 27*(2), 831–852.

Snyder, M., & Cantor, N. (1998). Understanding personality and social behavior: A functionalist strategy. In D. Gilbert, S. Fiske, & G. Lindzey (Eds.), *The handbook of social psychology: Vol. 1* (4th ed.), (pp. 635–679). New York: McGraw-Hill

Stebbins, R. A. (2002). Choice in experiential definitions of leisure. *Leisure Studies Association Newsletter, 63* (November), 18–20.

Stebbins, R. A. (2004). Introduction to volunteering as leisure. In R. A. Stebbins, & M. Graham (Eds.), *Volunteering as leisure, leisure as volunteering: An international assessment* (pp. 1–12). Cambridge, MA: CABI Publishing.

Tedrick, T., & Henderson, K. (1989). *Volunteers in leisure*. Reston, VA: American Alliance for Health, Physical Education, Recreation, and Dance.

Xing, X., & Chalip, L. (2009). Marching in the glory: Experiences and meanings when working for a sport mega-event. *Journal of Sport Management, 23*(2), 210–237.

Xing, X., & Chalip, L. (2012). Challenges, obligations, and pending career interruptions: Securing meanings at the exit stage of sport mega-event work. *European Sport Management Quarterly, 12*(4), 375–396.

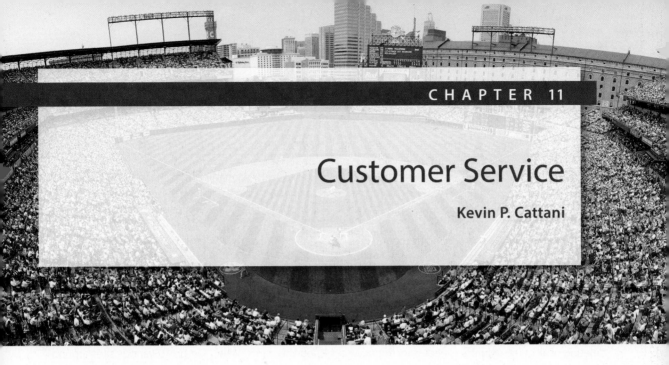

CHAPTER 11

Customer Service

Kevin P. Cattani

CHAPTER OBJECTIVES

Upon completion of this chapter, the reader will be able to:

1. Explain what customer service is and the qualities that are necessary to provide exceptional customer service.
2. Understand why service quality is important to sport managers looking to maximize their organization's standing in the sport marketplace.
3. Understand and create a customer service plan suitable for many small to medium sport organizations.
4. Identify and describe ways to measure customer service that are useful and easy to understand.
5. Identify and describe several positive and negative consequences of customer service in a sport business marketplace.

CHAPTER OVERVIEW

This chapter will review the various aspects involved with customer service in the sport marketplace. It will first discuss what customer service is and why it has become so important for sport managers. Next, it will discuss various ways to measure and better understand how an organization is attending to customer service. Additionally, it will discuss the elements of a customer service plan necessary for a lasting relationship with relevant stakeholders. Finally, it will discuss the consequences of customer service and why they are so vital in maintaining a competitive edge in an already-saturated marketplace.

IndustryVOICE

Rachel Wright—Championship Volunteer Operations Specialist, PGA of America

At the PGA of America, my current role consists of me helping to manage our nearly 10,000+ volunteers who we require for our spectator championships that we host around the country each year. Those events include the Ryder Cup, PGA Championship, KitchenAid Senior PGA Championship, and the KPMG Women's PGA Championship. At every host site for one of our events, we require a 50 to 60 person on-site planning team to assist in the recruiting and coordinating of all of the volunteers necessary to put on a Major Championship.

My path was one of learning by doing. I needed the experience to get to where I am currently and that takes time and patience at the end of the day. I started out as the Volunteer Operations Coordinator on-site at the 2015 Senior PGA Championship presented by KitchenAid. Being a member of our on-site team for that event, I had to live in French Lick, Indiana, a town with fewer than 1,500 people in total (we required more volunteers for the event than we had people living in town). On top of that, I was the only woman on our team; at times, I was outnumbered 50 to one when our vendors came on-site. To this day, I could not be more thankful for that experience. It made me tough. I learned a lot about myself and what I could do professionally. Unique situations such as those forced me to think. They forced me to adapt, because, if I didn't, I wouldn't be here. I look at my experience in French Lick as the catapult for the next position I was offered, which was managing all of our Volunteer Operations for our 2016 Senior PGA Championship presented by KitchenAid. I ended up managing 1,700 volunteers that year. It was the first time I truly realized that I

was never going to please anyone, regardless of my people-pleasing nature. For me, it was a hard lesson to learn. Managing that many people and that many personalities forced me to grow a backbone. Eat or be eaten. Learning this helped to propel me into my current role. I've learned traits that I've never had before because of this position. Although I can't please everyone, I learned how to talk to and treat those who aren't happy. That is my job at the end of the day: Managing personalities.

For my current organization, the PGA of America, the main goals are to grow the game of golf and to support our members. My job mostly focuses on growing the game. When we go to various sites around the country for our events, we create exposure not only for the city we are in but also for the game itself. It's an inherent part of hosting Major Championships. That's why there is so much that goes into picking one of our potential venues. There is a lot at stake. As you dig down deeper into my specific role, there are many times I work with a course and will negotiate a round of golf for each person who volunteers. In turn, we use the round of golf as a recruiting tactic to get the numbers we need and it encourages people to come back and play. That's a huge win for us! Our most tangible evidence of growing the game comes from our PGA Junior League. We have seen an annual average increase of 16 percent participation in junior golfers since 2012 and now there are over 50,000 participants. Currently, 25 percent of those participating in PGA Junior League are females.

One of the best trends that we are seeing is the increases in both women and juniors playing golf. The PGA of America recognizes these trends, so much so that we are giving women the opportunity to be in leadership positions. Starting this fall, the PGA of America will have our first-ever female President in Suzy Whaley. It is so empowering as a woman in this field to see another woman leading our team. I can't wait to see the effects that her tenure has on women getting involved in this game.

The best part about working for a sports organization such as the PGA of America is that we know how much noise we can make. We recognize how much power the media has and we try to capitalize on that notion. For example, we have Suzy doing as many TV interviews as we possibly can. She is the one handing out the trophy to our Champion on the 18th green. We want people to see her! We want women to see that they are represented!

The same goes for our PGA Junior League—we were able to partner with four of the biggest golfers in the entire world in Rickie Fowler, Rory McIlroy, Lexi Thompson, and Michelle Wie to be ambassadors for our PGA Junior League. Now, at each of our majors, we have PGA Junior League day, which usually consists of a surprise appearance from one of these four ambassadors among other world-class golfers. It draws positive attention! People are onboard with what we are doing and we need to do everything we can to keep that attention and help make it grow even more.

When hiring someone for the team, I usually look for two things:

1. How do you treat people?
2. How adaptable are you?

These questions can be used in a variety of ways. But when it comes down to it, this is what I am looking for. I can teach someone everything they need to know about their role, but I can't teach someone how to treat others and I can't teach someone how to handle stress or how to handle change, all of which are massively important.

For new hires coming into the work force, the biggest trend that I've noticed is a lot of new graduates who were never taught how to *work*. It's a vague statement, but many of them are underprepared for the time and dedication that this business asks of someone. To be able to physically and mentally handle starting work at 4 am only for it to end at midnight and waking up and doing it all over again for two straight weeks is exhausting.

I would encourage undergraduates to get as much experience as they can in as many different departments as they can. They need to figure out what they like and, more importantly, what they don't like. Gaining experience is one thing, but having a vast amount of experience makes you versatile. Employers see that and will utilize you in many different ways! Your skills are going to come in handy down the road as opposed to someone who only learned one aspect of this business.

In the sports business, every single organization has partnerships or sponsorships and the customer service that you give these individuals is just as important as what you give the patrons at your events. When you start working for a particular team or sports organization, learn as much as you can about your sponsors and their product(s). The dollars that they are giving your organization will affect your job and what is asked of your job in some way. Keeping them happy is key! You do not want to deal with unhappy partners. For instance, it could be something as small as if your organization has a partnership with Pepsi, you don't want to walk around the office with branded Coca-Cola products. You never know who is wandering around your office. Be cognizant of your brand and the partnerships your brand has with other brands. Trust me, it matters! When you are talking about the bottom line, there are very few things that will take precedence over that. Additionally, be ready to problem solve and ensure that any problems that come your way (whether they are under the umbrella of your job or not) are handled and that everyone walks away feeling good about the result.

Introduction

The spectator sport industry is a multibillion-dollar-a-year business that sees millions of fans attend events, spend their hard-earned money, and look to spend a few hours with family and friends away from their daily realities (Wysong, Rothschild, & Beldona, 2011). In the major spectator sport industry, competition has increased with the addition of rival leagues of same and/or different sports and the ongoing expansion of playing seasons. Many sport organizations also face resistance from their customers as a result of increased cost and heightened expectations for better performance and event quality (Howard & Crompton, 2004). As traditional revenue streams begin to stagnate and new sources of income are more difficult to come by, sport managers must look inward to understand how to maintain their standing in the marketplace while attempting to grow despite the glaring issues ahead of them. Because even the best

© dotshock/Shutterstock

teams in each league can no longer rest on their accumulated brand equity and identity, the notion of customer service is becoming more and more important in today's sport organizational landscape. Turban, Lee, King, and Chung (2002) define customer service as "a series of activities designed to enhance the level of customer satisfaction—that is, the feeling that a product or service has met the customer expectation." These organizational activities are designed to create and maintain relationships with your customers— relationships that should lead to many of the desired outcomes inherent to the organization— customer interaction: Satisfaction, loyalty, positive word of mouth, and repatronage.

Marketing literature suggests that the provision of high-quality services is critical to increase customer satisfaction and loyalty, which, in turn, increases the profitability of an organization (Anderson, Fornell, & Lehmann, 1994; Anderson & Sullivan, 1993; Dagger & Sweeney, 2007; Fornell, 1992). According to the work of Ko, Zhang, Cattani, and Pastore (2011), service quality has received attention from numerous scholars and is considered one of the most important issues in the sport and recreation landscape. They cite three main reasons for its perceived importance: (1) It is a measure of management performance, (2) it is related to the positioning of the organization, and (3) it is a key determinant of ultimate consumer behavior variables such as customer loyalty.

As we delve deeper into our discussion of customer service, it is of the utmost importance to first understand those qualities that sport managers should either look for when recruiting organizational personnel or work to train into current staff members. In no particular order, **Table 11-1** presents 15 qualities that are necessary in making sure that the needs and wants of an organization's fan base are attended to.

TIP

Since all employees in a sport organization share customer service responsibilities, organizations should consider regular training on relevant customer service skills (like the ones contained in the table below).

Table 11-1   Fifteen Qualities of Effective Customer Service

Customer Service Skill	What It Is	Why It Is Important
Patience	Quiet, steady perseverance; even-tempered care	Customers will require help of all kinds, and we must attend to each situation in a calm manner.
Attentiveness	Mindfulness and consideration of others; courteousness; politeness	It is imperative that we treat each concern as our own. A thoughtful approach will communicate genuine care and concern.
Effective Communication Skills	Sound written and oral skills replete with proper grammar and knowledge of situational communication	Dealing with agitation and frustration calls for an ability to communicate in a manner that will mitigate anxiety and solve issues.
Product Knowledge	A thorough understanding of the inner workings of your team, organization, and product	Every employee should know basic answers to common FAQs in the event of being stopped by customers during an event. This basic knowledge will communicate passion and excitement for your product.
Use of "Positive Language"	The ability to frame your response in an optimistic and customer-centered way	Small changes that utilize "positive language" have a significant effect on how your customers *hear* your response and create a perception of your organization.
Acting Skills	Skills necessary to maintain a cheerful and helpful persona in spite of customer frustration	While many concerns have simple responses, the more complicated ones require calm under pressure—either genuine or "created" through simple acting skills.

(continues)

Table 11-1 Fifteen Qualities of Effective Customer Service (continued)

Customer Service Skill	What It Is	Why It Is Important
Time Management Skills	An understanding of the time demands necessary to effectively handle customer concerns	Not *every* customer concern has an answer, no matter how much time we spend with the customer. Do your best with each customer, but know when to move on to the next one.
Ability to Read Customers	The skills (both in-person and electronic) necessary to understand the mood of your customer	Both in-person and electronic customer service have subtle clues that tip off a customer's mood state. It is imperative that we pick up on those clues in order to solve the issue in the best possible manner.
A Calming Presence	An external display of peace and composure	Many times, customers just want to have their complaints heard. The ability to remain calm and steady will alleviate many problems before they get out of hand.
Goal-Oriented Focus	The ability to direct the customer service issue toward one of several different organizational goals	While each customer service issue is different, the ability to understand the main idea of the issue and direct it toward an organizational goal increases the likelihood of a mutually beneficial conclusion.
Ability to Handle Surprises	The ability to think on one's feet when the customer service interaction takes an unexpected turn	While a customer service employee is expected to handle many different problems, one cannot prepare for and anticipate every issue. One must understand his or her support structure in order to send the issue to the right person.
Persuasion Skills	The ability to direct customers to your products and services and away from competitors	In some customer service situations, customers are merely curious of what you have to offer. Being able to direct these customers to your products and services will help your organization capture unplanned business in the face of a competitive marketplace.
Tenacity	Sound work ethic combined with a willingness to do what must be done—every time	Being able to put yourself into the customer's shoes will allow you to exhaust all angles so that, in the event that a direct solution is not possible, an amenable solution is possible.
Closing Ability	The ability to conclude a customer service interaction with confirmed satisfaction of all presented issues (not to be confused with the sales term "closing")	Taking the necessary time to ensure that all customer issues have been attended to is vital to continued patronage and customer loyalty. Do not take shortcuts when concluding a customer service interaction.
Willingness to Learn	The desire to use available feedback to make necessary changes that will improve service levels	Mistakes will happen when dealing with customers. Taking those mistakes in stride and learning from them will ensure that similar situations will be dealt with more appropriately next time.

Combining the skills outlined in Table 11-1 with the personalities of organizational employees is the starting point toward fostering relationships with all of your current and potential customers. According to the work of Gronroos (1990), relationship marketing endeavors "to establish, maintain, enhance, and commercialize customer relationships so that the objectives of the parties involved are met" and is accomplished through "a mutual exchange and fulfillment of promises" (p. 5). No matter the context (e.g., sport spectating, parks and recreation), the sport organization seeks the patronage of its customers and, in return, should provide products and services worthy of that patronage. The important notion to remember here is that relationship building is an ongoing process that goes beyond short-term gain and extends to repeated usage (along with additional potential uses from friends and colleagues) through the continued commitment to understanding the needs and wants of your customers and demonstrating an advancement of those needs and wants. Please consult the Consumer Behavior chapter for more information on these issues.

> **TIP**
>
> Similar to personal relationship building, business relationship building takes time and effort. In some cases, no actual business will be discussed in some meetings. The point is to better acquaint yourself with your supporters in order to understand how to better serve them in the future.

Marketing expert Mari Smith (www.marismith.com) has generated a list of best practices as a measuring stick for organizations of all kinds to gain a better understanding of how in touch they are with their customers and the relationships they have with their customers:

- **Conduct regular surveys with your customer database to ensure that you understand the current challenges and needs of your market**—maintaining a high level of contact with your customers not only helps you stay up with current trends but it also demonstrates a high level of care and inclusion to which many customers respond well.
- **Integrate customer feedback as much as possible in order to improve your products and services**—there are few things customers dislike more than spending time to provide feedback only to feel that no changes were made as a result…if you ask for feedback, use it.
- **Understand the power of social media (yes, even sport facilities and events should have a social media presence) and maintain active profiles on the major social networking sites**—a strong social media presence is not only an effective way to keep customers in the loop but it is also usually free to use—creating one to two posts a day should not be the reason why your relationships are lagging.
- **Have effective feedback systems in place**—many customers enjoy giving feedback (especially when there is an incentive attached to it) but get turned

off when those systems are difficult to use and interact with. Whether you outsource or create your systems in-house, be sure to regularly evaluate them for usability and ease of use.

- **Use a reliable customer relationship management (CRM) strategy**—based on your organizational capabilities and primary customer segments, a keen eye must be kept on the *technology* used for your CRM system, the *people* who manage the CRM system, the *process* used to access and interact with your customers, and the *knowledge* that your staff has to make the data useable and valuable.

- **Conduct regular training sessions for all members of your staff to ensure that proper customer service practices are being used in every customer encounter**—the chapter will touch on this later, but as all employees have the chance to interact with your customers, all employees must be up-to-date on organizational objectives and core messages in order to deliver excellent customer service.

- **Stay on the cutting edge of new technologies in your field**—it is no secret that technology is changing all of the time—ignorance is never an acceptable excuse; make it a priority to be a market innovator, not a market follower.

- **Embrace high tech, but *always* maintain "high touch" by personally (not via email, text, or social media message) reaching out to your partners, vendors, and customers**—as with many elements of life in general, communication is everything—transparency should not just be a word in your mission statement, it should be a lived ideal practiced at all levels of your organization.

  - **Strive for a high customer satisfaction rate**—repeated studies (both academic and industry) have shown that increased satisfaction leads to increased loyalty and repatronage—especially with the prevalence of consumer websites like TripAdvisor and Yelp; negative reviews can affect all levels of business.

  - **Consistently go out of your way to let your customers know how much your organization values them (beyond their financial contributions)**—events like a preseason fan appreciation day, promotional punch cards, and other appreciation-type events (these can be tailored to many segment types) continually let your customers know that you care about their role in your organizational success—this is especially true for smaller organizations that are more dependent on customer patronage.

TIP

Use your own sport-spectator experience as a foundation when analyzing your customers. Things like attending games as a fan, walking around the stadium during a contest, and spending some time in different seating sections talking with fans for perspective are all great ways to learn more about your customer experiences.

As an organization, the more of these best practices you regularly and effectively integrate, the more likely you will enjoy long-term success in your industry. For purposes of comparison, companies that are very well known for their exceptional customer service are Disney, Zappos, Starbucks, Southwest Airlines, and Ford Motor Company. Taking the above information into consideration, it should be more clear that customer service should not be an afterthought, but a proactive strategic management policy to make each customer feel special, accommodated, and taken care of.

The Customer Service Plan

Understanding that a majority of sport facility and event organizations rely on customers to keep their businesses going, excellent customer service cannot be an accident, rather, it must be planned. The following outlines the basic steps of a sound customer service plan that should provide a strong foundation for organizations of all sizes. It is important to note that a plan in and of itself is not enough for an organization to provide excellent customer service—you must train all employees, from top to bottom, on this plan and practice it often for it to become part of your organizational culture.

1. **Create a customer service vision**—as with other elements of organizational strategy, a sound vision and clear set of goals is necessary to achieve excellent customer service in every service encounter. This vision should be shared with all employees and every employee should be able to articulate that vision. To enhance this first step, consider allowing all employees to have some input into the creation of the vision and goals. When employees feel that their input is valued, organizational buy-in is typically much higher.

2. **Assess customer needs**—this step was discussed earlier in the chapter, but many small to medium organizations waste valuable resources by producing products and services that they think will sell and/or attract new customers without ever asking their customers for their input. While this step takes a

good deal of time and energy to effectively complete, a lack of attention to assessing customer needs and wants could lead to outright failure in a relatively short amount of time. For suggestions on how best to assess customer wants and needs, refer back to Chapter 9 on consumer behavior.

3. **Recruit the right employees**—a consistent message repeated in many sport facility and event organizations is that skills can be taught, but attitude and personality cannot. Richard Branson once said that where many company leaders think that customers come first, he believes that employees come first. He went on to say that if you properly train and take care of your employees, they will take care of your customers. The employees you recruit should embody the ideals of your vision and goals—if not, find potential employees who do.

4. **Set customer service goals**—these goals can vary depending on your organization and setting, but benchmarks drive performance. If your employees have no standard to match their performance to, there is no telling what your outcomes might be. Half of the battle in reaching goals is creating SMART (specific, measureable, attainable, relevant, and time-based) objectives for your employees to work toward. Furthermore, organizations should reward and celebrate the accomplishment of customer service goals. When employees know that these goals and objectives are being continually monitored, buy-in improves.

5. **Train, train, and train, again**—properly recruited employees should have the natural inclination to provide excellent customer service, but if your organization is undergoing an administrative change or a culture shift of some kind, training is vital. While many elements can be encompassed in your training plan, key issues like responding to customer complaints, meeting the needs and wants of customers, how to answer the phone/greet a customer in person, and when to perform service recovery should be a part of any customer service plan. Organizational administrators should also use game/event days as opportunities to manage and evaluate the customer service plan. When employees know that their work is being monitored, they are more likely to follow the plan and use the skills that you have taught them.

6. **Hold people accountable**—since every employee bears the responsibility of representing the organization and employees' actions have a direct result on organizational performance, it is of the utmost importance to hold all employees accountable to your customer service goals. Sharing customer service

data and coaching employees on standards are just two examples of how to maintain accountability to the customer service vision.

7. **Reward and recognize good service**—sport facility and event organizations can maintain excellent customer service practices by providing positive reinforcement for examples of excellent service. Methods for rewarding employees are varied, but having both internal (employee reporting systems) and external (customer reporting systems) methods have a better chance of creating a more positive environment. When these methods are integrated into the organizational culture, employees enjoy coming to work and customers have a better experience at your events.

While these steps leave plenty of room for customization, the important takeaway from this section is that all sport and recreation organizations should create a customer service plan as part of their larger strategy. When these practices are systematic and part of the culture, positive outcomes become the rule, not the exception.

Ways to Measure Customer Service and Service Quality

Having an understanding of what customer service is, why fostering relationships with our relevant constituents is important, and which items should be considered when attending to the needs and wants of your customers, you may be asking yourself how you can assess your organization's level of customer service. Adhering to the best practices recommended previously, having a realistic and up-to-date assessment of where your organization stands in terms of its customer service is an effective tool for maintaining your success in the marketplace.

To date, many attempts have been made to explore the concept of service quality in various segments of the sport and leisure industry. Researchers used one of two tactics: They either modified SERVQUAL to tailor it to the services of the sport industry (Crompton, MacKay, & Fesenmaier, 1991; Howat, Absher, Crilley, & Milne, 1996; Wright, Duray, & Goodale, 1992) or they developed scales based on unique characteristics of specific segments of the sport industry.

There have also been several attempts to measure service quality in the spectator sport setting (Kelly & Turley, 2001; Ko & Pastore, 2005; Theodorakis, Kambitsis, & Laios, 2001). For example, by modifying the five dimensions of SERVQUAL (reliability, assurance, tangibles, empathy, and responsiveness), McDonald, Sutton, and Milne (1995) developed the TEAMQUAL concept. McDonald and colleagues measured the performance of ticket takers, ticket ushers, merchandisers, concessionaires, and customer representatives by assessing both the expectations and perceptions of professional basketball fans. The researchers suggested that overall service quality could be measured by averaging the scores of the five dimensions.

Theodorakis et al. (2001) developed the SPORTSERV scale to assess perceptions of service quality among sport spectators. This scale is composed of the five dimensions of SERVQUAL: Tangibles (i.e., cleanliness of the facility), responsiveness (i.e., personnel's willingness to help), access (i.e., accessibility of the stadium), security (i.e., team provides high standards of security during games), and reliability (i.e., team delivers its services as promised). Additionally, Kelley and Turley (2001) developed a nine-factor structure that includes employees, facility access, concessions, fan comfort, game experience, show time, convenience, price, and smoking.

A more recent scale that measures both core and peripheral product elements is the Scale of Event Quality in Spectator Sports (SEQSS) (Ko, Zhang, Cattani, & Pastore, 2011). Remember that elements of the **core product** are those directly related to the event occurring on/in the field, court, track, or recreation center. These elements, unfortunately, are mostly out of our control. Elements of the **peripheral product**, in contrast, are those that occur in and around the stadium, arena, or recreation center. They are mostly under our control. The following description of this scale includes the scale-specific concepts. Elements that are central are labeled C, and those that are peripheral are labeled P. These elements are of great importance no matter the sport or leisure context:

core product The main product that is made by the company for the customer (i.e., the sport event or contest).

peripheral product An element of the core product that complements its existence (e.g., concessions, merchandise, dance teams).

- *Game quality* (C) refers to fan perceptions of game performance (e.g., excitement, drama), particularly with regard to the athletes/participants.
- *Augmented service quality* (P) refers to the quality perceptions of the secondary products offered in conjunction with the event (e.g., in-game entertainment, music, concessions).
- *Interaction quality* (P) focuses on how the product or service is delivered. It considers two dynamics:
  - Employee–customer—Perception of how the service is delivered during the service encounter in which the attitude, behavior, and expertise of service personnel are highlighted.

- Interclient—Perception of how the service is delivered during the service encounter in which the attitude and behavior of other clients are highlighted.
- *Outcome quality* (P) refers to what the consumer receives as a result of this interaction with a sport or leisure organization (e.g., socialization; overall evaluation of experience, which may be tied to the event's outcome; enjoyment).
- *Physical environment quality* (P) refers to perceptions of facility ambience, design features, and quality and use of signage/symbols.

> **TIP**
>
> Remember that it is easy to bring fans to your events when your core product is performing well, but attention to detail and sound customer service will manifest themselves when your core product is underperforming.

An obvious observation from reviewing these elements of sport and leisure service quality is that there are more peripheral (P) elements in this measurement tool than core (C) elements. Remember that sport and leisure organizations have significantly more control over the peripheral elements than the core elements. While many fans and spectators attend events for the core product, it should be overwhelmingly evident that their decision to come to another event is mostly determined by elements well within our control as a sport organization. To reiterate a previous point, this new information should reinforce the necessity to both hire and train your staff (everyone from the general manager or facility owner to the maintenance staff) in a manner that will help your organization to stand above your competition. To quote Booker T. Washington, "Excellence is to do a common thing in an uncommon way." While sport and leisure professionals can do little to help their teams and participants to be successful on the field/court/rink, they can certainly go the extra mile for each and every one of their customers in order to make them feel welcome and valued.

These varied attempts to accurately measure service quality benefit sport and leisure professionals in that there are many scales available that can help organizations to gauge their effectiveness in providing high levels of customer service. It is important to remember that no perfect instrument exists that fully encompasses all of the inherent concepts of service quality. Rather, each organization should attempt to utilize the method most appropriate for the questions it wants to answer. If any of the previously listed measures are too time consuming or your organization lacks logistical resources to conduct them, consider the often-overlooked word-of-mouth (WoM) analysis. Searching resources like your social media channels is a great way to get a usually unfiltered idea of what you are doing well and what can be improved. Remember that, on average, a satisfied customer will talk to two to five other people about his or her experience while an unsatisfied customer will tell 10 to 15 other people about his or her experience.

Outcomes of Service Encounters

Now that there is an understanding of what customer service is, why service quality is of vital importance to sport and leisure organizations, and how to measure service quality encounters, one must understand the outcomes of service quality in order to have a more complete picture of organizational success. While it can be argued that there are many outcomes in service encounters, this chapter will focus on a couple of negative outcomes of poor customer service, chief among them a damaged reputation and the loss of good employees, as well as the positive outcomes of satisfaction and loyalty. Throughout this section, overlap of concepts will be evident, as many of the same elements that motivate us to attend sport and leisure activities manifest themselves as potential outputs after the service encounter has ended.

A Damaged Reputation

Warren Buffet once said that it takes 20 years to build a reputation, but only 5 minutes to ruin it. Reviewing customer feedback from various sporting events, the number of things that they pay attention to is often different from what we might expect when implementing a sport or recreation event (i.e., wait times at concession stands and merchandise booths, out of place trash cans, lack of bathroom amenities, etc.). Especially in today's digital environment, news travels much more quickly than it did 15 to 20 years ago. Recalling an earlier thought from the chapter, with discretionary income shrinking in today's economic landscape, customers are relying more on reviews than ever before (especially those looking to travel to a new city). Sport and recreation organizations must dedicate time to monitoring both team and secondary review sites for negative word-of-mouth publicity, as this can lead to shrinking revenues and decreased attendance.

While sport and recreation organizations will never satisfy 100 percent of their customers, there are ways to fix a damaged reputation. The most effective way to do this is to make amends for instances of poor customer service. Many customers can be forgiving of poor experiences if the organization works to fix the issue. It helps to reach out to the customer directly. Small fixes can be attended to on a case-by-case basis, but if the issue is systematic, the organization must work to adjust its customer service plan to make the long-term fix.

A Loss of Good Employees

While many sport and recreation organizations focus on the external issues surrounding poor customer service, a more impactful internal issue is the loss of your better employees. A recurring issue in group settings is the effect of better employees working to pick up the slack of their poorly performing colleagues. This issue magnifies when it comes to situations of customer service. When weaker employees are identified, stronger employees tend to take over customer interactions for fear of a missed opportunity if a weaker employee gets there first. Continued repetition of this cycle often leads to decreased morale and less engagement from your higher-performing employees. What is worse is if these higher-performing employees do leave, they can now create negative word-of-mouth reviews, which may further damage your organizational reputation.

So, how can we avoid this issue? First and foremost, work to create an organizational culture that promotes fast, friendly, and effective customer service. Such a culture should hold average employees to a higher standard. Beyond creating and maintaining a customer service-friendly culture, merely rewarding examples of excellent customer service and terminating poorly performing employees are great ways to retain strong employees (keep in mind that these rewards do not need to be monetary—especially for smaller sport and recreational organizations).

Having reviewed a couple of the more damaging consequences of poor customer service, let us now focus on positive outcomes of excellent customer service.

Satisfaction

Beard and Ragheb (1980) define sport and leisure satisfaction as "the positive perceptions or feelings that an individual forms, elicits, or gains as a result of engaging in activities of his or her choosing." Years ago, satisfaction was the primary outcome sought by many sport and leisure organizations as the measuring stick of overall performance. Berry and Parasuraman (1991) suggested that customers evaluate their personal satisfaction in a service encounter by assessing the following five elements:

- *Reliability*—The ability to perform the promised service dependably and accurately
- *Tangibles*—The appearance of physical facilities, equipment, personnel, and communications materials
- *Responsiveness*—The willingness to help customers and to provide prompt service
- *Assurance*—The knowledge and courtesy of employees and their ability to convey trust and confidence
- *Empathy*—The provision of caring, individualized attention to customers

> **TIP**
>
> Ask yourself if meeting expectations is good enough.

While these elements are still relevant in today's service setting, one can see that attending only to these concepts in every service encounter is merely the starting point in striving for viability (where it was the endpoint in prior research). As researchers studied this issue more intently, it was determined that while a general contentment with products and services is important, simply meeting the needs and wants of customers did not necessarily lead to additional uses. While many authors still argue that satisfaction should be a chief goal for a product or service, 60 percent of consumers who switched to a competitor in the same product category said that they were satisfied with the prior product or service (Chitturi, Raghunathan, & Mahajan, 2008). As a result, sport and leisure organizations have looked to grow customer satisfaction into customer loyalty.

Loyalty and Repatronage

In a follow-up study to previous work on the subject, Oliver (1997) suggests that loyalty consists of four stages. The first stage is a cognitive stage, during which information about the product or service is evaluated and may be primarily cost-based. This first stage, while typically low on the spectrum, is vital to moving customers toward deeper levels of loyalty. Efficient informational channels, effective use of social media, and well-trained customer service personnel adept at answering questions will help attract customers to add a product or service to their consideration set. Initial awareness is paramount.

Oliver (1997) describes the next stage of loyalty as an affective stage, a combination of liking the service and experiencing satisfaction. Once adequate information about the product or service is gathered, a trial use typically follows and is used as the basis of comparison between a previously used product or service and this current one. While trial lessons, sample products, and free consultations can mean short-term loss of profits, the time and resources invested to move customers to this stage should go a long way toward establishing a solid relationship with that customer. At this point in the loyalty process, comfortability and familiarity are necessary for a second use (and third and fourth, for that matter).

As loyalty continues to increase, the individual progresses to the third stage, which is conative loyalty (Oliver, 1997). Oliver suggests that this is a behavioral intention stage. Individuals indicate an intention to purchase the product or use the service in the future. Once customers reach this stage, they have a positive level of satisfaction with the product or service, so much so that they are now willing to spend their resources with the organization. Referring back to the skills necessary to thrive in a customer-service encounter, the ability to close is one of the more important abilities. Many customers respond to questionnaires that they are willing to purchase a given product or service, but beyond that response, organizations have few ways of knowing if that intention ever comes to fruition. Knowing that your customers have intent to purchase your product or service combined with a suggested sound customer-relations management system and effective trained or inherent closing skills should equate to converting more "intentions" to actual behavior.

> **TIP**
>
> Remember that it takes hard work to provide excellent customer service, but the work doesn't stop once you've cultivated a good relationship with the customer. You must work to maintain it or another organization will take your customer.

According to Oliver (1997), the final and highest stage of loyalty is the action stage. This is where the individual's behavior toward the product is a consistent occurrence or habit. This sequence of quality of satisfaction to loyalty elicits consumption behavior by the individual. The important takeaway from this final stage (as mentioned earlier) is that as more and more outlets compete for the **discretionary income** of today's consumers, converting customers from satisfied to loyal must be an ongoing and evolving process. Sport and leisure professionals must heed the suggestions proposed earlier in this chapter to stay current on what their customers need and want. Once we think we know what our customers need more than they do, we *will* be surpassed by a competitor who attends to their actual needs and wants more effectively. Staying profitable and relevant in today's sport and leisure marketplace takes the diligent work of an entire organization, and once the focus shifts from customer-oriented to outcome-oriented, success will be hard to come by.

discretionary income
Monies left over once all financial obligations have been attended to by an individual or family.

SUMMARY

This chapter has provided insight into the concept of customer service. Customer service is attending to the needs and wants of your customers in a manner that works to solve each issue effectively while preserving the relationship created between the service provider and the individual. A large section of this chapter was dedicated to understanding helpful skills and abilities that current and potential customer service professionals should either possess or develop in order to be effective service providers. Exploring how to create a sound customer service plan will aid the organization in creating a strong culture of excellent customer service designed to provide positive experiences for both employees and customers. Being familiar with alternative ways of measuring service quality will not only set your organization apart from competition but it will also save your organization valuable resources in targeting external firms to provide those services for you. Finally, understanding primary positive and negative outcomes of customer service will help you to go above and beyond with every service encounter so that you keep your current customers coming back (in addition to bringing a friend or two along). While many organizations have turned a blind eye to this vital component of long-term success, more and more sport and leisure companies are beginning to realize that exceptional service quality must be built into the organizational mission and practiced from the top down.

DISCUSSION QUESTIONS

1. Choose a favorite sport or leisure organization. Identify and describe the core and peripheral elements of this organization. Highlight several ways that you can optimize the customer service of each element.
2. Many of the potential measures of service quality were not discussed in detail. Find a measurement tool mentioned in the chapter. Compare and contrast that measurement tool to the SEQSS. Which tool do you think is better for the sport or leisure organization you chose in Question 1?
3. Interview a staff member for a sport or leisure organization in your town. Provide the list of skills mentioned in the chapter to your interviewee. Ask that person to name three of those skills that he or she currently possesses and three that he or she has had to work to develop.
4. Review the elements of the customer service plan. Which step do you think is most important to sport and recreation organizations and why? What are some potential consequences for not executing the customer service plan effectively?
5. Think about a sport or leisure event that you have recently attended. Using the elements of the SEQSS, assess that event and evaluate your level of satisfaction and loyalty. Would you go back? Why or why not?

Case STUDY

Analyzing Sport Organization Social Media Presence as an Extension of Customer Service

As a way to extend themselves to their fans, sport organizations have embraced the splendor of social media and its wide-ranging power to deliver information and interactive content to those who follow them. Sport organization social media channels (Facebook, Twitter, Instagram, Snapchat, etc.) are often their window to the public. These portals contain information about the team, its upcoming contests, various team and league initiatives/hashtags, and fan-specific information such as promotions and giveaways, among other items. A poorly designed social media portal can sometimes be the difference between patronage and spending one's money elsewhere—in the same way that a poor interaction with a customer service representative can turn an individual away from a company. Because many sport fans cannot directly interact with their favorite sports team and their personnel, these portals are typically the best way to gather important information in a one-stop-shop setting. What basic information and news do you think should be communicated on these organizational platforms in order to satisfy a customer looking for information or interaction? Would you consider responses from the organization's social media platforms to be equal to a face-to-face response? How might these two types of responses be the same or different?

Before you begin, take some time to analyze the social media portals of the St. Louis Cardinals of Major League Baseball and the Gateway Grizzlies of the independent Frontier League. While exploring these social media portals, take special note of elements attributable to the core product and the peripheral product. What are the pros and cons of each portal? Does one seem better maintained than the other (more staff, better content, more resources), or are they relatively equal? Assuming that the portals are your only way to engage with the team, what are some elements contained within the portals to give you a realistic understanding of what you will encounter once you arrive at the respective stadiums? Do the portals offer the ability to communicate with a customer service representative? If so, which platform(s) are the most effective for customer-service interaction?

Once you have taken some time to arrange your notes, refer to the information regarding the SEQSS (game quality, augmented services, interaction quality, outcome quality, and physical environment quality). How well do the two highlighted social media platforms measure up to the SEQSS? Are any elements of the measurement tool difficult to assess based on the remote nature of the organizational portals? Does there need to be a specific tool to help measure the customer service efforts of sport organizations? How would you revise the SEQSS to better assess sport websites for their customer service qualities?

(continues)

Case STUDY (continued)

Once you have analyzed the websites with the SEQSS, answer the following questions:

1. What recommendations would you deliver to the Cardinals and Grizzlies to help improve their social media customer service?
2. Should teams even worry about how complete (or incomplete) their social media portals are?
3. Upon making your recommendations, how would you convince these teams (the "so-what?!" factor) that social media customer service is integral to their business operations?

REFERENCES

Anderson, E. W., Fornell, C., & Lehmann, D. R. (1994). Customer satisfaction, market share, and profitability: Findings from Sweden. *Journal of Marketing, 58*(3), 53–66.

Anderson, E. W., & Sullivan, M. W. (1993). The antecedents and consequences of customer satisfaction for firms. *Marketing Science, 12*, 125–143.

Beard, J., & Ragheb, M. G. (1980). Measuring leisure satisfaction. *Journal of Leisure Research, 12*(1), 20–33.

Berry, L. L., & Parasuraman, A. (1991). *Marketing services: Competing through quality.* New York, NY: Free Press.

Chitturi, R., Raghunathan, R., & Mahajan, V. (2008). Delight by design: The role of hedonic versus utilitarian benefits. *Journal of Marketing, 72*(3), 48–63.

Crompton, J. L., MacKay, K. J., & Fesenmaier, D. R. (1991). Identifying dimensions of service quality in public recreation. *Journal of Park and Recreation Administration, 9*(3), 15–27.

Dagger, T. S., & Sweeney, J. C. (2007). Service quality attribute weights: How do novice and longer-term customers construct service quality performance? *Journal of Service Research, 10*(1), 22–42.

Fornell, C. (1992). A national customer satisfaction barometer: The Swedish experience. *Journal of Marketing, 56*(1), 6–21.

Gronroos, C. (1990). Relationship approach to marketing in service contexts: The marketing and organizational behavior interface. *Journal of Business Research, 20*(1), 3–11.

Howard, D. R., & Crompton, J. L. (2004). *Financing sport* (2nd ed.). Morgantown, WV: Fitness Information Technology.

Howat, G., Absher, J., Crilley, G., & Milne, I. (1996). Measuring customer service quality in sports and leisure centers. *Managing Leisure, 1*, 77–89.

Kelly, S. W., & Turley, L. W. (2001). Consumer perceptions of service quality attributes at sporting events. *Journal of Business Research, 54*(2), 161–166.

Ko, Y. J., & Pastore, D. L. (2005). A hierarchical model of service quality for the recreational sport industry. *Sport Marketing Quarterly, 14*(2), 84–97.

Ko, Y. J., Zhang, J., Cattani, K. P., & Pastore, D. (2011). Assessment of event quality in major spectator sports. *Managing Service Quality, 21*(3), 304–322.

McDonald, M., Sutton, W., & Milne, G. (1995). Measuring service quality in professional team sports. *Sport Marketing Quarterly, 4*(2), 9–16.

Oliver, R. L. (1997). *Satisfaction: A behavioral perspective on the consumer.* New York, NY: McGraw-Hill Companies.

Theodorakis, N., Kambitsis, C., & Laios, A. (2001). Relationship between measures of service quality and satisfaction of spectators in professional sport. *Journal of Service Theory and Practice, 11*(6), 431–438.

Turban, E., Lee, J. K., King, D., & Chung, H. M. (2002). *Electronic commerce: A managerial perspective.* Upper Saddle River, NJ: Prentice Hall.

Wright, B., Duray, N., & Goodale, T. (1992). Assessing perceptions of recreation center service quality: An application of recent advancements in service quality research. *Journal of Park and Recreation Administration, 10*(3), 33–47.

Wysong, S., Rothschild, P., & Beldona, S. (2011). Receiving a standing ovation for the event: A comprehensive model for measuring fan satisfaction with sports and entertainment events. *International Journal of Event Management Research, 6*(1), 1–9.

Sponsorship

Amanda L. Paule-Koba

CHAPTER OBJECTIVES

Upon the conclusion of this chapter, students will be able to:

1. Define and distinguish between different levels of sponsorship in the United States.
2. Discover how to uncover possible sponsors and who is responsible for making the decisions.
3. Determine what a good sponsorship fit might be.
4. Understand how to obtain sponsorship for large and small events.
5. Write a sponsorship proposal letter.
6. Create a sponsorship agreement.
7. Activate strategies for sponsor partnerships.

CHAPTER OVERVIEW

This chapter will outline the main components of sport sponsorship and will help future sport facility and event managers generate ideas for forming successful relationships between sport properties and their sponsors. A definition of sponsorship will be provided, followed by a discussion of the various levels of events (from international to small local) and the various sponsorship opportunities possible at each level. The common sponsorship inventories available to both facilities and sport events will then be outlined. Finally, acquisition of sponsors, activation of the sponsorship, and relationship marketing will be reviewed.

IndustryVOICE

Lisa Murray, Global CMO, Octagon Sports and Entertainment Network

As Global CMO, I oversee marketing and communications for the Octagon brand worldwide, and I continue to consult with select, long-standing, global brands. My "specialty" since 1994 has been FIFA World Cup with this year marking my seventh one. Global platforms like FIFA World Cup and the Olympics allow me to leverage my expertise to assist our clients in making their next "right move" across some of the largest global sporting events. In addition, I lead marketing for our multi-agency organization that works across sports, entertainment, and culture. I also work to promote women's empowerment and professional development, and other strategic initiatives across the Octagon Sports and Entertainment Network.

My career path is unique compared with new graduates. Simply put, the industry as we know it now did not exist 30 years ago. It was just luck (and fate) that I had the privilege of joining Rick Jones and his newly developed firm called, *The Strategic Group*. Slowly but surely, we began to build a book of business, and with the announcement of Atlanta as host of the 1996 Olympic Games, our company grew quickly. Our agency was soon acquired by *Advantage* and then by Interpublic Group (IPG), and here I am today! It has been a privilege to call Octagon my home. I've worked with the best clients in the world at the most formidable sports and entertainment events around the globe!

Octagon is the leading global sports and entertainment marketing agency focused on helping our clients make the best decisions in a quickly changing marketing and media landscape. We help brands, properties, and athletes create partnerships, experiences, and content across the sports and entertainment world. From sponsorship evaluation to activation, we help our clients to leverage the world's biggest sports and entertainment events, creating incredible marketing platforms and hospitality experiences for a client roster that includes Mastercard, BMW of North America, Bank of America, Cisco, Delta Air Lines, AB InBev, Taco Bell, Allstate, and others. We manage major events including seven LPGA events, two PGA Champions Tour events, and eight culinary festivals. Our representation business—named 2018 Best in Talent Representation by SportsBusiness Journal—spans more than 800 athletes, broadcasters, and personalities including Stephen Curry, Michael Phelps, Simone Biles, Giannis Antetokounmpo, Hannah Storm, and more. Our global team of experts and in-house creators partner to weave technology into every aspect of our offering and to deliver total solutions for our clients.

The marketing and sponsorship landscapes are always evolving; as a marketer, it is my job to identify what consumers and fans are craving and help my clients bring that to their target audience. Millennials, and new technology companies are redefining how we consume sports and entertainment. Consumers want the ability to consume, curate, and create all at the same time—that is the new sports experience. When social platforms, like Twitter, live stream sports and entertainment content, it allows the content and the conversation to take place on one, singular platform.

Sponsorship, and the platforms they live across, are also fluid. As consumer habits and the media landscape evolve, so does the strategy and execution of the major global sponsorships. With that in mind, we create unique approaches for every client, to ensure that we're driving communications through the right technology and platforms.

Octagon also has an in-house strategy team that helps our clients to determine the right mix of investments, partnerships, and channels in order to generate business results for our clients. In order to do that, we use a number of tools and research platforms, as well as our own proprietary tools that have been developed and refined for the past 20 years. It is known as Passion Drivers®; the tool helps us to understand and quantify why fans care about certain sports or entertainment platforms. Most recently, we've expanded the tool to include an eSports Passion Drivers® study. Finally, we use social media research tools to develop insights that our clients can leverage around content creation and sharing.

For those trying to break into the industry, writing and communication skills are critical. The candidates that resonate with me are those who can clearly articulate themselves verbally and through their writing. It is a skill that will always serve you well, whether that's communicating internally, with a client, or across a varied group of stakeholders.

Sponsorship Defined

Sponsorship can be defined as "negotiated contracts between a corporation and another event, organization, or property, whereby the sponsor pays cash or provides in-kind services for rights to be commercial and marketable benefits associated with that property" (Mowen & Graefe, 2002, p. 32). In essence, a company or **sponsor** pays for the right to be associated with the sport organization or **property**. This can occur in a direct cash payment, by exchanging some service for these rights such as a local media outlet running television advertisements in exchange for tickets to games, or as an **in-kind donation** of product to help an event minimize their out-of-pocket costs. These relationships have become an increasingly valuable revenue stream for sport organizations. In 2017, total sponsorships for North America were projected to increase to $994 billion from $862 billion spent in 2016 (Andrews, 2017a). In 2016, total sponsorships for North America were $15.7 billion and sport sponsorship spending was projected to increase to $16.37 billion in 2017 (Andrews, 2017b). Sport sponsorship is considered the strongest of all of the categories including entertainment, causes, arts, festivals, fairs and annual events as well as association and member organizations.

Defining Each Level

Shani and Sandler (1996) created the Sports Pyramid that lays out five categories for sports events and organizations to describe the geographic reach and level of interest. Although there are also global and international scale categories, this chapter will focus on three: National, regional, and local. An additional component will be introduced for consideration and to assist

sponsorship It is a legal contract between a sport property and another entity exchanging something of value, whether cash or an in-kind service/product, wherein the sport property allows the sponsoring organization the rights to commercialization of its brand and the resulting benefits derived from these actions.

sponsor The organization purchasing the rights from the sport organization. This company may be a sport-oriented organization itself (e.g., a sport goods company) or may not be (e.g., financial entity).

property In reference to sport sponsorship, the sport organization being sponsored.

in-kind donation
In-kind donation or payment is the exchange of something of value other than cash currency for the purpose of entering a business relationship between a sports property and a sponsoring company.

categorizing sponsor levels. The area in which a sponsor wishes to buy will be part of the definition expansion. Currently, levels are determined mainly by how far a sport organization or event reaches in terms of geography and the distance that fans will travel or where the majority of the sport organization's fan base is located. In the current sports environment, more categories are needed to determine the sponsors' perspective and why companies might consider a property for determining its purchase decision.

National—large regional—regional—small regional—large local—local—small local

National-level sports involve interest from one or possibly two countries such as the NCAA Final Four, the NBA Finals, or the World Series (Shani & Sandler, 1996). These events have national television coverage, spectators who travel around the country, and are not focused only on the host city. If a company sponsors a sporting event at this level, it is able to reach more consumers than if they focused on regional or local events. However, this national reach often comes with a large price tag associated with the sponsorship.

Regional organizations or events are more geographically limited than national-level sports (Shani & Sandler, 1996). These events may generate less attention than the national organizations or events but they are still often extremely popular in their geographical region. This level may include individual professional teams such as the Houston Texans of the National Football League (NFL), the Nashville Predators of the National Hockey League (NHL), or college sports teams like Stanford University.

Local levels "have the narrowest geographic focus, usually a city or community, and usually appeal to a specific segment in the area" (e.g., high school sports, minor league sport, or local golf tournaments) (Shani & Sandler, 1996, p 6). Media coverage, if any, is confined to local sources and the interest in fan attendance does not expand very far outside of the local region. In the suggested new model, large local-level sports like high school football may be covered regularly in the local media and draw large crowds. Little League baseball games or softball tournaments, on the other hand, do not. Thus, a sponsor may wish to invest in the high school sport to make a more visible local impact, hence, a need for large local and small local should be defined further.

Recreational and leisure can be considered local but it depends on the size and scope of some well-organized and popular events that can reach, and do, much further, which is one reason that it cannot be categorized as simply local. An additional dimension will be included to more clearly delineate this additional category. The previously mentioned events tend to have some level of spectator focus that often far exceeds participant numbers. The emphasis of marketing this level shifts from increasing spectatorship to driving up numbers of active participants. While participation-oriented events are gaining regional and national status, this category is most certainly for people who are playing sport largely for pleasure and not simply watching, hence, the participant dimension. The obstacle races such as Muddy Buddy and Warrior Dash are excellent examples of a growing trend toward participation-oriented sports for fun.

Included in this definition are sports in which people will travel to participate. Golfing, water sports, and hiking are but a few examples that fit well here. These types of activities can be helpful toward generating tourism. Publically funded venues and property such as city parks are spaces in which sports at these levels often take place. Demands and expectations placed on publically funded community property and their sponsors can be very different from that of privately held businesses. Some of these considerations will be noted throughout the chapter.

Interconnectivity of Levels

One of the reasons why it can be difficult to clearly differentiate the levels is due to the marketing **activation** process. A company buying at a national level will still want to create platforms for activation, even down to specific local areas. Simply running a national television advertisement is not enough to engage consumers with the products or develop more personal relationships with them. Sports can be useful for these levels of activation. It is much more engaging when people can sample or try a product and interact with sponsoring a company's employees rather than just watching a television commercial telling them about products. This is why it is not uncommon to see a product sample of major brands being promoted, even at relatively small local events. The model in **Figure 12.1** illustrates interconnectivity of numerous levels that a sponsor may consider, as previously suggested. The arrows indicate activation direction. National companies with strategic marketing plans will potentially activate through the regional categories down to the small, local, recreational, or leisure level. Regional companies may also activate by using a variety of local sports platforms.

activation A specific action taken toward leveraging the sport-sponsorship relationship.

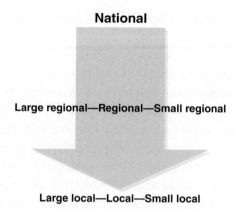

Figure 12-1   Model of Sponsorship Interconnectivity

Sponsorship Inventory

Facility Naming Rights: When trying to categorize the level in which to place facility-**naming rights**, one might at times find it very difficult to find a good fit. The level and consistency of coverage now seems much larger than the scope of just that one city. These brands now garner more national media attention and are shown on television nationally when a home game is played, which translates into powerful impression value. Visibility of the sponsoring entity as well as media mentions and brand association with teams and their conferences or leagues are powerful drivers for these investments.

Financial institutions are trending toward the practice of facility-naming rights where "nearly 20 percent of the teams in four major sports leagues have the name of a financial services affixed to their home building" (Bhasin, para 1, 2011). This may be a testament to the fit among institutions that specialize in how to handle large sums of money and properties with expenses and revenues in the multi-million dollar range. However, naming rights are not just for the national-level sponsors and properties. This is actually an area in which local-level sports, such as high school venues, can now capitalize. For those responsible for revenue generation at a local level, putting together a plan to indicate the amount of exposure and media mentions could go a long way toward helping a business consider this a worthy investment far beyond a simple philanthropic endeavor.

naming rights The nonsport entity's (sponsor's) exclusive ownership of the name of the venue where sport events occur (i.e., the stadium, arena, or ballpark); used interchangeably with title sponsorship.

VIGNETTE 12-1

Sponsors Help Fund High School Athletics

Jackson Township, Pennsylvania—In an effort to help fund their athletic department, the Seneca Valley School District officials have created a new sponsorship program. They produced a program that consists of one-, two-, three-, and four-year sponsorship agreements. Potential sponsors have the option of advertising on the fencing at the tennis court, baseball field, softball field, and athletic stadium and on the scoreboards at the baseball fields, softball fields, and the soccer/lacrosse field. In addition to the facility sponsorships, the athletic department also decided to sell the naming rights to their athlete of the month and scholar athlete programs. All of the sponsor proposals require that any text or images are in line with the school district's mission statement and values (Genco, 2016).

Any new sponsors who partner with the Seneca Valley School District will join NexTier Bank, which, in early 2016, reached an agreement with the school district to renew their facility-naming rights sponsorship. The new deal was for $100,000 over a 10-year period. The new programs to find sponsors were created in an attempt to find revenue to fund athletics from sources other than taxes. The athletic director stated that the sponsorship dollars would help fund new uniforms, facility maintenance, professional development of coaches, and equipment (Genco, 2016).

Local sport, recreational, and leisure should consider sponsorship as a means of generating revenue through venue-naming rights. The scenario in the vignette sounds ideal but sponsorship at these levels needs to be exercised with caution and an awareness of the limitation that local citizens may have toward sponsorship in certain areas. In the case of parks and recreation agencies, Mowen and Graefe (2002) uncovered citizens' attitudes that were situational and circumstantially more or less favorable to sponsors' facilities within the parks and recreation purview. Citizens did not have favorable attitudes toward corporate sponsorship purchasing "naming rights of specific park facilities and settings" (p 45). They speculated that this might have to do with permanency of visual noise in a setting considered to be "environmentally sensitive" (Mowen & Graefe, 2002, p 45). It seems as though properties may wish to maintain the outdoor natural setting to the best of their ability in order to better ensure public favor and to protect the environment. It may be a wise choice to determine whether there will be a negative reaction to a sponsor considering such a naming-rights purchase in cases involving schools and parks. These public-sector areas were of particular concern to the community with regard to whether sponsorship would be appropriate (Mowen, Kyle, & Jackowski, 2007).

Title Sponsorship. A title or presenting sponsor is an organization that has provided a large amount of financial capital, product, or other support in exchange for the sponsor's name to be attached to the event. The larger and more prestigious the event, the more money the title sponsorship would cost the sponsoring organization. This is often thought of as the most significant and impressive level of sponsorship. As the title sponsor, the logo and name of the organization that is sponsoring the event is on all print and visual materials associated with the event. The name of the sponsoring organization will go before the name of the event, such as Company ABC presents the Inaugural Golf Outing or Company ABC's Inaugural Golf Outing.

Food and beverage sponsorship. When planning a sporting event, the cost of food and beverages can be incredibly large. Finding sponsors to donate the needed food and beverages can be a tremendous relief to one's budget. The size, scope, and time of your event will dictate the number of food and beverage sponsors you will need. Also, whether you are including the food and beverages in the admission cost of your participants or if it is available for purchase will impact your food and beverage sponsorship decisions. Additional questions to consider can include: Is your event taking place at a time when people often eat a meal or meals? How long is your event? What is your target market and how will that impact the necessary food and drinks? For instance, if you are planning a golf scramble to raise money for a charity, you will want your expenses to be as low as possible. Potential sponsors you may try to get for your event would include a breakfast sponsor, a morning coffee sponsor, a lunch sponsor, and a beverage cart sponsor. You may also want to find a sponsor to provide snacks for a golfer amenity bag. These sponsors are often not necessary but obtaining them can significantly lower your expenses and provide a quality experience for your participants.

Event element sponsors. This type of sponsorship refers to finding organizations to sponsor contests or other areas of the event. If you are creating a youth basketball tournament, you could find sponsors to provide prizes for knockout games, a free throw contest, a skills challenge, etc. These types of sponsorships are often used to elevate the event and provide opportunities and prizes for participants that may not have been an option prior to the sponsorship.

Other Facility Inventory: The types of **sponsorship inventory** that are within and around sport facilities are numerous. Traditional on-site forms of inventory include perimeter advertising and logo placement around and throughout the facility and handout materials (Wishart, Seung, & Cornwell,

sponsorship inventory Any place or location, whether physical or digital, that can be exchanged for something of value (cash or in-kind service/product) with the purpose of a sponsoring organization being able to achieve its sponsorship objectives.

2012). Facility signage is certainly a significant and very visual sponsorship inventory but there are many other ways to generate revenues within facilities. Parts of the facility can be sponsored, such as concourses or even the field itself, as a separate buy. One study uncovered a possible new sponsorship space with the in-stadium game personnel. The facility or event staff impact fan experience can be powerful brand ambassadors for sponsors (Park & Choi, 2011).

New opportunities continue to present themselves as technology improves. The ever more advanced jumbo-trons and digital signage, such as ribbon boards, within stadiums and arenas, now offer new space to sell. Also, they can be changed frequently, allowing for reselling or multiple selling of the same space to different sponsors. This reduces visual clutter and enables completely new concepts to emerge such as sponsored in-game promotions. The flexibility trend does not end with digital technology. The physical setting has been developing toward this goal as well with further implications for emphasis on activation and onsite product sales.

While more ways and places to sponsor are becoming available, it is important to understand the value of the inventory. Research supports some commonly accepted ideas but continues to uncover less obvious answers as well. For instance, Park and Choi (2011) discovered that signs and banners located around the perimeter of the playing field and on center field, in the case of Major League Baseball, continue to be the most visible to fans. Furthermore, larger signs with strong contrasting colors tend to garner more attention. However, the televisions located near the restrooms in the hallways also drew attention as people did not want to miss the game and thus noticed attached sponsors (Park & Choi, 2011). Note that visibility alone does not necessarily translate into results for the sponsoring company. Activation plans should be developed to engage with the consumer on a more personal basis.

Unlike naming rights, facility signage is one that can generate cash flow for the property without many repercussions to the sponsoring corporation, even among the local levels of public sector entities. Attitudes by community members in one study were found to be more favorable toward indoor facility signage within facilities as opposed to outside in the natural setting (Mowen & Graefe, 2002). Mowen and Graefe (2002) suggested that the partnership takes care to "maintain the integrity and aesthetic quality of natural environments" (p. 45). Potential partnerships should be evaluated to determine which properties possess the best fit for the community, environment, and organization.

Finding and Acquiring Sponsors

Prior to beginning your search for sponsors, it is necessary to know the types of sponsors you need for your event through an analysis of the sponsorship inventory previously discussed. With the definitions outlined, the process for seeking out and acquiring can begin. Understanding one's own sport organization is critical to be able to establish the best sponsorship fit. Subsequently, it will be possible to identify companies that match in the way that the property can positively impact their business model.

match-up hypothesis
In reference to property and sponsorship, the belief that the more congruent the relationship, the more effectively the brands will connect in the minds of the consumers (e.g., a tire company sponsoring a race-car series).

Whether the potential sponsors have approached the property or the property is in search of new partnerships, the sport organization and potential sponsor need to examine the fit. The overview concept can be explained by the **match-up hypothesis**, which emphasizes a congruency between the sporting event and the sponsor results in connection with images in the minds of the fans. A local shoe store and pet store would be good matches for the New York City 5K Run/1 mile Walk/Dog Walk fundraiser. It makes logical sense to have shoes associated with the run/walk and pet products for the twist of getting to bring one's dog along for fun. The closeness of the sponsor and sport organization or event can make for a smooth brand transfer in the mind of the fans and consumers because there is already a similarity. An important question to consider is who ultimately makes the decision to buy the sponsorship? The process of finding and contacting potential sponsor decision-makers is likely to vary among the different levels. While there are commonalities among all of the levels and platforms, there will be some unique considerations for large events and smaller or new events.

Sponsorship for large events (existing entities such as a professional sport league, franchise, or university). At a national and regional level, there will more often be high level experts involved with these purchases and evaluations. Media buyers and companies specialize in how to plan and buy media or promotion-oriented outlets. Media Brokers International (MBI) claims sports marketing as one of the six categories that also include print, television, radio, out of home, and the Internet (www.media-brokers.com). Large companies may involve marketing agencies like these to handle this complex area of advertising under which sport sponsorship often falls.

There are many benefits for companies choosing to sponsor a large event. Research has shown that corporate sponsorship often produces a positive image for the sponsor (Gwinner & Eaton, 1999). The sponsoring organization may choose to do so because they want to be associated with the event to increase the favorable image of their company in the eye of their consumer or potential consumer (Gwinner, 1997). Additional benefits of sponsoring large events are direct access to your target market, an increase in sales, and increase in visibility. When choosing to sponsor an event, the organization has to understand its goals for the partnership. They may just want their name associated with an event to keep their brand in the minds of their target market. Other organizations may desire an increase in sales. It is important to understand your objectives and figure out if the return on investment (ROI) is worth the cost of the sponsorship.

An example of a company that has used sport sponsorship to change the perception of their business in a positive manner is Hyundai. Prior to sponsoring golf tournaments, Grammy Awards, and college sports, the public perception was that Hyundai was a lower-quality car brand. Once they became attached to golf tournaments, including the Hyundai Tournament of Champions PGA Tour stop, that perception changed. Hyundai even starting competing with, and in some cases, outselling top rivals Honda and Toyota (Higgins, 2017).

However, not every sponsorship partnership of large events is positive. There are, at times, negative aspects to companies choosing to sponsor sporting events. Copeland, Frisby, and McCarville (1996) stated that, "corporations are often inundated with requests for sponsorship funding yet cannot always ensure that events sponsored will be executed in a quality fashion or that an adequate return on investment will be achieved" (pg. 33). Additional negative aspects or risks include an athlete or team scandal and negative publicity associated with the scandal, injury and/or less than ideal performance, or the sponsor partnership causing a negative impact on sponsor brand. To help guard against scandals, many companies will put a morals clause into the sponsorship agreement, which allows the company to dissolve the partnership if a scandal or situation occurs that can damage the company's brand or image (Epstein, 2011, Sandler & Shani, 1989).

Elements of contracts. While there are a variety of elements that can be included in a sponsorship contract, three common elements are exclusivity, right of first refusal, and right of first negotiation. **Exclusivity** refers to a sponsor's desire to be the only sponsor attached to an event in their category. The sponsoring organization does not want any of their direct competitors associated with the event because it will reduce the impact of

exclusivity A sponsor's desire to be the only sponsor attached to an event in their category (e.g., a cell phone provider not wanting any other cell phone providers associated with the event).

the sponsorship. For example, if Coke is the official beverage sponsor of the event, the organizers should not also attempt to use Pepsi or any Pepsi products (such as Aquafina water or Gatorade).

Right of first refusal grants the sponsor the ability to match the terms of any other offer from competitors to be the sponsor of the event during a given period of time. A right of first refusal clause is considered by some to be the most restrictive clause because the organization must disclose to potential sponsors that this clause is in place. As a result, it may decrease another organization's desire to negotiate a sponsorship deal that may not come to fruition if the original sponsor matches the deal.

Right of first negotiation refers to the clause that event owners or organizers negotiate in good faith with the sponsors to renew the sponsorship agreement before they can offer the sponsorship to another company. While this clause is generally considered to be low risk, it is crucial that the event owner or organizers ensure that the right of first negotiation expiration date is prior to the conclusion of the sponsorship agreement. This ensures that there will not be a lapse in sponsorship.

Obtaining sponsors for smaller or new events. When running an event that is smaller in scale or brand new, it is important to locate and acquire sponsors who align with the event and the event mission. Given that you are most likely working with a finite amount of resources and capital, locating sponsors is important in order to successfully run your event.

It is important to choose the right sponsors for your event. The sponsoring organization and the event should "make sense." This means that their target markets should be similar and the missions should align. However, obtaining sponsors (especially for a new event) is not easy. The first step for the event owners is to create a wish list of sponsors. When doing this, you should consider the connections you have to other businesses, what companies in your area have a history of sponsorship, and what products or services your target market uses? All of these will help you develop a list of potential companies to target for sponsorship.

Before you contact the companies on your target list, it is important to research each individual company to assess whether you believe the organization is a realistic partner for your event. There are many tools at your disposal to help research the companies. First, you can examine the company website to get to know as much as you can about the organization. Conducting a Google search will help you to learn if the organization has

---

right of first refusal
The sponsoring organization has the ability to match the terms of any other offer from competitors that have a desire to sponsor the event.

---

right of first negotiation A clause that event owners or organizers negotiate that requires sponsors to renew the sponsorship agreement before they can offer the sponsorship to another company.

sponsored other local events. Finally, social media is a great way to find out what others are saying. You can search the organization by using a hashtag and the business name. LinkedIn can also be a helpful tool to see if you know anyone connected to the organization. This possible connection can make approaching the organization with the sponsorship proposal more natural and may yield a more positive result.

Once you have narrowed down your target list to a list of companies that you are going to approach, you must identify the individuals at each company who are responsible for handling sponsorships. Furthermore, look into whether the organization has a charitable donation or giving policy. Tailor each proposal to the organization and have a clear idea about what you are asking each company for in the proposal. If they have a charitable donation or giving policy, make sure that your request aligns with this policy. If you ask for specific items, you will be more successful than just asking for a check.

Writing a Sponsorship Proposal Letter

When you are writing your sponsorship proposal letters, it is important that the letters are specific and focused. Clearly convey your mission and why you need and/or want this partnership. If you can convey your passion and purpose in the proposal, it will help the person reading it to understand why this event is important.

In the proposal, be clear if you are asking for cash or an in-kind donation. Both of these are important and necessary to run events. While you may desire cash from all sponsors, that is often not realistic. Asking for a product or a donation of items at cost as a form of sponsorship can be very effective. If companies are willing to donate all of the print materials in exchange for being named a sponsor, that can save your organization money.

When drafting the sponsorship proposal letter, be sure to put the proposal on organization letterhead. Often, it is helpful to use a sponsorship letter template if you have never created one. Make sure that this letter is both specific to your event and to the company you are sending it to for potential sponsorship.

The letter should begin with an opening paragraph that introduces your company and event. Do not assume that the person you are sending the letter to knows who you are. Highlight any accomplishments of the organization or events that you have done in the past. This will show that you are legitimate and that you pose less risk.

In subsequent paragraphs, make your specific sponsorship requests. Why are you seeking the sponsorship? How will the money or in-kind donation be used? You can also provide different sponsorship options that will allow the potential sponsor to pick the sponsorship that best aligns with their organizational goals, objectives, and budget.

If this event has been done previously, what were the demographics of your participants? What was the turnout at the event? How are sponsors recognized? What was the impact of this event on the participants, community, and/or sponsors? Show details or data that can help you make your argument as to why this sponsorship is a good partnership for both you and the sponsoring company.

Once the letter is sent, it will most likely be necessary to follow up personally. Always be respectful and positive in all communication. It is important to remember that companies receive many requests for sponsorship so if you come across as pushy, rude, or difficult, the company may choose to spend its sponsorship dollars elsewhere.

How to Sell Your Event to Potential Sponsors

After you send your sponsorship letters, you will ideally need to set up meetings to discuss the details of the sponsorship with the potential sponsors. At this meeting, it is important to listen to what the potential sponsor is telling you about their organization, what they value, budget, and how they measure success. Use what they are telling you to help convince them why this is a good fit.

In this meeting, along with listening, you need to make this all about them. You need to convince them why sponsorship is a great idea for them and not just why you need them. What can they expect to get out of this relationship? Use what you learned about their goals during your conversation to explain how this event and sponsoring partnership can help them to achieve their goals. What is going to be their return on investment (ROI)? If there is going to be media coverage, explain the specific media coverage. If a logo is going to be on a shirt, how many shirts will be made? Specifics will not only convince the sponsors that you have done your homework but they allow them to see what their sponsorship is actually giving them in return.

Determining Objectives

Once the sponsors have been screened and commitment to budget has been established, the partnership can move forward. There are two main categories under which an array of objectives can be housed; direct and indirect. **Direct objectives** are intended to drive immediate sales. These objectives may provide an opportunity to quantify revenues. **Indirect objectives** are the larger group of ways to utilize sport sponsorship to achieve desired results; including influencing brand awareness, brand attitudes, and brand image (Shank, 2009; Coppetti et al., 2009). Objectives of this nature will take time to execute and can be difficult to establish clear returns with standard measurement tools. In facilities and sporting events, one can readily find large and colorful company logos displayed in prominent places such as scoreboards or along the outfield, which points to indirect objectives.

Whether direct or indirect, a good way to uncover and define what these should be can be found in the widely accepted SMART formula outlined earlier in this book (Doran, 1981).

Taking the time to meet with sponsors regarding this simple formula could amount to much better communication with the goal of more success. Staying coordinated will help to identify and prepare for the continually changing objectives as market opportunities allow (Farrelly, 2010). Seiferheld (2010) recommends meeting monthly or at least quarterly to stay on top of any inevitable changes. Beyond a simple recommendation, working more closely together is the direction of the future of sports business. As stated by Farrelly (2010), "Sponsorship has shifted from a marketing tool to a business platform where the need for strategic collaboration and mutually beneficial outcomes for both the sponsor and the sports entity is seemingly more vital" (p. 320). Due to the importance and need to understand more thoroughly, the relationship warrants a section of its own.

direct objectives
A business and marketing action specifically crafted toward increasing sales.

indirect objectives An outcome other than achieving immediate sales or gains such as increasing awareness to new market segments or a campaign to reposition a brand.

The Sponsorship Agreement

After a sponsor and a property have determined that they will be a good fit, the documentation and literal agreement must be created. Writing the sponsorship agreement can be complicated if you have never done one before. A good rule is to have a lawyer look over the document or help you draft it in order to ensure that you are covering all of your bases and that there is no way (without reason) for the sponsor to back out of their commitment.

The sponsorship agreement will vary largely across the national to recreation & leisure levels. Regardless of the number of specifics and length of document, there are certain areas that should be included at each level.

- Determining and defining the length of contract must be made clear, for example, January 1 to December 31.
- Benefits to the sponsor should be outlined. This may be challenging and focus mainly on the inventory being purchased, such as signage placement and media inclusion.
- Payment obligations of the sponsor. There must be an agreed-upon price, along with how to provide payment and consequences for late payments. Type of capital exchanged should be considered and outlined as well: monetary and/or in-kind (Mowen & Graefe, 2002, p 37).
- Responsibilities of the event organization. What items or publicity have been promised to the corporate sponsor? The event organization needs to ensure that each item that was agreed upon is executed in the manner that was agreed upon. For instance, if you are running a youth hockey camp and the sponsor is supposed to have a logo on the center ice board on the player side of the arena, you need to make sure that it is where the logo is placed. The little details are huge when fulfilling a sponsorship agreement and developing the contract.
- Contingency plans resulting in the partnership not taking place, termination, or an event not taking place. There are two main categories for this.
  - Indemnification—Noting that legal action can occur when a party is at fault, resulting in possible financial losses.
  - Force Majeure—Termination of agreement upon even cancellation when neither party is considered at fault due to causes beyond either party's control. Reed, Bhargava, & Kjaer explain that actions falling under this category are those rendering the event impossible, such as a labor strike. The authors note that since September 11, 2001, most contracts within the United States will include clauses for "act or threat of terrorism" (Reed, Bhargava, & Kjaer, 2010, p 87). Weather at outdoor events is considered foreseeable (that bad weather could result in event cancellation) in which case both parties should secure Cancellation Insurance. Responsibility for this can be included in the contract (Reed et al., 2010 pp 87–88).

Inventory is the more tangible benefits part that a sponsor is purchasing but there are some additional important concepts (see **Figure 12.2**) that influence the price for a sponsorship deal. Wishart et al., concluded that going beyond the visual logo placement, sponsors also value media coverage, hospitality, customer interactions, access to property offerings like sport celebrities and consumer databases, and technological sophistication (2012). These are all part of the on-site communication components but may fall within the negotiable territory.

One of the important price factors pertains to the target market offered by the sport property. If the property can deliver concentrated numbers of

---

Sponsorship Agreement Checklist

The Term and Parties
- Identify the length of time that the sponsorship will be in place and when it will expire
- Discuss the parties involved in the agreement and state how they will be referred to throughout the sponsorship agreement

Sponsorship Rights
- State the purpose of the sponsorship and/or the event with which it is associated
- Is there exclusivity?
- Does the sponsor have the ability to veto other potential sponsors?
- List all individual recognition components associated with the sponsorship

Responsibilities
- What is the sponsor responsible for in this agreement?
- What is the event organization responsible for in this agreement?
- What are the marketing and promotions that accompany the event?
- How will the sponsor be represented?

Financial
- What is the financial responsibility of the sponsor?
- What is the financial responsibility of the event organization?
- What are the terms of payment?
- When are the payments due?
- Is there a penalty for late payment or non-payment?

Trademark and Logo Licenses
- Sponsor should provide logo and details of logo use
- Sponsor must specify the dos and don'ts of logo use
- Is the sponsor responsible for quality control surrounding the logo?

Expiration of Sponsorship Agreement
- When does the sponsorship expire?

Signatures
- Who are the official signers and organization representatives?
- What date was the document signed?

Figure 12-2 Sponsorship Agreement Checklist

people highly desired by a sponsoring company, the price will potentially remain in the property's favor. This may be even more important than the actual numbers so long as it is a desired target audience (Wishart, et al., 2012). Thus, sport managers should take note, know one's self first, and then approach sponsors who seek what the property has to offer.

Activation

The best-laid plans mean absolutely nothing without proper execution. Activation is the portion of the sponsorship that engages with the fan, ideally with some sort of close interaction that enhances the fans' experience. Mayo & Bishop state clearly that, "…it is now known that the activation drives the greatest gains in ROI as it drives demonstrable purchase consideration increases" (Mayo & Bishop, 2010, p 11). What a sponsor does with and at the sport event or facility is vital to the entire relationship. However, a valid question to ask would be "Who sets the objectives and implements the plans of action?" The answer is not so simple. There appears to be ongoing debate not only regarding who is responsible for setting objectives as previously discussed but also as to who should finance and execute them, the sponsor or the property? The best answer, in an increasingly more relationship-oriented environment, is that both are responsible.

First and foremost, communication between organizations and education appear to be very important to setting the stage for success. One of the reasons many sponsors place responsibility with the sports team is because they may not understand the inventory being purchased and how it can be leveraged. Rob Hoffmann, Pittsburgh Penguins Corporate Sales Manager, reveals that several companies have official and exclusivity status to the Penguins marks and logos "and they don't do anything with them" (O'Keefe et al., 2009, p 50). Furthermore, O'Keefe et al., called for better planning between the property and sponsor as well as increased education by the sports property to the sponsor (2009). It is important for the sponsor to know what their own inventory is and how to use it.

It has been said previously: the sponsors must know their own objectives and what they want from the property. It is the sport event managers' responsibility to lead the way by helping the corporate sponsors in doing just this. It is not enough to just provide a list of inventory but to help them understand the how and why for activation. Upfront, the companies must also be educated about additional expenses and personnel that will need to be provided for these plans and their execution. When making recommendations for successful activation, the sport property should pay careful attention to involvement of the sponsor organization on-site as well as the types of activities offered. Standard sample giveaways are not the most desirable or successful way to activate. Coppetti et al. (2009) found that fans who "were provided the opportunity to participate in attractive sponsor activities, to interact with some of the sponsor's employees, and to meet other consumers, they are likely to evaluate the sponsorship more favorably due to these positive experiences" (p. 30). A fun social experience during an engaging activity that allows the fan to interact with sponsor employees directly is a good goal for on-site activations. Take, for example, the Zombie Mud Run and Carnival in College Station, Texas, which offers sponsors a chance to host game booths blending these objectives nicely. This makes sense for several reasons. People will have an affinity toward those who they have fun with and toward those who created the experience. Sponsors' employees are not only brand ambassadors who know the company and products for one but they are also a human extension of the company with whom fans can connect and develop a relationship bond. Sports fans may be more likely to want to purchase from a person than a faceless company.

SUMMARY

The chapter has defined sponsorship, its components, and trends within the industry that have important implications for sponsorship opportunities. Strategies for finding good property/sponsor fits and forming relationships that will result in success for every party involved should be followed, as doing so will help both the sponsor and the facility or event owner achieve their goals and objectives. The underlying theme is that creating a win-win relationship is accomplished by developing creative solutions to meet those goals and objectives. Remaining aware of this quickly-evolving aspect of sport business will enable sport managers to proactively ensure continued relationships with an ever-vital partner.

DISCUSSION QUESTIONS

1. What would be some new or unique ideas for sponsorship activation that fits the criteria, maximizing success? How can a sports organization, the fans, and the sponsors all benefit from these ideas?
2. Consider activation spaces in sports facilities or at sports events. Where would good locations be and why? Remember to consider the fan's experience from arrival at the location until they leave.

3. Take the view point from the sponsor's perspective and also the sport property's perspective. If a peer is available, ask him or her to take on one of these rolls for this discussion. Who should be responsible for what in this agreement and why? What does each partner bring to this relationship? Remember to think through and include leveraging and activation.

4. As stated in the chapter, companies receive many sponsorship proposals. The reality is that each organization has a finite amount of resources that they can dedicate to sponsorship. With that in mind, what unique elements do you think would enhance an organization to sponsor a youth athletic team? What would you include in a sponsorship proposal to convince the company to choose to sponsor your team instead of other events?

Case STUDY

Sponsorship and the Brazos Valley Senior Games

The Brazos Valley Senior Games (BVSG) were launched locally in 2006 in College Station, Texas, with several goals in mind. The competition was intended to provide individuals of age 50 years and older with an opportunity to compete in various sports, socialize with other seniors, and have fun. The games were created under the auspices of the National Senior Games Association, which is the overall governing body and highest level of competition for these athletes. Community wise, it made sense to utilize this sport event as a way to generate potential tourism. Thus, the Bryan–College Station Convention and Visitors Bureau (CVB) was a good fit to assist with starting and helping to support the competition. The CVB provided a meeting place and individuals to serve on the board of directors. This cooperation was vital toward the success and sustainability of the event over the next several years.

The initial leadership direction was more recreational competition in nature. In 2008, new leadership in the president position provided a vision of more intense competition with high-quality events and an ultimate goal to grow the games into a large annual community event. The new president was careful to build a strategic board of directors that included people connected to the major business facets around town. The aggressive plans began to work in a relatively short amount of time. From inception, the numbers of athletes grew substantially from less than 200 athletes to over 400. Close to 20 different types of events were offered in an effort to become the best local senior games in Texas.

The president was passionate about and highly committed to the growth of the BVSG, taking on many of the functions, such as sponsorship, himself. Growth continued and athlete feedback was quite good. Then, the next step in the vision came to pass when the state level granted the BVSG the bid to host the Texas State Games for 2010 and 2011. This opportunity should have been a good thing, but it proved to be the demise of the organization. As with many businesses (and nonprofits in particular), budgetary problems were pervasive.

The way in which revenue was generated was limited and did not readily produce enough income to support high-quality competition, venues, and prizes. Registration fees were collected but were often less than $30 per person. Thus, sponsorship was vital but was also sparse. The highly energetic president devoted most of his time and much of his own resources to providing high-quality events, several of which he organized and oversaw himself. It was ideal and encouraged that each event coordinator would generate his or her own sponsors for each event. Staffing events with unpaid volunteers, most of whom would be full-time employees elsewhere, would not be successful since their time and energies would be limited. Hence, the president did most of the searching for sponsors for the entire event himself, as he was retired and more fully focused on his vision for the games. While the occasional cash sponsor was signed, many of the partner sponsors were in the form of in-kind trade, which meant fewer hard dollars available to spend as needed. Some of the board members also contributed in this fashion, but it just wasn't enough.

In the first year hosting the State Games, overestimates and some very large bills for medals, t-shirts, and venues became problematic. Furthermore, due to the timing of the event, the athlete turnout was far lower than expected and the numbers estimated much higher than was usual for a standard local senior games event. Other parts of the BVSG also began to fall apart. With the massive growth also came increased time demands for nonpaid volunteers, who played crucial roles in the execution of successful events. The CVB had to move to an advisory role, and several other board members had to do the same. The BVSG simply could not recover. The second year was relinquished to a larger Games that had much better funding and was in a position to take on the demands of such an event. These damages were too great, and the local BVSG reached its breaking point and dissolved on the brink of achieving its greatest success to date.

Although the nonprofit organization was officially dissolved, the good news was that the City of College Station Parks and Recreation Department saw the importance of the event and elected to take it on. Back to the original goals of recreational competition, the local senior games would at least be available as one of very few left in the state of Texas. Having even a simple event is far more desirable than having none, which has been the trend in recent years. There are goals of being consistent with this event and growing the brand with time; however, simplicity and cost-effectiveness are at the root of each decision.

A systematic analysis of the area for sponsors with matching target markets and objectives would be the first step. Second, prospective large investment sponsors should have been approached a year in advance. These should have been the primary focus for the president and others on the board specializing in revenue generation. Ideally, each sport organizer should have been presented with the training and strategy to generate sponsors for his or her own events. However, there are also many other viable plans and solutions that could have saved the BVSG. Taking

(continues)

Case STUDY (continued)

concepts learned in this chapter and applied to this case study will assist the reader in preparing for this very real-world scenario. This would be a good time to reflect upon and develop some creative and innovative plans and techniques for sponsorship to ensure success for sport businesses and worthy endeavors such as the Brazos Valley Senior Games.

1. Consider some sponsors who may have been a good fit for this particular organization. Why were these selected? Feel free to utilize your local community as though these games were taking place there.
2. Given the specifics for this event, what might have been some strategies for the sponsors identified in Question 1 to leverage and activate this investment? Hint: Consider every party involved, not just the property and the sponsor.
3. Pretend to be the Senior Games president and restructure the organizational strategy so that a more organized or strategic approach could have been taken to increase sponsorship of this event. What could have or should have been done differently, by whom, and why?

REFERENCES

Andrews, J. (2017a). What sponsors want and where dollars will go in 2017. ESP Properties. Retrieved January 12, 2018 from http://www.sponsorship.com/IEG /files/7f/7fd3bb31-2c81-4fe9-8f5d-1c9d7cab1232.pdf

Andrews, J. (2017b). Sponsorship spending forecast: Continued growth around the world. *ESP Sponsorship Report.* Retrieved January 12, 2018 from http://www .sponsorship.com/IEGSR/2017/01/04/Sponsorship-Spending-Forecast --Continued-Growth-Ar.aspx

Bhasin, K. (May 18, 2011). Why do so many banks put their names on stadiums? Retrieved from http://www.businessinsider.com/banks-stadium-naming-rights-2011-2

Copeland, R., Frisby, W., & McCarville, R. (1996). Understanding the sport sponsorship process from a corporate perspective. *Journal of Sport Management, 10*(1), 32–48. https://journals.humankinetics.com/doi /10.1123/jsm.10.1.32

Coppetti, C., Wentzel, D., Tomczak, T., & Henkel, S. (2009). Improving incongruent sponsorships through articulation of the sponsorship and audience participation. *Journal of Marketing Communications, 15*(1), 17–34.

Doran, G. T. (1981). There's a S.M.A.R.T. way to write managements's goals and objectives. *Management Review, 70*(11), 35.

Epstein, A. (2011). An exploration of interesting clauses in sports. *Journal of Legal Aspects of Sport, 21*(1), 1–41.

Farrelly, F. (2010). Not playing the game: Why sport sponsorship relationships break down. *Journal of Sport Management, 24*(3), 319–337.

Genco, J. (2016, June 8). District program will raise sports funding. *The Cranberry Eagle*, Retrieved January 14, 2018 from http://www.thecranberryeagle.com/article/20160608/CRAN0101/706089791/-1/CRAN

Gwinner, K. P. (1997). A model of image creation and image transfer in event sponsorship. *International Marketing Review, 14*(3), 145–158.

Gwinner, K. P., & Eaton, J. (1999). Building brand image through event sponsorships: The role of image transfer. *Journal of Advertising, 28*(4), 47–57.

Higgins, R. (2017). 5 reasons brands want to sponsor your event. *Eventbrite*. Retrieved January 13, 2018 from https://www.eventbrite.com/blog/5-reasons-to-sponsor-your-event-ds00/

Mayo, D., & Bishop, T. (2010). Fixed rights to activation ratios can harm sponsorship ROI. *Journal of Sponsorship, 4*(1), 9–14.

Mowen, A. J., & Graefe, A. R. (2002). Public attitudes toward the corporate sponsorship of park agencies: The role of promotional activities and contractual conditions. *Journal of Park & Recreation Administration, 20*(2), 31–48. https://js.sagamorepub.com/jpra/article/view/1872

Mowen, A. J., Kyle, G. T., & Jackowski, M. (2007). Citizen preferences for the corporate sponsorship of public-sector park and recreation organizations. *Journal of Nonprofit & Public Sector Marketing, 18*(2), 93–118.

O'Keefe, R., Titlebaum, P., & Hill, C. (2009). Sponsorship activation: Turning money spent into money earned. *Journal of Sponsorship, 3*(1), 43–53.

Park, S. R., & Choi, A. J. (2011). Visual signs/logo-identity in the major league baseball facility: Case study of tropicana field. *International Journal of Applied Sports Sciences, 23*(1), 251–270.

Reed, M. H., Bhargava, M. N., & Kjaer, J. G. M. (2010). Terminating a sponsorship relationship: Conditions and clauses. *Journal of Sponsorship, 4*(1), 79–92.

Sandler, D. M., & Shani, D., (1989). Olympic sponsorship vs ambush marketing: Who gets the gold? *Journal of Advertising Research*, 9–14.

Seiferheld, S. (2010). Try a S.M.A.R.T. way to turn sponsorships into partnerships. *Street & Smith's Sportsbusiness Journal, 13*(31), 14.

Shani, D., & Sandler, D. (1996). Climbing the sports event pyramid. *Marketing News, 30*(18), 6.

Shank, M. D. (2009). *Sports marketing: A strategic perspective* (4th Edition ed.). Upper Saddle River, New Jersey: Pearson Prentice Hall. https://www.pearson.com/us/higher-education/program/Shank-Sports-Marketing-A-Strategic-Perspective-4th-Edition/PGM94577.html

Wishart, T., Seung, P. L., & Cornwell, T. B. (2012). Exploring the relationship between sponsorship characteristics and sponsorship asking price. *Journal of Sport Management, 26*(4), 335–349.

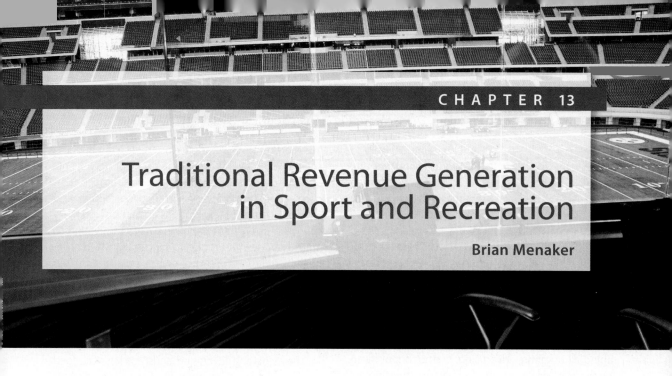

CHAPTER 13

Traditional Revenue Generation in Sport and Recreation

Brian Menaker

CHAPTER OBJECTIVES

Upon completion of this chapter, the reader will be able to:

1. Identify the types of revenues available in spectator sport, participation events, and recreation facilities.

2. Distinguish between facility revenues and event revenues.

3. Differentiate between methods of revenue generation in a variety of facilities and venues.

4. Consider how to utilize different facilities for revenue-producing events.

5. Articulate the strengths and weaknesses of the various revenue production strategies.

6. Identify multiple revenue opportunities for facilities.

7. Outline revenue generation strategies for participatory events.

CHAPTER OVERVIEW

This chapter will review the various techniques used to generate revenue through sport and recreation facilities and sport events. Techniques and principles of revenue generation from sport, and recreation facilities and participatory events are categorized and summarized. The difference between direct revenues from events and ancillary revenue will be explained. Categories of sources of revenue include venue-related revenue such as ticket sales, concessions, merchandise, event fees, and participatory event monies such as exposition-related income and registration fees.

IndustryVOICE

Brad Timberlake—Vice President, Event Marketing & Sales Southeast, Feld Entertainment

Feld Entertainment is a leading producer and promoter of live touring entertainment properties. As vice president of marketing and sales, I support the business development efforts of a talented group of marketing and sales professionals throughout our Southeast region with leadership through—among other things—coaching, mentoring, teaching, and strategic thinking. Furthermore, it is our team's responsibility to generate attendance at our events by managing all ticketing, advertising, promotion, publicity, public relations, community outreach, partnership, and sales activity for each marketplace visited.

Feld Entertainment is the worldwide leader in producing and presenting live touring family entertainment experiences that lift up the human spirit and bring people together. Properties include Monster Jam®, Monster Energy Supercross, *Disney On Ice*, *Disney Live!*, *Sesame Street Live!*, Marvel Universe LIVE!, *DreamWorks Trolls The Experience*, and, coming in the Fall of 2019, Jurassic World Live.

- Our Core Values: Quality, integrity, passion, and teamwork & collaboration
- Our mission statement: We create memorable experiences that bring people together and lift up the human spirit
- Our Vision: To bring joy to more people in more places around the world through innovative live experiences

Whether direct or indirect, competition has been and always will be a challenge in which to be knowledgeable and to stay ahead of with current industry and market research. Not only does Feld Entertainment focus on producing the highest quality, best-in-class, state-of-the-art, live events in our own space

like monster truck competitions and live family show spectacles, but we must also be aware of how events and venues like community festivals, amusement parks, concerts, professional and college sports, and in-home entertainment options impact discretionary spending as well as a fan's or family's motivation to attend our events. Producing high-quality and compelling content through our own popular and trusted brands as well as through our licensed brands is key. Everything we do with production and marketing must follow through on the brand promises and enhance the brand. This allows us to maintain consumer trust and loyalty.

The media and advertising landscape have changed significantly in a short amount of time as audiences continue to shift from traditional print, broadcast, and cable channels into the online environment with social media and streaming services. As a result, mass market advertising that created mass market awareness has become much more fragmented, ultimately diluting marketing resources. At the same time, this has also created the opportunity to be much more targeted with our message to specific demographics and allows for better evaluation of the return on marketing budgets.

The industry continues to migrate entirely into mobile, paperless ticketing. This move will help venues, promoters, and fans in a number of ways from addressing security concerns and secondary market activity with ticket brokers to providing better data to improve overall communication with fans. Additionally, sponsorships continue to become more integrated partnerships, allowing for more meaningful connections among the fans, the brands, and the events. From a live event perspective, more focus has been put on creating more immersive and interactive fan experiences. For example, advancements in video technology and projection mapping have allowed for more dynamic set design and storytelling opportunities.

When I consider a new hire for a position, above almost all other qualities, having the right positive attitude toward elements like the job responsibilities, learning process, communication and collaboration, and self-reflection is the most important—whether a candidate is a seasoned professional or a recent college graduate. In the sport and entertainment industry, you really have to love the work and the amount of time you spend on the job. You have to understand the difference between being a spectator and fan and being one who actually plans and executes the events. Also, practical experience in the business at some level is often more valuable than just having book knowledge and understanding theory. Being teachable is also critical. Someone who believes that he or she knows everything can rarely be helped. If you have a positive attitude and are teachable, you can usually fill in the gaps in your skillset along the way. Beyond that, qualities that I look for include: Emotional intelligence, mental toughness, honesty and integrity, leadership acumen, and an ability to think as well as gel with others.

Understanding one's own strengths and weaknesses is also important.

To better prepare for the workforce, I would recommend to anyone to put a greater emphasis on mastery of public speaking, understanding sales techniques and marketing, and gaining practical knowledge in your desired field through internships. Being able to stand up and speak confidently about your ideas in front of small and large groups is probably the single most important skill that one can develop for success in your professional and personal life, regardless of your specific occupation. The ability to understand others and influence them to your way of thinking is a key element in one's ability to successfully lead teams, groups, organizations, and your own family.

Regarding the different revenues involved in Facilities and Events, I would simply note that there are a lot of ways to generate revenue. However, from admission revenue to food and beverage to merchandise to sponsorship and beyond, one must always keep the fan top-of-mind. Fans drive the business, and they must find value in the product that is on the field or on the stage.

Introduction

Sport facilities and associated events provide owners, operators, managers, and other connected stakeholders with the opportunity to generate revenue through many forms of creative planning. All types of sport facilities and venues can be profitable by providing the assortment of services that make a variety of events viable and valuable revenue producers. Arenas, stadiums, convention centers, multipurpose facilities, event-specific venues, and other public assembly facilities can provide locations for sporting events, concerts, and other public assembly events. These facilities may also be used for participatory events to provide event-driven revenue. Public parks, fields, and roads can be used for road races, urban challenges, obstacle course races, and other revenue-producing physical activity events. This chapter highlights the revenues that can be accumulated using sport, recreational, and public facilities and other sport and physical fitness events.

Why Is It Important to Identify Sources of Revenue?

Sport and fitness venues are diverse and flexible spaces that have numerous uses. Large venues such as arenas, stadiums, field houses, and gymnasiums are used for only a finite time in hosting their primary tenants' contests. Unlike a typical commercial retail store, which may be open every day of the year, large-scale facilities are not used every day for sporting events. An empty venue does not produce revenue. Therefore, it is important to consider the multiple ways to utilize an arena, stadium, or other public assembly building beyond the primary intended use, whether that be football, baseball, soccer, basketball, hockey, or another sport. There are alternatives for raising revenue beyond sporting events, including using the facilities to supplement other events hosted outside or near the venue. This chapter is divided into two parts. The first part of the chapter will discuss the ways that sport and fitness-related facilities can be used to produce revenue. The second part will focus on event-related revenues.

Venue Revenue

TICKET SALES

gate receipt The sum of money received from ticket sales for a particular event.

season tickets A subscription for a series of tickets, usually lasting for one season of a sports teams' contests, which costs less than buying separate tickets to individual events.

Selling tickets for events is the most common and direct way for host facilities to ensure revenue from visitors. A ticket gives the visitor the right to a seat, or an area to stand if the ticket is general admission or standing room only, for the purpose of watching a game, concert, or other event. The **gate receipt** refers to the total amount of money received for tickets at a certain game. A venue can increase its gate receipt by offering visitors' options when it comes to ticket sales. The venue can offer single-game tickets, **season tickets**; and a subscription for a series of tickets, usually lasting for one season of a sports team's contests, which costs less than buying separate tickets to individual events, miniseason ticket plans, and group ticket sales.

Table 13-1   Average Ticket Prices

League	Average Ticket Cost	Average Premium Ticket
NFL '16	$92.98	$277.29
MLB '16	$31.00	$95.42
NHL '14 – '15	$62.18	$151.53
NBA '15 – '16	$55.88	N/A

The price of tickets is a considerable investment, as illustrated by an overview of the price offerings by the major North American sports leagues (see **Table 13-1**). According to Fan Cost Experience reports, the average ticket in a Major League Baseball (MLB) stadium in the 2016 season was $31.00, with the highest team average being $54.79 for the Boston Red Sox, with the Yankees offering the most expensive premium seats (tickets such as club seats that include at least one added amenity or is classified as premium by the team) for $305.39 and the lowest for $18.53 for the Arizona Diamondbacks (Team Marketing Report, 2016). The average National Football League (NFL) ticket price for the 2016 season was $92.98, with the Chicago Bears offering the most expensive ticket at $131.90 and the Jacksonville Jaguars offering the lowest at $61.36 (Team Marketing Report, 2016a). For the 2014–2015 National Hockey League (NHL) season, seats averaged $62.18 across the league, with the Toronto Maple Leafs' average ticket price being $113.66 and the Florida Panthers' tickets averaging $33.39 (Team Marketing Report, 2014). The average National Basketball Association (NBA) seat for the 2015–2016 season (excluding club seats, suite prices, and floor seats) was $55.88, with the New York Knicks having the highest average ticket cost of $129.38 and the Charlotte Hornets offering the cheapest average ticket of $30.60 (Team Marketing Report, 2016b)

While the average ticket price comes at a considerable cost to the consumer, there is clearly a large discrepancy of ticket prices among teams. Offering season ticket plans can serve as a way to discount the single-game face value of a seat to loyal fans and ensure that a large portion of seats are sold before the season. However, there are many other strategies beyond full-season ticket packages to increase revenue through ticket sales.

Ticket Sales Strategies

Teams and venues have identified a number of different ways to improve ticket sales, including differential pricing, flexible season ticket pricing,

money-back guarantees, web-based tickets, and secondary ticket exchanges (Howard & Crompton, 2005).

DIFFERENTIAL PRICING

differential pricing
Differences in pricing of a seat based on quality, time, and place. Quality refers to reputation, strength, and draw of the opponent. Time corresponds to the day of the week, time of day, or part of the season. Place is determined by location of seat.

Differential pricing is based on three variables: Quality, time, and place. Quality refers to the reputation, strength, and draw of the opponent. Time corresponds with the day of the week, time of day, or part of the season. Teams may raise prices based on which day of the week the game is played. For example, MLB teams charge higher ticket prices when traditional powers or rivals come to visit, such as when the Boston Red Sox visit the New York Yankees. For baseball teams, games in the months of April, May, and September are often discounted because children are in school and have less ability to attend games. Place is determined by location of seat (Howard & Crompton, 2005). Seats closer to the playing surface or those with special amenities, such as club seating, may be pricier than the seats near the ceiling rafters. Using club and other luxury seating to raise revenue will be discussed later in the chapter.

FLEXIBLE TICKET PRICING

Many teams use a scheme that offers flexible season ticket plans. For example, the NBA's Cleveland Cavaliers offer a partial season ticket plan that gives fans the opportunity to purchase tickets to 10 games that are determined by the team before the season. Included in the Cavaliers packages are the ability to use the Cavaliers Ticket Exchange to sell unwanted tickets, a 15 percent discount off of team shop purchases, priority to purchase tickets for the playoffs, and the ability to spread out payment over time. Often, tickets to the most desirable and popular games are included in the package along with games against teams that may not draw as well. This strategy is a way to entice fans to purchase tickets to less attractive games while offering discounts to popular games that are likely to sell out. During the 2017–2018 season, the NBA's San Antonio Spurs saw a decline in their season ticket sales after having a waiting list for tickets in previous years. Flexible ticket strategies included offering a Holiday Package, which gave fans the opportunity to buy five games from a selection of 20 that occurred between November and February, to serve as a possible enticement to include basketball tickets in holiday shopping. Their Stretch Run pack gave fans the opportunity to buy the last 22 games of the year and have playoff ticket purchasing priority, an opportunity that has generally extended to full-season ticket holders.

Flexibility can also come in the form of voucher programs. The Los Angeles Angels offer an eVoucher program. Fans can purchase 10 tickets for $200 and pick from a list of 65 games. They can redeem the vouchers for any of the eligible games. Additional ticket packages include family ticket plans. A typical family package could include four tickets, four hot dogs, four soft drinks, and a program for a discounted price.

MONEY-BACK GUARANTEES

A number of teams have included **money-back guarantee** conditions in their ticket packages or single-game tickets. While this strategy has not been used that much recently, the Jacksonville Sharks indoor football team, a former member of the Arena Football League (current members of the National Arena League), after a successful season winning their division, announced a money-back guarantee to all new season ticket holders in 2013. In the team's press release regarding the money-back guarantee, the Vice President of Ticketing, Steve Curran, gave the following reasoning for engaging in the program: "Like any business, we believe in our product. After three-plus years of positive feedback and helpful criticism, we guarantee that you will have a great time at Sea Best Field if you give us a try" (Jacksonville Sharks, 2013). The following year, they announced a guaranteed win game against the New Orleans Voodoo in which the team gave fans who purchased tickets to the game a free ticket to the next home game in their arena (Jacksonville Sharks, 2014). The Sharks lost and fans were entitled to a free ticket to the subsequent game.

Other teams have picked one game to offer the guarantee. For one game in December of 2012, the NBA's Phoenix Suns guaranteed a good time for all guests or a complete refund of the ticket price. Following the game, they received 365 refund requests but drew 17,517 fans, which was over 2,700 more than the team averaged the previous season and their highest attended game of the year to date (Soshnick, 2013). The team anticipated a higher rate of refund requests, so the promotion ended up being more successful than originally predicted. The money-back guarantee seems to be a good way to market to prospective new season ticket holders. The trade-off of having to refund the ticket price to the customer vs. adding ticket revenue works out in the venue's favor because it has been shown that fans are

money-back guarantee An agreement between the ticket seller and buyer that the buyer will receive a full refund if the event does not meet a standard of satisfaction for the patron.

unlikely to ask for a refund. It may be time for teams to consider the money-back-guarantee as a revenue-producing strategy in the future.

WEB-BASED TICKETS

Traditionally, customers would buy tickets from a team box office, over the phone, at retail stores, by mail order, or through Ticketmaster outlets. Now, the Internet has become a primary tool to purchase tickets. Preventing brokers or scalpers from selling and reselling tickets on the secondary ticket market has become a challenge for teams and venue owners and operators, especially with the development of relaxed secondary ticket market laws and websites such as StubHub. The question for teams is how to make revenue off of the secondary ticket market when a patron resells tickets. In 2000, the MLB's San Francisco Giants decreased no-shows by reselling tickets through their ticket exchange at a 50 percent reduction and generated half a million dollars in additional revenue (Dickey, 2000). Ticket exchanges offering season ticket holders an opportunity to resell tickets in a safe and legal environment have been offered. The major leagues now have their own official resale markets. In fact, StubHub is now the official secondary ticket sales market of MLB. Ticketmaster operates secondary ticket exchanges for the NBA, NHL, and NFL.

ELECTRONIC TICKET DELIVERY

Many venues and teams are using electronic and paperless ticket delivery as a more convenient way to deliver tickets to fans. The traditional ticket is also becoming a thing of the past with the emergence of new technologies, including smartphones. FanPass is the electronic ticketing delivery system developed and used by Major League Baseball. Industry giant Ticketmaster utilizes electronic ticketing as well. Flash Seats, owned by AXS, a company based in Los Angeles, is a ticketing system used by many college arenas (including those operated by Boise State and Texas A&M), professional venues such as Ford Field and Quicken Loans Arena, and the 2018 NCAA Basketball Final Four held in San Antonio, Texas (Flash seats, nd). The benefits of the electronic ticketing systems include fast entry into the venue, no tickets to forget, and a reduction in counterfeit tickets. Visitors can choose a credit card, driver's license, or other form of electronic identification, or they can use a Quick Response (QR) code or a mobile device application. The card is swiped or the code read by a handheld device operated by a representative at the entry gate. Seat holders are given a seat locator identifying their seats within the venue (Flash seats, nd).

Electronic ticket delivery can help limit lines into the venue and reduce the staffing required at ticket windows on game day. This ticketing capability can help raise revenue by making ticket purchases easier, offering the potential ability to deduct service charges from paper tickets, and allowing teams to add a service charge to paper tickets. Electronic ticket delivery is an innovative way to use technology to increase ticket revenue while minimizing the barriers to obtaining tickets from a team and reducing loss of revenue to the secondary ticket market.

UNIQUE GENERAL ADMISSIONS SEATING/STANDING ROOM SECTIONS

MLB
CLE

Offering **general admission** seating in unique market-like or food-court settings has become another strategy in major sports venues. In 2016, Cleveland's MLB team opened the Right Field District. The District ticket is $13 and includes the first drink (water, soft drink, or beer). A highlight of the District is food from local restaurants in the city of Cleveland. This serves as a cost-effective way to get fans into the stadium, instead of watching the game at local bars or restaurants. The idea is a low ticket price and providing a local pub or restaurant environment inside the stadium.

> **general admission** A fee paid for a seat in an unreserved seating or standing area in a public assembly facility.

Similarly, the 2015 north end of the AT&T Center has very few seats but instead has two rows of high top counter seats in the first and second row of the upper level. These provide first come, first served seats at a general admission price, subject to dynamic ticket pricing. In addition, the arena took out numerous rows of seats to add bars that had views of the floor. Patrons can purchase drinks and watch the game from the standing room bar area in the corner of the stadium, equal to the view of the third row of the upper deck.

LUXURY SUITES AND CLUB SEATS

Beyond the general seats in a large public assembly facility, luxury suites and club seating are often available. The highest-priced seats are often club and luxury suites. A primary reason for the stadium boom of the 1990s and 2000s was the lack of luxury seats in the older venues. The first venue to utilize luxury suites was the Houston Astrodome, which opened in 1965. The arena

HOUSTON

AUBURN

considered to be at the forefront of using suites was the Palace of Auburn Hills (former home to the Detroit Pistons). Club seats and luxury suites are often cited as the primary reason for building new arenas or stadiums.

Luxury suites are similar to a hotel room with seating areas to watch the action in the venue. Areas to serve food and beverages and to socialize are a benefit of these spaces. Food and beverages are often included with the price of the suite or are charged to the account holder. These suites are often leased for a season or multiple years to corporate entities that are team sponsors, who use the tickets for client development, or who use the space for game-day events or other purposes. Suite holders may be able to use the suite for functions during a game or on a non-game day.

Club seats are premium seats in a venue that have prime views of the game while providing extra amenities not available to other patrons. One part of the club seating at Cleveland's Quicken Loans Arena is the VIP club. The club seats are located behind the baseline. Seating is in the normal seating area, with a club area behind the seat. Amenities include five buffet-style food stations; complimentary drinks including beer, wine and soda; *CAVS* company or personal nameplate on your seats; and other club amenities (Cleveland Cavaliers, 2018). This seating area targets businesses that may want to combine business engagements with a sporting event.

LOADED TICKETS

Stored-value tickets have become commonplace at MLB stadiums. Patrons pay one price for a seat. The tickets include ballpark admission and an additional value that is programmed into the ticket, which can be used to purchase food, beverage, and merchandise. The stored value is accessible via a *PHILLIES* barcode scanned at the venues. MLB's Philadelphia Phillies call their package Power Tickets and sell and promote their stored-value tickets heavily on their ticket webpage. They estimate that patrons with Power Tickets spend 70 percent more on concessions and merchandise (Muret, 2009).

PERSONAL SEAT LICENSES   *ALBERT*

The personal seat license system traces back to the debenture system, which was first employed by Royal Albert Hall in London. When the hall was built in 1871, the builders offered 999-year leases for 1,200 of the 5,500 seats to help finance construction. Leases may be resold by the owners and have been

PSL'S ⤶

sold for as much as £1.2 million. The concert hall receives £960 for administrative fees from box holders. The box holder is able to attend most of the concerts. This system is also used for seats at the All England Lawn Tennis and Croquet Club in Wimbledon and Twickenham Stadium for Rugby Union Football (Daily Mail Reporter, 2008).

TENNIS - DICK

In the United States, the **personal seat license (PSL)** gives the holder the ability to purchase a specific seat in a stadium as long as the individual holds those seat rights. The idea of the first PSL is credited to Stanford University's tennis coach Dick Gould, who was trying to raise funds for a new tennis stadium for the school. Colleges used this strategy years before by exchanging better seats in their stadium for donations to the university. The strategy is also used at professional sports venues. For example, Churchill Downs, the famous horse racing track in Louisville, Kentucky, offers PSLs for the Kentucky Oaks and Kentucky Derby for a 3- or 5-year period. PSL license fees range for this racetrack from $3,600 to $135,000, and $290 to $1,400 for each ticket. The license fee must be paid in November, the year prior to the next year's racing season (Churchill Downs, 2013).

HORSE KENTUCKY

PSLs are most popularly used with NFL teams, which are limited to the amount of events they can sell tickets to due to a shorter season than that of most other professional leagues (ten home games, including preseason exhibition games). PSLs often are called by a promotional name unique to the particular team. For example, the Seattle Seahawks' PSLs are called Charter Seat Licenses, the Cincinnati Bengals' PSLs are called Charter Ownership Agreements, the San Francisco 49ers' and the Pittsburgh Steelers' PSLs are called Stadium Builder's Licenses, and the Dallas Cowboys' PSLs are called Seat Options (PSL Source, 2013).

SEATTLE

PSLs can account for a significant amount of revenue to pay for stadium construction costs. The two NFL teams of New York, the Jets and the Giants, expect to make $325 million and $400 million, respectively, from PSLs to put toward the $1.7-billion construction costs for MetLife Stadium. The highest-cost PSL under an agreement with the Jets costs $30,000, while the Dallas Cowboys have a PSL worth $150,000 (Nelson, 2012). Some argue that utilizing PSLs can price out fans who may be able to afford tickets but not the fee for the license. However, this has not seemed to be a deterrent to attendance, and attendances at NFL stadiums with PSLs remain steady. PSLs may be exchanged by the holder via the PSL source online exchange.

NFL) PSL's

personal seat license (PSL) A paid license that affords the buyer the right to buy season tickets for a specific seat in a stadium. The license is transferable and seat rights may be sold to another person once the owner decides not to purchase season tickets.

Promotions

Venues will often have special promotions or events in conjunction with a game day to help increase attendance. Many of these events are linked to a sponsor as a promotional opportunity. The concept of sport promotion is often associated with Bill Veeck, past owner of MLB's Cleveland Indians, St. Louis Browns, and Chicago White Sox from the 1940s through the 1970s. Veeck is regarded as one of the most innovative promoters in sport history. Some of his more famous promotions included "lucky chair" giveaways (with such prizes as 36 live lobsters), orchid giveaways on Mother's Day, and free admission days for cab drivers and bartenders. His efforts in 1959 yielded the best attendance for the White Sox since the 1929 season. Many of Veeck's concepts of promotions can be used to help improve attendance and gate receipts (Corbett, nd).

Free product or souvenir giveaways are some of the most common forms of promotions used by venue and team owners. Popular promotions include hat day, jersey day, dollar hot dog day, and soft drink day. Combining events can help create interest and improve attendance. Many college basketball teams have a local elementary school or community youth team play a shortened game at halftime. It is a way to entertain crowds at halftime and introduce parents and families to a form of inexpensive entertainment in the hopes of turning the halftime entertainment participants into future ticket buyers. Promotional days that honor or recognize certain groups can also be excellent forms of promotion. These groups may include youth sports leagues, camp groups, service industry professionals, Boy Scouts, Girl Scouts, and members of the military.

Loyalty Programs

loyalty program A structured, long-term program that rewards repeat customers for purchasing multiple units of an item or attending multiple events with incentives, gifts, or discounts.

Loyalty programs have become popular for marketers to develop patrons who exhibit brand loyalty through a structured long-term program that rewards repeat customers for purchasing multiple units of an item or attending multiple events with incentives, gifts, or discounts. AAdvantage by American Airlines was one of the first modern-day customer loyalty programs founded in 1981. Nowadays, almost every company has embarked on providing a loyalty program. This strategy has trickled down to the college sports level. One of the most well-known loyalty programs is the 12th Man Team Rewards program (TAMUS, 2005). This concept was created to help get fans to attend the

TEXAS A&M

other sports that populate Texas A&M Aggie athletic department events in addition to the major sports of football and basketball. Fans get a gift with as few as 12 events attended and can earn a watch valued at $250 for attending 100 Aggie events in a year.

Contemporary technology has helped make loyalty programs easier to incorporate at any level of sport. SuperFan, based in Louisville, Kentucky, is a company that produces an app that helps get college students excited and involved in university activities, particularly sports. SuperFanU is a loyalty and rewards platform intercollegiate athletics programs, powered by Super-Fan, an app for smartphones that allows fans to accrue rewards for event attendance. The app uses the company's proprietary mobile technology to boost an organization's attendance and revenue. It also provides analytics on fans and students to understand their profiles and what incentivizes them. This app has become popular to drive attendance at events at NCAA institutions of all divisions. (SuperfanU, nd)

LOUIE K

Ancillary Revenue

Ancillary revenue refers to the income generated from goods and services that enhance the primary product or service. Concessions, parking, and merchandise are some of the most common forms of ancillary revenue available at sporting events (see **Table 13-2**). While none of these services are necessary components to the sport spectating experiences, they are often expected by ticket holders and patrons.

ancillary revenue
Income generated from goods and services that enhance the primary product or service; examples include concessions, parking, and merchandise.

CONCESSIONS AND FOOD OPERATIONS

An integral part of the fan experience at spectator venues often revolves around food. Concession stands are small kiosks or locations in a venue that serve snacks or some other type of food. They are known as concessions

Table 13-2   Average Prices for Ancillary Items at Major League Venues

League	Beer	Soft Drink	Hot Dog	Parking	Program	Cap
NFL ('16)	$7.38	$4.86	$5.19	$32.58	N/A	$21.33
MLB ('16)	$5.90	$4.19	$4.52	$16.32	N/A	$16.48
NHL (14–15)	$7.45	$4.46	$4.94	$17.70	$2.60	$19.75
NBA (15–16)	$7.50	$4.49	$4.96	$17.15	$3.03	$19.74

because they are often operated by a third party independent of the venue. Venues may sell their own food or operate a concession company. Centerplate, Levy Restaurants, Delaware North, and Aramark are well-known food and hospitality concessionaires that run food operations in professional and college sporting facilities and venues.

Traditional food offerings in venues include hot dogs, soft drinks, popcorn, and candy. However, gone are the days when hamburgers, hotdogs, candy, popcorn, pretzels, and soda made up the totality of food and beverage options. In contemporary professional stadiums, sushi and other gourmet items (such as lobster rolls) are frequently offered—and, frankly, expected—as stadium fare. The stadium experience has become another form of food court by offering multiple restaurant choices. Often, the food of local restaurants and delis is featured. This partnership can provide revenue for a local business while offering fans food options they enjoy consuming outside of the venue. If individuals know they can purchase their favorite food inside the stadium, it may prove to be a positive revenue producer for the facility. Many new venues have added chain restaurants or fine dining to make their locations year-round destinations. For example, Miller Park in Milwaukee, Wisconsin, operates a TGI Friday's franchise, while Yankee Stadium in the Bronx, New York, has a Hard Rock Cafe open year round, game or no game. Including famous restaurants as part of the venue can help increase the gate receipt. The projected gross food and beverage revenue for one NFL stadium is over $5 million per game (AECOM, 2013).

One issue that stadiums and arenas face is alcohol sales. There has been debate about whether alcohol sales contribute to fan misconduct. Many stadiums around the world prohibit alcohol sales within the seating areas or in the stadium, period. In the United States, alcohol is a ubiquitous part of the concession offerings in professional venues. The potential for revenue production is significant for many venues. Nonetheless, the majority of facilities that reside on college campuses refuse to sell alcohol for any events. However, there is a growing trend of more college football stadiums introducing alcohol sales, including beer, wine, and liquor sales in their stadium as a way to increase attendance and add ticket revenue, and, in turn, add ancillary revenue. Darren K Royal—Texas Memorial Stadium began alcohol sales in 2015 and saw revenues of $1.8 million that year and $3.1 million in 2016. Professional stadiums have increased the selections of beer and even include hard liquor for sale.

When serving alcohol, it is important to be aware of a state's dram shop laws. The server, concessionaire, and team are liable if an individual whom the patron knows to be intoxicated is overserved on the premises and commits a crime or injures someone else in a traffic accident. Furthermore, all guests, regardless of age, must provide valid photo identification (Zullo, Bi, Xiaohan, & Siddiqui, 2013). Dram shop laws make the venue and servers liable for alcohol-related negligence. Also, venue operators should consider the type of event being played in the facility. If a venue has a liquor license and allows alcohol sales at many events, there may be event-specific restrictions on sale. It may not be appropriate to allow alcohol consumption at high school events, and many college conferences do not allow sales at their events. For example, the Southeastern Conference (SEC) prohibits alcohol at all conference-sponsored events.

PARKING

Depending on location, venues may operate their own parking facilities, contract to outside companies or **concessionaires**, or rely on surrounding areas and have no control over event parking. An example of a parking concessionaire

concessionaire An entity given the rights to operate and sell goods or services on premises that belong to another. Venues often enter into agreements to sell parking and food concessions on their premises.

VIGNETTE 13-1

Is Selling Beer at College Sporting Events Worth It?

A Division II school recently made headlines after deciding to be the first school in its state to sell alcohol at its games. Many colleges have grappled with the decision of whether to sell beer and mixed drinks at their events due to the potential institutional liability. The State University A&M—Universityville athletic program has seen its expenses increase as it continues to chase success as a Division II football powerhouse. Since more college football stadiums have started to commence alcohol sales, the athletic department at SUAM-U broached the subject of alcohol sales with its president and Board of Trustees. After some intense debate, beer sales were approved for the season.

Now came the hard part. The stadium operators needed to make sure beer sales would not lead to additional problems in the stadium. To limit liability, alcohol was sold in an area behind the end zone that was roped off from the rest of the venue out of a trailer owned by the third-party concessionaire. This allowed the university to be able to say they were not selling alcohol to their fans or students directly. Second, it kept alcohol in a contained part of the stadium. Individuals entering the area had to show identification that proved they were above the legal drinking age, 21 years old. At the end of the year, the university increased its football game-day revenue by $50,000. However, an average of ten more spectators per game were ejected from the venue, which became a concern to university officials. This shows how universities must balance the increase in revenue with the potential for bad public relations because of a potential increase in misconduct by fans.

is Central Parking, one of the world's largest parking facility operators. The company operates city, airport, and stadium parking lots. There are a number of advantages to operating facility-owned and -controlled lots. In addition to adding to overall profit of an event, it may serve as a way to lure patrons to the venue earlier in the day prior to a game to take part in pregame fan festivals, tailgating parties, or other events that complement the game. Including ample parking in the facility plan gives more flexibility and ability to raise revenue surrounding game day. However, it may be more cost-effective to have an outside dedicated concessionaire operate parking lots and not dedicate other facility personnel and energy to parking-related issues.

MERCHANDISE

Merchandise sales are another form of ancillary revenue. Whether it is a sporting event of the primary tenant, a special tournament event, or an outside group renting a facility, patrons often want to buy souvenirs to commemorate their experience. Teams may operate their own merchandise tables, booths, or stores or may contract to a concessionaire to manage and sell their merchandise. Many stadiums and arenas are home to club stores in which patrons may purchase products they cannot get anywhere else. These stores are open on game day and are often open all year long.

Event Revenue

ALTERNATIVE USES FOR SPORT-SPECIFIC STADIUMS

What uses are there for a baseball stadium when the team is on the road? How about in the winter months? An outdoor stadium with capacity for 80,000 people may not be appropriate for many types of outdoor events. Baseball stadiums have unique shapes that make them difficult to use for other events. Also, in what ways can an outdoor venue be rendered useful in cold and harsh climates? An indoor venue, in contrast, may be used every day of the year. In the off-season, indoor stadiums may still be used for sporting events, even in climates in which weather limits outdoor activities. Regardless of the type, large stadiums often present challenges for use outside of their intended sport or season.

Many venues have embarked on the strategy of hosting special events or events that are not traditionally hosted in that type of venue. Baseball stadiums have hosted international, friendly soccer matches when their primary tenant is on the road or in the off-season. Baseball stadiums such as Fenway Park and Yankee Stadium have also become the hosts of college football games. Yankee Stadium in New York has sought to host a college football game once a year including a Big Ten matchup between Rutgers and Maryland in 2017. During college bowl season, Yankee Stadium and AT&T Park (home to the San Francisco Giants) have been used for football games, even though they are oriented for baseball. Many baseball stadiums have started to host or plan to host college football postseason bowl games. Tropicana Field, home of MLB's Tampa Bay Rays, hosts the Beef 'O' Brady's St. Petersburg Bowl every December. An additional scheduling and revenue-producing opportunity is hosting concerts for national and international touring musical performers. Acts that draw crowds beyond the capacity of an indoor arena are often options for further facility use. Visits by major religious figures, such as the pope, have graced outdoor sport venues in years past, including Pimlico Race Course (in Baltimore, Maryland), Yankee Stadium, and Giants Stadium (former home to the NFL's New York Giants), among others (United States Conference of Catholic Bishops, nd).

BEEF

In frigid winter months, large venues often transform their stadiums into public ice rinks or host ice hockey competitions for the NHL and college teams. Since these games are thought of as novelties and played in stadiums with larger capacities, they are able to draw a considerable number of fans over the average crowd for a typical regular season game. The NHL has had much success with their Winter Classic hockey game held on or around New Year's Day in a football or baseball stadium. This event began in 2008 and was expanded in the 2013–2014 season as the NHL Stadium Series, with a series of games in New York and Los Angeles. Television ratings for the outdoor games have yielded five of the six highest-rated regular season games. The 2014 version of the game was played at Michigan Stadium in front of a crowd of 105,491 (Shea, 2014). The 2018 and 2019 versions are respectively scheduled to be played in New York City at Citi Field (a baseball stadium) and in South Bend, Indiana, at Notre Dame Stadium (college football stadium). Additionally, when the game is played in a baseball stadium, which is guaranteed not to be used by its primary tenant in January; college, high school, and alumni games can be held in the venue and yield additional ticket revenue.

HOCKEY

NOTRE DAME

Tennis venues have also sought to bring in visitors and revenue through scheduling concerts and other untraditional events. The U.S. Tennis

Association's (USTA) Billie Jean King National Tennis Center in Flushing Meadows, New York, hosts the qualifying and main draws of the U.S. Open tennis tournament for 3 weeks each year. The other 11 months of the year, the operators pursue other events to fill the tennis center. While the facility hosts USTA, NCAA, and high school tournaments throughout the year, Arthur Ashe Stadium (which is the main stadium of the tennis center) is often too large to be a useful venue for youth tournaments, and team matches require six courts at a time. In 2008, Arthur Ashe Stadium was host to a Women's National Basketball Association (WNBA) game between the New York Liberty and the Indiana Fever for the first-ever regular season basketball game played outdoors (Brill, 2008).

HOSTING CHAMPIONSHIPS

Numerous effective uses of available space exist for venues of all shapes and sizes, ranging from alternative competitive events on open dates to hospitality events. Renting a facility to high school or college teams for tournaments or games is a great option for professional, municipal, college, and high school venues. Professional and college sports facilities are used to host high school championships. These stadiums are often the largest venues the athletes will play in during the year and give them the chance to feel like they are playing in a big-time atmosphere. AT&T Stadium in Arlington, Texas, a retractable roof stadium, hosts the 12 UIL football championship games annually in late December. The University of Northern Iowa's UNI-Dome and Syracuse University's Carrier Dome (in New York) host the state championship football games for their respective states because they are large-capacity facilities and protect players and fans from inclement weather that is likely in those states in late November when the championship games are played.

HOSPITALITY EVENTS

Hospitality events are also a great option for venues, whether during an event, on a day without a scheduled event, or in the off season. For example, Citi Field, home baseball stadium of the New York Mets, offers many hospitality and event options when the stadium is not in use for games, during the 6 months when MLB is not in session. Citi Field lists 19 locations within their stadium that can be used for hospitality purposes during games or are completely independent of game day or in the off-season. These events can include

HOSPITALITY EVENTS

academic conferences, business meetings, trade shows, birthday parties, bar/bat mitzvahs, fundraisers, corporate events, or other family events. For these events, venues offer a number of potential event services, including appearances by former players, audiovisual displays, coat check, custom team apparel, gifts, furniture rentals, floral arrangements, décor options, lighting, menu selections, mascot appearances, personal event coordination, rentals, and parking packages. Providing each of these services can be included in different pricing packages for events. Utilizing these spaces, offering multiple party and event opportunities, and providing the resources to carry out these events can ensure that facilities are being used when the house is dark and brings in additional revenue to the organization. However, it is important to require that groups renting or using facilities have their own insurance policies and furnish proof of the policy (New York Mets, 2013). When serving alcohol in spaces rented at an event for hospitality or party events, venues will permit sales and consumption provided that their concessionaire is in control of the serving of alcoholic beverages.

In summary, stadium managers should seek to schedule or plan novel events such as bowl games or nontraditional sporting events for their sport-specific stadiums as a way to make use of the venue on an otherwise dark day. In addition to adding revenue, using these facilities can show that the organization is innovative and will likely lure other potential clients to rent or utilize the facility.

Multipurpose Sport Facilities

Spectator sport venues make up a large share of sport facilities, but multipurpose facilities may be used for spectator sports, participatory events, and physical fitness. Many municipalities or private entities have built indoor multipurpose facilities that can be used for fitness, recreation, and competitive sports. In addition, indoor and outdoor sports practice facilities built by SPIRE private entities have been developed. These facilities can be focused on one sport or can address the needs of multiple sports. Types include ice hockey rinks, indoor turf fields, sport court buildings, swimming pools, weight rooms, and training centers. SPIRE Institute in Geneva, Ohio, and Birmingham CrossPlex in Birmingham, Alabama, are two examples of large sports training and competition facilities that seek to draw local, regional, and national competitions with a wide variety of facilities. The types of events offered in these facilities include team practices, swim meets, track and field meets, youth and Amateur Athletic Union (AAU) basketball competitions, and road races.

SPIRE and CrossPlex collect membership fees, facility-use fees for practice usage, and entry fees for tournaments and invitational events. CrossPlex houses a 4,000-seat indoor track facility with a hydraulic banked track, an Olympic-size swimming pool with seating for 1,600, nine volleyball courts, a 5,000-seat basketball arena, and the ability to host other sports (Birmingham CrossPlex, 2013). SPIRE operates a training academy for postsecondary school athletes wishing to improve their skills and grades before enrolling in college (SPIRE Institute, nd). The facility is comparable to the CrossPlex facility and hosts collegiate conference championships in swimming, volleyball, and track and field. It is the yearly host of the Big Ten Conference championship in track and field, which has hosted NAIA national championships. The venue produces income from entry fees, spectator admissions, and concessions. Additionally, the public may use the indoor track, swimming pool, and fitness and weight facilities through membership programs or pay-by-use arrangements. Thus, these facilities operate as recreational and spectator sport venues.

Repurposed warehouses also provide potential opportunities as multipurpose sport venues. Spooky Nook Sports in Manheim, Pennsylvania, is a former industrial distribution center that offers 700,000 square feet of soccer fields, hockey fields, ten basketball courts, ten volleyball courts, indoor jogging track, full-size baseball field, under one roof and additional outdoor field space. The Nook also provides a fitness center, a rock climbing facility, meeting and party spaces, a food court, and a hotel. In addition to providing a space for sport practices and games, Spooky Nook markets itself as a location for corporate retreats.

PARTICIPATORY EVENTS

While spectator events in arenas or stadiums and recreational events in multipurpose complexes are lucrative revenue producers, participatory events are another part of the sport industry that is worth considering. These events, which are often defined by their novelty and/or physical difficulty, may appeal to endurance athletes and individuals who are motivated by health consciousness, fundraising, or a chance to try a new, fun fitness activity. Many of these events include professional, elite, and competitive components, but the vast majority of participants are not looking to win money; they simply wish to push themselves to complete the event. Road running races, triathlons, and other themed, noncompetitive races are options for raising money for charity or for-profit endeavors. This section will focus primarily on running races held on public streets.

INDIVIDUAL PARTICIPATORY EVENTS   ROAD RUNNING

Participatory events are a growing part of the sport industry. Road running has been one of the most popular participatory sports in the world, specifically mass participation road races. Running races comes in many sizes. Local 5K races may draw 100 runners, while a World Marathon Major event may draw 50,000 participants and 2 million spectators. Races of all sizes rely on registration fees. A **dynamic pricing** strategy is employed in many races. The earlier an individual registers, the lower the price. The New York City Marathon charges a registration fee depending on membership in the New York Road Runners (NYRR) and citizenship. NYRR members pay $255, while U.S. citizens pay $295 and International competitors (including citizens of Puerto Rico and other U.S. territories) are charged $358. In 2017, over 51,000 people finished the New York City Marathon.

Revenue is not always made simply through the individuals who compete. In addition to the race, major marathons host expositions, or expos, which charge exhibitors fees to display and sell their products. Expos are open to the public, and races sell race-related merchandise to competitors and other visitors. Runners are required to attend the expos to pick up their numbers and other complimentary items included in the race registration fees. Fees paid for these races are nonrefundable and are often due months ahead of time. For instance, the Boston Marathon, held the third Monday in April, has a registration deadline in September. Since marathon training often lasts 6 months, runners may have no idea what injuries or other issues will keep them from racing. Race organizers usually expect that 10 percent of the registered runners will not show up. No-shows can bring in over $1 million in revenue to a major marathon. Smaller races can learn a lesson from this strategy, as requiring preregistration for an event can boost revenue.

Other participatory events have become lucrative business ventures. Mud runs such as Tough Mudder, obstacle course races such as the Spartan Race, and adventure races such as the Urban Dare allow individuals to combine running skills with physical agility. These events can use parks, private property, local streets, or even professional venues such as stadiums and

dynamic pricing A process of pricing that is similar to differential pricing but concerned with the fluctuation of the price of a seat for an event based on demand. Determinants of dynamic pricing may include weather, quality of opponent, promotional offerings, or day of the week.

CROSS FIT

arenas. The CrossFit Games are often held in convention centers and arenas, with finals held at the StubHub Center in Carson, California. While these are participatory events and raise the bulk of their funds from entry fees, spectator admission and ancillary income are also used to increase revenue. The Open events that serve as qualifiers for the Games finals in California are $20 for entry while age-group athletes are charged $200 per entry to the CrossFit Games (CrossFit Games, 2017). As one of the fastest growing participatory events in the world, CrossFit continues to raise revenue through entry fees along with sponsor agreements with Rogue and Reebok.

Event Packaging

MARATHON

Participatory events like marathon road races such as the New York City Marathon and Boston Marathon always have more demand than supply of bib numbers. Event managers of smaller running events, however, are beginning to take advantage of the fact that the roads of a major city are being closed down for multiple days and multiple races of different distances can be run. Many road runners opt to participate in events because of the lure of finishers' medals. Packaging events into a "Challenge" can help increase revenue by getting likely participants to run more races in the weekend than they were intending to, in pursuit of a special medal for completing the challenge. In

DISNEY

the early 1990s, Walt Disney World theme parks in Lake Buena Vista, Florida, sought to lure visitors to its parks during the least busy time of the year, mid-January. As a result, they started the Walt Disney World Marathon in 1994, subsequently operated by RunDisney, a division of Disney Sports Enterprises, a unit of Walt Disney Parks and Resorts, which has evolved into four races over the course of a weekend:, the marathon, half-marathon, 5k, and 10k. RunDisney pioneered the concept of packaging races with a unique finisher medal for finishing multiple races. The medals are branded after Walt Disney Movie characters. A finisher of the half marathon and marathon on Saturday and Sunday earns the Goofy Challenge medal while a finisher of all four races completed earns the Dopey Challenge. To register for these events, Disney is able to charge the participant for each race entry, as well as an extra fee for the two challenges.

CINCI

Other races have adopted and adapted the event packaging concept. The Cincinnati Flying Pig Marathon combines the sponsorship of a Cincinnati culinary institution with multiple race events over the course of

VIGNETTE 13-2

Using Technology to Increase Registration Revenue

A table tennis club in South Texas was interested in raising money for their fledgling organization. As experienced players and tournament participants, they had traveled the world and had gathered knowledge about the ins and outs of the great table tennis competitions of the world. However, funds were limited and they sought to fill their coffers to fund a trip to the U.S. National Table Tennis Championship. Furthermore, South Texas lacked a table tennis event. Previous attempts at tournaments had been unsuccessful and lost money. Their question was, how could the club put on a successful tournament and maximize their revenue by putting on a tournament that would draw participants of all ages and abilities while potentially drawing repeat participants in future years? The event was held during the third week of March to coincide with Spring Break, a time when many converge on Texas to attend the beaches, and named it the Southern Beach Open to encourage participants to think about combining a table tennis tournament with their beach vacation. The club had traditionally utilized a Facebook site, Twitter, email, and word of mouth to spread their news, but decided other means were necessary to draw their goal of 200 participants. The tournament director registered the tournament with Omni-Pong, a table tennis tournament management service that offers online registration and publishes table tennis competition schedules from all around the country on their website. As a result,

individuals from other states entered the tournament, paying a $75 entry fee through the on-line registration service. A local bank put up $5,000 in exchange for naming rights to the men's and women's open divisions. This enabled the club to offer prize money to lure the best players from the region to attend. Local university sport management students marketed the tournament to sell tickets and some students became certified as officials. They volunteered their time to work the event, saving the table tennis club money on staffing.

Players of all different ratings: Singles and doubles registered for the mid-March tournament to take advantage of the well-marketed and planned event. To keep costs down, they utilized the space in the church gymnasium where they held their practices to host a tournament with six tables. Overall, the tournament drew 220 players, exceeding their goals. Entry fees raised $16,500. Concession sales raised another $2,000. In the subsequent weeks, they received fees for 20 no-shows, which added an additional $1,500 in revenue. Overall, the club received $20,000 in gross revenues. This event illustrates how collecting entry fees ahead of the event along with enabling online event registration can increase revenue. Through cooperation with community organizations, creative thinking with regard to the timing of the event, and web-based registration processes, a small group can put on a sporting event to support their endeavors.

the weekend (www.flyingpigmarathon.com, nd). The challenge is promoted on the website as follows:

In the celebration of the city of Cincinnati and the Flying Pig Marathon, Skyline Chili is proud to present the 3-Way and 4-Way Challenge in the Flying Pig Marathon weekend of events. (The events' namesakes are the Skyline 3-Way, a Cincinnati signature dish crafted from chili, spaghetti and cheese; and the Skyline 4-Way, crafted from chili, spaghetti, cheese, and onions.) To complete the 3-Way Challenge, a single runner must complete Saturday's 5K and 10K events, as well as Sunday's Half Marathon. To complete the 4-Way

Challenge, a single runner must complete Saturday's 5K and 10K events, as well as Sunday's Full Marathon. (flyingpigmarathon.com, nd)

In addition to the finisher medal for each race, the 3-Way and 4-Way challenge winner receives an additional medal for completing each respective challenge. So, event packaging can serve as a way to secure more sponsorship revenue, drive additional excitement for an event, increase participation-related revenue via entries, and promote a city's culture and pride.

SUMMARY

There are multiple ways that facility and event operators can raise revenue from their events. These methods range from ticket sales, which may involve running promotions, to ancillary revenue from concessions, to merchandise sales, to parking fees. Primary tenants are not the only ones who can bring revenue to a facility; concerts, high school games, college games, and championship events are also potential revenue sources. Utilizing suites, club seating, and other spaces within a venue during the season and out of season can add flexibility and ways to produce more revenue. Multipurpose venues and city streets can provide areas for participatory events, including road running events. Overall, the possibilities for producing revenue from sport facilities and events are endless. A little creativity and innovation can go a long way in helping venue and event operators produce income.

DISCUSSION QUESTIONS

1. List the multiple types of sport facilities, and describe how sport managers and event planners can produce revenue for each. Consider the versatility of each facility.
2. Does the type of facility impact the type of revenue that can be raised?
3. What are some ethical considerations with regard to serving alcohol at sporting events? Does the type of event impact whether alcohol sales are appropriate?
4. What is ancillary revenue, and what strategies can be used to increase it?
5. In what ways can revenue be raised at road races from participants and spectators?

Case STUDY

The 50/50 Raffle Goes Digital

The electronic raffle has become ubiquitous in professional sporting events lately as a driver of ancillary revenue, as a visitor to the Quicken Loans Arena in Cleveland, Ohio, can likely attest. In 2013, Cleveland sport fans saw a new feature unveiled at major sporting events. The Cleveland Cavaliers offer fans the ability to enter a 50/50 raffle, where half of the pot goes to the winner and the other half to Cavaliers Youth Foundation and other area charities. Other arena tenants, the Cleveland Monsters hockey team and the Cleveland Gladiators arena football team, partake in these raffles to support charities as well.

The ability to offer these raffles nightly is made possible due to technological advances. Pointstreak 5050, a Canadian company, has pioneered digital raffle capabilities, developing many advantages over traditional ticket raffles. This company has teamed with many professional teams, including those in the Cleveland area. Tickets are sold by employees who have handheld devices with ticket printers attached. This gives sellers the ability to walk throughout the arena to distribute tickets, while automatically entering patrons into the drawing. This system has increased the amount of revenue that can be taken in during a raffle. It allows fans and ticket sellers to know how much the pot is worth at all times through integration with scoreboard displays, provides the possibility of unlimited tickets to be sold, and produces instant sales and reconciliation reports. Additionally, a title sponsor of the raffle may represent another form of revenue for the team.

The other teams in Cleveland have seen similar success from their 50/50 raffles at Quicken Loans Arena, MLB's Cleveland Indians had adopted the same technology to provide raffles for the 2014 season. During the 2017 ALDS in Cleveland, one prize rose to $33,708, while the charity raised the same amount. Other teams across North America are utilizing this raffling technology. The Tampa Bay Lightning have seen success with their 50/50 raffles offering prizes that consistently reach over $20,000 while donating a portion of each game's proceeds will support cancer research at a local research center and other local charities. The 2018 NHL All-Star game in Tampa Bay set a record for the largest 50/50 raffle pot in U.S. history, $276,104, while raising money to build a state-of-the-art street hockey rink for the community. Many teams have seen their contributions to their charities increase significantly, especially the Phoenix Coyotes, who saw a 723 percent increase in contributions when compared with using paper tickets in previous years. Overall, this type of raffle offers excitement for fans, creates more awareness about team charities and title sponsors, provides more sponsorship opportunities, and supports charitable foundations. In the NHL's case, it can provide funding for a legacy project for a mega-event.

Pretend you are the manager of a multipurpose indoor sport facility and wish to capitalize on the revenue-generating possibilities offered by technological advances, such as those employed at Quicken Loans Arena. Consider the following:

1. In what ways can technology increase your ability to enhance revenue production and fundraising for your organization?
2. What revenue-producing opportunities might an electronic raffle provide?
3. How might the nonprofit versus for-profit status of your organization affect how you distribute the proceeds of your 50/50 raffle?
4. How might beacon technology enhance your ability to enhance revenue streams?
5. Detail the benefits and potential outcomes of using your chosen technology to enhance ancillary revenue.

REFERENCES

AECOM Technical Services. (2013). Coliseum city football stadium revenue study. Chicago. Retrieved from http://newballpark.org/2013/07/16 /coliseum-city-football-stadium-revenue-study/

Birmingham CrossPlex. (2013). Retrieved from http://www.birminghamcrossplex.com

Brill, L. (2008). Liberty players excited for Outdoor Classic. Retrieved from http:// www.wnba.com/archive/wnba/liberty/news/loc_celebs.html

Churchill Downs. (2013). Personal seat licenses. Retrieved from https://www .kentuckyderby.com/tickets/how-to-buy/personal-seat-license

Cleveland Cavaliers. (2018). Hard VIP Club. Retrieved from https://www.theqarena .com/premium/premium-locations/vip-club/

Cleveland Indians. (2013). Indians introduce Perfect 10 Flex Pack ticket option for 2013 season. Retrieved from http://m.indians.mlb.com/news/article/40415526 /indians-introduce-perfect-10-flex-pack-ticket-option-for-2013-season

Corbett, W. (nd). Bill Veeck. Retrieved from http://sabr.org/bioproj/person /7b0b5f10

CrossFit Games. (2017). Competition rulebook. Retrieved from https://s3.amazonaws .com/crossfitpubliccontent/2017CrossFitGames_Rulebook.pdf

Daily Mail Reporter. (2008). For sale: The Albert Hall with a £1.2m view. Retrieved from http://www.dailymail.co.uk/news/article-1023841/For-sale-The-Albert -Hall-box-1-2m-view.html

Dickey, G. (2000). Giants' new tickets plan a winner. Retrieved from http://www .sfgate.com/sports/article/Giants-New-Ticket-Plan-a-Winner-2755154.php

Flash Seats. (nd). Flash Seats is the future of ticketing today. Retrieved from http:// www.flashseats.com/

Flying Pig Marathon. (nd). 3-Way/ 4-Way challenge. Retrieved from http:// flyingpigmarathon.com/events/3-way-4way/

Howard, D. R., & Crompton, J. L. (2005). *Financing sport* (2nd ed.). Morgantown, WV: Fitness Information Technology.

Jacksonville Sharks. (2013). Sharks offer season ticket money-back guarantee. Retrieved from http://www.arenafan.com/news/?page=pressrel&article=10997

Jacksonville Sharks. (2014). Sharks announce guaranteed win ticket redemption information. Retrieved from http://www.jaxsharks.com/news/index .html?article_id=821

Muret, D. (2009). Royals, Indians will join MLB clubs selling stored-value tickets. *Street & Smith's Sport Business Daily.* Retrieved from http://www.sports businessdaily.com/Journal/Issues/2009/01/20090119/This-Weeks-News /Royals-Indians-Will-Join-MLB-Clubs-Selling-Stored-Value-Tickets.aspx

Nelson, T. (2012). NFL stadium personal seat licenses compared. *MPR News.* Retrieved from https://www.mprnews.org/story/2012/11/15/sports /nfl-personal-seat-licenses-compared

New York Mets. (2013). Metropolitan hospitality. Retrieved from http://mets.mlb .com/nym/metropolitanhospitality/index.jsp

PSL Source. (2013). Frequently asked questions. Retrieved from http://www
.pslsource.com/faq/psl_source

Quicken Loans Arena. (2017). VIP Club. Retrieved from https://www.theqarena.com
/premium/premium-locations/vip-club

Shea, B. (2014). NHL Winter Classic at Big House hits record for tickets, ratings.
Retrieved from http://www.crainsdetroit.com/article/20140102
/NEWS/140109988/nhl-winter-classic-at-big-house-hits-record-for-tickets-ratings

Soshnick, S. (2013). Money-back offer from NBA's Suns yields 365 refund requests.
Bloomberg. Retrieved from http://www.bloomberg.com/news/2013-01-07
/money-back-offer-from-nba-s-suns-yields-365-refund-requests.html

SPIRE Institute. (nd). Retrieved from http://www.spireinstitute.com

SuperfanU. (nd). SuperfanU. Retrieved from https://superfanu.com/

TAMUS. (2005). Fan rewards program contributes to record attendance at Texas
A&M athletic events. Retrieved from https://news.tamus.edu/fan-rewards
-program-contributes-to-record-attendance-at-texas-am-athletic-events/

Team Marketing Report. (2014). NHL fan cost index. Retrieved from http://www
.fancostexperience.com/pages/fcx/blog_pdfs/entry0000020_pdf001.pdf

Team Marketing Report. (2016). MLB 2016 Retrieved from https://www.team
marketing.com/

Team Marketing Report. (2016a). NBA 2015-2016 Retrieved from https://www
.teammarketing.com/

Team Marketing Report. (2016b). NFL 2016 from https://www.teammarketing.com/

United States Conference of Catholic Bishops. (nd). (2015). Pope Benedict XVI's
itinerary. Retrieved from http://www.uspapalvisit.org/itinerary_en.htm

Zullo, R., Bi, X., Xiaohan, Y., & Siddiqui, Y. (2013). *The fiscal and social effects of state
alcohol control systems*. Ann Arbor, MI: Institute for Research on Labor, Employment, and the Economy.

CHAPTER 14

Sustainability and Legacy

Kostas Karadakis, Trevor Bopp, and Thomas J. Aicher

CHAPTER OBJECTIVES

Upon completion of this chapter, the reader will be able to:

1. Demonstrate a comprehensive understanding of the immediate and long-term impact, or legacies, of events.

2. Account for and give consideration to the numerous and integrative infrastructures and developments that can accompany the hosting of medium- and small-scale events.

3. Capitalize on the economic, social, emotional, promotional, and capital benefits to be derived from the proper management of medium- and small-scale events.

CHAPTER OVERVIEW

Facilities are too often left empty or underutilized, and many events do not make it past the inaugural year. This chapter will outline the strategies and techniques that organizations employ to create sustainable facilities and events that have a positive impact on the facility, event, and community.

IndustryVOICE

Maxilis Triantafyllidis—Owner/Operator Triantafyllidis Beach Arena

Triantafyllidis Beach Arena (http://www.beacharena .gr/index.php/poioi-eimaste /mixalis) is the first full-service indoor beach volleyball facility in Greece that is privately owned and operated. It is open to people of all ages with the goal of providing those interested in playing/having access to sport and providing them with a safe place to play. This facility includes multiple courts, training areas, academies, and camps for members to use. In addition, this private facility provides many additional amenities such as training rooms, video rooms, changing rooms, bathrooms, etc., and all of these are ADA compliant.

Prior to opening this facility, I was a successful volleyball player and coach. Playing for the Greek national volleyball team in 1987, I won 26 titles and a bronze medal. In total, I was proud to amass 365 international participations, ten championships, and seven cups with Olympiacos, two championships with Panathinaicos, and was a two-time MVP in Greek championships. In beach volleyball, I won King of the Beach in 1994, three championships in 3×3, and three championships in 2×2. I served on the Women's Greek national beach volleyball team as head coach in 1997, was Panathinaicos' head coach from 1997 to 1998, and was the Greek national team assistant coach from 2000 to 2004. In addition to these experiences, I developed the "Volley & Beachvolley Camps," managed a beachvolley tournament, and served on a number of municipal organization committees.

My passion and lifelong experience with beach volleyball was why I entered into this industry. Following my competitive playing career, I moved into the owner/ business side of beach/indoor volleyball. Through this experience, I enjoyed the ability to coach and train athletes. However, a business like this one is not common in Greece. Even with the economic conditions/crisis in the

last 5 to 6 years in Greece, I took a risk by starting something in an industry that had a lot of demands, but no offerings. So, I decided to become the business owner/ president/trainer and coach for the beach volleyball industry and start it up. My goal is to continue to grow the interest in the Greek youth and general population to have the desire to continue to participate in beach volleyball at the recreational level. Additionally, I'd like to grow to host international competitions, as well as hosting and traveling to organized tournaments for athletes of all ages. There is a recreational beach volleyball tourism market that I'd like to pursue to offer more opportunities to my members and attract new participants.

I believe that the goal is to offer competitive sport and access to sport for all ages, as everyone is in need of exercise, especially those individuals who are older and can benefit from being able to engage in sport and exercise as it serves as a way to escape the everyday routine and serve as a therapeutic release for people in Greece. When you think of the condition of the economy in Greece, beach volleyball has been therapeutic in releasing some of the citizens' frustrations rather than seeing a therapist.

One of the biggest challenges that I have ever faced was the process of opening the facility. First, I had to attain approval for the land for the facility, which, in Greece, is unique because I cannot build on or uncover any archeological/historically significant lands/artifacts. This process alone took approximately 11 months to complete, with numerous roadblocks and bureaucracy to manage. Additionally, attaining financial support from loans and investors was challenging given the length of time to begin to generate any revenue. I had several strategies to navigate this process, including patience! Most important, I kept the passion, stayed motivated, and was very persistent—even when I hit a roadblock. Being transparent with all of the different groups that needed to be included in order to move through the bureaucracy and get the appropriate licenses and permits was critical to success. Taking the time to do the research to know where to go for approvals is not easy—there are multiple meetings, lawyers, banks, and municipalities that required my attention. It is not a one-stop shop. I was constantly running from one person to the next to get the signatures and approvals.

I think beach volleyball and beach volleyball tournaments in the form of sport tourism have a big following and an untapped market to be exploited. However, while it is still at a recreational level, it has grown at a rapid pace. In the past, there was a high level of competition, but in the last 15 years and with the current situation in Greece, there has been a drop in the competitive/professional level. It is the recreational level (for all ages) at which there is a lot of potential and the direction in which future trends are moving. This is why I have begun to capitalize on the youth and continue to support and grow the sport over their life span. It is still in its infancy as there are not enough resources to support the production of an elite athlete, and the competitive level is still behind other sports. However, the passion, desire, and interest in playing beach volleyball for participants of all ages is there and; therefore, I aim to do my part to further develop the niche.

To grow the sport, there are several strategies that may be employed. For example, social media is essential to promoting events and programs and to generating awareness in order to target future participants. This has proven invaluable, as the youth are more interested and more apt to use these tools for information searches and sharing with their followers. I use a lot of daily posts, doing different things that target relationship building. There is a large emphasis on capturing milestones of the athletes to grow the brand and to create unique content to share with those participating and following. Some of the things may be simple, like showing a birthday party and wishes of current players. Developing symbiotic relationships with sponsors has also proven to help benefit the sport, as well as growing the brand and awareness of the organization's efforts to grow the sport. Word of mouth is also heavily relied upon to increase awareness and create excitement and to market events and tournaments.

When hiring someone for an entry-level position, I pursue candidates with very specific traits. First, trust in the individual is critical. In Greek culture, it is common to build a business for the family and have it continue in the family into the future. So, if I bring in an outside individual, I need to be able to trust that person like family. Next, if that person can be trusted, I find a suitable, important role in the organization for that person. Again, gathering recommendations from those within the organization is a key step. I look for loyalty and someone who is interested in the long-term growth of the business and industry. Someone who is respectful and understands or truly wants to learn the business and have a passion for it is highly important. I do not want someone who is only looking to get his or her foot in the door or only collect a paycheck because that person will leave whenever he or she wishes to do so on a whim. I realize that this is a risk, but I try to eliminate this type of candidate quickly.

When considering professional development, my advice is to follow this Steve Jobs quote as guidance and inspiration, "Have the courage to follow your heart and intuition." You should know what you truly want to become; make your dreams a reality. From a small child going to international sporting events and seeing the facilities, the clubs, the spectators, the players interacting, and post-game events have truly inspired me to make my dream of owning a facility a reality. It took 30 years to get to a position that would allow me to make these dreams a reality. But it finally happened! So, don't give up on your career goals. Take your dreams and make them your everyday vision and always use this idea to influence your attitude.

Finally, my organization is a great example of positive change and long-term legacy. The Triantafyllidis Beach Arena advocates and represents all generations and represents strong core values, meanings, and a purpose for a sport facility's existence and function. Success, competition, challenge, but, most importantly, sport development and wellness and health are the elements that make my legacy most worthwhile.

Introduction

Countries, states, communities, and local residents compete to host sporting events for a variety of positively perceived reasons (e.g., prestige, awareness, economic profitability, increased tourist activity, and infrastructure development). However, being awarded a sport event is almost certain to result in both positive and negative impacts on the host community and its residents. A positive impact can include new and updated roads, entertainment venues and other infrastructures, or increased tourism revenue, media exposure, commercial appeal, and civic pride. A negative impact can include overcrowding and increased travel concerns, disruption to the local environment, the building or renovating of uneconomical and unsustainable infrastructures, or unfavorable perceptions of the host community. Whether positive or negative, the greater the social, economic, and environmental impact of a sport event and the longer lasting its residual effects, the more likely a sport event legacy is to be created.

What Are Legacies?

Legacies are "the material and non-material effects produced directly or indirectly by the sport event, whether planned or not, that durably transform the host region in an objectively and subjectively, positive or negative way" (Chappelet & Junod, 2006, p. 84). Furthermore, legacies include "all planned and unplanned, positive and negative, tangible and intangible structures created for and by a sport event that remain longer than the event itself" (Preuss, 2007, p. 211). Legacies may be **tangible** or material, such as sports facilities, or they may be **intangible** or nonmaterial, such as sociocultural development. Tangible legacies, as indicated by the name, are easy to recognize, whereas intangible or nonmaterial legacies are more of a challenge to identify and measure (Chappelet, 2008).

As you can see from these descriptions, the term legacy is broadly defined and can encompass all facets of hosting an event. Examining the legacy of an event can be problematic in that different regions, cultures, and industries consider various outcomes of the event when examining legacies and the subsequent impacts. Simply put, legacies are the "things" left behind upon completion of an event. These things can be tangible, such as roads, venues, and housing; or intangible, such as memories from attending the event or the perception that the host community/region is a capable and experienced locale to

legacy The lasting direct or indirect effects generated from hosting an event that may positively or negatively impact the community.

tangible legacy Observable, easily identified, or physical changes to the host community that remain upon conclusion of the event.

intangible legacy Nonphysical changes associated with the transfer of knowledge, governmental reform, and emotional capital for residents, participants, and spectators, as well as psychological improvements to the city's image and social structure.

host future events. Legacies can be small or large, valuable or worthless, positive or negative, and can last an indeterminate amount of time, from days to years. Legacies can result from any and all sport events, ranging from small-scale (e.g., local charity race) to mega (e.g., Olympic Games or International Federation of Association Football [FIFA] World Cup) events.

Irrespective of size, community leaders believe that hosting a sport event can be the spark needed for urban development and, as a result, have pursued hosting various types and sizes of sport events to use as a platform to attract investors and tourists and to benefit their residents (Misener & Mason, 2008). Thus, the ultimate objective for event organizers and community leaders should be to determine how to develop and market sport events in ways that promote a host city (Misener & Mason, 2009). The resulting impact of such development and marketing efforts could lead to the establishment of sustainable sport venues and events in the local community, increases in sport tourism, improved infrastructure, and the progression of a legacy for both the sport event and host city/community.

Growth in Sport Tourism

As interest in sport and the consumption of sport have increased, so too has the need for more sport options, whether as a participant or as a spectator, when traveling. The tourism industry, as well as the sport industry, has witnessed growth in vacations in which a sporting event, ranging from youth recreational leagues to the professional ranks, is the main attraction or catalyst for the trip. In fact, a number of sporting events, such as the Daytona 500, National Collegiate Athletic Association (NCAA) national championships, FIFA World Cup, and Olympic Games, have themselves become vacation destinations. Sport event tourism has played a primary and central role for host destinations, evidenced by the inclusion of sport events in their tourism marketing plans (Chalip & Leyns, 2002; Higham & Hinch, 2002). However, the type (i.e., size) of sport events that take place in certain destinations is often contingent upon the ability of the host community to accommodate the influx of tourists, the current or prospective infrastructure, and the desired impact(s). Sport events can range from mega-events such as the FIFA World Cup and the Olympic Games, to large- or medium-size sport events such as national championships and college and high school tournaments, to small-scale events such as local charity walks/runs and recreational sport leagues. Again, it is important to consider the size of each event because of its impact on the community (Chalip & Costa, 2005).

(handwritten margin note: small vs mega vs medium)

Sport Event Sizes

The size of a sporting event is an important consideration in the discussion of legacies. As various events range in size, so too does their impact on the host community, participants, and spectators. Mega-sporting events garner the most attention and media exposure on a global scene, and as such, could be argued to result in the greatest and most impactful legacies. Given the large number of spectators, often a worldwide audience, it is understandable for event organizers and host communities to expect a positive long-term impact from their investments. For instance, anecdotal evidence supports the claim that the cities of Sydney, Australia, (host of the 2000 Summer Olympic Games), and Vancouver, British Columbia, Canada (host of the 2012 Winter Olympic Games), witnessed positive legacies regarding their cities as sport-event and tourist destinations. Specifically, one of the lasting legacies used on a daily basis by Vancouver residents and tourists is the new Sea to Sky Highway, which has made it faster and safer for individuals to travel from Vancouver to Whistler. However, mega-sporting events have been critiqued in recent years regarding the sustainability of their positive legacies (Smith, 2010). The best support of this argument would be the 1976 Summer Olympic Games hosted by Montreal, Quebec, Canada. The city of Montreal amassed millions of dollars of debt and fell so far behind schedule that the construction of one of the primary venues was not completed until after the games. In fact, it took the city 30 years to pay off the debt for Montreal's Olympic Stadium, with residents finally paying it off in 2006. Additionally, the Athens Organizing Committee did such a poor job of planning for the postevent use of the venues developed for the 2004 Olympic Games hosted in Athens, Greece, that many of them are empty and go unused and have become **white elephants**. Thus, scholars have suggested that the hosting of medium- and small-scale

(handwritten margin notes: olympics / Sydney / vancouver / SKY HIGH / 1979 MONTREAL CANADA / ATHENS GREESA)

white elephant In reference to event legacy, a stadium, arena, or other facility constructed to host an event that remains underutilized after the event has occurred.

sporting events could be more beneficial in the pursuit of a positive legacy (Higham, 1999; Gibson, Kaplanidou, & Kang, 2012; Misener & Mason, 2006). As such, the primary focus of this chapter will center on medium- and small-scale events.

Medium- and Small-Scale Events

Medium- and small-scale events are currently being utilized more often in community development strategies as host communities are becoming more proactive in the planning and managing stages of hosting an event to ensure that they allow for and attain the numerous potential benefits of doing so. Event hosts and organizers have recognized the opportunities to advance their image via increased media attention, promote their community's distinguishing features, draw tourists (as well as participants), and enhance investment opportunities for outside and local businesses (Misener & Mason, 2006). Not only is the size of an event an important consideration but the type of event is also important.

SIZE + TYPE important

Depending on the event, host communities may need to plan for an influx of spectators or participants, each bringing with them different needs, expectations, and outcomes. Higham (1999) suggests that there is more tourism development potential in small-scale events given that some of these small-scale events will draw spectators, while others, such as marathons, due to their features (i.e., competition) are more likely to attract participants. Furthermore, Higham (1999) suggests that small-scale sport events can have a more positive impact on residents, as they "comply with the principles of **sustainable tourism**" (p. 87). That is because the infrastructure to host the event already exists; such events require minor investment of public capital, and the resultant negative impacts (i.e., crowding and congestion) are more manageable.   ECONOMIC BENEFITS

Higham (1999)

MARATHONS

sustainable tourism
Development of the infrastructure in the host community to generate a continual flow of tourist activity.

While economic benefits appear to be of prime consideration when discussing the expected benefits of any event, social benefits can be extremely important to local and small-scale events. Small-scale events can often bring about a sense of civic pride, allowing local residents and volunteers to claim a sense of ownership and responsibility for the event. Walo, Bull, and Breen (1996) report that residents were more likely to volunteer for events that were perceived as bringing the community together, demonstrating the potential bond that can exist between a small-scale or local event and the host community.

CIVIC PRIDE

WALO, BULL, BREEN 1996.

VIGNETTE 14-1

✳ Lake Myrtle Sports Complex ✳   AUBURNDALE, FLORIDA

SOCCER
BASEBALL

© Sean Pavone/Shutterstock

In 2009, the city of Auburndale, Florida, opened a multipurpose sports complex consisting of soccer and baseball fields with the capabilities of hosting a variety of sport events such as lacrosse, rugby, and flag football. The sports complex is used to attract tourists by hosting various sporting events organized by the Polk County Tourism and Sports Marketing Headquarters. Some of the recurring events that are hosted include Florida State Soccer Association's Florida Classic, RussMatt Central Florida Baseball Invitational, and Florida State Soccer Association's State Cup. The sports complex is also home to the Florida Youth Soccer Association headquarters and host to the Florida Sports Hall of Fame. The sports complex provides the city of Auburndale with the opportunity to host various sporting events to attract local communities as well as tourists to attend tournaments. By hosting regular tournaments, the city of Auburndale and the organizers can leverage the tournaments to create an economic impact for the community. Furthermore, the complex provides an opportunity for residents to volunteer at the various sporting events, provides children with a place to play sports, and allows residents to come together and get to know one another, either through volunteering or by watching the children from the sideline. Thus, the complex provides residents of Auburndale a social, economic, and infrastructure legacy. Students should do some research to determine who is in charge of their state's and county's tourism and sport event initiatives to identify which sporting events occur on a regular basis in their given communities. Doing so will provide them with the opportunity to identify any legacies generated from hosting events in their community.

Why Is Legacy Important?

Given the increases in sport event destination traveling and sport tourism, interests have turned to the impact of hosting a sport event on the local community. The potential legacy that can be left with the host community, as well as with a particular sporting event, has drawn substantial consideration in the planning and organization of a sport event. Furthermore, investments made toward hosting an event have become an important component of community resources and infrastructure development. As a result of this increased awareness and desire to host events, experts have become more interested in gaining a better understanding of how to measure legacies so as to maximize positive legacies and minimize negative legacies. Additional interests lie in helping communities and event hosts to better plan sporting events and sport tourism destinations, as well as to address questions with regard to the postevent use of infrastructures and facilities developed or improved for the event (Karadakis & Kaplanidou, 2012).

It has been suggested that event organizers are responsible for utilizing sport events for the long-term development of a host community, which has directed attention to the legacy phenomenon (Weed & Bull, 2004). For instance, when awarding the Olympic Games, the International Olympic Committee (IOC) is concerned with the lasting impact on the host city. More specifically, the IOC has indicated three reasons that generating positive legacies is important to a variety of sport events:

- To prevent the host community from criticizing the organizers of the event for any potential shortcomings
- To substantiate the use of public resources for the potential sport-event-related infrastructure(s)
- To stimulate interest for the community and/or surrounding communities to host future events, helping to ensure the continuity of the event

As it relates to the sport industry, the term legacy is fairly new, and there is no clear definition of what legacy means in the sport event framework (Preuss, 2007). The IOC explains that difficulties in defining the term legacy can be attributed to the fact that different cultures can, and often do, interpret the meaning of legacy in a variety of ways. As defined previously, legacies are "the material and non-material effects produced directly or indirectly by the sport event, whether planned or not, that durably transform the host region in an objectively and subjectively, positive or negative way" (Chappelet & Junod, 2006, p. 84). Similarly, Preuss (2007) offers a similar definition: "Irrespective of the time of production and space, legacy is all planned and unplanned, positive and negative, tangible and intangible structures created for and by a sport event that remain longer than the event itself" (p. 211).

[Handwritten margin notes: K + K 2012; WEED + BULL 2004; OLYMPIC GAMES; IOC; 3 REASONS; NO CLEAR DEFINITION; PREUSS 2007; IOC EXPLAINS DIFICULTY; LEGACY DEFINITIONS]

Notice in these definitions that a legacy consists of effects that are tangible and intangible, are planned and unplanned, have a direct or indirect outcome, can be assessed objectively as well as subjectively, and can be both positive and negative. The contradictory nature of this definition clearly demonstrates the complexity associated with attempting to determine just what a legacy entails and just how it is produced. Thus, Preuss (2007) further explains that there are five dimensions of legacy incorporated into its definition:

5 DIMENTIONS OF LEGACY ↳

- Degree of planned/unplanned structure
- Degree of positive/negative structure
- Degree of tangible/intangible structure
- Duration and time of a changed structure
- Space affected by changed structure

Components of Legacy Impacts

★ TANGABLE

OLYMPICS ATLANTA

280

At this time, it is important to note a component of legacies that seems ambiguous but covers a spectrum of resultant impacts of hosting an event: tangible and intangible legacies. Tangible legacies are observable, are easily identified, include programs and initiatives, are measured by infrastructure (consisting of infrastructures either related to sport or not), consist of technological and environmental improvements to the community/city, and offer networking opportunities for local and international businesses to expand. Looking back at the 1996 Olympic Games in Atlanta, Georgia, infrastructure developed for the Games such as the Athletes' Village was given to the local university to serve as dorms for the students once the games were over. Furthermore, relationships and networking established during the Games resulted in 280 more international businesses in Atlanta (International Olympic Committee Factsheet, December 2013).

★INTANGABLE

K+K 2010

"CAN DO"

Conversely, intangible legacies are a little more difficult to identify and measure. Intangible legacies can be associated with the transfer of knowledge, governmental reform, and emotional capital for residents, participants, and spectators, as well as psychological improvements to the city's image and social structure. According to Kaplanidou and Karadakis (2010), examples of emotional capital experienced at the Vancouver Olympics included inspiration, pride, "can do" attitude, feelings of empowerment, excitement and feelings of togetherness, and gratitude for created opportunities for business and collaboration. As indicated by the Tourism BC Vice President of 2010 and Corporate Relations, "What a great way to build confidence in Vancouver for us, that we could pull off something this big. It builds an air of confidence and, you know, it can only be good for us." (p. 115)

Legacy Event Structures

While it may be difficult to determine exactly which tangible and intangible legacies to expect from hosting and/or organizing an event, there are several types of legacies that are more substantive. In examining characteristics of legacy types and in an attempt to classify the variety of legacies, Preuss (2007) suggests six event structures that can be created as positive offshoots from hosting an event: (1) infrastructure, (2) know-how, (3) networks, (4) culture (created both during the preparation stages of hosting the event and postevent), (5) emotions, and (6) image. The following section will present further details on each of the various event structures (from Gratton & Preuss, 2008, p. 1926).

6 EVENT STRUCTURES

INFRASTRUCTURE

Infrastructure refers to the sport facilities and subsequent surrounding areas needed for training and competition. Depending on the size of the event, this may include improvements and developments to airports, roads, hotels, telecommunication networks, housing (for athletes, media, and officials), entertainment facilities, fairgrounds, parks, etc. Organizers should fit all of these different types of infrastructures into their plan, as they will remain long after the event has ended. For example, an upcoming cycling race in a local community may request that roads be resurfaced to ensure that riders can safely ride along the route, or the postrace venue may receive significant upgrades to improve the appeal and amenities of the facility.

infrastructure The sport facilities and subsequent surrounding areas needed for training and competition.

cycling race

KNOWLEDGE, SKILL DEVELOPMENT, AND EDUCATION

As sport events take place, local area residents and other stakeholders are exposed to the necessary knowledge and skills associated with organizing an event. Furthermore, employees and volunteers associated with the host organization should have the opportunity to develop skills and knowledge that may be used for future event organization, human resource management, security, hospitality, service, and other industries. In addition, the spectators, participants, and volunteers are afforded the opportunity to use public transportation (potentially recently developed or improved) and might enjoy increased awareness of different projects, such as environmental sustainability. Finally, opportunities to boast and inform people about the local community's/ city's history and culture can be recognized. For example, in Alachua County, Florida, the Gainesville Sports Commission annually facilitates more than 30 sport events. Through its staff and trained volunteers, the organization has successfully hosted numerous events, contributing more than $20 million to the local economy. Volunteers who acquire skills after hosting these events can move on to other sectors and apply what they have learned, such as volunteer and event management.

IMAGE

Hosting a sport event can produce symbolic meaning, lead to change, or even help to establish the local city's image. When successful, this can provide positive imagery. However, host cities and communities must concern themselves with a potential negative impact. For instance, potential problems such as hooligans, unfriendly local residents, an unwelcoming atmosphere, and organizational shortcomings can have a negative impact on a host's image. Similar to positive imagery, negative perceptions can last for years to come. For example, when people are asked about the Atlanta Olympic Games, they think of the traffic problems that occurred and still associate Atlanta with poor transportation infrastructure. Looking back at the Montreal Olympic Games, people think of the debt that the Olympic Stadium cost the local citizens for 30 years. However, there are positive images that can be generated as well, and hosting events can serve as a way to change a city's image. For example, Turin, Italy, was able to rid itself of its long-standing reputation of being little more than an industrial city and became viewed as a tourist and business destination as a result of hosting the Winter Olympic Games in 2006 (International Olympic Committee Factsheet, December 2013).

EMOTIONS

There is also a psychological dynamic to hosting a sport event. When a community or city hosts a sporting event, it is afforded opportunities to create local pride, develop identification, and promote positive vision, optimism, and motivation for the residents. As with image, negative emotions can also be felt, and host organizations and cities need to be cautious of this potentially detrimental outcome. For instance, residents and local-area constituents may develop negative emotions about the event if the construction of new facilities exceeds time expectations and/or displaces local citizens, potentially resulting in the local residents feeling as though they lost their social environment.

NETWORKS

For an event to be successfully organized and executed, numerous organizations need to be involved from the beginning, working together and supporting one another. Depending on the type and size of the event, these organizations can include international sport federations, media, local tourism departments, and political groups, to name a few. The positive impact or legacy of successful networking among these organizations and the host community can lead to the development of grassroots coaching programs, new or improved educational facilities, the advent of sport programs designed for all ages and skill levels, and the potential to host additional sport events. Additionally, individual employees, volunteers, and participants might have the opportunity to socialize and grow their interpersonal networks.

grassroots

CULTURE

When discussing legacies, culture is a concept that includes the creation; development; potential enhancement; and promotion of local ideas, identity, and products. Hosting a sport event allows the host city to showcase its cultural identity, which can produce a positive image, increased awareness, new infrastructure, and additional tourist products. This notion of culture as an event structure can be witnessed in the Olympic Games. The opening ceremonies have been grounds for the host country to educate viewers on its history, promote positive characteristics of the country and its residents, and showcase the country's culture and history. Local events may also represent the community's culture. For instance, in some southern U.S. communities, adult softball is a big part of the culture. Several fields, teams, and leagues exist to meet the demands of these individuals. Therefore, hosting a championship tournament through the United States Specialty Sports Association may have a positive impact on the community's cultural identity.

ADULT SOFTBALL

EVENT LEGACIES

CASHMAN 6

CHAPPLET 5

K+K 6

Event Legacies

Beyond the event structures discussed previously, researchers have identified and classified legacies with some common themes. Cashman (2005) has suggested that event legacies are not generic and can be organized into six specific categories: (1) sport, (2) economics, (3) infrastructure, (4) information and education, (5) public life, politics, and culture, and (6) symbols, memory, and history. Similarly, Chappelet and Junod (2006) suggest that there are five types of legacies, categorized by their effects: (1) sporting, (2) urban, (3) infrastructural, (4) economic, and (5) social. More recently, Karadakis and Kaplanidou (2012) have used six themes in researching legacies: (1) economic, (2) tourism, (3) environmental, (4) sociocultural, (5) psychological, and (6) knowledge development. What is common in all of the proposed sets of legacy themes is that they center on sport as a means to promote and encourage development of infrastructure, improve psychosocial aspects of the host city/community, increase awareness and knowledge of culture, and produce a positive economic return. As can be seen by the numerous studies that have classified legacies, the three pillars of sustainability are always present (i.e., economic, social, and environmental legacies).

THREE PILARS

Pruess (2007) also recognizes the need to distinguish among legacies, using the terminology of "hard" and "soft" legacies in his classification of event structures. Preuss suggests that **soft structures** include knowledge (e.g., organizational, security, technological), networks (e.g., political, sport federations, security), and cultural goods (e.g., cultural identity, cultural ideas, and common memory). He categorizes **hard structures** as those consisting of primary structure (e.g., sport infrastructure and training sites), secondary structure (e.g., villages for athletes, technical officials, and media), and tertiary structure (e.g., security, power plants, cultural attractions, and telecommunication networks).

soft structure An element of event legacy relating to knowledge, networks, and cultural goods that are developed from the hosting of an event.

hard structure An element of event legacy relating to primary structure (e.g., sport infrastructure, training sites), secondary structure (e.g., villages for athletes, technical officials, media), and tertiary structure (e.g., security, power plants, cultural attractions, telecommunication networks).

As the discussion has shown thus far, there are numerous examples of the positive legacies produced by a sport event, including those that are easy to identify (e.g., urban planning and sport infrastructure) and those that are difficult to identify (e.g., urban regeneration, increased tourism, improved public welfare, opportunities for city marketing, renewed community spirit, improved inter-regional cooperation, production of cultural values, opportunities for education, and emotional experience). However, as the various definitions of legacy indicate, hosting a sport event can produce negative legacies, including debts from construction, opportunity costs, unneeded

EASY VS DIFFICULT
LEGACIES

infrastructure, temporary crowding, and loss of returning tourists (Cashman, 2005; Gratton & Preuss, 2008; Mangan, 2008; Preuss, 2007; Solberg & Preuss, 2007).

Measuring Legacies

Now that we have discussed the broad definition of a legacy, examined the many ways in which a legacy can be manifested through event structures, and introduced the three pillars of sustainability, it is time to provide insight into how legacies are measured. In other words, how do we quantify lasting effects of a sport event? Measuring legacies involves examining the changes that occur as a result of having hosted or through the continual hosting of a sporting event over time. This section will discuss three traditional methods of measuring legacies—benchmarking, the top-down approach, and the nontraditional bottom-up measure. Traditionally, measuring legacies has been carried out by conducting economic impact studies. This approach was once deemed the method of choice due to its tangible components and its use of easily defined dollar amounts. Furthermore, an economic impact study was seen as a means to help justify the use of public resources for infrastructure development related to the event (Preuss, 2007). However, most case studies currently aimed at measuring legacies make use of benchmarking and/or the "top-down" approach.

[handwritten margin note: QUANTIFY]

[handwritten margin note: 3 TRADITIONAL METHODS]

BENCHMARK AND TOP-DOWN APPROACHES

In accordance with the **benchmark approach**, there are three scenarios under which legacies can be produced: (1) the same city hosts the same sport event over time, (2) the same city hosts different sport events over time, and (3) the same sport event is hosted by different cities over time (Preuss, 2007).

In the first scenario, the same host city can develop different legacies as a result of hosting the same event twice or on a regular basis. Depending on the size and frequency of the event, new infrastructure or improvements to existing infrastructure may be needed.

In the second scenario, different events in the same city can also create different legacies. Having a portfolio of events that a community hosts may require additional infrastructure requirements, as well as addressing various social concerns, and allow for the use of the distinguishing geographic characteristics of said location in developing a legacy unique to the event.

benchmark approach A method of evaluating an event's legacy in which an event held in one city is compared with an event held in another to determine the impact generated from the events.

synergistic

Furthermore, if an event strategy is present, the organizers can leverage other events to create a similar legacy for both the host community and the event. Preuss (2007) suggests that "synergistic effects are possible when a legacy of one event is a prerequisite for another event (e.g., sport facilities)" (p. 214).

The same event in different cities can create different legacies as every community is unique and may have different infrastructure needs and community agendas, resulting in different legacies from the same event. The intent here is to consider the characteristics of a community when developing a legacy. There are caveats with using a benchmark approach, in that this manner of measurement attempts to compare an event held in one city with an event held in another. This is a difficult task because sport events are unique and complex and occur in a fast-paced changing environment, making it difficult for benchmark studies to identify and measure legacies for future events (Preuss, 2007).

Conversely, the **top-down approach** of measuring an event legacy aims to isolate event-related impacts from general municipal developments that may occur even if the event were not to be held. Thus, the top-down approach aims to compare the economic indicators of the event with the same indicators of the host city if the event had not taken place (Preuss, 2007). The legacy is essentially the difference between these two indicators (having hosted the event vs. not having hosted the event).

CONTROL-CASE APPROACH

A similar approach to, or subset of, the top-down method is that of the control case. In the **control-case approach**, attempts are made to compare the infrastructure developments that a city or community would incur as a result of hosting an event to the potential alternative infrastructure development that the city would undertake if the event were not to occur. In this situation, the legacy would result from the difference found between the event case and the control case (Preuss, 2007). Likewise, there are caveats to using this approach. Legacies are not limited to just economic growth for a host city. Sport events are complex, multifaceted events that go beyond economic impacts. As such, it is important to consider intangible sporting, recreational, political, psychological, and promotional outcomes from hosting an event that are difficult to measure (Preuss, 2007).

BOTTOM-UP APPROACH

The **bottom-up approach** responds to the limitations of the other legacy-measuring methods in that all relevant changes to infrastructures and the

---

top-down approach A method of evaluating an event's legacy that compares the economic indicators of the event with the same indicators of the host city if the event had not taken place.

control-case approach A method of evaluating an event's legacy in which attempts are made to compare the infrastructure developments that a city or community would incur as a result of hosting an event to the potential alternative infrastructure development that the city would undertake if the event were not to occur.

bottom-up approach A method of evaluating an event's legacy in which all relevant changes to infrastructures and the host city are considered as well as potential, long-term development for the city.

host city are considered as well as potential long-term development for the city (Preuss, 2007). You may recall from earlier in the chapter that sport events have both "soft" and "hard" structures. Two soft structures that are considered in this approach are image and emotions—primarily because they undoubtedly have an impact on the host city. Image has the ability to form, reposition, or strengthen the image of a city, while emotion can instill pride and motivation for residents (Preuss, 2007). Thus, using the bottom-up approach to measure a legacy takes into consideration the fact that structures created for the events may have different and sometimes conflicting goals. For example, trying to improve the city's tourism industry requires increased media coverage, flawless organization, and extraordinary sport facilities. However, the building of sport facilities does not always take into account use of the facilities after the event and into the future. Therefore, it is important to develop a clear strategy of how legacies will be developed and why it is important to understand legacies, because what may seem to be a positive legacy for organizers may actually be a negative legacy for residents (Preuss, 2007).

An additional point to be made about development plans is that they can result in three types of legacies. First, the host city can develop event structures more expeditiously because of the event. Second, a political consensus is often needed to finalize development plans, and thus helps ensure investments from public resources. Finally, resources for the development of city infrastructure and/or event infrastructure can be funded by autonomous capital suppliers such as sport federations, central government, or private firms (Preuss, 2007, p. 219). This means that in some cases, independent corporations or organizing bodies take the burden to build infrastructure that will be used for an event. This occurred in 1984, when Los Angeles held the Summer Olympic Games. To pay for the Los Angeles Olympic Games, organizers relied on corporate sponsors and the use of existing facilities to host the event. This resulted in a profit being generated and influenced the model used for bidding and hosting the Olympic Games today.

SUMMARY

As demonstrated in this chapter, hosting a sport event requires specific "soft" and "hard" structures and an infrastructure that remain after the event. These developments have been found to have the ability to change the quality of the host city as well as leave a positive and/or negative legacy (Gratton & Preuss, 2008; Preuss, 2007) in the minds of the host community, spectators, participants, and other stakeholders, including the general public. Legacies of events are complex; they can be influenced by various local and global factors. Most publications focus on single-event legacies or, at best, focus on only one or two legacies resulting from an event (Preuss, 2007). Despite the multifaceted uniqueness of legacies, the most common legacy that is cited and researched centers on the resultant sport facilities (Chalip, 2002) and transportation infrastructure developed for an event. Thus, it is imperative that host communities and event organizers strategically plan for legacies. In doing so, the long-term development of the host community must be at the forefront of any projects. If not, justifying the use and investments of public funds and resources may be difficult (Bohlmann, 2006).

It is possible for the impact of a legacy to diminish overt time and ultimately disappear if long-term efforts are not taken seriously and infrastructures (both hard and soft) are not maintained (Terret, 2008). Thus, an objective of studying legacies is to attempt to ensure and secure benefits from hosting a sport event that will not fade away long after the event is over (Gratton & Preuss, 2008). This is why studying and understanding legacies is such a critical component of the sport tourism industry. In order to identify if legacies have a lasting effect on the host cities, it is recommended that studies be conducted 15 to 20 years after the event has occurred (Gratton & Preuss, 2008). However, there are few studies that try to scientifically measure these long-term benefits.

To date, there has been no attempt to conduct a research study to evaluate the net, long-term legacies of a sport event. This deficiency can be the result of three critical issues that need to be addressed. First, it is extremely difficult to factually determine potential projects that a city would invest in had it not hosted the event. Instead, most studies focus on the "gross" legacy. Second, it is difficult to distinguish whether a legacy is positive or negative. While this may not affect the tangible measurement of the legacy, how a legacy is interpreted is important to perceptions of the host community.

There is always the potential for discrepancies between perceptions of a legacy for a host community's event organizers and investors compared with the realities of the legacy for a city's residents. The third issue deals with measuring a legacy over time (Preuss, 2007). Preuss (2007) introduced the "bottom-up" approach, which helps identify a legacy that is left after an event has passed, but the difficulty that is common in all legacy studies is determining the particular impacts of a legacy over time. Consider that a legacy is what remains long after an event has passed; studies must continually be conducted in an attempt to measure and evaluate the definitive impact, or even the perception, of a legacy.

DISCUSSION QUESTIONS

1. How different and similar are the two legacy definitions suggested in the literature of this chapter? Using both definitions, discuss/create your own definition of the term legacy.
2. What legacy aspects are more useful in the marketing of a sport event to a host city, the tangible or the intangible? Explain your answer.
3. If you were the chief operating officer of the bid committee for an event, which legacy aspects would you focus on to market this event successfully to stakeholders, such as the federal or state/provincial governments or the public, to gain their support?
4. How can you incorporate the concept of legacies in solicitation of sponsorships, ticket sales, and license merchandizing for a sporting event? (It is probably more beneficial to focus on large-scale events for this question such as the Super Bowl, FIFA World Cup, or Olympic Games.)
5. Develop a model of the potential legacies that can be generated in a given city from hosting a sport event. Can the model be applied to other cities that are planning to host sport events? Or do you think it should change from city to city? What should one take into account?
6. Are there legacies that are unique to the Olympic Games vs. other sport events? Are legacies easier to identify/plan for in mega-events, medium-scaled events, or small-scaled events? Explain your answer.

Case STUDY

Legacy Impact of RAGBRAI

In 1973, a group of friends got together for a casual ride across the state of Iowa. This inaugural event was organized by two newspaper column writers who were also avid cyclists and thought of the expedition as a potential idea for a column. The event was rather disorganized as no one had prepared the course or developed campsites or rest areas along the way. The two columnists simply selected five different cities throughout

(continues)

Case STUDY (continued)

Iowa to serve as overnight resting destinations. In total, approximately 300 individuals started the ride and 114 finished the entire event. Currently, the race, now known as Register's Annual Great Bicycle Ride Across Iowa (RAGBRAI) limits the number of riders to 8,500 to ensure that they do not overwhelm the host communities.

The event has grown over the years and has received major national and international attention. In the late 1980s, for instance, *NBC Nightly News*, the *Today Show*, and *CBS News* broadcast features about the race and highlighted some of the host communities. In the 1990s, the ride had reached international appeal and was broadcast on a television station in Germany. These broadcasts and the newspaper and other media outlets reporting on the event not only helped increase the awareness and levels of participation for the event but they also highlighted the wonderful state of Iowa.

From a tangible outcome perspective, the event has led to the increase in bicycle lanes throughout the host communities, which rotate every year of the event. The roads are repaved for the safety of the riders, and part of the expense is shared by the state and the event. There are also various charitable organizations associated with the ride, enabling people to raise thousands of dollars each year. Finally, 10 different bike shops across the state are affiliated with the ride, and they each see an increase in riders and provide new riders with helpful tips, bike maintenance training, and ride training plans. Overall, this event has established a positive, long-term legacy in its 42-year existence.

RAGBRAI has demonstrated both positive tangible and intangible legacies, as have other events, some likely in your community. Knowing the importance of legacy, you will want to make sure that your event is a financial success and a credit to your community, not just now but long into the future. Review a local facility or event in your community to determine if it has developed a positive or negative legacy for the community. The following exercises will help get you on the right track:

1. Select either a sport event or facility and review the history of the event.
2. Evaluate the event's or facility's long-term impact on the host community, including both tangible and intangible benefits.
3. Identify methods you would use to evaluate the success of the legacy of the event.
4. Outline two new strategies that you would use to create an additional legacy for the event or facility.

REFERENCES

Bohlmann, H. R. (2006). Predicting the economic impact of the 2010 FIFA World Cup on South Africa. Pretoria, South Africa: Department of Economics, University of Pretoria. *International Journal of Sport Management and Marketing.*

Cashman, R. (2005). *The bitter-sweet awakening. The legacy of the Sydney 2000 Olympic Games.* Petersham, Australia: Walla Walla Press.

Chalip, L. (2002). Using the Olympics to optimise tourism benefits: University lecture on the Olympics [online article], from Barcelona: Centres d'Estudis Olimpics (UAB). International Chair in Olympism (IOC-UAB). Retrieved from http://olympicstudies.uab.es/lectures/web/pdf/chalip.pdf

Chalip, L., & Costa, C. A. (2005). Sport event tourism and the destination brand: Towards a general theory. *Sport in Society, 8*(2), 218–237.

Chalip, L., & Leyns, A. (2002). Local business leveraging of a sport event: Managing an event for economic benefit. *Journal of Sport Management, 16*(2), 132–158.

Chappelet, J.-L. (2008). Olympic environmental concerns as a legacy of the Winter Games. *The International Journal of the History of Sport, 25*(14), 1884–1902.

Chappelet, J.-L., & Junod, T. (2006). A tale of 3 Olympic cities: What can Turin learn from the Olympic legacy of other alpine cities? In D. Torres (Ed.), *Proceedings of workshop on major sport events as opportunity for development* (pp. 83–90). Valencia, Spain: Society for the Advancement of Library & Information Science; Madras School of Social Work; and United Nations Educational, Scientific, and Cultural Organization.

Gibson, H., Kaplanidou, K., & Kang, S. J. (2012). Small-scale event sport tourism: A case study in sustainable tourism. *Sport Management Review, 15*(2), 160–170.

Gratton, C., & Preuss, H. (2008). Maximizing Olympic impacts by building up legacies. *The International Journal of the History of Sport, 25*(14), 1922–1938.

Higham, J. E. S. (1999). Commentary - Sport as an avenue of tourism development: An analysis of the positive and negative impacts of sport tourism. *Current Issues in Tourism, 2*(1), 82–90.

Higham, J., & Hinch, T. (2002). Tourism, sport and seasons: The challenges and potential of overcoming seasonality in the sport and tourism sectors. *Tourism Management, 23*, 175–185.

International Olympic Committee Factsheet (December, 2013). *Legacies of the Games.* Retrieved from http://www.olympic.org/Documents/Reference_documents _Factsheets/Legacy.pdf

Kaplanidou, K., & Karadakis, K. (2010). Understanding the legacies of a host Olympic City: The case of the 2010 Vancouver Olympic Games. *Sport Marketing Quarterly, 19*(2), 110–117.

Karadakis, K., & Kaplanidou, K. (2012). Legacy perceptions among host and non-host Olympic Games residents: A longitudinal study of the 2010 Vancouver Olympic Games. *European Sport Management Quarterly, 12*(3), 243–264.

Mangan, J. A. (2008). Prologue: Guarantees of global goodwill; Post-Olympic legacies—Too many limping white elephants? *The International Journal of the History of Sport, 25*(14), 1869–1883.

Misener, L., & Mason, D. S. (2006). Creating community networks: Can sporting events offer meaningful sources of social capital? *Managing Leisure, 11*(1), 39–56.

Misener, L., & Mason, D. (2008). Urban regimes and the sporting events agenda: A cross-national comparison of civic development strategies. *Journal of Sport Management, 22*(5), 603–627.

Misener, L., & Mason, D. (2009). Fostering community development through sporting events strategies: An examination of urban regime perceptions. *Journal of Sport Management, 23*, 770–794.

Preuss, H. (2007). The conceptualisation and measurement of mega sport event legacies. *Journal of Sport & Tourism, 12*(3–4), 207–228.

Smith, A. (2010). Theorising the relationship between major sport events and social sustainability. *Journal of Sport & Tourism, 14*(2–3), 109–120.

Solberg, H. A., & Preuss, H. (2007). Major sport events and long-term tourism impacts. *Journal of Sport Management, 21*(2), 213–234.

Terret, T. (2008). The Albertville Winter Olympics: Unexpected legacies—failed expectations for regional economic development. *The International Journal of the History of Sport, 25*(14), 1903–1921.

Walo, M., Bull, A., & Breen, H. (1996). Achieving economic benefit at local events: A case study of a local sports event. *Journal of Festival Management and Event Tourism, 4*(3/4), 95–106.

Weed, M., & Bull, C. (2004). *Sports tourism: Participants, policy and providers.* Oxford, UK: Elsevier.

CHAPTER 15

Measurement and Evaluation

Thomas J. Aicher

CHAPTER OBJECTIVES

Upon the completion of this chapter, the reader will be able to:

1. Explain the importance of continuous measurement and evaluation of facility and event organizations.

2. Identify stakeholders who may provide valuable information for organizations to understand their performance.

3. Differentiate measurement and evaluation techniques and the impact that each measure has on the organization's various internal and external stakeholders.

4. Define and articulate the strengths and weaknesses of the various internal and external measurement techniques.

CHAPTER OVERVIEW

This chapter will review the various techniques to measure the performance of the event or facility from a multi-stakeholder perspective. First, it will establish the importance of continuous evaluation of the organization and its performance from pre-event to post-event to ensure that all stakeholders' expectations are met. It will outline the major components of SERVQUAL—economic, environmental, and social—along with other methods of evaluating the organization's performance.

IndustryVOICE

Jen Jorgensen—Director of Quant, Egg Strategy

I am a marketing research and consultant working with a range of clients from a variety of industries including entertainment, beauty, consumer packaged goods (CPG), finance, and sports. I started working with FOX Sports in 2017, doing custom qualitative and quantitative market research to help them better understand the nature of sports fandom and its intersection with entertainment.

I went to New York University for undergraduate studies, where I majored in economics and minored in math. While I love numbers and models, I dreamed of a career with color and creativity. In my sophomore year, I stumbled upon an internship at a boutique qualitative market research firm in the SoHo neighborhood of New York City. I fell in love with the idea of a job that centers around asking people interesting questions. Since then, I've moved between New York; Colorado; and Sydney, Australia; working for both quantitative and qualitative market research consultant agencies. I get to work with some of the most exciting brands out there, answering some big, heady questions. It is a fun and rewarding career.

Egg Strategy is a consultancy that creates business and innovation strategies for some of the world's most iconic brands. We use methods that combine creativity and rigor to inspire new thinking across three areas of expertise: Consumer insights, brand strategy, and innovation. Our clients are diverse but tend to be the big names you've heard of in CPG, Health, and broader Lifestyle categories, including sports.

Egg Strategy's mission is finding true paths forward. We fight against the distractions and paralyses that keep people and companies from making progress and inspiring actions that move them forward. Our company values are: Genuine collaboration, courageous thinking, creativity with purpose, and infectious leaders.

In our research, we at Egg are observing some stark differences in how the various generations interact with sports. The challenge is knowing what differences are inherent in a particular generation (e.g., Millennials or Gen Z behave this way) vs. what differences are caused by a life stage (e.g., all 22 year olds behave this way, which could change when they are 33 years old). My dream is to mirror Harvard's longitudinal study of happiness, *The Grant Study*, with a focus on sport fandom and sport consumption over time. I posit that half of our behavior stays the same and the other half changes in ways that we can't even begin to predict.

Another interesting challenge is that fandom is in the eye of the beholder. Said another way, measuring one's fandom is like measuring love or pain—it's all personal. It is very difficult to have a subjective measurement of avidity, especially when we consider that fan avidity and how often we watch the sport event are increasingly disjointed.

The way we consume all entertainment is rapidly changing. Netflix launched streaming services in 2007, and this year Netflix is reported to have nearly 118 million subscribers globally. Cord-cutting and streaming services have changed our relationship with television. This fundamental shift in how we access entertainment—on demand, according to our own schedules, cutting through commercials—has a big impact on our relationship with sports and the live game. I'm excited to see how the live game evolves in reaction to how we're consuming media. It feels like a sink-or-swim moment.

At Egg Strategy, the first thing we look for in a new hire is a deep level of curiosity and a desire to roll up your sleeves and tackle a challenge. As a marketing consultant, you're asked to view problems through multiple lenses—from the point of view of the fan, the league, the team, the athlete, the TV network—and we want people who are genuinely and enthusiastically interested in navigating through all of the complexity.

In terms of skills, a solid statistics class and basic fluency in Excel can take you a long way! I always look for candidates who are eager to learn new things and aren't afraid of Googling their way through a challenge from time to time. Finally, for people who are interested in a career in market research or any other industry, internships are a fantastic, low-risk way to try out the industry.

At Egg, we leverage qualitative and quantitative market research methods, along with desk research, to gather a consumer-centric point of view (POV) on sports, specifically fandom. We source our quantitative data from online surveys, and our go-to analyses include descriptive statistics, factor analysis, regressions and correlations, cluster analysis, and correspondence analysis. For qualitative research, we use traditional methods such as focus groups and in-depth interviews, as well as mobile ethnographies and online communities. For desk research, we kick off the beginning of a project by reading articles, academic papers, books, etc., that are relevant to our clients and that keep us up to date on the industry.

Having a job where you research sports is a fun excuse for you to talk about what you would be talking about anyway…but now you have the data to back it up!

Introduction

The facility and event industry faces many challenges and serves a variety of stakeholders who each play a significant role in the success of the organization. It is, therefore, very important that facility and event organizations measure their organizations' operations based on the objectives that serve as a guide for the facility or event. For instance, Hall (1992) suggests that evaluation is not an afterthought for event management; rather, it is a strategic necessity for the organization to be able to evolve and be successful in the future. As we detailed previously with planning, measurement and evaluation are integral to the organization's success.

Why Are Measurement and Evaluation Important?

Getz (2007) articulated seven reasons why facility and event organizations should incorporate measurement and evaluation into their procedures. These include the following:

1. To identify and solve problems.
2. To find ways to improve management.
3. To determine the value of the facility or event.

4. To measure success or failure.
5. To identify and measure impact.
6. To satisfy sponsors and other stakeholders.
7. To gain acceptance, credibility, and support.

Each of these items assist the organization in measuring its performance compared with the objectives it has set forth. For instance, if a cycling event were attempting to expand its revenue source through its current and potential consumers, it would be extremely important for the event managers to assess the current participants' perceptions of the event. In doing so, they would be able to determine what attracted the participants and use that information in subsequent marketing materials. Similarly, if a volleyball facility were attempting to generate additional revenue through sponsorship, it would be very important for the facility to measure the success of its current sponsors. With this information, they would be able to potentially expand the current relationships and use the information to attract new partners. In both examples, the measurement should be developed to evaluate the organization's success or process of attaining its overall objectives. In the following sections of this chapter, I will outline various methods to measure organizational performance toward these types of objectives.

What Are Performance Measurements Used For?

performance measurement An outcome that describes how well the organization is using its internal and external inputs to produce the desired output.

Performance measurements can serve to evaluate numerous functions within facility and event organizations. Behn (2003) suggests that there are eight common purposes for performance management: Evaluation, control, budgeting, motivation, promotion, celebration, learning, and improvement. These measurements describe how well the organization is using its internal and external inputs to produce the desired output. These types of measures can be used to determine how well the facility or event is performing and allow the organization to evolve as it moves forward. For instance, a running festival may evaluate participation rates, expenses, and partnership relationships to determine if the event was a success this year as well as how to improve for the following year. Another example would be the sport complex using these measurements to improve the management of the facility in order to attract additional events to the complex. The focus of the measurement may be on capacity management strategies, employee training, and improvement to demonstrate the facility's ability to host numerous events.

How and When to Measure Performance

When measuring organizational performance, most facilities measure performance annually and utilize a single measurement to determine their overall performance, which has severe limitations. Typically, events will only perform a **post-event analysis** to measure performance and will focus on a single outcome of the event (e.g., participant satisfaction). When conducting performance studies, the impact of time on the memory may be detrimental to measuring the organization's performance accurately. Over time, stakeholders will likely remember only the very good (i.e., halo effect) or the very bad (i.e., horn effect), which will bias any information collected from these individuals. In addition, financial measurements may not be as accurate over time. For instance, if a soccer facility runs a special in August for the upcoming season, its level of sales may be increased for the month of August; however, because they are selling these items at a lower rate than normal, this promotion could impact their annual sales performance. Furthermore, sales may also fall in September as they lead up to the October indoor season and the individuals who normally register at this time may have taken advantage of the reduced rates. In either case, it would be more effective for facilities and events to measure performance using a continuous and multifaceted approach.

> **post-event analysis**
> Measurement of a specific variable of interest after the event has occurred.

To ensure that they are accurately measuring performance, organizations should first vary their data sources. Concentrating on one group of stakeholders will only paint a part of the picture from the event. The best way to understand this concept is through a brief illustration. A local community submitted a bid for, was selected, and hosted a junior international triathlon championship event. At the end of the event, the facility and event managers met to discuss the notes that they took during the event, and overall, they found that there were numerous issues with logistics and timing to consider for future events. Upon conclusion of their review, they sent summative reports to both the sponsors and the organizing committee of the event (in this case, the United States Triathlon Association) according to their original agreement and made suggestions for future improvements.

After receiving the feedback from the management team, both groups, sponsors, and event owner were quite surprised, as both groups were pleased with the event and thought that it was a resounding success. For instance, what the management team saw as a logistical issue, the sponsors of the event thought was a great plan because it ensured that all of the participants and spectators flowed through the sponsors' area, which allowed them to successfully market their

products. The event organizing committee felt that the timing of the event was consistent and even more efficient than the events that they had hosted in the past and were also pleased. This brief example demonstrates the importance of measuring various individuals' opinions of the event to ensure that all groups are satisfied with how the event was managed. If the facility management team had not elicited feedback from these groups, they may have made changes to future events that would have had an adverse impact on sponsor and event owner satisfaction.

Organizations will also want to vary the techniques they use to collect data. Broadly, data are collected in two distinct forms: **Qualitative** and **quantitative**. Each form brings value and understanding to the facility's or event's overall performance. Some of the most common sources for quantitative data include attendee statistics, sales figures, financial reports and accounts, economic impact analyses, environmental impact analyses, and social impact analyses. Quantitative data develop a numerical analysis of the organization's performance, while qualitative data offer a deeper understanding of the stakeholders' perceptions, attitudes, and other information. For instance, qualitative data come in the form of attendee perceptions, interviews with attendees and staff, management notes and commentary, and interviews with external stakeholders (e.g., sponsors, community members), among other forms. The two broad techniques allow the organization to develop a broader understanding of how well the organization is achieving or progressing toward its objectives. In the following sections, I will outline more specific methods of data collection that organizations may employ to measure performance.

qualitative Research methodology used to develop a more in-depth description of behaviors and experiences.

quantitative Research methodology used to provide a numeric analysis of the organization's performance.

What to Measure

When measuring organizational performance, the default for most organizations is to measure financial performance. This may be an effective approach for the organization to determine how well it is performing financially, but it does little to measure other variables that should be considered equally important (e.g., customers/participants, sponsors, external stakeholders). Therefore, rather than using a single measurement approach, facility and event organizations should employ the **triple bottom-line approach**, in which they measure the impact that the event has on (1) its consumers, (2) internal business operations, and (3) external business operations. Each prong should be evaluated with the overall business objectives as a framework to indicate success. Additionally, rather than using a single measurement, facility and event managers should maintain a continuous evaluation approach and measure the three prongs of the triple bottom line. An outline of each prong follows, including a strategy of how to measure each performance indicator.

triple bottom-line approach A method of measuring organizational performance focused on the impact that the event has on its consumers, internal business operations, and external business operations.

CUSTOMERS/PARTICIPANTS

Facility and event organizations cease to exist if they do not have customers or participants using their facility or partaking in the events they host. There are several key variables that organizations should concentrate on when evaluating customers' perceptions of the organization. Some of the most common variables include service perceptions, overall satisfaction, attitudinal changes, and lifestyle change.

Ko and Pastore (2007) developed a conceptual framework for sport and recreation organizations to better understand service quality in recreational facilities. Using Bitner and Hubbert's (1994) definition, service quality refers to "the consumer's overall impression of the relative inferiority/superiority of the organization and its services" (p. 77); Ko and Pastore developed the Scale of Service Quality in Recreational Sports (SSQRS). This measurement approach focuses on four main categories: (1) program quality (i.e., range of programs, operating times, and program information), (2) interaction quality (i.e., employee–client and client–client interactions), (3) outcome quality (i.e., physical and social benefits), and (4) physical environment (i.e., ambience, design, and equipment). Finally, they include a measurement of overall customer satisfaction with the facility.

Each item of the SSQRS can be operationalized (i.e., defined in the context of the study) and measured to determine if the facility can improve in the SSQRS dimensions. For example, a recreation center could survey individuals who frequently use the facility to determine their level of satisfaction with the facility. The SSQRS would measure attributes about the facility (e.g., cleanliness, safety, benefits sought) to determine if areas exist in which the facility is considered deficient. Furthermore, they may want to measure how well the facility users were treated by the employees and other members, as well as how pleased they are with the array of equipment provided by the facility, among other variables. In doing so, the recreation center managers may find that individuals are very pleased with the staff and range of activities but feel that the lighting needs improvement and that the services provided do not meet the demands of the organization. This may also highlight issues with space utilization as well as areas such as the racquetball courts, which may be underutilized while the cardio and free weight sections are overcrowded. This knowledge would allow the managers to improve these areas, which would lead to higher customer satisfaction and potentially increased usage.

Facility and event managers may use the SSQRS findings from their evaluations to develop stronger customer segmentation strategies. Facility and event organizations typically segment their customer or participant bases into three categories: Goods or services sought, customer relationship, and image and reputation. The first category, goods or services sought, differentiates the customers or participants based on the attributes that the individuals value the most about the facility or event. These attributes may be price, quality, options available, and benefits sought from participation, among many others. For example, running events may differentiate according to the distance that individuals must complete, and in doing so, they may vary the cost to participate. This strategy will allow individuals who are not well conditioned to participate in a shorter event, while others have the opportunity to challenge themselves with a longer distance. The price of each event should be directly related to the distance and level of support associated with the participants' expectations so they will feel satisfied with their purchase.

The second way in which organizations may use SSQRS findings is to differentiate themselves through the relationships they have with their customers. This strategy involves evaluating the relationship or interaction between the customer and the staff in the facility. For instance, suppose parents take their child to participate in the local recreational soccer league. While there, they encounter a rather unpleasant person working at the concession stand. Although the child really enjoys the team and playing soccer, the parents may consider an alternative recreational league to participate in because of this encounter. Additionally, the relationships that an organization creates with the participants may impact the longevity or continued participation in an organization's events. The longer individuals participate in an organization's events, the more accustomed they become to the organization's processes, and the expectations of organizational performance may be increased. For example, each time individuals receive a greater level of treatment than they have in the past, they may expect the same or better each time they return. This may take a toll on an organization if they do not continually assess and train their employees to perform at a high level. Failure to maintain the high level of service may lead to a negative event or relationship with the customers, and thus, they may go to another league.

The last way in which organizations may use the SSQRS is to assist in the development of their strategies to manage their image and reputation of the facility. Similar to word-of-mouth advertising, the image and reputation of a facility and event may have either a positive or negative impact on the customer segmentation strategies. For example, a cycling studio may define itself as wealthy, challenging, exclusive, and with a high level of service. This would minimize the number of consumers who may be able to afford to attend the classes that the studio provides; however, it would provide the level of exclusivity and amenities that some individuals may seek. Another example could be a small softball tournament. This event could take on a reputation of being a lively, fun, family-friendly event, in which everyone is welcome to participate, or it may be billed as a competitive tournament that teams use to test their abilities against other elite teams. In either case, the strategies used to develop and maintain the image and reputation should be consistent with the organizational objectives, and thus, the measurement will focus on those variables.

INTERNAL OPERATIONS

Facility and event organizations employ **financial measurement** approaches to determine how well the organization is contributing to the bottom line. If not directly tied to the organization's overall business objectives, using these measurements may potentially have a negative effect on the long-term health and viability of the facility or event. Organizations commonly use traditional financial measurements (e.g., return on investment, debt vs. equity, gross profit) developed from the financial statements to outline the financial

financial measurement
An outcome used to determine how well the organization is contributing to the bottom line.

standing of the organization. While these measurement approaches do help the organization understand how it is performing, other approaches may provide greater insight into the organization's financial performance and the impact on organizational objectives.

revenue growth and mix measurement An outcome used to denote how well the organization is performing toward organizational objectives such as market share, increased markets, or expanding its revenue sources.

Revenue growth and mix measurements denote how well the organization is performing toward organizational objectives such as increasing market share, increasing markets, or expanding its revenue sources. For example, a tennis club may measure its overall gross profit and find that it is doing well as an organization. However, if the organization's stated objective is to increase the number of members or broaden its sources of revenue, this measurement would not provide the information that it needs to correctly determine how well it is performing toward this objective. Rather, the organization would want to break down its sales and sources of revenue to determine how much it is generating from each business category (e.g., gift shop, concessions, trainings, memberships), and it may notice that it has undervalued certain categories in which it may enhance the revenue streams.

Instead of evaluating and improving revenue streams, facilities and events may turn to cost reduction or efficiency measurements to determine if they may enhance the organization's performance. For instance, an ice skating facility may evaluate its marketing strategy to bring in new customers. With the various media that it uses to reach potential clients, it could measure which methods are generating the greatest number of new or interested members, hockey players, or spectators of their events. This approach would provide the organization with the information to determine which platforms are most effective and then eliminate or reduce spending on the underperforming methods. Other options may include using technological advancements (e.g., online ticket or mobile ticket sales for events), which would eliminate the need for certain staff, although an unpopular choice.

Finally, organizations may evaluate how well they manage their assets to generate a return on the resources they currently possess. Management of assets may come in a variety of forms—capacity management, space utilization, and event performance, to name a few. These types of measurements allow organizations to develop an understanding of how much return they are getting for the use of the space or other assets. A local YMCA, for example, may evaluate the current setup of the facility. With the focus on developing new workout trends and an alternative desire for individual- and group-based training, they may want to eliminate certain sections that are underutilized. Doing so would allow the YMCA to maximize its use of space, eliminate some of the equipment in the facility, and reduce the cost of maintenance. Additionally, it may schedule classes that have demonstrated greater popularity than others, which would lead to greater profitability.

The second major component of internal operations is **human resources measurements**. This element can be very challenging for facilities and events to measure because of the dependence on volunteer staff to manage events. Common measurement approaches that organizations may use to measure their full-time staff members would be employee retention through frequency of turnover or attrition. They may also find value in measuring employees' job satisfaction, organizational commitment, motivation, productivity, role clarity and competency, and other factors. These measurements would allow the organization to develop a better understanding of its employees' perceptions of the organization and to assist with the human resource management component. Ultimately, and to use a cliché, our organizations are only as strong as our weakest link. Similar to financial measurement approaches, these approaches should be consistent with the organizational objectives and provide support and guidance to the employees so they may help the organization to reach those objectives.

human resource measurement An outcome that allows the organization to better develop an understanding of an employee's perception of the organization.

EXTERNAL OPERATIONS

Facility and event operations impact the host community in three common ways: Economically, environmentally, and socially. The United Nations World Tourism Organization suggests that organizations monitor these three impacts to ensure a sustainable tourism destination by ensuring that each impact has been brought to a level consistent with the local residents, visitors, and business interests. The most commonly discussed measurement approach of the three is the economic impact analysis; however, the latter two are gaining momentum as economic impact studies are called into question quite often. Facility and event management organizations use these studies to gain public support or recognition for what they bring to, or do not take from, the community. For instance, if managers of a local sport team are attempting to pass a public referendum to use tax dollars to build a facility, they would want to use the economic impact study to demonstrate the positive growth that the facility will generate for the local community and economy. The environmental impact study will outline how the organization will minimize the impact that the construction may have on the local environment, as well as how they will minimize the impact of the harsh chemicals they use on the field. Finally, they may want to report how the new facility will create greater civic pride or social cohesion in the community; thus, elevating the city's reputation and image in the broader community. A further discussion of each technique follows.

Economic Impact Analysis

Economic impact is used to measure the effect of a facility or an event on the local community. An economic impact study measures the organization's ability to generate new revenue for the host community, increase impact on individual-level income within the host community, or produce new jobs within the host community. Each of these measurements will generate a continuous impact, which has led to the use of multipliers to estimate the overarching impact of a single dollar spent at a facility or an event. The multipliers measure both direct impacts (e.g., spending on hotels, restaurants, event participation) and indirect impacts (e.g., event suppliers, employees spending their earnings, local government taxes). For instance, an individual traveling to Knoxville, Tennessee, for the sole purpose of participating in a basketball tournament generates new spending in the local community, which would not have existed without the event. The money that the individual spends during the trip on hotels, restaurants, and shopping then turns over through the local community as it is used by the businesses to pay its employees and replenish their supplies and as it becomes tax revenue for the local government, for example. The revenue will continue to travel through the local economy, with some money being lost at each stage of the spending cycle.

To estimate this relationship, organizations use three common multipliers: Sales, income, and employment. The use of these multipliers should be carefully interpreted to ensure that a more accurate estimate of the event's or facility's impact has been calculated. Howard and Crompton (2005) outline the details and how to properly employ the multipliers, and more importantly, the five inviolable principles of economic impact analyses. Failure to follow these principles will lead to an overestimation of the event's or facility's impact. The principles also shed light on the various economic impact analyses provided by organizations when attempting to attain government support mentioned previously. These inviolable principles are listed in **Table 15-1** with examples of how they may affect the estimated impact.

The most common method used by facility and event organizations is surveying the participants/customers to determine spending levels while the

Table 15-1   Five Inviolable Principles of an Economic Impact Analysis

No.	Principle	Reasoning
1	Exclusion of local residents and deflectors	These two groups do not generate new money. Locals would have spent money elsewhere within the community.
		Deflectors are local residents who would have spent money outside of the community but remained local because of the event. While considered new money, the amount is negligible.
2	Exclusion of "time switchers" and "casuals"	Time switchers are nonlocal spectators who were planning a visit to the community but changed the timing of their visit to coincide with the sport event.
		Casuals are visitors already in the community, attracted by other features, who elected to go to the sport event instead of doing something else.
3	Use of income rather than sales output measurements of economic impact	Sales multipliers inflate the numbers but do not tell the local public how much they will truly benefit; sales do not guarantee more jobs.
4	Use of multiplier coefficients rather than multipliers	Coefficients attribute an increase to the injected change created by visitors.
		Multipliers attribute an increase to income generated.
5	Careful interpretation of employment measurements	Are the positions full- and part-time jobs?
		Are the "new" jobs really new or just a transfer of time between workers?
		Are the positions seasonal?

individual is visiting the community. An example of this method is provided in **Figure 15-1**. If you review the questions carefully, you will see how to ensure that you do not violate any of the inviolable principles. For instance, the questions listed will determine who should be considered a local vs. a nonlocal person, whether the person should be considered a casual or time-switching visitor, and how much the person spends on various activities during the trip. Once the data are collected, services such as IMPLAN (which stands for IMpact analysis for PLANning) are utilized to generate the multipliers to estimate the impact of the initial spending. For a full explanation of how to perform an economic impact analysis, review Howard and Crompton's *Financing Sport*, which is listed in the references.

Umstead Trail Marathon

Visitor Survey

AT Consulting Services is requesting your support in determining the economic impact of the Umstead Trail Marathon. The information provided will allow us to assist the Umstead Trail Marathon organizer with the information needed to ensure quality future events, as well as assist with future negotiations for the development of trails. We greatly appreciate your support!

What is your home zip code? _____

How many people are traveling in your party? Be sure to include yourself. _____

Approximately how much will your traveling party spend IN TOTAL during your entire stay in the Raleigh Area for the following categories:

Lodging: _____	Marathon Expo: _____
Food and Beverage: _____	Tourist Attractions: _____
Local Transportation: _____	Entertainment: _____
Retail Shopping: _____	Other Expenses: _____

Figure 15-1   Example of an Economic Impact Survey

VIGNETTE 15-1

Projecting Economic Impact of a Local Sport Facility

In Hays, Kansas, a group of investors and Fort Hays State University (FHSU) developed a proposed sport complex to be constructed by using some public funds. The facility was designed to include eight baseball/softball fields, four football fields, and four soccer fields. Additionally, the facility would include maintenance building, picnic areas, playground facilities, concessions, warm-up areas, and ample parking to host the events. In addition to these fields, a new soccer complex was planned for development and use by FHSU next to the new sport complex. Combining these two projects into one specific location allowed for shared infrastructure improvement (e.g., roads, utilities). The estimated cost of the entire project is $8 million dollars and a ½ cent increase in sales tax over the next four years to pay back the bonds

associated with the construction of the facility was requested.

To help justify this expense and increase in sales tax, the group commissioned a consulting firm to conduct an estimated annual impact analysis of the sport complex. The study assessed the direct and indirect effects on the local economy of hosting tournaments for regional baseball, softball, soccer, and football organizations. These events typically require an overnight stay from out-of-town teams and participants, and, therefore, through spending on accommodations, transportation, food, and entertainment, should have a positive economic impact on the local community.

First, the consultants had to estimate the number of tournaments likely to be hosted annually, the number of teams that would participate, and the average number of participants and supporters for each team. To do so, the group analyzed various seasons from regional sport facilities and leagues to develop an accurate projection of these variables. Next, the group distributed an online survey to adult participants and parents of youth participants to estimate the amount of spending on accommodations, food, entertainment, and transport when these individuals travel for tournaments.

The results of this analysis projected that the facility would be able to host 16 adult softball tournaments, 12 baseball tournaments, seven youth softball tournaments, two youth soccer tournaments, and one youth football tournament annually. Based on the average size of the team and number of parents, coaches, and supporters who travel with the team, the group estimated that these tournaments would account for an estimated, slightly over 25,000 visitors. The average amount spent per respondent on the total categories listed above was $92.81/day, which generated an estimated $2,368,642 annual direct economic impact on the city. While these numbers appear to present a good case for spending on the sport facility, costs were not included and employment projections were not included either.

Environmental Impact Analysis

The large numbers of people who participate in our events or use our facilities generate an **environmental impact**. Additionally, the construction, maintenance, and resources that our facilities use to operate may have a deleterious impact on the local environment. The chemicals and fertilizers we use to maintain the green spaces (e.g., fields, golf courses) may also negatively impact the environment. Moreover, the larger events hosted within our communities cram several thousand people into small areas, and the travel, trash, noise, and other by products generated by these individuals may harm the local environment. Some events may harm the local flora and fauna through erosion and negative effects on the watershed. For instance, a trail-running event may damage the local environment because of the repetitive flow of runners following the same path, and the spectators walking along the course may have a similar impact. This trampling of the grasses and underbrush may lead to greater erosion of the soil.

When evaluating the environmental impact of a facility or an event, it is important to remember that there is no such thing as a zero impact. Every facility and event will have a negative impact on the local environment, so it is imperative that event and facility managers develop strategies to minimize or counterbalance the impact. For example, a charity cycling event hosted in a local community will have individuals traveling to the event, which will release greenhouse gas emissions. Trash from the event, including the cups and wrappers at the rest stations, will be placed in the local landfills, along with countless

environmental impact
The negative effect that the construction of or the existence of a facility or event has on the local environment.

other by products of the event. In this situation, the event could support mass transportation options to reduce the number of individuals traveling to the event or give a reward to those who carpool. The cups used at the rest stops could be recycled as long as they are paper and do not have a wax coating. These strategies would not negate the event's impact on the environment but would at least lessen it.

The event may employ other strategies to decrease environmental impact. For example, facilities could reduce their energy consumption by using energy-efficient lighting (e.g., fluorescent or high-intensity discharge lighting) and cooling/heating systems. The facilities may also benefit from having large windows to increase the amount of natural light, which may reduce lighting costs. Those facilities that use chemicals to treat their green spaces or pools could adopt environmentally safe products that would reduce the harsh chemicals normally used. Facilities may also provide electronic options for ticketing, marketing, and other facility operations that utilize a tremendous amount of paper. When paper must be used, the organization should make sure that it is recyclable and print on both sides to minimize the total number of pages. A newer strategy in facilities is the use of rooftop gardens as they provide a unique aspect to attract visitors, may produce food, and most importantly, serve as an extra level of insulation, which can enhance the efficiency of heating and cooling the facility.

To further manage the environmental impact of the Olympics, the International Olympic Committee (IOC) created the IOC Sport and Environment Commission. This was established in 1995 in response to the 1992 Albertville, France, Winter Olympics. In those Games, the construction and running of the events associated with the Games had a devastating impact on the local community. The conditions outraged several environmental groups, prompting the IOC's response. In addition to the creation of the Sport and Environment Commission, the IOC added the environment as the third dimension of Olympism (along with sport and culture). For more information and to learn more helpful environmental protection strategies, visit the IOC Sport and Environment Commission website (www.olympic .org/sport-environment-commission).

SOCIAL IMPACT

Recently, owners have begun to evaluate the impact that their facilities and events have on the local community's social norms, roles, and customs. Facilities and events have been found to generate both positive and negative impacts on the host community. Similar to environmental and economic impact analyses, **social impact** analyses are important for organizations to employ so they have a strong understanding of local communities' perceptions of their organizations. It is integral to the success and sustainability of the organization to maintain a positive social impact on the community. Outlined next are some of the potential negative and positive social impacts that facility and event organizations may have on the host community.

Evaluating the impact of hosting mega-events, such as the Summer and Winter Olympic Games or the International Federation of Association Football (FIFA) World Cup, on the host community, researchers have largely pointed to two negative outcomes: Crime and displacement of the working poor. Factors that may contribute to increased levels of crime include the following:

- The nonlocals do not have a strong understanding of the formal mechanisms of social control
- These visitors also do not act as good guardians of the rental properties
- Criminals may choose to go to the area because of the perception of "easy marks"

Evaluation of the 2002 Winter Olympics hosted by Salt Lake City, Utah, demonstrated the opposite impact of hosting. In their investigation, Decker, Varano, and Green (2007) found a brief reduction in the crime levels during the event, and once the games concluded, crime rates returned to their normal levels. Alternatively, other research studies have demonstrated that local residents perceived the crime rate to have increased during the event, and their perception (whether accurate or not) may be more meaningful in generating local support for the event.

The second major concern of hosting mega-events is the negative impact on the working poor and the housing available to these groups. When determining where to build the stadiums and other facilities to host such events, communities typically turn to the most affordable land options. Additionally, the pressure of meeting fixed deadlines leads to the bypass of normal decision-making processes, which leads to the demolition of "eyesores" and the displacement of many urban poor (Lenskyj, 2000, p. 228). In doing so, individuals are relocated from these areas, and those who are not directly impacted by the construction of the facility may be forced from the community because of the increasing costs of living in the area. This was on full display in the lead up to the FIFA World Cup hosted in Brazil. Butler and Aicher (2015) evaluated the media reports during the protests leading

social impact The effect that facilities and events have on the local community, social norms, roles, and customs.

up to the event. The community was frustrated with the exorbitant spending on the venues to host the event when they had healthcare, education, and other basic services that could be improved.

Facilities and events may also have negative impacts on the local residents' daily lives. For instance, facilities and events typically generate greater levels of noise, traffic, pollution, crowding, and other undesirable variables. These activities may lead to less support from local residents because their routines have been hindered due to the hosting of the event. For instance, individuals who live near a baseball complex may have increased levels of frustration when the facility hosts a fireworks Friday promotion. With the increased traffic in the community, individuals parking along the streets, and the loud firework display, the local residents may become frustrated with the event organizers because they are not able to navigate the area as they normally would and the noise may scare their animals or prevent them from sleeping.

The effects of a facility or event on the local community need not be negative, however. Through proper management, facilities and events may generate a positive social impact within the local community. One example of a positive impact is psychic income. With the lack of economic impact found in most facility economic impact studies, organizations have turned to the notion of psychic income to bolster community support. Psychic income is the method by which the city expresses its identity, personality, and status to the rest of the world. Generated in the local community through the production of major facilities and events, psychic income has a strong social bonding impact on the local community because it develops a shared identity that breaks through all other social barriers (e.g., race, sex, political affiliation, religion). Facilities and events can enhance psychic income through (1) increasing social interactions between the community and the facilities or events through community-specific events, (2) cultivating common group interests through small events in which various stakeholder groups may interact, and (3) developing a strong and trusting relationship between the facility and event managers and the local community. Each of these strategies costs the facility or event organization very little yet may have a significant impact on the local community. For instance, a local recreational facility adds a rock-climbing wall. To generate a buzz, the facility owners decide to allow nonmembers access to the facility to check out the new equipment. Rather than just having anybody come in, the facility could send invitations to those in the area who may be adversely impacted by the other large events they plan to host. Treat them to a meal and maybe a small instructional session about rock climbing. This open-door invitation will demonstrate to the local residents that the facility understands them and their needs and is attempting to reach out.

Additional social outcomes generated by facilities and events include community cohesion, educational development, support from families, and regional development. These outcomes will engender greater support from the local residents because they feel that hosting such events is of value to the local community. For instance, the city of Indianapolis, Indiana, has made large investments in their sport facility infrastructures. They now host several major sport events (e.g., National Football League [NFL] Combine, National Collegiate Athletic Association [NCAA] men's and women's basketball tournament championships, the Indianapolis 500), two professional franchises (the NFL's Colts and National Basketball Association's [NBA's] Pacers), and a minor league baseball team. This does not include the level of investment made in the local parks and recreation system as well as other sport events hosted in the community. With this level of events in one community, the city of Indianapolis has enjoyed considerable support for investing in additional sport facilities and events by those who see the positive impact generated from hosting such national and worldwide spectacles.

The social return on investment (SROI) model provides a framework for facility and event managers to understand the social impact that they have on the local community. The purpose of the SROI model is to estimate the financial amount of social value generated from the facilities or events in the host community. The basic formula to calculate the SROI model is to divide the value of the social impact by the value of spending. To do so, Rotheroe and Richards (2007) outline four distinct areas on which organizations should focus to determine the level of social impact. The first is stakeholder engagement, which is the level to which stakeholders' objectives are identified and integrated into the organizational processes. Second, the event analysis is centered on the stakeholders' interests (i.e., materiality). For example, if sponsors and local residents are considered integral to the success of the event or facility, measurement of their perceptions of the event would be paramount to other stakeholder groups. Next, organizations will develop an impact map that depicts the pathways to understand how the facility or event causes changes in the external environment. Finally, facility and event managers should develop an awareness of deadweight. This calculates the proportion of outcomes that would have occurred in the community regardless of the existence of the facility or event.

An alternative approach to the SROI model is the basic social impact assessment. These assessments measure the local residents' attitudes, perceptions, and behaviors as well as the health standards of the local residents, number of local fitness organizations, and lifestyle of the local residents based on a facility or event. The social impact analysis is derived directly from the objectives of the facility or event operations. For instance, in DeKalb, Illinois, an annual cycling event is held called Biking with Beanzie. Proceeds from the event are used to support the community bike pathway projects. Through the efforts of this event, several miles of bike pathways have been created throughout the city and connect to other municipalities, which have allowed for more individuals to use the path for running, cycling, walking, and cross country skiing. This increased level of physical activity may subsequently affect the local community in a positive manner.

VIGNETTE 15-2

A Marathon Event with a Focus on Positive Impact

The Flying Pig Marathon, was founded on Mother's Day in 1999 and 5,297 people completed the marathon. Over the years, the event added a half marathon, marathon relay, 10K, 5K, 1-mile run, kids' mile, and a dog run. In 2017, the event hosted its largest to date with 37,244 participants with an estimated 150,000 spectators. The event attracts participants from every state in the United States and 16 other countries. With the high level of out-of-town visitors who participate in the event, the Flying Pig generates an estimated $14 million dollars of economic activity annually and generates approximately 260 new jobs. In 2017, the Flying Pig continued its focus on greening the event to minimize the environmental impact. Each water stop was provided with recyclable cups to use, and the post event used volunteers to help participants either compost, recycle, or dispose of their waste. Through these efforts, they were able to divert more than 10 tons of waste from the landfills, 1,600 pounds of heat sheets were recycled, 1,800 pounds of clothes were donated, 3,618 pounds of food was donated to local food pantries, and 596 carpool cars were used. Socially, the Flying Pig impacts the local community in numerous ways; however, two are especially worth mentioning. First, the event was used by approximately 329 charitable organizations to raise funds either through volunteering for the event, selling the "piggiest raffle ever" tickets, or runners who use pledges to donate to the organizations. In total, the 2017 event accounted for almost $610,000 in charitable giving. Another major impact is the kids program in which younger kids run their 26th mile at the Flying Pig Marathon and others "Fly up to the 5K." These programs not only teach children the benefit of running but they also provide them with nutrition facts and healthy living resources to help them to lead a healthy lifestyle. Overall, these impacts generated by the Flying Pig Marathon have a positive effect on the city of Cincinnati.

SUMMARY

Facility and event managers should evaluate performance through a continuous and multifaceted approach. Outlined in this chapter are various strategies and sources of information that organizations can use to measure how well they are performing in terms of their overall business objectives. These different measurement approaches allow facility and event managers to better understand the impact of the event on customers and participants and on the organization's internal and external business operations. This type of evaluation is consistent with the triple bottom-line approach to measuring organizational performance. This approach enables the organization to generate a much fuller understanding of the various factors that may impact its performance within its environment and community.

DISCUSSION QUESTIONS

1. Explain the importance of measuring the facility's or event's performance, and outline the basic strategies that managers may use to continuously measure performance.
2. Who are the different stakeholders who can give the organization information to determine its performance? What approaches could be used to measure these aspects?
3. How can an organization alter the Scale of Service Quality in Recreational Sports (SSQRS) to determine the satisfaction level of the users of the facility or participants in an event?
4. What measurement approaches can be used to determine the financial performance of a facility or event? What are the strengths and weaknesses of the different approaches?
5. What are the five inviolable principles of an economic impact study, and how can a facility or event avoid violating these principles?
6. What adverse environmental impact could events and facilities have? What strategies can managers employ to minimize these impacts?
7. Explain the positive and negative social impacts that an event may create for the local community. What strategies can event organizers use to maximize the positive impacts while minimizing the negative?

Case STUDY

Play Foley: Creating a Sport Tourism Destination

In the summer of 2017, Foley, Alabama, became the home of a private/public partnership to drive tourism in the area. First, funded through various private and public funds, the city of Foley created a new sport complex to capture the rapidly growing youth sport tourism market. This new sport facility is home to 16 open-air fields, which can be used for numerous events such as soccer, football, lacrosse, and ultimate Frisbee. The outdoor space is anchored with a 2,000-seat stadium, expandable to 10,000, and fully equipped for television capabilities. The indoor space at the complex boasts 90,000 square feet of

(continues)

Case STUDY (continued)

space including 50,000 square feet, which can be used for basketball, cheerleading, gymnastics, and many other activities. The second major facility was developed through a private organization call OWA. This complex includes several accommodations, an outlet mall, an amusement park, and a 14-acre lake. Combined, these two facilities, and their proximity to the Alabama Gulf Shore, make this a unique and marketable destination.

As the facility continues to market and develop a portfolio of events, it is proving to be successful with the amount of tournaments and events that it is hosting. The popularity of OWA as a destination has also proven beneficial when the Foley Sports Commission successfully bids on national competitions. In 2016, they hosted 62 events, which demonstrates a potentially positive economic impact on the host community; however, they are currently unsure of the actual impact. In addition, they would like to create a level of customer service and value that brings tournaments back to their destination annually, as well as those teams that compete in the events that they self-manage.

Given the lack of awareness of the potential impact that the facility may have, they have hired a research consulting firm. They would like to develop a strong understanding of how the organization is operating as well as the impact that it has on the local community. Specifically, they asked the firm to determine what the impact of the facility was on the host community, what the key drivers for success are, and how they can improve organization efficiencies. A secondary concern is how much the sport tourist utilizes the OWA facility or if large events prevent individuals from going to the facility.

1. Establish key performance indicators that could be utilized to determine the facility's efficiency in each of the components of the triple.
2. Based on the new indicators, outline who the appropriate stakeholders would be to determine the current organizational performance.
3. Outline the steps and instrumentation you will use to measure this group of stakeholders.
4. Provide a few strategies based on your expected results that the sports commission director can use to improve the facility's efficiency and overall financial performance.
5. Determine and explain the impact of large sport events on the OWA facility.

REFERENCES

Behn, R. D. (2003). Why measure performance? Different purposes require different measures. *Public Administration Review, 63*(5), 586–606.

Bitner, M. J., & Hubbert, A. R. (1994). Encounter satisfaction versus overall satisfaction versus quality: The customer's voice. In R. T. Rust, & R. L. Oliver (Eds.), *Service quality: New directions in theory and practice* (pp. 72–94). Thousand Oaks, CA: Sage.

Butler, B. N., & Aicher, T. J. (2015). Demonstrations and displacement: Social impact and the 2014 FIFA World Cup. *Journal of Policy Research in Tourism, Leisure and Events, 7*(3), 1–15.

Decker, S. H., Varano, S. P., & Green, J. R. (2007). Routine crime in exceptional times: The impact of the 2002 Winter Olympics on citizen demand for police services. *Journal of Criminal Justice, 35*(1), 89–101.

Getz, D. (2007). *Event studies.* Oxford, UK: Butterworth-Heinemann.

Hall, C. (1992). Adventure, sport and health tourism. In B. Weiler & C. M. Hall (Eds.), *Special interest tourism* (pp. 141–158). London: Bellhaven Press.

Howard, D. R., & Crompton, J. L. (2005). *Financing sport* (2nd ed.). Morgantown, WV: Fitness Information Technology.

Ko, J. Y., & Pastore, D. L. (2007). An instrument to assess customer perceptions of service quality and satisfaction in campus recreation programs. *Recreational Sports Journal, 31*(1), 34–42.

Lenskyj, H. J. (2000). *Inside the Olympic industry: Power, politics, and activism. SUNY series on sport, culture, and social relations.* Albany, NY: State University of New York Press.

Rotheroe, N., & Richards, A. (2007). Social return on investment and social enterprise: Transparent accountability for sustainable development. *Social Enterprise Journal, 3*(1), 31–48.

act of god   An instance of uncontrollable natural forces (often used in insurance claims).

activation   a specific action taken toward leveraging the sport-sponsorship relationship.

administration domain   The event management domain that includes the finance, human resources, information, procurement, stakeholders, systems, and time elements of an event.

affective dimension   The emotional response to the experience.

altruism   Individual's selfless desire to help improve others' welfare.

ancillary event   An event that occurs in conjunction with another type of event.

ancillary revenue   Income generated from goods and services that enhance the primary product or service; examples include concessions, parking, and merchandise.

arms race   As it relates to the sport event industry, the competition among sport organizations to have the best facilities, resources, revenue-generating amenities, and other event features to ensure an advantage in the marketplace.

assessment   Identifying and analyzing the environment to assess the needs of the event.

audit   A systematic critical examination of the facility or event to identify key risks or safety issues.

behavioral involvement   The action one takes in sport, whether as a participant or a spectator.

benchmark approach   A method of evaluating an event's legacy in which an event held in one city is compared with an event held in another to determine the impact generated from the events.

bid   It is a competitive process in which the objective is to win the right to organize a specific sporting event.

bonds   A debt security in which the issuer owes the bondholder a designated amount; payment, interest, and maturity date details are provided.

bottom-up approach   A method of evaluating an event's legacy in which all relevant changes to infrastructures and the host city are considered as well as potential, long-term development for the city.

breakeven analysis   An assessment used to determine at what point the event can cover all of the expenses and begin to make a profit.

burnout   Result of physical or mental exhaustion from the workload.

capital project   A long-term investment project that will increase the organization's assets.

capital projects   A project that maintains or improves upon an asset, like a sport facility.

change order   A document used to record an amendment to the original scope of construction work.

checklist   A preventive control tool that ensures that each individual is performing all tasks essential for to the success of the event.

closure/shutdown   The final stage of event planning to ensure that nothing is lost, equipment is returned properly, and the flow of those involved occurs seamlessly.

cognitive dimension   Making sense of an experience through awareness, perception, memory, learning, and judgment.

cognitive involvement   The acquisition of information/knowledge about a sport.

commitment   The frequency, duration, and intensity of attachment to sport.

communication   the open and transparent channels of discussion about the processes.

communitas   A special place where event attendees share a heightened sense of community and belonging.

community event   A relatively small-scale event that appeals to a specific geographic region.

competitive factor   A rivalry or event meant to measure ability in relation to another.

conative dimension   The behavior, or physical responses, of event attendees.

concessionaire   An entity given the rights to operate and sell goods or services on premises that belong to another. Venues often enter into agreements to sell parking and food concessions on their premises.

consumer involvement   A blend of the individual's interest in sport and the degree of importance that sport has in his or her life.

consumption   The active use of a product or service.

contractor   A firm that contracts directly with the owner for the construction of a project.

control-case approach   A method of evaluating an event's legacy in which attempts are made to compare the infrastructure developments that a city or community would incur as a result of hosting an event to the potential alternative infrastructure development that the city would undertake if the event were not to occur.

core product   The main product that is made by the company for the customer (i.e., the sport event or contest).

critical path   An analysis of the most efficient scheduling of tasks and subtasks.

cues   A feature or element of the event that is perceived and interpreted by the attendee with the intended outcome of a lasting (hopefully positive) impression or memory.

customer profile   A description of the customer or set of customers based on their demographics, psychographics, media preferences, and purchasing behavior.

data-based marketing (DBM)   A comprehensive system that captures critical demographics, psychographics, media use, and purchasing behavior information on customers and potential customers in order to enable direct marketing strategies.

decision-making process   The process of weighing the factors to determine the best option for purchase.

demographics   The categorization of consumers based on age, gender, ethnicity, education, income, socioeconomic status, profession, geographic location, religion, type of sport played, and other such identifiers.

design domain   The event management domain that contains the event's content, theme, program, environment, and production, entertainment, and catering needs.

differential pricing   Differences in pricing of a seat based on quality, time, and place. Quality refers to reputation, strength, and draw of the opponent. Time corresponds to the day of the week, time of day, or part of the season. Place is determined by location of seat.

differentiation   The positioning of a product in the minds of the consumer by highlighting the important attributes and benefits.

direct objectives   A business and marketing action specifically crafted toward increasing sales.

discretionary income   Monies left over once all financial obligations have been attended to by an individual or family.

divestment   The disposal/removal of the items associated with consuming a product or service and/or the ceasing of the relationship with the organization altogether.

documentation   recording, reporting, and maintaining assessments of progress in order to collect valuable data for current and future event processes.

domain   As used by the International Event Management Body of Knowledge, a division of the labor required at an event.

duration   The length that the experience stays present for the individual.

dynamic pricing   A process of pricing that is similar to differential pricing but concerned with the fluctuation of the price of a seat for an event based on demand. Determinants of dynamic pricing may include weather, quality of opponent, promotional offerings, or day of the week.

egoism   Fulfillment of personal needs as the primary motivating factor

emotional factor   The excitement, enjoyment, and self-fulfillment individuals gain from participating in sport.

emotional involvement   The effect that a sport event produces in the individual.

environmental/destination factor   The attractiveness of a destination or the environment in which an event is hosted that can impact individuals' motivations to attend or participate in an event.

environmental impact   The negative effect that the construction of or the existence of a facility or event has on the local environment.

environmental protection agency (EPA)   The U.S. federal agency responsible for protecting the environment and human health as it relates to the environment.

episodic volunteer   Short-term volunteers who require lower levels of commitment and are non-specialist in nature.

errors & omissions insurance   A form of liability insurance that protects the service-providing companies from claims made by clients for inadequate work or negligent action.

event feasibility   The likelihood that an event can be executed at the desired level given the resources at the event organizer's disposal.

exclusivity   A sponsor's desire to be the only sponsor attached to an event in their category (e.g., a cell phone provider not wanting any other cell phone providers associated with the event).

experience   In the sport event industry, the meaning attached to the event through the perception of the competition, atmosphere, social interactions, food, and entertainment, among other factors.

experience economy   The consumer's reaction to an event beyond the goods or services of the event alone.

extrinsic rewards   External drive to perform tasks within the organization.

feasibility study   An assessment that is conducted to determine key market characteristics.

financial measurement   An outcome used to determine how well the organization is contributing to the bottom line.

fixed cost   An expense that does not change as a function of the business activity.

floor plan   An illustration of where equipment or items are to be placed within the event venue.

flow diagram   A graphical representation as to how attendees will move through the event and venue.

formal communication   Information generated by the facility or sport event owner.

gantt chart   A bar chart that illustrates the various tasks that must be completed for the event in a time-sequence order.

gate receipt   The sum of money received from ticket sales for a particular event.

general admission   A fee paid for a seat in an unreserved seating or standing area in a public assembly facility.

general obligation bonds   Bonds that are secured by state and local governments' authority to levy income, property, or sales taxes.

generic experience   An experience that is commonly found at every event.

geotechnical report   A report of the soil conditions that dictate what materials are necessary to support the foundation for the proposed building as well as provisions for drainage of surface and runoff water that can affect the drying time of certain materials.

gift   A donation provided to an organization to finance a project that is tax deductible.

guerrilla marketing   A marketing strategy that uses unique methods to gain large effects at low expenses.

hard cost   A direct cost specifically related to the project.

hard structure   An element of event legacy relating to primary structure (e.g., sport infrastructure, training sites), secondary structure (e.g., villages for athletes, technical officials, media), and tertiary structure (e.g., security, power plants, cultural attractions, telecommunication networks).

heterogeneous   Relating to perceptions of an experience that are widely dissimilar.

human resource measurement   An outcome that allows the organization to better develop an understanding of an employee's perception of the organization.

impervious surface   A surface, such as cement pavement, that prevents precipitation from naturally soaking into the ground, causing water to run rapidly into storm drains, sewer systems, and drainage ditches.

implementation phase   The execution of the event plans.

incremental budgeting   Budgeting system that makes slight changes to the previous period's actual revenues and expenses.

indirect objectives   An outcome other than achieving immediate sales or gains such as increasing awareness to new market segments or a campaign to reposition a brand.

informal communication   The information we receive from our friends, family, or groups of people we interact with socially.

infrastructure   The sport facilities and subsequent surrounding areas needed for training and competition.

initiation phase   The stage in event planning that allows sport event organizers to define the event, set objectives, and determine the sport event's feasibility.

In-kind   Donation or payment is the exchange of something of value other than cash currency for the purpose of entering a business relationship between a sports property and a sponsoring company.

intangible legacy   Nonphysical changes associated with the transfer of knowledge, governmental reform, and emotional capital for residents, participants, and spectators, as well as psychological improvements to the city's image and social structure.

integrated marketing communication (IMC) A delivery strategy that ensures that brand positioning, personality, and key messages are delivered synergistically across every element of communication.

intensity The strength of the experience.

intrinsic rewards Internal drive to perform tasks within the organization.

learning factor The desire to learn about or explore the facility and destination of a sport event.

LEED certification A green building certification program that recognizes best-in-class building strategies and practices. LEED stands for Leadership in Energy and Environmental Design.

legacy The lasting direct or indirect effects generated from hosting an event that may positively or negatively impact the community.

liminal zone A zone within a sacred, ritualistic event that creates meaning that transcends the person and creates meaning outside of normal everyday life.

liminoid zone A zone within an unsacred, secular event that creates meaning that transcends the person and creates meaning outside of normal everyday life.

line-item budget Revenues and expenses are estimated and grouped together into categories.

loyalty program A structured, long-term program that rewards repeat customers for purchasing multiple units of an item or attending multiple events with incentives, gifts, or discounts.

marketing domain The event management domain comprised composed of the event's marketing plan, marketing materials, merchandize, promotions, public relations, sales, and sponsorship.

mastery factor A factor relating to the skill, learning, and personal challenge of participating in sport.

match-up hypothesis In reference to property and sponsorship, the belief that the more congruent the relationship, the more effectively the brands will connect in the minds of the consumers (e.g., a tire company sponsoring a race-car series).

meaning The perception and interpretation of the event elements that make the event significant.

media preference and use The categorization of consumers based on the type of media consumed and how it is consumed.

mega event The most complicated type of event to execute because it is often international in nature and requires years of planning to implement.

memorabilia   Tangible goods that support theme cues and that are available for purchase or as free takeaways.

memorability   The ability of an experience to remain an intense and enduring memory.

mission statement   A statement defining the purpose of the organization (or event).

money-back guarantee   An agreement between the ticket seller and buyer that the buyer will receive a full refund if the event does not meet a standard of satisfaction for the patron.

monitoring   The systematic tracking of the progress of a task.

monitoring and control system   The controls that are implemented to ensure that performance standards are achieved as the sport event is executed.

municipal bonds   Tax-exempt bonds issued by the local or state government to support capital projects.

naming rights   The non-sport entity's (sponsor's) exclusive ownership of the name of the venue where sport events occur (i.e., the stadium, arena, or ballpark); used interchangeably with title sponsorship.

need   A state of perceived deprivation.

nonstandard labor   Anyone who engages in part-time, temporary, and contract work.

op-down approach   A method of evaluating an event's legacy that compares the economic indicators of the event with the same indicators of the host city if the event had not taken place.

operating budget   Authorizes the funds necessary for the day-to-day operations of the facility or event.

operation and maintenance manuals (O&M manuals)   A collection of documents that contain pertinent information to maintain the building by providing detailed information on the management of the new systems in addition to the maintenance and repair of equipment.

owner   The party, whether public or private, responsible for getting the project financed, designed, and built.

operations domain   The event management domain that consists of communications, event infrastructure, logistics, the venue, technical needs, participants, and attendees.

organizational culture   Set of shared values, beliefs, and assumptions that guide behavior

organizational factor   An element that differentiates one event from another and influences a participant's motivation to attend an event.

outsourcing   Using a third-party organization to manage a component of the organization's services.

performance measurement   An outcome that describes how well the organization is using its internal and external inputs to produce the desired output.

peripheral product   An element of the core product that complements its existence (e.g., concessions, merchandise, dance teams).

personal seat license (PSL)   A paid license that affords the buyer the right to buy season tickets for a specific seat in a stadium. The license is transferable and seat rights may be sold to another person once the owner decides not to purchase season tickets.

pervious material   A material that allows water to soak naturally into the ground.

place   The location of the sport product where the product is distributed; the geographic location of the target market and other channels that might be relevant to the sport product.

planning phase   The proactive and dynamic stage in event planning in which the various suggested options suggestion in the initiation phase are reviewed for the best course of action and preparation of the event.

positioning   Developing and delivering a product that is perceived as more valuable and distinctly different than the other products.

post-event analysis   Measurement of a specific variable of interest after the event has occurred.

price sensitive   Susceptibility to variations in price.

procurement   The ordering, expediting, and delivering of key equipment and materials required for the construction project.

product extension   An additional event component that creates an atmosphere and experience for an event.

pro forma   A statement that summarizes the projected future status of a company and that is used as the foundation for financial planning for an organization or project.

program budget   Funds are allocated for specific programs or projects.

program evaluation and review technique (PERT) chart   An illustration of the tasks, duration, and dependency information, which can be useful in defining the critical path for the project.

project   A temporary and one-time venture undertaken to create a unique product with specific outcomes and benefits.

project management   The dynamic process of organizing and managing appropriate resources in a controlled and structured manner to deliver the clearly defined work required to complete a project within the given scope, time, and, often, cost constraints.

project management triangle   The cost, time, and scope constraints that impact the final quality of an event.

project outputs   The transformation of resources (human, financial, physical) into new assets through a defined deliverable.

promotion   The communication of the marketing message.

promotion mix   The varied use of a number of promotional methods to create a message.

property   in reference to sport sponsorship, the sport organization being sponsored.

psychographics   The categorization of consumers based on the consumers' interests, beliefs, and attitudes.

pulsating organization   An organization that creates a cycle where they radically expand their labor force and operations around the time of the event and then contract to a more modest core staff.

purchase   The act of making a final selection.

purchasing behavior   The frequency with which individuals consume a product and the manner in which they use the products and services.

qualitative   Research methodology used to develop a more in-depth description of behaviors and experiences.

quantitative   Research methodology used to provide a numeric analysis of the organization's performance.

realtor   An expert in real estate who can assist in identifying land options, demographics, and traffic volumes of an area, as well as zoning requirements for specific areas.

recurring event   An event that happens on a regular basis; it is the "easiest" type of event to execute because it occurs consistently.

referendum A direct vote in which an entire electorate (i.e., voting public) is asked to accept or reject a proposal put forward by the community leadership.

relationship marketing A marketing strategy that seeks to develop and maintain relationships with customers, while using information gathered from them to attract new customers; the client–consumer relationship is emphasized over a more purely transactional behavior.

retained earnings Revenues generated by the sport organizations that are reinvested for financial improvements and additions.

revenue and expense statement Financial statement that presents budgeted and actual revenues and expenses in summary form for a given period of time.

revenue bonds Issued for a specific project and are secured through the project's revenues.

revenue growth and mix measurement An outcome used to denote how well the organization is performing toward organizational objectives such as market share, increased markets, or expanding its revenue sources.

right of first negotiation A clause that event owners or organizers negotiate that requires sponsors to renew the sponsorship agreement before they can offer the sponsorship to another company.

right of first refusal The sponsoring organization has the ability to match the terms of any other offer from competitors that have a desire to sponsor the event.

risk The probability that a hazard will lead to a loss.

risk acceptance A method of managing risk that involves preparing for the risk through budgeting, deductibles, or self-insurance.

risk analysis Categorization of the levels of risks based on the severity and likelihood of occurrence.

risk avoidance A method of managing risk that involves discontinuing the component of the activity considered to be a risk.

risk domain The event management domain that consists of compliance issues, emergency plans, health and safety plans, insurance needs, legal concerns, security needs, and any risk-related decisions.

risk evaluation A process of determining the acceptability of the risk through a cost–benefit analysis.

risk identification Evaluation of the environment, structures, and marketplace to determine the sources of risk associated with the sport facility or event.

risk management   A sound framework to minimize the potential and severity of the risk.

risk monitoring   The continuous assessment of the risk associated with facilities and events, as well as the management strategies to reduce those risks.

risk reduction through proactive measures   A method of managing risk that involves establishing a series of controls to reduce either the likelihood of occurrence or the consequences associated with the risk.

risk retention   A method of managing risk in which the organization does not employ any risk management strategies.

risk transfer   A method of managing risk that involves moving the risk to another entity.

risk treatment   A method of managing risk that involves minimizing the impact and/or occurrence of the risk.

role ambiguity   Lack of clearly defined job duties

run sheet   A detailed schedule of the sequencing and timing for each element of the event.

schematic drawing   A drawing that exhibits the size of the facility and assists in defining the maximum capacity of land needed to build.

season tickets   A subscription for a series of tickets, usually lasting for one season of a sports teams' contests, which costs less than buying separate tickets to individual events.

securitization   When sport organizations use contractually obligated income as collateral for debt.

segmentation   The breaking of consumers into smaller clusters or groups identified by certain characteristics rather than attempting to sell to everyone.

selection   the decision point of the planning process.

silt fencing   Temporary fencing used to keep any debris from passing from the site to any areas beyond the construction zone.

SMART goals   An acronym used to describe the goals of an event; stands for specific, measurable, attainable, relevant, and time-based.

social identity   A sense of belonging or membership to a wider social group.

social impact   The effect that facilities and events have on the local community, social norms, roles, and customs.

socialization   The process whereby individuals learn skills, traits, values, attitudes, norms, and knowledge associated with the performance of present or anticipated social roles.

soft cost   A cost that is not directly related to the physical construction of the project and commonly occurs prior to the project; also called indirect cost.

soft structure   An element of event legacy relating to knowledge, networks, and cultural goods that are developed from the hosting of an event.

special tax bonds   Bonds that are secured by local taxes typically in the form of bed, car rental, or sin tax.

specific expectation   An expectation or belief that one holds about an event.

sponsor   the organization purchasing the rights from the sport organization. This company may be a sport-oriented organization itself (e.g., a sport goods company) or may not be (e.g., financial entity).

sponsorship inventory   Any place or location, whether physical or digital, that can be exchanged for something of value (cash or in-kind service/product) with the purpose of a sponsoring organization being able to achieve its sponsorship objectives.

sponsorship   is a legal contract between a sport property and another entity exchanging something of value, whether cash or an in-kind service/product, wherein the sport property allows the sponsoring organization the rights to commercialization of its brand and the resulting benefits derived from these actions.

stakeholder   A person or entity that has a vested interest in the event.

subjective   A unique and personal venture undertaken by an individual, who attaches his or her own meaning.

sustainable tourism   Development of the infrastructure in the host community to generate a continual flow of tourist activity.

SWOT analysis   A tool used to assess the internal and external strengths and weaknesses of an event; SWOT stands for strengths, weaknesses, opportunities, and threats.

SWOT   analysis A tool an organization can utilize to identify the internal strengths and weaknesses, and assess the opportunities and threats facing the organization.

tangible legacy   Observable, easily identified, or physical changes to the host community that remains upon conclusion of the event.

target market   The consumer most likely to purchase the product or service.

television blackout   The National Football League's policy stating that if the nonpremium or luxury suite tickets have not been sold out, the game will not be televised in the local market.

theming   Alteration of the attendees' sense of time and reality through tangible and memorable cues that leave lasting impressions.

topographical report   A survey of the land that identifies any existing buildings, site surface evaluations, and availability of electrical, sewer, water, and gas services.

traveling event   An event that occurs on a regular basis but in various locations.

triple bottom-line approach   A method of measuring organizational performance focused on the impact that the event has on its consumers, internal business operations, and external business operations.

USGBC (united states green building council)   An organization that promotes Green Building through Leadership in Energy & Environmental Designs (LEED) certifications.

variable cost   An expense that changes based on the volume of business activity.

viral marketing   The use of social networks to increase brand awareness through self-replicating processes.

vision statement   A statement of what the organization would like to achieve or accomplish.

want   The form taken by human needs as they are shaped by culture and individual personality.

waste diversion   The prevention/reduction of generated waste through recycling, reuse, or composting.

white elephant   In reference to event legacy, a stadium, arena, or other facility constructed to host an event that remains underutilized after the event has occurred.

work breakdown structure (WBS)   Project tasks broken down into manageable parts.

zero-based budgeting (ZBB)   Requires that each line item from a previous budget be reviewed and approved and starts from a zero amount.

Note: Page numbers followed by *f* or *t* indicate material in figures or tables respectively.

A

absorption, spectrum connection, 134
act of God, 55
action stage, loyalty, 229
activation process,
    sponsorship, 239, 252–253
administration domain, 30
AES motives, 206
aesthetic realm, 135
affective dimension, 134
affective stage, loyalty, 228
AFL. *See* Australian Football League
agreements, of sponsorship,
    249–252, 251*f*
alcohol sales, in sports stadiums, 272
altruism, 205
altruistic motives, 205
America Scores, 205
American Recovery and
    Reinvestment Act, 93
ancillary events, 119
ancillary revenue, 271
    concessions and food
        operations, 271–272
    merchandise, 274
    parking, 273–274
Archeological evidence, 5
arms race, 6
    in intercollegiate athletics, 7
Arthur Ashe Stadium, uses for, 275–276

assessment, 23
assets, management of, 318
attainable goals, SMART goals, 109
audit, 70
augmented service quality, peripheral
    product, 224
Australian Football League (AFL), 126

B

Banks, Omar, 82–83
baseball stadium, uses for, 274–276
behavioral involvement, 173
benchmark approach, 301
benefits, 244–245
bid process, 114–116
Billie Jean King National Tennis Center,
    uses for, 275–276
bombings, 65–66
bonds, 90–95
Boston Marathon bombing, 63
bottom-up approach, 302–303
Brazos Valley Senior Games (BVSG),
    case study, 254–256
breakeven analysis, 153
budget
    approaches, 97–99
    estimation of, 43–45
    for facility, 96–97
burnout, 199
business operations, 64

C

capital campaigns, 88–89
capital projects, 40, 84–86, 94
CDP model. *See* consumer decision
process model
Central Parking, 274
championships, hosting, 276
change order, 52
checklists, 33
closure/shutdown, 29
club seats, luxury suites and, 267–268
co-creation, 140, 141*t*
cognitive dimension, 134
cognitive involvement, 173
cognitive stage, loyalty, 228
college athletics departments, 273
commitment, consumption factors, 173
communication, 23
communitas, 138, 140
community events, 119–120
Company ABC, 242
competitive factors, motivation, 179
conative dimension, 133
concessionaires, 273
concessions, 271–272
connection, 134
construction-related injuries, 55
consumer behavior
consumption factors of, 171–173
decision-making process, 182–186
motivating factors of. *See* motivating
factors, consumer behavior
consumer decision process (CDP)
model, 182
information search, 183–184
consumer involvement, 172–173
consumer profile, case study, 186–187
consumption evaluation, 185
contingency plans, 250
contractor, 51
contractor's pricing proposal,
review of, 51–52
control-case approach, 302

core product, 224–225
core staff, 196–197
cost constraint, 20
cost–benefit analysis, 71
costs, estimation of, 43–45
critical path, 32
CRM systems. *See* customer relationship
management systems
CrossFit Games, 280
CrossPlex, 278
cues, 135
cuju, 3
culture, event structures, 299–301
customer participation spectrum, 134
customer profile, 156
customer relationship management
(CRM) systems, 157–158
customer service, 213, 230
case study, 231–232
damaged reputation, 226–227
definition of, 216
effective, 217*t*–218*t*
loss of good employees, 227
outcomes of service encounters, 226
satisfaction in, 227–228
service plan, 221–223
service quality measures, 223–226
customers, relationships
with, 219–221
customers/participants, performance
measurement, 315–317

D

damaged reputation, 226–227
data-based marketing (DBM), 157
day-of-event timeline, 121, 122*f*
debt finance, 89
bonds, 90–95
loans, 89–90
decision-making process, 182–186
capital projects, 86
consumption and postconsumption
evaluation, 185

information search, 183–184
 need recognition, 182
 prepurchase evaluation and
       purchase, 184–185
DeMeo, James A., 62–63
demographics, 155–156
design domain, 30
design firm, 48, 49, 53
 hiring of, 48–49
differential pricing, 264
differentiation, 158
direct costs. *See* hard costs
direct objectives, 249
discretionary income, 229
divestment, 185–186
documentation, 23
domain, 30
 feasibility areas by, 25*t*
donations, 88
duration of experience, 132
dynamic pricing, 279

E

economic impact analysis, 320–323, 322*f*
 inviolable principles of, 321*t*
education, event structures, 297–298
educational realm, 135
effective customer service,
       qualities of, 217*t*–218*t*
egoism, 205
egoistic motives, 205
electronic ticket delivery system,
       266–267
emotional connections, 200–201
emotional factors, motivation, 180–181
emotional involvement, 173
emotions, event structures, 298–299
enjoyment, emotional factors, 180
entertainment realm, 135
environmental impact analysis, 323–324
Environmental Protection Agency
       (EPA), 55, 57

environmental sustainability, 298
environmental/destination factors,
       motivation, 176–177
EPA. *See* Environmental
       Protection Agency
episodic volunteer, 204
equity finance
 gifts, 88–89
 retained earnings, 88
 sale of stock, 87–88
errors and omissions insurance
       (E&O), 55
escapism, emotional factors, 180
escapist realm, 135
event feasibility, 110–112, 113*f*
event management domain, 30
event packaging, 280–282
event structures, legacy, 297
 culture, 299–301
 emotions, 298–299
 image, 298
 infrastructure, 297
 knowledge, skill development,
       and education, 297–298
 networks, 299
event timeline, 120–121, 122*f*
events
 execution of, 108
 implementation stage, 76–77
 reasons for, 108–110
 sponsors of, 313
 timelines for, 120–121, 121*f*, 122*f*
 types of, 108, 116–120
exclusivity, 245
execution phase, 28–29
experience, 128, 129
 dimensions of, 133–135
 duration of, 132
 economy, 128
 intensity of, 132
expo, 130
external factors, events, 26–27

external operations, performance
measurement, 319–328
economic impact analysis, 320–323,
321*t*, 322*f*
environmental impact analysis,
323–324
social impact analysis, 324–328
extrinsic rewards, 203

F

Facebook, 156, 184
facilities' recurring event
organizations, 196
facility and event budgets, common
expenses in, 100–101
facility and event organizations, 191
case study, 208–209
culture, 195–196
customers/participants, 315–317
external operations. *See* external
operations, performance
measurement
factors, 193
internal operations, 317–319
managing volunteers, 201–207
measurement and evaluation of,
311–314
organizational forms, 194–195
staff management
motivation and emotional
connections, 200–201
sources of labor, 196–198
stress, burnout, and retention,
198–200
facility design and construction, 40
case study, 58–59
construction costs estimation, 45–46
construction process, 51–54
costs and budgeting estimation, 43–45
design process, 48–51
feasibility, 41–42
green construction and
LEED certification, 55–57

insurance, 54–55
procurement, 41
site selection, 46–47
facility management tragedy, 70
Fan Commerce, 170
FanPass, 266
feasibility areas by domain, 25*t*
feasibility study, 111, 152–154
feedback control, 29
FIFA World Cup, 12
financial measurement, 317, 319
fixed costs, 43
Flash Seats, 266–267
Flavian Amphitheater, 4
floor diagrams, 33
floor plans, 33
food and beverage sponsorship, 242
food operations, 271–272
force majeure, 250
Forest City Ratner Companies
(FCRC), 45
formal communication, 184
for-profit sport organization, 85
Futterman, Matt, 192–193

G

game quality, core product, 224
Gantt chart, 31–32
Garden Square, 139
gate receipt, 262
general admission, 267
General obligation (GO)
bonds, 93–94
generic experiences, 132
geotechnical report, 48
gifts, 88–89
Greater Cleveland Sports
Commission (GCSC), 18
Green Bay Packers, 87
green construction, 55–57
Griesmer, Becky, 18–19
guerrilla marketing, 163
Gutierrez, Ignacio, 126–127

H

hard costs, 45
hard structures, 300
heterogeneous experience, 129
heterogeneous, sport, 151
hippodrome, 4
hospitality events, 276–277
host communities, 290–292, 302,
    304–305
hosting championships, 276
hosting mega-events, 325
human resources
    measurements, 319

I

image, event structures, 298
immersion, spectrum connection, 134
IMpact analysis for PLANning
    (IMPLAN), 321
impervious surfaces, 57
IMPLAN. *See* IMpact analysis for
    PLANning
implementation phase, 28
implementation phasefiscal policy,
    28–29
incremental budgeting, 97–98
indemnification, 250
indirect costs. *See* soft costs
indirect objectives, 249
individual participatory events, 279–280
informal communication, 183–184
initiation phase, 24–30
in-kind donation, 237, 238
in-kind payment, 237, 238
insurance policy, 54–55, 73–74
intangible legacy, 290, 296
integrated marketing communication
    (IMC), 161
intensity of experience, 132
intention stage, loyalty, 229
interaction quality, peripheral product,
    224–225

intercollegiate athletics, arms race in, 7
interest, 89
internal factors, events, 28
internal operations, measuring
    performance, 317–319
International Event Management
    Body of Knowledge
    (EMBOK), 30
International Olympic Committee
    (IOC), 295
    Sport and Environment Commission,
    324
International Trade Union Confederation
    (ITUC), 53
intrinsic rewards, 202
inventory, sponsorship, 240–243
involvement, consumption factors,
    172–173
IOC. *See* International Olympic
    Committee

J

jewel box design, 7
job insecurity and retention, 199–200
job satisfaction, 206–207
Jorgensen, Jen, 310–311

K

Klein, Alexandra, 2
knowledge, event structures, 297–298
Kyle Stadium, 7

L

lacrosse, 3
Ladies Professional Golf Association
    (LPGA), 236
Lake Myrtle Sports Complex, 294
large facilities, construction of, 52
Leadership in Energy and
    Environmental Design (LEED)
    certification, 55–57
learning factors, motivation, 181
LeBlanc, Franzter, 38–40

legacies, 287–306
    case study, 305–306
    categories of, 300
    definition of, 290
    dimensions of, 296
    event structures. *See* event structures,
        legacy
    impacts, components of, 296–297
    importance of, 294–296
    introduction of, 290
    measuring, 301–303
        benchmark and top-down
            approaches, 301–302
        bottom-up approach, 302–303
        control-case approach, 302
    themes in, 300
    types of, 297
leisure satisfaction, 227–228
levels of sport
    definition of, 237–239
    interconnectivity of, 239–240
leveraging, 239
Levi's Stadium in Santa Clara,
    California, 7, 8
liability insurance, 55
light-colored roofing materials, 56–57
liminal zone, 138
liminality, creation of, 137–140
liminoid zone, 138, 139
limited-liability coverage, 73–74
line-item budget, 96
loaded tickets, 268
loans, 89–90
local convention and visitor's
    bureaus, 116
local government agencies, 46
local level sports events, 238, 243
longevity, 52
loss of good employees, 227
loyalty program, 270
loyalty, stages of, 228–229
LPGA. *See* Ladies Professional
    Golf Association
luxury suites and club seats, 267–268

M

Major League Baseball (MLB), 7, 263,
    267, 268
marathons. *See* road running races
marketing, 161
    case study, 165–166
    domain, 30, 31
    relationship, sponsorship, 248–249
    strategy and plan, 154–155
mastery factors, motivation, 93–94, 180
Match Day, Events & Hospitality, Sydney
    Swans Football Club, 126–127
matchup hypothesis, 244
material legacy. *See* tangible legacy
maturity, 89
MBI. *See* Media Brokers International
meaning, experience, 133
measurable goals, SMART goals, 109
Media Brokers International (MBI), 244
media preference and use, 156
medium-scale events, 293–294
mega-event organizing committee, 198
mega-events, 116–118
    hosting of, 325
memorabilia, 137
memorability, 132
merchandise, ancillary revenue, 274
message, communicating, 161–164
MetLife Stadium, 269
Michaels, Nick, 148–150
mission statement, 154
money-back guarantees, 265–266
monitoring, 23
monitoring and control systems, 28–29
motivating factors, consumer behavior
    competitive factors, 179
    emotional factors, 180–181
    environmental/destination
        factors, 176–177
    learning factors, 181
    mastery factors, 180
    organizational factors, 174–176
    social/group factors, 178–179

motivation, 200
multipurpose sport facilities, 277–278
multivenue sport event, case study,
     35–36
municipal bonds, 90–93
    advantages, 92
    economic benefits, 92–93
    security for, 93–95
Murray, Lisa, 236–237

N

naming rights, facility, 240–241
National Association of Intercollegiate
     Athletics (NAIA), 278
National Association of Sport
     Commissions (NASC), 12, 184
National Basketball Association (NBA),
     264
National Collegiate Athletic Association
     (NCAA), 6, 291
    championship, case study, 123–124
National Football League (NFL), 263
    policy, 9
    PSLs and, 268–269
    security policy, 67
National Hockey League (NHL), 263,
     275–276
National Multiple Sclerosis Society, 181
national-level sport events, 238
NCAA. *See* National Collegiate Athletic
     Association
need recognition, CDP model, 182
negative cues, 136, 137
networks, event structures, 299
NFL. *See* National Football League
NFL G-4 program, 90
NHL. *See* National Hockey League
noncash support for sport facilities, 91
nonmaterial legacy. *See* intangible legacy
nonporous soils, 48
nonprofit sport organizations
    decision making, capital projects, 86
    gifts, 88–89

retained earnings, 88
    revenues for, 98–99
nonsporting events, hosting of, 120
nonstandard labor, 197
Noosa Surfing Festival, 136
nostalgia, emotional factors, 180

O

off-site parking, 46
    accessing, 46
O'Leary, C.J., 106–107
Olympic Games, 4–6, 117–118, 135
one-off event organizing
     committees, 194
one-off organizing
     committees, 195–196
on-site communications, 242
operating budget, 96
operating modes, 28
operation and maintenance manuals
     (O&M manuals), 54
operational revenues, 95–96
operations domain, 30, 31
organizational culture, 195–196
organizational factors, motivation,
     174–176
organizational forms, 194–195
organizational performance,
     measuring, 311–314
    customers/participants, 315–317
    external operations. *See* external
     operations, performance
     measurement
    internal operations, 317–319
outcome quality, peripheral product, 225
outsourcing, 197
owner, 40

P

Pan American Games in Canada, 199
Panathenaic Stadium, 5–7
parking, ancillary revenue, 274
participatory events, 278–279

performance measurements, 312
peripheral product, 224–225
personal seat licenses (PSL), 268–269
pervious materials, 56
phases of project management, 23
    closure/shutdown, 29
    implementation, 28–29
    initiation, 24–30
    planning, 26–28
Philadelphia Eagles, 148–150
Phoenix Suns, 265
physical environment quality,
        peripheral product, 225
Pierce, Chris, 170
place, 160
planning phase, 26–28
    for facility design, 46
planning team, 26
Plunkett Report (2014), 12
Populous, 48–49
positioning, 158–159
positive cues, 136
postconsumption evaluation, 185
post-event analysis, 313
potential sponsor, sport
        organization and, 244
prepayment provision, 89
prepurchase evaluation, 184–185
preventive control, 29
price, 159–160
    four Cs of, 160*t*
price sensitive, 159
pro forma, 43, 44*f*, 45, 46
proactive stage in event planning, 26
processes, 23–24
procurement, 41
product extension, 152
professional and college sport
        projects, 84, 85*t*
program budget, 97
program evaluation and review
        technique (PERT) chart, 32
project, 20

project management, 20–22
    monitoring/control, 28–29
    phases of, 23
    tools of, 21, 23, 33–34
project management triangle, 20, 20*f*
project outputs, 21
project triple constraint, 20
project-based volunteering, 204
promotions, 161
    mix, 161
    of sports, 270
property, 237
property exposures, 64
proposal letters, sponsorship, 247–248
proposed construction project,
        costs of, 46
PSL. *See* personal seat licenses
psychic income, 326
psychographics, 156
public liability
    caused by negligence, 64
    excluding negligence, 64
public sector sport organizations,
        decision making, 86
pulsating organizations, 194–195
purchase, 185
purchasing behavior, 156, 157

Q

Qatar World Cup 2022, 53
Qualcomm Stadium,
        operating budget, 97
qualitative data, 314
quality of event, 20
quantitative data, 314

R

realms of experience, 135
realtors, 47
record-keeping process, 33
recreation landscape, 217
Recreation Management, 11

recreation organizations, conceptual framework for, 315
recreation projects, 94
recreational events, 278–279
recurring events, 118
recycled materials, purchasing, 57
Red Bull 400 event, case study, 143
referendum, 8
regional level sports events, 238
Register's Annual Great Bicycle Ride Across Iowa (RAGBRAI), case study, 305–306
registration revenue, technology to increase, 281
relationship marketing, 156–158
relevant goals, SMART goals, 110
repatronage, customer service, 228–229
retained earnings, 88
return on investment (ROI), 245, 248
revenue and expense statement, 97
revenue bonds, 94
revenue generation in sports and recreation, 259–283
    ancillary revenue, 271
    case study, 282–283
    event packaging, 280–282
    individual participatory events, 279–280
    multipurpose sport facilities, 277–278
    participatory events, 278–279
    sources of revenue, 262
    sport promotions, 270
    sport-specific stadium, alternative uses for, 274–276
    ticket sales, 262–263
    ticket sales strategies, 263–269
revenue growth and mix measurements, 318
right of first negotiation, 246
right of first refusal, 246
risk
    definition of, 64
    types of, 64–65, 65t

risk acceptance, 73
risk analysis, 70–71
risk avoidance, 72–73
risk domain, 30, 31
risk evaluation, 71–72
risk identification, 69–70
risk management
    benefits of, 68–69
    defined as, 68
    description of, 68
    steps in, 69–78
risk monitoring, 76–78
risk reduction through proactive measures, 73
risk retention, 76
risk transfer, 73–76, 74t, 75f
risk treatment, 72–76
road running races, 279
ROI. See return on investment
role ambiguity, 199
Roman Colosseum, 5
Round Rock Sports Center (RRSC), 100
Royal Albert Hall, personal seat license, 268
run sheet, 32

S

sale of stock, 87–88
satisfaction, customer services, 227–228
Scale of Event Quality in Spectator Sports (SEQSS), 224
Scale of Service Quality in Recreational Sports (SSQRS), 315–317
scale of sport event industry, 12
schematic drawings, 46, 49
scope, 21
sea battles, 4
season tickets, 262
securitization, 95
segmentation, 155–156, 157t
selection, 23
senses, engaging, 140–142

SEQSS. *See* Scale of Event Quality in
    Spectator Sports
service plan
    assess customer needs, 221–222
    employees accountable, 222–223
    goals setting, 222
    good service, 223
    recruiting employees, 222
    training, 222
    vision and goals, creation, 221
service quality
    definition of, 315
    measure customer service and,
        223–226
SERVQUAL, 224, 309
signage, facility, 243
silt fencing, 50
sin taxes, 95
site layout plan, 50
site schematics, 48
site selection, 46–47
skill development, event structures,
    297–298
small-scale events, 293–294
SMART goals, 109–110
Smith, Mari, 219
social identities, 178
social impact analysis, 324–328
social media, 184
social motives, 205–206
social networking sites, 164
social return on investment (SROI)
    model, 327–328
social/group factors, motivation,
    178–179
socialization, concepts of, 172
soft costs, 45
soft structures, 300
software, 33–34
Spartan Race, 279
Special Olympics Texas (SOTX), case
    study, 102–103
special tax bonds, 95
specialist volunteer, 204

specific expectations, 132
specific goals, SMART goals, 109
spectator sport industry, 216
spectator sports, multipurpose
        facilities for, 277–278
SPIRE Institute, 278
sponsor activation spaces, 243
sponsors
    definition of, 237
    employees, 253
    of event, 313
    finding and acquiring, 244–247
    payment obligations of, 250
    title, 242
sponsorship, 235
    activation, 252–253
    agreement, 249–252
    case study, 254–256
    definition of, 237
    interconnectivity of levels, 239, 240*f*
    level of sports, 237–240
    marketing relationship, 248–249
    objectives, 249
    potential sponsors, 248
    proposal letters, 247–248
sponsorship inventory, 240–243
    event, 242–243
    types of, 242
sport capital projects, 94
sport event, 19
    hospitality, 276–277
    medium-and small-scale, 293–294
    participatory, 278–279
    sizes of, 292–293
    structures. *See* event structures, legacy
sport event experience
    case study, 143
    characteristics of, 131–133
    co-creating, 140, 141*t*
    creating, 129–131
    designing, 135–140
    dimensions of, 133–135
    meanings attached of, 141–142, 142*t*
sport event industry, scale of, 12

sport event management, 12–13
sport facilities
    construction of, 40
    evolution of, 5–7
    hosting nonsporting events in, 120
    local
        case study, 329–330
        trends in, 10–11
    multipurpose, 277–278
    potential revenue streams for, 45
    role of, 10
    trends in, 7–10
sport facility to enhance tourism,
        case study, 58–59
sport industry, 223
sport landscape, 217
sport managers, 252
sport mega-events, 115
sport organization, 237, 244–245
    websites, case study, 231–232
sport products and services, 219, 221
sport promotions, 270
sport satisfaction, 227–228
sport socialization, 172, 172t
sport tourism, growth in, 291–292
sports
    conceptual framework for, 315
    terrorism and, 65–67
sports pyramid, 237
SPORTSERV scale, 224
sport-specific stadium, 274–276
sport–sponsor relationship, 248
SROI model. See social return on
        investment model
SSQRS. See Scale of Service Quality in
        Recreational Sports
SSQRS. See Scale of Service Quality in
        Recreational Sports
staff management
    motivation and emotional
        connections, 200–201
    sources of labor, 196–198
    stress, burnout, and retention, 198–200
stakeholder, 326, 327

stakeholder experiences, 130–131
standard operating procedure (SOP)
        manual, 73
statutory regulations, 27
stored-value tickets, 268
stress, 198–199
subjective experience, 129
sustainability. See also legacies
    environmental, 298
    of legacy, 292, 301–303
sustainable tourism, 293
SWOT analysis, 112–114, 153, 154t
symbolic elements, 140

T

tangible legacy, 290, 296
target market, 156
tax exemption, rationale for, 91
TEAMQUAL, 224
terrorism and sport, 65–67
Texas A&M, 8
theming, 135–137
ticket pricing, flexible, 264–265
ticket sales
    average price, 262–263, 263t
    loaded tickets, 268
    luxury suites and club seats, 267–268
    money-back guarantees, 265–266
    PSL, 268–269
    strategies
        differential pricing, 264
        electronic ticket delivery system,
            266–267
        flexible ticket pricing, 264–265
    web-based tickets, 266
Timberlake, Brad, 260–261
time constraint, 20
time-based goals, SMART goals, 110
title sponsors, sports, 242
Toledo Mud Hens and
        Toledo Walleye, 106–107
top-down approach, 302
topographical report, 48

topography, 177
Tort Claims Act, 63
Tough Mudder event, 279–280
Township, Jackson, 241
traditional marketing, 162
traveling events, 118–119
Triantafyllidis, Maxilis, 288–289
triple bottom-line approach, 315
Twitter feeds, 184

U

UMBC, 38
unique building materials, 52–53
Urban Dare, 279
U.S. Bureau of Labor Statistics, 12, 202
US Green Building Council (USGBC), 55

V

variable costs, 43, 45
variance analysis, 99, 99*t*
viral marketing, 163
Virginia Tech Athletics, 82–83
vision statement, 154
VOLSports, case study, 208–209
volunteer demographics, 204–205
volunteer expectations, 208–209
volunteering as casual leisure, 204
volunteering as serious leisure, 203–204
volunteers management
    contributions, 201–202
    defining, 202–203

demographic characteristics, 204–205
job satisfaction, 206–207
motivational theories, 205–206
project-based volunteering, 204
volunteering as casual leisure, 204
volunteering as serious leisure,
    203–204

W

waiver of liability, 75–76, 75*f*
wants, CDP model, 182
warrior dash tragedy, case study, 79–80
waste diversion, 57
web applications,
    project management, 33
web-based tickets, 266
White City Stadium in London, 5
white elephants, 292
Winter Olympics, 292, 324
word-of-mouth communication, 183
work breakdown structure (WBS), 32
work plan, example, 27, 27*f*
World Trade Center attack, 65
Wright, Rachel, 214–215

Y

Yankee Stadium, uses for, 274–275

Z

zero-based budgeting (ZBB), 98–99